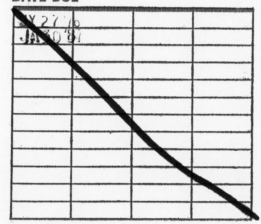

INTERNATIONAL BEHAVIOR

A Social-Psychological Analysis

Edited by

Herbert C. Kelman

DEPARTMENT OF PSYCHOLOGY AND CENTER FOR RESEARCH
ON CONFLICT RESOLUTION

THE UNIVERSITY OF MICHIGAN

Published for the Society for the Psychological
Study of Social Issues

Holt, Rinehart and Winston

NEW YORK · CHICAGO · SAN FRANCISCO · TORONTO · LONDON

To Rose

Rabbi Eleazar quoted Rabbi Hanina who said:
Scholars build the structure of peace
in the world.

Foreword

By custom, the President of the Society for the Psychological Study of Social Issues writes the foreword to volumes appearing during his term of office. Since the editor of *International Behavior* will be President when it appears, the privilege of introducing it devolves on the next incumbent of the office.

Though as dedicated to rigorous thinking and experimentation as their colleagues, members of the Society for the Psychological Study of Social Issues have always selected problems for study solely by the criterion of importance for human welfare, regardless of the difficulties they present. Among these vital but refractory areas, international relations ranks high both in importance and in difficulty. Continuance of the human adventure depends on nations mastering techniques of dealing with each other without recourse to war. The urgency of accomplishing this grows each year as national boundaries become ever more meaningless and the overload of destructive power ever larger and more diffused. At the same time every aspect of international relations bristles with difficulties for research, including how to gather valid and reliable data and how to conceptualize phenomena ranging from the individual to the nation in their complex interactions.

So the psychologist who dares to work in this field is haunted by misgivings based on the recognition that his special field of competence—the individual or small group—is only one part of the picture. At the same time he has had to contend with criticisms from some members of his own and other disciplines who insist on a priori grounds that his approach and information are largely irrelevant.

These obstacles have never daunted the members of this Society. From its inception it has sponsored studies on international relations, and in 1945 its third yearbook, edited by Gardner Murphy, dealt with "Human Nature and Enduring Peace."

Now, twenty years later, the time is ripe for another effort to review the contributions that students of human nature can make to this topic. In the interval new, ingenious methods of data collection have developed and conceptualizations have become more sophisticated and more pertinent. Concomitantly a new discipline seems to be emerging —the social psychology of international affairs—and the contributors to this volume are among its first practitioners. Though each retains his conventional professional affiliation—psychology, anthropology, sociology, or political science—each incorporates relevant aspects of other fields into his own presentation. Furthermore, the contributors not only present summaries of relevant literature and reports of original research but also attempt to apply their findings to the contemporary scene.

Believing that the state of development of the field warrants it, the editor and the contributors have aimed higher than the production of a collection of independent papers. They have striven to integrate the individual contributions into a coherent whole. The editor is unusually well qualified for this task by years of work at home and abroad on transcultural problems.

This volume contributes significantly toward an applied social science of international relations. We may hope that, along with other disciplines, this new science will supply the concepts and facts from which statesmen can construct an international system of stable peace before it is too late.

Jerome D. Frank

President-Elect,
Society for the Psychological Study
of Social Issues

April 1965

Preface

For several years a local workgroup, affiliated with the Society for the Psychological Study of Social Issues, met in the Boston area to discuss various topics in international relations. In 1958–1959 the group devoted a series of meetings to discussing the possibility of a volume on social-psychological approaches to international relations, which would provide some integration and direction for that budding area of research. It is out of these discussions that the conception of the present volume developed. The members of the workgroup, during the period that these discussions were held, were Curtis Barker, Norman Berkowitz, Inge Schneier Hoffmann, Helen Perry, Stewart Perry, Thomas Pettigrew, Victor Sanua, and myself.

The original proposal for the volume was presented to SPSSI Council in 1959. Council voted to sponsor the volume as a SPSSI publication, asked me to serve as its editor, and, in consultation with me, appointed the Editorial Committee. I proceeded to develop a detailed outline for the volume and to line up contributors. In this process, I benefited greatly from the advice of the members of the Editorial Committee; the members of the Boston area workgroup, particularly Inge Schneier Hoffmann and Helen and Stewart Perry, with whom I spent many hours of private conversation about the emerging outline; and a number of other individuals, particularly Gordon Allport, Walter Mischel, David Singer, and Kurt Wolff.

The outline was completed in January 1960. It constituted an attempt to spell out in some detail the domains of the various chapters and to place them within a general, if rudimentary, conceptual framework. It was hoped that this would facilitate the unity and integration of the volume as a whole. Perhaps I can indicate most effectively what we were trying to achieve by quoting from the introductory section of the 1960 outline, in which our conception of the volume was reviewed:

1. The book will consist of a series of chapters by different authors, written especially for this volume. Despite the fact that different authors will be involved, it will attempt to approximate, as much as possible, an integrated text with maximal continuity between different parts of the book. To achieve this goal, a general conceptual framework will be developed that will underlie the entire book. This framework will not be intended as a formal comprehensive theory, but rather as a more or less systematic structure out of which a series of questions emerge, and in terms of which answers or potential answers can be organized.

2. Substantively, the volume will be concerned with social-psychological variables involved in international interactions—real or symbolic, among members of various elites or of the populations at large. Emphasis will be on problems for which some empirical materials are available, or which are potentially translatable into empirical research. When there are no relevant data or concepts, the gaps will be pointed up and an attempt will be made to develop concepts and researchable hypotheses. The volume is not intended as a handbook: The emphasis will not be on a comprehensive review of research, but on a selective and interpretive one. Hopefully, each chapter and the volume as a whole will tell a story, make a point, develop a thesis. Theorizing and speculation are definitely in order —when these center around the focus of the volume: international behavior as a research problem.

3. The focus of the volume is defined as research on international behavior, rather than "psychological research relevant to war and peace." The problem of war and peace is, of course, of central concern in this volume, and explicitly or implicitly it will be raised throughout. But the volume will not represent a deliberate, systematic attempt to explain psychological causes of war or proposals for peace. Rather, it will concentrate on the study of the social-psychological processes that occur when nationals and governments interact. It will attempt to bring together those problems that are directly amenable to social-psychological investigation, in an effort to contribute to the development of international behavior as a special area of research within social psychology. Any research in this area is, of course, potentially relevant to problems of war and peace, but there will be no attempt to demonstrate this at every point. The study of international behavior will be viewed as an area of concern in its own right, and the organization of the volume will be dictated by its inherent demands.

4. The book can probably serve as a text for special courses on international behavior, whether these are given by psychology, sociology, or political science departments. As a matter of fact, it is our hope that the existence of such a book might encourage the development of new courses in this area. The book could also serve as a source of additional readings for courses in social psychology, political behavior, and international relations. It might also be a useful summary of social-psychological approaches for people in related disciplines, particularly political science and international relations, as well as for people who are professionally involved in foreign service, exchange of personnel, adult education in foreign affairs, etc. Accordingly, the book should not require too much psychological knowledge of a technical nature on the part of the reader. At the same time, we hope that the book will serve as a stimulating integration for the researcher or potential researcher in this field.

It has been a long time since these words were written, but they still represent a fair description of the purposes of this volume. The reader will be able to judge for himself how close the finished product comes to achieving these original goals. That they were not completely achieved goes without saying. For example, it turned out—much to my dismay—that the contributors had their own ideas about what they wanted to put into their respective chapters! And so, inevitably, each chapter represents an individually negotiated compromise between what the original outline demanded and what the authors were willing to supply. The resulting chapters have the great advantage of constituting statements about the status of various specialized problems, as seen by specialists who are actively involved in conceptualizing and investigating these problems. At the same time, it seems to me that the volume does approximate the kind of integration that we hoped to achieve.

As part of our effort to achieve integration, a two-day conference of chapter authors and members of the Editorial Committee was held in Cambridge, Mass., in May of 1960. To make this conference possible, it was necessary to obtain financial support in addition to the funds made available by SPSSI Council. I am very grateful, in this connection, to the Human Ecology Fund and to James Monroe, the Fund's Executive Secretary at the time, for their prompt, generous, and delightfully nonbureaucratic response to my request.

There have been some changes in the roster of contributors to the volume since May 1960: Some authors have withdrawn, and others have come in; some chapters have been dropped, and others added. Nevertheless, a large proportion of the final contributors did participate in the conference. They thus played an important role (along with the Editorial Committee) in shaping the definition of the volume. The conference contributed, moreover, to the development of a shared image of the volume and its purposes, and of the place of each chapter in the larger framework.

There are many individuals, some of whom have already been mentioned, who have made valuable contributions at various stages of the development of this project. I want to express special gratitude to the members of the Editorial Committee and to Wayman Crow, Irving Janis, Judith Long, Anatol Rapoport, John Raser, James Robinson, and David Singer, for their critical reading of various individual chapters and their helpful comments on them. I could not have done without the dedicated administrative and secretarial help of Mary Lynne Bird during the earlier phases of this project and of Catherine Hoch during the later phases. I am also greatly indebted to Catherine Hoch and Judith Long for their extensive work in the preparation of the index.

A large part of the final editorial work on the volume was done in the spring and summer of 1964, while I was a Visiting Fellow at the Western Behavioral Sciences Institute in La Jolla, California. I am very grateful to Richard Farson, Director of the Institute, and to the entire staff, for providing me with the atmosphere and the facilities that I needed for completing this work. My conversations at the Institute with Wayman Crow, Robert Noel, John Raser, and Richard Snyder were especially stimulating in connection with my work on this volume. The excellent secretarial assistance of Patricia Falck was indispensable.

Finally, I want to thank my wife, Rose, not only for her concrete assistance, but also for her patience and encouragement throughout the years that this volume was in progress. Her faith in the viability and value of this enterprise kept me going on the many occasions when I was about to give up. I am sure that my fellow-contributors will approve of my decision to dedicate this volume to her.

H.C.K.

Ann Arbor, Michigan
April 1965

Contents

Part Two: Processes of Interaction
in International Relations

Conclusion

Introduction

Social-Psychological Approaches to the Study of International Relations

DEFINITION OF SCOPE

Herbert C. Kelman

During the past decade or so, ever-increasing attention has been paid to the systematic analysis of the psychological aspects of international relations. There has been a steady growth of theory and empirical research on problems of international behavior in general, which has included the concerted use of psychological—and particularly social-psychological—concepts and methods. Part of this development has involved the attempt to define certain aspects of war and peace as researchable problems, to which the tools of behavioral science can be applied. At the same time, psychologists and social scientists in related fields have increasingly addressed themselves to matters of policy in the field of international relations: They have questioned some of the psychological assumptions underlying various approaches to foreign policy and have developed policy recommendations based, at least in part, on psychological considerations.

We are witnessing the beginnings of what seems to be a new and rather vigorous area of specialization. It is impossible to define exact boundaries for this emerging field, which of necessity spans several disciplines, but it might loosely be called the "social psychology of international relations."

THE DEVELOPMENT OF A SOCIAL PSYCHOLOGY OF INTERNATIONAL RELATIONS

Before attempting to define the scope of this new area of specialization, let us examine some of the historical antecedents of the more recent developments.

Earlier Approaches

The concern of psychologists with problems of international relations is by no means an entirely new development of the past ten years. Research efforts in this general area go back at least to the early 1930s. It was at that time, for example, that some of the associates of L. L. Thurstone at the University of Chicago initiated studies of attitudes toward war and related matters (for example, Droba, 1931). In the early 1940s Ross Stagner and associates published a series of studies on attitudes toward war, nationalism, and aggression in other areas of social life (for example, Stagner, 1942 and 1944), as well as attitudes toward war prevention (Stagner, Brown, Gundlach, & White, 1942). Much of this work was done under the auspices of the Society for the Psychological Study of Social Issues Committee on the Psychology of War and Peace. There were various other studies during these years, particularly in the areas of national stereotypes, attitudes toward international relations, and sources of aggressive attitudes. The entire domain of research on social-psychological aspects of international relations, through 1949, was thoroughly reviewed by Klineberg (1950). Reviews of specific problems within this field can be found in some of the chapters of a volume edited by Pear (1950), especially the chapter by Eysenck (1950). One must also note the steady development of public opinion research, which led to an accumulation, over the years, of data relevant to national images and attitudes toward foreign policy issues. Many of the findings based on American samples were brought together and integrated by Gabriel Almond in his study of *The American people and foreign policy* (1950).

In addition to these research efforts, there were various attempts to develop theories of war and peace based on psychological concepts. Some of these were formulated primarily in psychoanalytic terms (Glover, 1946; Durbin & Bowlby, 1939; Waelder, 1939). Others were rooted in general-psychological frameworks, particularly in theories of learning (Tolman, 1942; May, 1943). Finally, psychologists and social scientists in related disciplines addressed themselves to the psychological barriers to peace and determinants of tension, in an effort to develop recommendations for action conducive to tension reduction and international cooperation. Thus, the third yearbook of the Society for the Psychological Study of Social Issues, edited by Gardner Murphy (1945), was devoted to a detailed analysis of obstacles to peace and an attempt to carve out a concrete program toward world order. In two later volumes (Cantril, 1950; Kisker, 1951), psychological and social scientists from different parts of the world analyzed various aspects of national and international tensions. These efforts were direct expressions of the value orientation that also motivated most of the other activities of psychologists in this area.

Despite this activity, one certainly could not speak of an area of specialization in the social psychology of international relations. The total volume of research on these problems was exceedingly small, and it focused almost entirely on national stereotypes, attitudes toward war, and public opinion on foreign policy issues. While the study of these factors is and continues to be a central contribution of a social-psychological analysis, it touches only indirectly on the actual interaction between nations or their nationals. There was hardly any research on the processes that are set into motion when persons of different nationalities interact with each other, on either an official or an unofficial basis. Nor was there any research designed to trace the psychological processes involved in international politics. It is interesting that the only research on interaction between nations presented in the Pear (1950) volume was done by a physicist, L. F. Richardson, whose work has attracted a great deal of attention with the growth of this field of research in recent years (see Chapter 11 and elsewhere in this volume). Even the work on images and attitudes was largely of a descriptive nature. In particular, very little if anything was written before 1950 attempting to link images and attitudes to the interaction between nations—in other words, to assess how such images and attitudes develop out of the relationship between two nations, and what role they play in the foreign policy process. Those studies in which correlates of international attitudes were explored tended to focus on their relationship to other social attitudes, to personality characteristics, and to demographic variables, rather than to features of the international system.

None of these observations is intended as criticism of the earlier work in this area. It would be unreasonable to criticize this area of research for what it has *not* done, particularly if one keeps in mind that this line of work was just in its beginnings and that investigators were working with extremely limited resources. But it should be evident that social-psychological aspects of international relations did not constitute an area of specialization in its own right. What work was done on problems in this area was largely done in the context of the general study of social attitudes, and sometimes in the context of personality research, rather than in the context of the study of international relations.

It is not surprising, therefore, that much that was written by psychologists and psychiatrists on questions of war and peace tended to be at a level removed from the interaction between nations. It did not grow out of specialized study of the psychological aspects of international relations, but rather involved the application to the international situation of psychological principles derived from other areas of work. Such applications can be highly relevant insofar as they deal with general psychological assumptions that might influence international policy. An example of a relevant application of this kind is the conclusion, reached by most psychologists and other social scientists, that psychological and anthropological research offers no support for the assumption that war is rooted in human nature and hence inevitable (see Allport, 1945; Murphy, 1945, p. 455; Cantril, 1950, p. 17). Similarly, it is possible to apply psychological principles derived from work in other areas to certain specific problems in international relations—such as the effects of stress on decision-making processes. Any attempt, however, to conceptualize the causes of war and the conditions for peace that starts from individual psychology rather than from an analysis of the relations between nation-states is of questionable relevance.

Thus, some psychological writers, starting from individual behavior, have tended to overemphasize the role of aggression. They seemed to reason that, since war represents aggressive behavior on the part of nation-states, one can understand its causes by examining the determinants of aggressive behavior in individuals. Occasionally this reasoning was by analogy, but most commonly it was based on the assumption that the behavior of states consists, after all, of the behaviors of individuals. This assumption, however, ignores the fact that the behavior of nations is the aggregation of a variety of behaviors on the part of many individuals, representing different roles, different interests, different degrees of influence on final decisions, and contributing in very different ways to the complex social processes that eventuate in a final outcome such as war. One cannot, therefore, expect that the behavior of a nation will be a direct reflection of the motives of its citizens or even of its leaders. While war does involve aggressive behavior on the part of many individuals, this behavior is not necessarily at the service of aggressive motives. Leaders may engage in aggressive behavior for strategic reasons, for example, and the population at large for reasons of social conformity. Even where aggressive motives are involved in predisposing national leaders to precipitate war and segments of the population to support it enthusiastically,[1] their role in the causation of war cannot be understood without an examination of the societal (and intersocietal) processes that are involved in the decision to engage in war, and of the way in which different elements of the society enter into these processes. There are certainly things to be learned from the psychology of aggression that are relevant to international relations, but they cannot be applied automatically; only by starting from an analysis of international relations at their own level can one identify the points at which such application becomes relevant.

The personal motivations that play a part in people's preference for war or willingness to accept it are manifold. The motivations of fear and distrust, for example, are likely to be far more relevant to modern warfare than is personal aggression. Even a more complex analysis of the motivational patterns of individuals, however, which takes the entire range of motives into account, is not a proper starting-point for the study of war. War is a societal and intersocietal action carried out in a national and international political context. What has to be explained is the way in which nations, given various societal and political conditions, arrive at various international policies, including war. Part of this explanation involves the motivations and perceptions of different individuals—both decision-makers and various publics—who play different roles in the larger societal process. But only if we know where and how these individuals fit into the larger process, and under what constraints they operate, are we able to offer a relevant psychological analysis. Thus, the study of psychological processes is highly relevant to a full understanding of the causation of war, *if* it recognizes that societal and political conditions provide the framework within which the motivations and perceptions of individuals can function.

Some of the conceptualizations of war and peace that take individual psychology as their point of departure have been marked by another characteristic, related to the emphasis on aggression and other personal motives. This is the tendency to use the language of psychopathology, and to treat war as a form of deviation comparable to psychotic behavior in individuals. Now, war may be an extremely irrational form of societal behavior, in terms of the balance between costs and gains; certainly very few observers today would regard *nuclear* war as an instrument of policy that one would deliberately choose on the basis of rational considerations. But

---

[1] It is interesting that most of the psychological analyses of war that stress the role of aggression were written with an eye to Nazi Germany, where the assumption about aggressive motives in many leaders and perhaps large segments of the population may have been more justified than is usually the case.

this does not mean that the causes of war are in any way comparable to the etiology of pathological behavior in individuals. Such an analogy is likely to obscure the societal and intersocietal dynamics that generate conflicts between nations and that favor particular mechanisms for their resolution.

Insights derived from the study of behavior pathology are certainly relevant to the way in which individuals—decision-makers and members of the population at large—react to other nations and to foreign policy issues. Thus, for example, projection and other forms of perceptual distortion, denial in the face of threat, or rigidity in a situation of stress, are behavior mechanisms that often occur in response to international situations. But—in line with our discussion of psychological processes in general—whether and how these mechanisms contribute to the causation of war can only be understood in terms of the larger societal processes that serve as their context.

A clear implication of the preceding observations is that it makes little sense to speak of *a* psychological theory of war or of international relations. There cannot be a psychological theory that is complete and self-contained and can in any way be proposed as an alternative to other theories, such as economic or political. There can only be a general theory of international relations in which psychological factors play a part, once the points in the process at which they are applicable have been properly identified. Within such a framework, however, psychological—and, particularly, social-psychological—analyses can potentially make a considerable contribution to the study of international politics, and of international behavior in general. This is the conviction on which the present volume is based.

The tendency, particularly in some of the earlier psychological and psycho-analytic writings on war and peace, to focus on aggression and other motives of individuals and to emphasize irrational and pathological processes, without taking the societal and political context into account, has caused some specialists in international relations to question the relevance of psychological contributions. There is no inherent reason, however, why psychological analyses must ignore the environmental context within which behavior occurs, or must focus on irrational processes at the expense of rational ones. In recent years, the trend in psychology in general has been to move away from this kind of orientation. Psychological analyses of international relations, in particular, have tended increasingly to start at the level of international relations itself and to observe behavior within the context thus provided. Similarly, they have increasingly tended to use conceptual approaches in which neither rationality nor irrationality is a built-in assumption, but in which, instead, both cognitive and affective factors are integral parts of a common explanatory scheme.

Recent Developments

The social-psychological study of international relations in recent years certainly has not overcome all the shortcomings of earlier work in this area. In absolute terms, the amount of research on these problems is still very small, and the amount of dependable evidence that has been amassed is smaller yet. As the present volume will indicate, our ability to pose questions is not always matched by our ability to answer them. We have to consider seriously the possibilities—raised by some critics—that some of the current research and conceptualization may have only limited relevance to international politics, and especially to the issues of war and peace; that they may pay insufficient attention to the political realities that set constraints on psychological processes; that they may overemphasize the role of attitudinal and personal factors in national behavior; and that they may not focus their analysis on the right people and the right settings. Some of these issues are taken up in several of the chapters in this volume, and I shall return to the whole problem of the relevance of social-psychological research in the final chapter. There is no question, though, that many fundamental methodological and theoretical issues must be clarified as this field develops, before we can begin to resolve the problem of relevance.

Nevertheless, there has been a change of such proportions in the social-psychological study of international relations during recent years that one is justified in describing this area as having reached a new stage in its development. The volume of work has greatly increased and there has been a concomitant growth in quality and sophistication. The earlier work on international attitudes and public opinion has continued, at a greater rate and with greater methodological refinement, and with increasing attempts to link it more closely to the foreign policy process. There have been quite a number of studies focusing directly on cross-national contact and interaction. There have been various attempts to study international conflict and its resolution experimentally and thus to deal more concretely with issues of foreign policy-making. Many of the investigators in this area are acutely aware of the problems of generalization that this kind of research entails, and make serious attempts to grapple with them: to explore the international situation to which they hope to be able to generalize, and the conditions that would have

to be met in order to permit such generalization.

There is, in general, a concern with the theoretical and methodological issues involved in the psychological analysis of international relations, including the questions of what role psychological variables play in internation behavior and what constitutes a proper unit of analysis. In recent theoretical formulations, there is a greater tendency to start with questions derived from an analysis of international conflict and the interaction between nations, and to introduce psychological concepts whenever they can contribute to answering these questions. This has meant a decline in global approaches to the psychology of war and peace, with greater attention to the psychological analysis of specific subproblems. Similarly, psychological contributions to policy questions have tended to be more specific and more directly related to concrete issues in foreign affairs.

All these activities have taken place within a climate that has become increasingly favorable to research on problems of war and peace. Until recently, war and peace "has not been a respectable, meaningful target of rigorous inquiry" for most students of human behavior (Snyder & Robinson, 1961, p. 13). But the situation has changed, probably due to a combination of forces within and outside the social-science community. The external forces no doubt include the advent of nuclear weapons and the consequent change in the meaning of war; the occurrence of various crises engendered by the Cold War; and the gradual relaxation of Cold-War tensions and, in the United States, of the pressures of the McCarthy era. The internal forces probably include the steady growth of behavioral approaches in political science; the development of more complex theoretical models in psychology; and the emergence of an interdisciplinary behavioral science.

Whatever its sources, this new climate is clearly evident. In the early 1950s, the *Bulletin of the Research Exchange on the Prevention of War*—published by a small group of social psychologists who believed that the problems of war and peace were susceptible to social-science research—had a very small readership and practically no research to report. The Bulletin's successor, however, the *Journal of Conflict Resolution,* soon became a vital and vigorous interdisciplinary publication, with a steady flow of empirical and theoretical contributions reflecting the greatly accelerated rate of activity. There are now a number of research centers and research programs, focusing partly or entirely on social-psychological aspects of international relations. There are committees in professional associations and symposia at professional meetings; there are research conferences and societies. There are inventories of research needs—such as those sponsored by the Institute for International Order (see especially Pool, 1961; and Snyder & Robinson, 1961), and abstracting services for literature on peace research—such as the one sponsored by the Canadian Peace Research Institute. There are undergraduate courses and graduate seminars and—what is perhaps the most promising indicator for the future—the number of doctoral dissertations in this area has increased considerably.

Since all of these developments are extremely recent and still very much in progress, it is difficult to gain the necessary distance to assess them properly. Yet it does seem that these developments include the emergence of a new area of specialization—a social psychology of international relations that begins with the problems of interaction between nations and the individuals within them at their own level, rather than as extensions of individual psychology. It is a young field, an underdeveloped field, a field with many basic issues unresolved and with few concrete conclusions to its credit—but it does have the characteristics of a field of specialization in its initial phase.[2] The present volume is an attempt to assess the status of this field at the moment—to point up what we know, where the gaps are, what approaches are available for filling these gaps, and what problems can and cannot be handled by the use of these approaches.

It will be quite apparent from this volume that the use of social-psychological concepts and methods is by no means restricted to psychologists and sociologists. Much of the work in this vein is done by political scientists, and some by anthropologists, economists, mathematicians, and an occasional historian. It would probably be more accurate to speak, not of the development of a social psychology of international relations, but of the development of approaches to the study of international behavior in which social-psychological concepts and methods play an integral part. It is one of the key characteristics of the behavioral study of international relations that it cannot possibly be linked to a single discipline. The disciplinary background of a large proportion of the contributors to this field is, of necessity, political science with a

---

[2] It is important to note that the chapters in this volume are written by specialists, on their specialized problems, rather than by people who address themselves to these problems from the perspective of work in other areas. Ten or fifteen years ago it would have been difficult to gather together such a roster of specialists, because of the relative absence of research directly in this area.

specialization in international relations. But they are supported by investigators with a variety of disciplinary backgrounds, and all of these investigators draw very heavily on all of the behavioral sciences. There is, moreover, an increasing number of workers in this field who completely defy classification in terms of the standard disciplinary categories.

The development of social-psychological approaches has to be seen in the context of this broader interdisciplinary development of the behavioral study of international relations. The social-psychological aspects are by no means coterminous with the field as a whole, but it is neither possible nor desirable to draw sharp lines between them. The nature of the problems in this field is such that they generally require a combination of different levels of analysis (cf. Snyder, 1962). It becomes impossible, therefore, to divide them in terms of the usual disciplinary categories. Indeed, it is in large part the embeddedness of current psychological work on international relations in this larger interdisciplinary effort, and particularly its close ties with political science, that make it qualitatively different from the work of earlier years.

In addition to its interdisciplinary character—interdisciplinary not only in the sense that it represents a collaboration of investigators based in different disciplines, but also in the sense that its concepts and methods represent a genuine pooling of the resources of different disciplines—there are two other features that distinguish the behavioral study of international relations. One is the variety of methods that are used —laboratory experiments, simulation studies, surveys, observational studies, content analyses of historical documents, organizational studies, interviews with informants—and the readiness with which investigators combine different sources of data and shift from one to the other. While some investigators tend to prefer one or another method, there appears to be little tendency for the field to be divided along lines of methodological preference. The other distinguishing feature is the apparently comfortable combination of different purposes. There are no sharp divisions between concern with theory-building and concern with practical application, between an interest in the development of a methodology and an interest in addressing policy issues. Very often, the same investigator will shift from one to the other of these emphases on different occasions.

THE NATURE OF SOCIAL-PSYCHOLOGICAL CONTRIBUTIONS

Within the broader context of the behavioral study of international relations, what are the special contributions of social-psychological approaches? The efforts to which social-psychological approaches have contributed during the past few years can be described in terms of four categories: (1) the study of the "international behavior" of individuals; (2) the study of international politics and foreign policy; (3) the development of theory and methodology in international relations; and (4) the formulation of policy recommendations. While these categories are highly overlapping, each one points to a different type of function that can be performed by a social-psychological analysis.

The Study of the "International Behavior" of Individuals

This category involves, essentially, what Klineberg calls "the human dimension in international relations" in the title of his recent book (1964). The concern here is with the ways in which individuals relate themselves to their own nation and other nations, to the international system as a whole, to problems of foreign policy, and to the broader issues of war and peace; and with the study of actual interactions between individuals across national boundaries.

The research that falls into this category has varying degrees of relevance to international politics and the behavior of nations. Much depends, for example, on whose attitudes and whose interactions are being investigated. The study of attitudes and interactions of diplomats and national decision-makers obviously has more direct relevance to international politics than the study of average citizens contemplating foreign policy questions or traveling abroad. But regardless of its degree of relevance to international politics (a question to which I shall return later), the research in this category is meaningful and justified in its own right. It focuses on the special kinds of problems that arise when individuals confront—directly or indirectly—other nations and the international system. The contributions of social psychology are most obvious and most direct here, for the problems in this category are specifically and inherently of a social-psychological nature in that they concern social interaction (under a special set of circumstances) and the relation of the individual to social institutions.

Some of the types of research in this category that have been conducted in the past ten to fifteen years will be summarized in the following paragraphs.

1. *Attitudes toward International Affairs.* There have been some attempts, recently, to supplement data from opinion polls, which generally use only one or two structured questions on a given issue, with more intensive and exten-sive surveys. Thus, there have been some studies of national samples in the United States (for example, Withey, 1961) and in Canada (Paul & Laulicht, 1963) in which questions on a whole range of foreign policy issues were asked. Such studies make it possible to explore the relationships between different sets of attitudes and images, between general policy orientations and reactions to specific issues, and between attitudes and various demographic variables. There have also been a number of studies, usually focusing on special samples (such as students or residents of a particular geographical area), assessing attitudes in response to a specific international situation, such as the Cuban crisis in 1962 (for example, Chesler & Schmuck, 1964); or in relation to a specific policy issue, such as civil defense (for example, Barton, 1963; Ekman *et al.*, 1963; Rose, 1963). In such studies it is possible to examine in greater detail the way in which reactions to specific issues are linked to the more general attitudes toward foreign affairs held by individuals and groups.

General attitudes toward foreign affairs have also been examined in a number of studies, with particular emphasis on individuals' readiness to adopt a belligerent stand in international relations. Such attitudes have been related to the social characteristics (for example, Putney & Middleton, 1962) and personality dispositions of the respondents (Christiansen, 1959; Levinson, 1957), as well as to their reactions to communications about international events (Gladstone & Taylor, 1958). Finally, there is research underway to develop scaling procedures for international attitudes that, among other things, would permit periodic attitude measurement as one indicator of the state of the international system (Levy & Hefner, 1964).

One crucial line of research, which is just beginning to take shape, is the investigation of the dynamics of attitudes on international affairs, focusing on the psychological and social processes involved in the development of general orientations toward foreign policy issues within a society and the crystallization of reactions in specific cases. The specific application of research on communication and attitude change to the area of international attitudes is a related research need.

2. *National and International Loyalties.* A key area for social-psychological research is the study of the relationship of the individual to the nation-state, which in turn defines his relationship to the international system. There have been some studies of psychological aspects of nationalism (for example, Doob, 1962; Terhune, 1964), and the research on ethnocentrism certainly has some relevance here. But very little has been done on the nature of the commitment of the individual to the nation-state, on his definition of the rights and duties of the citizen, on the kinds of satisfactions that he derives from his relation to the state, and on his conceptions of the position and purposes of the nation in the international system. What is needed here is research on national ideology, as it is communicated by the national system and as it is interpreted by individuals and groups; on the way this ideology develops; and on the kinds of behaviors it calls forth under various conditions of arousal (including various national symbols). Theoretical analyses in terms of national role (Perry, 1957), social communication (K. Deutsch, 1953), and political ideology in general can be applied to research on this problem.

One type of research that has been gaining momentum recently is the study of special subgroups within the population—such as the extreme right (cf. Proshansky & Evans, 1963)—who, among other things, have special definitions of the role of the national vis-à-vis the nation-state, and of the nation vis-à-vis the international system. Similar questions can be posed with respect to the peace movement, in which there has also been an increasing research interest.

Different kinds of national ideology have different implications for international cooperation, participation in international organizations, and the willingness to surrender sovereignty to international bodies. A closely related area of research, therefore, is the study of the determinants of an international-ist ideology, and particularly of the conditions for the development of multiple loyalties (Guetzkow, 1955). Other problems to which social-psychological research will increasingly address itself are the developing nationalism in emerging nations, the problems of dual loyalty for employees of international organizations, and the ideological underpinnings for such supranational agencies as the European Economic Community.

3. *Images and Stereotypes of Other Nations.* The earlier work in this area has been continued, but also has pushed forward in various directions. There have been various attempts to study images cross-nationally (cf. Duijker & Frijda, 1960; Campbell & LeVine, 1961); to explore their development in children (for example, Lambert & Klineberg, 1959); to discover, through intensive interviews, their sources and the way in which they function (for example, Isaacs, 1958); to show their relationship to the political alignments between the nations in question (Buchanan & Cantril, 1953; cf. also Bronfenbrenner, 1961); and to study their effect on the perception of individuals belonging to these nations (Bruner & Perlmutter, 1957). Personality disposi-

tions to like or dislike foreign nations in general (Perlmutter, 1954, 1956) and the personal meanings that images of a particular nation may have for different individuals (Smith, Bruner, & White, 1956) have also been explored. Finally, a number of studies have investigated effects of cross-national contact on images (see later).

There has been only little systematic effort so far to relate images to national and international events; and, in particular, to explore in detail the way in which they are affected by and in turn affect the relations between nations. This is certainly an area requiring more research, as is the relationship between images of other nations and images of their nationals, which are obviously interdependent, but not completely so.

4. *Cross-National Contacts.* In recent years there have been numerous studies of cross-national contact, dealing with the processes of interaction between nationals of different countries, the problems of adjustment in a foreign culture, and the effects of personal contacts on images and attitudes. Most of the studies have dealt with foreign students in the United States (see M. B. Smith, 1956; Coelho, 1962; and Lundstedt, 1963, for reports of many of these studies). There have been some studies, however, of students and scholars in countries other than the United States (cf. Danckwortt, 1959). And there have also been studies of various groups of Americans traveling abroad, including students participating in special programs (for example, H. P. Smith, 1955; Isaacs, 1961), Fulbright grantees (Gullahorn & Gullahorn, 1963), Peace Corps volunteers

(Smith *et al.*, 1963), and businessmen (Pool *et al.*, 1956). Various applied problems in this area have also been investigated, such as the evaluation of international exchange programs (Kelman, 1963), the selection of personnel for overseas work (cf. Torre, 1963), and the conduct of international conferences.

It would be very useful to link research on cross-national contacts with research on national and international loyalties by studying interaction among representatives of different countries in more official contexts, including international and supranational organizations, and the effects of such interactions on their integration into an international network.

The Study of International Politics and Foreign Policy

This category refers essentially to the behavior of nations, or of decision-makers acting for their nations. The concern here is with the determinants of policy and with their effects on the national and international systems. Of special interest are international conflict and its resolution, and the conditions under which outcomes in the form of war become more or less probable. Clearly, research in this category—unlike the preceding one—is by no means specifically social-psychological. Social-psychological approaches can, however, *contribute* certain concepts and methods that promise to be of some value in a concerted attack on these problems from different vantage points. The relevance of these contributions to the study of international politics may be open to some questions[3]—a matter to which I shall return in the final

---

[3] It should be noted, of course, that the researches in this category are of interest in their own right, whether or not they are relevant to international politics. Many of them have direct and obvious relevance to certain other problems. For example, an experimental study of bargaining in a two-person game may or may not be relevant to the understanding of international negotiation, but it is certainly relevant to the investigation of interpersonal trust.

chapter—but many specialists in international relations see them as potentially useful tools for grappling with the thorny problems of their field. Let us review briefly some of the types of research in this general category that have been conducted in the past ten to fifteen years.

1. *Public Opinion in the Foreign Policy Process.* Public opinion research has a great deal of relevance to the study of internation behavior, provided deliberate attention is paid to the way in which public opinion (in general, and on specific kinds of issues) affects the formulation and conduct of foreign policy. This in turn requires an analysis of the broader assumptions and purposes that serve as the context within which foreign policy is carried out and within which public opinion can therefore influence the probability of various choices; and of the roles played by different segments of the public in the policy process.

Studies on the distribution of attitudes toward foreign policy issues in the population at large can be useful, insofar as they give an indication of general "moods" that decision-makers are likely to share and to take into account (cf. Almond, 1950). Public opinion studies become more directly relevant if—as is increasingly true—they focus in whole or in part on certain elite groups (for example, Free, 1959; Paul & Laulicht, 1963). Some recent studies have explored in detail the attitudes of special elite groups toward specific foreign policy issues, and have investigated both the sources of these attitudes and the way in which they feed into the decision-making process (for example, Bauer, Pool, & Dexter, 1963; Rosenau, 1963).

In addition to opinion studies per se, there has also been some research on the ways in which different segments of the public—including the "mass public," the "attentive public," and the policy and opinion elites or the "opinion-making public" (cf. Almond, 1950; Rosenau, 1961)—relate themselves to foreign policy issues. Such research has focused on the distribution of information, interest, and activity relating to foreign affairs within the general population; the characteristics of those who constitute attentive publics and opinion leaders; and (to a lesser extent) the way in which opinions on foreign policy matters circulate within the public. (See Hero, 1959a, 1959b, and 1960, for comprehensive reviews of relevant research at all levels of the public.)

There is a need for more detailed research on the actual processes whereby public opinion affects foreign policy decisions. One specifically social-psychological aspect of such research would concern the conditions that generate a particular mood in the public, that determine the choices the public perceives, and that mobilize certain segments of it into various kinds of action. Another would involve decision-makers themselves and explore their general conception of the role of public opinion in the policy process, the way in which they assess the shape of public opinion in any given situation, and the impact it has on their decision behavior.

2. *Individual Actors in the Foreign Policy Process.* A recent focus for conceptualization and research in international politics has been the behavior of the individual actors who are involved in the formulation and execution of foreign policy. Particular emphasis has been placed on the psychological and social processes that come into play when responsible decision-makers choose between alternative actions to be taken by the state (cf. Snyder, Bruck, & Sapin, 1962). This line of research is often—though not necessarily—based on

the assumption that the decision-makers in any given situation *are* the state and that the study of the decision-making process is therefore the most direct way of studying state behavior.

This assumption is particularly appropriate where research focuses on specific major decision cases. Thus, the Snyder-Bruck-Sapin model has been applied to an extensive and detailed study of the United States decision to resist aggression in Korea (Snyder & Paige, 1958). On the basis of interviews with the participants in this decision and examination of relevant documents, the attempt is made to reconstruct the interactions in the decisional unit, within the larger organizational system. This approach concerns itself with both the intellectual and the organizational processes involved in decision-making—with the definition of the situation, the problem-solving procedures, the exercise of leadership, and the flow of communication and influence.

A somewhat different approach to the study of international decision-making has been used by another group of researchers, who have developed detailed methods of content analysis in terms of a number of psychological dimensions (North *et al.*, 1963). This approach has been applied, for example, to a reconstruction of the events culminating in the decision to go to war in 1914, through content analysis of all available personal communications from the key decision-makers in different countries during the weeks preceding the outbreak of war (Zinnes *et al.*, 1961; Zinnes, 1962). The emphasis here is on the relationship of the perceptions and emotional reactions of authoritative individual actors to policy outcomes, in contrast to the Snyder model, which stresses interactional and organizational variables.

Both approaches generate hypotheses about the process and outcome of deci-

sion-making under varying conditions. They can also be applied outside of the context of specific decisions, in the study of the assumptions and perceptions of individual decision-makers that underlie their policy orientations (for example, Holsti, 1962) and in the study of the goals and decision processes that characterize organizational units with foreign policy responsibilities.

Research on individual actors in the foreign policy process, in addition to representing a way or operationalizing the behavior of states, may also be designed to explore some of the links in the chain that eventuates in certain state acts. Here the assumption is not that the individuals observed constitute the state for the purposes in question, but that they are important participants in and contributors to state action. By the same token, such research need not focus on the key decision-makers, but could deal with diplomats and other officials who play a variety of roles in the total process. Thus, there has been some research on individual participants in the foreign policy process both within national foreign policy organizations, such as the U.S. Department of State (Pruitt, 1962), and within international organizations, such as the U.N. (Alger, 1961). The research has concerned itself with the kinds of assumptions and role definitions that these individuals bring to their tasks, the kinds of actions and interactions in which they engage in the course of their work, and the ways in which these feed into the foreign policy process and—directly or indirectly—have an impact upon it.

3. *Processes of Interaction in International Conflict and Conflict Resolution.* A research area that has blossomed within the past few years is the experimental study of interaction between individuals or groups, with an

eye to illuminating processes of conflict and bargaining, of competition and cooperation, in the international arena. The underlying logic of this work involves the creation of experimental situations that are analogous, in certain fundamental ways, to the international situation, and that permit controlled observation of some of the interaction processes that also characterize the relations between nations. The assumption is that there is at least some basis for generalizing from the behavior of experimental subjects to the behavior of national decision-makers and negotiators. The validity of this assumption does not necessarily rest on the degree to which the real-life situation has been reproduced exactly in the laboratory, but on the degree to which the crucial variables in the real-life situation have been identified and incorporated in the experiment. Moreover, much depends on how the results of such experiments are used—particularly, as Snyder (1963) has indicated, on whether they are used for the purpose of verifying propositions or discovering new relationships.

Three types of experimental studies in this area can be distinguished. The first is best exemplified by the Inter-Nation Simulation (Guetzkow *et al.*, 1963), an ambitious attempt to simulate an international system—to create, in the laboratory, contrived "nations" with varying characteristics and assign the roles of national decision-makers to the subjects. In the Inter-Nation Simulation, the subjects do not behave as individuals, as in small-group experiments, but play the roles of decision-makers representing their nations. Feedback from their constituents actually enters into the simulation through the programming of intranational consequences of various decisions. Various foreign policy moves on the part of decision-makers—such as armament–disarmament, trade, aid, or alliance—and

various outcomes for the international system—such as tension level, international cooperation, and the outbreak of limited or nuclear war—can be observed. With the introduction of experimental interventions into the natural flow of the process, laboratory simulations can provide tests of specific hypotheses about the effects of various strategies, various military and political conditions, and various states of the international system (cf. Brody, 1963; Crow, 1963). Recent studies have used experimental variations in balanced designs to investigate the effects of certain weapons systems (Raser & Crow, 1964), and of crisis conditions (J. Robinson, C. Hermann, & Margaret Hermann, as described in Higgs & Weinland, 1964) on decision-making and on outcomes for the international system. Work currently underway also explores the effects of different values, as reflected in personal and cultural characteristics of the decision-makers.

The second type of experimental study is more removed from the level of international relations, but tries to incorporate some of the crucial variables involved in the interaction between nations. It takes the form of relatively simple two-man games, so structured that mixed (cooperative and competitive) motives are brought into play (cf. M. Deutsch, 1958; Deutsch & Krauss, 1962; Rapoport, 1963; Schelling, 1961). Choices of strategy in this type of conflict situation, processes of explicit and tacit bargaining, and outcomes for each party can be observed in these experiments. They have been studied as a function of such independent variables as the nature of the payoffs, the characteristics of the players, the definition of the situation, the opportunity for communication, and the availability of threats. The players in these games behave as individuals, but the kinds of choices that they have to make have some structural similarities to those with which national decision-makers are confronted. Recently, various procedures for extending experimental games of this sort so as to incorporate an ever-greater number of the characteristics of international conflict have been developed (Pilisuk & Rapoport, 1964).

The third type of experimental study involves the investigation of intergroup conflict, its manifestations, and its resolution in deliberately devised laboratory or field situations (cf. Sherif et al., 1961; Mouton & Blake, 1962; Bass & Dunteman, 1963). In these studies, subjects actually behave as members and representatives of their experimentally created groups, engaged in intergroup conflict, but these groups are, of course, at a level different from that of the nations to which one would hope to generalize. Among other things, the experimental groups, unlike nations, involve face-to-face interaction both within and between groups. Nevertheless, one can gain some insights into international relations by observing interactions between groups at different levels, provided some of the relevant variables are built into the experiment. By the same token, naturalistic studies of intergroup conflict and conflict resolution at different levels—such as studies of industrial or racial conflict—can serve as sources of insight about international conflict. Particularly germane are studies that focus on negotiation and bargaining processes in labor-management relations and other types of intergroup conflict (cf. Douglas, 1957; see also Blake & Mouton, 1962). These must, of course, be supplemented with observations and detailed study of negotiations at the international level itself (cf. Jensen, 1963), if full cognizance is to be taken of the unique features of international conflict and the limits of generalization from other levels.

The Development of Theory and Methodology in International Relations

Traditionally, the discipline of international relations has tended to place its emphasis on historical, descriptive, and normative approaches. In recent years, however, many scholars in the field have become increasingly oriented toward the formulation of general propositions about internation behavior, grounded in empirical observations. This has led to the development of theoretical models and to a general concern with the problem of theory construction in international relations and with the search for suitable methods (cf. Fox, 1959; Hoffmann, 1960; Claude, 1960; McClelland, 1960; Knorr & Verba, 1961; Singer, 1961a). Social-psychological approaches (along with others based, for example, in economics or sociology) have contributed to this process and are continuing to do so.

There have been a number of attempts by social psychologists to formulate certain limited aspects of international relations in terms of concepts derived from the study of small groups, social attitudes, role behavior, or intergroup relations (for example, Guetzkow, 1957; Kelman, 1955; Perry, 1957; Sherif, 1958). But, more than that, social-psychological processes—such as those relating to motivation, perception, trust and suspicion, definition of the situation, stress, communication, leadership, influence, norm formation, role prescription, group cohesiveness, loyalty—enter importantly into various general conceptualizations of the interaction between nations and foreign policy-making. Typically, these conceptualizations focus on the behavior of individual actors and their interactions for two interrelated reasons: (1) This focus gives investigators some leverage for analyzing the behavior of states in their relations with other states (cf. Snyder *et al.*, 1962; North *et al.*, 1963; Singer, 1961b). That is, it permits the application of certain conceptual schemes, such as the decision-making approach, to a detailed analysis of the generally elusive processes of state behavior. A formulation in terms of individual actors may also reveal certain characteristics of the international system itself, which do not emerge when the state is treated as the primary actor (Alger, 1963). (2) Conceptualization at this level facilitates the translation of theoretical variables into operational terms and hence the empirical testing of propositions (Schelling, 1961; Snyder, 1963).

The use of social-psychological concepts has gone hand in hand with the use of social-psychological methods, such as survey research, intensive interviewing, systematic observation, laboratory experiments, and content analysis in terms of psychological variables. There are many unresolved issues surrounding the role of social-psychological concepts and methods in international relations—such as the question of the proper unit of analysis in this area and the question of generalization from the laboratory to real life—but they do represent potentially useful tools at the present stage of theoretical and methodological development.

The Formulation of Policy Recommendations

Psychologists and other behavioral scientists have taken an increasingly active part in the foreign policy process during recent years, by bringing their specialized knowledge or analytic approach to bear on concrete policy issues (cf. Russell, 1961; Rose & Laulicht,

1963). Thus, social psychologists have examined some of the psychological assumptions underlying Cold-War policies, such as the doctrine of deterrence (cf. Milburn, 1961), and have recommended alternative policies on the basis of this examination. Other kinds of asumptions that could profitably be subjected to social-psychological analysis and research are assumptions about effective negotiation procedures (such as the notion that it is always best to negotiate from strength) or about the role of public opinion (such as the view that the public would not tolerate certain policy innovations). Psychologists have also examined some of the psychological mechanisms that reinforce Cold-War tensions by blocking adaptive responses to the situation (Frank, 1960) and creating distorted perceptions (Bronfenbrenner, 1961), and they have proposed ways of counteracting these mechanisms. Moreover, there have been analyses, from a social-psychological point of view, of the implications of certain specific policies (existing or proposed), such as the development of a national civil defense program (Waskow, 1962), or of certain general policy directions, such as those embodied in the programs for foreign aid and international exchange (Kelman, 1962a).

Psychologists, along with other social scientists, have developed specific proposals for new approaches to international relations, designed to promote disarmament, tension reduction, and international cooperation, and based, at least in part, on psychological considerations. The most influential contribution of this kind has been Osgood's (1962) proposal for graduated reciprocation in tension-reduction (GRIT), a carefully developed strategy based on unilateral initiatives by one side in the Cold War under conditions that are likely to lead to reciprocation by the other side. There have been other proposals, rooted in social-psychological analyses, for the development of activities involving international cooperation and interdependence, and conducive to the strengthening of values necessary to a peaceful world (M. Deutsch, 1962); and for the development of institutional arrangements and concomitant patterns of loyalty conducive to international security (Kelman, 1962b). Some attention has also been paid to the all-important problem of the psychological and social conditions on which the viability of a disarmed world depends (M. Deutsch, 1962; Frank, 1960).

Policy recommendations made by social psychologists can have varying degrees and kinds of relationship to relevant research evidence.

1. Some proposals may be based on extrapolations from general theoretical principles and the research evidence related to them, rather than on research specifically focused on the policy issue in question. The advocacy of specific policies on this basis is an entirely appropriate activity for the social scientist, not only because he is also a citizen, but because his specialized background enables him to make unique and valuable contributions to the policy process. He is able to bring to it a set of concepts, fund of information, and analytic approach that may provide a needed new perspective. The relevance of this contribution is particularly evident when one keeps in mind that all policies and policy proposals, whatever their source, involve certain basic psychological and sociological assumptions. Certainly the social scientist is in the best position to speak to these assumptions, even in the absence of specific research on the policy issue in question.

In making policy recommendations on the basis of extrapolations from general social science knowledge, how-ever, it is particularly important to be clear about the distinction between research evidence and value preference. There should be no implication that the mere fact that a policy is advocated by a social scientist endows it with scientific validity. Insofar as possible, recommendations should be supported by existing research evidence; and where there is no relevant research, this should be clearly communicated. Policy recommendations based on social-psychological principles cannot wait until all the data are in, but the ultimate value of such contributions rests on the extent to which they can be backed up by research that is directly relevant. The feasibility of such research is demonstrated, for example, by the recent efforts to put some of the implications of Osgood's GRIT model (1962) to the experimental test (Crow, 1963; see also Pilisuk & Rapoport, 1964).

2. Policy recommendations may be based also on extrapolations from a specific body of research that has fairly direct relevance to the policy issue in question. Examples of this kind of approach would be recommendations for the planning of international exchange programs, derived from the research on students and scholars sojourning in foreign countries; recommendations for the conduct of international negotiations, derived from experiments on bargaining and negotiation; and recommendations for the formulation of American policy toward the Soviet Union, derived from an analysis of Soviet public opinion data. Policy recommendations in these cases involve a relationship to research that is intermediate between extrapolation from general principles, on the one hand, and conducting research specifically focused on a particular policy issue, on the other. The recommendations are rooted in research that is directly relevant to the issue, but they involve integration

and interpretation of diverse research findings. Inevitably, this process will be influenced by the value preferences of the social scientist who does the integration and interpretation.

3. Finally, some of the potential contributions of social-psychological approaches to the policy process take the form of research specifically designed to answer policy-related questions. Such research can be done at the request of the agency responsible for a particular policy decision, or it can be done at the investigator's own initiative and then fed into the policy process. It can test assumptions that underlie existing policies, or provide new data that would be relevant to the formulation of policy, or check out the implications of alternative policy proposals. Research in these cases represents an integral part of the policy process, though it may range from being entirely within the existing framework of policy goals to pushing toward a radical redefinition of goals. An example of a research program that is somewhere in the middle of this continuum is Project Michelson (Milburn, 1964; Higgs & Weinland, 1964), a series of interrelated studies that are linked directly to the process of formulating American deterrence policy. Based on the assumption that deterrence is to a very large extent a social-psychological process, it attempts to develop relevant social-psychological thinking and evidence and to feed these directly into the formulation of specific deterrence policies. Research that is now being initiated to determine the degree to which American public opinion would tolerate various innovations in foreign policy exemplifies the possibilities for social-psychological contribution to the formulation of new policy directions. Policy-oriented research in general faces many barriers (cf. Dror, 1964), and policy-oriented research in the area of international conflict, in particular, is subject to a variety of special problems (cf. Archibald, 1963). In the long run, however, such research represents the primary contribution that the social psychologist qua social psychologist can make to the policy process.

THE SOCIAL-PSYCHOLOGICAL LEVEL OF ANALYSIS IN INTERNATIONAL RELATIONS

A central feature of the more recent work on psychological aspects of international relations—in contrast to some of the earlier work—is that it starts at the level at which the problem under investigation occurs, rather than at the level at which the greatest amount of psychological information is already available.[4] These attempts may not always be successful: psychologists may sometimes lack the political sophistication necessary for the task, and even political scientists using psychological concepts may display a tendency to overpsychologize. Nevertheless, there is an awareness of the problem and a serious attempt to come to grips with it. Thus, psychologists working in the area of international relations have become increasingly aware of the danger of translating all problems into psychological ones and then seeking to eluci-

---

[4] The term *level* is used in several different ways. Richard Snyder has suggested that at least three meanings could be distinguished: (a) the level at which a phenomenon occurs; (b) the level at which an explanation is formulated; and (c) the level at which data are collected. These three do not necessarily coincide in any given case. In the title of this section, the term is used with meaning (b) and to some extent meaning (c). On the other hand, in the first sentence it is used with meaning (a). In general, the term *level* is ambiguous, but it seems rather difficult to do without it.

date them in psychological terms—for example, of defining war as a form of aggression and then turning to the psychology of aggression for its explication. Instead, the tendency more and more is to start out with an analysis of the situation that we are trying to understand, at its own level, and to bring in psychological variables as they become relevant on the basis of this analysis.

For example, an analysis of foreign policy decision-making may reveal that it has a different character in crisis situations as compared to non-crisis situations; to explore these differences, one can then turn to some of the psychological work on cognitive processes under conditions of stress. An analysis of deterrence strategies may reveal certain assumptions about the control of an opponent's behavior through threat of punishment, to which some of the experimental work in the psychology of learning would have obvious relevance. To take another example, after examining in detail the social processes by which a population is mobilized for war, one can begin to specify the kinds of psychological dispositions (habits, motives, and the like) that make such mobilization possible. Or, finally, an analysis of cross-national contacts may point up the frequent occurrence of misunderstandings, which could be elucidated by what is known about the conditions that underlie perceptual distortions.

In an analysis of specific problems in international relations, along the lines exemplified, one could certainly draw on much relevant information from individual psychology. Without wanting to minimize these potential contributions, I would like to propose, however, that a *systematic* application of psychological concepts, starting at the level of international relations itself, must of necessity be *social*-psychological in

nature. In making this point, I have no interest in splitting hairs and no intention to reject insights, whatever their source. My sole purpose is to provide a handle for clarifying the oft-debated question of where and how psychological analysis can be relevant to the study of international relations.

The examples given above were deliberately chosen to illustrate the potential relevance of general-psychological work in such areas as cognition, learning, motivation, and perception to certain specific problems in international relations. But even in these examples, the usefulness of a psychological analysis would be greatly enhanced if it were informed by a social-psychological perspective. Thus, the foreign policy decision-making of our first example takes place in a complex situation of interaction—among the decision-makers themselves, between the decision-makers and other elements of their own society, and between the decision-makers and their counterparts in other governments. The process involves not merely problem-solving, but various social phenomena, such as mutual reinforcement, meeting the expectations of certain reference groups, anticipating and evaluating the reactions of others, and the requirement of achieving consensus. What is known, therefore, about the effects of stress on the cognitive processes of an individual, while certainly relevant, can illuminate only a small part of the behavior of decision-makers in this situation. Similarly, in the deterrence example, general experimental work on reactions to the threat of punishment does not tell us much about the social setting in which this threat occurs. Such factors as the credibility of the threat, the threatened person's evaluation of the threatener, his interpretation of the intent of the threat, and the possibility of mounting a counter-threat, are major determinants of action and reaction, which in turn are rooted in the nature of the relationship between the two parties. In the third example, our understanding of the psychological dispositions that make mobilization for war possible can be greatly enhanced if we view these not simply as parts of the habit and motive structures of individuals, but as manifestations—at the individual level—of the political ideology and national role prescriptions that characterize the nation-state as a system. And, in our final example, the nature of perceptual distortions that occur in cross-national contacts can be conceived most readily, not in terms of characteristics of the individual participants, but in terms of such variables as the relative status of the nations involved, cultural differences in interaction patterns, and the social context in which the interaction occurs.

The review of these examples was designed to illustrate, somewhat loosely, why a systematic analysis of some of the psychological aspects of international relations has to be a social-psychological analysis, even though certain specific insights can, of course, be derived from individual psychology. In order to clarify the basis for this point of view, let me proceed (a) to define briefly my conception of social psychology, (b) to outline the relationship of the conceptual foci of social psychology to the analysis of international behavior, and (c) to point up the relevance of a social-psychological approach to the study of state behavior.

A Definition of Social Psychology

Social psychology—which is a subfield of psychology as well as of sociology—is concerned with the intersection between individual behavior and societal-institutional processes. It follows from this concern that the primary focus for social-psychological analysis is social interaction, which is, par excellence, the area in which individual and institutional processes intersect. Social interaction is thus the level of analysis that is most purely and most distinctively social-psychological.

By social interaction I do not simply mean the behavior of individuals in one another's presence, but their mutual attempts to assess and affect one another's goals, images, expectations, and evaluations, as they act and react vis-à-vis each other.[5] Thus, the study of social interaction requires, on the one hand, attention to what the individual brings to the interaction situation—the goals he is trying to maximize, the self-concept he is trying to enhance, his images of the other, and his view of the expectations adhering to his own role and the role of the other. On the other hand, the study of social interaction requires attention to the larger societal context within which the interaction occurs—both the general cultural framework and the specific organizational setting that define the purpose of the interaction, the roles of the participants, the normative expectations and rules that govern the interaction, and the action choices that are available.

---

[5] This follows, more or less, the definition of social interaction offered by Swanson (1963), who speaks of it as "the conception of individuals trying to take account of each other's minds, that is relating to their fellows' motives, needs, desires, means and ends, knowledge, and the like" (p. 4). "This means that they take into account something of the specifically instrumental character of one another's behavior" (p. 6). Swanson contrasts social interaction with "behavioral interaction" which refers to the behavior of individuals toward each other "as they might toward any other objects in the environment" (p. 7).

In this sense, then, social interaction is precisely the point at which individual and institutional processes come together. Interaction processes—such as group problem-solving or informal communication—can be understood more thoroughly if they are explored as a function of the dispositions that the participants bring to them and of the organizational context within which they take place. At the same time, one would focus on interaction in order to understand the processes whereby social institutions shape the behavior of individuals—as in the study of socialization and social influence; and the processes whereby individuals produce institutional and societal outcomes—as in the study of decision-making and negotiation.

While social interaction represents the level of analysis that is uniquely social-psychological, it is not the only level on which social-psychological research focuses. In a great deal of social-psychological research—the broad area involving the study of social attitudes, opinions, images, beliefs, and values— the basic unit of analysis is the individual. The concern here is with the way in which the individual conceives of and relates himself to various components of the social system. The social system in question may be the society of which he is a part, with its various subgroups and institutions; but it may also be the international system, or a specific organization to which he belongs. The social-psychological study of attitudinal variables views these not merely as manifestations of individual personality, but also as manifestations of the social system to which these attitudes refer. The attitudes of any given individual, for example, toward an organization in which he is a member must be understood in the light of the nature and functions of this organiza-

tion, the kinds of member behavior that are required if the organization is to carry out its functions, and the social processes whereby members are informed of these behavioral expectations and socialized with respect to organizational norms. There is, of course, considerable variation in the way in which individuals and subgroups interpret and meet these expectations, and in the precise nature of the attitudes they develop. All of these variations, however, represent at least in part a response to the demands inherent in the social system. The relationship between individual attitudes and the social system is mediated through social interaction. It is through interaction with others that an individual develops his attitudes. (This interaction may be indirect, via the mass media, but even the effects of the mass media seem to operate to a large extent through face-to-face interaction.) It is also through interaction with others that an individual's attitudes have their impact on the social system. The mediating role of interaction, however, is often left implicit in the study of attitudes.

A third focus for social-psychological research is at the level of the organization or the society. Social-psychological studies at this level are concerned with the relationship of organizational or societal variables to individual variables. They might explore, for example, the effects of interpersonal relations on certain organizational outcomes, such as productivity; or, conversely, the effects of the authority structure characterizing an organization on the satisfaction of its members. The relationship between individual and organizational variables is, of necessity, mediated by social interaction. At times, however— as, for example, in some of the research on the relationships between personality and social structure—the role of social interaction in mediating these two levels is not brought explicitly into the analysis.

From this definition of social psychology as the study of the intersection between individual and institutional processes it should be apparent why the most relevant and systematic psychological contributions to international relations are likely to come from *social* psychology. It is inherent in the nature of a social-psychological approach to view individual behavior in its societal and organizational context, and to take deliberate account of the institutional processes that shape the behavior of individual actors and are in turn shaped by it. A social-psychological analysis that seriously attempts to live up to this definition of its task would be more likely, therefore, to do justice to the political realities of the national and international systems as it addresses itself to the psychological aspects of international behavior.

In line with our definition of social psychology, a social-psychological analysis of international behavior would concern itself with the ways in which individuals and groups (with varying positions in the decision-making structure) (a) conceive of their own nation, other nations, and the international system, of the relationships between these systems, and of their own relationships to them; and (b) interact—officially or unofficially, directly or symbolically—with other nations, their representatives, and their individual nationals. Two interrelated foci for social-psychological conceptualization thus emerge: (a) national and international images; and (b) processes of interaction in international relations.

Clearly, these cannot be separated from one another. National and international images must be seen as products of interaction among nations and among their nationals. Conversely, interactions across national boundaries can only be understood in terms of the underlying conceptions or images that govern them. One can, however, focus on one or the other—imagery or interaction—as the primary object of study in a given case. The present volume is organized, therefore, around these two conceptual foci, although the arbitrary aspects of this division are clearly recognized. Let me proceed to characterize the issues that these two foci are intended to encompass, and, in doing so, to give a brief overview of the entire volume.

National and International Images

The term image, as used in this volume, refers to the organized representation of an object in an individual's cognitive system.[6] The core of an image is the perceived character of the object to which it refers—the individual's conception of what this object is like. Image is an inferred construct, however, rather than a mere designation of the way the object is phenomenally experienced.

In large part, the individual's conception of the object is encompassed by the points on various descriptive and evaluative dimensions at which he would place it. In line with Boulding's (1956) broader use of the term *image*, however, we would want to include not only the individual's conception of the object at present, but also his view of its past and future. Thus, associated

---

[6] More detailed definitions of the concept are offered by Scott in Chapter 3, and by Deutsch and Merritt in Chapter 5. Their definitions are phrased in somewhat different terms (in line with the conceptual schemes on which their respective chapters are based), but they are completely consistent with and in fact have greatly influenced the definition offered here.

with the image of an object, would be various specific memories and expectations, various generalized beliefs and opinions regarding the object. Images differ not only in terms of the specific elements they contain, but also in terms of the nature of these content elements and the way in which they are related to each other—in short, in terms of their cognitive structures. Thus, images may vary in the number of elements of which they are composed, and particularly in the number of details and nuances; they may be more or less rich and refined, more or less complex and differentiated. Moreover, images can be characterized in terms of the affect toward the object that they carry—the degree to which the individual tends to approach or avoid, to like or dislike, to favor or oppose this object. This general affective orientation toward an object is what the term *attitude* usually refers to. Typically, the attitude associated with an image has both positive and negative components. If an image is relatively complex and differentiated, then it would be more appropriate to speak of a number of attitudes; that is, the individual may be more or less favorable or unfavorable, depending on the aspect of the object to which he is relating himself.

When we speak of an image as an organized representation of an object, we do not wish to imply that all images are consistent and well defined. The term *organized* is merely meant to convey that images have some coherent structure, that there is at least some tendency to relate different impressions of the object to each other so that they hang together in a unified whole. In other words, the image is not just an accumulation of discrete components, but a grouping of these components into a more efficient structure. This implies that there will be some push toward consistency—among the elements that constitute the image, as well as between the cognitive and affective components. The degree of consistency of images, however, can vary widely; the representation of an object can be coherent and organized even though it contains contradictions and ambiguities.

This leads us to a further qualification. Neither the view that images have some coherent structure, nor the emphasis on the perceived character of the object is meant to restrict our definition of images to conceptions that are clearly articulated and conscious. Many components of an image may be the products of direct and indirect experiences that the individual cannot recall; these components may be vague and incapable of verbalization, but they may nonetheless play an important role in the individual's conception of the object and behavior toward it. Thus, we are interested not only in the individual's verbalizations about what the object is like, but also in the conceptions of the object that are *implicit* in the ways in which he relates himself to it. It follows that, in the assessment of images, one would ideally want to supplement the individual's phenomenological descriptions of the object with observations of (or questions about) his behavior toward the object and with certain indirect devices. On the basis of these one can then make further inferences about the images that govern his relationship to the object.

In selecting national and international images as one of the two major foci of this volume, our intention is not to be restrictive, to use image in a very precise way that would differentiate it sharply from such related concepts as attitude and opinion. Rather, the concept is meant to be broadly representative of the whole family of attitudinal variables. We are concerned with the conceptions that individuals have of their own nation, of other nations, and of the international system as a whole. Directly linked to these conceptions are a variety of attitudes, opinions, and beliefs, with varying degrees of generality; for example, general attitudes toward conciliation vs. belligerence in international affairs, or national sovereignty, or international organization, and opinions on specific foreign policy issues. All of these are relevant to our discussion of national and international images, and the chapters in Part One bring in data on image-associated attitudes and opinions whenever these pertain to the argument. Some chapters, in fact, draw more heavily on data about attitudes toward policy issues than they do on data about images of nation-objects.

In short, no sharp distinction between images and related concepts is intended. We will usually speak of images when we refer to the way in which nations or international systems are perceived, of attitudes when we refer to general policy orientations, and of opinions when we refer to positions on specific issues. It is recognized, however, that these various concepts are closely linked to each other and, to a certain extent, interchangeable. Thus, some recent conceptualizations of attitude and opinion (Smith, Bruner, & White, 1956; Katz, 1960) provide broad and functional definitions of these terms that are completely consistent with the definition of image used here. We were primarily concerned with selecting a term to characterize conceptions of nations and international systems that takes the individual's definition of the object—the way it is seen, the properties with which it is endowed—as the starting-point of analysis. The use of such a starting-point seems particularly appropriate to the study of international behavior, because it makes it easier to link behavior toward nation-objects directly

and specifically to the perceived characteristics of these objects; and to deal with the cognitive structures of people's conceptions of nation-objects (which vary widely) and with the existence of mixed and often contradictory evaluations of these objects. The term image lends itself quite readily to this cognitive emphasis, although it is certainly not the only term that could have been employed.

In the study of international behavior it is also useful to have a concept that links perceptions of nation-objects to the characteristics of these objects. Again, the concept of image seems to facilitate this kind of linkage. The image can be seen as a joint product of the characteristics of the object and the characteristics of the perceiver (Kleining, 1959). One can use the same descriptive dimensions to characterize the image and the object and therefore move more readily from the nature of the object to the perception of the beholder. It thus becomes possible to integrate within the same conceptual scheme the "public image" of an organization, as Boulding (1956) calls it, and the images of the organization as held by its members, as long as one keeps in mind, however, that "the image is always the property of the individual persons, not of the organization" (Boulding, 1956, p. 28).

For example, the nation-state as a system conveys—through its institutional structures, basic documents, and elite communications—a certain definition of its character and functions and of the roles that its nationals must enact if the system is to carry out its functions. Individual nationals in turn adopt, as part of their personal belief systems, certain images of the state and of their own roles in relation to it; typically these images will be some variant of the "public image." The term image can thus be useful in conceptualizing political ideology in a way that bridges the system level and the individual level, since comparable dimensions can be used to describe both the definition that is communicated and the image that is adopted.

Similarly, in the study of the mutual images of two nations, one can develop a common set of dimensions, not only to compare various images held by A and B (A's image of B with B's image of A; A's self-image with B's image of A, and vice versa; A's self-image with his image of B, and vice versa), but also to compare the way in which each nation tries to present itself with the way in which it is perceived. This latter possibility, unfortunately, has led to some perversion of the concept of image when used in a public relations context. One often hears references, nowadays, to the need for some product, organization, or political candidate to "project" a certain image. This not only is questionable on ethical grounds, in that it implies an attempt to change the perception of an object by manipulating the perceiver rather than the object perceived, but it also misuses the term image. It treats image as if it were a deliberate creation of the object rather than a property of the individual who beholds the object. This is definitely not the way in which the concept is used in the present volume. At the same time, the possibility of using the same dimensions to characterize the object as represented in the cognitive system of the perceiver, and as presented in communications directed to him, makes the concept of image useful in the effort to relate individual and societal processes.

The concept of national and international images is used, to varying degrees, in both parts of this volume, but it represents the central focus of attention in Part One. For the chapters in Part One, national and international images are the objects of study, while in Part Two they are brought into the discussion (along with other concepts) as explanatory variables. Perhaps one way of putting it—though this is only an approximation—is that images are the *dependent* variables in Part One, while they are typically *independent* or *mediating* variables when they are used in Part Two. The seven chapters in Part One explore, from different vantage points, the *determinants* of national and international images. They can be grouped into three categories:

1. Chapters 2 and 3 are concerned with the sources of national and international images in the psychological structure of the individual, the social structure of his society, and his own place within that social structure. In Chapter 2, Robert LeVine draws on ethnographic data from preindustrial societies to explore the ways in which intersocietal images develop in the course of socialization, and the effect of the social structure of the society into which the individual is socialized on the nature of these images. In Chapter 3, William Scott examines data from industrial societies that bear on the structure of images and their relationship to various personality and demographic characteristics of the individual.

2. The next three chapters are concerned with the effects of various specific experiences on the formation of images and their modification. Chapter 4, by Ithiel de Sola Pool, focuses on the effects of direct cross-national contacts that occur in the course of travel in foreign countries. Chapter 5, by Karl Deutsch and Richard Merritt, deals with the effects of external events, both national and international, and messages about these events. Chapter 6, by Irving Janis and Brewster Smith, focuses on the effects of deliberate attempts to modify images, through education and persuasion.

3. The last two chapters of Part One are concerned with the ways in which images and associated positions on foreign policy issues are related to the nature of the interaction between two nations and the foreign policy process. In particular, they deal with the kinds of images and attitudes that tend to be manifested in the context of a conflictual relationship between two nations. In Chapter 7, Ralph White uses data on Soviet citizens' images of their own society and of the United States as a case in point, and examines these in terms of the dynamics of intergroup conflict. In Chapter 8, Milton Rosenberg draws on data about American public opinion regarding Cold-War issues to illustrate the way in which images and attitudes flow out of the process of foreign policy formation and execution. Of the contributions to Part One, these last two chapters have the most direct relevance to the study of international politics. The other chapters do have some very definite implications for international politics, but they must be viewed primarily as contributions to the study of the international behavior of individuals.

Processes of Interaction in International Relations

The term interaction, like the term image, is used rather broadly in the present volume and is meant to encompass a whole family of processes that can be subjected to a social-psychological analysis. The empirical focus and the basic unit of analysis of all of the chapters that are subsumed under this rubric is the social interaction of individuals. In some chapters, the focus is directly on processes of social interaction—for example, the process of bargaining, or joint decision-making, or informal communication. In other chapters, the focus is on certain societal processes that represent aggregations of social interactions occurring throughout the population—such as the evolution of a mood or the arousal of an ideology. In all cases, however, the basic data are the behaviors of individuals in interaction with one another.

Social interaction has already been described (see p. 22) as the pattern of mutual actions and reactions of two or more individuals who are engaged in a continuing attempt to assess and affect one another's goals, images, expectations, and evaluations. I have also indicated that social interaction is, par excellence, the area in which individual and institutional processes intersect, and must be studied with an eye to the larger societal context within which it occurs. Thus, when we speak here of processes of interaction in international relations, we refer to social interactions for which the national and international systems serve, at least in part, as the defining context. An international relations context would characterize almost any situation in which nationals of *different* countries interact with each other—certainly when they interact as representatives of their respective countries, or when they interact within the framework of an international organization, but also (to varying degrees) when they interact as private individuals.

Similarly, when nationals of the *same* country interact with each other around matters of foreign policy—whether they be national decision-makers planning a course of action for their government in its dealings with another government, or a group of private citizens who have come together either to build fallout shelters or to oppose building them —we again have an instance of social interaction in an international relations context. Finally, another instance would be those processes of reverberation and reinforcement within and sometimes across national populations that yield a state of readiness for particular kinds of international action—whether it be a climate of hostility or *détente*, a feeling of outrage or sympathy toward some other nation, a sense of national pride or national shame.

We have defined our focus as the social interaction of individuals within an international relations context. This is, indeed, the appropriate focus for social-psychological conceptualization, which must ultimately derive its data from the behaviors of individuals. Yet the designation "processes of interaction in international relations" suggests another possible focus, namely the interaction between *nation-states*. This degree of ambiguity or surplus meaning has some real justification, however, for it calls attention to another level of interpretation of the materials presented.

As far as the basic unit of analysis is concerned, we are indeed dealing with the interaction between individuals rather than nation-states. The situations of interaction themselves, however, can be seen (to varying degrees) as aspects of the behavior of states and the interaction between them. This is most obvious with respect to the study of decision-making in foreign policy: our data consist, to be sure, of the interactions between individuals, but we are certainly observing an aspect of state behavior. Some analysts, in fact, would say that the behavior of the key decision-makers *is* state behavior. It is also clear that the interactions of national representatives in international negotiations or international organizations can be seen as aspects of the interaction between states. It is least clear when we study cross-national contacts of private individuals, but even here it must be kept in mind that international exchange represents one component—albeit a minor one—of the foreign policies of most states. Thus, even the interactions between travelers in foreign countries and their hosts can be seen, in some sense, as manifestations of the interactions between nations.

In short, then, the conceptual focus of Part Two of this volume can be defined at two levels. The actual object of study is the social interaction of individuals in an international relations context. Insofar as these interaction situations constitute aspects of state behavior, however, their investigation has some relevance to the study of interaction between nation-states. This is not to say that one can equate the behaviors of the individuals observed with those of the state. Conclusions about state behavior as such can only be drawn if one specifies the precise links between the individuals and groups observed and the loci of state action.

The seven chapters in Part Two explore different processes of interaction in different settings. In line with some of the distinctions that have already been made, they can be grouped into three categories:

1. Chapters 9 and 10 are concerned with some of the processes of interaction that are widely distributed across the elites and publics of a national population and serve to create a state of readiness for certain kinds of international action. What we are dealing with here are essentially societal processes formed by the aggregation of social interactions among many individuals and groups throughout the population. In Chapter 9, Harold Lasswell discusses the development of widespread moods within a population at certain historical junctures, which provide a climate conducive to particular kinds of action in the international arena. In Chapter 10, Daniel Katz discusses the development and arousal of different kinds of nationalist ideology within different kinds of national sys-

tems, and relates these to the orientations toward international relations—
particularly to the strategies of international conflict resolution—that these
national systems are likely to adopt.

2. The next two chapters focus on
interaction processes involved in the
on-going conduct of foreign affairs—in
the determination of the actions and
reactions of two or more nations vis-
à-vis each other, in specific cases and
over a more extended period of time.
The emphasis here is largely, though
not exclusively, on interactions among
the decision-makers within a national
government who are responsible for
international action. In Chapter 11,
Dean Pruitt examines the processes of
perception and orientation, occurring
simultaneously and sequentially among
the decision-makers (and publics) of
two interacting nations, that lead to
different kinds of definition of the situation—and thus, in turn, predispose to
different kinds of international action.
In Chapter 12, James Robinson and
Richard Snyder examine both the processes of deliberation and the organizational processes in which national
officials engage, as they develop and
execute foreign policy decisions.

3. The final three chapters of Part
Two focus on three different kinds of
situations in which individuals of different nationalities engage in direct,
face-to-face interaction. In Chapter 13,
Jack Sawyer and Harold Guetzkow
examine processes of negotiation and
bargaining in international relations,
which involve direct interactions between different nationals as *representatives* of their respective governments.
In Chapter 14, Chadwick Alger presents data on personal interactions in
intergovernmental organizations—such
as the United Nations—which include
not only national representatives but
also a supranational secretariat, and in
which even the national representatives

often enact nonnational or supranational roles. Finally, in Chapter 15,
Anita Mishler examines cross-national
interactions that occur in the context
of international exchanges, which involve interactions between different
nationals as private *individuals*, although in a certain sense they may see
themselves and be seen by others as
representatives of their nations.

Relevance to International Politics

A considerable portion of the material to be presented in this volume, as
has already been noted, is intended to
have some bearing on the study of international politics. This is true to some
degree for Part One, and to a much
greater degree for Part Two. While the
basic units of analysis are typically the
behaviors of individuals and their interactions, a number of chapters are
directly and others indirectly concerned with the effects of these individual behaviors on the behavior of
nation-states and with the way in which
they mediate certain societal outcomes
for national and international systems—
outcomes that are ultimately linked to
the probability of peace or war. Let
us take another look, therefore, before
concluding this introduction, at the
whole question of the relationship of
the social-psychological level of analysis in international relations to the
study of international politics.

It should be clear, from our delinea-
tion of the scope of social-psychological
approaches to international relations
and of the coverage of this volume, that
we are dealing with a research area
that is both broader and narrower than
the study of international politics. It is
broader because it includes not only the
study of international politics, but also
what we have designated—for lack of
a better term—as the study of the "international behavior of individuals."

The empirical focus of social-psychological approaches in this field is almost always, and almost by definition, the international behavior of individuals. In some of the research, however, this focus is used for the purpose of illuminating the behavior of nations, while in other studies it is an end in itself. That is, the study of people's images of other nations and of the international system, of the sources of their attitudes toward foreign affairs, of the nature of their involvement in national roles, or of their experiences in cross-national contacts, may be remote from the questions of war and peace, but it represents a legitimate and fascinating area of social-psychological research in its own right.

In the long run, this kind of research may have some real contributions to make to questions of war and peace by building up our understanding of the psychological and social processes that run parallel to the operations of national and international systems. In the short run, however, this work can stand by itself and does not need to be justified by its relevance to international politics. In this sense, then, our concern is *broader* than the study of international politics.

Our concern is *narrower* than the study of international politics in the sense that a social-psychological analysis, where it does address itself to questions of international politics, can deal only with part of the picture. It can *contribute* to the study of international politics, along with other analytic approaches, but it can never *be* the study of international politics. I have already emphasized that, when we deal with war or peace, we are dealing with behaviors of nations, carried out in a historical context and within the terms of a national and international political structure. This must be the starting-point of our analysis. Such an

analysis can then reveal certain problems that can be handled most adequately through the use of social-psychological concepts and methods. In other words, a social-psychological approach is not a total approach to the study of international politics, which can serve as a substitute for alternative approaches. Rather, it is part of a total approach to which it can contribute once relevant points of application have been identified.

Ideally, we would want to have a broad conceptual framework for the analysis of interstate behavior. Such a framework would yield the kinds of questions that need to be answered, and would help us to identify those questions that can be answered most appropriately in social-psychological terms. To the extent to which such a procedure is approximated, we would be able to maximize the relevance of social-psychological research that is undertaken and see precisely where it fits into the larger picture and contributes to rounding it out. In an earlier paper (Kelman, 1955, reprinted in Hoffmann, 1960, pp. 209–222) I attempted to sketch out the beginnings of such a framework. While it is extremely tentative and rudimentary, it may help to illustrate the point that social-psychological considerations can fit into a larger framework but certainly not substitute for it.

The framework uses as its starting-point the following question: "Given a particular level of interaction between two nations, what is the probability that the sequence of events initiated by a given situation of interaction will produce war or peace or some other final outcome?" (Kelman, 1955, p. 55). The framework is designed as a scaffolding in terms of which this question can be broken down and answers to it can be sought. Thus, it suggests an analysis of the sequence of events initiated by a given situation into five steps: (a) communication about the situation to the elite and other segments of the population; (b) definition of the situation and perception of choices; (c) development of a climate or state of readiness for certain actions; (d) commission of specific acts relevant to the interest of the other nation; and (e) achievement of a new level of interaction or return to the initial equilibrium. Furthermore, the framework suggests "a distinction among three types of factors which are likely to affect each step in the sequence and hence the final outcome of the interaction: societal, attitudinal, and structural factors. These three types of factors differ in terms of the units of analysis and levels of theorizing to which they refer: societal factors describe characteristics of nations, attitudinal factors characteristics of indi-

viduals, and structural factors characteristics of structures or aggregating machineries. Societal factors set limits on international relations; attitudinal factors determine predispositions towards certain decisions and actions and thus modify the effects of societal factors; and structural factors determine who influences decisions and how this influence is exerted and thus prescribe the way in which societal and attitudinal factors are channelled into action" (p. 54).

The framework can thus be visualized as a fifteen-cell matrix, in which the five steps in the sequence of events represent the rows and the three types of determining factors represent the columns. Table 1.1 presents this matrix in summary form. Each cell in the table contains an illustration of a variable that might affect one of the steps in the

TABLE 1.1
Examples of Societal, Attitudinal, and Structural Variables That Might Affect the Outcome of an Interaction between Two Nations

Steps in the sequence of events initiated by a given situation of interaction	Societal variables	Attitudinal variables	Structural variables
Communication about the situation	Stability of regime	Expectancies in relation to other nation	Degree of centralization of mass media
Definition of the situation	Vulnerability of industrial apparatus	Level of trust vis-à-vis other nation	Power of military-industrial complex
Development of a climate for action	Level of unemployment	General level of optimism-pessimism	Diversity of opinion-making elites
Commission of specific acts	Military capability	Risk-taking propensity	Authority structure of decision-making organizations
Achievement of a new or return to initial level of interaction	Cohesion of alliance system	Responsiveness between the two nations	Effectiveness of international arbitration machinery

sequence of events initiated by a given situation of interaction, and thus the final outcome of that interaction.

Let us say, for example, that a naval vessel belonging to nation A opened fire against a fishing boat belonging to nation B. How this event is communicated to the population of B—and thus, in part, the final outcome of the sequence of events thus initiated—will depend on a variety of variables. An example of a societal variable that will affect this communication is the stability of the regime of nation B (row 1, column 1): If the regime is unstable, the decision-makers may be more likely to play up this event as a way of focusing on an external enemy and thus increasing internal cohesiveness. An example of an attitudinal variable that will affect this communication is the set of expectancies about nation A that are commonly held in nation B as a result of the prevailing level of interaction between the two nations (row 1, column 2): If B expects hostility from A, then it is more likely that this incident will be communicated as an act of deliberate provocation; if B expects friendliness, then the event is more likely to be communicated as an exception or an accident or a misunderstanding. Finally, an example of a structural variable that will affect communication of this event to B is the degree of centralization of B's mass media (row 1, column 3): If the mass media are highly centralized, only one version of the event is likely to be communicated and thus to dominate the definition of the situation; if the control of the mass media is decentralized, then several interpretations are likely to be communicated and a wider range of choices in response is likely to be perceived. It should be noted that the illustrative examples in each cell of Table 1.1 are not necessarily unique to the row in which they are placed, but

each example was selected to illustrate a variable that might determine what happens at the step in the sequence of events represented by that row.

A social-psychological analysis would be most directly appropriate to the five cells in the second column of Table 1.1, which refers to the effects of attitudinal variables on the interaction between two nations. Part One of the present volume is devoted to an exploration of the nature of these variables. A social-psychological approach has some relevance to the study of societal and structural variables as well, particularly in providing some methods for assessing these variables and their effects. For example, one might use opinion data (along with other types of data) in order to measure such societal variables as the stability of the regime, the extent of internal conflict within a national system, or the degree of polarization of the international system. Similarly, one might use interview techniques in the study of the power structure and the communication structure within a nation, aimed at establishing who is involved in the foreign policy process and by what means their influence feeds into the final decisions. Societal and structural variables can also be built (and in fact have been built) into such laboratory approaches as the Inter-Nation Simulation (Guetzkow *et al.*, 1963; see especially Chapter 3 by Robert Noel). Nevertheless, the contribution of a social-psychological analysis to the identification and conceptualization of societal and structural variables is less direct than its contribution to the study of attitudinal variables. If we recognize the role of these different variables and the interaction between them in determining internation behavior, we can develop a clearer view of where and how social-psychological research fits into the larger picture.

As for the rows of our fifteen-cell matrix, each step in the sequence of events can be analyzed in social-psychological terms—that is, in terms of the processes of social interaction engaged in by decision-makers, elites, and publics. This is essentially the concern of Part Two of the present volume. An analysis restricted to this level, however, would be patently incomplete. What happens at each step in the sequence is heavily determined by societal and structural factors, along with attitudinal ones. For example, how a given international situation is defined in a particular country may depend to a large degree on such factors as the existence of an economic recession in the country or the role of veterans' organizations and groups of superpatriots in its communication structure. These factors are essential parts of the input into the social interaction processes that lead the public to develop a certain climate of opinion and the decision-makers to select a certain course of action. Societal and structural factors also serve as major constraints to the processes that occur at each step, for example to the nature of the communications that can take place and the nature of the decisions that can be made. Finally, societal and structural factors constitute the important outcomes at each step, such as changes in the rate of armament or development of new international organizations. The general level of interaction between two nations, which is the end-point of any particular sequence of events, can be described in terms of such an attitudinal factor as "responsiveness between nations" (Pruitt, 1962, and Chapter 11 in this volume), but this is of necessity associated with certain societal and structural conditions.

In short, in order to understand what happens at each step in a sequence of interaction between nations, we must take into account the societal and structural, as well as attitudinal inputs into the process and constraints upon it. In order to understand the effects of one step in the sequence upon the next, we must also take into account the societal, structural, as well as attitudinal outcomes at each point. Moreover, it may often be possible to gain insights into internation behavior by remaining entirely at the macroscopic level—establishing relationships, for example, between such variables as rate of urbanization in a society and level of arms production (cf. Russett *et al.*, 1964). Relationships of this sort may suggest the operation of important societal processes, with major impacts on international relations, that might be difficult to assess or might even be obscured by a microanalysis of the decision to increase armaments.

This brief presentation of one framework for the study of internation behavior was designed to illustrate both the potentials and the limits of a social-psychological analysis. All one can claim for such an analysis—if it is carried out with due regard to the historical and political context of international relations—is that it can illuminate some aspects of the larger problem of international politics. The relevance of a social-psychological approach, even in this limited sense, is certainly open to question, because of difficulties due, for example, to the problem of generalization from one level of analysis to another, or the existence of severe constraints on the actions of decision-makers, or the limited role of public opinion in the foreign policy process. I shall return to these issues and to the whole question of relevance in the concluding chapter. In the meantime, however, I invite the reader to examine, in the chapters that follow, the illustrations of possible applications of social-psychological concepts and methods to the study of international behavior, including some aspects of international politics.

REFERENCES

Alger, C. F. Non-resolution consequences of the United Nations and their effect on international conflict. *J. Confl. Resol.*, 1961, 5, 128–145.

Alger, C. F. Comparison of intranational and international politics. *Amer. pol. Sci. Rev.*, 1963, 57, 406–419.

Allport, G. W. Human nature and the peace. *Psychol. Bull.*, 1945, 42, 376–378.

Almond, G. A. *The American people and foreign policy.* New York: Harcourt, Brace, 1950.

Archibald, Kathleen Social science approaches to peace: Problems and issues. *Soc. Problems*, 1963, 11, 91–104.

Barton, A. A survey of suburban residents on what to do about the danger of war. *Council for Correspondence Newsl.*, March 1963, No. 24, 3–11.

Bass, B. M., & Dunteman, G. Biases in the evaluation of one's own group, its allies and opponents. *J. Confl. Resol.*, 1963, 7, 16–20.

Bauer, R. A., Pool, I. de S., & Dexter, L. A. *American business and public policy: The politics of foreign trade.* New York: Atherton Press, 1963.

Blake, R. R., & Mouton, Jane S. The intergroup dynamics of win-lose conflict and problem-solving collaboration in union-management relations. In M. Sherif (Ed.), *Intergroup relations and leadership.* New York: Wiley, 1962. Pp. 94–140.

Boulding, K. E. *The image.* Ann Arbor: Univer. Michigan Press, 1956.

Brody, R. A. Some systemic effects of the spread of nuclear weapons technology: A study through simulation of a multi-nuclear future. *J. Confl. Resol.*, 1963, 7, 663–753.

Bronfenbrenner, U. The mirror image in Soviet-American relations: A social psychologist's report. *J. soc. Issues*, 1961, 17 (3), 45–56.

Bruner, J. S., & Perlmutter, H. V. Compatriot and foreigner: A study of impression formation in three countries. *J. abnorm. soc. Psychol.*, 1957, 55, 253–260.

Buchanan, W., & Cantril, H. *How nations see each other.* Urbana: Univer. Illinois Press, 1953.

Campbell, D. T., & LeVine, R. A. A proposal for cooperative cross-cultural research on ethnocentrism. *J. Confl. Resol.*, 1961, 5, 82–108.

Cantril, H. (Ed.) *Tensions that cause wars.* Urbana: Univer. Illinois Press, 1950.

Chesler, M., & Schmuck, R. Student reactions to the Cuban crisis and public dissent. *Publ. Opin. Quart.*, 1964, 28, 467–482.

Christiansen, B. *Attitudes toward foreign affairs as a function of personality.* Oslo: Oslo Univer. Press, 1959.

Claude, I. (Ed.) The place of theory in the conduct and study of international relations. *J. Confl. Resol.*, 1960, 4 (3).

Coelho, G. V. (Ed.) Impacts of studying abroad. *J. soc. Issues*, 1962, 18 (1).

Crow, W. J. A study of strategic doctrines using the Inter-Nation Simulation. *J. Confl. Resol.*, 1963, 7, 580–589.

Danckwortt, D. *Probleme der Anpassung an eine fremde Kultur.* Köln: Carl Duisberg Gesellschaft für Nachwuchsförderung, 1959.

Deutsch, K. W. *Nationalism and social communication.* New York: Wiley, 1953.

Deutsch, M. Trust and suspicion. *J. Confl. Resol.*, 1958, 2, 265–279.

Deutsch, M. A psychological basis for peace. In Q. Wright, W. M. Evan, & M. Deutsch (Eds.), *Preventing World War III: Some proposals.* New York: Simon & Schuster, 1962. Pp. 369–392.

Deutsch, M., & Krauss, R. M. Studies of

interpersonal bargaining. *J. Confl. Resol.*, 1962, *6*, 52–76.

Doob, L. W. South Tyrol: An introduction to the psychological syndrome of nationalism. *Publ. Opin. Quart.*, 1962, *26*, 172–184.

Douglas, Ann The peaceful settlement of industrial and intergroup disputes. *J. Confl. Resol.*, 1957, *1*, 69–81.

Droba, D. D. Effect of various factors on militarism-pacifism. *J. abnorm. soc. Psychol.*, 1931, *26*, 141–153.

Dror, Y. The barriers facing policy science. *Amer. behav. Scientist*, 1964, *7*, 3–7.

Duijker, H. C. J., & Frijda, N. H. *National character and national stereotypes.* Amsterdam: North-Holland Publishing Co., 1960.

Durbin, E. F. M., & Bowlby, J. *Personal aggressiveness and war.* London: Kegan Paul, 1939.

Ekman, P., *et al.* Divergent reactions to the threat of war: Shelter and peace groups during the Berlin crisis. *Council for Correspondence Newsl.*, March 1963, No. 24, 11–25.

Eysenck, H. J. War and aggressiveness: A survey of social attitude studies. In T. H. Pear (Ed.), *Psychological factors of peace and war.* London: Hutchinson, 1950. Pp. 49–81.

Fox, W. T. R. (Ed.) *Theoretical aspects of international relations.* Notre Dame, Indiana: Univer. Notre Dame Press, 1959.

Frank, J. D. Breaking the thought barrier: Psychological challenges of the nuclear age. *Psychiatry*, 1960, *23*, 245–266.

Free, L. A. *Six allies and a neutral.* New York: Free Press, 1959.

Gladstone, A. I., & Taylor, Martha A. Threat-related attitudes and reactions to communications about international events. *J. Confl. Resol.*, 1958, *2*, 17–28.

Glover, E. *War, sadism and pacifism.* London: Allen & Unwin, 1946.

Guetzkow, H. *Multiple loyalties.* Princeton: Princeton Univer. Press, 1955.

Guetzkow, H. Isolation and collaboration: A partial theory of inter-nation relations. *J. Confl. Resol.*, 1957, *1*, 48–68.

Guetzkow, H., Alger, C. F., Brody, R. A., Noel, R. C., & Snyder, R. C. *Simulation in international relations.* Englewood Cliffs, New Jersey: Prentice-Hall, 1963.

Gullahorn, J. T., & Gullahorn, Jeanne E. An extension of the U-curve hypothesis. *J. soc. Issues*, 1963, *19* (3), 33–47.

Hero, A. O. *Americans in world affairs.* Boston: World Peace Foundation, 1959. (a)

Hero, A. O. *Opinion leaders in American communities.* Boston: World Peace Foundation, 1959. (b)

Hero, A. O. *Voluntary organizations in world affairs communication.* Boston: World Peace Foundation, 1960.

Higgs, L. D., & Weinland, R. G. *Project Michelson status report I.* China Lake, California: U.S. Naval Ordnance Test Station, 1964.

Hoffmann, S. H. (Ed.) *Contemporary theory in international relations.* Englewood Cliffs, New Jersey: Prentice-Hall, 1960.

Holsti, O. R. The belief system and national images: A case study. *J. Confl. Resol.*, 1962, *6*, 244–252.

Isaacs, H. R. *Scratches on our minds.* New York: John Day, 1958.

Isaacs, H. R. *Emergent Americans: A report on "Crossroads Africa."* New York: John Day, 1961.

Jensen, L. Soviet-American bargaining behavior in the post-war disarmament negotiations. *J. Confl. Resol.*, 1963, *7*, 522–541.

Katz, D. The functional approach to the study of attitudes. *Publ. Opin. Quart.*, 1960, *24*, 163–204.

Kelman, H. C. Societal, attitudinal and structural factors in international relations. *J. soc. Issues*, 1955, *11* (1), 42–56.

Kelman, H. C. Changing attitudes

through international activities. *J. soc. Issues,* 1962, *18* (1), 68–87. (a)

Kelman, H. C. Internationalizing military force. In Q. Wright, W. M. Evan, & M. Deutsch (Eds.), *Preventing World War III: Some proposals.* New York: Simon & Schuster, 1962. Pp. 106–122. (b)

Kelman, H. C. (with Victoria Steinitz) The reactions of participants in a foreign specialists seminar to their American experience. *J. soc. Issues,* 1963, *19* (3), 61–114.

Kisker, G. W. (Ed.) *World tension: The psychopathology of international relations.* Englewood Cliffs, New Jersey: Prentice-Hall, 1951.

Kleining, G. Zum gegenwärtigen Stand der Imageforschung. *Psychologie und Praxis,* 1959, *3*, 198–212.

Klineberg, O. *Tensions affecting international understanding.* New York: Social Science Research Council, 1950.

Klineberg, O. *The human dimension in international relations.* New York: Holt, Rinehart and Winston, 1964.

Knorr, K., & Verba, S. (Eds.) *The international system: Theoretical essays.* Princeton: Princeton Univer. Press, 1961.

Lambert, W. E., & Klineberg, O. A pilot study of the origin and development of national stereotypes. *Int. soc. Sci. J.,* 1959, *11*, 221–238.

Levinson, D. J. Authoritarian personality and foreign policy. *J. Confl. Resol.,* 1957, *1*, 37–47.

Levy, S. G., & Hefner, R. Multidimensional scaling of international attitudes. *Peace Research Society (International) Papers,* 1964, *1*, 129–165.

Lundstedt, S. (Ed.) Human factors in cross-cultural adjustment. *J. soc. Issues,* 1963, *19* (3).

May, M. A. *A social psychology of war and peace.* New Haven: Yale Univer. Press, 1943.

McClelland, C.A. The function of theory in international relations. *J. Confl. Resol.,* 1960, *4*, 303–336.

Milburn, T. W. The concept of deterrence: Some logical and psychological considerations. *J. soc. Issues,* 1961, *17* (3), 3–11.

Milburn, T. W. *Studies in deterrence: I. Design for the study of deterrent processes.* China Lake, California: U.S. Naval Ordnance Test Station, 1964.

Mouton, Jane S., & Blake, R. R. The influence of competitively vested interests on judgments. *J. Confl. Resol.,* 1962, *6*, 149–153.

Murphy, G. (Ed.) *Human nature and enduring peace.* Boston: Houghton Mifflin, 1945.

North, R. C., Holsti, O. R., Zaninovich, M. G., & Zinnes, Dina A. *Content analysis: A handbook with applications for the study of international crisis.* Evanston, Illinois: Northwestern Univer. Press, 1963.

Osgood, C. E. *Alternative to war or surrender.* Urbana: Univer. Illinois Press, 1962.

Paul, J., & Laulicht, J. *In your opinion: Leaders' and voters' attitudes on defence and disarmament.* Clarkson, Ontario: Canadian Peace Research Institute, 1963.

Pear, T. H. (Ed.) *Psychological factors of peace and war.* London: Hutchinson, 1950.

Perlmutter, H. V. Some characteristics of the xenophilic personality. *J. Psychol.* 1954, *38*, 291–300.

Perlmutter, H. V. Correlates of two types of xenophilic orientation. *J. abnorm. soc. Psychol.,* 1956, *52*, 130–135.

Perry, S. E. Notes on the role of the national: A social-psychological concept for the study of international relations. *J. Confl. Resol.,* 1957, *1*, 346–363.

Pilisuk, M., & Rapoport, A. Stepwise disarmament and sudden destruction in a two-person game: A research tool. *J. Confl. Resol.,* 1964, *8*, 36–49.

Pool, I. de S. *Communication and values in relation to war and peace.* New York:

Institute for International Order, 1961.

Pool, I. de S., Keller, Suzanne, & Bauer, R. A. The influence of foreign travel on political attitudes of American businessmen. *Publ. Opin. Quart.*, 1956, *20*, 151–175.

Proshansky, H. M., & Evans, R. I. (Eds.) American political extremism in the 1960's. *J. soc. Issues*, 1963, *19* (2).

Pruitt, D. G. An analysis of responsiveness between nations. *J. Confl. Resol.*, 1962, *6*, 5–18.

Putney, S., & Middleton, R. Some factors associated with student acceptance or rejection of war. *Amer. sociol. Rev.*, 1962, *27*, 655–667.

Rapoport, A. Formal games as probing tools for investigating behavior motivated by trust and suspicion. *J. Confl. Resol.*, 1963, *7*, 570–579.

Raser, J. R., & Crow, W. J. *WINSAFE II: An Inter-Nation Simulation study of deterrence postures embodying capacity to delay response.* La Jolla, California: Western Behavioral Sciences Institute, 1964.

Richardson, L. F. Threats and security. In T. H. Pear (Ed.), *Psychological factors of peace and war.* London: Hutchinson, 1950. Pp. 219–235.

Rose, P. I. Citizens' opinions on civil defense. *Council for Correspondence Newsl.*, March 1963, No. 24, 25–37.

Rose, P. I., & Laulicht, J. (Eds.) The threat of war: Policy and public opinion. *Soc. Problems*, 1963, *11* (1).

Rosenau, J. N. *Public opinion and foreign policy.* New York: Random House, 1961.

Rosenau, J. N. *National leadership and foreign policy: A case study in the mobilization of public support.* Princeton: Princeton Univer. Press, 1963.

Russell, R. W. (Ed.) Psychology and policy in a nuclear age. *J. soc. Issues*, 1961, *17* (3).

Russett, B. M. (with Alker, H. R., Jr., Deutsch, K. W., & Lasswell, H. D.) *World handbook of political and social indicators.* New Haven: Yale Univer. Press, 1964.

Schelling, T. C. Experimental games and bargaining theory. In K. Knorr & S. Verba (Eds.), *The international system.* Princeton: Princeton Univer. Press, 1961. Pp. 47–68.

Sherif, M. Superordinate goals in the reduction of intergroup conflict. *Amer. J. Sociol.*, 1958, *63*, 349–356.

Sherif, M., Harvey, O. J., White, B. J., Hood, W. R., & Sherif, Carolyn W. *Intergroup conflict and cooperation: The Robbers Cave experiment.* Norman: Univer. Oklahoma Book Exchange, 1961.

Singer, J. D. The relevance of the behavioral sciences to the study of international relations. *Behav. Sci.*, 1961, *6*, 324–335. (a)

Singer, J. D. The level-of-analysis problem in international relations. In K. Knorr & S. Verba (Eds.), *The international system.* Princeton: Princeton Univer. Press, 1961. Pp. 77–92. (b)

Smith, H. P. Do intercultural experiences affect attitudes? *J. abnorm. soc. Psychol.*, 1955, *51*, 469–477.

Smith, M. B. (Ed.) Attitudes and adjustment in cross-cultural contact: Recent studies of foreign students. *J. soc. Issues*, 1956, *12* (1).

Smith, M. B., Bruner, J. S., & White, R. W. *Opinions and personality.* New York: Wiley, 1956.

Smith, M. B., Fawcett, J. T., Ezekiel, R., & Roth, Susan A factorial study of morale among Peace Corps teachers in Ghana. *J. soc. Issues*, 1963, *19* (3), 10–32.

Snyder, R. C. Introduction. In R. C. Snyder, H. W. Bruck, & B. Sapin (Eds.), *Foreign policy decision-making.* New York: Free Press, 1962. Pp. 1–13.

Snyder, R. C. Some perspectives on the use of experimental techniques in the study of international relations. In H. Guetzkow *et al., Simulation in international relations.* Englewood Cliffs,

New Jersey: Prentice-Hall, 1963. Pp. 1–23.

Snyder, R. C., Bruck, H. W., & Sapin, B. Decision-making as an approach to the study of international politics. In R. C. Snyder, H. W. Bruck, & B. Sapin (Eds.), *Foreign policy decision-making.* New York: Free Press, 1962. Pp. 14–185.

Snyder, R. C., & Paige, G. D. The United States decision to resist aggression in Korea: The application of an analytical scheme. *Admin. Sci. Quart.,* 1958, *3,* 341–378.

Snyder, R. C., & Robinson, J. A. *National and international decision-making.* New York: Institute for International Order, 1961.

Stagner, R. Some factors related to attitude toward war, 1938. *J. soc. Psychol.,* 1942, *16,* 131–142.

Stagner, R. Studies of aggressive social attitudes. *J. soc. Psychol.,* 1944, *20,* 109–140.

Stagner, R., Brown, J. F., Gundlach, R. H., & White, R. K. A survey of public opinion on the prevention of war. *J. soc. Psychol.,* 1942, *16,* 109–130.

Swanson, G. E. The structure of a social psychology. University of Michigan, 1963. (Dittoed)

Terhune, K. W. Nationalism among foreign and American students: An exploratory study. *J. Confl. Resol.,* 1964, *8,* 256–270.

Tolman, E. C. *Drives toward war.* New York: Appleton-Century, 1942.

Torre, M. (Ed.) *The selection of personnel for international service.* New York: World Federation for Mental Health, 1963.

Waelder, R. *Psychological aspects of war and peace.* New York: Columbia Univer. Press, 1939.

Waskow, A. I. *The shelter-centered society.* Washington: Peace Research Institute, 1962.

Withey, S. B. *The U.S. and the U.S.S.R.* Ann Arbor: Survey Research Center, University of Michigan, 1961.

Zinnes, Dina A. Hostility in international decision-making. *J. Confl. Resol.,* 1962, *6,* 236–243.

Zinnes, Dina A., North, R. C., & Koch, H. E. Capability, threat, and the outbreak of war. In J. N. Rosenau (Ed.), *International politics and foreign policy.* New York: Free Press, 1961. Pp. 469–482.

Part One

National and International Images

2

It seems appropriate to begin our exploration of national and international images with the process of childhood socialization. The culture into which the individual becomes socialized makes available to him certain national self-images, images of the outsider in general, images of specific other nations, and images of an intersocietal order. In modern societies these images are transmitted, to a large extent, via the readers and textbooks contained in the school curriculum; and via literature, art, plays, movies, and various forms of popular culture to which the individual is exposed. How does growing up in a particular society, and exposure to these various media, shape the person's images? How are these images related to what the child learns about the structure of his own society and its relationship to other societies, near and far? These are some of the questions that Chapter 2 is designed to illuminate.

There is another sense, however, in which this chapter begins at the beginning. It draws its data about the role of socialization in image formation from ethnographic studies of preindustrial and preliterate societies. We are thus able to gain a better picture of the total society than data from more complex industrial societies can provide; and we can see more clearly the relationship between the internal structure of the society and the intersocietal images that it fosters. The acquisition of intersocietal images is presented as part of the process of socialization into a society with a particular social structure. This approach is certainly relevant to the understanding of image formation in modern societies, as will be seen especially in Chapter 10. Moreover, it is useful to start out with an examination of images of one's own and other societies in a context more general than that provided by the modern nation-state. Chapter 2 will bring in materials from modern societies only indirectly and occasionally, but the reader will be able to make his own extrapolations. Research that is currently underway in several industrialized countries, on the development of national and international images in children, will provide a firmer empirical basis for such extrapolations.

The author of Chapter 2, Robert A. LeVine, is Associate Professor of Anthropology with the Committee on Human Development, University of Chicago. He also holds a Research Career Development Award from the National Institutes of Health, and is a Fellow of the Foundations' Fund for Research in Psychiatry. He has written on socialization and African ethnography; and his current research focuses on culture and personality, and on ethnocentrism among tribal societies.

H. C. K.

Socialization, Social Structure, and Intersocietal Images*

Robert A. LeVine

*T*he cultures of the world as described by anthropologists are a potential laboratory for the systematic study of intergroup conflict and hostility and of ethnocentric imagery. Hypotheses developed by social scientists concerning such phenomena in the context of industrial societies and the contemporary international system can be tested in this cross-cultural laboratory to assess their applicability to the full range of human social behavior. However, while existing ethnographic accounts contain much material that is of interest to students of international behavior, the intersocietal relations of indigenous peoples within an area have rarely been a focus of anthropological investigation. This chapter is a preliminary attempt to develop theoretical formulations at the cross-cultural level that might guide future investigations of non-industrial societies.

Four propositions are basic to the argument of this chapter and are presented here as the assumptions from which the more specific assertions follow.

1. Most human populations are ethnocentric (i.e., hostile to some outgroups and carrying negative images of them) to some degree, but the intensity and generality of the hostility as well as the specific contents of the images are widely variable cross-culturally.

2. The intersocietal behavior of a population is functionally related to its social system and varies concomitantly with it.

3. Customary patterns of intersocietal behavior are transmitted from one

* This chapter is in effect a working paper of the Cooperative Cross-Cultural Study of Ethnocentrism directed by Donald T. Campbell and myself under a grant from the Carnegie Corporation of New York to Northwestern University. (See Campbell and LeVine, 1961.) For helpful comments on an earlier version of this chapter I am grateful to William A. Scott, Paul Rosenblatt, Donald T. Campbell, Eleanor E. Maccoby, M. Brewster Smith, and Herbert Kelman, although responsibility for its present content is entirely mine.

generation to the next, and each individual acquires the customary attitudes and images in the course of his socialization and personality development. Thus, certain aspects of childhood experience covary with certain patterns of intersocietal behavior.

4. When there is a high degree of functional congruence between personality and social system, the performance of customary intersocietal behavior is functional for collectivities at some level in the social system and gratifying to the individual.

SOCIALIZATION OF THE CHILD AND INTERSOCIETAL BEHAVIOR

The acquisition of intersocietal behavior patterns can be considered within the general framework of social learning. Sears, Maccoby, and Levin (1957) have suggested that children learn to make novel social and emotional responses by three means: trial-and-error, direct tuition, and role practice. All of these are relevant to the learning of cultural behavior patterns concerning outgroups, and they direct our attention to specific aspects of such learning. Trial-and-error learning would seem to be most relevant to motivational sources of ethnocentric behavior, direct tuition to cognitive sources, and role practice to "habitual" or social-structural sources.

Motivational Sources of Ethnocentric Behavior

The motives that appear to be most clearly involved are aggression and dependency (or affiliation). Every child in his early years manifests approach, avoidance, and aggressive responses with respect to others in his interpersonal environment. These may be viewed as trial-and-error in the course of social adaptation, for parents and other elders reinforce some of these tendencies and discourage others. The typical individual grows to adulthood with a structure of motives that are socially valued and for which intergroup behavior, along with other kinds of social behavior, may provide opportunities for satisfaction.

The linkage between socialization of the child and customary social behavior is most conspicuous in the case of the aggressive motive. Whiting and Child (1953) have found cross-cultural confirmation for a hypothesized relationship between severity of aggression training of children and belief in sorcery, which they take as an index of projected aggression. Following Dollard (1938) and Dollard, Doob, Miller, Mowrer, and Sears (1939), they discuss customary aggressive behavior in terms of displacement and projection. Their analysis is applicable to intersocietal behavior although they do not devote much attention to that structural level.

Recent anthropological studies provide some evidence for the operation of displacement at the intersocietal level. Murphy (1957) describes the Mundurucú, a Brazilian tribe characterized by peaceful cooperation among its male members, who in the past expressed the antagonisms generated by their social structure through predatory warfare and head-hunting directed against other tribes. He refers to Mundurucú warfare as a "safety valve institution" and claims that it drained off aggression that would have weakened social solidarity had it been allowed intrasocietal expression. Under contemporary conditions, in which warfare is impossible, community fission within the society has resulted. In a recent volume on tribes of the Purari delta of New Guinea, Maher (1961) discusses the importance of intertribal warfare and cannibalism for each of the groups before World War I. By the end of the war, governmental intervention had drastically diminished such activity and eventually eradicated it. Summarizing historical and contemporary evidence on the Purari peoples, Maher states, "The data on this behavior over the long term are not as full or as clear as one would like, but they suggest that there has been a rising tide of aggression through intratribal fighting and sorcery, and that this is correlated with, and is probably a function of, the suppression of intertribal warfare" (p. 16). It might be added that, among the Gusii of southwestern Kenya, a similar phenomenon has occurred. The pacification of the area in 1907 and the prohibition on intertribal and interclan feuding were associated with a considerable rise in aggression among neighbors and close kinsmen, expressed, as among the Purari, in an increase in accusations of sorcery.

These studies from South America, Africa, and the Pacific on the displacement of aggression onto outgroups do not demonstrate that this is related to the aggression training of children; it is possible to accept displacement explanations of intergroup conflict patterns and reject any connection between these patterns and childhood experience. However, the displacement concept implies that warfare and other culturally patterned forms of aggression serve psychodynamic needs for individuals, and it is not far-fetched to assume that the intensity and quality of these needs depend on the manner in which they are handled in childhood. Whiting and Child (1953) have hypothesized that the tendency to displace aggression onto objects in cultural fantasy is strengthened by anxiety resulting from severe aggression training. It may well be that the same applies to physical combat and the tendency to

maintain hostile images of alien groups. For the nonliterate societies from which data have been drawn in this discussion and in cross-cultural studies like those of Whiting and Child, one can safely make the assumption that intersocietal behavior requires participation by a large proportion of group members and that most of these are interested and involved in intersocietal relations. Given this situation, an expectation of close correspondence between the motivational state of the population and the patterns of intersocietal action is entirely reasonable. In large-scale, differentiated societies, however, where only a small elite may be deeply involved in international problems while the largely nonparticipant masses are apathetic, it might be a mistake to expect such a correspondence. There are also many more organizational obstacles to translating personal aggressiveness into war in a large industrial nation than in a small New Guinea tribe. Nevertheless, the study of such nonliterate groups gives us an opportunity to see a heightened version of a phenomenon that may exist only in attenuated form in our own society. Furthermore, it may be that the same motivational factors that result in war and feud in nonliterate societies lead to prejudice against foreign nations and peoples in the populations of industrial nations.

Cognitive and Evaluative Sources of Ethnocentric Behavior

All peoples have some images and evaluations of other peoples of whose existence they are aware. Although the intensity of the feelings involved in the images and evaluations is a motivational problem, the content of the images and their validity can be viewed from a cognitive perspective. The images may be complex or undifferentiated, accurate or distorted; evaluations may be positive or negative for each of the peoples recognized as separate entities. In other words, each group with a common culture has a cognitive map of other groups and their traits as part of this common culture. A good deal of this cognitive map is transmitted to each generation of children by means of direct tuition; that is to say, parents or other elders give children instruction in the names, locations, attributes, and accepted evaluations of other groups both near and far. Some of this information may be conveyed to children informally, as when they overhear adults discussing other groups. In some cultures, the very names children learn to use for other groups imply the opprobrium with which adults regard them or refer to specific attributes of those groups. In the course of child training, parents may hold up certain alien groups as positive or negative role models for the child. It is not uncommon in many societies for adults to label misbehaving children with the name of a despised group; such metaphors undoubtedly contribute to the child's acquisition of the culturally standardized images of the groups concerned.

However, it would be a mistake to assume that the child simply absorbs from adults a coherent and socially acceptable set of outgroup images in the course of development. A simplified picture of this kind may approach validity in an isolated small group with a stable cultural and intercultural environment, although even here various motivational and experiential factors might cause discontinuities and deviances in the transmission process. In large-scale, complex societies with highly differentiated and efficient communication systems, however, there are many extrafamilial sources of images and information about outgroups for the child: mass media, school teachers and textbooks, religious teachings, personal contact with foreigners or travellers who recount their experiences. Since these sources are not necessarily consistent with one another, differential exposure across individuals can result in a wide range of images and evaluations in a single population of children, while differential exposure of children in different age groups can lead to discontinuities in the development of outgroup orientations.

The problems of age trends in the development of national self-identification, national self-images, and international images and attitudes in children has been investigated in a systematic cross-national study (see Lambert & Klineberg, 1959; Klineberg, 1962). Preliminary findings indicate that there are few universal age trends among ten countries of Europe, Asia, and America. Among these few is an increase in knowledge and differentiated images of other peoples between the ages of six and ten (Sato, 1962), and an increase in the tendencies to perceive other peoples as similar to one's own and to proclaim affection for other peoples during the same period (Lambert, 1962). The notion that increasing age necessarily means an increase in ethnocentric prejudice does not seem to be supported (Lambert, 1962). The developmental complexities and discontinuities revealed so far may well be a function of the different and inconsistent sources of international images for children of different ages; they may also, as Lambert has suggested, be related to the influence of generalized social habits that are not necessarily consistent with explicitly transmitted international images (this kind of influence is discussed later). Clarification of some of the knotty problems involved in the development of ethnocentric imagery in children may be expected from future findings of this ongoing cross-national study.

Insofar as the intergenerational transmission of ethnocentric images is a matter of the child's absorption of a culturally standardized cognitive map, it is essential to know the cognitive attributes of this map. One hypothesis suggested by some convergent cross-cultural findings is that it is possible to maintain (or at least to entertain seriously) more inaccurate images of groups with which one has had less experience. Swartz (1961) reports that those people of Romónum, Truk, in the Caroline Islands who know of New Guinea "consider the inhabitants of this place to be unregenerate cannibals whom they group together with sharks and other fearsome and hateful life forms" (p. 77). Lévi-Strauss (1961) states that Spaniards of the early sixteenth century were not certain that the Indians of Hispaniola were humans rather than animals or creatures of the devil, and that, according to one account, Indians of Puerto Rico would drown captured Europeans and then watch them for weeks to see if the corpses would putrefy. According to Shepperson and Price (1958), there was a widespread belief among East and Central Africans during the second half of the nineteenth century that Europeans, whom they were meeting for the first time, generally engaged in cannibalism with respect to Africans. Intensive contact between groups usually tends to eliminate the more fantastic images, although superordinate groups sometimes maintain them as a rationalization for keeping other groups in subjection.

Where populations differ in conspicuous physical features, it may take a long period of intensive contact to provide sufficient reality-testing for inaccurate and distorted images to disappear. It is often reported in contemporary Africa that unschooled Africans who have seen Europeans on numerous occasions are curious about whether the latter have the same skin color on those parts of their bodies that are concealed by clothing. This suggests that a great deal of information and experience is required before an accurate perception of the attributes of different racial groups is acquired. Ordinarily, this process seems to begin with a small number of group members who acquire a great deal of knowledge about outsiders through direct experience and then pass information on to other members of the group. Eventually, more realistic images of the outsiders become part of the group culture, although if the groups do not become socially mixed, quite distorted images are likely to be stabilized.

In sum, the images of an outgroup that adults pass on to children are affected by the amount of direct experience the adults have had with members of the outgroup and by the amount of conspicuous difference (in physical features, dress, language, and occupational specialization) between the ingroup and the outgroup. This notion leads to the hypothesis that a group will maintain more accurate images of groups with which it has frequent contact than with groups with which it interacts only rarely, as well as more accurate images of groups that are less conspicuously different than ones that are more so. It should be noted that some distorted and negative images are self-maintaining in the sense that each new generation that learns them tends to avoid contact with the group concerned and thereby loses the opportunity for the reality-testing that might alter the images in the direction of greater accuracy (though not necessarily less negative valence). These statements are familiar propositions in the literature of ethnic relations, but they have been neither systematically applied to the interaction of political-territorial units nor tested cross-culturally.

Habitual Sources of Ethnocentric Behavior

Outgroups, particularly those with which contact is infrequent, are somewhat ambiguous stimuli which may be variously organized into cultural images. Other things (such as displacement motives and actual known characteristics of the outgroup) being equal, a people can be expected to react to an outgroup with responses that are high in their social habit hierarchy. William A. Scott (1958), in a discussion of international attitudes, has made this very point:

A particular frame of reference which the individual applies successfully to adjustment within his realm of familiar events may, because of its rewarding character, find strong emotional attachment within the person and hence be applied indiscriminately to the interpretation of new events concerning which information is inadequate (p. 14).

He describes one form of nonrational international attitude in the following terms:

When a cognitive frame of reference is forcibly brought to bear on an attitude, it is likely to be a set of values and related elements which has been found serviceable in meaningful areas of the individual's lifespace, such as his relations with job, family, or friends, or other realm of intense interest to him (p. 15).

In other words, it is suggested that the phenomenon of habit transfer is at work, particularly in constructing images of international relations after the pattern of interpersonal relations. If this were applied to all kinds of ethnocentric behavior, we might hypothe-

size that groups with high levels of internal suspicion or self-hatred or sociability would act with suspicion or hostility or sociability, respectively, to outgroups. Thus stated, such a hypothesis generates expectations that are contradictory to a displacement hypothesis, which involves complementarity in ingroup–outgroup behavior. However, it may well be that the critical factor determining whether a generalization or displacement type of effect operates is a concept of dissimilarity or boundedness with the outgroup in question. If the group is viewed as similar to the ingroup, generalization would be expected to operate, whereas if it is viewed as dissimilar, then a displacement expectation would be reasonable. Thus the choice of behavior mechanisms would hinge on the stimulus equivalence of ingroup and outgroup for ingroup members. The stimulus equivalence is established or prevented by the social structure of the group. (Cf. Christiansen, 1959, for a discussion of the displacement vs. the generalization hypotheses.)

Elsewhere (LeVine, 1960) I have suggested that certain social structures facilitate the transfer of social habits learned as appropriate in the family to larger sociopolitical units. Societies that have large extended kin groups with many corporate functions but lack a specialized central government appear to be most susceptible to this tendency. In such a situation family behavior is a reasonable model for behavior in the wider social system and there is no need to acquire a special set of differentiated "political" habits. Among the Gusii of southwestern Kenya, who fall into this category of society, the stimulus equivalence of social and political units at all levels is symbolized by the use of a single word, *egesaku*, which literally denotes the door into an ordinary house from the adjacent cattle pen. The elders of a man's patrilineage must enter his house through this door rather than the front door. In its social usage, *egesaku* is usually translated as "lineage," but within Gusii society it can refer to a group comprised by a man and his sons, to lineages equivalent in size to a small community, to clans numbering in the thousands, to tribal sections numbering in the tens of thousands, or to Gusii society as a whole (many of these units have special names as well). In terms of the subject of this chapter, it is most significant that the Gusii characterize each of the other Kenya tribes as *egesaku* and also use the word to mean "nation," as when they talk of Kenya, the United Kingdom, or any other contemporary country. Thus in Gusii society the images and behavioral expectations that persons have of the interaction of groups at any level, including intercultural and international, are derived in part from patterns operative in the interaction of the smallest patrilineal kin groups. This is not to say that they do not recognize differences in behavior at different levels, but rather that they tend to use kin group interaction as the primary model for ordering events and relationships in wider settings.

The possibility that interpersonal relationships learned relatively early in life may serve as models for intergroup behavior directs our attention to the means by which children acquire generalizable interpersonal habits. One of the means is the type of learning that Sears, Maccoby, and Levin (1957) call role practice—"the discovery and learning of new actions by observing what others do, and then practicing it by pretending to *be* the other person" (p. 369). Once we accept as given that this observational learning of roles goes on, then all role behaviors that the child observes become possible models for imitation by him, even if such imitation

is covert and in fantasy. Presumably, however, the probability of his habitually imitating a given role is in direct proportion to the amount of his opportunity for observing it, the frequency of his practice of it, and the amount of reward provided for such imitation. This view leads to the expectation that the child's membership in a few primary groups of kin and peers, which give him most opportunity for role observation, most active participation, and most social rewards, is critical for the acquisition of generalizable role behaviors.

We may extend this view and assert that the group membership of the child leaves him with a residue not only of a particular role with which he identifies, but with a preference for certain valued patterns of dyadic interaction. This kind of reasoning played a large part in the developmental hypotheses of *The authoritarian personality* (Adorno *et al.*, 1950), especially in terms of the learning of dominance–submission as a pattern so that the individual who had internalized the pattern could play either dominant or submissive roles. Carrying this a step farther, it is possible to suggest that the entire set of interaction patterns or role structures in the primary groups to which the child is exposed leaves him with values about how groups should be composed and how they should operate and how persons in various roles should relate to one another. In other words, the social participation of the child may give him some ideal images of human interaction that are high in his social habit hierarchy and that he is likely to apply to novel and relatively unstructured social situations later in his life.

The above line of reasoning leads to the examination of several aspects of child social life as relevant to the formation of general habits, values, and images that might condition ethnocentric behavior. These aspects can be indicated by the following ethnographic questions: What is the range of groups in which children participate? What is the authority structure of such groups? To what extent do parents encourage participation in children's peer groups and allow children in such groups autonomy? To what extent do parents and children's groups encourage sociability (that is, a general quality of friendliness), sharing goods, and generalized trust of others, as personal traits? The significance of these childhood variables is brought into clearer focus in a discussion of empirical data below. At this point, however, it should be emphasized that the impact of such child-training experiences on ethnocentric behavior is likely to be diminished when there is subsequent learning that is more specialized in the sense of being explicitly applicable to intersocietal affairs and when this subsequent learning is at variance with the more general lessons of early social life.

To summarize, I have argued in this section that intersocietal behavior patterns can be thought of as modal personality characteristics which have their ontogenetic sources in the socialization process. Like other complex modal personality characteristics, they are affected by the development in the individual of particular motives, cognitions, values, and habits. I have suggested that the intersocietal behavior characteristic of a people may depend on (a) their early training in aggression and dependency, (b) the information on outgroups that socializing agents are capable of providing children and that they select to transmit to them, and (c) the kinds of habitual dispositions in sociability and interpersonal behavior generally that are reinforced in the childhood environment and transferred

to wider social situations met later in life.

In the remainder of this chapter I shall generate, through ethnographic comparisons, a theory of the relationships between social structure, socialization of the child, and intersocietal behavior in politically uncentralized societies. This theory states that certain internal features of social structure (specifically, the integrative or divisive tendencies of component groups within the society) determine certain norms of interpersonal conduct which in turn affect the ways in which adults socialize the young. Through this normatively organized socialization process, individuals acquire certain motives, images of themselves and others, and interpersonal response patterns, which affect the way they view outgroups and behave toward them. The argument that follows begins with the end points, the hypothesized linkage between internal social structure and intersocietal behavior, illustrating by an extreme contrast between a Brazilian tribe and Bedouin Arabs the possible relations between the two sets of variables. A further comparison, between two neighboring East African tribes studied by the author, illustrates the hypothesized role of socialization in mediating between social structure and intersocietal behavior.

SOCIAL STRUCTURE AND INTERSOCIETAL BEHAVIOR

Each social system, from the viewpoint of individual loyalties, may be considered a structure of ingroups and outgroups. Political sociology, in analyzing social systems in terms of their major group cleavages and the effects of such cleavages on political behavior, has made this kind of structural perspective familiar. The analyses of political sociologists have ordinarily been limited to social systems in which the major groups, no matter how opposed to one another, are politically amalgamated in a national state and in which intergroup violence within the state is unusual and directed toward changing the leadership or form of the national government.

When one brings in the full range of human societies, it is necessary to consider those that, in terms of cultural and linguistic homogeneity, occupation of a continuous territory, self-recognition as an entity distinct from surrounding groups, and certain social and ritual bonds, deserve to be thought of as single social systems although they have no central government at all. In many such societies, the major groups may engage in armed combat against one another on a regular basis since there is no society-wide monopoly of violence. Societies of this kind can be found among the indigenous inhabitants of North and South America, Africa, Oceania, and some parts of Asia, although in most cases they have come under the political control of a national or colonial government which has put an end to their internecine violence. In their traditional forms, these societies present an interesting challenge to political analysis, for their "internal" relations often resemble contemporary international relations more than they do the internal structure of a politically amalgamated social system.

There are, however, wide variations in the intergroup structures of these uncentralized societies, and the amount of internecine violence is variable among them as well. Some of them approximate what Deutsch (1954) has called "pluralistic security communities," since they maintain interunit peace in the absence of political amalgamation. Others do not constitute security communities at all, since their component units have a mutual expec-

tation of warfare which is more or less frequently fulfilled. The hypothesis presented here is that these variations in intergroup relations at the *intra*societal level cause variations in imagery and behavior patterns at the *inter*societal level. I shall attempt to demonstrate the plausibility of this thesis and the place of child training in the causal chain by means of a series of ethnographic cases representing ideal types.

Social Structure and Intersocietal Behavior among the Mundurucú and the Arab Bedouins

The first ethnographic case is an unequivocal example of a pluralistic security community: the Mundurucú of the Brazilian rain forest, which have already been mentioned. Although they had no central government, the Mundurucú as described by Murphy (1957) did not war among themselves and were extremely aggressive toward other peoples. The social basis for internal peace was a set of cross-cutting ties established by the dispersion of forty-odd patrilineal clans (sibs) throughout various villages. Each man moved at marriage to the household of his bride, and this was frequently in a different village. He became a member of the men's house in his wife's village, and this was the military unit to which he belonged. War with other villages was repugnant to him because it would bring him into conflict with members of his own clan, yet the clan was too widely dispersed to be a functional military unit. Thus each man had dual loyalties, to his kin group and to his village, and since these did not coincide geographically, they acted to prevent open warfare among the Mundurucú. As Murphy puts it:

Despite the diversity of their local and lineal origins, the men of a village, and ultimately the whole tribe, were expected to maintain harmonious and cooperative relations. Cooperation in economic activities transcended the minimal necessities of their ecological adaptation, and any open show of aggression between men was strictly prohibited (p. 1020). . . . Tribal feeling was highly developed and conflict between villages was totally absent (p. 1021).

Murphy suggests that matrilocal residence at marriage inevitably distributes men, the primary political role-players in all societies, among territorial units other than the ones to which they owe loyalty through birth and early contact, and that the multiple loyalties in such a situation lead to the repression of intrasocietal aggression. He cites evidence to indicate that matrilocal societies of Brazil are characterized by a much higher degree of internal peace than closely related patrilocal societies in the same area.

Thoden van Velzen and van Wetering (1960) have tested Murphy's hypothesis on a sample of fifty-one socially unstratified societies, most of them nonliterate, drawn from all over the world. They obtained statistically significant positive relationships between matrilocality (as opposed to patrilocality, in which men remain with their natal families after marriage) and various indices of internal peacefulness (rarity of fighting and murder, aversion to intrasocietal bloodshed as a principal value, and absence of retaliatory blood feuds). This is a striking confirmation of the hypothesis that the multiple loyalties of individuals can have a pacifying effect on intergroup relations. In this sense, it supports theoretical formulations by Simmel (1955), Coser (1956), Gluckman (1955), Guetzkow (1955), and other social scientists who have seen the cross-cutting ties of individuals to several groups as a politically integrating structural pattern. It should be noted, however, that in the type of societies for which the specific hypothesis holds, community and kin relations operate within the context of relatively small, face-to-face groups, and membership in such groups tends to be functionally diffuse and permanent rather than limited to specific functions or contractual relationships. For this reason, the phenomenon cannot be regarded as identical with the group loyalty structures of the most urbanized industrial societies. Nevertheless, there is ethnographic evidence to indicate that in some politically centralized nonliterate societies, the control maintained by the central authority rested on a social underpinning of cross-cutting kin and territorial ties; this is true of the Iroquois, a conciliar federation in which matrilineal clans (sibs) and tribal territories cross-cut one another, as well as for Buganda, an African monarchy with spatially dispersed patrilineal descent groups. Thus the pacifying effect of multiple loyalties, although seen in clearest form where a central authority is absent, may be operative in a politically amalgamated group as well.

Murphy's interpretation of the relation between Mundurucú residence patterns and intrasocietal peace has thus been confirmed. It is now possible to return to his analysis and examine the effects of intrasocietal patterns on intrasocietal relations and images among the Mundurucú.

The human world was seen by the Mundurucú to consist of two distinct spheres; there were "people" or Mundurucú, and *pariwat*, a term referring to any non-Mundurucú human. With the exception of the neighboring Apiacá Indians and the white men, all pariwat were enemies. An enemy was not merely a person to be guarded against but was a proper object of attack, and the Mundurucú pursued this end with extraordinary vigor and stamina (Murphy, 1957, p. 1021).

The men and women of enemy groups were killed and decapitated; the heads were later ceremonially shrunk. Any warrior who took a trophy head was specially honored and referred to as *Dajeboiši,* literally "mother of the peccary," "an allusion to the Mundurucú view of other tribes as equivalent to game animals" (p. 1024). Enemy children were captured, incorporated into the kinship system through adoption and grew up as normal Mundurucú rather than being treated as inferiors. Murphy emphasizes the point that Mundurucú warfare was not carried out for material gain, out of a necessity to defend their territory, or even in response to provocation by other groups. They enjoyed warfare and looked upon the mere existence of other groups as inviting attack. "The enemy was looked upon as game to be hunted, and the Mundurucú still speak of the pariwat in the same terms they reserve for peccary and tapir" (p. 1028). Thus, for the Mundurucú, the high degree of internal peace and extreme bellicosity toward outside groups is associated with a simple dichotomy of ingroup and outgroups, almost all of the latter being grouped together under a single term, regarded as inferior beings, and deemed worthy of attack.

The second society to be considered as an ethnographic case is not a security community at all and is characterized by a high degree of internal violence. This is Arab Bedouin society as analyzed by Murphy and Kasdan (1959). In one perspective, all Bedouins are members of the same patrilineal (agnatic) descent group and can trace genealogical connections. At the same time, patrilineal relationship, no matter how close, is no guarantee of peaceful rela-tions. Murphy and Kasdan describe it as follows:

> In its underlying principle, the process of segmentary opposition between patrilineal sections corresponds closely to the Arab proverb: "Myself against my brother; my brother and I against my cousin; my cousin, my brother and I against the outsider."
>
> In this system, it is almost impossible to isolate a solidary ingroup, and groupings are continually being activiated or redefined through struggles that may even pit members of the nuclear family against each other (p. 20). . . .
>
> The seeming disorganization of the Bedouin family is of course simply a part of the fundamental structure of Arab society. Just as there is structural opposition between agnatic sections of several generations' depth, so also is there opposition within the family, for the agnatic units differ only in scope and not in organization. That Bedouin society follows fundamentally the same principles at all levels of organization can be seen when one considers the maximal units of the society. Ideally, all Arabs, whether nomadic or sedentary, form a single superlineage, the member units of which trace common ancestry to the prophet Abraham. . . . Hostility characterized relations between the two branches [of Arabs] during the Ummayad dynasty of Islam, and opposition between the two great groupings today rationalizes intertribal wars and the commonly encountered split of peasant villages into antagonistic factions. It is noteworthy that these comprehensive agnatic units are structured in the same way as small groupings of but a few generations in depth, and they are defined and maintained by the same oppositional process (p. 21).

By and large, the function of the agnatic (patrilineal) groups is military; they are not multifunctional. Hence it is possible to build a huge alliance of such units for a specific military purpose, only to have it fall apart again when that purpose is attained or no longer relevant. As Murphy and Kasdan put it, "Cohesive relations between and within sections do not have an enduring continuing quality, but are situational and opportunistic" (p. 21). The most stable unit is the "tribe," whose members have corporate rights in grazing lands and water holes, but even this unit is subject to realignment of its component sections. All other forms of wealth are owned by individuals. Thus there is a high degree of consistency in the principles of alliance and conflict at levels ranging from the family to the entire ethnic group, and the shifting scope of alliances does not allow an individual to consider himself permanently bound or opposed to any particular group in the society. Each conflict situation defines the structure of ingroups and outgroups differently; thus today's ally may be tomorrow's enemy. However, the genealogy provides a clear hierarchy of loyalties, which are multiple but not conflicting at any point in time. A man stands with those who are closer to him in patrilineal relationship against those who are genealogically more remote. When the large-scale conflict against more remote groups is over, then he is free to engage in conflict with those more closely related to him. The most important feature of such a system is that groups at any level attain social solidarity primarily through opposition to other such groups, and that the participants are aware that alliances are temporary expedients rather than enduring bonds.

It would be expected on the basis of Murphy's hypothesis that a society as full of internal strife as that of the Bedouin Arabs would be patrilocal, and it is. But there is an additional social mechanism that works against the development of conflicting loyalties among the Bedouins—the endogamous pattern of parallel cousin marriage. When a man marries the daughter of his father's brother, as is preferred, he does not acquire a tie to a patrilineal unit other than the one into which he was born. In fact, endogamy within small patrilineal kin groups tends to isolate them from one another socially, so that there are no cross-cutting bonds of marriage and in-law relationship to temper conflicts between the groups. Thus the Arab Bedouins not only have the tendencies toward societal divisiveness characteristic of uncentralized patrilocal societies generally (that is, the clustering of patrilineally related males in local groups capable of united military action), but they also lack the somewhat pacifying effect, found in many patrilocal societies, of dual loyalties resulting from intergroup marriage. In this structural arrangement, group loyalties do not act as a brake on intergroup conflict; thus conflict is pervasive and frequent.

The contrast between the Mundurucú and the Bedouin Arabs suggests that sociopolitical organization has determinate effects on certain cognitive and evaluative properties of group images. The Mundurucú have no armed combat within their own ethnic group, due in part to the cross-cutting ties created by their multiple overlapping loyalty groupings. They are, however, extremely warlike toward most other ethnic groups. Consistent with this set of sociopolitical relations are their group images: a sharply bounded, highly esteemed ingroup surrounded by despicable outgroups who are classed together as enemies, similar to game animals, and legitimate to attack. The Arab Bedouins, on the other hand, have considerable internecine group violence, facilitated by the social isolation of inbreeding local groups of patrilineal kinsmen. As the Mundurucú gain societal unity through the territorial dispersion of mutually loyal patrilineal kinsmen, so the Arab Bedouins promote divisiveness by marriage and residence patterns that reinforce local ties at the expense of wider ones. The sharply dichotomous group images of the Mundurucú are not possible among the Arab Bedouins. For the latter, ingroup–outgroup boundaries vary according to circumstance; conflict is possible within any unit and genealogical proximity is used to legitimize temporary alliances for military purposes. The Arab Bedouins must remain ambivalent about all group relations since they know they may be (or have been) pitted against their fellow members on another occasion. Unlike the Mundurucú, they cannot esteem "their own group" in an unqualified and enduring way, since no matter what the scope of the group involved, it contains potential enemies.

Thus the Mundurucú have a fixed set of ingroup–outgroup images that reflect the integrated organization of their society and its hostile relations with other societies. The Arab Bedouins view ingroup–outgroup relations relativistically, reflecting the divisiveness and shifting scope of loyalty groupings within their own society. In congruence with these images, we would expect the Mundurucú to be highly sociable among themselves and to displace their aggression onto the despised outgroups; Murphy indicates that this is what takes place among them. The Arab Bedouins, however, would be expected to have a generalized suspicion in social relationships at all levels (though varying in intensity), and to use projection as well as displacement in the handling of aggression since the temporary nature of alliances engenders an exaggerated fear

of the hostility of others. It is also plausible to expect that children in each of the societies would be socialized to quite different patterns of social interaction. In the absence of detailed information on socialization patterns in the two societies, it is necessary to turn to a different comparison, derived from ethnographic data collected by the present writer.[1] Before examining socialization patterns in the two ethnic groups to be compared here, let us look at their social structures and the intersocietal behaviors that seem to be linked to these.

Social Structure and Intersocietal Behavior among the Kipsigis and the Gusii

The Kipsigis and the Gusii inhabit adjacent sections of the southwestern highlands of Kenya, where they have been in contact for approximately two hundred years. Despite their common environment and many cultural similarities, the Kipsigis and Gusii have retained structural differences that stem from their divergent origins. The Kipsigis speak a Sudanic language and are part of the "Nilo-Hamitic" group of peoples in Kenya, Tanganyika, and Uganda. Like other Nilo-Hamitic peoples, their most important sociopolitical units are age-graded groups of adult males. The Gusii are part of the huge Bantu-speaking majority of subequatorial Africa and, like many other East African Bantu, have patrilineal descent groups as their primary sociopolitical units. This major structural contrast between Kipsigis and Gusii forms the basis of the comparative analysis attempted below, but it should be borne in mind that the two societies have the following culture traits in common: an

---

[1] The field work on which the data are based was carried out in Kenya during 1955–1957 with the support of a Ford Foundation fellowship.

economic base combining agriculture and animal husbandry, dispersed settlement pattern, polygyny, the mother-child household, patrilineal descent and inheritance, and intermittently warlike relations with surrounding groups, including each other. Furthermore, both have populations between 300,000 and 600,000 that were politically uncentralized (as well as smaller) before the advent of colonial administration at the turn of the century.

A major dimension of contrast between the pre-colonial Kipsigis and Gusii is that the Kipsigis maintained peace within their ethnic group despite the absence of a central authority, while the Gusii were subject to internecine group violence. To a great extent the internal peace of the Kipsigis seems attributable to cross-cutting ties resulting from four independent types of group organizations: (a) the entire society was divided into four *territorial units,* which were in turn subdivided down to the level of village—the most important level—and beyond to individual homesteads; (b) there were also four *military regiments* in which membership was hereditary in the male line; (c) at or around puberty, men were initiated into *age groups* which progressed through a series of age grades; the entire male population was stratified into seven such age groups; and (d) there were *patrilineal clans* and their segments, the largest exogamous segment having obligations regarding mutual economic assistance and the payment of compensation for homicide. The military regiments, age groups, and clans were territorially dispersed, so that they cross-cut the territorial units and made unified military action by one village or area against another virtually impossible. Family residence patterns

gave rise to even more cross-cutting ties. Kipsigis men tended to set up their own homesteads after about a year of patrilocal residence. Since the entire society was a peaceful unit, and since land was plentiful, it was possible for sons to move anywhere in tribal territory, and most often they moved far away from their fathers and brothers. Furthermore, polygynists kept wives as much as twenty or thirty miles apart, in different territorial units. By taking advantage of the internal peace in their society to disperse themselves spatially, Kipsigis families made it even more difficult for group violence to break out. Disputes were settled by the adjudication of local elders in institutionalized judicial roles with community consent and much informal pressure for settlement.[2]

The Gusii had only one principle of group organization: patrilineal descent traced to a common ancestor. The entire society was thought of as a single lineage subdivided at six or seven levels into a myriad of component lineages (see page 51). A major division was into seven "tribes," which were territorial units that conducted warfare against one another. Each tribe was made up of numerous "clans" which also engaged in group combat with one another, over trespass of territory, cattle theft, and the abduction of women. Within some clans there was military action between subclans, and sometimes even among component lineages, although these local combats tended to be with clubs rather than spears. As in the case of the Arab Bedouins, any of the units that fought one another could combine for conflict with outgroups, and the Gusii as a whole sometimes fought against the Kipsigis. The social isolation of local groups was not as ex-

---

[2] This analysis of Kipsigis social structure is based on the introduction by E. E. Evans-Pritchard to the ethnography by Peristiany (1939, pp. xix–xxxiv).

treme as among the Arab Bedouins, since marriage within the clan was not permitted. The Gusii have a proverb, "Those whom we marry are those whom we fight," but it seems likely that intermarriage between clans had some mitigating effect on conflict. Patrilocal residence prevented men from becoming loyal to their in-laws, but married women, though they were excluded from political and military participation, were sometimes used to communicate between two feuding clans, since they had affiliations with both. Despite intermarriage and the existence of more cohesive localized descent groups than the Arab Bedouins, the Gusii also recognized as similar the divisive tendencies of equivalent social segments at any level ranging from brothers within the family to tribes within the total Gusii society. It was the role of wealthy men and elders to prevent these divisive tendencies from breaking out into open conflict. This required authoritarian action, such as the threat of supernatural sanctions and military coercion (by the armed sons of leaders), and these actions were much more effective within small units than they were at the clan and interclan levels where there was little institutionalized leadership. It is notable, however, that violence could break out within small communities, even within families, if the leaders of such units were not capable of fulfilling the authoritarian role. The Gusii were keenly aware of such possibilities, but alliance for defense of land and property against outsiders aided local leaders in their efforts to contain the divisive propensities of lineage segments.

Thus the Kipsigis and Gusii afford a comparison similar to that of the Mundurucú and Arab Bedouins, of a society in which widespread political unity is cemented by the territoral dispersion of loyalty groups versus one in which localized patrilineal descent groups allow internal violence and shifting alliances within the society. One other point of divergence is relevant to the content of interpersonal behavior in the two societies: unlike the Kipsigis, the Gusii practiced sorcery against one another, and witchcraft accusations appear to have been much more frequent among them than among the Kipsigis. This suggests that the Gusii were not only more hostile than the Kipsigis, but also more suspicious of their fellow men. Given this contrast in behavior within the ethnic group, the intersocietal relations of the two societies may now be considered.

According to Peristiany (1939), "The Kipsigis are inordinately proud of their social divisions and of the mass of tradition and myth with which they are associated, and they show an aloof and overbearing disposition towards *punik* (strangers)" (p. 4). They dichotomized surrounding peoples into "brothers" (or "members of the same family") and *punik*, which is translated as either "strangers" or "enemies." Those tribes considered brothers were other Nandi-speaking groups (for example, Nandi, Tugen, and Keyo) whose dialects were intelligible to the Kipsigis and who had the same age group system. The Kipsigis intermarried with these peoples, maintained peaceful relations with them, and even paid them compensation in homicide cases. The cultural similarities among all these groups were very great, although they were territorially separated, and this was recognized by the Kipsigis, who regarded them as virtually identical to themselves. All other tribes were *punik*, but those enemies speaking unintelligible languages were evaluated according to their similarity to the Kipsigis. The major division among *punik* was into those who accepted the wartime custom of *saiset*, in which an individual could ask for mercy in battle by snatching a handful of grass and throwing it at his opponent, and those who did not. The Masai and Luo followed *saiset* and were for that reason respected opponents in warfare, whereas the Gusii did not and were said to be *kou ngogi*, "like dogs" (Peristiany, 1939, p. 171). The observance of a number of other courtesies in battle was associated with this distinction, but *saiset* epitomized it. The Masai, who are more closely related in language and culture to the Kipsigis than other *punik* tribes, were preferred to the Luo because the Masai respected Kipsigis shrines and had a similar code for behavior in warfare. Thus the Kipsigis evaluated surrounding groups in terms of their degree of similarity to themselves, preferring those more like themselves in language, culture, and intersocietal behavior. The fundamental dichotomy was one between their cultural brethren, with whom peace was permanent, and all others, but the images of enemy groups were differentiated in terms of resemblance to the Kipsigis self-image.

Although the Kipsigis had contempt for those who were unlike them, they did not regard them as irredeemable. On the contrary, they regularly took *punik* women and children as captives in battle and incorporated them into the society on an equal status with other Kipsigis. Even *punik* men were sometimes "naturalized" in this way. A whole group of Gusii, fleeing from the Masai warriors and isolated from their own people, were taken in by the Kipsigis. The latter insisted that the Gusii settle in a central section of Kipsigis country so that they would be quickly assimilated to their new culture. An eminent contemporary Kipsigis chief is said to be descended from these fugitives. Gusii men living on the margins of Kipsigis country sometimes married Kipsigis women and were natu-

ralized. The major requirement for becoming a Kipsigis was undergoing the elaborate male initiation, including circumcision. This provided the newcomer with knowledge of Kipsigis culture, loyalty to those who had undergone the process with him, and membership in an age group.

The Gusii were for the most part surrounded by peoples of different linguistic stocks and, although they recognized their kinship with more distant Bantu peoples, they did not expect friendship or peace to be maintained among them. They evaluated neighboring peoples more in terms of their domestic morality than on the basis of their intersocietal behavior or other characteristics relevant to war and peace. They disparaged the Luo for their immodest nudity, the Kikuyu for their custom of having women thatch the roofs of houses, the Kipsigis for their licentious sexuality. The Kipsigis were considered superior to the Luo because the former practiced circumcision of boys and clitoridectomy of girls, like the Gusii, whereas the latter did neither. In spite of this, the Gusii took the Luo as allies against the Kipsigis in a very important battle. The acceptability of the outgroup's customs was less important to the Gusii than the strategic advantage they might gain from such an alliance. Furthermore, the Gusii did not think of rating hostile groups in terms of their friendliness or adherence to a code of honorable behavior because they did not expect this friendliness or honor of other groups within their own society. They expected all outgroups to be hostile, and they concentrated on defending themselves against the stronger groups like the Kipsigis and preying on weaker groups like the Luo. The strategic considerations were not modified by evaluative images of the outgroup's behavior.

Nothing is more characteristic of the differences in intersocietal behavior between Kipsigis and Gusii than their traditional attitudes toward cattle theft and raids. Cattle were of great importance in the prestige economies and rituals of both groups. The Kipsigis considered theft of cattle from another Kipsigis as a heinous offense, worse than murder and as unnatural as incest. The theft of cattle from *punik*, however, was not only allowed but regarded as admirable and imperative. In the Kipsigis view, their enemies had no right to have cattle and it was only right and proper that the Kipsigis conduct raids to take them away. The Gusii had no such rigid dichotomy; cattle theft was considered a crime (though not of the most immoral type) when committed within units which had enough internal order to try the offender and enforce compensation. Between clans, such theft was certain to provoke a feud. Many Gusii preferred to go into the lowlands and raid the Luo for cattle, because it was more difficult for the Luo to retaliate and because other Gusii could be depended upon to help them fight the Luo, but theft within the ethnic group was neither unknown nor horrifying. The Kipsigis viewed both stealing cattle from enemies and restraint of such theft within the ingroup as moral imperatives, whereas the Gusii were typically relativistic and opportunistic about cattle theft altogether.

The Gusii did not have institutionalized means of incorporating and assimilating outsiders into their society. They were willing to take Kipsigis women as wives, since they had undergone clitoridectomy, although they claim nowadays that such women introduced the "evil eye" (*okobiriria*) among them. Women could take the patrilineal affiliation of their husbands, but men from outside were not welcome because membership in Gusii society was through one's patrilineage and such affiliations were not fictionalized. Even when a fragment of a Gusii clan fled from interclan warfare in one Gusii tribe and was allowed to settle in another, it remained a distinct group, subordinate in status to the clans already resident there. Individual settlers were always known as *abamenyi*, "dwellers," whose right to live on land granted them by another clan or tribe remained tenuous. The Gusii social structure was particularistic and compounded of parochial groups; this is well illustrated by their version of male initiation, very different from that of the Kipsigis. While the Kipsigis initiated simultaneously sixty or seventy boys from different parts of the country at a secluded place in the forest, Gusii initiation (after a large-scale circumcision) brought together two or three boys, often related, from the same local community in a specially built hut near the dwellings of one of their families. Thus initiation, which for the Kipsigis was an introduction to a wider loyalty than that of the family and locality and could be used to naturalize young men of alien birth, was organized along narrow kinship and local lines in Gusiiland.

The most relevant contrasting characteristics of the two societies are as follows: The Kipsigis ethnic group constituted a security community based on social allegiances that cross-cut territorial units. Within the security community, social solidarity was high, as indicated by the rarity of witchcraft accusations, the absence of sorcery, and the moral restraint on cattle theft. The security community itself and the social behavior patterns associated with it were extended to those groups who were, in the Kipsigis image, their brothers, with a culture and social structure identical to their own. Other neighboring peoples were viewed as enemies against whom homicide and theft—criminal offenses within the security community—were commendable. Each enemy group was respected in proportion to its perceived degree of conformity to the Kipsigis code of honorable behavior in warfare, and was despised if, like the Gusii, it did not conform at all. Being a Kipsigis was regarded as a behavioral characteristic, attainable by those enemy individuals who were willing to alter their behavior by undergoing initiation, observing Kipsigis customs, and becoming a member of one of their universalistic age groups.

The Gusii ethnic group was not a security community but a territorial grouping of clans and other patrilineal descent groups which fought each other but also joined forces against outsiders. Loyalties were most enduring within the smallest groups, and decreased rapidly with increasing social (that is, genealogical and territorial) distance. Even within solidary groupings, divisive tensions were recognized and expressed in witchcraft accusations and the use of sorcery; cattle theft among Gusii was not viewed with alarm. The Gusii were aware of cultural differences among surrounding peoples and had different negative images of each, but they had no expectation of varying patterns of intergroup behavior. For them, every *egesaku*, from an extended family to a great nation, contained rival groups that distrusted each other and would attempt to destroy or unite with their opponents according to their own advantage in a particular situation; only the exercise of strong superordinate authority could alter this. The Gusii expected, therefore, that surrounding peoples would use every available means to defeat them, and they intended to reciprocate. Being a Gusii was regarded as a matter of descent from a Gusii ancestor and membership in a particular Gusii lineage rather than as an acquired behavioral characteristic; thus it could not be achieved by an outsider.

THE ROLE OF SOCIALIZATION IN MEDIATING BETWEEN SOCIAL STRUCTURE AND INTERSOCIETAL BEHAVIOR

We have seen that the Kipsigis, like the Mundurucú, are characterized by structural arrangements and interpersonal behavior patterns that might be termed *socially integrative,* while the comparable aspects of Gusii culture (like those of the Bedouin Arabs) might be termed *socially divisive.* As we have seen, the two peoples with socially integrated societies make a sharp dichotomy between themselves and other ethnic groups, whom they despise and toward whom they feel free to express hostility. In the two socially divisive societies, on the other hand, no sharp boundaries for aggressive action are present and hostility may legitimately be expressed between various groups inside and outside the ethnic boundary.

If it is true that intersocietal images and behavior patterns are transmitted in the socialization process, then it should be possible to find differences in socialization practices between integrative and divisive societies, corresponding to their different types of intersocietal behavior. Such differences do seem to characterize Kipsigis and Gusii socialization.

Socialization of the Child among the Kipsigis and Gusii

An analysis of ethnographic data on child training practices of the two societies suggests that there are a number of ways in which Kipsigis and Gusii children acquire the culturally appro-

priate images and behavioral dispositions. These are presented below under
headings that parallel the motivational, cognitive-evaluative, and habitual sources of ethnocentric behavior,
but the order is reversed for easier
comprehension.

Habitual Aspects of Socialization.
Under this heading falls the shaping of
the social behavior of the child in directions that facilitate his acquisition of
the traditional intergroup behavior patterns of his culture. The differences between Kipsigis and Gusii concern (a)
food sharing and (b) sociability. The
Kipsigis punish a child severely for
exhibiting gluttony and attempting to
take more food than his siblings. Jealous grumbling about food apportionment is not tolerated, and a child who
complains may find his food taken away
by his mother. Gusii mothers tolerate
gluttony and allow a greedy child to
take more than the others. Children
who are habitually greedy in this way
are called "black-stomach children" and
are given a separate dish with more
food than their siblings get. It is expected that an older child will deprive
the others of any valuable thing, and
mothers appear to reward the younger
ones for complaining by giving them
something as compensation only when
they do complain. These methods of
handling sibling behavior may be seen
as antecedents of social behavior in
the adult community. The Kipsigis
child learns habits of restraint in the
presence of equals and is encouraged
to get on with them rather than complain about them to authority. The
Gusii child, on the other hand, does not
learn to inhibit his acquisitiveness but
to regard peer relations as a competition in which the stronger takes all and
the weaker attempts to recoup through
a jealous appeal to authority.

The Kipsigis allow and encourage
their children to form groups that are
active day and night. Every child over
seven years old participates in such a
group, which is comprised of all the
children of a locality regardless of
family. The groups range far and wide
and meet children from other localities.
In the evening a group of boys frequently goes out to pick up food that
women leave for them in baskets outside houses; afterwards they sleep together in one of their parents' houses.
To punish a boy, parents will not let
him out with his friends at night. The
children's groups have their own leaders and exert control over their members' behavior, punishing those who are
deviant. The Gusii have no such organized groups, in large measure because parents prevent their formation
and development. Gusii parents consider the child's part in the family labor
force his primary obligation and they
do not allow him to wander far from
home. With their isolated homestead
pattern, this means that many children
grow up associating only with their
own siblings and perhaps a few neighboring cousins. Parents encourage them
to avoid contact with children other
than siblings who quarrel with them or
cause them any other difficulty. Gusii
children who were interviewed expressed reluctance to play with a
strange child whose kinship affiliations
were unknown. Closely related boys
who herd together, and girls of about
the same age who have been initiated
together, do form working groups, but
parents ignore such groups and think
nothing of interfering with their own
children's participation in them. These
peer groups are regarded by children
and parents as a temporary escape from
parental discipline, and they never develop the cohesion and internal self-
discipline of their Kipsigis equivalents.

The differences in peer group organization and values between the two societies are nowhere more clearly seen than among male adolescents who have undergone initiation together. For the Kipsigis, mutual respect among such agemates is mandatory, and there are rules restricting the verbal abuse they can engage in. For the Gusii, the hallmark of the "pal" (*omokiare*) relationship established by simultaneous initiation is the permissibility of engaging in joking and verbal abuse of the most obscene kind, something that is strictly forbidden between a man and anyone of his father's generation. The typical joke of Gusii agemates is to call one another "uncircumcised boy," which would be a grave insult among Kipsigis agemates. At the same time, Kipsigis agemates constitute one of the most important cohesive groups in their society, so much so that the father of a misbehaving youth will appeal to his age group to discipline him rather than doing it himself. Gusii men who were initiated together form no functioning group at all, and a man remains under direct paternal control after initiation. Thus the Kipsigis develop peer relations characterized by solidarity, cooperation, and control, whereas Gusii relations between social equals lack order and control, which characterize intergenerational relations in their society.

Kipsigis child training, as described here so far, favors the acquisition of habits of sharing, general sociability, and solidarity among social equals. In the same childhood situations, Gusii socialization favors dominance rather than sharing, parochial social contact rather than general sociability, and suspicion rather than solidarity among social equals. These contrasts may be seen as correlates of the differences in over-all social solidarity in the two societies.

Cognitive and Evaluative Aspects of Socialization. Among both Kipsigis and Gusii, children learn about neighboring peoples and acquire the culturally standardized images their parents have of them. There is an important difference, however, in the kind of salience these images have for them because of the difference in images of peers and neighbors in general that they have acquired. The Kipsigis child grows up in a community in which neighborhood relations are relatively good and, for the most part, free of suspicions and accusations of witchcraft and sorcery. When he learns about the enemy peoples and their evil attributes, the contrast between them and other Kipsigis, as he has observed them, is very great. Among the Gusii, however, children are raised on malicious gossip; they learn at an early age to view various neighbors with whom their parents are quarrelling as enemies attempting to kill their family through sorcery and witchcraft. When they hear of foreign enemies, the contrast effect is slight, since their concept of the enemy is based on intimate local relations. The Gusii child, then, learns that there are enemies everywhere, near and far, while the Kipsigis child acquires a clear image of enemies being foreign and remote.

For the Kipsigis individual this learning experience eliminates stimulus equivalence between ingroup and outgroups, thereby informing him that the positive social habits mentioned above are not generalizable to relations with the enemies. For the Gusii, a rough stimulus equivalence between all groups is established, due both to the linguistic equivalence of the word *egesaku* applied to groups at all levels and to the inculcated belief that potential enemies are everywhere, not restricted to the alien portion of the environment. This equivalence facilitates a transfer of the ambivalent attitudes toward peers in the immediate environment to more remote peoples.

Motivational Aspects of Socialization. Several aspects of child training in these two societies appear to increase the strength of motives that are appropriate to their respective patterns of ethnocentric behavior. These aspects are the use of praise, the inculcation of fear, and aggression training.

Praise is not only used by Kipsigis mothers but also institutionalized. A child is given the praise-names of warriors, and at a number of points in childhood and adolescence, his mother and other women of the house literally sing his praises, reciting not only his praise-names but a variety of good qualities about him. For example, if a young boy has been sent to relatives for a few months to herd their cattle, his praises would be sung on his return. A Kipsigis informant said, "That makes you feel good; you almost shed tears." Gusii adults do not believe in praising their children, for they think that praise will make them conceited and disobedient. Mothers reported that they refrained from praising their children in their presence even when the children were exceedingly well behaved and pleased their parents. The use of praise would seem to strengthen need affiliation, and this difference between Kipsigis and Gusii may be related to their differences in sociability and peer group behavior.

Gusii parents, particularly mothers, deliberately condition their children to be fearful of many aspects of their environment, including domestic and wild animals, strangers, the father and other male elders, and witches. This is done at first in order to control the child by threatening him with punishment by one of these agencies, but there is much behavioral evidence indicating that it

has permanent effects on the individual. The Kipsigis do much less of this, and they use imaginary animals that the child later finds out do not exist. The differential effects of these training patterns are evident from the fact that older Gusii children (and many adults) are terrified of the dark and remain indoors at night, while Kipsigis children play outside in the dark, looking for the food scraps that have been left for them. Gusii men learn to master this fear in its most extreme form, but they are convinced that witches run at night and present serious dangers to anyone walking in the dark. This fear of the environment intensifies interpersonal suspicion among the Gusii, as evidenced by the number of stories involving accusations of witchcraft and sorcery against neighbors that have a nocturnal setting.

Both Kipsigis and Gusii mothers disapprove of fighting among children and make some efforts to stop it, but the peer group organization makes a critical difference in the amount of aggression children have an opportunity to indulge. Among the Kipsigis, the relative independence of the children's groups, and their wide-ranging mobility, make it impossible for mothers to enforce their prohibition. A great deal of fighting is reported to go on, both within and between groups, and the best fighter often becomes the leader of a group. Boys try to show their bravery by asking others to beat them with sticks and demonstrating their ability to withstand blows before retaliating. Fathers encourage their sons to fight courageously, and they become concerned if they hear that their boys are always losing fights. The Gusii have more direct control over their children and punish them more frequently for fighting. Parents also indicate to the child that they prefer him to report being attacked rather than to retaliate, and that they look more kindly upon his

verbally insulting his peers than assault-
ing them. Often, Gusii parents complain bitterly to the parents of a child
who has assaulted their own child. This
attention to and punishment for fighting reduces the amount of fighting
among children but appears to result
in a preoccupation with hostility, and
the encouragement of reporting attack
and verbal abuse may be seen as shaping aggressive behavior in the direction
of projection and verbal attack, respectively. The Kipsigis handling of
aggression, especially the lesser amount
of punishment, seems to lead to less
suspicious social attitudes and less
divisive group behavior.

The differences in motivational development discussed here may well
have a direct impact on differences in
intersocietal behavior. The greater
strengthening of the sociable or affilia-
tive motive in Kipsigis socialization may
be seen as contributing to their greater
willingness to incorporate foreigners
into their society. The greater inhibition on aggression in Gusii socialization and the greater development of
projection as an intrapersonal defense
against hostility may contribute to their
defensive posture in making war as
opposed to the overt offensive militancy
of the Kipsigis.

This comparison illustrates that theoretically plausible concomitants for
variations in intersocietal behavior can
be found in the habitual, cognitive-
evaluative, and motivational aspects of
socialization. In the following section
some testable generalizations are drawn
out of this comparative analysis, in the
form of a polar typology.

Structural and Psychological Correlates of Intersocietal Images and Behavior

Table 2.1 presents two ideal types
which stand at opposite ends of a continuum. These ideal types are based on

the comparisons of Mundurucú with
Bedouin Arabs and of Kipsigis with
Gusii, and they serve to illustrate hypothesized linkages between social
structure, ethnocentric images, intersocietal behavior patterns, and socialization. The typology refers only to
uncentralized, non-industrial societies,
but many of the linkages may be generalized to other settings.

Obviously, these are extreme types,
but each of the variables is conceived
as continuous, so that many intermediate cases are expected in an examination of actual societies. Although this
framework may be viewed as a set of
functional hypotheses, generating predicted associations of variables across
societies, it has a distinct causal direction. The basic structural features—the
territorial arrangements of groups to
which loyalty is owed—are the independent variables, causing a certain
intrasocietal structure of group relations, including alliances and antagonisms. The intrasocietal structure favors
certain types of interpersonal behavior
over others, and parents attempt to
socialize their children so as to adapt
to the favored norms of interpersonal
conduct. Insofar as the socialization
process is effective in this regard, individuals are produced whose images
of their own and other groups are congruent with the demands of intrasocietal functioning. These shared images
act as premises for intersocietal behavior, that is, for warfare and immigration policies.

It should be noted that this hypothetical framework does not assume
that interpersonal images will necessarily be extended to intersocietal behavior; such generalization is assumed
to be a characteristic of socially divisive
societies but not of integrated societies,
which see different cultural groups as
opposite to themselves. Furthermore,
the differential evaluation of internal
and external groups is not equally

TABLE 2.1

A Typology of Social Structure, Socialization, and Intersocietal Dispositions

	Socially integrated societies	*Socially divisive societies*
Ingroup structure and behavior		
Basic structural features	Cross-cutting ties and conflicting loyalties created by territorial dispersion of loyalty groups through matrilocality, residential mobility, or nonlocal recruitment	Clear hierarchy of male loyalties, with local group loyalty paramount, fostered by patrilocality and/or endogamy
Intrasocietal group relations	Society is one security community; no internal warfare, permanent solidary bonds	Shifting scope of alliances for military activity at various levels within society: relations between groups are contractual, functionally specific
Interpersonal behavior patterns	Sociable, cooperative	Suspicious; projecting hostility generally onto interpersonal environment, as in witchcraft-sorcery accusations
Socialization practices		
Training in interpersonal behavior patterns	Emphasizes sharing, sociability, organized peer groups	Low on sharing and peer sociability; emphasizes dominance and obedience
Manipulation of motives	High on use of praise, low on inculcation of fear, mild aggression training	Low on use of praise, high on inculcation of fear, severely punitive aggression training
Images		
Evaluation of own ethnic group	Extremely positive; regarded as superior people	Ambivalent, dependent on present state of alliances and ingroup conflicts
Images of culturally contrasting outgroups	Inferior, weak, dishonorable, inviting attack and plunder (opposite of ingroup image)	Hostile, threatening, possibly powerful (similar to ingroup image)
Intersocietal behavior		
Warfare patterns	Offensive, courageous, foolhardy	Defensive (either actually or in belief), cautious
Immigration policies	Open; contingent on acquisition of ingroup behavior patterns	Restrictive; particularistic criteria of group membership

essential to both types. Socially integrated societies use the evaluative dimension to polarize ingroups and outgroups, but people in divisive societies —though they may rate their own way of life higher than that of others—do not distinguish groups in absolute moral terms, for they are ready to engage in alliance or conflict with any group on the basis of strategic advantage.

CONCLUSION

It is hoped that the typology presented here, and the hypotheses implicit in it, will provide theoretical guidance for cross-cultural studies of intersocietal images and behavior. Although the empirical validity of these hypotheses remains in question, three implications of possible relevance to contemporary international behavior may be drawn from the discussion in this chapter.

1. Societal divisiveness leads to generalized dispositions of suspicion, paranoia, and defensive hostility in a population. Hence the internal solidarity of societies is highly relevant to the behavior of their members in intersocietal situations, and especially to their capacity for forming stable alliances and cooperative relationships. Attention must be paid to serious internal conflicts within nations in order to alleviate certain kinds of pervasive xenophobia.

2. The institutionalization of multiple affiliations and loyalties, particularly through residential dispersion of members of the same primary groups, leads to cultural norms and behavioral dispositions of a positive, sociable kind within the limits of such dispersion; however, persons and groups outside these limits may be despised and attacked. Thus there appears to be a correlation of internal solidarity, trust, and sociability with external hostility.

This picture is mitigated by a look at the broad outlines of political history during the last 7,000 years, which shows humans capable of widening the limits of solidarity, trust, and sociability through the development of larger scale societies, increasingly complex forms of interrelationship, and technological-economic systems that demand and facilitate interlocal mobility. Furthermore, the principle of multiple affiliations and residential dispersion can be applied in the modern world, and it would argue for increasing the movements of peoples across international boundaries, particularly in noncompetitive situations. The cross-cutting structural arrangements resulting from such moves can act as a brake on international conflict even without eradicating the motives that lead to war.

3. Insofar as socially integrated societies do in fact have a concept of membership as something that can be achieved by outsiders, they allow the possibility not only of naturalizing immigrants but also of creating a superordinate order based on a similarly open criterion of membership. Although they have tended to define themselves *against* outgroups, their concept that outsiders could become members by following certain behavior patterns leaves open a door that in societies organized along lines of ascribed membership groupings and associated parochial sentiments is shut. If outsiders are redeemable, the possibilities of their redemption may be examined. Admittedly, a concept of conversion or naturalization did not seem to mitigate outgroup hostility in the cases of medieval Christendom, Islam, nineteenth century United States, and Soviet Communism, but each of these ideological "nationalisms" was associated with a concept of a political grouping that would unify diverse and scattered peoples. This argues that the search for world unity must go hand in hand with

a search for some wider values or ideologies, the acceptance of which acts as a condition of membership in a grouping of worldwide scope open to all peoples.

REFERENCES

Adorno, T. W., Frenkel-Brunswik, Else, Levinson, D. J., & Sanford, R. N. *The authoritarian personality.* New York: Harper, 1950.

Campbell, D. T., & LeVine, R. A. A proposal for cooperative cross-cultural research on ethnocentrism, *J. Confl. Resol.*, 1961, 5, 82–108.

Christiansen, B. *Attitudes towards foreign affairs as a function of personality.* Oslo: Oslo Univer. Press, 1959.

Coser, L. A. *The functions of social conflict.* New York: Free Press, 1956.

Deutsch, K. W. *Political community at the international level.* Garden City, N.Y.: Doubleday, 1954.

Dollard, J. Hostility and fear in social life. *Soc. Forces*, 1938, 17, 15–26.

Dollard, J., Doob, L., Miller, N. E., Mowrer, O. H., & Sears, R. R. *Frustration and aggression.* New Haven: Yale Univer. Press, 1939.

Gluckman, M. *Custom and conflict in Africa.* New York: Free Press, 1955.

Guetzkow, H. *Multiple loyalties: Theoretical approach to a problem in international organization.* Princeton: Princeton Univer. Press, 1955.

Klineberg, O. A cross-national comparison of peoples considered "like us" and "not like us" by children. *Proceedings of the Sixteenth International Congress of Psychology.* Amsterdam: North-Holland Publishing Co., 1962. Pp. 592–600.

Lambert, W. E. A cross-national comparison of ethnocentrism, perception of similars, and affections vis à vis other peoples. *Proceedings of the Sixteenth International Congress of Psychology.* Amsterdam: North-Holland Publishing Co., 1962. Pp. 612–619.

Lambert, W. E., & Klineberg, O. A pilot

study of the origin and development of national stereotypes. *Int. soc. Sci. J.*, 1959, 11, 221–238.

Lévi-Strauss, C. Tristes tropiques; from an anthropologist's memoirs. *Encounter*, February 1961, 16 (2), 7–23.

LeVine, R. A. The role of the family in authority systems: A cross-cultural application of stimulus-generalization theory. *Behav. Sci.*, 1960, 5, 291–296.

Maher, R. F. *New men of Papua.* Madison: Univer. of Wisconsin Press, 1961.

Murphy, R. F. Intergroup hostility and social cohesion. *Amer. Anthropologist*, 1957, 59, 1018–1035.

Murphy, R. F., & Kasdan, L. The structure of parallel cousin marriage. *Amer. Anthropologist*, 1959, 61, 17–29.

Peristiany, J. G. *The social institutions of the Kipsigis.* London: Routledge, 1939.

Sato, K. A cross-national comparison of peoples considered attractive and repulsive by children. *Proceedings of the Sixteenth International Congress of Psychology.* Amsterdam: North-Holland Publishing Co., 1962. Pp. 610–612.

Scott, W. A. Rationality and non-rationality of international attitudes. *J. Confl. Resol.*, 1958, 2, 8–16.

Sears, R. R., Maccoby, Eleanor E., & Levin, H. *Patterns of child rearing.* New York: Harper, 1957.

Shepperson, G., & Price, T. *Independent African: John Chilembwe and the origins, setting, and significance of the Nyasaland native rising of 1915.* Edinburgh: The Univer. Press, 1958.

Simmel, G. *Conflict and the web of group affiliations.* New York: Free Press, 1955.

Swartz, M. W. Negative ethnocentrism. *J. Confl. Resol.*, 1961, 5, 75–81.

Thoden van Velzen, H. U. E., & van Wetering, W. Residence, power groups, and intrasocietal aggression. *Int. Arch. Ethnography*, 1960, 49, 169–200.

Whiting, J. W. M., & Child, I. L. *Child training and personality.* New Haven: Yale Univer. Press, 1953.

3

The next chapter continues our exploration of the psychological and social sources of national and international images by turning to data from modern societies. The research on which this chapter draws consists largely of attitude studies and public opinion polls conducted in English-speaking countries. The chapter presents a conceptualization of images in terms of a theory of cognitive structure, and then proceeds to examine some of the personal and social correlates of these images. This examination includes a review of personality factors and demographic variables that are associated with the particular content and structure of images held by individuals. By studying the ways in which national and international images fit into the personality and value structures of different individuals and are distributed across different subgroups of the population, we can gain considerable insight into the psychological and social processes out of which such images typically develop.

William A. Scott, the author of Chapter 3, is Professor of Psychology at the University of Colorado, and Research Associate in the International Relations Program, Northwestern University. He is co-author of *The United States and the United Nations: The public view* (1958), and *Introduction to psychological research* (1962); and author of *Values and organizations: A study of fraternities and sororities* (1965). His current research interests include the study of personal values; cognitive structure and social structure; and attitude development and change.

H. C. K.

Psychological and Social Correlates of International Images*

William A. Scott

This inquiry into some social and psychological correlates of international images will proceed from two vantage points, theoretical and empirical. The theoretical effort represents an interpretation of international images in terms of some general formulations of cognitive structure and process. (For a review of some of these see Scott, 1962a.) The empirical sections will report some published studies of international attitudes based on selected groups of subjects (primarily college students), and also some unpublished public opinion data from Australia, Canada, and the United Kingdom. Although the poll data were generally not collected within a theoretical context, they have the advantage of coming from cross-sectional samples of large national populations; these are the populations to which theories of international attitudes typically refer, but for which precious little systematic data are available. Wherever possible, the findings will be interpreted in terms of the proposed theoretical framework. However, most of the empirical ma-

* In the preparation of this chapter I was immensely aided by the following persons and institutions: Ruth Scott and Donald Miklich, who made many runs on IBM cards kindly loaned by the Roper Public Opinion Research Center; the University of Colorado's Committee on Research and Creative Work, which provided funds for borrowing these data cards; the Western Data Processing Center, which provided free computer time for correlational and factor analyses; Walter Klein, who prepared excellent abstracts of some of the literature; and Barbara LeVine and Paul Rosenblatt, who helped in construction, administration, and analysis of some measures of international cognition. The Program of Graduate Training and Research in International Relations, of Northwestern University, has generously made research, writing, and thinking time available to me. I am indebted to the Program's co-directors, Harold Guetzkow and Richard Snyder, for their contributions to many of the ideas presented here.

terials can in no sense be regarded as "tests" of the theoretical formulation; rather they will be used to illustrate some common varieties of international images, together with their empirically found correlates.

THE CONTENTS OF INTERNATIONAL IMAGES

Conceived within the framework of cognitive theories, an image of a nation (or of any other object) constitutes the totality of attributes that a person recognizes (or imagines) when he contemplates that nation. In abstract terms, one may describe an image as consisting of three analytically distinct aspects: First and primary is the set of *cognitive* attributes by which the person understands the object in an intellectual way. This is his view of its "inherent" characteristics, which he regards as independent of his own response to them. Second, the image may contain an *affective* component, representing a liking or disliking for the focal object. This is usually associated with perceived attributes that the person either approves or disapproves. Finally, the image may carry an *action* component, consisting of a set of responses to the object that the person deems appropriate in the light of its perceived attributes.

Though the traditional distinction among cognitive, affective, and behavioral aspects of an image is made here for convenience in exposition, it is quite unlikely that these three components can be distinguished empiri-

cally in most people (see Harding *et al.*, 1954; D. T. Campbell, 1947). Beliefs about nations, feelings toward them, and notions of what ought to be done in relation to them are probably closely intertwined in the typical image structure; it is only by posing questions to subjects in a particular way that the analytical components can be isolated for study.

Affective Component: Liking and Disliking of Nations

Although the affective reaction to any single nation depends, in part, on the characteristics attributed to it, there is substantial evidence of a widespread disposition either to like or to dislike foreign countries in general. For instance, a study by Kosa (1957) of Hungarian immigrants to Canada showed a correlation of .71 between their liking for the British and their liking for Canada. Though the magnitudes of correlation were less, the same tendency was found in a national cross-section sample of Canadian adults[1] with respect to their attitudes toward Germany, France, Italy, and Japan. A favorable attitude toward any one of these countries was associated with a favorable attitude toward all others. And two different Canadian surveys (CIPO #252, October 1956; CIPO #254, November 1956) found a correlation between respondents' feelings that U.S. foreign policy was losing her friends and comparable feelings concerning British foreign policy.

Among British respondents in a June 1946 poll (BIPO #134), reported

---

[1] CIPO study #274, March 1959. Here and elsewhere in the chapter are reported previously unpublished results of public opinion surveys by the Australian Gallup Poll (AGP), the British Institute of Public Opinion (BIPO), and the Canadian Institute of Public Opinion (CIPO), conducted with large, national, adult samples in their respective countries. The IBM cards containing the data were made available on loan from the Roper Public Opinion Research Center (Williamstown, Massachusetts); all analyses were performed by the present author, with the assistance of Ruth Scott and Donald Miklich.

changes in attitudes toward the United States during the preceding year were correlated with corresponding changes in their attitudes toward the Soviet Union. People who said they had become more favorably disposed toward one of these countries were likely to report increasingly favorable feelings toward the other as well. When Australians were asked to indicate the acceptability of seven different national groups as immigrants to their country,[2] there were positive intercorrelations among all pairs of nations (the average intercountry correlation was .23); there was a negative correlation between the acceptability of each of these national groups and the general feeling that there were too many immigrants in Australia already. Somewhat earlier, another poll in Australia (AGP #69, December 1949) showed that respondents opposed to non-British immigration in general were also opposed to Japanese participation in the Olympic Games in Melbourne that year. Thus there is uniform evidence in all three countries polled of a general tendency toward xenophobic or xenophilic reactions, regardless of the nation involved. Such a general tendency either to like or to dislike all countries might be expected to color certain cognitive aspects of the person's image of any particular nation.

Cognitive Component: Threatening and Benign Images; Perceived Power

One commonly found cognitive dimension of international images is the benevolence or malevolence attributed to the nation-object. This, too, appears to have its generalized aspects: the same quality may characterize a person's image of various nations, and also —expressed as an expectancy for war or peace—of the international arena as a whole. For example, Canadian respondents who in August 1953 (CIPO #231) felt that the Soviet Union might start a war unprovoked were more likely than others to believe the United States would do the same thing. Canadians who expected atomic war between the West and Russia by 1980 were much more likely than others to believe that the year 1960 would be troubled internationally, while those who expected to see Russia and the West peaceful by 1980 expected 1960 to be peaceful as well (CIPO #279, November 1959).

There is some tendency for war expectancy to be associated with a dislike of nations or the perception of them as dangerous. In Canada (CIPO #244, September 1955) the expectation of war was negatively correlated with the belief that the Soviet Union had been "more sincere lately" and also negatively correlated with respondents' attitudes toward having European immigrants for neighbors. People who foresaw an early war tended to disapprove of both Russia and immigration. The latter result was duplicated in an Australian poll (AGP #79, March 1951), in which war expectancy was associated with a desire for reduced immigration. In 1953 (CIPO #231) Canadian respondents who felt that the United States might start a war on its own were less optimistic than the rest about the outcome of a projected "summit" meeting. (However, there was no correlation between expectations of the summit meeting and beliefs concerning Soviet belligerency.) The inference to be drawn from these correlations is that some people display a general tendency to see the entire foreign world as either threatening or benign, regardless of the specific events that are focused on.

---

[2] AGP #79, March 1951. The countries named in the question were France, Germany, Greece, Holland, Italy, Sweden, and Yugoslavia.

There is also some evidence that the attribute of power—including both strength and success—is a subjectively enduring aspect of a nation-image and that this quality too may be generalized over a variety of nation-objects. Among Canadians in 1959 (CIPO #279) the expectation of increased Russian power during 1960 was negatively correlated with the belief that Russian Communism would collapse by 1980; and the belief that Russia had had a successful past decade was associated with an expectation of its continued increase in power during 1960. The Canadians showed comparable correlations among the same attitudes expressed with respect to Britain and the United States. Moreover, expectations concerning the future success of Russia, the United States, and Britain were all positively correlated. People who expected one of them to get either stronger or weaker tended to expect the same fate for the other two.

It is not at all certain that these findings would be duplicated in other nations; in the United States or the Soviet Union they would very likely not be. There is a distinct possibility that citizens of minor powers, not intensely embroiled in big-power conflict, may view the world in terms quite different from the perspectives of major participants. Americans are used to believing that an increase in Soviet strength will threaten the peace of the world, and no doubt Russians feel similarly about the United States. Canadians quite possibly agree with both, for a number of different questions included in the same study (CIPO #279) all showed positive correlations between the expectation of either a Russian or a United States power increase and the expectation of war. People who thought that 1960 would be peaceful, rather than troubled, tended to expect a decrease in United States, British, and Russian power during the year. The expectation that Russia and the West would be at peace by 1980 was associated, not only with an expectation of decreased United States and Russian power during 1960, but also with the belief that Russian Communism would have collapsed by 1980—and with it Western Capitalism.

This is not to say that Canadians find the two major antagonists equally malevolent. Rather the findings indicate that the greatest apprehensions concerning one side are held by people who are *also* most apprehensive about the other side. In other words, Canadians have not tended strongly to take sides in the "cold war," by believing that their own national interest lies unambiguously with the United States against the Soviet Union. It is more probable that the average Canadian citizen's feelings about both these countries reflect his general tendency to be either favorably or unfavorably disposed toward *all* other countries in the world. A power struggle is apt to be most salient for its direct participants, who can readily view their own nation as angels and the opposition as devils. But any such dichotomous, black-and-white thinking in which citizens of outside nations indulge is likely to be channeled into a preference for their own country over all the rest—the latter category being rather poorly differentiated.

Action Component: Associated Response Repertories

The perception of a nation as strong or weak can be expected to interact with the judgment of its intention (benevolent or malevolent) in determining the action component of the image. The kinds of international actions that people deem appropriate in light of their nation-images can be classified, for convenience's sake, along a scale ranging from extremely competitive to extremely cooperative. At one end of this scale is war; at the other end, political unity such as Commonwealth membership. Between lies a gradation of increasingly cooperative policies, such as national defense, collective defense, peaceful coexistence, the sharing of information, and economic aid. Not that this is a unidimensional continuum of mutually exclusive actions; it will be seen shortly that even to an unsophisticated public various combinations of them are compatible. The gradation presented here is also rather coarse; this is partly because only a limited variety of action possibilities have been posed in studies of international attitudes.

War. During either peace or war aggressive measures in foreign policy tend to be regarded by the general public as incompatible with overtures toward peace. In June 1939 (BIPO #66) British respondents who advocated fighting Japan to protect England's interests in China tended more than others to oppose calling a world peace conference at that time. After the beginning of war with Germany (BIPO #62, September 1939) there was a strong negative correlation between approval of attempted peace talks and the desire to continue fighting until Hitlerism was eliminated.

In May 1940 (BIPO #69), respondents who advocated bombing Germany "even if it means that they might bomb us in return" were more likely than others to believe (a) that the entire German people, rather than just Hitler, was the real enemy and (b) that Britain would win the war. A comparable association between approval of military action and confidence in the power of one's own side was shown a decade later in a Canadian survey (CIPO

#214, October 1951): people who felt then that the West could win a war with Russia were more likely than others to believe that the Korean war was worthwhile; also, they tended to be more in favor of using German troops in an allied (NATO) army.

National and collective defense. The advocacy of primarily defensive measures appears to be associated with an image of the enemy as strong and dangerous, though not invincible. In Canada (CIPO #274, March 1959) dissatisfaction with national defense preparedness was most pronounced among those who felt that the West was "dropping behind Russia" in international power. Somewhat earlier (CIPO #243, July 1955), opponents of continued testing of atomic weapons by the United States were found most commonly among people who believed that Russia's current peace talk was "sincere" rather than just propaganda.

While there is no evidence that approval of defensive measures is associated with belligerent tendencies, it does seem connected with a desire to protect that which is "rightly" one's own or someone else's. For instance, in 1939 support among Britons for a military alliance with France and Russia was associated with a desire to see Britain's China interests protected (though not necessarily by war), and also with a willingness to guarantee the independence of small European countries (BIPO #60, June 1939; BIPO #57, April 1939).

Peaceful coexistence. In time of peace, the policy of "peaceful coexistence" represents minimal normal intercourse with nations, which merely excludes violence as a course of action. In time of war, the desire to reestablish normal relations with the enemy, or to explore this possibility through truce negotiations, amounts to about the same degree of cooperativeness—though by contrast with the on-going state of war it may appear to go much further. In March 1940 (BIPO #68) at a time when Great Britain was fighting Germany, but Russia had not yet entered the war, British respondents who favored peace talks were much more likely than others to advocate "friendly" relations with the Soviet Union (a German ally at that time) as well. Though the desire for such friendly relations tended to be negatively correlated with jingoistic sentiments, it was not at all incompatible with defensive courses of international action. For instance, in March 1939 (BIPO #56) approval of friendly relations with Russia was positively correlated with the feeling that Britain should fight rather than give up her colonies. And support for a world peace conference was correlated with support for a military alliance with France and Russia (BIPO #60, June 1939). There is a hint of low confidence in one's own power, however, in two other correlates of peace-oriented responses: Early in the war (BIPO #62, September 1939) there was a substantial association between the desire for peace talks with Germany and the belief that England would not win. Echoing this result is the finding two decades later in Canada (CIPO #279, November 1959) that respondents who named world peace as their most important wish for 1960 were most frequently those who thought Russia had had a successful decade, but that Canada had not.

Active peaceful interchange. Public opinion polls do not often give respondents the opportunity to "vote" on the host of potential policies involving international cooperation. Nevertheless, the respondent can entertain or evaluate rather grossly a spectrum of acts that imply cooperation and seem consistent with a benign image of the other country. Here again, for the average citizen there appears to be a general tendency either to approve or to disapprove such policies toward a variety of nations. In the United States, people who advocate close relations with the countries of Western Europe or who approve economic aid to developing nations also tend to want a foreign policy that relies on the United Nations or on alliances with other democratic nations, rather than on armed might in isolation from the rest of the world (Scott & Withey, 1958, pp. 194–200). During the United Nations police action in Palestine there was a positive correlation in Canada (CIPO #248, May 1956) between willingness to contribute Canadian troops to help maintain order and approval of continued membership in the British Commonwealth of Nations. An earlier study (CIPO #239, November 1954) also found desire for Commonwealth membership associated with the belief that coexistence between capitalist and communist nations is feasible. Thus it appears that people who approve one kind of cooperative international interchange are likely to approve other kinds.

Advocating such policies of peaceful involvement tends to be associated with benign images of the relevant nations or of the total international environment. For example, Canadians who approved of President Eisenhower's proposal to exchange military information with the Soviet Union tended to report favorable opinions of that country and also tended not to expect an early war (CIPO #244, September 1955). Similarly, in England (BIPO #134, June 1946), respondents who favored worldwide sharing of atomic "secrets" were more likely than others to report an improved attitude toward Russia (though there was no significant correlation with their reported changes in attitude toward the United States). Again, in a Canadian sample, attitudes favorable toward Germany, Italy, Japan, and France were all associated with a desire for increased trade with the Soviet Union (CIPO #274, March 1959). In the United States, people who approved of both economic and military aid to friendly countries were less inclined to regard United States and Russian interests as irreconcilable than were people who approved of military aid only (Fisher & Belknap, 1952). Canadian respondents who favored continued membership in the British Commonwealth were more likely than others to believe that the prospects for peace were improving (CIPO #239, November 1954), and less likely than opponents of Commonwealth membership to feel that the United States wielded undue influence over their country (CIPO #248, May 1956).

Cultural vs. Psychological Interpretations

The import of these public opinion studies for the understanding of international images would appear to be at least threefold: First, they tend to support, at a cultural level, the psychological view that there is some degree of consistent relationship among cognitive, affective, and action components of images. Second, they indicate that response dispositions associated with the nation-images may be conceived as somewhat flexible clusters of functionally equivalent, mutually compatible acts. Third, since the correlations noted among the various image components do not always depend on reference to a single nation, there is the suggestion that many different specific images may be colored by common themes reflecting the person's general world-view, or perhaps more basic characteristics of his personality.

Such data as these, however, have limited usefulness for understanding the psychological bases of nation-images. One major problem stems from the very representativeness of the samples polled: This is advantageous for generalizing results to some definable population. However, it has the attendant limitation of including in the sample a heterogeneity of subjects, whose image structures may be quite diverse. For example, a large national sample will necessarily include a preponderance of poorly informed individuals whose cognitive differentiation with respect to international affairs is quite rudimentary. Generalizations from the total sample may thus be inapplicable to the small proportion of sophisticated people, who constitute the focus of reference for most discussions of international images.

Even if the sample limitation could be overcome by including a sufficient number of internationally sophisticated respondents to permit separate analysis of their images, there would still remain an epistemological difficulty in inferring the psychological structure of images from data on their cultural structure. Psychological structure refers to a relationship among cognitive components that exists within the individual, while cultural structure represents a correlation among image components across a group of people.

It is the latter type of structure that is typically assessed through public opinion polling, or through the usual correlational analysis across samples of subjects. One can discover from such analyses what types of image content tend to be found together within the population. But the covariation of image contents across people does not warrant inferences concerning a corresponding covariation across objects perceived by the individuals in this population.

If, for example, one found a cross-individual correlation between hostility toward the Soviet Union and perception of her as belligerent, a tempting interpretation would be that people tend to attribute benign qualities to objects they like and malevolent qualities to those they dislike. But the same cross-individual correlation could have resulted from a division of the population into two types of respondents: (a) those who are hostile toward *all* countries and regard them all as belligerent and (b) those who feel kindly toward *all* countries and perceive them as friendly. Thus, the result is ambiguous with regard to the underlying psychological dynamics. In order to infer that image components covary within individual people, one would have to confront subjects with a set of nations, and ask them to judge each one on belligerence and also to express an attitude toward it. Then, for each person, a correlation would be computed over the nation-objects between attitude and perceived belligerency. Though such procedures for data collection and analysis are not, in principle, excluded from public opinion polling, they have not been undertaken in any of the polls reviewed here. Thus, when we conclude, for example, that affective and cognitive components of images are associated in a particular way, the meaning of that conclusion must generally be limited to cross-individual, rather than intraindividual, association.

It should be noted additionally that cross-individual analyses may obscure intraindividual processes that are systematically structured for each person, but not in the same way from one person to another. For instance, respondents who admire belligerency may display positive correlations over the nation-objects between liking and per-ceived belligerency, while respondents who deplore this trait will display negative correlations. If a sample consists of equal numbers of both types of respondents, the correlation across subjects between these affective and cognitive components, as applied to a single nation, is likely to be zero. Thus, a culturally shared image structure would fail to appear, even though meaningful psychological structures exist.

THE PSYCHOLOGICAL STRUCTURE OF IMAGES

Since public opinion data do not permit a clear interpretation of the structure of international images for an individual, we shall introduce a theoretical model which, though plausible in the light of the findings, is by no means demanded by them. Our reference here will be to the phenomenal world of a particular individual. The specific image contents of this phenomenal world may be quite different from one person to another, but the terms we shall use to describe the cognitive structures in which these contents are embedded are assumed to be applicable to all people, regardless of specific content.

The meaning of a phenomenal object is provided by the cognitive structure in which it is embedded. The basic units of a cognitive structure consist of the attributes a person applies to a given domain of objects (such as nations of the world). If Russia is seen in terms of its size, climate, geographical location, scientific accomplishment, and military power, this particular image implies that these concepts exist, in the mind of the viewer, as attributes that can potentially be applied to all nations. The attributes conceived by an individual as applying to nation-objects may be represented as a set of lines in multidimensional space, and the nation-images to which they are applied may be regarded as intersections of the lines. In Figure 3.1, image A is defined by the intersection of attributes 1, 2, 3, and 4. B, a less

image is significant only insofar as it consists of attributes along which several nations may be compared, and an attribute is significant only insofar as it serves to compare two or more nations with one another.

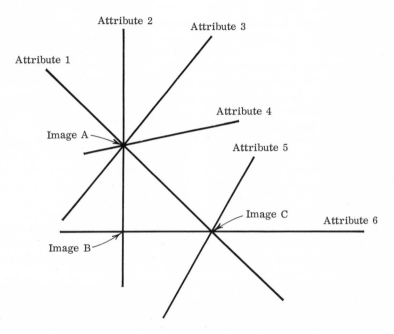

Fig. 3.1. Two-dimensional projection of attributes and images in a multi-dimensional cognitive space.

"rich" image, includes only attributes 2 and 6. Attribute 1 is defined in this subspace by two points, A and C; attribute 6 by points B and C. Attributes 3, 4, and 5 are not sufficiently defined in this subspace, though they might intersect images in other subspaces that are not shown here. Just as a point in geometrical space has no meaning apart from the lines that intersect at it, and a line means nothing more than the locus of points that constitute it, so the two kinds of cognitive units—images and attributes—have no meaning apart from one another. A particular nation-

The structure of attributes for conceptualizing nations develops, of course, through experience with particular nations (or norms about them); but, once established, it serves as a framework into which any new nation can be placed and in terms of which it can be understood. A new placement can occur in at least two ways—through direct information about how the nation stands on a particular attribute, or through inferences that the person makes, based on correlations among his cognitive attributes. Just as people seem to entertain "implicit theories of personality" (Bruner & Tagiuri, 1954), which enable them to judge others on an ancillary trait, given information about a primary trait, so they may also utilize the correlations among cognitive attributes for viewing nations in order to fill in aspects of an image that are not directly perceived (for example, that communism implies totalitarianism or that economic dependence implies laziness).

Correlations among cognitive attributes can also provide the basis for enhancing the contrast between nations that are seen as different in one important respect. A perceived contrast on such a "central attribute" might be generalized to all attributes subjectively associated with it. What constitutes a central attribute would depend to some extent on the person, but perhaps, within a given culture, certain attributes are commonly held in central determining positions. Just as the "warm–cold" dimension appears to be of crucial importance in filling in images of people (Asch, 1946; Kelley, 1950), so attributes like "hostile–friendly" and "strong–weak" may strongly influence other components of national images.

Dimensional Complexity

A complex nation-image demands a complex attribute structure for viewing it. An attribute structure is complex to the extent that it comprises a large number of independent dimensions for describing objects. Two dimensions are independent if they serve to distinguish nations in distinct (that is, uncorrelated) ways. Thus, one way of measuring dimensional complexity of an attribute structure is to ask subjects to group nations into as many different combinations as seem meaningful to them. Some subjects produce groups that are nearly identical, even though they may identify them by distinct words (such as

"Communist" and "totalitarian"). Others may produce nonoverlapping groups, implying negatively correlated attributes. The most independent groups are those that overlap partially but not completely; there is an optimal degree of overlap for maximum independence (Scott, 1962b, 1963). The more independent the groups, the greater is the complexity of the structure of attributes they represent and, correspondingly, the more highly differentiated are the nation-images for the subject.

Assumed Adequacy of Images

Any image of a nation is necessarily oversimplified. The nation itself includes various types of people and displays diverse behaviors in the international arena; yet the image that any person holds of it is marked by a relative coherence and consistency. It serves both to highlight presumed modal tendencies and to contrast these with the characteristics of other nations. Such image processes might readily be deemed stereotypic. But any image is perforce stereotyped in the trivial sense that it oversimplifies reality. The relevant question for purposes of structural analysis is whether the person who holds the image is aware of this limitation.

Many subjects (see, for example, Gilbert, 1951) display a reluctance to characterize entire groups in general terms, but this does not necessarily mean they lack even vague, uncertain images of these groups. Moreover, subjects who check particular attributes as characterizing a designated population are not necessarily implying that they regard these as adequate or complete characterizations. In order to apply the term stereotype, with its usual connotations of assumed inclusiveness and assumed adequacy, it would seem necessary to ascertain whether or not the subject thought that his particular image in fact represented all the important characteristics of the nation referred to.

From this point of view, the essential feature of a stereotype is not its oversimplification or even its resistance to refutation, but rather its structural "openness" or "closedness" (cf. Harvey, Hunt, & Schroder, 1961)—whether or not the image admits the possibility of additional, independent attributes for describing the object. An image is "closed" to the extent that the person regards the attributes included in it as completely defining the object (with the possible exception of synonyms or closely correlated characteristics). The more "open" the image, the more is the person willing to entertain the possibility that essential features of the object have not yet been recognized by him, and that these additional attributes would reveal new similarities and differences in relation to other objects. It is as if the cognitive region representing the phenomenal object contained some "empty space" or undefined areas that the person explicitly recognized. This definition of "stereotype" in terms of openness–closedness is intended to distinguish one of its meanings from other meanings commonly employed—such as "rigidity" (see immediately following) and "degree of sharedness" (see p. 94).

Rigidity of Images

Closely tied to the subjectively assumed adequacy of an image is the person's notion of the relative permanence or mutability of the assigned attributes. The assumption of fixed qualities will dispose one to react unvaryingly to the object, and an outside observer will thereby infer a rigid image; whereas the assumption of changeable qualities will permit one to react to a nation as it might become, or as one wants it to become. The rigidity of an image over time is often taken as a definition of stereotypy. Mace (1943), for example, states that "Current usage tends to restrict the term [stereotype] to ideas that are fixed when fixity is inappropriate, or appropriate on other than intellectual grounds. It implies most frequently fixity of ideas or invariability of response in circumstances which call for plasticity or adaptability" (p. 30).

We prefer to define stereotypy in structural terms (see preceding section) and to treat the correlation between stereotypy and rigidity as a matter of hypothesis, not of definition. In fact, the whole question of the relation between structural features of image systems and their temporal dynamics is a central problem raised by the present formulation. Not much research has been done that would clarify relationships that are often implicitly assumed here. One seemingly relevant finding is provided by Mischel and Schopler's (1959) investigation of the relationship between authoritarianism and resistance to change in beliefs about the Soviet Union after her second Sputnik launching. If the F Scale measures a general tendency toward closedness of cognitive systems (as is often assumed), then these data suggest that closed systems tend to be more rigid over time than open systems. More direct evidence is provided by Scott's (1962b) study, in which people with complex attribute structures (see p. 80) were able to alter these more readily than people with simple structures, and to increase their discrimination among nation-objects when required to do so.

Images and Their Associated Affect

Besides lending meaning to a cognized object, images usually contain an affective response to it. Conceptually, one might view the affective component as an attribute that consists of value-qualities. An affective or evaluative attribute constitutes a central dimension of image structures for a wide range of objects (cf. Osgood *et al.*, 1957). To the extent that any cognitive attribute is correlated with the affective attribute, an image that includes the former will elicit an affective response. Probably the tendency to ascribe qualities of "good–bad" is an exceedingly primitive one that is never wholly absent from any image structure, however elaborated with additional dimensions. Particularly if the dimensional complexity is fairly low, the available attributes may readily engage an affective association. Conversely, the greater the dimensional complexity of an attribute space, the greater should be the capacity for nonaffective cognition (see Scott, 1963).

A considerable body of research evidence on national and ethnic attitudes confirms the association of affect with cognitive attributes of images. People tend to attribute favorable characteristics to nations (or groups or individuals) they like and unfavorable characteristics to those they dislike. Katz and Braly (1935) were among the first to present systematic evidence of a similarity between the mean preference rank assigned by a sample of subjects to a national or ethnic group and the favorableness of traits most frequently attributed to that group. (Favorableness of traits was determined from the mean rank assigned by subjects in a separate task.) Child and Doob (1943) similarly reported high correlations between the proportion of favorable traits assigned to a nation and the preference rank assigned to it. Vinacke's (1956) study of mutual images among ethnic groups in Hawaii suggested that, in general, traits assigned to one's own group tend to be more favorable than traits assigned exclusively to other

groups. Buchanan and Cantril (1953), in one of the few systematic cross-national studies, found that more favorable traits are attributed, on the average, to nations liked by a large proportion of the respondents in a particular country than to nations liked by a smaller proportion of the respondents.

The last authors' interpretation of their results suggests the primacy of affect in generating the particular contents of images. They maintain that, since views of Russians, Germans, and Japanese change with the fluctuations of international relations, "stereotypes are less likely to govern the likes and dislikes between nations than to adapt themselves to the positive or negative relationship based on matters unrelated to images of the people concerned" (Buchanan & Cantril, 1954, p. 203).

Though it is clearly possible, and presumably quite common, to find such an influence of the affective on the cognitive aspect of an image, it would be misleading to assume only one direction of influence. Carlson's (1956) study of the effect of persuasion on attitudes can readily be interpreted as demonstrating the dependence of affect on cognitive components. Conversely, Rosenberg's (1960a, 1960b) experiments on hypnotic attitude reversal demonstrate directly the dependence of image content on affect. It is clear, therefore, that one's emotional response to an object and the qualities ascribed to it must be treated as interdependent, with either class of component capable of affecting the other. This mutual interdependence follows from the principle of *cognitive balance* (Heider, 1946).

A state of balance seems particularly applicable to univalent attitudes of either clear liking or clear disliking, rather than to ambivalent attitudes, which include some degree of both. If the image of an object includes both favorably and unfavorably evaluated attributes, then it is reasonable to expect that the affective resultant will represent a neutral, or ambivalent, compromise between liking and disliking. The more general state of correspondence between affect and cognitions has been called *cognitive consistency* (Scott, 1958, 1959). Though people appear to differ in degrees of cognitive consistency with respect to any particular attitudinal object, a consistent state can be predicted at least as a first approximation to the relation among image components.

A maximally balanced image structure would occur if to each nation were attributed only favorable, or only unfavorable, characteristics and if it were liked or disliked accordingly. Such.extreme balance for all nation-images could be found only in a cognitive structure with high intercorrelations among the liked and disliked attributes. This would imply a fairly low degree of dimensional complexity for the structure as a whole (though, of course, additional, nonevaluated attributes might be conceived independently of the principal affective component). Essentially this result appeared in a study by Scott (1963): the best balanced classifications of nations tended to come from subjects who displayed simple cognitive structures for viewing nations. The simplest, purest form of such an attribute structure would presumably be found in people who made just one primary distinction—between domestic and foreign. Their own nation would represent one category of the dimension, with positive affect, and all other nations would be lumped together in the other category, with a negative affect loading. Such a unidimensional structure would normally be termed "ethnocentric." Certain empirical findings on the relation between ethnocentrism and intolerance for ambiguity (for example, Block & Block, 1951; Taft, 1956)

can be well interpreted within this formulation, if one assumes that both these traits are manifestations of dimensionally simple cognitive structures. It may thus be that an extreme tendency toward cognitive balance in viewing nations in the world is associated with ethnocentric attitudes, and oversimplified, fallacious images of the nations concerned.

Images and Their Associated Response Repertories

It is useful to consider international images as capable of containing, either explicitly or implicitly, some conceptions of appropriate responses to the nation. Not that all images necessarily involve such an action component, but many of them consist of attributes that forcefully suggest a relevant response (such as, for example, the attribute-combinations "poor, starving, helpless" or "dangerous and invincible").

Certain associated response repertories appear to follow almost directly from the image content, whereas others require an additional set of associations or calculations that depend primarily on the experiences and goals of the perceiver. The former kind of repertory might be designated "reactive," since it consists primarily in responding, almost reflexively, to the stimulus itself. It may be assumed that certain patterns of response (such as withdrawal or approach) are either innately associated with a particular class of stimuli, or else associated through early learning processes that are so widespread as to make the stimulus-response association quite dependable in the species. Particularly in rather simple, primitive world-views one is likely to find image contents of this type. For example, the attribute combination "bad, strong" immediately suggests the reactive response of "flight," whereas "bad, weak" may indicate "fight"; the image, "good, strong" seems to impel some response pattern like "follow, obey, subordinate one-self," while the attributes, "good, weak," call forth a response repertory including "love, nurture, protect." Such simple images and associated response patterns are direct analogues of attribute systems that children use to discriminate parents' and children's roles (Emmerich, 1959).

It is possible that these and other response repertories associated with nation-images in fact derive, through stimulus generalization, from response repertories for dealing with human objects who manifest the same qualities. Thus, if a nation is seen as self-seeking, one may wish to counteract with competitive or blocking responses similar to those he would apply to a person who showed the same attribute. To the extent that response repertories associated with nation-images are generalized from the domain of interpersonal relations, these still constitute reactive responses, but they are perhaps less appropriate to the immediate stimulus, since their effect on the nation's behavior may be quite different from that on a human object.

Contrasted with reactive responses, which tend to be bound either to the immediate stimulus or to subjectively related stimuli, are what might be called "anticipative" responses. The latter depend as much on the person's goals for the nation-object as on his notion of what it is doing at the moment. Thus, the image may include, not only concepts of what the object is actually like, but also concepts of what it might be like, or of attributes that one desires it to have. With such an anticipative image, a person can entertain a repertory of responses aimed at shaping the nation's behavior toward the desired goal, rather than simply reacting to it as it is now. He can con-

sider the expected consequences of any response, both for the nation-object and for his own nation in relation to it. This may encourage reinforcement for actions of the nation that approximate the desirable, in much the same manner as is attempted in operant conditioning (cf. Skinner, 1953, pp. 62–68; Milburn, 1959).

PSYCHOLOGICAL CORRELATES OF NATION-IMAGES

To conceptualize nation-images, a structural representation has been proposed, based on two sets of cognitive units, subjective attributes and the phenomenal objects at which they intersect. Within the framework of this structural formulation we may consider some selected empirical findings concerning certain correlates of international images that have come from national samples and from more restricted groups of subjects. For the most part, the available data are only vaguely suggestive of the interpretations to be placed on them; we must therefore go beyond the empirical results in many instances to propose other relationships implicit in the theoretical model.

Information and Awareness

Results from a number of studies support a preliminary generalization that benign images of the world and a desire for cooperative involvement in it will more frequently be found among the well-informed segments of the population than among the poorly informed. In the United States it has often been shown that people who are well informed about world affairs are more likely than the ignorant to espouse internationalist foreign policies in general and to support the United Nations in particular as a mechanism of cooperative involvement (Scott & Withey, 1958, pp. 160–164, 178–180). Other surveys taken in Australia and Canada indicate that a variety of positive orientations— such as approval of membership in the British Commonwealth, optimism concerning the prospects for peace, favorable attitudes toward immigrants and toward the Soviet Union—tend to be correlated, not only with level of information about world affairs, but with other kinds of knowledge as well, and with knowledge-seeking behavior, such as reading.[3]

An interpretation of these results can be made within the structural theory proposed earlier. One possible effect of information about world affairs may be an increase in the number of attributes that a person can bring to bear in assessing any nation. And, if the information is of fairly wide scope and reasonably accurate, an increase in the number of attributes would presumably be accompanied by an increase in dimensional complexity of the attribute system. This assumption was supported by a study conducted with a sample of students at Northwestern University: a positive correlation was found between level of information about world affairs and a measure of dimensional complexity (Scott, 1962b).

With a dimensionally complex cognitive structure it is more difficult to maintain a dichotomous, ethnocentric view of the world that regards the foreign as essentially different and dangerous. Of course, new information does not necessarily increase dimensional complexity. It is possible to acquire information that is simply redundant with the pre-existing image structure—in other words, that adds no new dimensions to what is already known. Such information would presumably not re-

---

[3] In AGP #79, March 1951, the average number of books read per year correlated positively with a favorable attitude toward admission of immigrants from seven different nations. In CIPO #214, October 1951, ignorance of the meaning of inflation and ignorance of the Russian occupation zone in Germany were both associated with the belief that the Soviet Union wanted war. In CIPO #231, August 1951, there was a positive correlation between awareness of the forthcoming "summit" meeting and the belief that it would result in decreased world tensions. However, there was no correlation between either knowledge of Syngman Rhee or awareness of the forthcoming "summit" meeting and belief that Russia or the United States would start a war unprovoked (exceptions to trend). In CIPO #239, November 1954, there was a correlation between awareness of foreign compact cars and the belief that Premier Khrushchev was sincere in proclaiming his good intentions on his current visit to the United States. In CIPO #243, July 1955, there was no correlation between awareness of the Salk vaccine and belief in the sincerity of Russia's peace overtures (exception to trend). In CIPO #244, September 1955, the recency of respondents' reading correlated with a willingness to accept European immigrants as neighbors; also recency of reading correlated with a desire to visit the Soviet Union. In CIPO #248, February 1956, awareness of fluoridation was associated with approval of increased U.S. investment in Canada and also with approval of continued Canadian membership in the British Commonwealth of Nations. Awareness of the recent Arab-Israeli dispute correlated with approval of Commonwealth membership, but not with attitudes toward U.S. investments (exception to trend). In these, as in other survey results referred to in this chapter, there are occasional exceptions to the general trend reported. Whether these are due to inadequate measures of the intended variables or to an imprecise understanding of just what the relevant variables are, cannot be determined without further study. If, however, out of fourteen different tests of a particular kind of relationship, ten outcomes occur significantly in the same direction, and the rest are merely nonsignificant departures from zero, then this constitutes preliminary evidence for the generally observed direction of relationship. Presumably it would appear more dependably if the measures were better or if other kinds of influences could be controlled.

duce prejudice, but might instead increase it, since it tends to add affective support to the initially simple structure. Thus, from the present point of view, the relationship between information and the nature of international images should be qualified as follows: Minimal information about the world will yield a simple, unidimensional cognitive structure, which is most conducive to an ethnocentric attitude of maximum psychological distance from things foreign. This can manifest itself in isolationism, a disliking of foreign nations, a fear of them, or a desire to fight them with slight provocation. To the extent that additional information increases the complexity of the cognitive structure for viewing nations, it will counteract the simple ethnocentric dislike of the foreign, and affect will come to be differentially associated with more specific attributes of particular nations.

This formulation implies that complex image systems grow out of simple ones through prolonged contact with relevant events. But it might also be argued that different people are predisposed to perceive particular classes of events in either a simple or a complex fashion. Amount of contact with relevant events might, therefore, not affect the complexity of people's images since, from the moment of initial contact, they would apply their preferred structures. According to this view, dimensional complexity may be a general trait reflected in a variety of cognitive domains. Bieri and Blacker's (1956) research suggests this, and if the perceptual tendencies toward sharpening and leveling represent related processes, then the results of Holzman (1954) seem to favor a predispositional interpretation. However, Ulehla (1961) and Wyer (1962) did not find consistent levels of cognitive complexity (differentiation) across different domains of objects. Whether these results simply reflect inadequacy of the instruments employed or whether they should be interpreted as implying that structural complexity is not a general trait, but instead depends on experience with a particular class of objects, cannot be decided at the moment.

Of course, increase of dimensional complexity is not necessarily easy to achieve, for pre-existing characteristics of the cognitive structure will presumably limit the nature of any new information that can be incorporated. The present conceptualization implies that change of a particular attribute in an image would affect the total attribute structure, altering the likelihood that the same set of attributes would subsequently be associated in any new image. It should also follow that the more independent a group of cognitive attributes, the more selectively can they be associated with, or dissociated from, any particular image. This would permit relative flexibility in responding to the changing characteristics of nations. By contrast, a structure of highly correlated (redundant) attributes should be maximally attuned to information affectively congruent with what is already present, and hence tend to resist incorporation, not only of contravalent material, but also of affectively neutral information, since it demands cognitive differentiation along an unaccustomed dimension.

Some suggestive evidence for this hypothesis is provided by recent research among adults in Evanston, Illinois (Scott, 1962b). Following an initial task in which subjects arranged nations into groups (see p. 80), they were asked to indicate which additional nations on a list might be included in each of the groups they had provided. Those subjects who displayed an initially high level of information yield (high dimensional complexity) performed the regrouping task in such a manner as actually to increase that level to a greater extent than did subjects with an initially low level of complexity. Such an increase in information through the forced cognitive reorganization presumably required a selective alteration of nation images, rather than either rigid adherence to the initial structure or wholesale, indiscriminate change. This result therefore suggests that the more complex the existing cognitive structure, the more readily can particular attributes be associated with, or dissociated from, the image of any nation; hence the more easily can the person entertain information requiring new kinds of discriminations.

The above formulation is admittedly speculative and may represent excessive seduction by the proposed geometrical model. However, it does suggest some hypotheses that permit the content of information to be treated in a formal fashion (that is, in terms of its dimensionality in relation to the pre-existing cognitive structure), and that explicitly allow for varying consequences of particular kinds of information in conjunction with particular kinds of image structures.

Sense of Personal Security

A completely different kind of psychological variable, which correlates fairly consistently with the content of international images, is one that may be called a "sense of personal security." This name seems to summarize appropriately an entire set of empirical variables that correlate similarly with certain aspects of international images to which they have been related. The questions by which these variables have been assessed are of at least three types. The first, and most readily interpretable, refers directly or indirectly to the respondent's satisfaction with some aspect of his own life. The second type of question, from which a sense of security or insecurity may be inferred, elicits feelings of optimism or pessimism about various kinds of personal and national events. Finally, there is a group of questions that seems to reflect feelings of anxiety or extreme fear of dangers from the world outside. These again are only labels applied from a subjective interpretation of the question content; their empirical distinctiveness does not matter in this context, since all correlate with international images in approximately the same manner.

One of the earliest studies of this kind was by Angus Campbell (1947), who found a positive correlation between anti-Semitism and dissatisfaction with one's job. Kosa's (1957) intensive study of Hungarian immigrants to Canada explored various characteristics associated with their attitudes toward the British. In general, favorable attitudes tended to appear in those who were most satisfied with their lives in Canada and who had made the best economic and social adjustment to their new surroundings. Spilka and Struening (1956) obtained comparable results on a sample of college students: negative correlations between ethnocentrism (California E Scale) and (a) a sense of personal worth and (b) total self-adjustment, both as measured by the California Test of Personality.

National interview surveys in Canada show somewhat broader—though not entirely consistent—relations. In general they suggest that personal happiness may be associated, not only with favorable attitudes toward foreign nations, but also with optimism concerning world events.[4] The sprinkling of negative outcomes may be due to the

---

[4] In CIPO #214, October 1951, married women who felt that the wife gains more from marriage than the husband were more likely than other women to believe that the West could win a war with Russia. No comparable correlation appeared for married men (exception to

less precise measures employed (single questions, rather than multiple-item scales). But they may also represent a better sampling of the population of possible outcomes; negative results from samples of college students are rarely reported in the psychological journals.

A different kind of question, which might be presumed to tap the sense of personal security in a more indirect way, refers to people's judgments about the way things are going at present and their expectations about the future. These are perhaps best assessed by multiple-item measures such as Srole's (1956) anomie scale. Srole, as well as Roberts and Rokeach (1956), have found a correlation between anomie and ethnocentrism. Farris (1960), using a different measure, reported a correlation between anomie and war expec-

tancy, also between anomie and a scale of jingoism. Douvan and Walker's (1956) measure of "personal effectiveness" appears to represent the opposite of this construct; it was shown to correlate with the respondent's ability to offer solutions to the problem of war. The last two results are echoed by Farber's (1951) finding that students who advocated an immediate show-down war with Russia were less likely than others to report a satisfactory outlook for their future personal lives.

The relevant public opinion data come mainly from a single Canadian study; they tend to show a correlation between optimism–pessimism concerning economic and social trends within the country and optimism–pessimism about the future course of international relations.[5] These expectations are measured by a variety of questions; though

---

trend). In CIPO #254, November 1956, there was a negative correlation between respondent's report that 1956 had been a good year for him and the belief that Britain's foreign policy was losing her friends. There was no comparable correlation with the belief that U.S. foreign policy was losing her friends (exception to trend). In CIPO #279, November 1959, there was a positive correlation of professed marital happiness with (a) the belief that by 1980 Russia and the West would be peaceful, (b) the belief that by 1980 the manufacture of hydrogen bombs would have ceased, and (c) the belief that Canada had had a successful time in the 1950s. Professed marital happiness was negatively correlated with (a) the belief that capitalism and the Western way of life would have collapsed by 1980 and (b) the belief that civilization would be in ruins by 1980. In the same study there was a positive correlation of professed personal happiness with (a) the belief that the manufacture of hydrogen bombs would have ceased by 1980 and (b) the belief that Canada had had a successful time in the 1950s. Personal happiness did not correlate with (a) the belief that by 1980 Russia and the West would be peaceful, (b) the belief that capitalism and the Western way of life would have collapsed by 1980, or (c) the belief that civilization would be in ruins by 1980 (exceptions to trend).

[5] In BIPO #138, September 1946, there was an association between expectation of a future business decline and belief that the wartime alliance of Britain, the United States, and Russia had deteriorated. In CIPO #254, November 1956, the belief that family life is more successful nowadays than a generation ago was negatively correlated with the belief that U.S. foreign policy was losing her friends, but not with the belief that British foreign policy was losing her friends (exception to trend). In CIPO #279, November 1959, the expectation that 1960 would be peaceful internationally was positively correlated with the expectations that (a) there would be domestic industrial peace in 1960, (b) taxes would be down in 1960 (c) prices would remain stable in 1960, (d) 1960 would be a year of full employment, and (e) the world would be a better place to live in "for people like yourself" ten years hence. The expectation that by 1980 Russia and the West would be peaceful correlated with the beliefs that (a) the world would be a better place to live in "for people like yourself" ten years hence, (b) life expectancy would reach 100 by 1980, (c) Canadians' honesty, health, attitudes toward sex, and attitudes toward religion were "improving." The belief that Russian Communism would have collapsed by 1980 was associated with the expectations that (a) the living standard would be

there are a number of exceptions to the general trend, taken together the data indicate the presence of a generalized optimism–pessimism variable that may color one's views of the world. Not that either pole of this dimension is necessarily realistic; replies to some of the questions seem to range all the way from wishful thinking to unrestrained gloom. The fact that such an attitudinal dimension appears at all suggests that personality variables may be operating in many instances to detract from the objectivity of international images.

In a number of other Canadian surveys, feelings of pessimism almost appear to take on a paranoid tone; it is from these that one may infer feelings of anxiety or threat from the person's surroundings. Opposition to scientific technology, the belief that dangerous things are going on in the world, or that other people have too much power—these kinds of feelings tended to be associated with malevolent images of nations.[6] In many cases, of course, the gloomy outlook on foreign affairs might be entirely justified on objective grounds—as the belief of some British in 1946 that relations among the war-time allies were deteriorating—but the fact that this belief correlated with a concern over good sanitation, for example, indicates that for many people a generalized threat orientation might well intrude upon a dispassionate assessment of the degree of danger present in a particular world situation.

---

doubled by 1980, (b) a cancer cure would be found by 1980, (c) life expectancy would reach 100 by 1980, (d) prices, taxes, and unemployment would be down in 1960. The expectation that unemployment would increase in 1960 was correlated with the expectations that (a) capitalism and the West would have collapsed by 1980 and (b) civilization would be in ruins. Beliefs that Canadians' honesty, happiness, attitudes toward sex, attitudes toward religion were improving correlated with the belief that Canada had had a successful time in the 1950s. Expectations of industrial strife and increased taxes in 1960 correlated with the expectation of increased Soviet power during 1960. Exceptions to the trend found in this study were: No correlations between the beliefs that Canadians' health and intelligence were improving and the belief that Canada had had a successful 1950s; no correlation between the expectation that 1960 would be a year of industrial strife and the expectation that capitalism and the West would have collapsed by 1980; no correlation between the expectation of increased unemployment during 1960 and the expectation of increased Soviet power during 1960.

[6] In BIPO #138, September 1946, the belief that food sanitation laws were inadequate was associated with the belief that the wartime alliance of Britain, the United States, and Russia had deteriorated. In CIPO #214, October 1951, the belief that other economic groups than the respondent's own gained most from inflation correlated with the perception of hostile intent on the part of the Soviet Union. In CIPO #244, September 1955, the belief that the weather was being affected by atomic explosions correlated with the expectation of war; also with unwillingness to accept European immigrants as neighbors; but not with the belief that Russia had been more sincere lately or with professed improvement in attitude toward Russia (exceptions to trend). A discrepancy between the respondent's perceived and desired loci of domestic power correlated with a reported worsening of feelings toward Russia; also with the belief that Russia was not being sincere. In CIPO #248, February 1956, disapproval of fluoridation was associated with the belief that the U.S. influence on Canada was excessive. In CIPO #254, November 1956, the belief that personal rights were endangered in Canada was associated with the beliefs that U.S. and British foreign policies were losing them friends. In CIPO #278, September 1959, expressed distrust of science was correlated with the expectation of an early war; but not with suspiciousness of Khrushchev (exception to trend). Disapproval of space exploration correlated positively with expectation of an early war and also with suspiciousness of Khrushchev. Apprehension over Earth satellites was associated with the expectation of an early war; not with suspiciousness of Khrushchev (exception to trend).

These various attitudes and beliefs concerning the surrounding world represent quite a hodgepodge of content, and it is undoubtedly an oversimplification to interpret them as reflecting some common underlying theme, such as feelings of personal security or insecurity. However, there is no basis at the moment for offering a more refined interpretation of the data reviewed. Perhaps this gross characterization may provide a useful orientation for future studies aimed at defining the relevant variables more precisely.

Personal Aggressiveness

Another psychological trait which can be inferred from a variety of single- and multiple-question measures is that of personal aggressiveness or hostility in one's orientation toward people. In a number of studies on restricted samples, this kind of measure has been found to correlate with certain kinds of international attitudes, though relevant public opinion data from large representative samples are scant. Perhaps the international attitudes to which the psychological trait of aggressiveness corresponds can appropriately be identified as image-associated response repertories involving extremes of competitiveness (see p. 75), such as ethnocentrism, nationalism, xenophobia, and jingoism.

The best-known personality correlate of ethnocentrism is "authoritarianism," as measured by the F Scale. In fact, the F Scale was developed by Frenkel-Brunswik and her associates (Adorno et al., 1950) specifically as a correlate of ethnocentrism (measured by the California E Scale). Though the content of the F Scale is diverse, one of its principal components would appear to be the kind of personal aggressiveness that is of concern here. Eysenck (1953), for example, interprets its content as

consisting of two factors, tough-mindedness and conservatism; the former is very similar to what is meant here by aggressiveness.

A number of investigators have used the F Scale in conjunction with studies of international attitudes. Levinson (1957) reports that it correlated .60 with his scale of nationalism. Sampson and Smith (1957) found a correlation of $-.46$ between the F Scale and their measure of "worldminded" attitudes. MacKinnon and Centers' (1958) survey of adults in Los Angeles County found that high scorers on the F Scale were less likely than low scorers to feel that Americans benefit from information about the Soviet Union, and more likely to approve atomic bombing to stop propaganda coming from Russian ships at sea. Modified measures of "authoritarianism" have been used by Fensterwald (1958) and Farris (1960). The former study reports a correlation with nationalist and isolationist sentiments, while the measure of authoritarianism in the latter study was found to correlate with both war expectancy and jingoism. (See Katz, 1960, and Titus and Hollander, 1957, for a review of other studies relating "authoritarianism" to international attitudes.)

Comparable results have been obtained by researchers working with other measures of aggressiveness. Gladstone (1955) found that a belligerent orientation toward nations is associated with interpersonal belligerence, while pacifism at the international level tends to go with nonviolent attitudes toward people. Christiansen's (1959) study of Norwegian cadets showed a tendency for subjects manifesting "threat-oriented extrapunitive" (that is, aggressive) responses in interpersonal relations to advocate a comparable foreign policy for their nation. (See also Chapter 6 in this volume.)

In the public opinion surveys reviewed four separate studies included questions that appeared to tap aggressive, or at least repressive, attitudes toward people. In England during World War II people who advocated interning all aliens were much more likely than others to approve of both press censorship and the proposed law against "despondency statements" (BIPO #71, July 1940). Australians who doubted the sincerity of Russia's peace campaign tended also to be in favor of banning the Australian Communist Party and limiting the importation of Japanese toys (AGP #83, September 1951). Another Australian study (AGP #114, October 1955) showed a positive relation between opposition to exchanging farm visits with the Soviet Union and opposition to allowing prisoners week-end passes. Finally, the feeling that foreigners should speak English in public was associated with approval of compulsory union membership for all workers (AGP #135, November 1958). Undoubtedly responses to these questions represent other traits besides aggressiveness. The reported correlations stood up, however, even when political party and socio-economic status were held constant, so alternative explanations will have to be sought outside of these obvious demographic variables.

Personal Values

The last class of psychological characteristics to be considered here have been called "personal values" or "moral ideals" (Scott, 1965). These represent the individual's standards for judging the "goodness" or "badness," the "rightness" or "wrongness," of his own and other people's actions. In a study of

college students (Scott, 1960), scales assessing eight different personal values were administered together with scales designed to measure attitudes toward eight corresponding goals of U.S. foreign policy.[7] Since the predicted correlations emerged between the pairs of personal values and international goals, one may broaden the interpretation of the studies of aggressiveness just reported: The kind of foreign policy advocated for one's nation bears some correspondence to the kind of interpersonal relations advocated for individual humans.

In speculating about the implication of these results for the theory of cognitive structure previously presented, one might say that the image structure for viewing nations may bear some degree of correspondence to that for viewing people. Specifically, the correspondence appears to lie in the kinds of desired relationships envisaged and in notions of appropriate means for achieving those end-states. Just why such similarities should occur, or what conditions should maximize them, is not at all clear at this writing. Previously it was suggested (Scott, 1960) that relatively high correspondence between interpersonal and international goals would occur for people who are quite ignorant about foreign affairs; but in a recent study of students at Northwestern University, I found no difference in the magnitudes of correlations between well-informed and poorly-informed subjects. The patterns of intercorrelations between personal values and advocated goals of U.S. foreign policy were nearly identical with those previously found among University of Colorado students (Scott, 1960), regardless of the level of information about world affairs. Perhaps the

---

[7] The pairs represented were: self-control (personal value)—pacifism (international goal), intellectualism—cultural development, kindness—humanitarianism, social skills—coexistence, religiousness—religiousness, independence—independence, status—power, loyalty—nationalism.

correspondence depends more on the nature of the knowledge acquired than on sheer amount, or on some kind of individual disposition toward communication among various cognitive domains.

SOCIAL SOURCES OF INTERNATIONAL IMAGES

The social system within which a person moves can have at least three kinds of effects on the images of nations that he entertains. First of all, it may expose him directly to the nations, and hence encourage development of images in accord with his own experiences. Secondly, the social environment may provide norms about an object that serve to mold an image of it in the absence of direct contact. Finally, development of an individual's cognitive structure and total personality within a particular social setting may engender basic psychological dispositions, which in turn affect the content and structure of his nation-images.

The social system can be analyzed in units of varying size, from dyadic relationships to entire nations or large cultural groups. As the size of the unit increases, the difficulty of studying its influence on individual members becomes more pronounced, first because of the sheer problem of sampling its components adequately, and second because the impact on individuals of a large social structure is often attenuated by transmission through its mediating parts. Often, too, the large units chosen for study may be quite inappropriate for distinguishing image types, since they are not functionally relevant to image development. All these difficulties have probably inhibited cross-national studies of nation-images. It is rare to find a study that even comes close to providing a repre-

sentative sample of citizens in any one country. More often, conclusions about cross-national differences are based on samples of college students, whose psychocultural characteristics probably bear only a remote resemblance to the rest of the society from which they come.

The few published reports of systematic surveys that have gone beyond student samples (for example, Aubert et al., 1954; Buchanan & Cantril, 1953, 1954; Eysenck, 1953) have not yielded many interpretable internation differences, but have instead focused on similarities of image content or on the similarities of their correlates within the various countries. The fact that all the nations represented in these studies were either Western European or of English heritage, and maintain close cultural and politico-military ties today, probably increased the degree of cross-national similarity.

Even if cross-national research, based on representative sampling of the appropriate units, were to yield significant differences between particular pairs of nations, there would still remain the problem of interpreting those differences—of attributing them to specified characteristics of the nations concerned. Just as the finding of a difference between the behaviors of two persons provides inadequate grounds for inferring its basis, so a difference between two countries does not permit one to infer a general basis for it, or even to predict that it would be replicated in another similar pair of countries. In cross-national studies the unit of analysis is an entire nation. A description of a single nation, or a comparison of two of them, can provide an interesting source of hypotheses—much as the clinical description of one or two individual human beings can generate hypotheses for nomothetic research—but it cannot support a cross-national generalization about the basis for differences in an entire population of nations.

In order to generalize the correlates of nation-differences it is necessary to study a sizeable sample of nation-units, preferably representatively selected from the population of nations that is of interest. Then, if the national characteristics that are to be compared refer to shared or modal traits of people within them, information about these shared traits is preferably obtained from appropriately representative samples of the people referred to. (They may be the entire population of the country, or some subgroup—such as children or the power elite—within it.) The kind of cross-cultural research that is done through the Yale Human Relations Area Files and other ethnographic sources (see Whiting, 1954) aims at the first of these sampling criteria (cross-national representativeness), but intranational sampling is generally inadequate to lend confidence to measures of central tendency for any particular culture, unless its members are remarkably homogeneous with respect to the trait under study.

Cross-national assessment of international images encounters another difficulty in the variability of language and culture patterns from one nation to another. Although some attributes can be operationally defined by a standard measure that is applicable to any nation, subjective traits like nation-images very likely cannot. For instance, the manifestations of aggressiveness in one society may be different from those in another, so that it is difficult to find a single description of an aggressive nation that would carry the same meaning in the two instances. It may therefore become necessary to devise higher-level measures of image content that are not bound to a particular culture, but convey similar meanings to respondents with differing histories and thought patterns.

Undoubtedly the cross-national level of analysis deals with social units that are of greatest interest in connection with the problem of international images. However, aside from the paucity of relevant empirical studies, the exceedingly great methodological difficulties entailed even in designing such research (see Jacobson, 1954) encourage one to restrict attention to more limited social units. At present it can only be assumed rather gratuitously that whatever social dynamics are encountered at a lower level of analysis will account for differences among nations as well. So here we shall simply consider in a very general fashion three ways—object contact, norm contact, and psychological mediation—in which any social unit may influence the kinds of images its members develop.

Contact with the Object

Common sense, together with most of the available research data, suggests that the more contact one has with a group, the more clear one's image of it becomes. When respondents in seven different nations were asked to pick adjectives describing people in the United States, Great Britain, and France (Buchanan & Cantril, 1953), citizens of these three countries were less likely to say that their own nationalities were "impossible to characterize" than were respondents in the other countries represented.

There is also some evidence that contact with the object tends to produce an image of it that is shared with others who have had similar contact. Taft's (1959) review of relevant research findings indicates that the better known an ethnic group is, the more uniformly is it likely to be characterized by a given sample of respondents. His own empirical study showed a high correlation between the degree to which his Australian subjects were familiar with a particular national group and their degree of consensus in choosing descriptive characteristics.

Taft also found a substantial positive correlation between the mean familiarity of the national groups and the mean preference value accorded them. However, this relationship has not always obtained in other studies reviewed by him; it would seem to depend on the circumstances under which familiarity is acquired and the kind of interdependence (for example, cooperative or competitive) that the groups maintain (see Harding *et al.*, 1954; Katz, 1960, pp. 191–195; Sherif & Sherif, 1956, pp. 287–331).

These findings seem to contradict two other, perhaps equally compelling, common-sense dicta—that stereotypes will develop with respect to those objects that are only vaguely known, but will tend to diminish as direct experience accrues; and that stereotypes will most readily be attached to disliked, rather than to liked, objects. However, it should be noted that the word *stereotype*, as commonly employed, refers to oversimplified, overgeneralized images (see p. 81); whereas, the measure of "stereotypy" used in Taft's study (as well as in many others) is simply the number of respondents who share a common image.[8] This really constitutes a measure of social sharedness, rather than of stereotypy, so the interpretation of Taft's study, and others reviewed by him, had best be restricted to the former meaning.

It may seem reasonable to presume that the increasing consensus accompanying familiarity with an object reflects an increasing accuracy of the image. Vinacke (1949), for example, found that Hawaiian subjects tended to hold images of various ethnic groups within the society much like those that the groups held of themselves, even with regard to unfavorable traits. But consensus alone is not sufficient evidence for accuracy, even if it happens to agree with the self-image of the group being judged. Borg's (1955) study indicated that, although fine arts students agreed with other students on their collective image of the artist, neither of these agreed with the results of personality tests administered to the former sample. Of course, accuracy is a slippery concept when used with reference to images, which are, of necessity, incomplete abstractions from reality. Perhaps one should therefore limit inquiry to the conditions that produce consensus of images or agreement with the group's own self-image, and sidestep the question of accuracy entirely.

Studies in interpersonal perception (for example, Manis, 1955; Newcomb, 1961) indicate that interaction between two people leads to increasing correspondence between each person's image of himself and the other's image of him. In fact, one would suppose that interpersonal interaction can be stable and mutually rewarding only insofar as this condition develops with respect to attributes relevant to the interaction. Such an increasing consensus is only in part due to changes in one person's impression of the other. It often happens that, in crucial respects, one's own self-image is molded by the reactions of those around him, which in turn are based on *their* views of him. This may even occur if the view is unflattering (see Newcomb, 1956).

---

[8] More complexly, the degree of "stereotypy" may be defined as the reciprocal of the number of traits on a list that are required to include a specified proportion (for example, 50 percent) of all subjects' choices (cf. Katz & Braly, 1933).

However, other avenues of cognitive reorganization are available in interpersonal relations. One may try to present himself in such a way as to elicit a favorable image, especially if the co-respondent is a prestigeful person; or reduce one's attraction to a negative evaluator, or minimize the subjective importance of his evaluation (Steiner & Peters, 1958). Also it is possible to effect a compromise solution, which incorporates another's unfavorable view of oneself without explicitly accepting it. My own reanalysis of Vinacke's (1949) published data on Hawaiian ethnic groups suggests that the response to unfavorable "stereotyping" by others may be to enhance one's view of them, rather than to degrade one's own self-view. For instance, Filipinos, who were regarded unfavorably by other ethnic groups, tended to see these other groups in relatively flattering terms; whereas the Japanese and Hawaiian respondents, who represented high-status ethnic groups, tended to hold relatively lower opinions of the others. In general, the absolute favorableness of the image assigned by a group to itself was not correlated with the average favorableness others assigned to it; but the relative favorableness (its self-view in relation to its other-view) was positively correlated with its status in the eyes of others. Thus, contact with an object may have consequences, not only for one's image of the object, but also for one's own self-image.

Contact with Norms about the Object

It is rare, even in interpersonal interaction, for direct experience with an object to be unaided by knowledge of others' views concerning it. When people travel abroad, they tend to do so in groups of fellow countrymen; they discuss their individual experiences with one another, and come to share a collective image of the country that reflects as much an internalization of their own group norms as a direct perception of the object being viewed (cf. Herman & Schild, 1961). Such norms may serve either to reinforce or to distort the effects of direct contact.

More commonly, international images are developed in complete absence of contact with the object—except, perhaps indirectly through acquaintances, lectures, or the mass media. In such circumstances, people cannot employ the mechanism of cognitive or behavioral adjustment described above in connection with interpersonal perceptions. The holder of an image is restricted in the kinds of testing action he can take. Similarly, the object of the image is restricted in the actions he can take to change the view of the image-holder. If the ideologies of two groups are antagonistic, they provide strong forces toward the development of unrealistic images. Here, particularly, one would expect forces toward cognitive balance to be reinforced both by isolation from the object of the image and by the way in which information about it is presented through the available channels of communication. The favorable attributes of a liked object are accentuated, and so are unfavorable attributes of a disliked object. The affective component thus becomes most salient in the resulting images, and this tends to exaggerate any inherent structural tendencies toward a maximally balanced cognitive system. Newcomb (1947) has noted the circularity of such a reaction pattern by reference to "autistic hostility," in which antagonism produces a disruption of communication between two hostile groups, which in turn lessens the opportunity for favorable alteration of their respective images, and thereby in-

creases the degree of mutual antagonism felt.

The norm-providing groups within a
society are many. First, of course, is
the family of orientation. A study by
Helfant (1952) showed significant correlations between parents' and their
children's attitudes toward Russia, war,
and internationalism, even though the
children were college students away
from home. Schools and other socializing agents also have their effects.
Though the evidence is less direct,
studies by Jahoda (1959) and by Prothro
and Melikian (1955) suggest that
Ghanaians and Arab students had
adopted images of various national
groups that corresponded closely to
those maintained by their colonizers or
teachers.

In some countries political parties
may set norms about international
images for their membership. For example, in the study of school teachers'
attitudes in six European countries by
Aubert *et al.* (1954), it was found that
members of the conservative and center
parties were more likely to be concerned about the Soviet threat, whereas
socialist, social-democrat, and labor
party adherents tended more to focus
on the dangers of war. At the beginning of World War II, members of the
Conservative Party in Great Britain
tended to express greater sympathy for
Germany over Russia, Franco over the
Spanish Loyalists, and Fascism over
Communism, while the Labor Party
adherents tended more to support the
opposite side in each case (BIPO #53,
December 1938; BIPO #54, January
1939; BIPO #56, March 1939; BIPO
#68, March 1940). After the war, sup-
porters of the British, Australian, and
Canadian labor parties (the last of these
being the Cooperative Commonwealth
Federation) maintained relatively
greater sympathy toward the Soviet
Union than did adherents of the other
major parties in these countries (BIPO
#134, June 1946; AGP #83, September
1951; CIPO #214, October 1951; CIPO
#243, July 1955; CIPO #244, Septem-
ber 1955; CIPO #278, September 1959;
CIPO #279, November 1959). Of
course, the Cooperative Commonwealth Federation in Canada was very
small compared to the Liberal and Pro-
gressive-Conservative Parties during
the period of the studies reviewed
(1951–1959); and the latter two differed
not at all on most of the international
attitudes represented in these polls.
Thus the dominant political situation
in Canada appears much like that found
in the United States (see, for example,
Scott & Withey, 1958, pp. 134–146):
ideological differences between the two
major parties do not generally extend
to the realm of foreign affairs.[9]

In those countries where political
parties serve as reference groups for
international attitudes, one might expect nation-images to constitute more
salient features of their citizens' cognitive structures than in countries without enduring political cleavages with
respect to foreign affairs; for in the
former, political propaganda would
constantly remind party adherents of
characteristics of the international arena
to which they should attend. Such political cleavages might also increase the
vulnerability of the country's government to internal criticism regarding its
conduct of foreign affairs, since among
the diverse international images created by political agitation would surely
appear some that would be offended by
almost any conceivable act in foreign
relations.

---

[9] Except, perhaps, in very special cases, such as the Korean War (see Scott & Withey, 1958,
pp. 144–145); this, however, appeared to reflect, not an ideological difference between the
parties, but rather an attempt by the party out of power to take advantage of a frustrating
international situation to focus antagonism against the party in power.

Regardless of the sources of social norms for international images—be they family, school, political party, religious institutions, or communications media —it is generally in the interest of such agents to develop fairly simplified, undifferentiated image structures. These increase the chances that desired response repertories will be elicited from the people who hold the images. Complex, multidimensional concept structures have certain social disadvantages in that they are more difficult to communicate, leave considerable latitude for emotional and behavioral reaction, and do not provide the strong basis for group solidarity that black-and-white in-group–out-group distinctions do (see Chapter 7). It is quite likely, therefore, that group norms generally serve not only to increase the homogeneity of their members' images, but also to keep the cognitive structures in which these are embedded relatively simple.

Inculcation of Mediating Psychological Dispositions

To the extent that international images reflect more basic personality traits, one might expect that social conditions giving rise to the latter would indirectly affect the images themselves. It has been suggested, for example (Lasswell, 1933), that Hitlerism, with its attendant collective image of anti-Semitism, represented a response to socially induced feelings of frustration in lower middle-class Germans. Scapegoat theories of prejudice (see, for example, Adorno et al., 1950; Allport, 1954; Bettelheim & Janowitz, 1950; Lindzey, 1950; Miller & Bugelski, 1948) involve the notion that frustrations encountered during socialization or daily social life induce aggression which is displaced onto a convenient out-group. Harding et

al. (1954) provide a thorough review of theories and research findings concerning personality correlates of prejudice. Most of the evidence on social antecedents of these personality dispositions is quite indirect and unsystematic, but it points vaguely to childhood socialization practices that require submission to authority and limit exploration of the interpersonal environment, and to consequent development of "closed" and "rigid" cognitive structures (see p. 81).

One may suppose that performance of ascribed or achieved roles within the society may reinforce in the incumbent, not only certain role-specific attitudes (cf. Lieberman, 1956), but also a variety of diffuse personality dispositions. Some of these may be expressed in incidental ways—such as in attitudes toward foreign affairs (cf. Smith, Bruner, & White, 1956). A previous section of this chapter reviewed some cognitive and personality characteristics that have been found correlated with international attitudes. These included level of cognitive awareness, personal security, and aggressiveness. It is not difficult to think of particular roles that, in a given social context, tend to engender these and other traits that may be reflected in international attitudes.

For example, sex-role differentiation within Western society has traditionally tended to foster interpersonal aggressiveness in the male and passivity in the female. Such a tendency toward contrast in interpersonal roles appears to be reflected in the sex differences in international attitudes found in Australia, Canada, and Great Britain. On the one hand, women are less likely to advocate aggressive international relations;[10] on the other hand, they may also exhibit more fear of the world (war expectancy) and a greater tendency toward withdrawal even from certain

---

[10] In BIPO #56, March 1939, males were more likely to favor Britain's fighting to prevent return of her colonies. In BIPO #61, August 1939, males were more in favor of fighting to defend Poland. In BIPO #67, February 1940, females were more in favor of discussing peace

peaceful interactions in it.[11] The greater tendency of males to advocate aggressive international relations has also been found among samples of college students in the United States. Farber (1951) found his male subjects more likely than the females to advocate an immediate show-down war with the Soviet Union; and Smith (1942) reports that female students over a twelve-year period scored consistently more pacifistic than males on Thurstone's scale of attitudes toward war. Eysenck (1951), in a study of political attitudes among members of three major British parties, found that women uniformly scored lower than men on his "toughminded" factor, which represents a general ag-

gressive orientation toward a wide range of attitudinal objects.

It is possible that certain of the regularly obtained differences among socioeconomic classes in attitudes toward foreign affairs can be interpreted as resulting from generalized, role-engendered expectancies and response-dispositions. It would appear, for example, the members of the lower class in Australia, Canada, Great Britain, and the United States are likely to display greater hostility toward foreign nations and greater pessimism concerning the prospects for peaceful international relations than are middle and upper class respondents.[12] Along the same lines is Eysenck's (1951) finding that

---

with Germany. In BIPO #68, March 1940, females were more in favor of discussing peace with Germany; males were more likely to believe that Britain would have to fight Russia someday. In CIPO #214, October 1951, males were more in favor of using German troops in an allied (NATO) army. In CIPO #238, males were more likely to believe that the West should go to war with Russia now, and more likely to believe that arming Germany would improve the prospects for peace. In CIPO #243, July 1955, females were more likely to advocate stoppage of the U.S. tests of atomic weapons; the same finding appeared in CIPO #268, March 1958.

[11] In AGP #69, December 1949, males were more likely to favor non-British immigration, and more likely to favor Japanese participation in the Olympic Games. In AGP #79, March 1951, females were more likely to believe that war was imminent, and more likely to believe that Australia had too many immigrants already; males were more likely to approve admission of immigrants from seven specified countries. In AGP #83, September 1951, females were more likely to favor a limitation on the import of Japanese toys. In AGP #114, October 1955, males were more in favor of exchanging farm visits with Russia, more in favor of increased immigration, and more in favor of import cuts (reversal of trend). In CIPO #214, October 1951, females were more likely to believe that the Soviet Union wanted war. In CIPO #231, August 1953, females were more likely to believe that Russia would start a war unprovoked; but there were no sex differences in the belief that the United States would start a war (exception to trend). In CIPO #244, September 1955, males were more in favor of President Eisenhower's proposal to share military information with Russia, and more likely to want to visit Russia; males were more likely to believe that war was imminent (reversal of trend); there was no sex difference in willingness to have European immigrants as neighbors (exception to trend). In CIPO #268, March 1958, females were more worried about the possibility of atomic war. In CIPO #274, March 1959, males were more likely to favor trade with Russia. In CIPO #278, September 1959, females were more likely to believe that war was imminent. In CIPO #279, November 1959, males were more likely to believe that 1960 would be peaceful internationally; females were more likely to expect atomic war between Russia and the United States by 1980, and more likely to expect capitalism and the West to have collapsed by 1980; there was no sex difference in belief that civilization would be in ruins by 1980 (exception to trend).

[12] In AGP #69, December 1949, income and occupation correlated positively with favorable attitude toward non-British immigration; positively with approval of Japanese participation in Olympic games. In AGP #79, March 1951, income and occupation correlated positively with

lower-class members of three political parties in England tended to be more "toughminded" in their political attitudes than middle-class respondents.

Of course, without more thorough studies, which include direct measures of the allegedly revelant role characteristics, it is not possible to tell just what it is about these social roles that is responsible for the differences in international attitudes—or, indeed, if role characteristics are responsible at all. Sex and social class are, after all, fairly gross role typologies—representing very crudely a number of differences in way of life, in consequent perceptions of the world and orientations toward it. So a variety of mediating psychological processes may be operating jointly: information level, anomic tendencies, notions regarding the appropriateness of interpersonal aggressive behavior, and other value orientations. What is needed ultimately is a better analysis of role types in terms of the kinds of psychological characteristics that they are likely to engender, and then an assessment of these characteristics in relation to international attitudes. Such an analysis would allow us to determine the nature of the psychological processes that mediate the presumed role differences in attitudes.

SUMMARY AND CONCLUSIONS

The images people hold of foreign nations can be analyzed into their cognitive, affective, and behavioral com-

---

willingness to admit immigrants from seven specified countries; negatively with belief that there were too many immigrants in Australia already. In AGP #114, October 1955, income and occupation correlated positively with approval of increased immigration rate. In AGP #135, November 1958, income, but not occupation, correlated negatively with the belief that foreigners should speak English in public. In BIPO #68, March 1940, there was no correlation between income and the belief that Britain would have to fight Russia sometime (exception to trend). In BIPO #71, August 1940, there was no correlation between income and the belief that enemy aliens should be interned (exception to trend). In BIPO #134, June 1946, income level correlated positively with professed improvement in attitude toward the Soviet Union. In CIPO #244, September 1955, education and income correlated positively with willingness to accept European immigrants as neighbors; not with reported improvement in attitude toward Russia or with belief that Russia had been more sincere lately (exceptions to trend). Education level correlated with desire to visit Russia. In CIPO #274, March 1959, income, but not education, correlated with favorable attitudes toward France, Germany, Italy, and Japan.

In AGP #79, March 1951, income level correlated negatively with the expectation of an early war. In CIPO #231, August 1953, income level was positively correlated with the belief that a "summit" meeting would bring about a decrease in world tensions. In CIPO #239, November 1954, education level correlated positively with the belief that prospects for peace were improving; also with the belief that coexistence between East and West was possible. In CIPO #244, September 1955, there was no correlation between education level and war expectancy (exception to trend). In CIPO #268, March 1958, education level was negatively correlated with respondent's professed worry over the possibility of atomic war. In CIPO #278, September 1959, education and income levels were negatively correlated with the expectation of an early war. In CIPO #279, November 1959, education, income, and occupation levels were negatively correlated with the expectation of atomic war between Russia and the United States by 1980; also negatively with the expectation that civilization would be in ruins by 1980. Education and occupation, but not income, were positively correlated with the belief that Russia and the West would be peaceful by 1980. Education, but not income or occupation, correlated with the belief that 1960 would be a peaceful year internationally.

For social class correlates of international attitudes in the United States see Scott and Withey (1958), pp. 113–129.

ponents. The first represent perceived characteristics of the nations, the second a liking or disliking for them, and the third a set of actions or policies toward them that the person deems appropriate. There is considerable evidence, at both psychological and cultural levels of analysis, for a tendency toward correspondence among these image components. Favorable characteristics tend to be attributed to liked nations, and unfavorable characteristics to disliked nations. Such relationships reflect at least two basic kinds of psychological processes: tendencies toward cognitive balance, which involve differential perceptions and affect within the same person concerning the various nation-objects that he recognizes; and interperson differences in tendency to be favorably or unfavorably disposed toward all foreign nations.

The degree to which individuals display tendencies toward cognitive balance depends in part upon the complexity of their image structures; people who perceive a variety of independent bases for differences among nations are less likely to hold balanced ("black-and-white") attitudes. Image complexity depends, in turn, upon the person's level of information about world affairs.

Generalized xenophobic attitudes tend to be associated with feelings of threat from the international environment and also with the advocacy of international policies that are competitively, rather than cooperatively, oriented. There is also some evidence that generalized threat-oriented image contents may be found most frequently among poorly informed, insecure, and personally aggressive individuals.

The social determinants of image contents and structure can be only vaguely interpreted from the present evidence. In fact, systematic data on cross-cultural differences in international images are virtually unavailable in the published literature. Certain demographic correlates found in four Western nations may be interpreted as reflecting different social circumstances of the groups.

The data from which these inferences have been drawn come in part from published studies of restricted groups (usually college students), and in part from hitherto unpublished results of public opinion surveys in Australia, Canada, and the United Kingdom. The obtained correlations between international images and psychological or social variables frequently serve to raise more questions than they answer. Considerable liberty has been taken in interpreting findings in the context of a structural formulation of images; but linkage of data to theory has been tenuous at many points, and in a number of instances conceptual interpretation was foregone in favor of mere reporting, since the theory could add little to the reader's own common-sense understanding. In concluding, therefore, it may be appropriate to re-emphasize a point made earlier to justify an analysis in terms of the structural characteristics of images: The variety of contents of international images is nearly limitless. They may be shaped by actual happenings in the world or by normatively regulated information that the person encounters. What the individual himself contributes to the interchange is a receiving and selecting capacity, which is inherent in his own cognitive and psychological make-up. If crucial characteristics of this receiving system can be described in sufficiently general terms, then it may be possible to overcome some of the obstacles to understanding posed by the extreme diversity of image content.

REFERENCES

Adorno, T. W., Frenkel-Brunswik, Else, Levinson, D. J., & Sanford, R. N. *The authoritarian personality*. New York: Harper, 1950.

Allport, G. W. *The nature of prejudice*. Reading, Mass.: Addison-Wesley, 1954.

Asch, S. E. Forming impressions of personality. *J. abnorm. soc. Psychol.*, 1946, *41*, 258–290.

Aubert, V., Fisher, B. R., & Rokkan, S. A comparative study of teachers' attitudes to international problems and policies. *J. soc. Issues*, 1954, *10* (4), 25–39.

Bettelheim, B., & Janowitz, M. *Dynamics of prejudice*. New York: Harper, 1950.

Bieri, J., & Blacker, E. The generality of cognitive complexity in the perception of people and inkblots. *J. abnorm. soc. Psychol.*, 1956, *53*, 112–117.

Block, J., & Block, Jeanne An investigation of the relationship between intolerance of ambiguity and ethnocentrism. *J. Pers.*, 1951, *19*, 303–311.

Borg, W. R. The effect of personality and contact upon a personality stereotype. *J. educ. Res.*, 1955, *49*, 289–294.

Bruner, J. S., & Tagiuri, R. The perception of people. In G. Lindzey (Ed.), *Handbook of social psychology*, Vol. 2. Reading, Mass.: Addison-Wesley, 1954. Pp. 634–654.

Buchanan, W., & Cantril, H. *How nations see each other: A study in public opinion*. Urbana: Univer. Illinois Press, 1953.

Buchanan, W., & Cantril, H. National stereotypes. In W. L. Schramm (Ed.), *The process and effects of mass communication*. Urbana: Univer. Illinois Press, 1954. Pp. 191–206.

Campbell, A. Factors associated with attitudes toward Jews. In T. M. Newcomb & E. L. Hartley (Eds.), *Readings in social psychology*. New York: Holt, Rinehart and Winston, 1947. Pp. 518–527.

Campbell, D. T. The generality of a social attitude. Unpublished doctoral dissertation, University of California, 1947.

Carlson, E. R. Attitude change through modification of attitude structure. *J. abnorm. soc. Psychol.*, 1956, *52*, 256–261.

Child, I. L., & Doob, L. Factors determining national stereotypes. *J. soc. Psychol.*, 1943, *17*, 203–219.

Christiansen, B. *Attitudes toward foreign affairs as a function of personality*. Oslo: Univer. Oslo Press, 1959.

Douvan, Elizabeth, & Walker, A. The sense of effectiveness in public affairs. *Psychol. Monogr.*, 1956, *70*, No. 22.

Emmerich, W. Young children's discriminations of parent and child roles. *Child Developm.*, 1959, *30*, 403–419.

Eysenck, H. J. Primary social attitudes as related to social class and political party. *Brit. J. Sociol.*, 1951, *2*, 198–209.

Eysenck, H. J. Primary social attitudes: A comparison of attitude patterns in England, Germany, and Sweden. *J. abnorm. soc. Psychol.*, 1953, *48*, 563–568.

Farber, M. L. The Armageddon complex: Dynamics of opinion. *Publ. Opin. Quart.*, 1951, *15*, 217–224.

Farris, C. D. Selected attitudes on foreign affairs as correlates of authoritarianism and political anomie. *J. Politics*, 1960, *22*, 50–67.

Fensterwald, B., Jr. The anatomy of American isolationism and expansionism. II. *J. Confl. Resol.*, 1958, *2*, 280–309.

Fisher, B. R. & Belknap, G. *America's role in world affairs*. Ann Arbor, Mich.: Survey Research Center, 1952.

Gilbert, G. M. Stereotype persistence and change among college students. *J. abnorm. soc. Psychol.*, 1951, *46*, 245–254.

Gladstone, A. I. The possibility of predicting reactions to international events. *J. soc. Issues*, 1955, *11* (1), 21–28.

Harding, J., Kutner, B., Proshansky, H., & Chein, I. Prejudice and ethnic relations. In G. Lindzey (Ed.), *Handbook of social psychology*, Vol. 2. Reading, Mass.: Addison-Wesley, 1954. Pp. 1021–1061.

Harvey, O. J., Hunt, D. E., & Schroder, H. M. *Conceptual systems and personality organization.* New York: Wiley, 1961.

Heider, F. Attitudes and cognitive organization. *J. Psychol.*, 1946, *21*, 107–112.

Helfant, K. Parents' attitudes vs. adolescent hostility in the determination of adolescents' sociopolitical attitudes. *Psychol. Monogr.*, 1952, *66*, No. 13.

Herman, S. N., & Schild, E. O. The stranger group in a cross-cultural situation. *Sociometry*, 1961, *24*, 165–176.

Holzman, P. S. The relation of assimilation tendencies in visual, auditory, and kinaesthetic time-error to cognitive attitudes of leveling and sharpening. *J. Pers.*, 1954, *22*, 375–394.

Jacobson, E. Methods used for producing comparable data in the OCSR seven-nation attitude study. *J. soc. Issues.*, 1954, *10* (4), 40–51.

Jahoda, G. Nationality preferences and national stereotypes in Ghana before independence. *J. soc. Psychol.*, 1959, *50*, 165–174.

Katz, D. The functional approach to the study of attitudes. *Publ. Opin. Quart.*, 1960, *24*, 163–204.

Katz, D., & Braly, K. W. Verbal stereotypes and racial prejudice. *J. abnorm. soc. Psychol.*, 1933, *28*, 280–290.

Katz, D., & Braly, K. W. Racial prejudice and racial stereotypes. *J. abnorm. soc. Psychol.*, 1935, *30*, 175–193.

Kelley, H. H. The warm-cold variable in first impressions of persons. *J. Pers.*, 1950, *18*, 431–439.

Kosa, J. The rank order of peoples: A study in national stereotypes. *J. soc. Psychol.*, 1957, *46*, 311–320.

Lasswell, H. D. The psychology of Hitlerism as a response of the lower middle classes to continuing insecurity. *Pol. Quart.*, 1933, *4*, 373–384. (Reprinted in G. E. Swanson, T. M. Newcomb, & E. L. Hartley, Eds., *Readings in social psychology.* New York: Holt, Rinehart and Winston, 1952.)

Levinson, D. J. Authoritarian personality and foreign policy. *J. Confl. Resol.*, 1957, *1*, 37–47.

Lieberman, S. The effect of changes in roles on the attitudes of role occupants. *Hum. Relat.*, 1956, *9*, 385–402.

Lindzey, G. An experimental examination of the scapegoat theory of prejudice. *J. abnorm. soc. Psychol.*, 1950, *45*, 296–309.

Mace, C. A. National stereotypes—their nature and function. *Sociol. Rev.*, 1943, *35*, 29–36.

MacKinnon, W. J., & Centers, R. Social-psychological factors in public orientation toward an out-group. *Amer. J. Sociol.*, 1958, *63*, 415–419.

Manis, M. Social interaction and the self-concept. *J. abnorm. soc. Psychol.*, 1955, *51*, 362–370.

Milburn, T. What constitutes effective deterrence? *J. Confl. Resol.*, 1959, *3*, 138–145.

Miller, N. E., & Bugelski, R. Minor studies in aggression: The influence of frustrations imposed by the ingroup on attitudes expressed toward outgroups. *J. Psychol.*, 1948, *25*, 437–442.

Mischel, W., & Schopler, J. Authoritarianism and reactions to "Sputniks." *J. abnorm. soc. Psychol.*, 1959, *59*, 142–145.

Newcomb, T. M. Autistic hostility and social reality. *Hum. Relat.*, 1947, *1*, 69–86.

Newcomb, T. M. The prediction of interpersonal attraction. *Amer. Psychologist*, 1956, *11*, 575–586.

Newcomb, T. M. *The acquaintance process.* New York: Holt, Rinehart and Winston, 1961.

Osgood, C. E., Suci, G. J., & Tannenbaum, P. H. *The measurement of meaning.* Urbana: Univer. Illinois Press, 1957.

Prothro, E. T., & Melikian, L. H. Studies in stereotypes: I. Familiarity and the kernel of truth hypothesis. *J. soc. Psychol.*, 1955, *41*, 3–10.

Roberts, A. H., & Rokeach, M. Anomie, authoritarianism, and prejudice: A replication. *Amer. J. Sociol.*, 1956, *61*, 355–358.

Rosenberg, M. J. Cognitive reorganization in response to the hypnotic reversal of attitudinal affect. *J. Pers.*, 1960, *28*, 39–63. (a)

Rosenberg, M. J. A structural theory of attitude dynamics. *Publ. Opin. Quart.*, 1960, *24*, 319–340. (b)

Sampson, D. L., & Smith, H. P. A scale to measure world-minded attitudes. *J. soc. Psychol.*, 1957, *45*, 99–106.

Scott, W. A. Rationality and non-rationality of international attitudes. *J. Confl. Resol.*, 1958, *2*, 8–16.

Scott, W. A. Cognitive consistency, response reinforcement, and attitude change. *Sociometry*, 1959, *22*, 219–229.

Scott, W. A. International ideology and interpersonal ideology. *Publ. Opin. Quart.*, 1960, *24*, 419–435.

Scott, W. A. Cognitive structure and social structure: Some concepts and relationships. In N. F. Washburne (Ed.), *Decisions, values, and groups*, Vol. II. New York: Pergamon Press, 1962. (a)

Scott, W. A. Cognitive complexity and cognitive flexibility. *Sociometry*, 1962, *25*, 405–414. (b)

Scott, W. A. Cognitive complexity and cognitive balance. *Sociometry*, 1963, *26*, 66–74.

Scott, W. A. *Values and organizations.* Chicago: Rand McNally, 1965.

Scott, W. A., & Withey, S. B. *The United States and the United Nations: The public view.* New York: Manhattan Publishing Co., 1958.

Sherif, M., & Sherif, Carolyn W. *An outline of social psychology.* (Rev. ed.) New York: Harper, 1956.

Skinner, B. F. *Science and human behavior.* New York: Macmillan, 1953.

Smith, M. War attitudes in peace and war. *School and Society*, 1942, *56*, 640–644.

Smith, M. B., Bruner, J. S., & White, R. W. *Opinions and personality.* New York: Wiley, 1956.

Spilka, B., & Struening, E. L. A questionnaire study of personality and ethnocentrism. *J. soc. Psychol.*, 1956, *44*, 65–71.

Srole, L. Social integration and certain corrolaries: An exploratory study. *Amer. sociol. Rev.*, 1956, *21*, 709–716.

Steiner, I. D., & Peters, S. C. Conformity and the A-B-X model. *J. Pers.*, 1958, *26*, 229–242.

Taft, R. Intolerance of ambiguity and ethnocentrism. *J. consult. Psychol.*, 1956, *20*, 153–154.

Taft, R. Ethnic stereotypes, attitudes, and familiarity: Australia. *J. soc. Psychol.*, 1959, *49*, 177–186.

Titus, H. E., & Hollander, E. P. The California *F*-scale in psychological research: 1950–1955. *Psychol. Bull.*, 1957, *54*, 47–64.

Ulehla, Z. J. Individual differences in information yields of raters. Unpublished master's thesis, University of Colorado, 1961.

Vinacke, W. E. Stereotyping among national-racial groups in Hawaii: A study in ethnocentrism. *J. soc. Psychol.*, 1949, *30*, 265–291.

Vinacke, W. E. Explorations in the dynamic processes of stereotyping. *J. soc. Psychol.*, 1956, *43*, 105–132.

Whiting, J. W. M. The cross-cultural method. In G. Lindzey (Ed.), *Handbook of social psychology*, Vol. 1. Reading, Mass.: Addison-Wesley, 1954. Pp. 523–531.

Wyer, R. S. A model of cognitive structure. Unpublished doctoral dissertation, University of Colorado, 1962.

4

So far we have been looking at more general determinants of national and international images—their sources in the psychological structure of the individual, the social structure of his society, and his own place within that social structure. In the next three chapters, we shall examine the effects of various specific experiences on the formation and change of images.

One type of experience that is likely to have a pronounced effect on national and international images is direct, face-to-face contact with nationals of other countries. Research has focused in particular on the cross-national contacts that occur in the course of foreign travel, study abroad, and international exchange of personnel. What effects do such contacts have on the images of the visitor and the host? What kinds of experiences increase or decrease the extent of these effects, both in the short run and in the long run? What are the conditions that maximize openness to the new experiences and readiness to abandon preconceptions? Under what conditions does travel increase internationalism and world-mindedness, and under what conditions does it strengthen nationalist orientations? These are some of the questions to which Chapter 4 addresses itself. In Chapters 14 and 15 we shall continue our examination of personal cross-national contact from a different point of view: whereas Chapter 4 focuses on the *effects* of contact, the later chapters will be concerned with the *processes of interaction* that tend to occur when persons of different nationality meet under various circumstances.

The author of Chapter 4, Ithiel de Sola Pool, is Professor of Political Science at the Massachusetts Institute of Technology and director of the research program in international communications at MIT's Center for International Studies. He has been a member of the Scientific Advisory Board of the United States Air Force and chairman of the Research Board of Simulmatics Corporation. Recent publications of which he is a co-author include *American business and public policy*

(1963), *The people look at educational television* (1963), and *Candidates, issues, and strategies: A computer simulation of the 1960 presidential election* (1964). His major current research interest is the computer simulation of social systems.

H. C. K.

Effects of Cross-National Contact on National and International Images

Ithiel de Sola Pool

*T*he subject of this chapter is travel and how it affects certain images: images of the foreigner and of the self; images held by the traveler and by his hosts. Thus the subject is the effects of travel on four sets of images: (1) The traveler's image of himself, his home country, and his own culture. (2) The host's image of himself, his country, and his culture. (3) The traveler's image of the outside world, particularly but not exclusively of the country he visits, its inhabitants and culture. (4) The host's image of the country from which the traveler comes, its inhabitants and culture.

Note what is omitted. First, we are not considering the two-step effect of the traveler on his compatriots back home and on their images of the world. For example, the ex-tourist at a picnic dressed in *Lederhosen* may somehow affect his neighbors' images of Europe. The ex-missionary to China or Africa may be an organizer of lectures and re-

lief meetings in his home town. The Peace Corpsman's parents may acquire a deep interest in the Philippines or Tanganyika. Such effects we do not consider here.

Second, we will not be treating in a detailed way the diffused effect of foreign contacts via the traveler who is a writer. China had effects on Marco Polo; those are within the terms of reference of this chapter. But Marco Polo, and via him China, had a profound effect on millions of Europeans in the Renaissance; those effects are beyond this chapter's limits. This is a somewhat arbitrary limitation, for behind every mass media message that conveys images of foreign lands there lies an event of personal contact by a traveler. A story on sacred monkeys in India diffused through the wire services originates with a foreign correspondent. He expresses thereby what he as a traveler saw through his own prism of prejudices as he looked around him in a foreign land. But the impact of his perceptions is multiplied manifold by the power of the pen. And so, as we draw the line of our attention at the effect of foreign travel on the traveler himself and on his immediate host, we cut the chain of causality almost at its start.

Yet somehow we must draw limits. So we shall deal here only with the effects of travel contacts on those individuals who participate in the contact event in person.

Thus, four sets of images—the traveler's image and his host's images of self and others—are our dependent variables, and travel is our independent variable. But travel is of many kinds. And so we start by considering the variety of types of travel.

KINDS OF TRAVEL

Let us consider some of the dimensions along which trips may vary. We list dimensions that can make a great deal of difference in the impact of a trip. One could certainly add to the list, yet even the combinations of only the noted variables would yield an astronomic number of kinds of trips, no two of which would affect a traveler alike.

1. Clearly, a first question to ask about any trip is its *purpose:* is it undertaken primarily for business, tourism, education, government service, news reporting, lecturing, attendance at meetings, health, family affairs, or for some other purpose? The effect of a trip is apt to differ depending upon the main purpose behind it.

Some trips involve responsibilities; many trips are undertaken for pleasure only. The vacation trip is a form of escape. It is a release from the pressures of normal duties. Not so the work trip,

which engenders responsibilities of its own.

Some trips are undertaken in order to acquire information. Images are formed of those very objects about which information was sought. Such images are apt to be quite different from those acquired incidentally.

We might be interested, for example, in the images travelers to Germany acquire about the peaceful or warlike character of that country today. Consider first a trip by a newsman taken explicitly to investigate this question, in the course of which he interviews ex-Defense Minister Strauss, conducts a taxi-driver poll recording the replies, and engages in other purposive activities to get at relevant facts. Contrast that with a trip by a tourist visiting museums and beerhalls. The tourist, too, may acquire an image of Germany as peaceful or warlike. Asked after his return whether Germany can now be trusted, he may recall an evening of Schubert songs and an affable conversation on a train and report an image of Germany as a peaceful country. Or he may recall a rude ticket collector and a heel-clicking guide and may perceive it as warlike. Images come casually and all of the time from such adventitious experiences that have no logical relation to the object of the images. Clearly such effects must be distinguished from the effects of purposive information-seeking.

Yet in real life the distinction cannot always be sharply drawn. Foreign correspondents, whose professional job is to engage in purposive information-seeking, still gain many of their impressions from the casual events of their lives. Unfortunately, this is particularly true of their impressions of public opinion. Few reporters use the objective data available. Their assessment of the mood of a country is most often an interpretation of casual experiences and suffers thereby from the biases that arise from their round of life. But even if such impressions are formed in events having other purposes than information-seeking, the interpretation of such casual events may be affected by the fact that the event occurs to a man whose mind is tuned to seeking answers to predetermined questions.

Up to now most social science studies of the effects of foreign travel have dealt with incidental effects of travel, not with its intended object. Thus, studies of student exchange programs have usually surveyed persons who came to the United States to acquire information on such matters as how to build bridges or how to irrigate deserts, but the studies have most often asked about the incidental images acquired of America as a country and of Americans as a people!

One particularly important kind of responsibility that a traveler may carry is the responsibility to report back his experiences to someone else. In studies of "debriefing" this responsibility has been found to have a particularly significant effect on the images acquired. The man who expects to write something, whether it is a progress report to the boss, a dispatch to his paper or foreign office, or even a piece of *belles lettres* for an unknown audience, carries on his shoulders all the time his imagined reader. The perception of every experience is colored by the expectation of telling it and by a fantasy of what the reaction to the story will be (Zimmerman & Bauer, 1956. See also Pool & Shulman, 1959; Bauer, 1958; and Bauer & Pool, 1960).

2. The effects of a trip are conditioned by a number of *temporal and spatial facts.* Is it the traveler's first, second, or Nth trip abroad (Pool, Keller, & Bauer, 1956)? Is it a permanent migration or will there be a return? If not permanent, how long will the whole

trip last—three days, two weeks, or five years? Within that total period, will one place be visited for the whole time, or will it be a series of short stops with little depth but opportunity for comparison between them, or some mixed combination of these patterns (Kelman, 1963)?

3. The nature of the *traveler's relations to the people he meets,* especially to members of the host society, also shape the effects of a trip.

What is the traveler's relation to fellow travelers? Is he traveling alone, in a pair, in a family group, in a travel group, or in large formations such as an army? If he is in a group, does it consist entirely of co-nationals, is it mixed with host-nationals, or is it multinational?

What is the traveler's residential relation to the host society? Is he part of a joint living group with his hosts—staying, for example, with a local family or in a university dormitory or a youth camp; does he live in a normal part of the community—for example, renting an apartment and shopping in local stores; is he in a traveler's milieu, staying in hotels and eating in restaurants; or is he in a foreign enclave such as an army camp, embassy, or compound?

What is the traveler's functional relation to host nationals? Is he engaged in a joint task effort with his hosts (if so, as superior, peer, or subordinate)? Is he trying to sell them something, be it a commodity or a policy? Is he seeking information or enlightenment from them? Does he have personal introductions to some of them (be it through friends, family, business, or profession)? Or does he have only the incidental contacts that arise with service personnel and in public places—contacts with hotel employees, taxi drivers and neighbors on a train? Moreover, does the traveler know the host's language, and how well (Deutsch & Won, 1963)?

The factors just mentioned have been frequently examined in social science studies of intercultural contact. For example, living arrangements of students have, not surprisingly, been found to affect significantly the amount and the quality of the interactions between foreign students and their American hosts. The Indian student, coming from a culture where living with a mother is not expected to end at eighteen, may often find in his landlady the key to how at home he feels. Selltiz *et al.* (1963) found that foreign undergraduates at small colleges interacted with Americans more than those at metropolitan universities. Further analysis revealed "that the difference between kinds of school in the interaction of foreign students with Americans can be accounted for largely on the basis of living arrangements provided at the different institutions" (p. 97). There can be no doubt that jointness of living arrangements is a very important factor (see also Lambert & Bressler, 1956, especially pp. 23–28). Even more important in shaping the total impact of the trip are the functional relations between the visitor and the host. These have been studied especially with reference to the varied professional roles involved when the visitor feels highly competent or feels inadequate, is allowed an opportunity for satisfactory professional development, or is subordinated (see Bailyn & Kelman, 1962; Mayntz, 1960).

4. The *relation of the culture visited to the traveler's own culture* is a further factor conditioning the effects of a trip. The traveler may go to a land much like his own (for example, an American to Canada) or to one with a very different culture (an American to Japan). He may have been prepared for what he meets or he may not. He may have been informed about the conditions there or they may come as a shock.

It makes a profound difference whether the traveler goes from a homeland he regards as more advanced to a land he regards as more backward or whether he goes from a homeland he regards as more backward to a land he regards as more advanced. One may also ask if the host concurs in that rating.

Various studies have dealt with the problem of inferiority feelings by Asian and African students in Europe and America and the resulting forms of defensive behavior (see Isaacs, 1958; Bennett *et al.*, 1958; Morris, 1960; Selltiz *et al.*, 1963; Lambert & Bressler, 1956). A lot of attention has also been given to the problem of the foreign student who wishes never to return home because he finds in his host country the land of his professional and personal dreams (Mayntz, 1960, p. 736; Coelho, 1958).

5. The *ease or hardship* a traveler experiences is another factor affecting his reactions. Most generally, we may ask, does the trip turn out to be a pleasure or a pain? Obviously reactions to places enjoyed will be different from reactions to places suffered.

One can easily list a number of special factors that play a role in the enjoyment of voyages: Is the trip to a place where travel facilities are well organized, or to one where hotels are bad, information hard to obtain, transportation schedules unreliable, and so forth? Is the traveler well financed? Does he live as well as at home, better, or worse (Cleveland *et al.*, 1960)? Often this depends on whether the cost of living at prevailing exchange rates is higher or lower than at home. Is the traveler going at his own expense or on an expense account? Is life physically comfortable where he is abroad? Is the climate good or bad? Is the country clean or dirty (Isaacs, 1958), noisy or quiet, attractive or ugly? Is the food and drink palatable to the visitor (Isaacs, 1958)? Are the recreational facilities enjoyable? Is the traveler in good health or beset by illness? Is the trip made voluntarily, with some reluctance, or under compulsion? Examples of compulsory trips are the movements of armies or the flights of refugees; the images they acquire are quite different from those of the voluntary traveler.

6. Finally we may note that the changes experienced by the traveler are very much a function of *the person he was when he started.*

What were the expectations with which his trip was undertaken? Did the traveler have unrealistic hopes—of going to a utopia or finding a husband on the voyage? Or did the traveler expect the trip to be unpleasant and burdensome? Or did he have reasonable positive expectations?

What were the family status and other primary group attachments of the traveler? Did he leave behind family or a fiancée? Was he traveling alone and free from home ties? Or was his family with him? How old is the traveler: is he a child, an adolescent, or an adult?

One could further classify travelers on an endless list of other social variables including such standard categories as sex, occupation, level of education, ethnic origin, and place of residence. Among those demographic facts that are of great and obvious importance in conditioning response to travel experiences are sex and level of education.

Social research on the effects of international contact has been conducted on only a few of the many kinds of travel situations that could be defined by the parameters we have just reviewed. Often, reports of such research have failed to recognize the specificity

of the results to the parametric peculiarities of the situation and have generalized about the effects of *travel,* when in fact all that was justified was generalization about the effects of *travel of some particular kind.* Thus, for example, the conclusion that travel produces a more sophisticated perception of the host country, which can be supported by studies of student travelers, may not hold up for soldiers serving in foreign theatres. The conclusion that travel abroad tends to strengthen identification of the traveler with his home culture can be supported by studies of Americans taking trips abroad, but probably does not always hold up for persons coming from less advanced to more advanced countries, nor does it hold up among immigrants.

Another conclusion widely accepted among specialists on exchange programs is that six-week trips are of very dubious value. The reason for this feeling is that the period is too short for the traveler to get over his initial culture shock. It is a period long enough for him to get homesick, disoriented, and puzzled, but not long enough for him to acquire any perspective on the host culture. But these conclusions tend to be based on first trips to the United States by persons from underdeveloped countries. A transatlantic trip by a European or American businessman or public official who has been abroad often before is a long trip if it lasts six weeks. He can seldom spare more time without disrupting his career role; and six weeks may be plenty of time for him to become thoroughly oriented to a situation much easier for him to adjust to than that of the Asian or African in the West for the first time.

So it is only with caution that we can generalize about foreign travel as such. What are the specific travel situations on which social research has shed some light?

One may distinguish six main travel situations on each of which a body of literature exists. There are studies of

a. foreign students, trainees, and others on trips to learn,
b. technical assistance personnel,
c. tourists and summer travel groups,
d. businessmen abroad,
e. armed forces overseas, and
f. immigrants.

Each of these is a peculiar situation readily characterizable in terms of the parameters listed above. The foreign student is a purposive traveler, usually responsible to someone at home for accomplishing certain objectives. Typically he is young and on his first trip, during most but not all of which he stays put. He tends to travel alone and must function in the language of the host country. Since his reason for studying abroad is that the foreign country can offer him something that his home country cannot, he concedes some partial superiority to the host country, though the concession may vary greatly in extent and avowedness. He is a willing if not an eager traveler, often but not always with unrealistic hopes. Usually intelligent and ambitious, he suffers some competitive handicaps in winning recognition in an unfamiliar environment, which is nevertheless one he prizes enough to have traveled abroad to partake in it.

Those are uniformities of travel for study. Such travel may vary, however, on other dimensions. The duration of the trip may vary between the three months' course for a specialized trainee and the ten-year leisurely pursuit of the Ph.D. by the acculturated or semi-refugee student reluctant to return home. The student may live in a solitary room, as a boarder, in a hostel or dormitory. He may be either in a coun-

try much like his own or in a very different culture. Typically, he enjoys his student years despite a stringent budget, mediocre food, and physical discomfort, partly because he has the irresponsible camaraderie of premarital life. Yet examples of rich students, unhappy students, married students, and so forth, are also numerous.

In the same way we can characterize the specific parameters of each travel situation that has been studied. For reasons of space and tedium we do so only incompletely.

The technical assistance situation is typically one characterized by an ambiguous superiority over subordinates in a joint task effort. While many advisors come on quick trips, the ones who have been studied are mostly ones who spend at least two years abroad, living at an unaccustomedly high standard of living in a backward, often hot and dirty, and otherwise uncomfortable environment. Variations in some of the other parameters, such as degree of residential isolation from the host culture or family status, and the ways in which these variations affect adjustment, have been main foci of many of the studies that have been made.

Tourists are the archetypes of the pleasure tripper without responsibilities. Off on one- to three-month trips, usually to pleasant places and in the lap of the travel industry, the tourist often, but by no means always, has only incidental contacts with his hosts. There are, of course, some tourists with personal friends in the host country and others who live, as in The Experiment in International Living, in host country homes; but they are the minority. The tourist more often goes from a rich country to a poorer country to take advantage of the buying power he can thus command. There is the reverse pattern of tourism too, of the visitor from the poor country to the rich, though it has not been much studied. The tourist is most often a repeated traveler.

Business travelers are also often persistent travelers. With the heads of American corporations making an average of a trip abroad every other year, there are obviously many (perhaps one fifth or one sixth) who go abroad regularly, perhaps twice a year. Nowadays, men who make monthly business trips to Europe are by no means unknown. There are, of course, in addition executives stationed overseas. Typically, business travelers are trying to sell something and so they are anxious to please and understand their hosts. Typically also, they have close working relations with colleagues in the host country. Thus, contrary to the usual stereotype, the business traveler resembles the rich tourist in only a few respects, one of course being his comfortable travel budget. He is much more strongly motivated than the tourist needs to be to develop a sophisticated understanding of the country in which he operates.

Foreign troops (with some exceptions, such as guerillas or military government officers) are at the opposite extreme in terms of need for understanding of the country in which they are stationed. Often, indeed, they are really at home away from home, living in camps isolated in every possible way from the host population. Responsibility is almost entirely to fellow nationals, not to citizens of the host country. The duration of the overseas assignment and its other characteristics are usually such as to make it undesirable in the soldiers' eyes and to make a return home eagerly sought. In addition, usually, though by no means invariably, the soldier has a certain contempt for the host country and its culture; he is young, without family present, and most of whatever

contacts he has with the host occur in the course of pleasure seeking.

Finally, as we turn to immigrants we find a very different travel situation, or rather two situations which may be distinguished as immigration and colonialization. The difference lies in the migrant's attitudes toward the culture from which he comes and that to which he is going. Which carries the more prestige with him? The Frenchman going to Algeria had no intention of becoming an Arab, even if he settled there permanently. Nor does the typical American missionary going to Africa expect to give up his citizenship and adopt African ways, even if he too intends to stay for his whole career. On the other hand, the European immigrant who came to the United States quickly dropped his old country identity. He wanted to be an American. Sometimes in the first generation the transition was hard and he continued to live in a linguistic and cultural enclave, but there was never any doubt as to the direction of aspiration (see Handlin, 1951; Thomas & Znaniecki, 1918–1920). Only rare groups such as the Hutterites continued to evaluate their original culture above that of the host country. Perhaps the point can be emphasized by noting that early settlers of the American West from non-Anglo-Saxon origins were often mixed cases of colonizers and immigrants. With regard to the Indians, they were colonizers. It never occurred to them to become Indians, for they confidently felt superior in their culture. Simultaneously, they were dropping their German or Scandinavian or Slavic or other ways in favor of the English language and American practices.

In the above illustrations, the migrants and the hosts implicitly shared the evaluations of the two cultures, though those of inferior status would, of course, never admit it. But in practice the shared evaluation is evidenced by the fact that a Westerner settling in Africa would not assimilate, while an African settling in Europe would. A most interesting case arises when there is mutual condescension, when each group implicitly as well as verbally prefers its own culture to the other. That situation may be found where communities live side by side for generations, even centuries, without assimilation. The Hutterites and their American and Canadian neighbors are an example. Other examples are in the cities of Asia where side by side for centuries have lived communities with different dress, different customs, and different cultures. Ghettos of Arabs, Greeks, Kurds, Jews, Gypsies, and Indians may live next to each other indefinitely, without one trying to assimilate to another.

The situation that has been studied is that of the immigrant who does wish to acculturate, who moves from one country to another where he sees the promise of a more advanced and better life.

THE TRAVELER'S IMAGES OF THE HOST: FAVORABLE AND UNFAVORABLE

Travelers in the variety of situations noted above respond to their foreign experiences in different ways. Depending upon circumstances, their images of their hosts may be favorable or hostile, simple or complex, accurate or inaccurate.

Among the dimensions on which images may differ, favorability has been a major focus of past research. Does the traveler end up with a friendly or hostile feeling toward his host? Does he acquire sympathetic understanding of the country visited or become prejudiced against it? This, it should be

emphasized, is a very limited way of looking at images. Does every image have to be friendly or hostile? We may have much more interest in the differences in cognitive content between, say, an image of Paris which is the Left Bank and an image of Paris which is the Right Bank than in whether one is more favorable than the other. Clearly, to characterize them only by which image is more favorable is to miss most of the interesting differences between them.

The evaluative dimension, while only one of those on which images can be located, still is an important one. The cross-cultural work of Osgood and associates (1957) using the semantic differential has demonstrated that the evaluative dimension is virtually always the first factor in the pragmatic definition of concepts. So it is not surprising that much of the work on travelers' reactions to the places they visit has focused on evaluative changes in their images.

Evaluations of many things may change as a result of travel, but most research has focused on the effect of the travel experience on favorableness or unfavorableness toward the host county—which in most studies was the United States. Financial support for exchange programs was wrested from the United States Congress in large part by the argument that seeing the U.S.A. would result in liking it and that the outcome of such favorableness would be political support. Experience has proved this assumption too simple.

Also too simple is the less ethnocentric "assumption that getting to know the people of another country will lead to liking them; this assumption underlies the expectation that exchange-of-persons programs will increase international good will. In its simplest form, this hypothesis would lead one to expect that, on the whole, visitors to a country will leave with more favorable views than they held before their arrival, and that their views after the trip will be more favorable than those of their compatriots who have not visited the country in question. The entire body of research on cross-cultural education, however, suggests that this expectation is oversimplified and overly optimistic" (Selltiz & Cook, 1962, p. 10).

The findings on the effects of visiting on favorableness toward a country are actually contradictory. Most measures at most times show increased favorableness toward the host country by the visitor, but some studies do show decreased favorableness (Riegel, 1953; Watson & Lippitt, 1955; Langley & Basu, 1953; Selltiz & Cook, 1962). The differences between studies cannot be explained by the national origin of the students. True, there are great differences in favorableness toward the United States by students from different countries, but these differences do not follow a simple pattern, nor are the findings of different studies always the same for particular countries. Richard Morris' *The two-way mirror: National status in foreign students' adjustment* (1960) shows how complex are the variables involved. In his study it turned out that a foreign student's favorableness towards the United States was not significantly related to the average status actually accorded to the visitor's country by American students; that is, how the foreign student evaluated the United States was not related to how American students evaluated his country. On the other hand, the foreign student's evaluation of the United States was inversely related to how he himself ranked his own country. If he thought his own country backward he thought better of the United States. But the relationship of evaluation of

the United States to any objective measure of development was too weak to be documented.[1] One cannot generalize that Caucasians are more favorable, nor is there any other easy generalization, not even that English speakers are more favorable.

Foreign policy does have something to do with how favorably a student views the United States. He is apt to reflect his government's policies. The way in which a visitor judges a country is often colored somewhat by the antagonisms and friendships manifested in international political alignments (Selltiz & Cook, 1962, p. 13; Buchanan & Cantril, 1953; Bauer, Pool, & Dexter, 1963). Accusations of colonialism or militarism or racism are not just high politics. They do get internalized by millions of people. But foreign relations account mostly for the basal attitude toward the United States with which the student starts his visit here, not for whether the experience leaves him more favorable or less favorable at the end than he was at the beginning.

More relevant to how the student's images change during his visit to the United States is the extent to which he has established close and friendly personal relations with Americans. Selltiz and Cook (1962) found "an association between having one or more close American friends and liking American life" (p. 18). But they point out that there is a problem in interpreting that result, having to do with time sequences and causal relationships. For example, in other studies (such as Morris, 1960), the data were gathered at only one point in time, when most of the students questioned had been in the United States a year or more. From a correlation, at a single point in time, between having friends and liking American life one

---

[1] Selltiz and Cook (1962, p. 17) indicate different results from different studies.

cannot tell which way the causality goes. To try to meet this difficulty, Selltiz *et al.* measured attitudes toward the United States both early in the student's stay and toward the end of his first academic year in this country. Their finding suggests that causality does go both ways. Students who reported at the end of the first academic year that they had at least one close American friend were more favorable in their attitudes toward the United States than those who said they had no close American friends. But they "found in addition that the former group had also been more favorable than the latter when they were first asked their attitudes, at the beginning of the year. Perhaps those who were initially most favorable were the most likely to make friends with Americans, rather than vice versa" (Selltiz & Cook, 1962, p. 19).

From many studies it is clear that adjustment correlates highly with the number and intensity of social contacts made by the foreign student in the United States (Selltiz & Cook, 1962, p. 18; Morris, 1960; Scott, 1956). Adjustment, in turn, is associated with giving vent to fewer angry remarks about the host. But the finding that satisfaction correlates with contact is of limited use, since the evidence is weak on the direction of causality. A priori it is just as possible that well-adjusted students make more contacts as that students who have more contacts become happier. It is not clear that a student temperamentally unsuited to making contacts will be happier if he is pushed into them. The Selltiz study coped with this issue by comparing students in institutions offering different degrees of opportunity for contact (and it is not likely that this was the basis on which students selected institutions), but the resulting data are still not conclusive. So we are still left unable to specify

simply the degree to which contact through travel under any given circumstances will make the traveler more or less favorable toward the host. (For further discussion of these issues, see Chapter 15.)

Ultimately, many of the diverse data on favorableness of attitude toward the United States jelled in the observation of the now familiar U-shaped curve of changing attitudes. The general finding was that the visiting student typically started with very positive attitudes toward the United States; then, during the first year, he had problems of adjustment and tended to become disillusioned; but beyond a certain time he gained a deeper and more sophisticated insight and became increasingly favorable toward his host country. This was a finding replicated in many studies, highly general in its application to exchange and student programs, and of great practical importance for the design of such programs (Coelho, 1958; Lysgaard, 1955; Morris, 1960; Selltiz & Cook, 1962).

The general finding of the U-shaped curve revealed a norm around which cultural variation took place. The nadir was reached and more favorable attitudes began to be restored more quickly among students who came from cultures more like that of the United States and more slowly where the culture shock was greater.

Unrealistic expectations will intensify the disappointment manifested in the downward slope of the first half of the U-curve. The Indian student, for example, as described by George Coelho (1958) in an earlier period of intense political conflict, reached New York full of hopes and expectations. He anticipated opportunities for learning, new experiences, and human relationships. He knew that there were tensions in the situation arising from Indo-American frictions. He knew that many Americans regarded Nehru as a dupe of the Communists and Indian neutralism as evil. These attitudes, the student felt, could only arise from ignorance. Americans simply did not know much about India. He felt that he could easily explain that India was not anti-American or pro-Communist, and that her only aim was peace. He felt a mission to explain these clear and simple facts as he saw them. He was quickly disillusioned. He found that while Americans may indeed be ignorant of much about India, their political views had firmer roots and more tenacity than he had realized. He discovered people holding to their views with the same unquestioning intensity as he did to his. Each found opposite truths to be self-evident.

The would-be visiting corrector and teacher now found his own view of the world challenged and doubted. The welcome he had foreseen from people glad to have the "correct" facts given them had turned into annoyed criticism by obdurate people. And so the hopes of the first week turned into an increasingly unhappy first six months.

Not dissimilar is what happens to xenophiles (described by Howard Perlmutter, 1954 and 1956) when they actually go abroad. Xenophiles, as Perlmutter defined them, are people who score high on a test consisting of sentences comparing favorably foreign with domestic objects. They agree with such statements as "Most European girls make better wives than American girls" or "The British use the English language better than do most Americans." Among the high xenophiles will be found certain kinds who are apt to carry through their feelings by

actually going to live abroad either in overseas jobs or as expatriates.[2] But these people, who had fantasies about a better world abroad while they lived complainingly at home, tended to isolate themselves in an American enclave once they actually got to live abroad. They literally became expatriates from America, but psychologically were equally expatriate from their foster-fatherland. It could not live up to their unrealistic expectations.

Unrealism of expectations, the individual's personality, the extent of culture shock, and the hard facts of reality all affect the detailed shape of the U-curve. It can go down slowly or steeply, reach its nadir early or late. And, along with other and perhaps more subtle causes, its shape is certainly affected by whether the visitor lives in comfort or squalor, and whether he is treated hospitably or not.

Finally, it should be noted that the favorableness of reaction to the foreign host is partly determined by what happens to the traveler when he returns home, for his permanent image of his overseas experience does not become crystallized until the completion of the process of readjustment (Useem and Useem, 1955; Scott, 1956; Bennett et al., 1958; Gullahorn & Gullahorn, 1963).

Thus the extent to which contact produces favorable images turns out to depend on a complex of several things. It depends on the traveler's initial psychological adjustment and his interpersonal relations. It depends on the moment in the cycle of his stay at which the measure of attitude is taken or his stay cut short. It depends upon how he views his experience in retrospect. And

---

[2] These are apt to be high authoritarians among the xenophiles rather than low authoritarians if a small study of student tourists by this author and his wife, Jean MacKenzie Pool, can be trusted. Those who thought seriously about returning for a length of time were the high-xenophiles, high-authoritarians. It should be noted that Perlmutter has established the existence of a positive correlation between xenophilia and authoritarianism.

it depends, but as a second derivative, on the extent of cultural differences experienced (that is, cultural differences affect the rate at which the process determined by other factors takes place). The answer to the question as to how contact affects attitudes cannot be given in one sentence. Let us summarize, even if loosely and cryptically, what it is that we do know. We know that those individuals who are most favorable toward foreign countries from afar are not necessarily the ones whose reaction to a travel experience will be most favorable. We can predict that those individuals who have most and deepest contacts with the host will be most favorable, but we cannot be sure how far pushing people who avoid such contacts into having them will produce the same result. We also know that a deeply understanding favorable attitude takes some time to produce. A quick trip may leave shallow favorable attitudes, but these are likely to be stereotyped and to wear off, unless one has allowed time enough for understanding to develop. And finally we know that anything that can be done to make the return home easier and less traumatic is apt to let favorable attitudes to the host survive better.

THE TRAVELER'S IMAGES OF THE HOST: SIMPLE AND COMPLEX

Beyond the points considered in the last section, there are some further fundamental considerations that challenge not only the answer but even the relevance of the question as to whether closeness makes the heart grow fonder. Favorableness need not be a unitary trait; and if it is not, favorableness may not be of much political relevance. Study after study has indeed found no particular relationship between liking

for Americans and support of American foreign policy positions (see DuBois, 1956). An outstanding study, that of John and Ruth Useem (1955), found that Indian students who had studied in the United States liked Americans but did not particularly respect them, whereas Indian students who had studied in England respected the English but did not particularly like them. Other studies have found that in many situations contact moved people toward neither more favorable nor less favorable attitudes, but from both the favorable and the unfavorable extremes toward the middle (Bauer, Pool, & Dexter, 1963; Cherrington, 1934). That result is related to another and very general finding: that the effect of first-hand experience is reduction of stereotyping—the shifting of the traveler's images from simple black and white perceptions to more qualified perceptions of the foreign reality.

Miscellaneous findings on such points were put into longitudinal perspective by George Coelho (1958) in his study of Indian students in the United States, in which he established a growing differentiation and specificity of images over time. The global like–dislike dimension, which can also be equated to support–oppose, is characteristic only of the most naive and inexperienced person, that is, the newly arrived foreign student. As time passes the visitor develops differentiated attitudes toward specific Americans, American domestic political practices, American foreign policy, American institutions of one sort or another (see also Selltiz et al., 1963).

Insofar as there is a global positive–negative dimension, Coelho's study implies that it is nothing more than a symptom of the student's general state of adjustment to life. This is strongly suggested by his remarkable finding that attitudes toward India correlate positively with attitudes toward the United States, that is, that during the initial phase of the student's stay, when he is becoming more and more disillusioned in regard to the United States, he is simultaneously becoming more and more unfavorable toward his own homeland. Later, when his attitude toward America improves, his attitude toward India simultaneously improves. This demonstrates to what extent evaluation of a country is a matter of projection and has little to do with the country itself.

Such global responses, when they occur, are thus of less interest as an international relations phenomenon than as a measure of holism in human behavior. They are an evidence of the power of what Abelson and Rosenberg (1958) call psycho-logic or the need to maintain balance. Fortunately, human cognitive processes are often subtle and allow for various modes of resolution of imbalance, including the conscious acceptance of affectively imbalanced beliefs and also including differentiation of entities into subentities.

It is the latter process that increasingly takes place during at least the first few years of a foreign contact experience. Coelho's (1958) results suggest that after a while (three or four years with his sample) a reversal sets in. The newly arrived student had a number of simple preconceptions about America and Americans. He soon began to discover that there were Americans and Americans. There were whites and Negroes; rich and poor; friendly and unfriendly; informed and ignorant. And he found that individuals had complex views on even those items on which the foreign stereotype of Americans assumes a completely simple image: Communism, materialism, race.

Not only does experience enable the visitor to say that Americans are *both* friendly and obsessed with Communism, but it even allows him sometimes to recognize that many Americans have highly complex views as to the significance of the existence of Communist movements in the world and what to do about them. True, most foreign student surveys have found that even returning students at the end of their stay are highly critical of American attitudes on Communism and race, but even if critical, they are apt to have somewhat less simple notions of what these views are.

Discovering these complexities is an exciting experience. It is the heart of the exploratory process of discovering America. The process goes on for at least a couple of years. The student is intensely attentive to all the differences and nuances he finds in the culture and will talk about them endlessly. But if he stays much longer (Coelho says more than four years) he begins to take America for granted. It is no longer an object of study; it is simply the environment in which he lives. His becomes the fish's attitude toward water rather than, as before, that of the land animal thrown into it. He thinks of his life in relation to his neighbor, not his life as a foreigner in relation to Americans. His interests become personalized. He may, as a result, become less attuned to subtleties in national characteristics. In that sense he may revert to a small degree to simpler national images.

It would be interesting to study this process in immigrants. There is no reason to assume that the sequence of complexity and simplicity of images is the same for immigrants as for sojourners. It might be the same or it might be different. Unfortunately, the process of image development we have been describing here as observed in studies of foreign students has been almost entirely overlooked in the large literature on immigrants. There are hundreds of studies of the acculturation of different ethnic groups. Almost none has documented the changing images that the migrants held of their new country. Passing remarks in memoirs and diaries are numerous, but the job remains open for someone to compile these and to document what happened to the image of the migrant's new homeland as he experienced the transition from stranger to native (see Hansen, 1940a, 1940b; Handlin, 1951; and Thomas & Znaniecki, 1918–1920).

THE HOST'S IMAGES OF
THE TRAVELER

In the last two sections we have followed the existing literature where it has led us. Wherever that has been one-sided, our treatment has also been one-sided. We have considered how the traveler changes in his perceptions of the country he visits. But earlier we defined our subject more broadly. We said that we were interested in the effects of contact upon the images of host and of traveler held by host and by traveler. This gives us four possible topics, of which only one—the traveler's image of his host—has been extensively studied. There remains a panoply of fascinating questions about the rest of the relationships. With two of these— the host's image of the traveler and the traveler's image of himself—we shall deal in the present section and the next.

How does the host's image of the traveler change? In what ways do contacts with tourists and foreign students shape their hosts' images of the visitors' homelands? Harold Isaacs, whose pioneer work on images stands almost alone in its focus on this aspect of image formation, documents the extent of such impact of travelers on the host. Isaacs, whose work appropriately to its hypothesis-forming role in an unexplored field is partly anecdotal, tells

us in *Scratches on our minds* (1958) of various ways in which Indian and Chinese travelers have shaped the images of their countries that are held by influential Americans. He describes the Indian student in a rooming house who, by failing to clean his hairs out of the bathtub, left an indelible scratch on the mind of an American fellow student destined to an ultimate role of international importance. He notes the impact of Vivekenanda and other writing swamis; of Lin Yu Tang, of Nehru and Mme. Chiang in their visits to the United States, of Krishna Menon in New York. And then there is the repeated and oft documented experience of Americans with Indian visiting students, wherein the host finds the visitor arrogant, opinionated, hypercritical.

Writers comment on such transmissions of images through a traveler, usually, when the results are bad. They note the problem case among foreign students. They write about obnoxious American tourists, who are noisy, boastful, and indifferent to the sensitivity of their hosts (Garraty & Adams, 1959). They analyze relations of troops overseas to the local population, usually when incidents of sex and violence have acerbated tensions. They comment on difficulties of absorbing refugee or immigrant populations.

It is these atypical situations that have been studied and observed. And they are probably very atypical. In the absence of systematic research there is no solid evidence, but there is good reason to suspect that the net impact of the ordinary traveler on his host, like the impact of his host on the traveler, is primarily to increase the complexity and differentiation of the images held. The consequence is undoubtedly sometimes favorable, sometimes regressive toward the middle, as well as sometimes unfavorable. The patterns that determine which outcome occurs are unknown and may perhaps differ from those bearing on the images of the host received by the visitor.

In one respect the image of his country conveyed by a traveler is most often inaccurate. Travelers are not a representative cross-section of their home populations. That type of Indian student whose querulousness has entered into the American image of India is in the first place an educated Indian. His education is essentially British in content, at the hands of British-educated scholars. He is of high or medium-high caste, from a prosperous family, used to commanding service in all menial activities. Expectations of respect and unwillingness to give it, reluctance to do normal chores, and condescension to American culture, when they do occur, reflect the kind of person he is in his home country rather than global characteristics of his country itself, but they get communicated as part of the national image.

While the foreign student is an abnormally high-status sample of his society, the immigrant is often an abnormally low-status one, and either distortion creates problems. The turn of the century American image of the Irish or the current New York image of Puerto Ricans arises from observing a population of men who did not make a go of it in their homelands. The old Yankee image of crude and ignorant Irish bumpkins could hardly encompass a milieu that could produce a Noyes, an O'Flaherty, and a Joyce. Nor does the prejudiced New York image of Puerto Ricans encompass the facts of Operation Bootstrap, of a country developing to a modern society faster than any other in Latin America.

The traveler may be unrepresentative for other reasons too. Travelers act differently when abroad than they do at home. The problem here is the weakening of control by relevant reference groups. Good conduct, if not internalized, is often enforced by awareness of the ways in which important "others" will react. Travel is a way of escaping these censors. The traveler puts his usual reference persons at a distance. The foreigners close at hand do become new reference persons for travelers with sharp sensitivity, a broad sense of humanity, or high need for affiliation; but foreigners do not serve this role for everyone. For some types of persons the only "others" who count are those in his own in-group; the feelings of outsiders do not matter even when they are physically present. By confining the scope of his sensitivity to censors at home, whom he has temporarily escaped, the tourist permits himself the indulgence of misconduct abroad. The man on a spree at a resort, the one who shouts at waiters and clerks, the woman who wears shorts into a cathedral, the traveler who talks disparagingly about the country he is visiting, might never at home so contravene the demands of etiquette.

Such kicking over of the traces may not always be negative. For a few individuals the foreign environment provides a freedom from censorship which opens up their initiative and creativity. Missionaries and colonizers have often felt a readiness to take command of "little brothers" toward whom they felt superior, in a way they were incapable of at home. Asian students abroad have often felt free to disregard traditional taboos when away from their families.

Release from authoritative controls can have many consequences and take many forms. Whatever the form, however, it makes the traveler an unrepresentative sample of his society. Yet he is read most often not as an individual, not as a sample of his class or social group, but as a sample of his nation. Experiments by Perlmutter have shown that observers code the behavior of foreigners primarily in national categories and only secondarily in terms of other available categories (Perlmutter, 1957; Bruner & Perlmutter, 1957). Subjects in these experiments were asked to predict characteristics of men described on a series of dimensions. One man might be described by occupation (a businessman), by personal attributes (intelligent), by nationality (a Frenchman). The most variance in the predictions was accounted for by nationality if the nationality was foreign. Telling Americans that a man was an American did not help them at all to predict what he would do or be like. That was treated as irrelevant information and other items, such as his occupation or intelligence, were used as indicators. In predicting the behavior or traits of foreigners, on the other hand, nationality was used as the dominant clue.

In line with these findings one may suspect that the traveler is most often read not as a sample of the generic stranger; nor as a sample of his sex, or age group, or social class; nor as a sample of his profession, or his personality type, or skill group; but as a sample of his nation. The things he does become part of the observer's image of the country from which the traveler comes. The new information may add only a small part to the image; it may only complicate the image and make it less black and white. But whatever the perception does, it is to the national image that it does it.

There is a good reason for this dominance of the coding by nationality in the interpretation of the behavior of foreigners. It is not just chauvinism. It is because typically the person doing the coding has less prior information on that category than on other likely ones. Let me illustrate the point by an anecdote. I once took a charming, petite, Japanese woman schoolteacher to a restaurant. She ate two forkfuls of a large steak and then set it aside, protesting it was very good but too much. My image of the eating habits of women was not changed. I was already familiar with enough examples to have a stable image of that distribution. Nor was my image of the eating habits of small women, or of schoolteachers, or of small schoolteachers or even small women schoolteachers changed. For all these categories I had more than adequate information to dismiss this case as an exception. The only obvious category on which I was ignorant (and in fact remain ignorant to this day) is the nationality one. For several years there has been a question in the back of my mind about the facts on eating habits in Japan (or more likely of some possible subcategory of these, such as habits of educated Japanese women in eating meat). This is something less than a fixed or well-formed image, but it is at least the ghost of an image. It is a large part of my stock of knowledge on this subject.

Nationality plays such a key role in the coding of images about foreigners precisely because of the widespread initial ignorance of them. If that is so, then the growth of travel and of all forms of international communication may have a profound effect. The peculiarities we have been describing in the way in which people handle foreign information are in large part the peculiarities of information processing in the presence of ignorance. But the incorporation of information gradually erodes ignorance. The very information processed reduces ignorance and changes thereby the special peculiarities of the information-processing situation we have been describing. With more information the foreign becomes less foreign. We described this sequence before when we noted the increasing complexity of images that comes with experience. These more complex images are also more stable. And in a sense they are less psychologically powerful; they are less apt to provide the illusion of all-encompassing and adequate explanations. The more we really know about foreign nationalities the less clear-cut our images become.

THE TRAVELER'S IMAGES OF HIMSELF AND HIS OWN COUNTRY

Profound as the impact of travel may be on people's images of foreigners, it is even more profound on the traveler's image of himself. Contact with people of another culture is a way to discover one's own identity.

A number of studies have been made of youthful American tourist groups—groups such as The Experiment in International Living and Crossroads Africa. Uniformly they find that the student has returned with a greater appreciation of America and an intensified identification with America (Smith, 1954; Thanas; Pool, 1958; Isaacs, 1961). The same type of finding has emerged in studies of foreign students in the United States. In many cases the most profound effect of their stay in a strange land is a better appreciation and understanding of their home country—a firmer attachment to its values.[3]

This reidentification with his homeland by the traveler abroad takes many forms. It shows up, for example, in increased support of his government's foreign policies. Thus John and Ruth Useem (1955) found that Indian students who went to England and America returned closer to the basic Nehru foreign-policy viewpoint. Those leftists who started out more critical of American policy than Nehru became less anti-American while in the United States. But those individuals who started out more pro-American than Nehru became less pro-American while in the United States. Being abroad solidified them with their own national policy.

The same thing was found in a study of American businessmen who traveled abroad (Bauer, Pool, & Dexter, 1963). The foreign trade policies supported by businessmen who had not traveled much were largely determined by their companies' special interests. But the highly traveled respondents—those who had made five or more trips abroad and at least one in the previous five years—arrived at their views in quite a different way. They were not in general more liberal on trade matters than their less-traveled colleagues, nor were they more protectionist. However, their views on tariff policy were less predictable from knowing the industry in which they were engaged than were those of their more provincial colleagues. For those businessmen who had not traveled much, if we knew what their firms produced, we could make a reasonable prediction of where they as individuals would stand on tariff policy. For those who had traveled, however, better predictions could be made, not by knowing what they manufactured, but by knowing the nation's foreign policy. From either atypical extreme, the travelers moved to support that norm.

---

[3] Kelman and Bailyn (1962) distinguish two patterns of behavior of Scandinavians who spent a year in the United States. Both these patterns involve increased identification with their home countries, but in one pattern this identification appears to take a defensive form, while in the other it takes the form of greater differentiation of images and understanding of the country.

Summarized in a sentence, the political effect of travel on tariff attitudes was to counteract the force of self-interest. It made a man see the trade issue in national terms, rather than in the parochial terms of his own industry.

Foreign travel made the businessman increasingly aware of international political problems and America's relationship to them. As he traveled, he found himself being role-cast, not as the representative of a particular industry, but as an American. He found himself playing at being Secretary of State and talking for his country, not for his firm.

The influence of travel was not primarily to bring European or other foreign ideas to the traveler, leading him to diverge from his national norm. On the contrary, it moved him toward that norm. There was a shift in center of gravity away from narrow parochial interests toward international interests, but with views quite close to the national standard. Thus, foreign travel broadened the frame of reference in which the businessman considered the foreign-trade issue to one which took account of world political and economic circumstances. But the responses he gave to the facts that he learned abroad were ones that his own domestic reference group would approve. The reference group perceived as relevant changed from a parochial to a national one, but it remained a *domestic* one.

Thus the very partial and often irrelevant experiences of foreign travel, either on the Lido or in an office, did affect the broad foreign-policy conclusions reached by businessmen. Whether the traveler acquired his sense of responsibility to an American role in an argument with a perverse waiter or in a study of foreign production costs perhaps made little difference. Whatever the stimulus, its effect was to shake established convictions and to make the traveler think about himself in a national, and often more statesmanlike role—defined, it is true, as the American business community sees that role.

The way in which foreign travel related to public-affairs attitudes was illustrated in a most striking way by data on political party affiliation of our respondents. The theory we have just stated about the way in which new information affects old attitudes postulates that, if any shift of opinion on matters of substance occurs as a result of a challenge to previous views, its direction should be toward the standard position of the individual's reference group, not toward the view expressed in the stimulus. Insofar as businessmen's travel fits that theory, the effect of travel should be to push deviant businessmen to the standard business view—in this case, toward the Republican Party. Though this prediction follows from the theory we were using, we cannot claim advance wisdom. Like most of our colleagues, we expected that travel would liberalize and that liberals would be less often Republicans. We were wrong. We found, as our theory should have led us to expect, that the most traveled businessmen are most uniformly Republican (Bauer, Pool, & Dexter, 1963, pp. 168–170).[4]

These findings also help us to understand that minority of cases in which travel alienates the traveler from his homeland; of course such cases do exist. What usually distinguishes the immigrant or defector or other person whose identity is shaken is a transfer of reference groups. Before travel can undermine his attachment to his home-

---

[4] The authors consider and give data for rejecting the most obvious noncausal explanations of the correlation.

land he normally has to find a sense of belonging in a group in the host country that can partially replace his original reference persons. For a student this new reference group often consists of his scientific and professional colleagues in the host country, especially in those instances where his profession has no significant cadre in his home (Bennett *et al.*, 1958; Watson & Lippitt, 1955; Coelho, 1958; Lambert & Bressler, 1956). But these conditions of disaffection are far less often realized for the traveler than are the conditions of patriotic reinforcement. Renewed attachment to the homeland is the normal effect of travel.

Such a process of growing support for their own country and its policies by travelers overseas has been studied most closely by Harold Isaacs (1961 and 1963). It is dramatically illustrated by the case of American Negroes who have gone to Africa.

In their search for identity, many American Negroes have gone to what they felt to be a homeland. Some had called themselves Afro-Americans before going to see. Many had felt themselves rejected children of the United States and in turn rejected those who rejected them. But in Africa they discovered that, oppressed or not, they were more American than they knew. They were eaters of hamburgers, not of fufu. They were not even dark enough in most cases to pass as African. They talked English like Americans not like Englishmen. Many discovered that if Africa was home they could not go home again.[5]

It should be no surprise to discover that foreign travel is a profound psychological experience. The travel in-

dustry is able to sell tours to millions of people who spend on these trips amounts of money comparable to what they spend on cars, homes, and education, even though vacation travel is a sheer luxury. Clearly it must be a deeply meaningful luxury.

Testing one's identity against alternative ways of life, and in that way rediscovering one's identity, is a deeply meaningful experience. But anything as personally significant as travel seems to be must mean different things to different people. It must be a shell into which can be poured whatever is most salient in the particular individual's resolution of his psychic conflicts. It must provide a variety of very different people an opportunity to act so as to produce very different desired images of themselves.

Travel does that. It creates all sorts of opportunities for people to act out their self-images and, in so doing, to confirm or modify them.

Let me illustrate that point by closing with a report of a small study done by my wife, Jean MacKenzie Pool, and myself on a Council for Student Travel ship to Europe and back.

The study explored how each of forty-two students used his summer abroad to work out his own identity problems. The students, who were members of The Experiment in International Living, each filled out a battery of questionnaires on the way over and the identical battery on the way back. In addition, we had a two-hour interview with each on the way back. The battery included authoritarianism items, Perlmutter xenophilia items, sentence completions, and (on the way back only) projective stories (comparable to the

---

[5] What makes this experience and that of summer tourists different from that of immigrants who do change their identity is a subject well worth studying. Could it be that we are in the presence of a dissonance phenomenon in which the old identification has to become all the stronger the more it is challenged until there is a quantum jump and the individual reverses sides?

Thematic Apperception Test) with a verbal stimulus.

The population we studied was far from a typical one. It was liberal and xenophilic and our cutting points on the appropriate scales were certainly all at one end of the general population distribution.

It was a youthful population, with its mode in the years eighteen to twenty. Their problems were problems of adolescence. If need for affiliation burst through many protocols (and it did), if identity conflicts were salient (and they were), it is partly because these are above all the problems of youth. What can be problems for older travelers too, burst forth in undisguised magnitude among these adolescents.

The group was in many ways homogeneous; but the point of interest is not the ways in which they were alike, but the ways in which they differed. They all were delighted with their summer. All used the summer's experience in the search for identity, but since they were different persons and personalities, they did it in different ways. Indeed, as we tried to explore the range of meanings and uses that a summer in Europe could have even for a homogeneous population engaged in a common program, we had no difficulty in differentiating a number of different patterns among these forty-two students.

We can differentiate four patterns in terms of the dominant motivation or need served by the trip. First, there were those for whom the trip was an escape. Second, there were those for whom it was a chance to test their adulthood, their ability to cope. Third, there were those for whom the gratification of a trip to Europe was status enhancement. Finally, there were those for whom the trip was an opportunity to satisfy various instinctual impulses.

Consider those for whom the trip was an escape. They told us that they felt freer, more relaxed, less anxious abroad than they do at home. Sometimes they told us on the return trip that their anxiety levels were building up as they were coming closer to the realities of life.

This pattern contrasts sharply with the reactions of youngsters for whom the trip was a way of proving that they could cope all alone in a strange foreign place. To these timid souls it would be inconceivable to think of abroad as a place to relax. They reported greater anxiety abroad. They were often consciously breathing a sigh of relief as the ship was taking them closer to home. They were proud of themselves for having successfully pulled the summer off. They regaled the interviewer with stories of how they had found their destination in cities where they could not speak a word. They were pleased and happy that they had done it all, but several of them said explicitly that they had had their traveling now. Having proved that they were now adults and no longer children needing a parent's knee, they were done with traveling for at least several years.

That was not so for the other two groups. They, especially those for whom the trip was a chance for status enhancement, contemplated with pleasure the prospect of further trips abroad.

Those for whom the trip was an escape were intermediate in their inclination to contemplate another trip soon. It was not that they enjoyed the trip less. On the contrary: they were the most successful Experimenters. They are the people whom the selectors should be looking for. Yet they are less apt to return soon than some of the others. To understand why, we must consider those persons rather more closely. What is it that they are trying to escape from?

These are people who are trying to escape from a driving sense of duty, and they never really do escape. They are people who at home are constant doers. They work very hard. They have high ideals. At their universities they are activities men and joiners. (In our own small sample almost every one of the "escapers" came from a home in which there had been a disruption of their parental identification and they narcotized their personal problems in work.) For these people the trip was an escape from the pressures of over-commitment and of group relations. But the escape was only a partial one, for they soon made the same life for themselves on the Experiment, though with lesser responsibility since the Experiment was only temporary. On the trip they did everything, talked to everybody wherever they went, enjoyed it enormously. They were full of reports of the wonderful people they had met. They were group-oriented in their own Experimenter groups. They cared primarily for the human contacts they made with foreigners. They were often contemptuous of cathedrals and museums, for they were heavily socially conscious thanks to their grinding consciences.

The reason these people could not indulge too often or too much in the escapist pleasure of travel was precisely that they recognized it as escapist. They were returning to purposeful careers in "the real world" and while that made them anxious, they knew they had to do it. Most of them had well-laid plans for some years ahead. In principle they would be all in favor of engaging in overseas work as a contructive kind of activity, but in practice they were committed in one way or another for some time to come.

It was the young men and women who saw travel as enhancing their status who were seriously discussing the idea of going abroad for a year or two soon. They were the ones most likely to take overseas jobs or to marry abroad. (The Peace Corps with its hair-shirt ideology had not yet appeared on the horizon and would presumably not have appealed to them.) This group included a number of high-xenophile, high-authoritarians.

The ways in which these thirteen individuals saw European travel as conferring status on them were varied. For some this occurred in the most obvious ways; travel to the high spots of Europe is after all a well-recognized symbol. For others the mechanisms were more subtle. They might appreciate the formality of European manners as a drama in which they liked to participate. They might aspire to the great tradition of culture. They might look down on the backward Europeans. Some of them filled their interviews with reports of their contacts with great persons. But however they managed it, the events they reported somehow demonstrated their status.

Such travelers can indulge in the xenophilic fantasy of expatriation because they are not kept to their lasts by conscience. They dream of enhancing themselves by becoming part of the great life of Europe or by enjoying the good life of the American in Europe. They have actually traveled more often than any of the other types. They correspond more with European friends. It is from this group that a disproportionate share of our professional international communicators will tend to come, whether for the State Department or for other public or private agencies.

Finally we mentioned the group for whom the great gratification of the foreign is release of instinctual impulses.

That statement may give a misleading picture of our respondents, for they were, after all, youngsters from good middle-class homes. So we must distinguish between those few who got this satisfaction directly and overtly in their own behavior and those inhibited ones who obtained it only in the fantasy of liberation. Those who are inhibited might merely observe with admiration what they consider to be the great warmth and emotional freedom of Europeans. They may talk of women kissing each other or of boy chums. A few who were less inhibited had gone on a minor spree in taverns and brothels, somehow feeling that that is Europe in contrast to the United States. But whatever they do the symbolic significance of Europe to them is an assuaging of guilt and a testing of dependency.

They are at one with all our respondents, and indeed with all adolescents, in that central to their behavior is the question of acceptance. Proof that one is accepted takes a variety of forms. Whether the form was finding a lover, group activity, or social life, all these young people were looking in Europe for evidence that, cut off as they now were from their parents' apron strings, they were nonetheless welcomed and loved, even by foreign strangers. The interviews are loaded with tedious pathos about wonderful ways in which their foster families accepted them (or occasionally failed to), the way in which they found friends in strange places, the kindness shown them by complete strangers on the street. With all due deference to the validity of the sentiments, they began to verge on an obsession.

In this connection, we can distinguish a fifth group, consisting of shy souls who could not bring themselves to seek evidence of their acceptability directly. These painfully timid youngsters, while no less preoccupied with being loved, did not dare press the issue directly. They retreated into watching—a very legitimate occupation for tourists. Some of these people were brilliant observers. They did not take pictures. To face a camera toward a person is an aggressive act, much more common among those whose primary gratifications were status enhancement and instinct release than among shy observers or for that matter among those escaping an overruling conscience.[6] But they could describe a cathedral rose window in detail. These people walked, often alone, and looked at the physical glories of Europe. Yet for all their escapism they were just as concerned as anyone with how far people accepted them.

At this point we can summarize what it means when we say that the travel experience enables the traveler to see *himself* in a new image. Each one of the five groups we have just examined acted out a different drama in their trip abroad, but some things they all had in common. In each instance the circumstances of travel unshackled the traveler from the routines of normal life and enabled him to experiment with who he is. His images of himself and the world were expressed in these experiments. In that process the traveler (incidentally for him but of great interest to us) distorted his image of the host to make it fit his needs. The image of Europe became that of the distinguished, or the passionate, or the dangerous, or the beautiful, as needed.

---

[6] What people photograph is a very suggestive indicator. There are travelers who take people only, buildings only, or mixed scenes only. And there are those who take few pictures and those who take many.

At the same time the traveler acquired a deeper conviction of his image of himself as a person and as an American. In his contacts with foreigners he could establish a sense of his identity more clearly than he might have seen it before. And, of course, the images with which he experimented in perceiving his identity were those with which his psyche was most preoccupied.

REFERENCES

Abelson, R. P., & Rosenberg, M. J. Symbolic psycho-logic: A model of attitudinal cognition. *Behav. Sci.*, 1958, *3*, 1–13.

Bailyn, Lotte, & Kelman, H. C. The effects of a year's experience in America on the self-image of Scandinavians. *J. soc. Issues*, 1962, *18* (1), 30–40.

Bauer, R. A. The communicator and his audience. *J. Confl. Resol.*, 1958, *2*, 66–77.

Bauer, R. A., & Pool, I. de S. *The effects of audiences on communicators.* Cambridge: Harvard Graduate School of Business Administration and Center for International Studies, M.I.T., 1960.

Bauer, R. A., Pool, I. de S., & Dexter, L. A. *American business and public policy: The politics of foreign trade.* New York: Atherton Press, 1963.

Bennett, J. W., Passin, H., & McKnight, R. K. *In search of identity: The Japanese overseas scholar in America and Japan.* Minneapolis: Univer. Minnesota Press, 1958.

Bruner, J. S., & Perlmutter, H. V. Compatriot and foreigner: A study of impression formation in three countries. *J. abnorm. soc. Psychol.*, 1957, *55*, 253–260.

Buchanan, W., & Cantril, H. *How nations see each other.* Urbana: Univer. Illinois Press, 1953.

Cherrington, B. M. *Methods of education in international attitudes.* (Teachers College Contributions to Education, No. 5.) New York: Teachers College, Columbia University, 1934.

Cleveland, H., Magone, G. J., & Adams, J. C. *The overseas Americans.* New York: McGraw-Hill, 1960.

Coelho, G. V. *Changing images of America: A study of Indian students' perceptions.* New York: Free Press, 1958.

Deutsch, S. E., & Won, G. Y. M. Some factors in the adjustment of foreign nationals in the United States. *J. soc. Issues*, 1963, *19* (3), 115–122.

DuBois, Cora A. *Foreign students and higher education in the United States.* Washington: American Council on Education, 1956.

Garraty, J. A., & Adams, W. *From Main Street to the Left Bank.* East Lansing: Michigan State Univer. Press, 1959.

Gullahorn, J. T., & Gullahorn, Jeanne E. An extension of the U-curve hypothesis. *J. soc. Issues*, 1963, *19* (3), 33–47.

Handlin, O. *The uprooted.* Boston: Little, Brown, 1951.

Hansen, M. L. *The immigrant in American history.* Cambridge: Harvard Univer. Press, 1940. (a)

Hansen, M. L. *The Atlantic immigration, 1607–1860.* Cambridge: Harvard Univer. Press, 1940. (b)

Isaacs, H. R. *Scratches on our minds.* New York: John Day, 1958.

Isaacs, H. R. *Emergent Americans: A report on "Crossroads Africa."* New York: John Day, 1961.

Isaacs, H. R. *The new world of Negro Americans.* New York: John Day, 1963.

Kelman, H. C. (with Victoria Steinitz) The reactions of participants in a foreign specialists seminar to their American experience. *J. soc. Issues*, 1963, *19* (3), 61–114.

Kelman, H. C., & Bailyn, Lotte Effects of cross-cultural experience on national images: A study of Scandinavian students in America. *J. Confl. Resol.*, 1962, *6*, 319–334.

Lambert, R. D., & Bressler, N. *Indian students on an American campus.* Minneapolis: Univer. Minnesota Press, 1956.

Langley, Grace, & Basu, Sita Exchange of persons: An evaluation of the experience and training of Indian grantees under Fulbright and TCM programs. A study prepared for the Evaluation Section of USIA, India, 1953. (Mimeographed)

Lysgaard, S. Adjustment in a foreign society: Norwegian Fulbright grantees visiting the United States. *Int. soc. Sci. Bull.*, 1955, 7, 45–51.

Mayntz, Renate The visiting fellow: An analysis of an academic role. *Amer. sociol. Rev.*, 1960, 15, 735–741.

Morris, R. T. *The two-way mirror.* Minneapolis: Univer. Minnesota Press, 1960.

Osgood, C. E., Suci, G. J., & Tannenbaum, P. H. *The measurement of meaning.* Urbana: Univer. Illinois Press, 1957.

Perlmutter, H. V. Some characteristics of the xenophilic personality. *J. Psychol.*, 1954, 38, 291–300.

Perlmutter, H. V. Correlates of two types of xenophilic orientation. *J. abnorm. soc. Psychol.*, 1956, 52, 130–135.

Perlmutter, H. V. Stereotypes about Americans and Europeans who make specific statements. *Psychol. Reports*, 1957, 3, 131–137.

Pool, I. de S. What American travellers learn. *Antioch Rev.*, 1958, 18, 431–446.

Pool, I. de S., Keller, Suzanne, & Bauer, R. A. The influence of foreign travel on political attitudes of American businessmen. *Publ. Opin. Quart.*, 1956, 20, 161–175.

Pool, I. de S., & Shulman, I. Newsmen's fantasies, audiences and newswriting. *Publ. Opin. Quart.*, 1959, 23, 145–158.

Riegel, O. W. Residual effects of exchange of persons. *Publ. Opin. Quart.*, 1953, 17, 319–327.

Scott, F. *The American experience of Swedish students.* Minneapolis: Univer. Minnesota Press, 1956.

Selltiz, Claire, Christ, June R., Havel, Joan, & Cook, S. W. *Attitudes and social relations of foreign students in the United States.* Minneapolis: Univer. Minnesota Press, 1963.

Selltiz, Claire, & Cook, S. W. Factors influencing attitudes of foreign students toward the host country. *J. soc. Issues*, 1962, 18 (1), 7–23.

Smith, H. P. *Changes in attitudes resulting from experiences in foreign countries.* Unpublished Ph.D dissertation, Harvard University, 1954.

Thanas, Katherine Significance of social context for short term cross-cultural travel. Unpublished manuscript.

Thomas, W. I., & Znaniecki, F. *The Polish peasant in Poland and America.* (5 vols.) Boston: Gorham, 1918–1920.

Useem, J. & Useem, Ruth *The Western educated man in India.* New York: Holt, Rinehart and Winston, 1955.

Watson, Jeanne D., & Lippitt, R. *Learning across cultures: A study of Germans visiting America.* Ann Arbor: Institute for Social Research, University of Michigan, 1955.

Zimmerman, Claire, & Bauer, R. A. The effect of an audience upon what is remembered. *Publ. Opin. Quart.*, 1956, 20, 238–248.

5

The next chapter continues our exploration of the effects of various specific experiences on the formation and change of national and international images. It is concerned with the impact of external events—domestic and international, spectacular and cumulative—on public images. Under what conditions do existing images determine the interpretation of new events so that the images can remain unaltered by them? Under what conditions do events produce temporary shifts in images, followed by a return to earlier levels? Under what conditions do external events actually produce a reorganization of images with far-reaching consequences? And—since the effects of events are inevitably mediated by communications about them—what roles do governments and the mass media play in the selection and interpretation of events? These are some of the questions to which Chapter 5 is addressed. Since there is very little research that has dwelled systematically on these issues, the chapter makes use of a variety of public opinion polls that provide data on trends over time and shifts in the wake of major events. These are interpreted in terms of a theoretical model for the relationship between events and images.

Both authors of Chapter 5 are members of the Department of Political Science at Yale University.

Karl W. Deutsch is Professor of Political Science at Yale. He is also President of the New England Political Science Association (1965–1966). He is recipient of the Sumner Prize in Political Science from Harvard University and the Benton Prize from the Yale Political Union. He is author and co-author of a number of books, including *Nationalism and social communication* (1953), *Germany rejoins the powers* (1959), *The nerves of government* (1963), and *The process of political integration* (1964). His current research interests focus on the study of large-scale political communities, and the testing of political theories with the aid of quantitative data.

Richard L. Merritt is Assistant Professor of Political Science and Director of the Political Science Research Library at Yale University.

He is author of *The growth of American community, 1735–1775* (1965), and co-editor of and contributor to *Comparing nations: The use of quantitative data in cross-national research* (1965). He is currently involved in research on large-scale political integration; arms control and disarmament concepts in the Western European environment; and political behavior in postwar Germany.

H. C. K.

Effects of Events on National and International Images

Karl W. Deutsch and Richard L. Merritt

*T*he tasks of this chapter are several. First, though both advertisers and social scientists are familiar with the general concept of "images," we shall sketch out more precisely what we mean by images, and what we think may be their possible links to the statistical distribution of attitudes as measured by public opinion data and survey research. Second, we shall propose rough classifications of several relevant aspects of images—such as focus, periphery, cognitive and evaluative cues —and of several kinds of external events —such as spectacular, cumulative, government-manipulated, and their combinations—that may impinge upon them. Third, by combining these classifications, a table of hypothetical possibilities of such effects will be generated, so as to permit an overview of possible strengths of relationships between events and images as estimated very roughly on the basis of a general familiarity with relevant historical and political experience.

In the fourth place we shall discuss a number of specific case studies and data that throw some light on the relationships listed as theoretically possible in our general table. Finally, we shall compare the actual relationships found in the data with those surmised in theory, and draw some conclusions from the findings.

IMAGES AS COMBINATORIAL CONSTRUCTS AND THE BIAS TOWARD CONSISTENCY

An individual normally carries in his memory a collection of images of the world in its various aspects. These images are combinatorial constructs, analogous to visual experiences. They are interdependent to varying degrees, both in the sense that the structure of some images can be inferred or predicted from the structure of others, and in the sense that changes in some images produce imbalances tending toward change in others.

To the extent that images are highly interdependent they resemble Boulding's notion of "the" image (1956, pp. 5–6; cf. Wiener, 1964, pp. 31–32), that is, an aggregative image of the whole world, built up "as a result of all the past experiences of the possessor of the image," and defined as the totality of his subjective knowledge or of what he believes to be true. At the other extreme there are many relatively independent images, among which the effects of mutual interaction are below the level of noise or triviality.

A certain minimum level of interdependence among the most salient images is needed for a functioning personality. The person whose images are completely independent is no better off than the lifeless movie camera that records whatever comes into its view without being able to integrate the images into a meaningful whole—a condition suggested by the title of the play *I am a camera*, based on Christopher Isherwood's short story "Goodbye to Berlin" (1939).

That a person's images are above the minimum level of interdependence, however, is by no means an indication that the images are internally consistent. Clearly the internal consistency both within and among images varies from one person to the next. The person who recognizes that his images are internally inconsistent, finding his situation psychologically uncomfortable, will not only "try to reduce the dissonance and achieve consonance," but also "actively avoid situations and information which would likely increase the dissonance" (Festinger, 1962, p. 3).

As images vary in their interdependence and their internal consistency, so too they vary in their operational content. If one stresses, with Boulding, the strong behavioral effects of aggregate images, one should also note that some types of images may lead to no action whatsoever, and that some actions may occur that were not mediated by images.[1] And even where images have operational content, it may be self-contradictory or ambivalent, resulting in psychological cross-pressures that leave behavior unchanged. Or else the cross-pressures may have such strong inhibitory effects as to make the individuals or groups more immobile than they were before.

All images by their nature have cognitive content, but only some of them contain explicit evaluative elements that imply such notions as good or bad: "the grass is pleasant," "this man is good-looking," or similar cues to some form of approach or avoidance behavior. Other images, such as "the grass is short" or "this man is dark-haired," may be nonevaluative in and by themselves. Images of the latter type may nonetheless yield a latent evaluative content in response to additional external *cues for evaluation:* In the United States a widespread social convention makes well-cut lawns a symbol of suburban respectability, and a less acceptable prejudice ascribes to dark-haired people lower incomes and less restrained passions.

Something similar holds for the cognitive content of images. Much of the manifest informational detail in an image may require external *cues for orientation* before it can be connected with the cognitive content of other images, so as to yield a fuller amount of meaning and knowledge. Questions like

---

[1] Examples of this type of behavior include simple stimulus-response processes in physiology, or the creation of automatic missile systems that could respond devastatingly to certain types of radar blips or, what is worse, to mechanical or electronic malfunction of their parts without any image of an "enemy."

"Which side is up?" in first looking at an abstract painting, "Who has done the most research on this topic?" in quickly appraising a scientific controversy, or "Which side could become allied with us?" in considering a Southeast Asian guerrilla war are all examples of requests for such cues for orientation.

Similar to visual experiences, mental images usually contain a small set of sharply defined elements in the *focus of attention* and many more elements only dimly and sketchily perceived at the *periphery*. We remember only a fraction even of the selective details that are reported to our brains by the process of macular vision. As time goes on more of the peripheral detail is forgotten, and fewer and simpler features are remembered. In this sense information loss in the process of forgetting resembles the loss of information in the transmission of rumors. If one plots the number of distinct details retained over time, the curves for both of these processes, as Allport and Postman (1947, pp. 75, 86) have shown, are similar. Simultaneous with this elimination or "leveling" of details, an opposite process also takes place—the process of "sharpening," or "the selective perception, retention, and reporting of a limited number of details from a larger context." This latter process is functionally equivalent to bringing these details to, or retaining them in, the central part of the remembered image.

Images serve as screens for the selective reception of new messages, and they often control the perception and interpretation of those messages that are not completely ignored, rejected, or repressed. At the same time, however, new messages sometimes change the images that an individual already holds, as well as the images held in the common culture and communication system of a community. External messages then change such images in many ways,

some of which will be discussed in a later section of this chapter.

External messages are by no means the only ones that change images. Internal messages may have equal or even more powerful effects. Such messages may arise from the dissociation of an image in memory into several separate elements and from the recombination of some of these elements into new patterns and their further recombination with other images, or with elements of other images; and from the various internal feedback processes between old memories and images, new recombinations, current messages, and the internally stored and temporary priorities regarding their reception, transmission, and recall, including finally such higher-order feedback processes as consciousness and will (Deutsch, 1963; Hebb, 1949; Wiener, 1950 and 1961).

Images thus can change autonomously through internal combinatorial and feedback processes. In most cases, therefore, images are best understood as elements and stages in such developing internal programs of information feedback and recombination rather than as products of organic growth. It seems undeniable that organic inputs play a role in the formation of many images. Scientists in the fields of psychiatry, neurophysiology, and psychopharmacology study the role played by adrenalin in rage, by hormones in what is sometimes called libido, and generally by chemical messages in human emotions and by drugs in influencing people's attitudes and actions. This chapter will not deal with such organic inputs, nor will it concentrate to any great extent upon internal combinatorial and feedback processes in image formation and change. Rather, it will focus upon the effects on images of events mediated by external messages.

THE KINDS OF EVENTS IMPINGING UPON IMAGE FORMATION AND CHANGE

An event is an occurrence in the real world, regardless of whether it is of short duration (a hurricane or the assassination of an archduke) or takes place over a longer period of time (the Industrial Revolution). In considering some of their possible effects upon images, three types of external events seem especially significant to us: spectacular events, cumulative events, and shifts in the policy of governments or mass media. Any of these may act alone or in combination with other types of events to affect the sources of image formation and change.

Spectacular Events

Single events can be defined and located fairly well in space and time. Not only do they occur in a specific place, but they have both a beginning and an end. In this sense a telephone call is a single event; and so is an automobile accident or the explosion of an atomic bomb. Such single events are generally of short duration. In the case of the assassination of an archduke or a president, the actual event may take place over the space of time of a few seconds or minutes, from the time the shot rings out until the victim is perceived to be dead. A hurricane lasts for several hours or even days; it takes one to two years to build an elementary school; and a war may last three, four, or even more years (but if it lasts more than four years, we shall assume that we are dealing chiefly with the cumulative effects of attrition rather than with those of any spectacular single battle or campaign). If the lifetime of an individual is used as a measuring rod, such events consume a relatively short period of time, and may be viewed as single entities in the broader panorama of his life-history.

In this chapter we shall restrict ourselves largely to the more spectacular varieties of single events, primarily since the events themselves as well as their effects (if any) seem to be more easily observable. This is not, however, to discount the fact that events that seem trivial to an outside observer may nonetheless have tremendous impact upon the lives of some individuals at some places and in some times. We shall also ignore the type of event that, even though spectacular in itself, does not affect human society, such as the eruption of a volcano on an uninhabited island.

One type of spectacular event is externally imposed. Earthquakes or tidal waves stem from natural rather than human causes. Decisions by a foreign government to devalue its currency, or to attack our own country, result from human rather than natural causes. Our own country may have done nothing to prompt either type of situation. In all such cases individuals may be affected by natural or human events in which they themselves played no part.

Still other occurrences with the character of spectacular events may have been generated originally by ourselves or our own government, but since then have gained a life of their own. Proponents of World War II's Manhattan Project could comment on the feasibility of the project and make some generalized predictions about outcomes; but they could not retain control over all ramifications of the situation once they had decided to set the spectacular event in motion. They could not, for example, control the effect upon man's thinking about war or the changed structure of the international system (such as the acceleration of the Soviet atomic energy program) that would stem from the explosions at Hiroshima and Nagasaki.

What are some of the types of effects upon the sources of image formation and change that such spectacular events can have? One important source consists in the *messages* about the event —both public and private messages— in the communication net of a society. The person who experiences an event directly will receive a fairly straightforward set of sensory messages, distorted only by physical or psychological factors in his own make-up. Others, however, must experience the event only at second or third hand by means of messages communicated to them. Moreover, in the normal course of life a variety of messages about events are competing for people's attention. In terms of public messages, a spectacular event such as the explosion of an atomic bomb or the successful flight of an astronaut may crowd most other routine news off the front pages of our daily journals and become the main topics of presidential news conferences. To the extent that such an event receives widespread public attention it will also, in all likelihood, become a main topic for private communications or for discussions with family and friends.

A second source of image formation and change comprises the sets of individual and collective *memories* that the event may call into play. The occurrence of a spectacular event often leads a population to search its collective memory for types of information (such as analogies) useful in understanding or dealing with the new event. Conversely, a population may forget or repress information that runs counter to the information presented by the spectacular event: The outbreak of a war sometimes causes a population to reject the cultural masterpieces of the new enemy or memories of historic

friendship with him. Some events also produce a personal trauma that may cause a person to repress those parts of his private memory that make him uncomfortable (Grinker & Spiegel, 1945).

Finally, spectacular events at times bring about changes in opinion leadership. Wars, assassinations, the divulging of a government scandal, and the like may lead to the removal of informal or formal leaders from positions of influence. Or the population may simply feel that the old leaders are not capable of handling the crisis resulting from the event, and turn from their discredited leaders to new ones, as did British public opinion when it shifted from Chamberlain to Churchill in June of 1940.

Cumulative Events

Cumulative events we shall call those that take place over a long period of time, such as four years or more. They comprise a myriad of lesser events or day-to-day happenings, the full effects of which are not really felt until the process is well under way. The invention of a labor-saving machine is a single event. (If the machine revolutionizes the production of certain items it could even be considered a spectacular event.) But, just as one swallow hardly makes a summer, the creation of a new machine, however remarkable in itself, did not constitute the Industrial Revolution. The latter event was cumulative in that it encompassed not only the invention of numerous new machines, but also new modes of production, changes in the structure of society, and the development of new attitudes toward man and his environment. Other examples of cumulative events include the gradual pauperization of a population, the depletion of a country's soil, changes in the age structure of a population, the mobilization of new groups into the polity, growing feelings of separateness among peoples divided by geographic or other boundaries, or the development of a sense of community consciousness among groups or peoples who find the experience of living together rewarding.

As in the case of spectacular events, cumulative events too may be generated from either without or within. The depletion of vital minerals from the soil by excessive rains or the gradual erosion by the sea of a country's littoral are examples of the former. Shifting tastes or preferences of a population are instances of the latter, as is a government measure (such as a conservation bill) that inhibits soil depletion and erosion.

The ability of a government is severely limited when it comes to halting or redirecting the flow of insignificant daily events that, like a glacier, increase gradually in scope and significance. First of all, the nature of governmental intervention is sectoral. As the experiences of the major dictatorships of our century suggest, a government is generally unable to intervene in every sector of public and private life. Hitler, for example, concentrated upon foreign policy and military strategy, giving the German economy only sporadic attention. Second, the frequency of governmental intervention is marginal compared with the frequency of the day-to-day situations in which the government does not or cannot intervene. Finally, the probability of successful governmental intervention is limited. Consider, for instance, the case of a dominant country trying to impose its own language upon a subordinate area. Unless the population clearly perceives the positive benefits to be derived from using the language, the result may well be that it will be spoken only in court or upon other occasions when the police-

men or sympathizers of the dominant country are present; but, in the absence of an informer following every individual every minute of the day (or watching him constantly over Orwell's television screen, an equally time-consuming and impracticable task), it seems unlikely that each individual would use the new language in every communication transaction.

Shifts in Governmental or Mass Media Policy

Thus far we have spoken of governments only in the sense that they may set spectacular and even cumulative events in motion. In this sense the government generates the events themselves. A government no less than the mass media of a country may play a separate but equally important role in mediating between the events, however they came about, and the sources of image formation and change. Both government and mass media can shift their attention to or withhold it from events (for example, recognizing or ignoring a new problem or set of problems); they can lend an impression of more or less salience to an event by the amount and kind of attention given to it, particularly in relation to the attention given to other events; or they can change the valuation that they place upon events, objects, and processes within the environment of other events and the messages about them.

Governments and communication elites are the managers of public messages about events, selecting out of the mass of competing messages those that they will transmit, those to which they will give special attention, and those that they will suppress. The management function may operate through news releases and press conferences at the White House, the editorial policy of a newspaper, or, in a larger sense, the entire system of public education.

To the extent that governments and mass media influence the flow and content of public messages about events, they also play a role in determining the character of private messages about these events. Public messages form a major part of the background of private communication interaction in a highly developed and politically well-integrated country. Such is particularly the case when the introduction of certain patterns of communication (as, for instance, quasi-military words, phrases, and slogans, styles of logic and expression) spills over into private life, becoming a part of the individual's style, imagery, and vocabulary (Lasswell, Leites, *et al.*, 1949, pp. 20–39). In the extreme case of George Orwell's fantasy of complete thought control, an omnipresent and omniscient Big Brother, immune to communication overload, is always on guard against private communications that might be incompatible with messages passed on by the regime. Modern totalitarian states seem to practice a somewhat different pattern of control over interpersonal communication by creating an atmosphere of mutual distrust and suspicion: The individual isolated from his fellow man often comes to rely ever more upon government-sanctioned messages, preferring to parrot them than to risk asserting contradictory messages that could expose him as a "traitor" or "enemy of the people" (Orwell, 1949; Deutsch, 1954). Democracies at war, or close to it, sometimes have created temporarily an only somewhat milder pattern of control. Their public messages, reinforced by popular consent, generated such overwhelming expectations of conformity as to isolate and stigmatize at once anyone who uttered deviant views. Rather than hold such deviant opinions even privately, many individuals soon came to internalize many of the images and beliefs demanded by their community and its rulers. Clearly, however, as we shall discuss later, such forms of control are highly imperfect under any and all political systems.

Governments and mass media also try to influence the organized or collective memories of a population. In the crudest sense this could involve rewriting history books, or possibly the post hoc rehabilitation or vilification of political or intellectual leaders. If such efforts are consistent, however, and practiced over a sufficiently long period of time, they may be effective in changing the public memory of an entire generation. A more drastic method is the forcible movement of populations. By removing them from the locus of their public memory—the rolling hills and farmlands of their native land, the church on the town square, monuments, cemeteries, and other symbols of the people's history—even the attempt of older generations to instill a common memory and sense of common identity into the youth is doomed to failure, *if assimilation into the new environment is made to appear attractive.* In the absence of this condition, migration may have the opposite effect of consolidating the original particular ideas or culture of the migrants or exiles that might have been under increasingly heavy pressure in the old environment. This was the experience, for instance, of the Jewish Diaspora, the American Pilgrim Fathers, the Mormons, and many others. Less obvious but more effective in the last analysis may be the government's use of criteria of selectivity to emphasize certain aspects of the public memory, greatly increasing the frequency with which these aspects are recalled, possibly even attaching positively valued connotations or secondary symbols to the memories it wishes to foster and offering social or economic rewards for their frequent use. Disfavored memories are not directly repressed under this procedure but drowned out by competition—with a similar or even stronger ultimate result.

As it is easier to influence public than private messages, so too it is easier to influence public than private memories. The government can rewrite the history books and public inscriptions, down to the monuments or tombstones of the dead; it can change place names, buildings, landscapes; and it can prescribe what may be publicly recalled from memory—all this without obliterating the memory of contradictory events from the minds of individuals. Attempts to change private memories would be successful only to the extent that individuals internalize changes in the public memory. In a limited number of people, of course, "brainwashing" can go far in reducing the salience of inappropriate memories (Lifton, 1961; Meerloo, 1956); but such measures have proved impracticable for the populations of entire countries—unless the governmental policies were themselves supported by major cultural beliefs, popular aspirations, and at least a measure of reinforcing experiences from reality.

Finally, through selection of individuals installed in or removed from positions of influence, tax laws designed to increase or reduce the income of certain groups, censorship of communications, court action, and even outright assassination, governments and mass media can influence the key personnel in a society—that is, its reference groups and its elites, its formal policy makers, its informal opinion leaders, and its human models for imitation. The character of the persons who transmit messages about events makes a difference in the quantity and quality of information in the messages that are trans-

mitted. A secretary of state who perceives a foreign country to be hostile to his own, for example, may view and interpret that country's behavior in quite a different light than would another man predisposed to view that foreign country in a kindlier light. The images of the foreign country that the population at large derives from the alternative sets of messages could vary correspondingly. Similarly, a government whose policy it is to tax a certain class of people virtually out of existence could not only alter the structure of its society but also transfer influence from that group to another; new images of the criteria of high status would emerge among the population; and new people would be placed in positions where they could influence the type of messages about events that are communicated to the public.

SOME KINDS OF POSSIBLE EFFECTS OF EXTERNAL EVENTS UPON IMAGES

Messages about external events, as these are communicated to the individual, may have many kinds of effects upon an image held by him. Such external messages may (a) reinforce the image, much as a message about British or Russian misdeeds in the international arena strengthens the image that we may already have of a perfidious Albion or Soviet Union; (b) produce no significant change in the image, either if the messages are not relevant to the image or if the person holding the image does not or chooses not to receive the messages; (c) add explicit information, perhaps of the sort that only extends or fills out the image without altering it in any significant way; (d) clarify the image by reducing uncertainty and thus adding information implicitly; (e) reorganize the image, increasing its internal consistency, perhaps, or making it more understandable by relating it to a context of other cues or images; or (f) change the importance of the image, that is, the dependence of other images upon it.

Furthermore, messages may have any of these kinds of effects not only on a single issue but on an entire cluster of related images and, in extreme cases, on the entire cognitive and value structure of the individual, that is, upon his mind and personality (as is sometimes the case in political or religious conversion). They may even have similar far-reaching effects over time upon entire cultures and political and social systems, as in the historical cases of major new religions or new modes of scientific, artistic, philosophic, or social thought.

The five kinds of effects just listed (omitting the "no change" case) could, in theory, impinge upon any one of the six aspects of images discussed earlier: (a) focus; (b) periphery; (c) cues for orientation; (d) cues for evaluation; (e) image clusters; and (f) major configurations of personality or culture. This interplay of five types of effects with six aspects of images creates an ensemble of thirty combinatorial possibilities. Each of these thirty specific effects—reinforcing the focus, adding detail at the periphery, and so forth—could be produced by messages manipulated by the government or mass media (G), or by the impact of spectacular events (S), or by the gradual effects of cumulative events (C); by the combined effects of any one pair of these three sources (GS, GC, SC); or finally by all three sources—government, spectacular, and cumulative events—acting together (GSC). If we thus distinguish seven sources or combinations of sources, each of which could produce any one of thirty specified changes, our ensemble of combinatorial possibilities

grows to 210. For purposes of a quick overview, these hypothetical possibilities are exhibited as rows 1–7 of Table 5.1.

The same table can also be used to indicate the implications of a few hypotheses embodied in a simple system of coding:

1. In going across the first three rows of the table we have made a total of ninety commonsense judgments about the degree to which each of our three basic sources of messages about external events might produce each of our thirty possible specified changes.

2. We then hypothesized that the effects of any pair of sources will be one step higher than the effects of the stronger one of its components.

3. We further assumed that where all three sources act together their joint effects will be yet one step higher than those of the strongest pair in the same column.

We made similar assumptions about the effects of cross-pressures:

4. We supposed that any single type of external event—or any combination of such types—will be weakened in its effects by two steps if another event is working in the opposite direction, and further:

5. That its effects will be diminished by three steps if two types of events oppose them. (We thus supposed that external events are somewhat more effective in inhibiting attitude change than in promoting it.)

These assumptions generated another twelve rows in our table (rows 10 through 21 of Table 5.1) and raised the total number of cells to 570. This scheme still assumes that each type of external event in its net effect will tend to have a clear impact in one direction rather than another. It makes no provision, for instance, for two spectacular events having wholly or partly opposite effects, as had the Suez and

Hungarian crises which occurred within a few days of each other in the fall of 1956. Where such cross-pressures occurred, we should expect them also to lower the impact of the most salient event by one step, but we have not represented this by any additions to our table. A total of 570 cells, not including averages, were the most we felt able to manage at this point.

Since we express our judgments in a five-step code ranging from very low to very high, as listed at the foot of Table 5.1, we get 570 hypothetical estimates of what approximate strength of relationship we expect to find between each combination of sources and each aspect of image and type of effect. Of the 570 expected changes, 249 (or 44 percent) are "very low," 110 (19 percent) are "low," 90 (16 percent) are "medium," only 48 (8 percent) are "high," but as many as 73 (13 percent) are "very high." Such a scheme, of course, tells us nothing more than the implications of our own assumptions and beliefs, made more explicit and exhibited for more convenient inspection.

If we should be able, however, to find at least a limited number of illustrations for some of the cells in the table, we can compare our findings from these scattered cases with our expectations as presented in the table. This would not be enough to confirm or disconfirm our hypotheses statistically, but it would at least give us some indication as to how far removed our intuitive judgments might be from reality.

To do this, it is desirable to translate our notions of images in the minds of individuals into some distribution of attitudes found in opinion polls. An assumption implicit in such a procedure is that the extent or intensity of a change in the image or attitude held by an average individual will be highly correlated with the frequency with which a change in the same direction will be observable in the group of which he is a member. Though it is easy to imagine exceptional cases and situations, our general assumption flows from the proposition that people have so much in common that sample surveys are acceptable sources of knowledge, bearing in mind, of course, all the limitations of survey data that have been discussed extensively in the literature. Data about the percentage of poll respondents who indicate a change in attitude will be used, therefore, as indicators of changes in the relevant images held individually by a large part of the members of the group from which the poll sample was drawn. In regard to such poll data, our five-step code might be interpreted very roughly to suggest expectable opinion changes of less than 5 percent for "very low" effects, 6 to 15 percent for "low" ones, 16 to 25 percent for cases of "medium" impact, 26 to 35 percent for effects expected to be "high," and 36 percent or more for "very high" ones.

An expected average percentage change in any cell in Table 5.1 then would simply mean that, if a set of survey questions could be drafted that would correspond to the kind of image change and external event in each cell in the table, and if such questions were given to many relevant samples, and if the hypotheses all should prove correct, then the average of the observed attitude changes would be close to the hypothetical averages given in each cell. Where images or attitudes are reinforced, of course, the shift would not be in the distribution and frequency of responses, but rather in the intensity with which attitudes are held, and thus in the distribution of responses to survey questions measuring intensity or permitting the application of scaling techniques.

TABLE 5.1
Some Possible Effects of External Events upon Images: A Schematic Presentation*

Type of effect / Aspect of image changed	Reinforce						No change	Add detail					
	Focus	Periphery	Cues for Orientation	Cues for Evaluation	Image Cluster	Personality or Culture		Focus	Periphery	Cues for Orientation	Cues for Evaluation	Image Cluster	Personality or Culture
	1	2	3	4	5	6	7	8	9	10	11	12	13
Sources of Change in the Absence of Cross-Pressures													
1. G	M	M	M	M	L	L	–	M	L	VL	VL	VL	VL
2. S	H	L	H	H	M	L	–	H	L	VL	VL	VL	VL
3. C	M	H	L	H	H	H	–	L	M	VL	VL	VL	VL
4. GS	VH	H	VH	VH	H	M	–	VH	M	L	L	L	L
5. GC	H	VH	H	VH	VH	VH	–	H	H	L	L	L	L
6. SC	VH	VH	VH	VH	VH	VH	–	VH	H	L	L	L	L
7. GSC	VH	VH	VH	VH	VH	VH	–	VH	VH	M	M	M	M
8. Avg. susceptibility to change	H	H	H	H	H	H	–	H	M	VL	VL	VL	VL
9. Avg. total of type of effect	H						–	L					
Sources of Change with Cross-Pressures (Barred Symbols) Opposed to Effects Indicated													
10. $G\bar{S}$	VL	VL	VL	VL	VL	VL	–	VL	VL	VL	VL	VL	VL
11. $G\bar{C}$	VL	VL	VL	VL	VL	VL	–	VL	VL	VL	VL	VL	VL
12. $S\bar{G}$	L	VL	L	L	VL	VL	–	L	VL	VL	VL	VL	VL
13. $S\bar{C}$	L	VL	L	L	VL	VL	–	L	VL	VL	VL	VL	VL
14. $C\bar{G}$	VL	L	VL	L	L	L	–	VL	VL	VL	VL	VL	VL
15. $C\bar{S}$	VL	L	VL	L	L	L	–	VL	VL	VL	VL	VL	VL
16. $GS\bar{C}$	M	L	M	M	L	VL	–	M	VL	VL	VL	VL	VL
17. $GC\bar{S}$	L	M	L	M	M	M	–	L	L	VL	VL	VL	VL
18. $SC\bar{G}$	M	M	M	M	M	M	–	M	L	VL	VL	VL	VL
19. $G\bar{SC}$	VL	VL	VL	VL	VL	VL	–	VL	VL	VL	VL	VL	VL
20. $S\bar{GC}$	VL	VL	VL	VL	VL	VL	–	VL	VL	VL	VL	VL	VL
21. $C\bar{GS}$	VL	VL	VL	VL	VL	VL	–	VL	VL	VL	VL	VL	VL
22. Avg. susceptibility to change	L	L	L	L	L	L	–	L	VL	VL	VL	VL	VL
23. Avg. total of type of effect	L						–	VL					

*KEYS: Types of Events

G = Shifts in governmental and communication media policy
S = Spectacular events
C = Cumulative events

Degree of Effect

VL = very low (less than 5%)
L = low (10% ± 5%)
M = medium (20% ± 5%)
H = high (30% ± 5%)
VH = very high (36% or more)

TABLE 5.1 (Continued)

Clarify						Reorganize						Change importance						Average total
Focus	Periphery	Cues for Orientation	Cues for Evaluation	Image Cluster	Personality or Culture	Focus	Periphery	Cues for Orientation	Cues for Evaluation	Image Cluster	Personality or Culture	Focus	Periphery	Cues for Orientation	Cues for Evaluation	Image Cluster	Personality or Culture	
14	15	16	17	18	19	20	21	22	23	24	25	26	27	28	29	30	31	32
M	L	M	M	L	L	M	M	M	M	L	L	M	M	M	M	M	L	L
H	M	H	H	L	L	H	M	H	H	L	L	H	M	H	H	M	L	M
L	M	L	L	L	L	H	H	H	H	H	H	H	M	H	H	H	H	M
VH	H	VH	VH	M	M	VH	H	VH	VH	M	M	VH	H	VH	VH	H	M	H
H	H	H	H	M	M	VH	VH	VH	VH	VH	VH	VH	H	VH	VH	VH	VH	H
VH	H	VH	VH	M	M	VH	VH	VH	VH	VH	VH	VH	H	VH	VH	VH	VH	H
VH	VH	VH	VH	H	H	VH	VH	VH	VH	VH	VH	VH	VH	VH	VH	VH	VH	VH
H	M	H	H	L	L	H	H	H	H	H	H	H	M	H	H	H	H	M

Clarify: M   Reorganize: M   Change importance: H

Clarify						Reorganize						Change importance						Average total
VL	VL	VL	VL	VL	VL	VL	VL	VL	VL	VL	VL	VL	VL	VL	VL	VL	VL	VL
VL	VL	VL	VL	VL	VL	VL	VL	VL	VL	VL	VL	VL	VL	VL	VL	VL	VL	VL
L	VL	L	L	VL	VL	L	VL	L	L	VL	VL	L	VL	L	L	VL	VL	VL
L	VL	L	L	VL	VL	L	VL	L	L	VL	VL	L	VL	L	L	VL	VL	VL
VL	VL	VL	VL	VL	VL	L	L	L	L	L	L	L	VL	L	L	L	L	VL
VL	VL	VL	VL	VL	VL	L	L	L	L	L	L	L	VL	L	L	L	L	VL
M	L	M	M	VL	VL	M	L	M	M	VL	VL	M	L	M	M	L	VL	L
L	L	L	L	VL	VL	M	M	M	M	M	M	M	L	M	M	M	M	L
M	L	M	M	VL	VL	M	M	M	M	M	M	M	L	M	M	M	M	L
VL	VL	VL	VL	VL	VL	VL	VL	VL	VL	VL	VL	VL	VL	VL	VL	VL	VL	VL
VL	VL	VL	VL	VL	VL	VL	VL	VL	VL	VL	VL	VL	VL	VL	VL	VL	VL	VL
VL	VL	VL	VL	VL	VL	VL	VL	VL	VL	VL	VL	VL	VL	VL	VL	VL	VL	VL
L	VL	L	L	VL	VL	L	L	L	L	L	L	L	VL	L	L	L	L	VL

Clarify: L   Reorganize: L   Change importance: L

= 249 entries (44%)
= 110 entries (19%)
= 90 entries (16%)
= 48 entries (8%)
= 73 entries (13%)

570   (100%)

This procedure implies an extensive use of poll data throughout most of this chapter. To be sure, such data are subject to many errors, such as sampling error; bias inherent in the wording of questions or the personalities of interviewers; errors in recording, coding, and tabulation; discrepancies between surface responses and more hidden and deep-seated feelings; and gaps between attitudes and actions. Despite all these weaknesses, poll data very often can be used to predict within an error range of less than 4 percent the distribution of votes cast in elections, the preferences of consumers, and other aspects of behavior. In fourteen national elections from 1936 to 1962, for instance, "the average deviation of Gallup Poll results from the actual division of the vote [was] 2.9 percentage points" (American Institute of Public Opinion [AIPO] press release, 7 June, 1964), and the size of the deviation seems to have declined during the last fifteen years. To aid the reader in allowing for the possible effects of inaccuracy and error, we shall indicate statistical significance levels that may be attached to the poll data we shall be summarizing. The results of a partial test of the extent to which the data confirm our argument as a whole will be given at the end of the chapter.

MINOR EFFECTS OF EXTERNAL EVENTS ON IMAGE FORMATION AND CHANGE

Reinforcement

First of all, messages about events and policies often reinforce images that people already hold, whether by long tradition or from recent experience. Thus Lerner (1958, p. 140) reports that, although 80 percent of "traditional" Turks have opinions on Soviet Russian foreign policies, these opinions "derived not from current information, but rather from the traditional stock of Turkish folklore." No more than 2 percent of these respondents actually claimed any current knowledge of Soviet policies.[2] In sum, "any question dealing with Russia is likely to evoke from Traditionals . . . stock responses under the guise of current opinions." Present-day Turkish government messages about national policy, such as military preparedness against Russia and membership in NATO, merely are apt to reinforce traditional attitudes that may stem more directly from the policies of earlier Turkish governments between 1853 and 1918, not to mention numerous Turkish-Russian military clashes during the seventeenth and eighteenth centuries. In this sense the traditional beliefs of peasants resemble a savings account of memories: Memories of current policies of past generations seem to accumulate, sometimes with interest, until they become the traditional peasant folk belief of later generations. When broader peasant strata then enter politics, they often do so as an electorate prepared to support as "national traditions" the artificial innovations—such as national flags, anthems, and other symbols, as well as military or monarchic institutions—of an earlier generation of their so-called "betters" (Friedrich, 1937).

External messages, even though they are about events that did not happen, can nonetheless reinforce relatively recent images no less than traditional

---

[2] This particular subgroup in Lerner's sample included only 49 respondents, but the difference between 39 cases and 1 is large enough to be significant at greater than the .0001 level, using a simple binomial test, and it accords well with other information about Turkish political behavior.

ones. In 1914 English images about the supposed Hun-like barbarism of the Germans were only about fifteen years old. Such images did not exist to any significant extent in British literature throughout the nineteenth century when, on the contrary, German letters and scholarship were held in the highest esteem. At the outbreak of World War I, however, Kipling could tell the English people, "The Hun is at the gate," and the largely untrue but widely credited accounts of German atrocities in Belgium greatly reinforced this image (Lasswell, 1938).

If messages or memories about past events do not directly reinforce a strongly held image, they may be selectively screened or distorted until they do so. Students of American public opinion and electoral behavior report that people misstate—and presumably misremember—their own behavior to make it more congruent with their images of social norms. Campbell, Converse, Miller, and Stokes (1960, p. 94) found that about 12 percent more persons claimed to have voted in the 1952 and 1956 presidential elections, and 3

percent more claimed to have voted for the victorious candidate, than had done so in fact. Similarly, Hyman (1944–1945) writes that as many as 42 percent of respondents in a survey during World War II distorted their actual record about such matters as war-bond purchases, the display of government posters, and absenteeism. In later studies, Hyman and his associates (1954, pp. 196–197, 255–256) found that interviewers tended to distort in the direction of their own policy preferences the statements of respondents on such topics as conscription and the Henry Wallace campaign of 1948. In some cases differences between the opinions recorded by two independent interviewer groups ranged from 3 to 18 percent, which suggests that biased interviewers can produce a distortion effect of roughly 1 to 7 percent.[3]

In the Kennedy-Nixon television debates of 1960, partisanship had an even stronger effect in reinforcing and exaggerating images based on current perceptions. In eight polls reported by Katz and Feldman (1962, pp. 175, 199), an average of 65 percent (69 percent in

---

[3] Survey data of this type raise difficult questions of statistical significance. Standard opinion polls, such as those of the American Institute of Public Opinion, are based on about 1500 respondents; many European poll data, including those used by the United States Information Agency, are derived from the answers of between 600 and 1800 respondents. Since the samples used often are selected on a stratified rather than on a purely random basis, a conservative procedure would be to count only one half these numbers for the computation of confidence intervals or levels of statistical significance. The finding of Campbell and his associates that about 3 percent of their respondents falsely reported having voted, when in fact they had not, was based on 3166 cases, that is, on an effective *n* of nearly 1600. Here a 3 percent difference is significant at about the .05 level. The statistical significance of Hyman's finding cannot be evaluated, since it is based on the number of statements reported by interviewers, rather than on the number of the latter, which was likely to be small. On other questions, however, Hyman and his associates report that interviewer bias made a difference significant at the .05 level or better for 8 out of 21 fixed-response questions (Hyman *et al.*, 1954, pp. 255–256). Despite its doubtful statistical basis and low strength of relationship inferred, Hyman's finding is worth noting since it was confirmed by later studies. The two cases illustrate the different qualities of statistical evidence one is apt to find in data of this sort. We are indebted to Professors Hayward R. Alker, Jr., and Donald J. Puchala for their statistical advice and their help in the computation of significance levels. Further details can be found in a forthcoming article by Professors Alker and Puchala on the statistical analysis of public opinion models.

the two polls among them based on representative national samples of 2200 and 2673 respondents, respectively) of Democratic or pro-Kennedy respondents indicated a belief that Kennedy had won the first of the four debates, whereas only 19 (13) percent of Republican or pro-Nixon viewers thought so. Similarly, victory for Nixon was perceived by 40 (56) percent of Republican or pro-Nixon respondents as against less than 5 (5) percent of Democratic or pro-Kennedy viewers. The effects of partisan distortion thus amounted on the average to about 40 (53) percentage points—or to 35 (51) percent among Republicans and 45 (56) percent among Democrats. It is striking that the relationship found by using eight polls with varying statistical bases becomes still sharper when only the two polls with large statistical bases are used. The findings are clearly significant at better than the .001 level. Democratic partisans, a number that includes a larger proportion of persons of lower levels of income and education, may have been somewhat more prone to emotional distortion. The fact that 19 percent of the Republicans conceded victory to Kennedy while only 4.5 percent of the Democrats did so for Nixon shows a pro-Kennedy differential of 15 percentage points as against the 10 percentage point difference between the two camps in regard to general differential perception. These 5 percentage points of additional difference may therefore measure in some sense the actual edge in Kennedy's performance, but it can be taken as statistically significant only at the .05 level.

The mechanism by which the reinforcement of preconceived images occurs has been studied in some detail by psychologists and others. Festinger, Riecken, and Schachter (1956, pp. 3–6, 193–233) report how holders of intense beliefs reinterpreted messages about the clear-cut failure of their prophecies until these reinterpreted messages became instruments of reinforcement. They add that, in addition to strong previous dispositions, the continued presence of strong social support for the original image or belief system, from at least a small group of nearby fellow believers, is essential for the process. More recently a content analysis (Holsti, 1962) of the writings and speeches of the late United States Secretary of State John Foster Dulles revealed how that statesman consistently reinterpreted both truculent and conciliatory messages from the Soviet Union so as to make them fit into an unchanging image of an aggressive, implacably hostile, and dynamic Russia.

Where all messages are likely to be reinterpreted so as to reinforce a previously held image, the best counterstrategy for a communicator may be message deprivation. If no messages on the sensitive topic are received, none is available for distortion; and fanaticism may be dulled by boredom. If the communicator controls the external environment of the image-holder, the effects of message deprivation may be broadened to sensory deprivation of varying degrees. The inclination to distort messages into reinforcements of previously held images may be weakened further by the absence of social support for the image-holder and by the cumulative effects of anxiety and loneliness. Reports on Chinese methods of brainwashing indicate the lengths to which this approach may be carried as well as the limits of its effectiveness (Lifton, 1961; Biderman & Zimmer, 1961).

In general the process of distorting incoming messages to reinforce preconceived images should be distinguished from the "self-fulfilling prophecy," familiar from the writings of William James and others. Both appear to be amplifying feedback effects, usually with decreasing increments up to some limit. The distorting effect, however, occurs in the mind of the individual or in the communication system of the group, whereas the reality-changing effect occurs in the outside world. Ordinarily, the distorting effect is much larger. The data reported in this section suggest that it can account for differentials in attitudes or perceptions of the order of magnitude of 20 to 25 percent. We have no data to offer at this stage on the reality-changing effect, but as a purely impressionistic and provisional judgment from our experience in observing international politics we should estimate the order of magnitude of changes produced by it only at 4 to 5 percent, or roughly at one fourth or one fifth that of the level or strength of the distorting effect. Data on the "bandwagon" effect in opinion polling—which might be considered a subspecies of the self-fulfilling prophecy—would fit in with these proportions: Lazarsfeld, Berelson, & Gaudet (1948, pp. 5, 45, 108) found that 21 percent of the 18 percent of respondents without voting intention in May 1948 appear to have been moved by the band-wagon effect —a net shift of about 4 percent of the total vote.

No Change: The Stability of Images

Images and attitudes often persist with little or no substantial change despite spectacular changes in the external world, or messages about such changes. In April 1961, shortly after the decisive failure of the United States-supported invasion of Cuba, 65 percent of American respondents to a Gallup Poll expressed their opposition to an invasion of the island by American troops.

One and a half years later, in early October 1962, at an early stage in the Cuban missile crisis, a virtually unchanged 63 percent reiterated this opposition. Four months after the climax of this extremely dramatic crisis, in February 1963, almost exactly the same proportion—64 percent—expressed once again their opposition to an American invasion of Cuba (AIPO, 7 May, 1961; 14 October, 1962; 27 February, 1963).[4]

Deterrence Effects. The respondents' perception of the likelihood of an all-out war with the Soviet Union as a result of such a United States invasion of Cuba had only limited effect upon this attitude. In October 1962, 51 percent of Americans polled thought that an all-out war between America and Russia would be likely if the United States should invade, whereas 37 percent considered all-out war unlikely in that event. Among those who considered all-out war unlikely, opposition to the invasion still remained at 57 percent; and among those who considered war likely—that is, those who ought to have felt themselves "deterred"—opposition to the invasion rose only to 69 percent (AIPO, 17 October, 1962). The deterrence effect, even among those who reported themselves fearful about the invasion, thus would seem to have increased the opposition to any such action by only 12 percentage points. The proponents of the invasion comprised 19 percent of those who believed all-out war to be its likely consequence, but almost twice as many (36 percent) of those who indicated that they feared no such risk. The deterrence effect from this reasoning would seem to have been of the order of 15 ± 3 percent.

---

[4] The supporters of the invasion remained at an unchanged 24 percent in April 1961 and October 1962, but dropped slightly to 20 percent in February 1963, whereas the percentage of unconcerned and undecided rose gradually from 11 percent in April 1961 to 13 percent in October 1962 and to 16 percent in February 1963.

A somewhat different picture emerges from a more detailed analysis of this same poll. It is possible to construct a matrix of the expectations and attitudes surveyed in it and to compute the percentage of respondents for each cell. The results are shown in Table 5.2. In such a matrix, the first two cells on the main diagonal (with entries in italics) contain the all-weather warriors and the all-weather believers in international law or in pacifism—that is to say, mainly those cases where preferences were strong enough to prevail regardless of incongruent or contradictory expectations. (There may also have been some respondents who considered World War III as a positive good, but their number was probably small.) The cells on the first off-diagonal (marked by asterisks) contain a large number of opportunists together with those who adjusted their perceptions to their preferences. Thus as many as 35 percent of the respondents thought war likely and

opposed invasion. If every one of these respondents had been an ice-cold realist and opportunist, the maximum effect of deterrence might have amounted to a full 35 percent. It seems plausible, however, that almost three fifths of these 35 percent, or about 20 percent, would have opposed invasion even if they had considered war unlikely, for among those who considered war improbable this proportion did oppose the invasion. The net deterrence effect thus emerges again at the same order of magnitude, 15 percent. The 13 percent of respondents who favored invasion and considered war unlikely must again be discounted by the 10 percent who favored invasion even though they thought that war was probable. The fact that they did not feel deterred increased their number by only 3 percentage points. As a result of this more detailed analysis, the original estimate of the deterrence effect in October 1962 as amounting to 15 ± 3 percent still appears plausible.[5]

TABLE 5.2
American Attitudes toward an Invasion of Cuba and the Possible Effects of Deterrence

	Should invade (%)	Should not (%)	No opinion (%)	Total (%)
All-out war with Russia if we invade				
Is likely	*10*	35*	6	51
Is not likely	13*	*21*	3	37
No opinion	1	8	*3*	12
TOTAL	24	64	12	100

Asterisks mark the percentages of holders of images or attitudes who may be influenced by contingencies, such as their images of a deterrent situation, while the italicized entries on the main diagonal mark the "all-weather" opinion holders.

Source of data: AIPO, 17 October, 1962.

[5] If one accepts this reasoning, one might have expected an increase in President Kennedy's popularity of about 15 ± 3 percent once the Cuban crisis was over. The percentage of those who approved of the way in which Kennedy was "handling his job as President" rose in fact by 13 points, from 61 percent in early October to 74 percent in December 1962 (AIPO, 5 December, 1962).

Image Fluctuations. Frequently attitudes shift by 10 or 20 percentage points in response to some spectacular event, only to return to their previous level after some time has passed, usually after other events have moved into the focus of attention. The Western European response to the ruthless Soviet suppression of the Hungarian uprising in November 1956 may serve as an example. Results of relevant public opinion data from four Western European countries for the period 1954–1961 are summarized in Table 5.3.

The data in Table 5.3 suggest several interesting points. The rates of change of positive (responses of "very good opinion" or "good opinion") and neutral ("fair opinion") images of the Soviet Union are considerably different in the four countries. The British image was the least stable, with average changes from one polling date to another of ±15 percentage points. By way of contrast, the French image changed ±9 percentage points on the average, and the German and Italian images only ±7 percentage points. Such a finding certainly contradicts the stereotypes about calm Englishmen and volatile Italians.

More important for the present study, the magnitude of the average Western European image shift was modest. Taking a shift of 10 percentage points in either direction as standard, there were only two really dramatic shifts during the seven years from October 1954 to July 1961. The more prominent of these was the downward shift of 19 percentage points that came in polls conducted during the weeks following the Hungarian crisis. If we consider the ratio of unfavorable ("bad opinion" and "very bad opinion") to favorable ("good opinion" and "very good opinion") responses, the shift in imagery at this point in time was similar in each of the four countries surveyed. For the first six polls included here, the

average was about 3.6 unfavorable responses for every favorable opinion about Russia; in December 1956 the ratio quadrupled to about 14.6 unfavorable for every favorable response.

Equally significant in looking at the data in Table 5.3, however, is the complete restoration of the original image of the Soviet Union. The average level of favorable and neutral responses from October 1954 to April 1956 in the four countries was 35 percent. Following upon the spectacular Soviet intervention in Hungary in November 1956, which was extensively and unfavorably publicized by the Western governments and media, this level dropped 19 percentage points. After falling to 16 percent in December 1956, however, it gradually rose again and, by October of 1958, was above the average for the two years prior to the Hungarian uprising. The level rose still higher during the ensuing three years. Similarly, the ratio of unfavorable to favorable responses, after climbing to 14.6 to 1 in December 1956, dropped to its previous average level of 3.6 to 1 before two years were out. The average from November 1959 to July 1961 was still lower—about 2.3 unfavorable opinions of the Soviet Union for every favorable response. In short, whatever prestige the Soviet Union had lost in Western Europe as a result of its actions in Hungary, it regained within two years.

The last seven rows of Table 5.3 also throw some light upon the effects of Soviet space achievements in the late 1950s. The launching of Sputnik I in October 1957 was followed by an average increase of the aggregate of favorable and neutral opinions about Russia of 8 percentage points in November 1957 and another 7 percentage points in October 1958. A more dramatic increase occurred during the course of the next year. In November 1959, only weeks after two successful Soviet moon shots, the second of which photo-

TABLE 5.3
Western European Attitudes toward the U.S.S.R., 1954-1961

Question: "Now about various countries. Please use this card to tell me what your feelings are about them. Russia?"
Responses: The following figures are the percentages of respondents responding to the above question with "Very good," "Good," or "Fair."

Date	Great Britain %	Change*	France %	Change*	Italy %	Change*	West Germany %	Change*	Average %	Change*	Comment
Oct. 1954	30		24		30		18		26		
Feb. 1955	H-69	+39	30	+ 6	25	− 5	23	+ 5	37	+11	
June 1955	42	−27	35	+ 5	33	+ 8	31	+ 8	35	− 2	"Normal" range = 34 ± 8
Aug. 1955	58	+16	45	+10	38	+ 5	26	− 5	42	+ 7	
Nov. 1955	38	−20	40	− 5	37	− 1	18	− 9	33	− 9	
Apr. 1956	46	+ 8	39	− 1	35	− 2	21	+ 3	35	+ 2	
Dec. 1956	L-13	−33	L-18	−21	L-20	−15	L-11	−10	L-16	−19	Soviet intervention in Hungary = −19
May 1957	23	+10	28	+10	29	+ 9	16	+ 5	24	+ 8	
Nov. 1957	38	+15	37	+ 9	34	+ 5	19	+ 3	32	+ 8	Maximum impact of Soviet space program = +37
Oct. 1958	38	0	35	− 2	47	+13	35	+16	39	+ 7	Net impact = 37 − 19 = +18
Nov. 1959	54	+16	H-61	+26	H-55	+ 8	H-41	+ 6	H-53	+14	
Feb. 1960	50	− 4	55	− 6	50	− 5	25	−16	45	− 8	Impact of Western mass media = −11
May 1960	46	− 4	55	0	41	− 9	25	0	42	− 3	Residual impact of Soviet space program = 18 − 11 = +7
July 1961	50	+ 4	47	− 8	48	+ 7	22	− 3	42	0	
Average	43	±15	39	± 9	37	± 7	24	± 7	36	± 8	
Total range	41	± 28	40	± 22	38	± 18	26	± 15	35	± 19	

* Change in percentage points from previous survey.

The highest and lowest points of each country's attitude toward the U.S.S.R. are marked "H" and "L" respectively. In sample surveys of 1600 respondents made by the same agencies in 1952, differences of ±3 percentage points were found to be significant at the .05 level (Parry & Crespi, 1953, pp. 139–146, especially pp. 142–143).

Source of data: Puchala, 1964, pp. 1–4.

graphed the dark side of the moon, the percentage of favorable and neutral opinions of Russia reached its peak for the seven years, 14 percentage points above the level of October 1958, and 18 percent above the "pre-Hungary" level of early 1956. These changes occurred although the Western governments and mass media endeavored to some extent to counter the impact of the Soviet performance and the claims of Soviet propaganda. By July 1961, however, the last date for which information is available, Western European opinion of the Soviet Union had dropped to a level not far above the average level from October 1954 to April 1956. Moreover, it seems reasonable to believe that the opinion level dropped to that of the earlier years in the ensuing months, after August 1961 when the Soviet Union permitted the East German regime to build a wall separating East from West Berlin.

In other respects the effects of Soviet feats in outer space may be more lasting. Consider, for instance, Western European judgments about scientific development in the U.S.S.R. The same polls cited in Table 5.3 (Puchala, 1964, p. 24) reveal that in November 1957, shortly after the launching of Sputnik I, 21 percent more people responded "Russia" than "the United States" in answer to the question, "All things considered, do you think the United States or Russia is ahead in scientific development at the present time?" Less than a year later, in October 1958, after four American space successes, the reverse was the case: scientific development in the United States was considered more advanced than in the Soviet Union, albeit by the small margin of 6 percentage points. The next survey took place in February 1960, not long after the third and most spectacular of the Russian Lunik moon shots. It indicated that 44 percent of the Western European population thought Russia ahead of the United States in scientific development, whereas only 32 percent thought that America outstripped the Soviet Union. By July 1961 this margin perceiving Soviet superiority had decreased from 12 to 8 percentage points. It would seem then that, toward the end of the fourth year of the Soviet-American "space race," Western European public opinion continued to see the Russians clearly as the leaders.

The long-range effect of Soviet space accomplishments may also have been appreciable in American no less than in Western European opinion. If 16 percent of American poll respondents had described the Russians as "intelligent" in 1942 when they were our allies, and only 12 percent saw them in the same way in 1948 when they were our Cold-War adversaries, the proportion of Americans that conceded that the Russians were intelligent had risen to 28 percent by 1961 (AIPO, 30 April 1961; Buchanan & Cantril, 1953, pp. 46–47).

These public opinion data illustrate the point that images fluctuate, now in a random and then in a countervailing fashion. But they nonetheless fluctuate within certain limits about a secular curve or pattern of images. Every action followed by an adverse shift in opinion toward, let us say, the Soviet Union seems to have close on its heels an event putting that country in a favorable light.

Perhaps this is another way of saying that people, individually or collectively, view the occurrence of events in a perspective formed as much by a prevailing climate or trend of opinion as by their past experiences and perceptions. If an event should not fit into the expected pattern, momentary doubt and confusion—even disillusion—may ensue, except possibly in extreme cases where images or information are distorted immediately, so as to reinforce strongly held beliefs. With time, one or both of two processes might take place: a new event occurs that does fit into the pattern, enabling the perceiver to term the previous nonconforming event an aberration; or such oracles as newspapers or leaders interpret the nonconforming event so that it does fit into the preconceived pattern. In either instance, confidence in the pattern itself will generally return. Individual events thus produce more or less sharp fluctuations in images; but these fluctuations are often more important in terms of their cumulative effects on the patterns of images and image changes obtaining over a longer period of time.

Lane's unusually thorough study (1962), based upon depth interviews of fifteen voters chosen at random from a public housing project in a New England industrial city, presents a similar picture of limited change in a context of long-term trends in political imagery.

Asked about historical events happening in their lifetimes, such as the Spanish Civil War or the Nazi-Soviet pact, or the Korean War, which had an impact on their thinking, their response is a kind of numbed and fumbling unresponsiveness. History is a flow of events (as the news is a flow of words) that erodes a predisposition or strengthens it, or offers a rationale for it, but does not offer, without special assistance and more effort than most men can make, memorable changes in orientation. As they talk about school and favored teachers, one sees that education, too, has this same characteristic. Influence is *glacial*, not climactic (p. 376).

Some particularly dramatic instances of the relative persistence of attitudes were found in the limited effects of strategic bombing on German civilian morale, as revealed by the United States Strategic Bombing Survey (1945, pp. 95–99). Expressions of "willingness

to surrender" by the end of the war seem to have been only moderately higher among the populations of bombed communities as against the populations of unbombed ones, at levels of 58 percent and 51 percent respectively. Similarly, in heavily bombed communities, 44 percent of the population continued to demonstrate high morale, as against 42 percent in moderately bombed towns and 59 percent in unbombed towns—reminding us once more of the order of magnitude of the deterrence effect of 15 ± 3 percent.

The study by Shils and Janowitz (1948) on the unwillingness of certain German soldiers to surrender to the Allies even late in World War II also shows high resistance to both demoralizing messages and actual experiences. Although completely cut off, primary groups of ten to fifteen soldiers would refuse to surrender until their supplies were exhausted, even at the price of considerable casualties. Allied leaflets and loudspeaker communications pointing out their hopeless situation or attacking their commitment to Nazi ideology—which for many soldiers was in fact weak—had only scant results. According to Shils and Janowitz, a decisive factor keeping the small units from surrendering was the feeling of solidarity or of social support within the primary groups comprising the units. A second crucial factor was the presence in every such squad of one or two highly indoctrinated and fanatical Nazi leaders, men who were internally motivated to resist surrender. The solidarity of the primary group then served as a transmission belt or amplifier from the motivation of these leaders to the behavior of their fellows.

Factors Favoring Stability. The evidence surveyed thus far accords well with the theory of mass communications put forward by Lazarsfeld and his associates (1948, pp. 150–158), Pye (1963, pp. 24–29), Pool (1963), and others. According to this theory, mass communication is usually carried on by a two-step process to which correspond two distinct but interrelated systems of social communication. The first of these is the system of mass media—newspapers, motion pictures, radio, television, and so forth; the second is the human network of opinion leaders, formal or informal, such as bankers, lawyers, teachers, preachers, chieftains, party secretaries, shop stewards, trade union organizers, politicians, and the like, all of whom play a key role in the informal oral communication processes of the society. It is this second human network of opinion leaders that decides to a large degree about the credibility and impact of the messages of the mass media. The human network accepts or rejects these messages, passes them on or lets them die, endows them with credibility and social support or destroys them by ridicule and skepticism. The mass media in turn may increase the social status of some or all of the opinion leaders in the human network. And the functioning of a stable and mutually reinforcing feedback process between the two communication networks is an essential characteristic of a well-integrated and highly mobilized society.

It is most likely that incongruities between the external events as reported by the mass media system and the informal human networks dominating their social reception and assimilation were involved in many of the phenomena we have surveyed. The ruthless Soviet behavior in Hungary in 1956 was reported thoroughly by most of the mass media in Western Europe; but most of the Communist Party members and sympathizers belonged to relatively stable human networks, both formal and informal, that resisted these

images and encouraged the restoration of a favorable image of the Soviet Union. If this line of reasoning is sound, we should expect stability in Soviet sympathies to be directly correlated with the known strength of a pro-Communist or pro-Soviet human communications network in each country. We should thus expect the stability of pro-Soviet attitudes to be strongest in Italy, only slightly weaker in France, much weaker in West Germany, and weakest in Great Britain. This is indeed the rank order that our figures in Table 5.3 suggest. The average swings in the aggregate of favorable and neutral attitudes toward Russia were 7 percent in Italy, 9 percent in France, and 15 percent in Great Britain. The exception to the rank order is West Germany, where the swings amounted to only 7 percent, but where there was a particularly strong *anti*-Soviet human communications network of refugees and others, and where favorable or neutral attitudes toward Russia were lower to begin with. The same sort of pattern may be observed in the change from April to December 1956, presumably as a response to the Hungarian crisis.

An interesting sidelight on some of the problems involved in creating these effects is provided by Cantril's study (1958) of the "politics of despair" in postwar France and Italy. His interviews with non-Communists as well as with Communist sympathizers and party members suggest that the Soviet suppression of the Hungarian rebellion really had little impact. Cantril writes:

When we asked people in France and Italy to indicate which of several words shown them on a card (or read to them) best described *their reactions to what had happened in Hungary,* Communist sympathizers were found to have little of the indignation and sorrow that characterized the reactions of non-Communist sympathizers. Among the Communist sympathizers in France, only 3 per cent chose "indignant" or "sick at heart." In Italy, among the Communist sympathizers, the percentages for "indignant" and "sorrow" were, respectively, 19 and 16; whereas among the non-Communist public the number selecting these two words rose to 45 per cent and 35 per cent respectively (p. 185).

In choosing among possible reasons for the uprising and deciding whether the U.S.S.R. was justified in suppressing it, the Italian and French respondents answered in the same vein. But what about the Communist party members who defected in response to the Soviet actions? According to Cantril, "the overwhelming majority of these defectors still regard themselves as Marxists and will probably still vote for the Communist Party" (p. 196). He concludes:

These survey data reveal that the Hungarian revolt unquestionably was something quite different for different people. What people believed the Hungarian uprising to be apparently depended upon the particular significances they saw. And these significances were determined by the assumptions they brought to the series of happenings that constituted the uprising for them (p. 187).

These conclusions seem to be entirely in accord with the findings from the more general Western European opinion surveys from 1954 to 1961.

The same mechanism may explain the remarkable stability of American attitudes toward the Civil War, which in many communities persisted for a century. Pro-Southern attitudes especially, either in the territory of the former Confederacy itself or in the "copperhead" communities of southern Ohio and Indiana, are maintained by networks of human relations and patterns of local opinion, leadership, and community power. After studying the voting performance of Ohio counties Key (1953) reported:

Local resistance to presidential tides seems to be based on local party groupings or loyalties with impressive capacities of survival. The analysis throws no light on the nature or mechanisms of these groupings save that they seem to maintain themselves over extremely long periods of time. . . . The systematic lag between local and presidential shifts supports the inference that, at least in rural counties, presidential candidates receive little help from their fellow partisans in county organizations. County cliques save themselves rather than stem the tide against their presidential candidate (p. 532).

Key's discussion, as well as a good deal of what is known about local politics, points to the much greater importance of social support through human networks of face-to-face communications in local politics in contrast to the somewhat greater influence on the presidential vote of general issues, mass media, and the more distant personal images presented by the presidential candidates. Ohio voting patterns between 1916 and 1948 indicate the magnitude of differences between relatively stable preferences in local politics and more loosely held national alignments: In this period the percentage of Ohio counties with Democratic presidential pluralities fluctuated between 3 per cent in 1928 and 76 percent in 1936, whereas the percentage of county offices captured by Democrats fluctuated between only 18 percent and 59 percent in 1928 and 1936 respectively (see Table 5.4). The midpoint of both ranges was in the neighborhood of 39 percent, but the greater stability of local politics, in part due to the more closely knit human networks on the local level, may

TABLE 5.4
Partisanship and County Offices: Ohio and Iowa, 1920–1948*

| | A. Shifts in Votes | | | | B. Shifts in County Majorities | | | |
| | Local: Percent votes cast for Democratic gubernatorial candidate[a] | | National: Percent votes cast for Democratic presidential candidate | | Local: Democratic percentage of county offices | | National: Percent of counties with Democratic presidential pluralities | |
Year	Ohio	Iowa[b]	Ohio	Iowa	Ohio	Iowa	Ohio	Iowa
1920	45.9	38.6	38.6	25.5	20.0	L 12.0	19.0	L 0.0
1924	H 54.0	L 27.3	L 23.7	L 16.7	27.0	15.4	19.0	L 0.0
1928	44.6	37.2	34.5	37.5	L 18.0	12.9	L 3.0	6.1
1932	52.8	H 52.8	49.9	H 57.7	58.0	H 36.5	65.0	H 93.9
1936	52.0	48.7	H 58.0	54.4	H 59.0	34.8	H 76.0	81.8
1940	L 44.5	47.1	52.2	47.6	45.0	21.9	31.0	35.4
1944	51.8	43.6	49.8	47.5	31.0	16.7	16.0	33.3
1948	53.7	43.7	50.1	50.3	40.0	20.3	25.0	53.6
Range 1920–1948	49.3±4.8	40.0±12.8	40.9±17.2	37.2±20.5	38.5±20.5	24.2±12.3	39.5±36.5	47.0±47.0
Rank of stability	1	2	3	4	2	1	3	4

* Top and bottom of each range are marked by H and L respectively.

[a] Gubernatorial voting data for non-presidential years (1922, 1926, etc.) have been omitted; their inclusion would increase the range of instability only slightly (to 46.6 ± 7.1 in the case of Ohio and to 40.8 ± 13.5 in the case of Iowa), but in neither case changing the rank order of stability shown in the table.

[b] Though only Ohio data have been discussed in the text, Iowa statistics have been added in the table to show that the greater stability of local votes is not limited to a single state. It should be noted that local politics in the two states were quite different, with the Democrats at their nadir in Iowa in 1924 when they were at their peak in Ohio, but that the greater stability of local politics applies to both states. Rank-order comparisons within Parts A and B confirm our findings.

Sources of data: Key, 1953; Key, 1956; Petersen, 1963.

be seen by the fact that its range of fluctuation (41 percentage points) was 32 percentage points less than the range of fluctuation (73 percentage points) of presidential alignments.[6]

The "two-step theory" of communication flow and attitude change could also lead us to a different, and yet equally striking and expectable, effect. Since attitudes toward foreigners—particularly favorable attitudes—are not sustained ordinarily by any tightly knit and stable network of human communication and opinion leadership, they are more likely to be unstable; and the swings of likes and dislikes for each group are likely to be wider, the weaker the human links are between them and the electorate. Much of the volatility of American opinion during the period from 1935 to 1949 regarding foreign events and populations could be accounted for in this manner. Similarly, attitudes toward West Europeans should be expected to be more unstable than those toward American groups, and attitudes toward Asians more unstable than those toward West Europeans. Quantitative studies by Almond (1960) on the volatility of American foreign policy attitudes and qualitative studies by Isaacs (1962) on American images of India and China suggest that this may actually be the case. It would be interesting to investigate whether the stabilization of a foreign policy mood of Americans, noted by Almond (1960, p. xxii) for the 1950s, was also correlated with the growth of informal social support for the foreign policy attitudes and perspectives that the majority of opinion leaders had come to adopt.

Added Detail and Reduced Uncertainty

This is a subheading that needs little elaboration at this time. It is well known that the knowledge of certain historical dates increases in most populations sometime after the introduction of compulsory education; and that World War II greatly increased the geographic knowledge of a generation of Americans. In May 1945, for instance, after the spectacular invasion of Okinawa, 33 percent of American respondents knew where that small island was, whereas only 26 percent knew the location of the much larger island of Java (Cantril, 1951, p. 266). Even the names of unfamiliar alphabetic agencies or organizations become known to ever larger sections of the population—as long as their salience persists either to the population directly or to both the mass media and the human communication networks of opinion leaders.

As this last example suggests, however, increased knowledge of detail is usually associated with reduced uncertainty about details that are salient in this sense. Correct knowledge of the meaning of the abbreviation "NATO" among German voters rose from 19 percent in November 1955 to 28 percent in December 1956—an increase in cognitive knowledge to which both the delayed effects of Germany's emergence as a sovereign partner in NATO in May 1955 and the shock of the Hungarian uprising in November 1956 may have contributed (Noelle & Neumann, 1957, p. 339). A more vague familiarity with NATO increased from 73 percent in September 1956 to 75 percent in March 1957 and to 83 per-

---

[6] Computed from data in Key (1953, p. 526, Figure 1); the computation is approximate and the percentages of counties and of offices are not perfectly comparable, even though Key did compare them.

cent in October 1957—a level which was retained as late as June 1960 (DIVO, 1962, p. 36).

MAJOR EFFECTS OF EXTERNAL EVENTS ON IMAGE FORMATION AND CHANGE

Internal Reorganization

Examples abound of the process by which persons reorganize their images in the direction of greater internal consistency or in the direction of a closer and richer relationship between the image and the larger context of other cues and images. Examples of the first kind of process are given by Festinger (1962) and form the basis of his theory of cognitive dissonance. Where a major inconsistency in an image cannot be resolved, action is likely to be inhibited, as Lazarsfeld, Berelson, and others have pointed out in their discussions of cross-pressures and American voting behavior (Lazarsfeld et al., 1948, pp. 60–64; Berelson, Lazarsfeld, & McPhee, 1954, pp. 128–132, 148; Hovland, Janis, & Kelley, 1953, pp. 283–284).

Moderate contradictions, however, need not induce such inhibitory tensions or apathy. Consider, for instance, the laboratory experiments by Rosenberg, Hovland, and their associates (1960, pp. 37–53; oral communications from Rosenberg, 1961–1962). In one test, subjects originally in favor of foreign economic aid by the United States were told under hypnosis that they had a strong dislike for such aid (and ordered to forget ever having received the suggestion), without being given any cognitive material for or against foreign economic aid. Awakened from hypnosis they experienced and exhibited "sudden and intense changes in their feelings and beliefs on the foreign aid issue" and proceeded to develop elaborate rationalizations in defense of their new views. Only after the experimenter released them from posthypnotic control one week later did the subjects return to their original attitudes. It is significant, however, that the hypnotic commands did not change all aspects of the relevant images of the subjects. Of "the typical subject" in these experiments, Rosenberg wrote:

Usually some of his original beliefs persist within the new structure and are inconsistent with its overall import, though typically the intensity with which these beliefs are held is reduced after the affect manipulation. But . . . it is not assumed that total and perfect consistency need obtain in a stable attitude structure; all that is assumed is that affective-cognitive inconsistency, if present at all, is at a level below the individual's tolerance limit (Rosenberg et al., 1960, p. 45).

The Inconsistent Images as Goads to Change and as Reality Controls. A political example of the apparent toleration of persistent inconsistencies is furnished by the widespread anti-Semitic image of the Jews, who are portrayed as being at one and the same time stand-offish, clannish, and pushily eager to join the associations and social life of their non-Jewish neighbors. Detailed analysis of responses given by anti-Semites suggests how they reduce the contradiction to a tolerable level: "seclusive" or self-segregating Jewish behavior is accepted at face value, but "intrusive" or joining actions are reinterpreted not as attempts at genuine communication or give-and-take but as one-way efforts to establish dominance and power (Levinson, 1950, pp. 75–76). A particularly striking example of the resolution of conflict is furnished by the views of many American anti-Semites that, since Hitler went to such great lengths to exterminate the Jews, they must have given some good reason to "provoke" such systematic large-scale killings (Adorno, 1950, pp. 629–637).

Other examples of selective distortion that reduces flagrant inconsistencies in a political image to a tolerable level are offered by the success of Nazi propaganda in the early 1930s. This propaganda interpreted the impact of the Great Depression as the outcome of a single Jewish plutocratic-bolshevistic conspiracy utilizing equally the facilities of Wall Street and the Kremlin for the destruction of the German people. In restructuring the images of the Great Depression held by a large part of the German lower middle class, Hitler made good on his earlier claim in *Mein Kampf* that the skill of a political leader could be gauged by his ability to make two greatly dissimilar enemies appear as one and the same so as to direct the unified resentment of the people against them.

This last case illustrates a frequent sequence of the process. For such a mass response, first of all, a shattering and pervasive external event—in this case the depression of 1929–1932—was necessary. Second, it was necessary to create or coordinate the output of a set of mass communication media, such as the Hugenberg press and the well-financed publicity apparatus of the Nazi party after the middle of 1930, to disseminate certain images of this event. In the third place there had to be a suitably predisposed face-to-face network of opinion leaders (particularly among the German middle classes) to lend social support, credibility, and reinforcement to these messages and, in turn, to gain through them an enhancement of their local social and political status. And finally there had to be a group of able and dedicated political leaders who would have prepared in advance for some of the opportunities created by the situation and

who would then be prepared to exploit their opportunities with the utmost zeal and skill. These leaders restructure the images of reality offered to the population.

The Nazi leaders, however, made their images so consistent and persuasive that their success became fatal to themselves. They were masters of the short-range feedback, particularly in domestic politics. External event, mass media, opinion leaders, and top-level ideological interpretation came to form a nearly closed system even before the Nazi dictatorship could reinforce it by police control—and still more so thereafter. At no level in this system, however, were there any substantial long-distance feedbacks of communication from areas and populations outside Germany. Consequently there were no international reality controls, or only extremely feeble ones, for participants in the psychological world of Nazidom. Even the top Nazi leaders could assimilate only the most scanty information about foreign powers. They could appraise the weaknesses and follies of individual Western or Russian leaders and groups, but they remained consistently ignorant of the economic, political, and military strength of the populations and countries that they were mobilizing against themselves to an increasing degree. The Nazi system thus functioned internally as an amplifying feedback system in regard to its domestic leaders, members, and supporters, but it was precisely its success in this direction that promoted the Nazi failure to function adequately as a negative feedback system that could have avoided wrecking itself upon the realities of the outside world. If the system had received its main start from the impact of an external event—the Great Depression—then its response to that event proved within a few years to be pathological to the point of suicide.

The Nazi episode brings to mind the well-known generalizations about the connection between intolerance of ambiguity and psychic handicaps, and between excessive insistence upon consistency and paranoia. It suggests once again that a *moderate level of inconsistency may be conducive to better reality orientation and more receptivity to new information and to greater combinatorial resourcefulness.* Here we may suspect a fundamental but not unproductive contradiction between the human drive to reduce cognitive dissonance and the human need to combine and balance at almost all times a plurality of different information flows. Some of the greatest triumphs of science sprang from the desire of some man to reduce some nagging contradiction in the evidence before him; while other triumphs had their origin in human boredom with all too consistent trivialities and by the human search for new messages and new experiences even if these might contradict greatly what had been known before. The difference between the fatal and the fruitful response to inconsistencies in mental images may well come to this: whether such inconsistencies are treated as occasions for distortion and denial or as opportunities for learning.

In considering some of the major effects of external events upon image formation and change, it would be helpful to discuss the aspects of images that such events (or messages about them) may affect. The particularly relevant aspects, as will be recalled from Table 5.1, are the focus and periphery of images, cognitive and evaluative cues for image formation and change, and the impact of external events at the levels of the individual's entire personality and the culture.

Changes in the Focus and Periphery of Images. There is some evidence that the stability of attitudes and behavior is closely related to the stability of the focus of attention. The study by Shils and Janowitz (1948), cited earlier in a different context, illustrates this point. They report that relations in their small primary groups continued to occupy the focus of attention of German soldiers surrounded by Allied troops in World War II; and that, as long as such primary groups continued to include one or two indoctrinated and committed Nazis who also enjoyed close personal relations with their less politically interested fellows, unit morale tended to remain high even in hopeless military situations. According to Shils and Janowitz, Allied communications designed to encourage surrenders were relatively unsuccessful because they touched only the periphery of the German soldiers' perceptual images of their situation and thus had next to no effect on their behavior. A similar effect has been described by the German writer Gerd Gaiser (1953), a former fighter pilot in the Luftwaffe, for the pilots and personnel of a German fighter squadron in World War II. The pilots of this unit knew very well that the war was lost and that their own squadron was doomed; most of them also hated Hitler and despised the Nazi regime as criminal and contemptible. All these matters, however, were at the periphery of their attention. What was central and salient to them was their commitment to one another and to their fellow soldiers, and so they continued to fly their outmatched planes until most of them were killed. According to another German novelist, Uwe Johnson (1959), the same mechanism characterizes the decision of East German technicians to continue serving a Communist regime to which they may be opposed.

At most times domestic matters tend to be at the focus of political attention of most Americans. Congress was seen by Lane's working-class and lower middle-class informants as the center of American government and as more powerful than the President; at the same time Congress was seen as more friendly and responsive to the needs and desires of the people, and the self-interest of congressmen was believed to coincide fairly closely with the interests of the people in their districts. In contrast to "this slightly lovable venality" of Congress and its members, the President and his office are seen as somewhat awesome, and as "a strong arm against the outside world . . . a national protector" (Lane, 1962, pp. 147–152). The interviews from which these images were gathered took place during the second Eisenhower administration. During this time foreign policy matters seemed peripheral indeed to Lane's fifteen informants—who, it should be recalled, were picked by random numbers from a public housing project in the New England city of "Eastport." Although references to Mussolini, the bombing of Hiroshima, and the Korean War occur in Lane's materials, only the Hiroshima bombing seems to have been the subject of extended comments. Less dramatic foreign policy issues of the 1950s, such as Germany, Berlin, the Hungarian uprising and the Suez crisis of 1956, the Soviet launching of Sputnik and the beginning of the dramatic space race in 1957, the Iraq crisis and the landing of American and British troops in Lebanon and Jordan in 1958, and the Tibetan uprising against the Chinese Communists in 1959, are not mentioned in the index. On the other hand, the respondents of "Eastport" were aware of the contest between the United States and

Russia and of the need for national defense, and they were concerned about the lags in American technology revealed by the Sputnik affair. There were more references to foreign affairs in the unpublished interview transcripts, but, for perhaps thirteen of the fifteen respondents, national affairs and particularly the state of the national economy clearly ranked ahead of specific foreign problems, in contrast to the general United States contest with communism, Russia, Red China, and Cuba, and to the interest of some respondents in the old country from which their families had come (communication with Robert E. Lane, 16 May, 1964).

External events, however, have produced substantial shifts in the focus of attention in the past and may well do so again in the future. During the era of Franklin D. Roosevelt, only 14 percent of the respondents to a public opinion survey in January 1939 named foreign policy issues as the most important problems facing the American people. For four such polls between November 1935 and January 1939, an average of less than 19 percent of the respondents held this view. The salience of foreign policy issues then rose to 35 percent in April 1939 and, after the outbreak of the European War in September of that year, foreign problems seemed most vital to 47 percent in December 1939 and 48 percent in August 1940, in the summer of the Battle of Britain. After World War II, under the presidency of Harry S. Truman, twelve opinion polls between February 1946 and October 1949 showed an average of 36 percent of the respondents holding foreign policy issues to be most vital, even though this view fluctuated widely between a low of 11 percent in June 1946 and a high of 73 percent in April 1948, after the coup in Czechoslovakia and during the debate in America over the Marshall Plan; by October 1949, however, primary attention to foreign policy had fallen again somewhat below the average level to 34 percent (Almond, 1960, p. 73).

Foreign policy interest increased only slightly in the course of the following decade. During the last years of the Eisenhower administration, seven polls between January 1958 and October 1960 showed a primary interest in foreign policy for an average of 40 percent of the respondents, rising from a low of 17 percent in May 1958 to a high of 70 percent in October 1960 in the final phase of the presidential campaign with its debate over the state of American prestige abroad and over American policies toward the communist regime in Cuba. By contrast to the 1950s, the Kennedy administration found for the first time what seemed to be a stabilization of primary foreign policy interest at a new high level. In five polls between March 1961 and October 1963 foreign policy issues were of primary interest to an average of 54 percent of the respondents; the fluctuations were somewhat less than in the preceding periods surveyed, and the low of 25 percent in October 1963—reporting responses given in the previous month and reflecting the pre-emption of attention by the domestic racial agitation and the civil rights march on Washington in late August—was still considerably higher than the previous lows of 1935, 1946, and 1958 (AIPO, 23 March, 1958; 1 October, 1958; 27 February, 1959; 16 October, 1959; 15 March, 1961; 29 April, 1962; 26 September, 1962; 3 April, 1963; 2 October, 1963).

If one accepts the evidence of these figures for a long-run shift in the average level of American foreign policy attention during the last three decades, it follows that the image of the presidency is likely to remain more central

in the focus of political attention also on this account. Taken together with Lane's findings, the opinion data suggest that Congress would have to change its public image in order to gain public support for an active congressional role in foreign policy-making.

Generally, minor and isolated upsets in foreign policy do not change the focus of attention, but the cumulative effect of repeated conflicts may do so, and so could more briefly the impact of short-lived spectacular crises, such as the one that preceded the adoption of the Marshall Plan in 1948.

A more subtle shift between the center and the periphery of people's general image of the world may also be brought about by spectacular events. Lifton's study (1963) on the psychological impact of the bombing of Hiroshima upon the survivors in that city offers a striking example. Ordinarily, Lifton suggests, the ever-present possibility or probability of death surrounding human life is kept at the periphery of our attention, if it is not repressed more thoroughly. Similarly, an attitude of basic trust, that is, a diffuse image of a not-unfriendly human and nonhuman environment, seems to be part of the periphery of the world image of most individuals in technologically advanced modern civilizations. For the survivors of the bombing, according to Lifton, the presence of death has moved permanently into the focus of attention, while its counterpart—the peripheral image of a world deserving basic trust—has been destroyed. Perhaps something similar has been reported about the psychological situation of important groups of the population on the eve of sweeping social changes and major social revolutions. *Memento mori* was a slogan of what has been called the Cluniac Revolution of the Middle Ages, and similar images of the death of the "old Adam," the old order, have appeared in many revolutionary movements. Likewise, a feeling of a "great fear," a loss of basic trust in the old order, seems to characterize the mood prevailing in certain early stages of such revolutions (Rosenstock-Huessy, 1931 and 1938).

Changes in Cognitive Cues and Evaluative Cues. These two kinds of cues are often interdependent. Thus cognitive cues on the "friend–enemy" dimension often are associated with changes in the evaluative "good–bad" aspects of the image. For instance, knowledge of actual Nazi atrocities in the death camps, revealed by the Allied conquest of Germany between March and May 1945, seems to have increased by 16 percent the proportion of Americans holding unfavorable views of Germans. The number of those who attributed responsibility or co-responsibility for these atrocities to the German people rose from 40 percent in September 1944 to 56 percent in July 1945 (Cantril, 1951, p. 1070). Interestingly enough, however, the number of Americans who agreed that "the German people will always want to go to war to make themselves as powerful as possible," rose only slowly through a total range of 18 percentage points—from 21 percent in February 1942 to 27 percent in late November 1944, jumping to 35 percent in December 1944 and then climbing only a little to 39 percent in July 1945, dropping again to 30 and 31 percent in November 1945 and May 1946 respectively (Cantril, 1951, p. 500). These findings suggest that the German Rundstedt offensive of early December 1944 may have had an even stronger effect upon American opinion than did the later knowledge of the atrocities.

Presumably under the impact of the Japanese attack upon Pearl Harbor, a much higher proportion of Americans imputed this same kind of aggressiveness to the Japanese people. The number of Americans holding this view— 41 percent as early as February 1942— rose by 16 percentage points to 57 percent in June 1943. By July 1945 this number had receded to 52 percent and, after the atomic destruction of Hiroshima and the Japanese surrender, dropped still further to 45 percent in November 1945 and to 35 percent in May 1946 (Cantril, 1951, p. 501). The greater stability of attitudes toward Germany as contrasted to the shifting American image of the Japanese people correlates well with the greater amount of social support available among the American public for both negative and positive views about Germany together with the relative absence of such support for either kind of view about Japan. This in turn would seem to agree with the two-step theory of communication and image maintenance that was discussed earlier.

Since messages about external events, rather than any event itself, often bring about changes in the value content of an image, messages about events that did not in fact occur can produce sizable results. A well-known example of such an image change took place during World War I, when widely publicized accounts of alleged German massacres of Belgian children significantly changed the value content of British and American images of Germans (Lasswell, 1938, p. 207).

Actual contact with events may produce similar results. Personal experiences in wartime, particularly the cumulative deprivations of prolonged warfare, can decisively change the value content of images of war. In a qualitative sense this has been documented in studies of the deteriorating morale of armies and populations subject to the attrition of World War I (Schuhmacher, 1928). Similarly, among American soldiers tested in the closing stages of World War II, in June 1945, roughly one half of the fresh replacements arriving in the central Pacific showed a critical level of anxiety without in fact having seen combat; among veteran replacements returning to combat after hospitalization, the percentage of those with at least the same anxiety level ranged between 71 and 86 percent, depending upon education. For the age group between 20 and 24, the experience of combat seemed to increase the share of those with acute signs of anxiety by an average of over 30 percentage points (Stouffer et al., 1949, p. 446). Several years after the war experience, in 1954, 64 percent of the respondents in a German survey described either the war (36 percent) or the immediate postwar period (28 percent) as the most difficult time of their lives (Fröhner, von Stackelberg, & Eser, 1956, pp. 322–326, 439–440).

It is rare that changes in cognitive cues can be separated from changes in evaluative ones, particularly in ex post facto analyses of published material or of opinion surveys of the usual type. In future surveys, however, the technique of Osgood's semantic differential (Osgood, Suci, & Tannenbaum, 1957)—which permits the separation of the "good–bad" dimension from such other dimensions as "strong–weak," "active–passive," and the like—might be adapted to this purpose.

An early application of this approach by Holsti (1962) to more than 3500 statements by the late John Foster Dulles shows that evaluative aspects of that statesman's image of the U.S.S.R. coded on a "good–bad" dimension varied only one fourth as much as his cognitive perceptions of Soviet capabilities and policy intentions. Despite the well-known tendency for people to distort their own perceptions so as to reduce the cognitive dissonance between their knowledge and their preferences, Holsti's data do suggest a limited but significant degree of independence between the two types of cues.

Large-scale survey data from the German Federal Republic likewise show a considerable degree of independence between cognitive and evaluative aspects of foreign policy images. Thus the number of Germans who believed that the United States was militarily stronger than the Soviet Union dropped between 1957 and 1961 from 38 to 26 percent, but the proportion of Germans who felt that their country should side with the United States rose from 63 to 77 percent during the same years (Puchala, 1964, pp. 6, 23; USIA, 1961, p. 14).

A historical example of unchanged evaluative cues together with a dramatic change in cognitive cues may be found in General S. L. A. Marshall's account (1953) of General MacArthur's disastrous advance to the Yalu River in the fall of 1950 and MacArthur's belated discovery of a strong Chinese Communist army in his rear: General MacArthur presumably considered Chinese Communists as enemies both before and after this discovery, but his statement "This is entirely a new war" showed how drastically he had to revise his factual notions both of their intentions and their capabilities.[7]

In many situations, overly familiar cognitive cues mask the evaluative content of current perceptions as well as of long-held images. This is a process that

---

[7] A nonhuman example of the failure of cognitive cues has been offered by Stevens (1963) in his summary of recent studies of the ways in which whales get stranded on gently sloping beaches which fail to reflect back the sonar-like waves emitted by whales and thus leave the animals without cues about their proximity to dangerously shallow water.

produces emotional numbing or callousness, similar to the psychic closure reported by Lifton and discussed in a different context above. Well-known examples are the ways in which rich people often claim that the poor are "used to" their poverty or in which many Southern whites believe that the Negroes in their communities accept and even like the traditional way in which they have been treated (Hunter, 1963). An imaginative countermeasure designed to make again salient the value aspects of an overly familiar image has been developed by creative writers through what Bertolt Brecht (1957) has called the *Verfremdungseffekt*, or the method of representational estrangement. This is a technique of making the familiar appear strange and fresh again by presenting it vividly in unfamiliar guise, and thus to restore its emotional impact upon the reader or beholder. As early as the seventeenth century, it must be added, Jonathan Swift used a similar technique; and it was a widely used device among French satirists in the eighteenth century.

More frequent are the cases in which interpretive cues have both cognitive and evaluative implications. External events may change the cognitive cues by which an image is interpreted in terms of the "friend–enemy" relationship. This in turn may then change the evaluative content of the image. A study by Kriesberg (1946) of Soviet news presented in the *New York Times* during eight test periods between 1917 and 1946 may illustrate the process. Kriesberg computed for each of these periods a score of general attention paid to the Soviet Union as well as a score of unfriendly attention and a percentage ratio of the latter to the former. He reported an average of 50 percent of unfriendly attention for the total of 118 weeks that made up his eight test periods, with fluctuations of about 22 percentage points upward or down-

ward of this average following closely upon the particular external events that made the Soviet Union appear as an adversary or ally in each period. Kriesberg's data, as reported in Table 5.5, thus show both the predominantly unfavorable image of the Soviet Union at all times as well as the magnitude of the shifts produced in the image by changes in international alignments.

Suggestive qualitative examples for earlier favorable changes in foreign images of Russia have been presented by Braunthal (1946) for the French press after the Franco-Russian alliance of 1890 and by Dorothy Brewster (1948) for English literary criticism during the decade of mounting Anglo-German rivalry after 1901 and of the Anglo-Russian agreement of 1907. A still earlier example of a favorable change in the image of the Turkish sultan as presented by the English press has been carefully documented by Martin (1924) for the eve of the Crimean War.

Australian politics in 1950 offered a striking example on the level of mass opinion:

During a period of much agitation about the dangers of the Communist party, a Gallup Poll survey reported that 80 per cent of the electorate favored outlawing the Communists. Shortly after this survey, the Conservative government submitted a proposal to outlaw the party to referendum. During the referendum electoral campaign, the Labor party and the trade unions came out vigorously against the proposal. Considerable shifting took place after this, to the point that the measure to outlaw the Communists was actually defeated by a small majority, and Catholic workers who had overwhelmingly favored the outlaw measure when first questioned by the Gallup Poll eventually followed the advice of their party and unions and voted against it (Lipset, 1960, p. 128, citing Webb, 1955).

TABLE 5.5

News of the U.S.S.R. in the New York Times, 1917–1946

Period		Number of weeks in period	Average total attention score[a]	Average anti-Soviet attention score[a]	Average percent, anti-Soviet to total	Dominant characteristic of period
Dec 1917–Apr	1918	19	30.2	20.2	66.9%	Brest-Litovsk Treaty
Apr 1935–Jun	1935	12	10.0	3.1	31.0	Collective security pacts
Aug 1935–Nov	1935	14	9.5	4.8	50.5	US–USSR diplomatic exchange
Dec 1936–Mar	1937	11	12.5	6.5	52.0	Treason trials begin in USSR
Apr 1937–Jun	1937	10	15.2	9.4	61.8	Soviet aid to Spanish Loyalists
Jun 1939–Oct	1939	16	20.6	13.7	66.5	Pact with Germany; invasion of Poland
Aug 1942–Jan	1943	21	32.0	9.1	28.4	USSR takes offensive on Eastern Front
Apr 1945–Jun	1945	10	40.4	15.7	38.9	USSR takes Berlin; UN conference
Apr 1946–May	1946	5	36.4	26.4	72.5	Paris Conference; deadlock on Trieste
TOTAL PERIOD		118	22.9	11.5	50.2%	

[a] Number of items weighted according to position in newspaper.

Source of data: Kriesberg, 1946, pp. 552–557.

In the Australian example, a proposed repressive measure became unpopular when it was opposed by the Labour party and trade unions, whom many workers considered their friends, and when it acquired in this manner an unfavorable evaluative context.

A Special Case: Dehumanized Images of Targets and Victims. The converse of this effect has also been reported. A severely repressive measure, which individuals might ordinarily oppose, can be made palatable to many of them if the image of its victims can be stripped of human detail and its evaluative connotations. In a series of experiments Milgram (1963) and his associates at Yale University induced the real subjects of their experiments to act in good faith as experimenters who were to test the effect of severe punishment on learning and who for this purpose were to push buttons administering increasingly severe electric shocks whenever the apparent subject of the "learning experiment" was making a mistake. The pushing of the "moderate shock" buttons was followed by realistic exhibitions of pain by the apparent subjects, who in some cases had told the naive "experimenters" that they suffered from severe heart conditions. About two thirds of the naive "experimenters" continued nonetheless to push buttons inflicting increasingly severe punishment upon the groaning victims, as instructed by the supervisors. They were found to be more willing to do so, however, if their victims were behind screens or one-way glass that greatly reduced the amount of human communication between "punishers" and "victims."

The Milgram experiments suggest the interplay of at least three factors. In a few of the naive "experimenters" they uncovered a streak of genuine sadism in their personalities which had been unknown even to themselves. All

the experiments showed the importance of social support, since the naive "experimenter" believed himself to be taking part in a legitimate experimental situation and was being reassured of the legitimacy of his actions by the name of Yale University and the presence of the supervisors. Finally, there was the dehumanizing effect of social and communicative distance between the naive "experimenter" and his "victim." It is to be hoped that eventually sufficient data will become available from experiments of this kind—performed, of course, under appropriate safeguards—to permit a quantitative appraisal of the contribution of each of these three factors as well as, perhaps, of others to the observed outcome.

A similar effect may have occurred quickly and on a large scale when pilots saw the image of the civilian population of enemy cities reduced to tiny dots in their bombsights or their radar screens. Cecil Day-Lewis (1954), in a poem, envisions Perseus as using a similar device to withstand the sight of the face of Medusa, writhing "like a furious ant-hill," whose aspect turned ordinary men to stone. Looking at her through the hollow of his shield, he saw her small and distant though still with precision and thus "pitying perhaps, he struck."

Sometimes the impoverishment of human associations and the removal of evaluative cues occur in an entire population in a gradual process. Thus there was scant popular acceptance in the Germany of 1933 and 1934 of outright cruelties inflicted upon Jews, who were still perceived as neighbors and as familiar human beings. But there was far more acceptance of such treatment of the same Jews from 1936 onwards, after they had been removed from their homes and deprived of their citizenship, their possessions, and much of their human context by a long sequence of Nazi measures, which in this manner prepared among Germans the psychological grounds for the widespread passive acceptance of their physical extermination (Riess, 1961). A lesser but not wholly dissimilar process of step-by-step dehumanization of the image of the enemy occurred among the populations of the Allied countries, and even, according to a recent study (Batchelder, 1962), among their moral theologians. Between 1938 and 1940 these men had protested against the killing of women and children in the Nazi air bombardments of Warsaw and Rotterdam, and later on of Coventry, but by 1942 many of them were beginning to accept the supposed military necessity of Allied "area bombardment" of German and Japanese cities, which claimed for the most part clearly civilian victims, and whose military effects were found after the war to have been scanty indeed. By 1944 and 1945 such bombardments of civilian populations—which Winston Churchill himself called "terror bombings" in a widely discussed memorandum—were tolerated by the preponderant part of Allied public opinion, both clerical and secular. Thus the psychological conditions were created for the widespread acceptance of the use of atom bombs against the cities of Hiroshima and Nagasaki, where they claimed predominantly civilian victims. The study comes to the conclusion that this use of weapons would have been unacceptable to British and American opinion in 1938 but that it took the cumulative effects of several years of war, and of the psychological dehumanization of the image of the enemy populations, to make possible the use of such weapons in 1945.

The Impact of External Events at the Level of the Entire Personality. External events are more likely to change particular images than to change the entire context of such images at the level of the personality as a whole. Nonetheless external events might change so many images that their cumulative effect can lead to a recognizable change in the personalities of individuals or the culture of groups. Thus a "Berliner" type of personality has emerged among the population of postwar West Berlin, which is in some ways rather different from the Berliner of prewar days as well as from the contemporary populations of large cities in West Germany. Opinion polls show the West Berliners to be far more intensely political and far less likely to admit to indifference or ignorance than are their metropolitan contemporaries in West Germany. Surveys conducted by the United States Army and private German polling agencies from 1946 to 1963 reveal that the proportion of West Berliners expressing "no opinion" in response to survey questions ranged between 5 and 15 percentage points less than the comparable proportion of respondents in other large West German cities (Merritt, 1965a). Berliners are far more militantly pro-Western, more intensely preoccupied with their own role and—even now, after the building of the Berlin Wall—with events in Communist-ruled East Germany. On nonpolitical matters, the views of West Berliners show the same distributions as those of their West German counterparts. In regard to politics, however, they have added a conscious self-image to their differences in attitudes and behavior. They see themselves as more aware, more tense, more committed, and more valuable in contrast to the West German *Bundesbürger* —whose name they pronounce with some of the connotations of "federal bourgeois" and whom they view as selfish, fat, complacent, timid, and out of touch with all the things that really matter (Weyrauch, 1961). It is a stereotype that bears a striking resemblance to the older one that many Germans between the two world wars affected to entertain in regard to the Swiss; moreover, it may have a similar function of defending the self-image of those who profess it.

If some aspects of the personalities of West Berliners seem to have been formed by their confinement to an uniquely secluded and beleaguered city, in many countries of the world human personalities are being changed by the cumulative impact of modern communication, monetization, and technology and by the unceasing exposure to new experiences and wider horizons that these changes bring. Lerner (1958) has summarized studies by himself and others that document the "constrictive self" of men who were still living in a traditional "courage culture," incurious toward knowledge and inhospitable toward change; and he has described the transition to the "ingenuity culture" of modern men:

> In the Modern milieu a man gets on by his wits in new opportunities, not by his inertia in familiar routines. In the perceptual apparatus of Modern men, all scales are in principle infinite until proved otherwise. He locates himself not at some fixed point in the rank-order of things known, but at some moving point of desire in a scale of things imagined (p. 134).

Specific efforts to manipulate the personality of individuals by severe deprivations applied in a crude or subtle manner, or by means of drugs or hypnosis, or by means of prolonged isolation or of overwhelming social group pressure, or by any combination of these, have relatively shallow and short-lived effects. They may do lasting damage to some of their victims, but they are extremely unlikely to produce lasting reorganization of a personality at the same level of mental and psychological capabilities; and even the pieces

of information extracted by such methods are notoriously unreliable (Lifton, 1961; Biderman & Zimmer, 1961; Kubzansky, 1961; Rosenberg *et al.*, 1960).

The most fundamental effect of external events upon individual personalities is likely to be indirect, at two removes. Such events not only affect gradually the periphery of their own images and memories during their adult life but also, at an earlier stage, the images, outlook, and behavior of their parents, and hence their own childhood experiences. Erikson (1958) has demonstrated this aptly by tracing how the social tensions and changes of late fifteenth-century Germany influenced the atmosphere in young Martin Luther's household.

In this manner external events may affect, quickly or more often gradually, an entire culture, including the ways in which children are raised and the experiences against which some of them later will react. Many writers have commented upon the striking similarity between the gregarious and equalitarian Americans of the age of Alexander de Tocqueville and their perceptive and other-directed successors in the age of David Riesman. What seems to have been commented upon less often is the intervention of at least two generations of "inner-directed" Americans from Andrew Johnson to Herbert Hoover. These generations stood under the impact of the examples of the great generals of the Civil War, steadfast under adversity and almost unyielding to criticism. The lesson was reinforced in later decades by the spectacular rise of the great barons of industry and finance of the type of Commodore Vanderbilt, Andrew Carnegie, John D. Rockefeller, and J. P. Morgan, whose single-minded concentration on their own goals and policies often made them impervious to the clamor of their competitors and their countrymen. Eventually the situation corrected itself. The populist revolt and the reform movement of the late nineteenth and early twentieth centuries eventually changed the atmosphere, although these movements were often led by men with personality types similar to those of the industrialists and financiers whom they attacked. The financiers in turn emphasized their interest in the welfare of the community, and an era of philanthropy and the establishment of the large foundations pointed toward a development beyond the bitter conflicts of the previous decades. Nonetheless, important aspects of American culture may have been more inner-directed, and perhaps authoritarian, in style and character between 1860 and 1910 than they were in the half centuries before and after. Woodrow Wilson, born in 1856, grew to manhood during these authoritarian decades as the son of a Presbyterian minister; and a recent study by Alexander and Juliette George (1956; cf. also Brodie, 1963) suggests that much of his personality and later behavior were determined by his need to react with an unperceptive and ineffective blend of self-justification and defiance against sarcastic older critics such as his father, Dean West at Princeton University, and Senator Henry Cabot Lodge. To be sure, not all men growing up in those years shared the experiences or showed the personality pattern of Woodrow Wilson. All that can be said plausibly is that such experiences and such personality types were more likely to occur at that period than in a later age when other external events, including a world war as well as the cumulative impact of many lesser changes, had brought about a major shift in American culture.

Changes in Culture. External events may have a variety of effects upon cultures. They may reinforce a culture, making it more resistant to future change than it otherwise might have been. They may clarify or decide contradictions or conflicts between different images, values, tendencies, or trends of behavior present in the old culture as it existed before the impact of the new events. They may accelerate or retard existing processes of change. By changing cognitive or evaluative cues, they may change the value orientations prevailing in the culture; or they may reorganize important parts of its cognitive content by reorganizing either the connections and compatibilities between different elements of the culture or else by changing major proportions between them, by making some elements relatively much larger or smaller, or stronger or weaker, than they had been before. External events could also change the importance of a culture at large for the behavior of smaller groups or even for the personalities and actions of individuals, for instance, by increasing or decreasing the amount of variance or deviance permitted for individuals and groups.

Much of culture change has certain general characteristics in common. According to Lane's "theory of ideological change" (1962, pp. 422–427), ideologies—and similar image systems—are most likely to be selected from a range of available alternatives in terms of their *function* in serving the needs of individuals and groups for orientation, goal-attainment, adjustment to others, and expression of existing psychic needs and tensions. They are also selected on the basis of their *congruence*—or cognitive consonance—with the experiences of individuals and groups, as well as with the images, ideas, and values already held by them; and with the unconscious needs and drives of individuals as they have developed in their particular culture, and also with their conscious programs for individual behavior and group action. According to Kluckhohn and Strodtbeck (1961, p.

45), cultures are less likely to change the greater the conformity that prevails in them, both in regard to value orientations, images, and symbols and to the conduct of groups and individuals. Conversely, cultures or parts of cultures are the more susceptible to change the greater the amount of variance or deviance that already exists within them. It is the variations in images and in behavior that provide the fertile soil for the seeds of change brought into the culture by the impact of outside events; and it is the variant or deviant persons in the culture who most often function as the innovators. This connection between variations within a culture and its capacity for learning and innovation echoes the similar relation between inconsistencies of images and the reality controls and learning capacity of the persons holding them.

In the light of these general characteristics it seems clear that even very powerful governments by themselves cannot manufacture major culture changes. Indeed, insofar as strong governments derive their power from the habits of conformity and obedience among their subjects, their very strength would make basic culture change more difficult. Even the modernizing dictatorships of Soviet Russia and Communist China, as well as the modernizing regime of Mustapha Kemal in Turkey, all had to find their main support within their countries. They had to base themselves upon at least some existing trends within their national societies and cultures, as well as upon the aspirations and interests of individuals, groups, and classes within their countries. *Only within the limits of these cultural and political givens have governments been able to control or at least influence the impact of external events upon their national culture.* They have done this most often by cutting down the reception of the flow of information and images from the outside world, by subjecting this flow to more or less rigorous screening and selection, but also at times by deliberately increasing national attention and receptivity to certain classes of external events so as to make their images loom larger in the national culture.

In this manner a government can make the national culture more national or more international, even within the limits of the officially preferred ideology or creed. If one considers the May Day slogans of the Communist Party of the U.S.S.R. as reasonably representative of a major aspect of Soviet culture, then it is interesting to note that the ratio of domestic-national slogans to international ones averaged about .9 from 1918 to 1925, but rose to more than 2.1 in 1926 and then to 3.4 in 1928, and remained at or above that level until 1939 when it stood at 4.5; thereafter it rose rapidly, from 6.6 in 1940 to a peak of 10.8 in 1946, and then declined to 6.8 in 1948, rose once more to 9.4 in 1949, and then declined swiftly to 4.0 in 1950, 3.4 in the two following years, and 2.5 in 1953, the year of Stalin's death. By April 1957, half a year before Sputnik, the ratio had declined to 1.4; and by 1961 it had further declined to 1.1, close to the level of the early 1920s. Thus, in that part of Russian political culture indicated by the May Day slogans, domestic affairs have loomed about as large as international affairs in the early 1920s and the early 1960s, while national concerns have outweighed international ones by ratios of 9 to 1 and 10 to 1 during much of the 1940s (Stafford & Flick, 1962). Changes of this magnitude suggest at least some of the changes that Soviet culture underwent up to the peak of the Stalin period in the late 1940s and perhaps some of the changes back toward a more international outlook since that time.

Spectacular events that are neither under the control of the government nor reinforced by its action, and that are not reinforced by the cumulative impact of smaller events, as a rule produce no major long-run change in the imagery and culture of large populations. The Lisbon earthquake in 1755 did not shake the basic outlook of the Age of Reason though it seems to have helped to discredit further the optimism of Leibniz in the eyes of Voltaire (1956). The spectacular assassinations of Presidents Garfield, McKinley, and Kennedy, which were not reinforced by other trends in the society, produced no major change in the political culture of the United States, nor in the continuing and conspicuous exposure of American presidents to hazards of this kind. (Even one of the most spectacular events ever reported in the Scriptures, the Flood, does not seem to have been reinforced in its impact by any cultural trend in Noah's family, and does not seem to have been followed by any major improvement in the moral behavior of most of Noah's descendants.)

The impact of cumulative events, however, can change a large culture, even without major reinforcement from governments or spectacular events. The cultural effects of the Industrial Revolution in many countries are an example of just this kind of process, and so are the effects of many of the broader processes of social mobilization (Ashton, 1948; Redford, 1936; Clapham, 1926; Deutsch, 1953; Deutsch, 1961; Russett et al., 1964; Merritt & Rokkan, 1965). A related example is the rise of the political subculture of the labor movement in many industrializing countries (Braunthal, 1961). Still another example is the development of an American culture and national character under the cumulative impact of economic abundance (Potter, 1954).

It is difficult to say much about the length of time over which cumulative changes have to pile up before producing a major change in the images and attitudes held by large numbers of people. The historical cases that can readily be recalled—some of which have been cited above and elsewhere in this study—tend to have ranged between at least fifteen and one hundred years, with many cases clustering about a mode of twenty-five to thirty years, that is, approximately one biological generation or two quasi-generations in bureaucracy, politics, and intellectual life.

Our three kinds of external events—government-induced, spectacular, and cumulative—need not operate in isolation. Governments can create spectacular events. The government of Colonel Nasser did so in 1954 when it nationalized the Suez Canal, and so did the government of Mr. Anthony Eden when it embarked upon the abortive Suez War two years later. The French government likewise helped to create spectacular events when it entered upon its wars in Indo-China and Algeria. In each of the last three cases the European governments concerned presented images of crucial national dependence upon some of the territories in question in the disputes. The Suez Canal in 1956 was presented by government quarters and by a part of the British press as "the jugular vein" of the Commonwealth. The French government made valiant efforts to conjure up an image of vast oil riches in the Sahara, the gain or loss of which would do much to decide the economic future of the French people. In the years after 1946 the Indo-China war was first presented by the French government as a mopping-up operation against local disorder; and later on as a war for the "integrity of the French Union" in which a bold strategy in accordance with the plan of General Navarre would lead to victory (Rosenbaum, 1958). Ultimately none of these government-influenced events and images prevailed against the cumulative pressure of mounting external difficulties and increasing domestic distaste. In each of these three cases of failure, governments had to contend with a highly resistant environment abroad and a divided society at home. Where, however, the spectacular action of a government paralleled a predominant trend within its own society and at the same time did not encounter frustrating difficulties in the international environment, it could indeed reinforce and restructure major images of a large part of the population. This may have happened in the case of President Jefferson's purchase of the Louisiana Territory, which strengthened the long-held popular image of the United States as a continental power. Nearly one and a half centuries later the explosion of nuclear weapons by the United States government greatly reinforced the image of the United States as a world-dominating power—an image held by many Americans for at least another decade and which was widely, though more briefly, accepted abroad. During that decade many Americans intently discussed how their government had "lost China," and by the mid-1950s they still had to be cautioned by a perceptive British critic against the "myth of American omnipotence" (Brogan, 1954). Not much later, the Soviet government initiated a series of spectacular events by demonstrating intercontinental rockets in 1956 and globe-circling satellites in 1957, to be followed in due course by successive—and successful—displays of space dogs, spacemen, space girls, and space rendezvous, all of which produced a temporary image of Soviet superiority and of an American "missile gap" until the early 1960s. Whether the effects of these spectacular events

will fade again, or whether they will be reinforced by already existing popular images and attitudes, and by the continuing impact of cumulative events, seems uncertain but may well vary from country to country.

A government is likely to be more effective in changing the images held by its citizens if it can change the impact of cumulative events upon them. Just this is one of the functions of a great deal of legislation. It is a tradition of political philosophy that a legislator is inevitably an educator of his people. The governmental decisions in favor of forced-pace industrialization in the U.S.S.R. and the less drastic decisions in favor of modernization of many aspects of Turkish life in the 1920s are cases in point.

In its own way the 1954 decision of the United States Supreme Court in the case of *Brown vs. Board of Education* and the stream of subsequent integration decisions and experiences that followed upon this precedent contributed significantly to a changed image of the legitimacy of interracial practices in the United States and to a change in the political climate of the United States. In 1954 President Eisenhower himself did not consider it wise to give any public personal support to the rightness of the Court's decision and he implied plainly that the slower pace of integration would seem to him the wiser one. Two years later seven out of ten voters preferred "a gradual approach to the problem of integration"; and in the South only 45 percent believed that integration would ever come. By July 1963 nearly twice as many southern voters—83 percent—believed that integration would come "some day" and 49 percent expected it to come within five years. In October 1963 throughout the nation 46 percent of the voters felt that integration was moving too fast while 43 percent thought that its pace was "about right" or "not fast enough." In the same month the percentage of voters approving the way in which President Kennedy was handling his job stood at 59 percent in the nation as a whole, 85 percent among Negro voters, and at 51 percent in the South, with only 31 percent disapproving of him even in that region (AIPO, 29 August, 1958; 28 June, 1961; 30 May, 1962; 16 June, 1963; 14 July, 1963; 11 August, 1963; 11 September, 1963; 13 October, 1963; 10 and 20 November, 1963). A combination of mounting Negro pressure and of cumulative experiences of government-backed increments in integration had produced a substantial change in the political climate of the country. The impact of President Kennedy's assassination and the impact of the political leadership succeeding him would inevitably be superimposed upon this longer trend, and the combined effect of the succession of judicial and political leadership from 1954 to 1964 remains to be seen. Yet a comparison of the outspoken statement on integration by President Lyndon B. Johnson, himself a Texan, with the cautious utterances of President Eisenhower in 1954 indicates the distance that the country has traveled.[8]

Spectacular events uncontrolled by governments have their strongest impact when they are superimposed upon an existing cumulative trend. Thus the Stamp Act crisis of 1765 dramatized and accelerated an already existing trend in the American colonies toward American self-consciousness and inter-colonial cooperation (Merritt, 1965b). The impact of money and modernity brought by World War II to certain South Pacific Islands substantially increased the processes of cultural change already at work among the native popu-

lations (Mead, 1956). The extreme insecurity experienced by young Germans toward the end of World War II and in the period immediately thereafter appears to have enhanced the trend away from ideologies and toward a greater concern with personal security which had been found at work in many industrial societies (Baumert, 1952, pp. 174–176; Sower et al., 1949, Appendix, Table 35; Schelsky, 1957; Lasswell, 1935; Schumpeter, 1963, pp. 143–163, 419–425). The nuclear explosion at Hiroshima greatly accelerated the increasing impression of defeat among the Japanese people; it may possibly have accelerated their revulsion from the warlike culture and tradition represented by their military rulers who had taken them into the war. In all these cases the combination of spectacular and cumulative events seems to have done more to bring about culture change than either element might have done singly, but the impression remains that the cumulative trend was the more important partner in the combination.

Governments or political leaders can add with considerable effect their own deliberate efforts to the combined impact of cumulative trends and spectacular events. Here we find the examples of great leaders in wars, revolutions, or the emergence of new states. They are often backed by the cumulative impact of events that strengthen their side in the conflict; they take advantage of spectacular events that help to break down past habits and traditions and leave populations in search of orientation and leadership; and they offer themselves as leaders, symbols, and selective re-interpreters of these trends and events until they appear in the role of charismatic leaders—a role that is

---

[8] Consider, for example, President Johnson's first address to Congress on November 27, 1963, when he said: ". . . no memorial oration or eulogy could more eloquently honor President Kennedy's memory than the earliest possible passage of the Civil Rights bill for which he fought" (*New York Times*, 28 November, 1963, p. 20).

sometimes created not so much by their own efforts as by the exigencies of the situation and the expectations of their fellows (Lipset, 1963, pp. 16–23, 315–316). Churchill and Roosevelt in World War II, Gandhi and Nehru in India's rise to independence, Lenin and Stalin in the Russian Revolution and forced industrialization, Sun Yat Sen in China, Thomas G. Masaryk in Czechoslovakia at the end of World War I, Atatürk in Turkey, Nasser in Egypt, Nkrumah in Ghana, and, last but not least, George Washington and Abraham Lincoln in the United States are all examples of the images and personalities of outstanding leaders who shape and interpret the impact of spectacular events in ages of rapid cumulative change.

In less dramatic fashion, governments may add their deliberate efforts to the impact of dramatic events in order to accelerate existing trends. This may have been done by both the American and the Soviet governments in 1955 when each of them encouraged in its own country the giving of wide publicity to the vast destructive potentialities of the new hydrogen weapons held by both, and thus accelerated the trend of public opinion in both countries away from the dangerously high level of tension in the years during and after the Korean War.

Finally, in the larger process of cultural change all these factors are likely to come together. In the course of two or three generations cumulative trends, spectacular events, and the deliberate policies of governments and leaders all may combine to produce major changes in the national culture. When Frederick Lewis Allen (1952) spoke of "the big change" in American culture between 1900 and 1950, he was describing the

results of such a combination of processes. And so did Thomas G. Masaryk (1927) when he described, in the original title of his book, World War I as "The World Revolution." After each such age of transformation, elements of continuity turn out to have survived in the culture, but not always to the same extent nor necessarily in their original form. The amount of change that finally results is perhaps most nearly related to the cumulative processes of change that have occurred. But the shaping and timing, the pace and style of cultural change may be more highly responsive to spectacular events and to deliberate decisions of the holders or claimants of political power.

Changes in Interdependence: The Ability to Dissociate Images

The concept of cognitive dissonance between images necessarily involves the concept of interdependence between them. If two images were completely unrelated, it seems unlikely that any contradiction between them would be perceived as salient. By contrast, *images are seen as important to the extent that other images depend upon them.* Thus the Western image of Russian scientific and technological competence had a great deal of bearing after 1945 upon the image of that country's long-run military capabilities, and these in turn upon the image of Russia's ultimate success in winning some sort of leadership in Europe or the world. If we piece together some fragmentary data from American and West German opinion polls, we find that respect for Russian intellectual competence has increased substantially;[9] respect for current Soviet military power has also increased, but less so; and the perceived

---

[9] As we noted earlier, the percentage of Americans describing the Russians as "intelligent" dropped from 16 percent in 1942 to 12 percent during a crucial phase in the Cold War in 1948, and rose again to 28 percent in 1961 (AIPO, 30 April, 1961; Buchanan & Cantril, 1953, pp. 46–47).

chance of ultimate Russian success in the East–West struggle has also risen but to a still lesser extent. The changes in the distribution of opinions in West Germany, pictured in Figures 5.1A and B, are sufficiently parallel to suggest that the relevant images are indeed interdependent. There is enough difference between them, however, to suggest also that roughly 6.7 percent of the respondents have learned to dissociate their images of the current power distribution from their images of long-run prospects.

This has been an example of moder-

ate interdependence, coupled with weak dissociation. The changed image of Soviet scientific and technological competence after the performance of Russian space satellites and astronauts, however, may in fact have been more strongly strategic than our West German series suggest. This at least is the impression gained from Almond's study (1963) of the impact of Soviet space feats upon international public opinion. From opinion surveys conducted in ten countries between February 1957 and February 1960, Almond concludes that even if the United States should attain

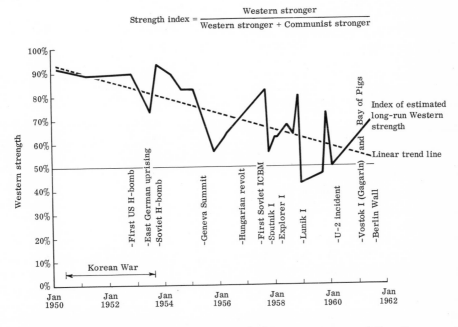

Fig. 5.1A. West German estimates of ultimate success of the Communist and Western Powers in the Cold War, 1950–1961. *Sources of data:* DIVO, 1959, pp. 10–12; DIVO, 1962, pp. 8–10; HICOG, 1950; HICOG, 1951; Neumann, 1961, p. 58; Puchala, 1964, pp. 23–24. The number of respondents (when given) for each of these polls ranged between 800 and 1975, corresponding roughly to significance levels between .05 and .01 for a change of 5 percentage points. Since the wording of the questions underwent some minor change, no significance level has been computed for the series as a whole. The trend appears too large, however, to be entirely fortuitous.

a more equal position with Russia in regard to space capabilities in the future,

we will have to reckon on the fact that one of the most significant components in the popular support of the American position in international politics—widespread popular conviction regarding American scientific and technical superiority—has been lost for the indefinite future and that all the expectations and attitudes that were based

only imperfectly mirrored by the far more "stubborn" United States opinion that quickly reverted to an image of American over-all military superiority. He reports that abroad, to the contrary, Soviet satellite superiority has tended to affect popular estimates of other components of military strength as well as long-run expectations of military capabilities.

The notion that the strategic impor-

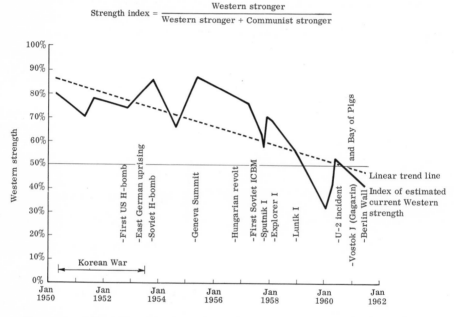

Fig. 5.1B. West German estimates of current strength of the Communist and Western Powers in the Cold War, 1950–1961. Sources of data: as for Figure 5.1A.

on this conviction have also been shaken for the indefinite future (p. 77).

The data about Western European opinions of American and Soviet scientific developments that were surveyed in an earlier section of this chapter would certainly bear out Almond's judgments. Interestingly enough, Almond also finds that the impact of Sputnik upon world opinion has been

tance of an image is positively related to the dependence of other images upon it implies that this importance will be inversely related to the facility of dissociation. The more easily a person or a group can dissociate two images, the less effect, all else remaining equal, should a change in either one of them have upon the other. What has been spoken of as the "life lie" by Henrik

Ibsen, the central political "myth" by MacIver (1947), or "patterns," "styles," or "configurations" of cultures by Ruth Benedict (1934) are all instances of varying degrees of inhibited dissociation. Hjalmar Ekdal in Ibsen's *Wild Duck* depends upon his unrealistic picture of himself as a great inventor because he cannot dissociate it from his motives for living; if the image were to break down, the motives would collapse with it. Lesser but still significant degrees of dependence have been asserted for some political systems in regard to their sustaining myth, and for certain cultures in regard to their central configurations of values and beliefs.

The opposite condition holds where the dissociation of different images from one another, and of parts of an image from the rest of it, have all become easy. To some extent the *ease of dissociation increases as a result of the process of modernization* in all its social, economic, cultural, and political aspects. The use of money is an exercise in dissociation; so is the use of alphabetic writing and of other abstract symbols; so is the use of most abstract rules or laws (Childe, 1946). Individuals dissociate some of their mental images more frequently with the broadening of their cognitive experience and the widening of their ranges of communication. Geographic and social mobility also tend to increase the likelihood of dissociation, since they decrease the social support from closely knit old groups for highly interdependent images and increase the opportunities for social support from new contexts and acquaintances for dissociated images or for new associations. Finally, formal intellectual training in many cultures, including all modern scientific cultures, teaches the art and practice of dissociation. It teaches men to separate those correlations that are merely familiar, and that are sometimes called "prej-

udices," from those old correlations that can be confirmed by operational procedures and that are often called "knowledge"; and it teaches men to distinguish both from new combinations of images that have not yet been tried out.

These three processes of facilitating dissociation need not all work at the same speed. For a member of a traditional culture (Lerner, 1958), or of the "underlying population" (Deutsch, 1953 and 1961), all three processes are at a minimum.

The possible effects of modernization are shown schematically in Figure 5.2. The ability to dissociate old images is represented as increasing along the horizontal axis of the diagram while the ability to integrate new combinations of images, and to establish new links of interdependence between them, is pictured as increasing along the vertical. Persons whom the social process of becoming uprooted has taught little else but the dissociation of their old images are likely to become anomic. They are likely to drift through life, responding to the interplay of stimuli from their environment with their own disjointed inner images and moods. Such persons would appear as having moved horizontally on the chart without moving upward toward higher capabilities for reintegration. A comparable movement on the vertical axis is unlikely to appear in practice. "Traditionals" can hardly move straight upward on our chart toward higher levels of integration without having to dissociate at least some of their earlier images or image clusters in the process, and they are likely to be prevented from this by the barrier of cognitive dissonance which has been described in so much of our material.

The most likely psychic movement of mobilized "Traditionals" toward modernity will occur along the diagonal from bottom-left to top-right, with balanced increases in the abilities to dissociate and to integrate accompanying the process of social mobilization and their psychic transformation into "Transitionals" and "Moderns" (Lerner, 1958, pp. 43–75).

It is even possible that this scheme might permit us to present the phenomenon of the fanatic, of Hoffer's "true believer" (1951), and of the "authoritarian personality" described by Adorno and his associates (1950). On

hence with an ever smaller range of new integrations from which to choose. At its pinnacle, such a pathological development leads once again to the unique and strategically all-important life lie of an individual or political system, and thus once again to the degeneration of the cognitive and combinatorial capabilities that we described earlier in the cases of Hjalmer Ekdal's life lie and of the Nazi system.

Another pathological process involves a decline in the ability to integrate images after modernization has been

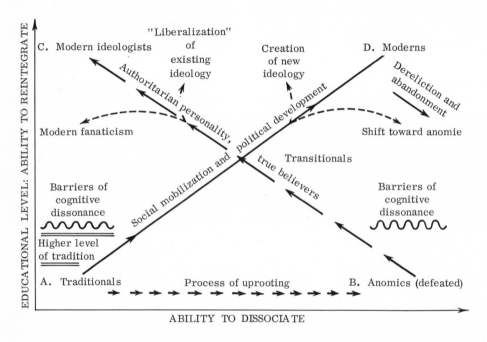

Fig. 5.2. A schematic overview of results of dissociation.

our diagram these psychic developments will appear as a movement along the secondary diagonal from bottom-right to top-left or from the state of anomie with its high dissociation and low integration toward a level of increasingly "modern" fanaticism with ever greater intensity of integration but an ever smaller ability to dissociate and

attained. According to Leites (1962, pp. 313–390), the ability to dissociate had reached almost pathological levels of "dereliction" and "abandonment" in French political culture in the mid-1950s. Such a return to lower levels of integration, with increasing ability to dissociate, would appear on our chart as a movement in a "southeasterly" direction, parallel to the secondary diagonal, and thus the exact opposite of the pathologically integrative movement of the "true believer." The efforts of President Charles de Gaulle in the years from 1958 to 1964 to establish again a more authoritarian style of political leadership would require for its lasting success a major change in the underlying political images and attitudes of a large part of the French people. By mid-1964 there was no clear evidence as yet that any such major changes had occurred.[10]

THE MODEL AS A WHOLE

The quantitative data that were readily available for this survey, and that were summarized in the preceding pages, are scanty indeed. They do not suffice to test in any serious manner the intuitive guesses and surmises shown in Table 5.1 (pp. 142–143). All that can be done here and now is to exhibit in descending rank order the ranges of attitude shifts and fluctuations observed in eighteen cases discussed earlier in this chapter, and to compare each of these with the intuitively expected strength of relationship from Table 5.1. A glance at Table 5.6, where these comparisons are shown, reveals that each of the eighteen results was within the range expected for it.

Some of these expectations, however, hinged upon estimating the effects of cross-pressures caused by efforts of governments to counteract the impact of external events upon popular attitudes. Our crude model assumed either that governments would make an all-out effort to offset the impact of external events which would tend to run counter to their preferred policies or

else that they would do nothing. We did not allow for the possibility that governmental efforts to mitigate the effect of such events might be moderate and at half-strength, so to speak, rather than at the level of a focused and sustained effort.

The case of the fluctuating image of the Soviet Union held by the Western European public involved the partial overlapping of the impact of two kinds of events. First, the Soviet intervention in Hungary in November 1956 drastically lowered the general level of favorable and neutral opinion about Russia. Then, after it had partly recovered from this impact in May 1957, the level of favorable and neutral opinion was pushed upward following the successful launching of the first Soviet Sputnik in October 1957 and other spectacular Soviet feats in space that ensued. The actions of the Western governments and media of mass communication generally amplified and reinforced the unfavorable impact of the Soviet intervention in Hungary; it was counteracted to some extent, however, by the cross-pressure effect of the cumulative events and experience that continued to maintain within each Western European country some formal or informal network of pro-Soviet or neutralist opinion. It had to be coded, therefore, as $G S \overline{C}$, as shown in line 8 of Table 5.6, with a predicted effect of "medium" that corresponded to the effect observed. The second group of events—the dramatic and repeated Soviet satellite launchings—was both spectacular and cumulative, but it was also counteracted at least to some limited extent by the Western governments and media. Accordingly, this set of events was coded as $S C \overline{G}$, as shown

---

[10] A "northwest" movement on this diagram, corresponding to that of Hoffer's "true believers," would thus appear as an antidote to the "southeast" movement described by Leites. Hoffer himself wrote admiringly in 1951 (p. 113), "de Gaulle is certainly a man to watch."

TABLE 5.6
A Summary of Predicted and Observed Changes in Images

Description of case	Text pages	Type of event (row & column in Table 5.1)
1. Foreign policy saliency, 1946–1949	160	GSC 28–29
2. Foreign policy saliency, 1958–1960	161	GSC 28–29
3. Foreign policy saliency, 1960–1963	161	GSC 28–29
4. Partisan distortion of TV debates, 1960	146	SC 1
5. Southern voters expect integration "some day," 1956–1963	172	GSC 20–22
6. Anxiety due to combat, 1945	162–163	S 29
7. U.S.–U.S.S.R. science race, 1957–1958	151	S 20–22
8. Impact on Western Europe of Soviet intervention in Hungary, 1956	149	GS$\overline{\text{C}}$ 20
9. Impact of Sputniks on West European image of U.S.S.R., 1957–1961	149–151	SC$\overline{\text{G}}$ 20–22
10. German morale loss from strategic bombing, 1944–1945	152	SC$\overline{\text{G}}$ 20–22
11. U.S. view of Russians as "intelligent," 1948–1961	151	SC$\overline{\text{G}}$ 20
12. Cuban crisis deterrence effect, 1962	147–148	SC$\overline{\text{G}}$ 20–22
13. Interviewer effects (Hyman), 1948	145	C 1
14. Germans valuing U.S. alliance, 1957–1961	163	GC$\overline{\text{S}}$ 28–29
15. German image of U.S. strength, 1957–1961	163	S$\overline{\text{G}}$ 28
16. German knowledge of NATO, 1956–1957	156–157	C 8
17. U.S. knowledge of Okinawa and Java, 1945	156	S 9
18. U.S. opposition to invasion of Cuba, 1961–1963	147	S$\overline{\overline{\text{CG}}}$ 1

TABLE 5.6 (Continued)

Observed range[a]		Approx. N of cases or respondents	Level of image change	
Net range	Shift from midpoint		Predicted (Table 5.1)	Observed
+62	±31	1500	VH	VH
+53	±27	1500	VH	VH
−45	±23	1500	VH	VH
+40	±20	159–8000 (2200–2672)	VH	VH
+38	±19	360	VH	VH
+31	±16	2800	H	H
+27	±14	800–1700	H	H
−19	±10	800–1700	M	M
+18	± 9	800–1700	M	M
−17	± 9	3800	M	M
+16	± 8	1015–1500	M	M
+15	± 8	1500	M	M
15	± 8		M	M
+14	± 7	800–1700	M	M
−12	± 6	800–1975	L	L
+10	± 5	1010–1950	L	L
(+ 7)	± 4	1500	L	L
+ 2	± 1	1500	VL	VL

[a] All changes in this table are significant at the .05 level, with the exception of row 18, in which absence of change is in line with the prediction.

in line 9 of Table 5.6, with a predicted effect of "medium" that corresponded to the effect actually observed.

A special problem arises in the case of the effects of interviewer bias as reported by Hyman and his associates (1954). If we assume that this bias was built up by cumulative events and pertains to the focus of the images held by the interviewer, and was not opposed by any significant cross-pressures, then we should expect its effects to be at the medium level. This in fact seems to have been the case. There is no indication that this bias was opposed by effective cross-pressures either from governmental efforts or spectacular events. It still seems plausible, however, that interviewer bias generally does not operate unchecked. Rather, it tends to be opposed by cross-pressures from the interviewing organization as well as from the network of social support that helps most respondents sustain their opinions. If we had assumed the existence of effective cross-pressures from the government or from any other sources, we should have expected only very low effects, and we should have been wrong in our prediction by two steps.

The theory as presented cannot, of course, be tested in any strictly statistical sense with the fragmentary data discussed above. Its component assumptions are too numerous, the data presented are too few, and their selection was not random but probably sub-ject to biases inherent not only in the availability and quality of data but also in the limited knowledge and interests of the investigators. If we should pretend for a moment, however, that the data were indeed random, then it would be possible to test the theory as a whole.[11] Let us make the worst possible interpretation of our findings and treat the three ambiguous cases that have just been discussed as disconfirmations. A model that produces 15 correct predictions in 18 cases would be significant at better than the .001 level on the conservative assumption of a .33 probability in each case of being right by chance. If we fully accept the three borderline cases, raising the number of correct predictions to 18 out of 18, then the significance level would be still better.

With these qualifications, it seems that our crude model of the impact of external events upon the change of images and attitudes has not been disconfirmed.

CONCLUSIONS

Our findings tally well with the research results summarized by Berelson and Steiner (1964, pp. 664–666) attesting to the resistance of human thinking and imagining to sudden environmental pressures. Men cling to their earlier memories and character. They call upon the support of their social groups

---

[11] One could treat the process of image formation and change as a black box, paying close attention to the input and output of the box. The input consists in certain properties of the events; and the output consists in the amount of image change or aggregate opinion shift observed. The properties of events may first of all be characterized in terms of the three types (G, S, and C), their combinations, and the positive or negative direction of each dimension within each combination. This would result in nineteen possible input states corresponding to rows 1 through 7 and 10 through 21 of Table 5.1. Further inputs consist in the aspects of the image affected and the expectable type of effect in each case. These would generate the 31 columns in Table 5.1. Ignoring the "no change" column, the model as a whole then would predict an output state for each of the 570 possible input states, represented by the 570 cells in the matrix. The output states can have one of five possible values—ranging from "very low" to "very high"—corresponding to classes of magnitude of expected change.

to defend their images and beliefs. They distort many of their perceptions and deny much of reality, in order to call their prejudiced souls their own.

Yet we must dissent from findings that make man seem too completely a creature of his fellows. Even the habits men have of conforming to their neighbors, of admiring reference groups of their betters, and of submitting to dominant elites are subject to the same limitations. Men conform, admire, and obey largely within the limits of the images and habits that they have learned earlier and that they have made into a part of their inner selves. If a dominant minority suddenly runs counter to these internalized images and beliefs of its followers, it may quickly cease to dominate.

Almost nothing in the world seems to be able to shift the images of 40 percent of the population in most countries, even within one or two decades. Combinations of events that shift the images and attitudes even of the remaining 50 or 60 percent of the population are extremely rare, and these rare occasions require the combination and mutual reinforcement of cumulative events with spectacular events and substantial governmental efforts as well as the absence of sizable cross-pressures. Most of the spectacular changes of politics involve a change in the attitudes of between one fifth and one third of the population, and almost all of these involve a combination of spectacular and cumulative events, although the combined impact of these may meet with limited opposition from governments. If the external events are less sustained and less dramatic or if cross-pressures are greater, the magnitude of opinion shifts declines to between 10 and 20 percent. Cumulative or spectacular events alone often shift less than 10 percent of public opinion.

Over longer periods of time, perhaps two decades or more, and particularly over the succession of generations, the impact of cumulative events tends to be much larger. Here again, the impact of spectacular events and of sustained efforts of governments and media of mass communication can speed the pace of large-scale change, but even so, many attitudes and images persist, or return at least part of the way toward their previous state, once the immediate external pressures slacken and so long as the main individual personality structures and supporting social networks have remained intact.

It seems almost impossible for the impact of any combination of external events and governmental efforts to reorganize all the main images and all their relevant aspects—focus, periphery, cognitive and evaluative cues, psychological and sociocultural contexts—as they are held in the minds of most of the population. The most that spectacular events or governmental efforts usually can accomplish is to change some important aspects of some important images, and some of their relations to their surrounding cues and contexts. Once this has happened, what will be important is the presence or absence of the continuing impact of cumulative events and the continued working of human personalities and social groups to assimilate the new image elements and to reduce the cognitive dissonance between the changed images and their environment of old ones within the mind of the individual and the culture of the group. Often it takes the replacement of one generation by another to let the impact of external changes take its full effect. The greater openness of adolescents and young adults to new images and impressions—not only in the negative sense of being less burdened with old images and hardened psychic structures, but also in the positive sense of greater sensitivity and ability to learn —is thus a major resource for the long-run learning process of their societies.

Within and across generations, external events can thus initiate or precipitate processes of psychological and cultural change, but these processes still remain to a very large extent autonomous. Perhaps the most limiting thing we can say about the impact of external events upon our mental images is at the same time the best: that they are most effective not in overwhelming but in eliciting the autonomous activity of man's individual and social mind.

REFERENCES

Adorno, T. W. Prejudice in the interview material. In T. W. Adorno, Else Frenkel-Brunswik, D. J. Levinson, & R. N. Sanford, *The authoritarian personality.* New York: Harper, 1950. Pp. 605–653.

Adorno, T. W., Frenkel-Brunswik, Else, Levinson, D. J., & Sanford, R. N. *The authoritarian personality.* New York: Harper, 1950.

Allen, F. L. *The big change: America transforms itself, 1900–1950.* New York: Harper, 1952.

Allport, G. W., & Postman, L. *The psychology of rumor.* New York: Holt, Rinehart and Winston, 1947.

Almond, G. A. *The American people and foreign policy.* New York: Praeger, 1960. (Originally published by Harcourt, 1950.)

Almond, G. A. Public opinion and the development of space technology: 1957–60. In J. Goldsen (Ed.), *Outer space in world politics.* New York: Praeger, 1963. Pp. 71–96.

Ashton, T. S. *The industrial revolution, 1760–1830.* London: Oxford Univer. Press, 1948.

Batchelder, R. C. *The irreversible decision, 1939–1950.* Boston: Houghton Mifflin, 1962.

Baumert, C. *Jugend der Nachkriegszeit: Lebensverhältnisse und Reaktionsweisen.* Darmstadt: Roether, 1952.

Benedict, Ruth *Patterns of culture.* Boston: Houghton Mifflin, 1934.

Berelson, B. R., Lazarsfeld, P. F., & McPhee, W. N. *Voting: A study of opinion formation in a presidential campaign.* Chicago: Univer. Chicago Press, 1954.

Berelson, B. R., & Steiner, G. A. *Human behavior: An inventory of scientific findings.* New York: Harcourt, 1964.

Biderman, A. D., & Zimmer, H. (Eds.) *The manipulation of human behavior.* New York: Wiley, 1961.

Boulding, K. E. *The image.* Ann Arbor: Univer. Michigan Press, 1956.

Braunthal, J. *The paradox of nationalism.* London: St. Botolph Press, 1946.

Braunthal, J. *Geschichte der Internationale.* Hannover: Dietz, 1961.

Brecht, B. *Schriften zum Theater: Über eine nicht-aristotelische Dramatik.* Berlin: Suhrkamp, 1957.

Brewster, Dorothy The Russian soul: An English literary pattern. *Amer. Scholar,* 1948, *17,* 179–188.

Brodie, B. A psychoanalytic interpretation of Woodrow Wilson. In B. Mazlish (Ed.), *Psychoanalysis and history.* Englewood Cliffs, N.J.: Prentice-Hall, 1963. Pp. 115-123.

Brogan, D. W. Can the Western three ride the storm? *New York Times Magazine,* 16 May, 1954, pp. 9, 53–56.

Buchanan, W., & Cantril, H. *How nations see each other: A study in public opinion.* Urbana: Univer. Illinois Press, 1953.

Campbell, A., Converse, P. E., Miller, W. E., & Stokes, D. E. *The American voter.* New York: Wiley, 1960.

Cantril, H. *Public opinion, 1935–1946.* Princeton: Princeton Univer. Press, 1951.

Cantril, H. *The politics of despair.* New York: Basic Books, 1958.

Childe, V. G. *What happened in history.* New York: Penguin, 1946.

Clapham, J. H. *An economic history of modern Britain.* Cambridge, England: Cambridge Univer. Press, 1926.

Day-Lewis, C. The image. In *Collected*

poems. Oxford: Jonathan Cape with Hogarth Press, 1954. P. 222.

Deutsch, K. W. *Nationalism and social communication: An inquiry into the foundations of nationality.* New York and Cambridge, Mass.: Wiley and Technology Press, 1953.

Deutsch, K. W. *Political community at the international level: Problems of definition and measurement.* Garden City, N.Y.: Doubleday, 1954.

Deutsch, K. W. Social mobilization and political development. *Amer. pol. Sci. Rev.,* 1961, *60,* 493–514.

Deutsch, K. W. *The nerves of government.* New York: Free Press, 1963.

DIVO-Institut. *Umfragen,* Vol. 2. Frankfurt: Europäische Verlagsanstalt, 1959.

DIVO-Institut. *Umfragen,* Vol. 3/4. Frankfurt: Europäische Verlagsanstalt, 1962.

Erikson, E. H. *Young man Luther: A study in psychoanalysis and history.* New York: Norton, 1958.

Festinger, L. *A theory of cognitive dissonance.* Stanford: Stanford Univer. Press, 1962.

Festinger, L., Riecken, H., & Schachter, S. *When prophecy fails.* Minneapolis: Univer. Minnesota Press, 1956.

Friedrich, C. J. The agricultural basis of emotional nationalism. *Publ. Opin. Quart.,* 1937, *1*(2), 50–61.

Fröhner, R., von Stackelberg, Maria, & Eser, W. *Familie und Ehe.* Bielefeld: Maria von Stackelberg Verlag, 1956.

Gaiser, G. *Die sterbende Jagd.* München: Hanser, 1953.

George, A. L., & George, Juliette L. *Woodrow Wilson and Colonel House: A personality study.* New York: John Day, 1956.

Grinker, R. R., & Spiegel, J. R. *Men under stress.* Philadelphia: Blakiston, 1945.

Hebb, D. O. *The organization of behavior.* New York: Wiley, 1949.

High Commission for Germany (HICOG) *German public opinion.* Series 2, No. 18, May 19, 1950.

High Commission for Germany (HICOG) *German public opinion.* Series 2, No. 83, June 12, 1951.

Hoffer, E. *The true believer: Thoughts on the nature of mass movements.* New York: Harper, 1951.

Holsti, O. R. The belief system and national images: A case study. *J. Confl. Resol.,* 1962, *6,* 244–252.

Hovland, C. I., Janis, I. L., & Kelley, H. H. *Communication and persuasion: Psychological studies of opinion change.* New Haven: Yale Univer. Press, 1953.

Hunter, Marjorie Race riot a shock to Lexington, North Carolina. *New York Times,* June 9, 1963, 61:1.

Hyman, H. H. Do they tell the truth? *Publ. Opin. Quart.,* 1944–1945, *8,* 557–559.

Hyman, H. H., with Cobb, E. J., Feldman, J. J., Hart, C. W., & Stember, C. H. *Interviewing in social research.* Chicago: Univer. Chicago Press, 1954.

Isaacs, H. R. *Images of Asia: American views of China and India.* New York: Capricorn Books, 1962. (Published originally as *Scratches on our minds.* New York: John Day, 1958.)

Isherwood, C. *Goodbye to Berlin.* New York: Random, 1939. (Reprinted in *The Berlin stories.* New York: J. Laughlin, 1945.)

Johnson, U. *Mutmassungen über Jakob.* Frankfurt/Main: Suhrkamp, 1959.

Katz, E., & Feldman, J. J. The debates in the light of research: A survey of surveys. In S. Kraus (Ed.), *The great debates.* Bloomington: Indiana Univer. Press, 1962. Pp. 173–223.

Key, V. O., Jr. Partisanship and county office: The case of Ohio. *Amer. pol. Sci. Rev.,* 1953, *47,* 525–532.

Key, V. O., Jr. *Statistics of gubernatorial election, 1900–1954: The Middle West.* Cambridge, Mass.: Election Statistics File, 1956. (Mimeographed)

Kluckhohn, Florence R., & Strodtbeck, F. L. *Variations in value orientations.* New York: Harper, 1961.

Kriesberg, M. Soviet news in the "New

York Times." *Publ. Opin. Quart.*, 1946, *10*, 552–557.

Kubzansky, P. E.　The effects of reduced environmental stimulation on human behavior: A review. In A. D. Biderman, & H. Zimmer (Eds.), *The manipulation of human behavior*. New York: Wiley, 1961. Pp. 51–95.

Lane, R. E.　*Political ideology*. New York: Free Press, 1962.

Lasswell, H. D.　*Propaganda technique in the World War*. New York: Peter Smith, 1938. (First published in 1927.)

Lasswell, H. D.　*World politics and personal insecurity*. New York: McGraw-Hill, 1935.

Lasswell, H. D., Leites, N., *et al.　The language of politics: Studies in quantitative semantics*. New York: Stewart, 1949.

Lazarsfeld, P. F., Berelson, B. R., & Gaudet, Hazel　*The people's choice*. New York: Columbia Univer. Press, 1948.

Leites, N.　*Images of power in French politics*. Santa Monica, Calif.: RAND Corp., Memorandum RM-2954-RC, 1962. 2 vols.

Lerner, D.　*The passing of traditional society*. New York: Free Press, 1958.

Levinson, D. J.　The study of anti-Semitic ideology. In T. W. Adorno, Else Frenkel-Brunswik, D. J. Levinson, & R. N. Sanford, *The authoritarian personality*. New York: Harper, 1950. Pp. 57–101.

Lifton, R. J.　*Thought reform and the psychology of totalism: A study of "brainwashing" in China*. New York: Norton, 1961.

Lifton, R. J.　Psychological effects of the atomic bomb in Hiroshima: The theme of death. *Daedalus*, 1963, *92*, 462–497.

Lipset, S. M.　*Political man*. Garden City, N.Y.: Doubleday, 1960.

Lipset, S. M.　*The first new nation: The United States in historical and comparative perspective*. New York: Basic Books, 1963.

MacIver, R. M.　*The web of government*. New York: Macmillan, 1947.

Marshall, S. L. A.　*The river and the gauntlet*. New York: Morrow, 1953.

Martin, B. K.　*The triumph of Lord Palmerston: A study of public opinion in England before the Crimean War*. London: Allen and Unwin, 1924.

Masaryk, T. G.　*The making of a state: Memories and observations, 1914–1918*. London: Allen and Unwin, 1927. (Originally published as *Světová revoluce za války a ve válce, 1914–1918* [*The world revolution*]. Prague: Čin a Orbis, 1925.)

Mead, Margaret　*New lives for old: Cultural transformation — Manus, 1928–1953*. New York: Morrow, 1956.

Meerloo, J. A. M.　*The rape of the mind: The psychology of thought control, menticide, and brainwashing*. Cleveland: World, 1956.

Merritt, R. L.　West Berlin: Center or periphery? In R. L. Merritt, & S. Rokkan (Eds.), *Comparing nations: The use of quantitative data in cross-national research*. New Haven: Yale Univer. Press, 1965. (a)

Merritt, R. L.　*The growth of American community, 1735–1775*. New Haven: Yale Univer. Press, 1965. (b)

Merritt, R. L., & Rokkan, S. (Eds.)　*Comparing nations: The use of quantitative data in cross-national research*. New Haven: Yale Univer. Press, 1965.

Milgram, S.　Behavioral study of obedience. *J. abnorm. soc. Psychol.*, 1963, *67*, 371–378.

Neumann, E. P.　*Public opinion in Germany, 1961*. Allensbach and Bonn: Verlag für Demoskopie, 1961.

Noelle, Elisabeth, & Neumann, E. P.　*Jahrbuch der öffentlichen Meinung, 1957*. Allensbach-am-Bodensee: Verlag für Demoskopie, 1957.

Orwell, G.　*1984: A novel*. New York: Harcourt, 1949.

Osgood, C. E., Suci, G. J., & Tannenbaum, P. H.　*The measurement of meaning*. Urbana: Univer. Illinois Press, 1957.

Parry, H., & Crespi, L. *Public opinion in Western Europe: Attitudes toward political, economic, and military integration.* Paris: Research Branch/SRE, January 1953.

Petersen, S. *A statistical history of the American presidential elections.* New York: Ungar, 1963.

Pool, I. de S. The mass media and politics in the modernization process. In L. W. Pye (Ed.), *Communications and political development.* Princeton: Princeton Univer. Press, 1963. Pp. 234–253.

Potter, D. M. *People of plenty: Economic abundance and the American character.* Chicago: Univer. Chicago Press, 1954.

Puchala, D. J. *Western European attitudes on international problems, 1952–1961.* Yale Research Memorandum in Political Science No. 1. New Haven, 1964.

Pye, L. W. (Ed.) *Communications and political development.* Princeton: Princeton Univer. Press, 1963.

Redford, A. *The economic history of England, 1760–1860.* London: Longmans, Green, 1936.

Riess, C. Wie wurde es möglich? *Die Zeit,* 4 August, 1961.

Rosenbaum, Susan B. The disengagement of the French from Indo-China. Unpublished manuscript, Yale University, January 1958.

Rosenberg, M. J., Hovland, C. I., *et al. Attitude organization and change.* New Haven: Yale Univer. Press, 1960.

Rosenstock-Huessy, E. *Die europäischen Revolutionen.* Jena: Diederich, 1931.

Rosenstock-Huessy, E. *Out of revolution: Autobiography of Western man.* New York: Morrow, 1938.

Russett, B. M., with Alker, H. R., Jr., Deutsch, K. W., & Lasswell, H. D. *World handbook of political and social indicators.* New Haven: Yale Univer. Press, 1964.

Schelsky, H. *Die skeptische Generation: Eine Soziologie der deutschen Jugend.* Düsseldorf: Diederich, 1957.

Schuhmacher, W. *Leben und Seele unseres Soldatenliedes im Weltkrieg.* Frankfurt/Main: Diesterweg, 1928.

Schumpeter, J. A. *Capitalism, socialism, and democracy* (ed. 3). New York: Harper, 1963.

Shils, E. A., & Janowitz, M. Cohesion and disintegration in the Wehrmacht in World War II. *Publ. Opin. Quart.,* 1948, *12,* 280–315.

Sower, C., *et al. Youth and the world of work.* East Lansing: Michigan State College, Social Research Service, 1949.

Stafford, Patricia S., & Flick, R. G. A content analysis of U.S.S.R. May Day slogans. Unpublished manuscript, 1962. (Publication forthcoming.)

Stevens, W. M. Why do whales become stranded? *Sea Frontiers,* May 1963.

Stouffer, S. A., *et al. The American soldier: Combat and its aftermath,* Vol. II. Princeton: Princeton Univer. Press, 1949.

United States Information Agency (USIA) Report WE-1, August 1961.

United States Strategic Bombing Survey *Over-all report (European war).* Washington, D.C.: Government Printing Office, September 30, 1945.

Voltaire Poem on the Lisbon earthquake. 1756. In H. M. Black (Ed.), *Candide and other writings.* New York: Modern Library, 1956. Pp. 193–202.

Webb, L. *Communism and democracy in Australia: A survey of the 1951 referendum.* New York: Praeger, 1955.

Weyrauch, W. *Ich lebe in der Bundesrepublik: Fünfzehn Deutsche über Deutschland.* München: List, 1961.

Wiener, N. *The human use of human beings.* Boston: Houghton Mifflin, 1950.

Wiener, N. *Cybernetics.* (ed. 2) New York: Wiley, 1961.

Wiener, N. *God and Golem, Inc.: A comment on certain points where cybernetics impinges on religion.* Cambridge, Mass.: M.I.T. Press, 1964.

6

With Chapter 6, we conclude our exploration of the effects of various specific experiences on national and international images. In the last two chapters we were concerned, by and large, with the more spontaneous effects of exposure to direct contacts and to external events, which may lead to the confirmation of old images or the "emergence" of new ones. In the next chapter, on the other hand, we are concerned with the more or less deliberate attempts to induce changes in images, in which governmental and nongovernmental organizations often engage. The distinction is far from perfect, in that direct contact may be a form of deliberate induction (as in various international exchange programs), and the effects of events are certainly often mediated by the deliberate manipulation that occurs in the communication of these events. In Chapter 6, however, the emphasis is on education and persuasion—the processes of influence through which the modification of images is attempted. The chapter draws primarily on the experimental literature on attitude change. Most of the research in this area has not dealt with attitude issues that are directly in the area of international relations, but some of the same general principles should apply (with perhaps minor variations) regardless of the specific issues involved. Moreover, the data reviewed in this chapter are interpreted with an eye to the special problems that arise in communications on international issues, whether they are addressed to domestic or to foreign audiences.

Both authors participated in the research of the Information and Education Division of the United States Army during World War II, and are contributors to *The American Soldier* (1949), the well-known product of this research.

Since 1947, Irving L. Janis has been at Yale University, where he is now Professor of Psychology and Director of Graduate Studies in Psychology. He is author and co-author of numerous publications from the Yale Communications Research Program, including *Communication and persuasion: Psychological studies of opinion change* (1953) and *Personality and persuasibility* (1959). He is also the author of *Air war and emotional stress: Psychological studies of bombing and civilian defense* (1951); and of *Psychological stress* (1958), for which he was awarded the Hofheimer Prize by the American Psychiatric Association in 1959. His current research interests include attitude change; decisional conflict; the influence of small-group processes on the individual's tolerance for deprivation; and the reduction of intergroup hostility.

M. Brewster Smith is Professor of Psychology and Associate Director of the Institute of Human Development at the University of California, Berkeley. He is a former president of the Society for the Psychological Study of Social Issues; and has served as editor of both the *Journal of Social Issues* and the *Journal of Abnormal and Social Psychology*. He is co-author of *Opinions and personality* (1956) and of *For a science of social man: Convergences in anthropology, psychology and sociology* (1954). His current research focuses on the overseas experience and performance of Peace Corps teachers in West Africa, and the development of intergroup attitudes and relationships among adolescents.

H. C. K.

Effects of Education and Persuasion on National and International Images

Irving L. Janis and M. Brewster Smith

*T*he years since World War II have seen, in American behavioral science, the burgeoning of empirical research on factors that influence the effectiveness of factual evidence, arguments, endorsements, and appeals—of attempts to induce changes in images or attitudes through persuasive communication. The novel ingredient in this active field of investigation has been the systematic use of controlled experimentation to specify the conditions under which a communication is likely to be effective or ineffective in influencing an audience. In these developments, the catalytic influence of the late Carl I. Hovland of Yale University has been immense. Many able investigators, working at numerous universities and research centers from a variety of theoretical perspectives, have now begun to contribute to the emergence of what Nathan Maccoby (1963) has called "the new scientific rhetoric." The purpose of this chapter is to extract some of the principal generalizations for which the existing research literature provides supporting evidence, in a way that brings them to bear on the problems involved in changing international images.

Because virtually all the research has been carried out in the United States, usually on readily available student audiences, and because the attitudinal content studied has rarely involved international imagery, our task is inherently one of extrapolation. The student or practitioner of communication in international relations must therefore regard our generalizations as suggestive leads rather than as established "laws."

If we are to extrapolate from the available evidence in ways that can be usefully suggestive to persons concerned with analyzing or modifying international images, we must first make explicit our assumptions about the social contexts in which people send and receive communications that bear upon the way they think and feel about other nations. Here we claim no special competence. Other chapters in the volume treat some of these aspects of international communication with appropriate documentation. We are presently concerned only with sketching a framework within which the ensuing sections can acquire relevance to our purpose.

SOME ASSUMPTIONS ABOUT CONTEXTS OF INTERNATIONAL COMMUNICATION

The educational and persuasive efforts with which this chapter is concerned fall into two major types: on the one hand, efforts by governmental or other agencies in a given country directed at the population of another country, designed to change aspects of the image of the "sending" country held in the recipient country; and, on the other hand, efforts by agencies in a given country directed at its own population, designed to change the prevailing imagery of their own country, of other countries, of international groupings, or of the world order. Obviously, the contexts of communication and the problems that must be solved, if relevant messages are to be effective, are different in the two cases. Different factors in the communication process are likely to become strategic, and relevant variables are likely to occur with different characteristic values, in the cases where the audiences are respectively "foreign" or "domestic," even though the same underlying social-psychological principles may be valid in both instances.

Consider first a communication that is addressed to a *foreign population,* intended to create a more favorable, a more accurate, or a more differentiated image of the sending country or of its policies and actions. In addition to the considerations arising from the unique

historical and contemporary relations between the particular sending and receiving countries, some general problems may be anticipated whenever communication is addressed to a foreign country.

In the first place, the mere fact that the communicator is alien from the point of view of the recipients has some obvious consequences. To the extent that nations are "in-groups," the communicator in this case belongs to an "out-group." If the communication challenges views that are prevalent in the recipient country and thus runs counter to in-group norms, it is likely to encounter special resistances along lines to be discussed subsequently. In any case, the source of communication is suspect almost by definition. The audience will be quick to attribute propagandistic intent, and the cluster of findings to be discussed under the heading of source credibility becomes strategically relevant.

The images and attitudes that communications of this sort are designed to modify are generally rather undifferentiated, tending toward gross black-and-white judgments rather than finer discriminations. Typically, such images have been developed with scanty informational support, on a basis of general consensus rather than of individual experience. By the same token, they are often held against a background of virtual unanimity in the social groups to which the individual recipient belongs, if not in the nation as a whole. Where each person believes as he does about a given country because "everybody else" shares the same beliefs, the communication from abroad may run counter to a social reality that leaves no ground for legitimate differences of opinion. People may see no possibility for entertaining any other point of view than their own. When the situation of communication is thus structured, a distinctive set of resistances and vulnerabilities to persuasion is generated.

A further set of considerations stems from the fact that the communicator from abroad has problems of gaining access to efficient channels of communication, problems that are different from and more difficult than those typical of domestic communication. Effective channels may be virtually nonexistent, as with some nonliterate populations in developing countries, or available channels may be "jammed" or otherwise closed to the communicator. And, from abroad, it is probably less feasible for the communicator to diversify his message to fit the predispositions of subgroups in the population; relatively indiscriminate beaming may be inherent in the available media of communication.

Finally, communications addressed to foreign populations can never hold the monopolistic advantage sometimes enjoyed by domestic communications, especially in totalitarian countries—except under special circumstances of military occupation or imprisonment that provide a literally "captive audience." Far from the conditions obtaining in "brainwashing" and thought-reform, the usual case in this type of internation communication requires each persuasive message to make its way in a field of competing counter-communications. Research findings that take the influence of subsequent counter-communication into account will therefore be especially relevant.

Communications to *domestic audiences* on international issues occur in settings having some of the same characteristics, but also involve other issues. Again, the attitudes and images that such communications are designed to modify are likely to be remote from people's daily lives, undifferentiated and loosely structured, and anchored primarily in perceived consensus among the person's reference groups rather than in his personal experience. In these respects there is little difference from the attitudes and images to which the foreign communicator addresses himself. But the communicator in the domestic setting is usually in a position to take a more differentiated view of his audience than is feasible in foreign communication. He has the opportunity to single out the "opinion leaders" of the groups in which people's international attitudes are anchored, particularly those with strong personal interests related to the foreign policy issues in question, and to orient his persuasive attempts directly to them.

The wide range of issues bearing on foreign policy with which the communicator to domestic publics may be concerned will include many that involve the capabilities of a potential enemy to launch destructive nuclear attacks, or other information of a threatening nature. Communications that arouse fear in the recipient can motivate him toward protective action, but we will encounter evidence that their effectiveness may be limited by inner defensive processes that they activate.

Since foreign policy is carried out in an ever-changing political environment, communications to the public must consider not only the requirements for getting immediate support for a given policy, but also the requirements for maintaining support for future policies, when the world situation may have shifted. Short-term considerations have to be weighed against long-term ones. In regard to these difficult matters, some suggestive guidelines are available from research findings to be reviewed on the effects of preparatory communications that anticipate a future action or event.

The foregoing discussion has made the simplifying assumption that foreign and domestic communication can be treated separately. The lives of policy makers and communicators are, of course, made sadder and more complicated by the fact that the two spheres of communication often merge in the real world, however convenient it would be to keep them apart. Thus, United States congressional debates on civil rights legislation, foreign aid, and the desirability of a test ban treaty, intended for domestic publics, create international news that is picked up and amplified by communicators abroad, reinforcing an unintended national image. Or "trial balloons" floated in international communication and aimed at the reduction of long-entrenched conflicts—say, in regard to Berlin or Communist China—get exploded prematurely as they are caught up in the domestic political fray. Unintended and unwanted consequences may often follow from the attentiveness of the wrong audience. Some of the general propositions to be presented in this chapter may be useful primarily for making accurate predictions concerning such consequences.

In both contexts that we have considered, communication may be directed at nations or publics, but if it is effective, it must first of all be received by individuals. A further set of assumptions that needs to be made explicit concerns the fact that these individuals are embedded in social structures that differentially affect their accessibility to communications on various topics from different sources and media. The flow of communication is neither random nor under the substantial control of the communicator. We are concerned here with social factors that shape its flow prior to the operation of the more psychological selective processes that are examined later in the chapter—that is, with the ecology of the informational environment.

The distinctive social niche that each person occupies makes it relatively probable that he will receive certain kinds of communication, and improbable that he will receive others. The American housewife is readily available to daytime programs on radio or television, as her husband is not. He, in turn, is differentially accessible to communications flowing from the world of work, and of labor or professional organizations. The resident of New York City has more ready access to information about international affairs than the Midwesterner of the Chicago *Tribune* belt: it costs him less initiative and effort to expose himself to relevant information. His counterpart in Accra or Kumasi, restricted to a two-sheet government-controlled newspaper, must have unusual resources and initiative to acquire any appreciable sampling of international news from the BBC or Voice of America. Traditionally, the farmer or peasant was essentially isolated from communications emanating from the larger world. Although the American revolution of country life—in which rural electrification, the car, the highway, and the mass media have virtually abolished its traditionally distinctive features—has incipient parallels in other parts of the world, rural and urban environments will continue to afford differential access to information for a long time to come.

Such factors of sheer accessibility to information merge in their effects with the results of habitual orientations to sources, media, and topics of communication that prevail in given social groups. The outcome is a marked subcultural patterning of the communication flow. Members of the working class, for example, are attentive to different media, respectful of different authorities, and interested in different topics from members of the middle class. These differences work heavily against their receiving and being responsive to communications from the United Nations and educational organizations that promote accurate and differentiated images in the realm of international affairs.

An important additional way in which the flow of communication is socially structured has emerged as an empirical finding in a number of field studies of the effects of mass communication (see E. Katz, 1963; Katz & Lazarsfeld, 1955). Converging evidence indicates that the principal impact of mass communications is often not direct, but mediated by face-to-face personal influence. In each relatively homogeneous social group, some people are particularly attentive monitors of what is being said by the press, radio, and television; they actively circulate those messages from the mass media that are of common concern to their group. These "opinion leaders" often function as innovators by taking their cues from outside sources in the public media, while others in the community are guided rather by their informal personal communication with the opinion leaders. Where this analysis of a two-step train of events set in motion by persuasive communication in the mass media is applicable, it has important implications for communication strategy. As noted earlier, it becomes important to identify the "opinion leaders," and to design communications that will reach and appeal to them. The evidence indicates that different persons emerge as opinion leaders in various areas of potential group concern.

SOME CAUTIONARY REMARKS

We have already emphasized that in bringing the findings of empirical research on persuasive communication to bear on modifying international images

and attitudes we must extrapolate to topics and populations for which direct evidence is not available. Some additional cautionary remarks are in order, before we turn to the principal substance of this chapter, about the evidential status of the generalizations to be reviewed, their relevance to communication about international affairs, and the limited effects that persuasive communication can hope to achieve in this area.

All the hypotheses to be discussed have the status of *partially established generalizations* that are directly supported by specific research evidence, mainly from experiments or controlled comparisons, and are consistent with what is generally known about communication effects. Although the hypotheses have been selected as promising leads, their generality has not yet been fully tested and they are therefore by no means fully confirmed. In order to establish the generality of any one of these propositions, a large number of replicating experiments would be necessary, each of which investigates the effects of the same variables but with different persuasive messages on a variety of social and political issues, presented to a different type of audience, in a different type of situation. In the absence of such multiple replications, we can only be sure that at least under some conditions the given proposition holds true.

In view of their tentative status, the hypotheses cannot appropriately be regarded as a firm basis for strategy and tactics in the planning and conduct of educational or promotional campaigns. They do, however, represent a considerable advance beyond "common sense" in suggesting factors that might profitably be taken into account in connection with various kinds of communication goals. They permit, we believe, a more sophisticated analysis than "common sense" makes available and serve primarily to sensitize and correct the communicator's practical judgment, even though they cannot replace it.

Many of the generalizations come from experiments that show the importance of a given factor in the short-term effects of brief communications given to classrooms or to other such "captive audiences" that are momentarily isolated from competing communications. In general, reasons of efficiency have led experimental work to focus on settings and topics in which maximal effects can be observed within a brief time span. The expectation is that many of the same factors will be relevant in the more complex, less efficient settings of communication in the international arena. Even if the same factors remain relevant, however, the effects may be disappointingly small, in comparison with those assessed under experimental conditions (see Hovland, 1959). The principal contexts of communication affecting international images and attitudes differ markedly from the usual experimental paradigm. Longer-term effects are usually of more interest to the communicator than immediate ones. The audience is rarely "captive": to the communicator, gaining access is likely to be more than half the battle. And, in the settings with which we are most concerned, the communicator can rarely give his message the advantages of monopoly. Thus, as is commonly recognized, rival countries and rival groups seldom succeed in influencing each other appreciably by large scale educational or propagandistic efforts.

Indeed, even when the source is regarded as fairly trustworthy and benign, the net effect of communications in the mass media seems to be mainly a matter of reinforcing pre-existing images and attitudes, as Klapper (1960) has emphasized in his recent review of the evidence, agreeing in this pessimistic appraisal with other authorities (see Berelson, Lazarsfeld, & McPhee, 1954; Schramm & Carter, 1959). Attempts at producing changes in social or political prejudices and stereotypes generally meet with an extraordinarily high degree of psychological resistance, the sources of which we are now beginning to understand. In fact, most of what we are able to learn from existing research is useful mainly for analyzing why attempts at education and mass persuasion *fail*. We are seldom able to extract fresh insights that might teach us something new about how to *decrease* psychological resistances, especially under conditions where the communications emanate from outgroups regarded by the audience with suspicion or distrust.

In the realm with which we are concerned, then, the "persuader," hidden or otherwise, is far from the powerful, perhaps sinister, figure that he is sometimes supposed to be. And anyone who looks to the existing social sciences to provide him with guiding principles and shining new psychological devices for substantially improving the effectiveness of communications in the mass media is bound to be severely disappointed. With only fragmentary and incomplete research findings at hand, we must be content with the more limited goals of delineating suggestive leads concerning: (a) the general conditions under which resistance to change will be relatively high or low; and (b) communication factors that help to instigate and reinforce the emergence of new images when resistances have been lowered sufficiently, for whatever reason, to permit at least a slight degree of modification in the audience's existing beliefs, prejudices, or stereotypes.

Simply to scotch the myth of the omnipotent propagandist would itself be a worthy contribution, since this myth tempts governments to substitute public relations "gimmicks" for needed policies and actions. To recognize that "actions speak louder than words," that dramatic events or consistently enacted policies which realign people's perceptions of their personal and national interests can have effects on international images and attitudes dwarfing any that can be produced by persuasive communication per se, is not to deny the relevance and potential usefulness of persuasive efforts; it is rather to view them from a perspective in which their range of real usefulness can begin to be identified. This perspective is surely one that sees persuasive communication in intimate contact with the shifting structure of events, not in isolation from them. As will be seen, preparatory communications may modulate the impact of events that might otherwise be disruptive. Interpretive communications, in turn, may reinforce desired aspects of images and attitudes when the cumulative pressure of changes in the real world has shaken the stability of previous stereotypes.

On this view, the primary fact with which an examination of generalizations about the modification of images and attitudes should start is their normal stability and resistance to change. We turn now to this topic.

RESISTANCE TO PERSUASIVE COMMUNICATION

It would be a mistake to attribute the general stability of attitudes and images entirely to psychological processes of resistance to change. Ecological factors that we have already noted restrict a person's encounters with discordant information and impose barriers that may be difficult for persuasive communication to penetrate, without any active defenses being called into play. By the same token, when a person's attitudes are congruent with the informational climate that prevails in his social milieu, they are likely to receive continual reinforcement. We are concerned in this section with more active modes of resistance that limit the effectiveness of attempts to bring about changes in international attitudes.

Modes of Resistance

In recent years, a number of experimental studies have been reported that supplement the large body of impressionistic observations concerning resistances to persuasive pressures. The findings repeatedly bear out the well-known generalization that whenever communications attempt to change pre-existing images or attitudes that engage important goals or values, strong resistances will arise at each step of the communication process. Thus, some communications will be so strongly resisted that they fail to achieve even the very first step of eliciting audience *exposure* to the message; others that are somewhat more successful at the outset may end up being just as ineffective because resistances are mobilized in members of the audience during the time they are exposed to the message, which interfere drastically with *attention, comprehension,* or *acceptance* (see Hovland, Janis, & Kelley, 1953, pp. 287–293).

When a political elite in one country issues messages on controversial topics to people in other countries or to rival political groups within their own country, the first manifestations of resistance may occur at the initial stage of *self-exposure* (Lazarsfeld, 1942; Lazarsfeld, Berelson, & Gaudet, 1948). If they are not a "captive" audience, people will resist being "captivated" by simply turning off a radio or television program as soon as they realize that it contains objectionable material. Similarly, if the title of a book, pamphlet, or magazine article cues the potential reader to expect disagreeable or unrewarding content, it will rapidly be relegated to the well-known *New Yorker* category of "items we never finished reading." For example, a survey by Cannell and MacDonald (1956) indicated that widely distributed pamphlets, posters, news stories, and magazine articles that publicized information about cigarette smoking as a cause of cancer were read by large numbers of nonsmokers but self-exposure to such reading matter was relatively infrequent among smokers in the same communities. Similarly, in the sphere of international communications, favorable publicity during a pro-U.N. campaign was found to have reached mainly those people who were pro-U.N. to begin with (Star & Hughes, 1950).[1]

Even if people have a tendency to avoid communications that are not in accord with their own preexisting beliefs and attitudes, exposure can often be induced, by a variety of "captivation" devices. But the seemingly effective use of such devices is certainly no guarantee of a successful net outcome with respect to modifying the audience's images or attitudes. No change at all or even "boomerang" effects may occur as a consequence of selective inattention to disturbing ideas, misperception of the message, or subsequent selective forgetting (Allport & Postman,

1945; Cooper & Jahoda, 1947; Hyman & Sheatsley, 1947; Kendall & Wolf, 1949; Levine & Murphy, 1943; Seeleman, 1941). Klapper (1960, pp. 19–25) calls attention to some twenty-odd studies that indicate that one or more selective processes occur in at least a sizable percentage of each of the various audiences. He points out, however, that in all instances there was always a substantial number of people within the audience who did not display any such selective process and who therefore absorbed the message.

Other authors have emphasized the characteristic forms of resistance that occur even when a persuasive communication is adequately perceived and correctly interpreted. Some typical examples of such resistances are to be found in a recent study by Janis and Terwilliger (1962), in which groups of smokers and nonsmokers were induced to read carefully a fear-arousing pamphlet on smoking as a cause of cancer. The subjects were asked to verbalize spontaneous associations after reading each paragraph, and these associations were classified according to a content analysis procedure designed to detect manifestations of resistance. The smokers gave some associations indicating that they tended to accept the arguments and evidence presented in the pamphlet but their associations frequently contained clear-cut manifestations of resistance, such as doubting the validity of the evidence cited, attributing propagandistic intentions to the communicator, and asserting that

---

[1] Although the principle of selective self-exposure, supported by the correlational evidence of field surveys such as those just cited, has been taken for granted as fully established by such authorities as Klapper (1960), recent controlled experimentation has called the conventional formulation of it into question. Evidence for the active seeking of concordant information is strong, but experimental evidence does not consistently support the corresponding hypothesis that people generally tend to avoid discordant information (see Brehm & Cohen, 1962, pp. 68–69). To the extent that people are less prone than had been assumed to avoid communications challenging their preexisting images, the opportunities for effective persuasion are of course greater. Research currently in progress should help to clarify this important issue.

the threat of cancer did not affect them in any way. A group of nonsmokers gave significantly more associations of the type indicating acceptance of the content and significantly fewer manifestations of resistances involving personal detachment from the threat (see also Janis, 1959, p. 215).

Hovland, Janis, and Kelley (1953, pp, 293–298), in their analysis of the conditions under which persuasion is successful and unsuccessful, point out that an essential difference between instruction and persuasion involves expectations that affect a person's motivation to accept or reject the communicator's conclusions. In the case of instructional communications, where high acceptance is readily elicited, the setting is typically one in which the members of the audience anticipate that the communicator is trying to help them, that his conclusions are incontrovertible, and that they will be socially rewarded rather than punished for adhering to his conclusions. In persuasive situations, on the other hand, interfering expectations are likely to be aroused that operate as resistances. The authors point out that the findings from experiments on communication effects seem to converge upon three types of interfering expectations that operate to decrease the degree of acceptance: (a) expectations of being manipulated by the communicator (for example, being exploited by an untrustworthy source who has ulterior economic or political motives for trying to persuade others to support his position); (b) expectations of being "wrong" (for example, making incorrect judgments on a controversial political issue or overlooking antithetical evidence that would be grounds for a more cautious or compromise position); and (c) expectations of social disapproval (for example, from members of the local community whose norms are not in accord with the communicator's position).

Although all three sources of resistance are recognized as important deterrents to successful persuasion, the third type has been most extensively investigated in the recent social-psychological literature. Here we refer to the numerous studies on the anchorage of images and attitudes in group norms, which point up strong resistances to change arising from fear of being criticized or rejected by one's family, friendship clique, work group, political organization, or some other reference group. (See the reviews of the literature in Kelley and Thibaut, 1954; Riecken and Homans, 1954; Newcomb, 1950; and Cartwright and Zander, 1960.) Such resistance is likely to be mobilized to a very high degree whenever educational or persuasive communications exert pressure on an audience to modify their stereotypes or traditional evaluations of other nations, and hence represents a major problem for international communication. Accordingly, we shall first examine this type of resistance in some detail before examining factors that affect the strength of other sources of resistance.

Resistance Due to Anchorage in Group Affiliations

It is generally recognized that the need to adhere to group loyalties and to maintain social approval from significant persons and groups in one's community often inclines a person to reject new ideas or to resist "thinking for himself" on political issues. This tendency is most apparent when the individual is a member of a primary or secondary group that prescribes specific ideological norms. In this section we consider factors affecting the degree to which an individual will resist changing attitudes and beliefs anchored in group norms. The principal research findings can be summarized in four propositions pertaining to "counter-norm" themes, that is, to communications that promote images, policies, or actions contrary to the norms of one or another group with which the audience is affiliated—family, community, party, nation, and so on. Although formulated in terms of group *membership*, the four propositions probably apply equally to people who merely *aspire* to membership—that is, those for whom a given norm-setting group is a positive reference group: (1) The degree of resistance to counter-norm communications varies directly with the strength of the formal and informal *sanctions* applied by the norm-setting group. (2) The more closely the group consensus on a given issue approaches *unanimity*, the greater will be the resistance of individual members to counter-norm communications on the issue. (3) Members of a group who are strongly motivated to maintain their membership status—or who place a high valuation on their membership—are likely to *internalize* the group norms and will therefore be highly resistant to counter-norm communications even on issues for which there is little expectation of surveillance or punishment. (4) When education or persuasion is intended solely to induce *immediate* actions or *temporary* changes in attitude that deviate from group norms, the persuasive arguments contained in the counter-norm communications will be more effective if presented under conditions in which the group symbols are *not salient*.

It is a truism that when a man is affiliated with a group, he is under constraint to avoid deviating from the value judgments and the ideology of that group. The first of the foregoing propositions takes account of the obvious fact that within any group it is harder to "get away with" certain deviations than others. Experimental findings concerning the forces exerted to bring deviating members back into line or to restore uniformity within the group by excluding or rejecting them (an ultimate sanction for any group) are discussed by Festinger (1950) and Schachter (1951). One of the few systematic cross-national experiments in the field of social psychology provides confirmatory evidence for this tendency to reject deviates (Schachter, Nuttin, De Monchaux, Maucorps, Osmer, Duijker, Rommetveit, & Israel, 1954). When exposed to communications that go counter to one of the norms of his group, the member will be most strongly inclined to reject the conclusions if he anticipates prompt detection and drastic punishment for deviating from the particular norm. His anticipations will depend, in turn, upon how the group has conveyed the sanctions that follow from deviance—the extent to which the norm is discussed within the group, the threats or incentives implied by group leaders, exemplary punishments of previous transgressors, and the degree of surveillance over verbal and overt behavior relevant to the norm.

The first proposition calls attention to the need for assessing sanctions and surveillance factors in order to decide *which* counter-norm appeals have some chance of being successful. Norms that are regarded as crucially relevant to the group's goals are likely to be buttressed by stronger sanctions than norms having more marginal status. In the United States, for example, attitudes toward Communist China are more strongly prescribed and sanctioned than attitudes toward Turkey (for many years the subject of unfavorable imagery), because of obvious differences in their relevance to national goals and international conflict.

Certain segments of the population may be potentially responsive to counter-norm communications because they are less exposed to communications within the group concerning norms and sanctions. In every nation there are those who have already become alienated and disaffected, who see little to gain from the official national goals and nothing to lose from rejecting them— the recruiting ground in the Western countries for Communist counter-norm appeals, as analyzed by Cantril in his *Politics of despair* (1958). Their vulnerability follows from both Proposition 1 (less awareness or fear of sanctions) and Proposition 3 (lower valuation of national membership). At the other social extreme are leaders in high power positions. Strong forces of a positive sort are likely to attach leaders to the norms of the group (Proposition 3), but their attachment to the official norms nevertheless gains a certain flexibility because they have less to fear from the application of group sanctions. Hollander (1958) has shown that leaders who have established a record of exemplary conformity earn a fund of "idiosyncrasy credits" that allows them to deviate with impunity when they decide to disregard one of the existing norms, which sometimes results in the entire group's shifting to a new norm. This may have been one of the aspects of General Eisenhower's role that gave him special advantages during the early months of his presidency, enabling him to extricate the United States from the Korean War at a time when strong norms against negotiation with the Communist adversary had created an acute crisis of policy.

The foregoing considerations lead us to expect that when communicators in one country are trying to change international attitudes and images in a rival country, their efforts will often be less effective if they diffuse the usual varieties of mass propaganda than if they prepare communications that are "hand-tailored" to appeal to the motives and level of insight of a highly selected audience—namely, those national leaders and elite groups who are most likely to regard themselves as being relatively immune to negative sanctions from others in their national group.

The second proposition takes account of empirical results indicating that the more closely the group is perceived by its members to be in full consensus, the more firmly they are bound to its norms, and, therefore, the less accessible they are to counter-norm communications. Several interrelated processes are likely to underlie and contribute to these findings. First of all, the mere perception that the vast majority of other members accept a given norm seems to operate as a powerful force on the individual to conform to it (Newcomb, 1950; Bennett, 1955). Many people are inclined to interpret a high degree of consensus among the members of any group to which they belong as a sign that deviations will be readily noticeable and will entail serious consequences. A second, and perhaps more important, force enters the picture when group consensus is perceived as completely unanimous (Asch, 1952, 1958). Unanimous judgment of one's fellows comes to constitute for each person a version of unquestioned "social reality" that carries the conviction of physical reality. Most of us "know" that the world is round on the same social basis that our ancestors "knew" it was flat. When convictions about the inherent villainy of another country are held with corresponding unanimity, they similarly acquire the status of fact, outside the sphere of questioning and controversy that pertains to matters of opinion.

Although any norm that is sustained by unanimity possesses a unique source of power, it also suffers from a unique source of potential weakness. Such norms are especially vulnerable to those communications that present irrefutable evidence of a break in the solidly unanimous front. Asch (1952, 1958) has shown how a single true witness can undermine the power of majority consensus to induce conformity with respect to judgments of simple perceptual stimuli, under circumstances in which the majority is maintaining a position at variance with the person's private experience. This type of vulnerability can be expected whenever the unanimity of a group or community is more apparent than real: One such state of affairs, called "pluralistic ignorance" (Katz & Schanck, 1938), arises when strong anticipated sanctions keep people who disagree with the norms from giving public voice to their deviant opinions. Under these circumstances, counter-communications that convincingly call attention to the existence of covert dissent can be strategically advantageous.

Even when a person is exposed to completely unanimous judgments in a group setting, as Crutchfield (1955) has shown, the tendency to conform is greater for supposedly factual issues than for issues commonly regarded as matters of opinion and personal preference. It seems reasonable to suppose that when communications run counter to near-unanimous stereotypes, they might gain in effectiveness by calling attention to the problematic, controversial aspects of the issue.

A further potential vulnerability of unanimous opinion is suggested by the work of McGuire (in press). He finds that "cultural truisms" that "everybody" agrees with (the ones he studied were in the health area and not subject to intensely held norms) are quite vulnerable to counter-argument, because people have never found it necessary to arm themselves with evidence and arguments in support of their position (see McGuire & Papageorgis, 1962). McGuire has shown that special types of communications can "immunize" people against such counter-arguments, but, in order to do so, it is necessary to

acknowledge the opposition and to shake the audience's faith in their judgments about the issue; otherwise there is no reduction in the potential vulnerability of the hitherto unchallenged "truism."

Our third proposition, which predicts that the members' adherence to the norms will vary with their degree of attachment to the group, is supported by converging evidence both from small group experiments (e.g., Festinger, 1950) and from surveys of American voters (e.g., Converse & Campbell, 1960). The motivational factors that attach a person to his group can be classified under four headings: (a) affection, friendship, and other positive ties toward group leaders and fellow members; (b) desire for prestige and self-esteem, special privileges, or other psychological gains from being a member; (c) desire to escape from social isolation, or other unwelcome consequences that are avoided by being a member; and (d) restraints that act to keep the person within the group regardless of his desires in the matter (cf. Hovland, Janis, & Kelley, 1953, pp. 134–149). Of these, the first two (involving positive or affectionate motives) probably contribute most heavily to the tendency to internalize group norms so that they are maintained even in the absence of external sanctions. (On internalization as a factor in social influence, see also Kelman, 1961, who would treat the present instance as a case of "identification.")

This proposition supports the widely accepted assumption that in times of crisis, when national cohesiveness is at a maximum, foreign propaganda that directly advocates counter-norm ideas (such as explicit attacks accusing the nation's leaders of corruption or immorality) will have little chance of being effective among the population at large, except among those dissident sectors least motivated to maintain their national affiliation. More subtle efforts to reduce the strength of the audience's motivation to maintain their group membership (for example, by calling attention to alternative ways that personal goals could be achieved independently of the group) might be much more effective, in the long run, in reducing the tendency to internalize group norms. In this way, some members of the audience might be prepared for accepting subsequent counter-norm communications that would otherwise be despised and avoided.

This implication is in line with observations on the effects of "Voice of America" broadcasts to European satellite countries during the early 1950s. According to a report by International Research Associates (1953), summarized by Klapper (1960), escapees interviewed within a few days of their crossing the border had evidently undergone a shift of reference groups before defecting. Frequently the change began with some specific incident, usually unrelated to ideology, that made their future seem relatively hopeless and caused them to look elsewhere. As their present lot became increasingly less tolerable, they apparently became more accessible to radio broadcasts from Western countries. "By the time they defected they had developed a set of attitudes totally out of keeping with their previous orientation, but in accord with the reference groups they had newly adopted. . . . The original group norms had ceased to hinder the influence of communications designed to convert, while at the same time, the attractions of the new group norms served to abet and reinforce the influence of the same communications" (Klapper, 1960, pp. 67–68).

The final proposition of the four under consideration concerns the effect of presenting persuasive arguments in counter-norm communications under conditions where the recipients' membership in the norm-setting group is made more or less salient. Several types of cues may come into play when a communication from the outside is presented, arousing resistances by reminding members of the audience of their affiliations with a group that is opposed to the new point of view. Among the potential cues are: a *source* of communication who is well known as an opponent of the group; the use of a *channel* (such as a particular radio station or newspaper) that is known to be affiliated with the opposition; as well as obviously biased features of the *contents* (appeals, arguments, and slogans) that are immediately recognized as violating the norms of the home group. Further research is needed to discover the more subtle cues occurring in international communications that induce heightened resistance to change in group-anchored attitudes and to find ways of reducing the prominence of such cues without having to mislead the audience about the source and purpose of the communication.

When group symbols are in the focus of attention, members of the group are most likely to take account of and conform to the norms of their group, and consequently will be most likely to resist counter-communications (cf. Hovland, Janis, & Kelley, 1953, pp. 155–165; Charters & Newcomb, 1958; Kelley, 1955). One of the obvious implications of Proposition 4 is that communications directed to members of a rival political organization would have a better chance of being taken seriously if the content were to avoid any mention of the organization and were presented in a nonpolitical setting—say, as a legitimate part of a cultural exchange program—where the audience is preoccupied with other loyalties and interests.

The proposition does not apply, however, when the goal of the counter-norm communication is to induce *sustained* changes in images and attitudes. The effectiveness of counter-norm propaganda presented under conditions of low salience is likely to be short-lived when the group symbols once again become salient in subsequent situations (cf. Brodbeck, 1956). After having been caught off guard and temporarily "seduced" into deviating from the norms of their group, people may experience guilt and social anxiety on realizing their error, and thereafter conform more rigorously than ever. Changes in images and attitudes induced under conditions of high salience, while much more difficult to produce, should have a better chance of persisting, inasmuch as the person has had the opportunity to resolve or to adapt himself to the conflict between the appeals of the communication and the powerful pressures of the group. Hence, the advantage of low salience is likely to be limited to short-run objectives.

Suggestive evidence for the more permanent effects of influence under high salience conditions comes from a report by Lesser and Peter (1957, pp. 188–191; see also Watson & Lippitt, 1958, for an account of the study on which this observation is based). The results indicated that among the members of several groups of German nationals visiting the United States as part of a post-war governmental program, those who kept their home-country membership salient during their American sojourn (having often posed difficult and critical questions to the team leaders) were more likely to show *persistently favorable* attitude changes after their return to Germany than those who fitted in more comfortably to their American experience, forgetting their back-home commitments during their sojourn.

The sources of resistance that stem from the anchorage of images and attitudes in group membership have particularly direct relevance, as we have seen, to the problems faced by a communicator who wishes to modify the images held by members of foreign audiences. But a person's attitudes are anchored not only in his social groups; they are also rooted in other ongoing motivational processes linked with important personality needs. The resistances that may arise from the personal anchorage of attitudes are our next topic.

Resistance Due to Anchorage in Personality Needs

A number of recent research investigators have started from the premise that there are concealed reasons why people hold particular images, opinions, and attitudes concerning foreign governments and international issues, inasmuch as their thoughts and feelings about such topics contribute to ongoing processes of personal adjustment. This "functional" approach is concerned with the degree to which responsiveness or resistance to persuasive attempts varies as a function of the motivational basis upon which the attitude in question rests. A personality-oriented approach to social and political attitudes is of interest from two perspectives. First, it may help us to clarify the nature and sources of *individual differences* in responsiveness to persuasive communications. In the present chapter, however, we shall not attempt a detailed examination of the literature from this standpoint, because educational and persuasive campaigns will rarely be in a position to tailor communications to take account of the personal characteristics of individual respondents; relevant differences in national character, to the extent that they can be documented, would involve us in special considerations that are idiosyncratic for each major national or cultural group and are out of place in this chapter. (The interested reader will find the relevant literature on national character and national stereotypes classified and reviewed in Duijker and Frijda, 1960. For an analysis of personality factors in persuasibility and relevant evidence, see Janis, Hovland, *et al.*, 1959; Janis, 1963.)

A second value of focusing on the personality needs satisfied by social and political attitudes is that we catch glimpses of some neglected sources of resistance or accessibility to persuasion that may lead to improvements in our ability to predict the outcome of educational and promotional campaigns.

Investigators who have analyzed the functions that ethnocentric, nationalistic, and authoritarian attitudes serve for the individual personality formulate their conclusions in somewhat different terms and draw on somewhat different theoretical premises, but seem to be in essential agreement. Smith, Bruner, and White (1956) offer one formulation, based on close study of the opinions about Russia held by a small number of adult men whose personalities were also studied intensively (see also Smith, 1947, 1949, and 1958). A slightly different version of the functional point of view is offered by Sarnoff and Katz (1954), with more explicit attention to hypotheses regarding the conditions of attitude change. A related and fuller treatment that differs in many details is given in Katz and Stotland (1959), who also provide a useful guide to much relevant research. Finally, Katz (1960) has reformulated the functional approach to attitude change in a way that probably has the greatest general usefulness in the present context. For the sake of simplicity, we shall seek to coordinate here only the first and last of these related approaches.

According to Smith, Bruner, and White's essentially clinical study, images and opinions about Russia and Communism appeared to serve three major functions in the economy of personality: (a) *object appraisal;* (b) *social adjustment;* and (c) *externalization.* Any persistent image is likely to serve all three functions to some extent, but there is considerable variation from one person to another with respect to the function that predominates.

The first function involves scanning and appraising the input of information from the external world for its relevance to the person's motives, goals, values, and interests, thus giving rise to the phenomena of selective self-exposure and attention to information. A person's stock of *existing* beliefs and opinions simplifies his task of scanning by providing him with already evaluated categories to which incoming information can be fitted. The authors found great individual variation in the extent to which their subjects' attitudes toward Russia reflected this function. At one extreme were those for whom the barest minimum of borrowed clichés sufficed to satisfy their need to put in order the modicum of information that filtered through to them; others showed quite different tendencies, ranging to the opposite extreme of being so strongly committed to religion, to liberal democracy, or to national interests that their view of every new item of information about Russia was shaped by the preexisting ideological matrix.

By "social adjustment" is meant the part played by a person's opinions in facilitating, disrupting, or simply maintaining his relations with significant others. Since attitudes may be organized in response to motivated nonconformity as well as to conformist motives, a better term for this function might be the *mediation of self–other relations.* In contrast with object appraisal, in which informational input *about the object* is selectively influential in accordance with the person's ongoing concerns, social adjustment pertains to the influence of information about *the way other people regard the object.* This information engages his motives to affiliate and identify himself with them or to detach himself and oppose them. At the time of the study, much of what Americans had to say about Russia seemed to be motivated by their wish to distinguish themselves from the Communists as a negative reference group. In a functional analysis of attitude change, this category provides a basis for taking account of individual differences in personality needs when dealing with the resistance phenomena we have already discussed under *group anchorage.*

The final class of functions, labelled *externalization* by Smith, Bruner, and White, involves response to an external event in a way that is colored by a person's unresolved inner problems. Outside events are treated as analogous to inner ones, and the attitude taken toward them is an overt symbolic substitute for covert attitudes taken in the inner struggle. Thus one of the men, personally greedy for his share of the world's goods and prestige to a greater extent than he could admit, conceived of the Soviet leadership with imagery of "pigs at the trough." Included under externalization are manifestations of the Freudian mechanisms of displacement and projection. Presumably the person, while seemingly attempting to appraise the object, is unwittingly carrying on some of the work of tension-reduction that is necessary in dealing with his inner problems.

Differentiation of these functions would seem to have considerable implications for the conditions under which images and attitudes will be resistive or responsive to informative communications. When *object appraisal* predominates, a rational, informational approach is indicated, which will be successful insofar as it can break through the scanning filter to reorient the person's appraisal of reality in its relevance to his needs, goals, and values. The frequently observed failure of educational campaigns (Hyman & Sheatsley, 1947) is probably due in part to the fact that attitudes often rest on other primary functional bases. When the *mediation of self–other relations* is the main basis for an attitude, information presenting a different picture of reference group norms and consensus is likely to be more effective. Finally, when an attitude is rooted primarily in *externalization,* it is likely to remain uninfluenced by information, but may respond to authoritative reassurances that alleviate anxiety, to changes brought about in self-insight, or to the uncovering processes that go on in psychoanalytic therapy, when deviations in reality-testing are recognized, resistances and transference attitudes analyzed, and new resources for strengthening the self-image discovered.

Katz (1960) groups the major functions that attitudes perform for the personality according to four motivational categories that are substantially congruent with Smith, Bruner, and White although with a different emphasis:[2]

---

[2] The *ego-defensive* function corresponds to *externalization,* a difference only in terminology. As for the other functions, Katz appears to have made his classification in terms of the respective traditions of psychological theory that seem most relevant, whereas Smith, Bruner, and White have been most concerned with differential ways in which informational input is relevant to the attitude. In result, *object appraisal* includes Katz's fourth category, the *knowledge function* (albeit less clearly differentiated), and also aspects of Katz's first and third functions, insofar as they work upon information concerning the nature and relevance of the

1. *The instrumental, adjustive, or utilitarian function* upon which Jeremy Bentham and the utilitarians constructed their model of man. A modern expression of this approach can be found in behavioristic learning theory.

2. *The ego-defensive function* in which the person protects himself from acknowledging the basic truths about himself or the harsh realities in his external world. Freudian psychology and neo-Freudian thinking have been preoccupied with this type of motivation and its outcomes.

3. *The value-expressive function* in which the individual derives satisfaction from expressing attitudes appropriate to his personal values and to his concept of himself. This function is central to doctrines of ego psychology which stress the importance of self-expression, self-development, and self-realization.

4. *The knowledge function* based upon the individual's need to give adequate structure to his universe. The search for meaning, the need to understand, the trend toward better organization of perceptions and beliefs to provide clarity and consistency for the individual, are other descriptions of this function. The development of principles about perceptual and cognitive structure have been the contribution of Gestalt psychology (p. 170).

Katz formulated the implications of his classification not only for the conditions of attitude change, but also for the conditions under which variously based attitudes are initially formed and subsequently aroused as determinants of a person's orientation and behavior. These implications are summarized in Table 6.1, which provides a rich source

of hypotheses for our present purpose. The items listed under "arousal conditions" may either enter into the mobilization of resistance or form the basis for receptivity to new information. While a major program of experimental research, under Katz's leadership, has been conducted to test hypotheses arising from this formulation, it has not as yet encompassed all of the suggested relationships and the table as a whole must be regarded, again, as a set of promising leads. Much of the relevant research is reviewed by Katz and Stotland (1959).

Before turning to evidence that brings the functional approach more directly to bear upon international images and attitudes, we shall attempt to carry the analysis one step further by introducing some additional tentative generalizations that supplement those from Smith, Bruner, and White and from Katz. First, it seems reasonable to assume that the more functions that an image or attitude serves, the stronger is the potential resistance to change. The idea here resembles the Freudian concept of "overdetermination": When an image derives support from a variety of motivational sources —contributing as a compromise solution to several adjustive problems—it should be more difficult to dislodge it by any single persuasive appeal.

A multidetermined attitude tends to be held with greater intensity or conviction than one less fully imbued with personal significance. A number of specialists in communications research (for example, Klapper, 1960; Tannen-

---

attitudinal object. *Mediation of self–other relations* likewise cuts across Katz's distinctions: it overlaps the *instrumental, adjustive* function insofar as the attitude serves the person by helping him to maintain a desired pattern of social relations, and also the *value-expressive* function, to the extent that holding the attitude contributes to the person's maintenance of a desired self-image, a valued self-identity. Playing these analytic schemes against each other is more than a mere scholastic exercise, as it may sensitize the reader to implications of the functional approach for the intentional modification of attitudes.

TABLE 6.1

Determinants of Attitude Formation, Arousal, and Change in Relation to Type of Function

Function	Origin and dynamics	Arousal conditions	Change conditions
Adjustment	Utility of attitudinal object in need satisfaction. Maximizing external rewards and minimizing punishments	1. Activation of needs 2. Salience of cues associated with need satisfaction	1. Need deprivation 2. Creation of new needs and new levels of aspiration 3 Shifting rewards and punishments 4. Emphasis on new and better paths for need satisfaction
Ego defense	Protecting against internal conflicts and external dangers	1. Posing of threats 2. Appeals to hatred and repressed impulses 3. Rise in frustrations 4. Use of authoritarian suggestion	1. Removal of threats 2. Catharsis 3. Development of self-insight
Value expression	Maintaining self-identity; enhancing favorable self-image; self-expression and self-determination	1. Salience of cues associated with values 2. Appeals to individual to reassert self-image 3. Ambiguities which threaten self-concept	1. Some degree of dissatisfaction with self 2. Greater appropriateness of new attitude for the self 3. Control of all environmental supports to undermine old values
Knowledge	Need for understanding, for meaningful cognitive organization, for consistency and clarity	1. Reinstatement of cues associated with old problem or of old problem itself	1. Ambiguity created by new information or change in environment 2. More meaningful information about problems

From Katz, 1960, p. 192. Reprinted by permission of publisher and author.

baum, 1956) have emphasized the inverse relationship between susceptibility to change and intensity of preexisting images and attitudes: The more intensely an image or attitude is held, the stronger the resistances evoked by any educational or persuasive communications that attempt to change it. As an empirical generalization, this proposition has wide support, although the vagueness of the term "intensity" leaves its implications in some doubt. One interpretation would regard the intensity of an attitude as a kind of summation of all the motivational vectors that enter into its significance to the individual.

Another suggestion is that an image may be more susceptible to change when there is *conflict* among the functions, as when reality testing is not well served by an image that effectively promotes the other two functions. Under favorable circumstances, a communicator might be able to heighten the conflict, increasing awareness of the deviation from good reality testing, and thereby inducing the opposing function to become dominant over the others. This line of reasoning calls attention to the assumption that although images and attitudes may be initially acquired at a time when they worked well for the individual, they may, nevertheless, subsequently become *dys*functional under changing circumstances. In such a case there should be greater readiness to relinquish the preexisting image, and an adaptive change can probably be accelerated by communications that make the dysfunctional aspects salient.

In referring to salience, we need to take more explicit account of the *degree of awareness* that is involved in the motivational basis of attitudes and images. Janis (1959, pp. 210–219) has called attention to the desirability of differentiating among conscious, preconscious, and unconscious sources of affective charges when analyzing the sources of decisional conflicts. The same distinction may be equally important for a functional analysis of the persistence and change of international images, particularly when the ego-defensive or externalization function is involved. If the primary function (such as bolstering one's self-image of being powerful or morally superior to others) is at the *preconscious* level, the person would be capable of recognizing it and discounting its influence if it were called to his attention by an impressive communication. But as Freud has repeatedly emphasized, there is much more resistance to change when a motive is kept at the *unconscious* level by processes of active repression.

Personality Factors and International Attitudes

Our discussion of the functional basis of attitudes and its implications for resistance to persuasive communications has thus far been cast in highly general terms. The sphere of international attitudes and imagery with which

we are specifically concerned seems peculiarly subject to the influence of the less rational of these personal determinants. As Scott (1958) has pointed out, such attitudes tend to be maintained in a context that does not compel rationality or cognitive consistency (see Chapter 3). With little opportunity for the more direct forms of reality-testing in personal encounters—and with the strong affects of hate, suspicion, and fear that are engendered in the still-Hobbesian world of nation states—people's imagery in the international sphere is likely to become tied to their inner problems in ways suggested under the concept of *externalization*. To put the matter in functional terms, the communicator who wishes to contribute to the reduction of international tension and to promote the peaceful organization of international relations often faces the task of shifting the motivational basis of attitudes from one rooted in externalization and social adjustment to one that facilitates object appraisal. In order to do so, of course, he must somehow gain attention to and acceptance of more valid information on which new, more differentiated and appropriate appraisals can be based. Suggestive leads from research concerning the nature of externalization processes in this sphere thus become highly relevant to understanding the sources of resistance to those persuasive attempts that promote the acceptance of tolerant, nonprejudiced, and pro-international attitudes.

One of the key hypotheses that is strongly suggested, but not yet securely established by existing evidence, holds that *persons who have strong latent needs to displace hostility toward remote social targets and to project their own repressed impulses onto them are less likely than others to be influenced by prodemocratic communications that attempt to break down ethnocentric attitudes.* The most influential statement of the underlying personality dynamics is that of *The authoritarian personality* (Adorno, Frenkel-Brunswik, Levinson, & Sanford, 1950). This series of studies has stimulated a large amount of research, but, because of methodological difficulties, has led to few incontrovertibly firm conclusions (see Christie & Jahoda, 1954).

The latent personality needs specified in the above proposition can be inferred from various observable characteristics of manifest behavior, as reported by many investigators. These characteristics include the following: (a) strong ideological acceptance of conventional mores combined with a high degree of concern about deviations from conventional moral standards; (b) unusually intense interest in "immoral" behavior of people in foreign countries and in other out-groups; (c) compulsive submissiveness to parents and to other authority figures combined with covert acts of defiance toward them; (d) inhibitions of normal sexual and aggressive activities in everyday social relations combined with indirect, devious forms of gratification; (e) exaggerated expectations of punishment or retaliation that will ensue from personal aggressive behavior toward positive objects. Individuals who show a constellation of personality characteristics of this kind appear to be especially responsive to totalitarian and nationalistic propaganda that advocates social prejudices toward various social classes, toward foreign countries, or toward minority groups. Because powerful personality needs are satisfied by adopting social prejudices, such personalities tend to be exceptionally resistant to any efforts to break down their ethnocentric attitudes.

The evidence for such a constellation has come primarily from American research on ethnic prejudice, rather than on international attitudes (cf. Allport, 1954 for a general review of research on prejudice; also Mussen, 1950; Hovland, Janis, & Kelley, 1953, pp. 205–206). In this sphere, Pettigrew (1958) has shown (with the much-used F Scale which purports to measure this "authoritarian" syndrome) that although authoritarianism correlates with anti-Negro prejudice in both the North and the South, the pronounced regional differences in prejudice cannot be attributed to differences in the personality variable. Socio-cultural factors rooted in group norms are presumably responsible for the regional differences. Pettigrew's study nicely illustrates how cultural norms and personality factors can operate conjointly in determining intergroup attitudes.

There is more direct evidence that authoritarianism, as measured by the F Scale, is related to attitudes in the international sphere. Levinson (1957) reports a positive correlation with a measure of nationalism (but unfortunately, the scales he correlated are similar in formal properties); Smith and Rosen (1958) find confirmatory evidence of the converse relationship, a negative correlation with "world-mindedness." Interviews with extreme respondents in the latter study also provide supporting evidence, indicating that the more world-minded individuals were more equalitarian in outlook, less stereotyped, and more likely to view various personal problems as internal rather than external in origin. They also tended to be more optimistic about solving society's problems. In a similar vein, Gladstone and Taylor (1958) found that general attitudes of belligerence, nonpacification, and feelings of threat in regard to international events are related to one another and to reactions to persuasive communications about international events. Furthermore, MacKinnon and Centers (1956) report, for a cross-section of Los Angeles residents, that "equalitarians" and "authoritarians" not only differed in expected ways in their attitudes toward trade with and education about Russia, but were also likely to give quite dissimilar types of reasons in support of their positions. Punitive considerations, for example, were mentioned more often by authoritarians as a reason against trade, whereas economic benefit was an argument distinctive of authoritarians who favored trade. The correlational evidence from these studies is open to alternative interpretations, however, and the findings retain the status of suggestive leads.

All the studies cited thus far were conducted with American respondents. Of particular interest, therefore, is Christiansen's study of *Attitudes toward foreign affairs as a function of personality* (1959), which was conducted with students at the Military and Naval Academies in Oslo. One of the hypotheses for which Christiansen presents confirming evidence is that a person's characteristic way of responding to conflicts of daily life will generalize to his attitudes toward international conflict situations. He constructed parallel scales to measure the reactions to conflicts in these two spheres. According to his schema, responses could either be *threat-oriented* or *problem-oriented;* within each of these types, reactions could be either passive or active, and, if active, directed either inward or outward. Generally positive correlations between corresponding scoring categories of the scales pertaining to everyday life and to international relations bear out the prediction that there is a substantial degree of generality of orientation across the two conflict areas. Such a relationship is compatible with the functional concept of "externalization," although the evidence is incomplete with respect to the underlying psychodynamics.

More pertinent to the latter are Christiansen's data concerning the "latency" hypothesis, which assumes that patterns characteristic of unconscious levels of personality will have their counterparts in manifest attitudes about international relations. Positive relationships were found between latent hostile tendencies, as revealed in two projective tests, and manifestly aggressive attitudes in foreign affairs. Personal insecurity did not turn out to be an important factor in international attitudes; nor was knowledge, as defined by agreement with expert judgment, at all related to any of the indices of international orientation. Adherence to an ideology of nationalism or chauvinistic patriotism, however, was shown to be an important factor in channelling personal aggressiveness into hostile attitudes on international topics. In the subgroups that were highest in nationalism, measures of latent aggression and of the tendency to blame others in daily life were found to be more highly correlated with the index of blaming other nations than in subgroups that were lower in nationalism. To the extent that a person's aggressive attitudes in foreign affairs are rooted in deep-seated hostile needs and in firm ideological commitments that encourage hostility toward out-groups, we would anticipate a very low degree of influencibility. Whenever attempts are made to induce such a person to adopt more cooperative or pacific attitudes toward the nations he scorns or despises, his resistances will be strongly mobilized and he is likely to react with aggression toward the communicator.

In the light of the available correlational evidence, it seems likely that extremist groups, who often attempt to disrupt organized efforts to ameliorate international relations, will prove to have more than their share of persons whose attitudes are anchored in personality needs and are relatively immune to rational persuasion. Since such persons are more likely to respect the "propaganda of the deed" than to be moved by persuasive words, it would seldom be profitable to plan the content of educational communications to meet *their* arguments.

OVERCOMING THE EFFECTS OF RESISTANCE

When one considers the variety of sources of resistance to change in international attitudes—resistances deriving both from group norms and from personal motives—one is left with a rather bleak picture. Conservative expectations concerning the power of persuasive communication to convert are certainly in order. But to redress the balance somewhat, we must take account of evidence that people's defenses can sometimes be penetrated or circumvented. We have yet to consider some promising approaches that may help to counteract the effects of resistance.

Evidence for Communication Effects in Spite of Resistance

Even when the audience remains highly suspicious of the source and is strongly motivated to resist being influenced, communications sometimes prove to be surprisingly effective. Perhaps the most dramatic evidence for this point comes from studies by F. H. Allport and Simpson (1946), conducted during World War II. These experiments involved exposing American students to recordings of broadcasts that had been sent by Nazi German shortwave radio. During the fourteen half-hour sessions, the students rated their degree of acceptance or rejection after each main point or thesis had been presented. In general, they rejected the blatant propaganda themes, including attempts to derogate U.S. war aims and to play up the alleged moral justification for the Nazi war effort. But the enemy broadcasts were nevertheless effective in inducing acceptance of "defeatist" themes conveyed by factual-sounding statements to the effect that the United States was weak and Germany was strong. The experimenters and their sponsors were so concerned about the unexpected success of the Nazi shortwave radio programs in changing images of the United States and Germany in this respect that they took the precaution of drastically restricting the circulation of the report until after the war was over. Apparently the allegedly factual material did not evoke the overwhelming resistances aroused by assertions that dealt with political aims, moral issues, or other controversial value judgments. Thus, if some degree of exposure can be achieved—as by the use of provocative "news releases"—even a despised communicator may exert an influence in the limited sphere of inducing acceptance of allegedly factual statements.

The dramatic case of the truly "captive audiences" of American war prisoners in Korea and civilian prisoners in Communist China provides further evidence concerning the relative success of alleged "facts." It is now well known that popular accounts of so-called "brainwashing" among American POWs have been overdrawn, so far as extensive attitudinal changes are concerned. But evidently the purported confessions by U.S. officers to the effect that they were guilty of employing germ warfare were widely believed. This captive situation, however, differs from almost all others in which communication is directed at international imagery, because the Communist cap-

tors had a total monopoly over all channels of communication for their messages, and were able to coordinate their
efforts at persuasion with total coercive
control over the prisoners' entire life
setting (cf. Biderman, 1963; Lifton,
1961; Schein, 1958, 1961).

Numerous experimental studies can
also be cited, which show that the apparently factual content of a communication is sometimes accepted even
though the communicator's evaluative
conclusions are rejected. A typical example is the experiment by Cooper and
Dinerman (1951) in which high school
students were exposed to an antidis-
crimination film that depicted Hitler
and the Nazi regime unfavorably. Comparisons with an unexposed control
group showed that the experimental
group accepted the information about
Nazi Germany but remained uninfluenced in their over-all attitudes concerning discrimination against racial
and ethnic minorities. Similar diver-
gences between the factual and attitudinal content have been emphasized
by Hovland, Lumsdaine, and Sheffield
(1949), on the basis of an extensive
series of carefully controlled experiments designed to test the effects of
the "Why We Fight" films on American soldiers during World War II. The
film on the "Battle of Britain," for example, succeeded in modifying certain
aspects of the image of the British people, such as their "heroism" in the
struggle against the Nazis and their important contribution to the Allied war
effort, but was ineffective in changing
general attitudes toward the British or
toward American participation in the
war, even though these themes received
strong emphasis as the main orientation
objectives of the film.

Some commentators on public opinion formation have interpreted the orientation film experiments with American soldiers as evidence of the failure

of mass media communications to produce the intended effects even when
facts are communicated successfully.
None of the available studies, however,
has followed up on the *long-run* consequences of influencing the audience to
accept pieces of information pertinent
to breaking down stereotyped images
and attitudes toward out-groups or foreign countries. There are possibilities
here paralleling the "sleeper" effect (to
be discussed in a later section) observed
when, over time, a remembered message is gradually dissociated from a distrusted or disliked source. From psycho-
therapists we repeatedly hear of
instances in which the patient progressively changes his basic attitudes toward significant persons or groups, after
a long series of very minor changes involving the acceptance of new information about the lack of reality-basis for
his suspicions or antipathies. There is
no reason to preclude the possibility
that similar cumulative long-run effects
on basic images and attitudes can come
from the acceptance of apparent facts
communicated by the mass media.

When the topic of a communication
is unfamiliar to the audience—as will
often be the case in communications
about remote foreign nations and newly
emerging leaders—studies have shown
that factual material can produce major
changes in political and social images.
For example, Annis and Meier (1934)
were able to induce sustained favorable
evaluations of the Prime Minister of
Australia among various groups of
American college students who were
exposed to "planted" editorials that
commented on this previously unknown
figure.

Perhaps because of their formative
state, the views of children seem to be
particularly susceptible to influence by
information presented in the mass
media. Himmelweit, Oppenheim, and
Vince (1958) found that British chil-

dren were markedly affected by television programs on matters about which they had little previous knowledge. For example, middle class children's conceptions of the upper classes were strongly influenced, although their images of their own class remained unaffected.

The Use of "Side Attacks" to Minimize Resistance

Although factual content bearing on international imagery has sometimes been found to be effective in spite of the expected arousal of resistance, there is little support for the view that the marshalling of factual evidence in a frontal assault on existing stereotypes is an ideal way to induce people throughout the world to be more tolerant. An alternative approach that can be expected to meet with much less resistance involves the use of "side attacks" (cf. Albig, 1939, p. 217; Klapper, 1960, pp. 90–91). Instead of assembling hortatory, polemical, or refutation arguments against widely accepted beliefs, the side attack judiciously selects minor or subsidiary issues on which relatively low resistance can be expected. For example, with audiences in countries like the Soviet Union and the United States, where stereotyped views of the East–West conflict incline each side to regard the other as being too hostile or treacherous to be trusted in any international agreement, a more differentiated and sophisticated image might gradually be substituted if side attacks were concentrated on literary, cinematic, and medical achievements, leisure time interests, and patterns of family life in the rival nations. After the image of a rival nation has become more differentiated in purely nonpolitical respects, the audience may come to take a somewhat more tolerant view that "after all, they are not really so very different from us." Thus, just as the accumulation of new facts may lead to a change in attitude, so the induction of a series of minor exceptions to the rule ("they are evil people") can lead to the eventual breakdown of the rule itself.

Side attacks may be similarly advantageous when the initial image of another nation involves a high degree of ambivalence. (Consider, for example, the U.S. public's image of the British, French, and other allies.) By concentrating on subsidiary issues, the "positive" components can be made more salient and gradually come to predominate over the negative ones in the overall image.

Piecemeal changes of the kind discussed here and earlier probably can be more readily introduced when the audience lacks a well organized, tightly articulated attitude structure regarding the given object. When the attitude structure is highly integrated (as simply structured and affectively charged stereotypes often are), the audience must be subtly taught to dissociate the piece from the whole, otherwise the piecemeal effort is likely to be completely lost. In terms of the so-called "balance" theories of attitude organization and change that derive from Heider (1958, pp. 174–212), the communicator's task is to replace simply balanced structures in which the person can afford to see nothing good in a bad object (a hated country), with more complexly balanced and differentiated ones in which both good and bad evaluations become simultaneously tenable without strain (see Abelson, 1959; Rosenberg & Abelson, 1960). The more differentiated view of the object, if attained, is likely to be stable because of its probably closer correspondence to presenting fact.

A further implication of the research cited earlier is that when factual material is used by the communicator, resistance to side attacks tends to be minimal. We have already noted that if selective exposure can be circumvented by special appeals, the degree of acceptance of a side attack will depend on the extent to which the audience perceives the content as factual rather than as argumentative or manipulative. But at this point there are large gaps in our knowledge about the cues that various audiences use to identify "factual" information. In some instances, the *source* of the information may be a crucial factor. For example, London and Anisimov (1956) claim that foreign broadcast listeners in the Soviet Union are inclined to listen to and take seriously talks about internal affairs in the Soviet Union if they are made by *former Russians,* including even those who are representatives of anti-Soviet emigré organizations. American or British political "experts," on the other hand, tend to be dismissed as "hired servants" of a government agency.

These authors also assert that certain content characteristics can play a crucial role in inducing Soviet citizens to accept the alleged facts put forth in foreign broadcasts. Accustomed to reading between the lines, to looking behind the informational façade to find the "true" meaning of the contents of the Soviet controlled media, the Soviet citizen approaches foreign communications with the same skepticism. But since he is accustomed to a closely coordinated informational front, failure to present such a front may reduce the effectiveness of plausible and impressive communications.

The failure to exercise responsible restraint in public speech-making, the failure to link action to word, the spectacle of speaking in a small voice, frequently in contrary voices, where the Soviet press and radio would sound forth loudly and in unison on many instruments, undermine the Soviet citizen's confidence in the Western message and can vitiate the effectiveness of the best of plausible appeals (London & Anisimov, 1956, p. 329).

Similar problems of communicator-identity and content consistency undoubtedly arise in other countries, even when the foreign country transmitting the messages is regarded as an ally or friendly nation.

Pinpointing Potential Waverers or Key Audiences

Even when the general public of a country lies beyond the range of influence, it may be possible to identify a subaudience of potential waverers—people who are somewhat disaffiliated from the national group or for other reasons are likely to display comparatively little skepticism about factual messages from rival countries (see Klapper, 1960, pp. 78–79). Communications may be especially designed to appeal to them.

From the standpoint of the communicator who is attempting to improve national images in connection with the intended settlement of international disputes, it is especially important to take account of the characteristic "interfering expectations" that prevent acceptance among the potentially influential sectors of the foreign country who will be receiving his message—for example, government officials who monitor and study foreign broadcasts and hence are bound to be exposed to them. Cues to authenticity and sincerity are sometimes crucial in the interchanges between national elites at moments of great crisis. Outstanding examples of the stark consequences of accepting or rejecting factual claims in wartime are provided by historical studies of the U.S. entry into World

War I following the British government's interception of the notorious Zimmerman telegram, in which the German foreign minister instructed a German ambassador to try to induce Mexico to invade the United States (Tuchman, 1958). Knowing that President Wilson and other leaders in the American Government would be highly skeptical about any British information seemingly calculated to obtain American entry into the war, the British leaders carefully confined their communications to information that would enable American officials to discover the incriminating telegram themselves. Thus, they induced American officials to search the files of the American Western Union offices for a telegram sent by the German ambassador in Washington to the German ambassador in Mexico. Once convinced of the authenticity of the Zimmerman telegram, Wilson and his cabinet, as well as the leaders of Congress, no longer had any faith in German official communications. From then on, all subsequent messages from the German ambassador in Washington were dismissed as mere propaganda, even though he was sincerely attempting to ameliorate the crisis and to convince his home government of the necessity for a negotiated "peace-without-victory" along the lines that Wilson had only recently been urging (cf. Bernstorff, 1920; Tuchman, 1958).

Role Playing as a Way of Circumventing Resistance

Role playing, as a device that circumvents resistances, may be applicable to limited types of international issues with selected domestic groups, although its more sensational achievements have been emphasized in reports about Chinese "thought reform" in captive audiences (Lifton, 1961; Schein,

1961). The central proposition, that has now received support from numerous experimental studies, is the following: *When exposed to persuasive messages, persons who are required to play a role that entails putting the content of the message in their own words to others will be more influenced than those who are more passively exposed.* This tendency toward "saying is believing" has been found to occur even when role playing is artificially induced, as in experiments dealing with the effects of communications designed to modify: (a) *expectations* about future scientific, economic and military developments (Janis & King, 1954; King & Janis, 1956); and (b) *evaluations* of previously disliked tasks, policies, or ethnic groups (Culbertson, 1957; Festinger & Carlsmith, 1959; Harvey & Beverly, 1961; Kelman, 1953; Scott, 1957). The tendency to accept personally the content of a message that one is required to verbalize to others has been found to increase as the amount of *improvisation* increases (King & Janis, 1956). Mere repetition of a persuasive message evidently has little effect as compared with an improvised restatement and elaboration of the arguments and conclusions.

The success of improvised role play might be attributed to several different psychological processes. Festinger (1957) suggests that the main gain from role playing comes about from efforts to reduce dissonance between what one is saying and what one actually believes. Since the new position that is verbalized becomes a matter of public fact, and one's knowledge that one has said it is not in accord with one's prior beliefs, shifting to the new position helps to restore inner equilibrium. An alternative explanation is in terms of self-persuasion: When attempting to put the message across to others, the role player is likely to think up new formulations of the arguments, illustrations, and appeals that are tailor-made to be convincing to himself (see Hovland, Janis, & Kelley, 1953, pp. 228–237). In accord with the latter view, an experiment by Janis and Gilmore (1965) showed that role playing under acceptable, benevolent sponsorship produces more attitude change than role playing under seemingly manipulative or exploitative sponsorship. Evidently, when a person is induced to role play under unfavorable sponsorship conditions he is more likely to make tacit interfering responses of doubt and distrust, which reduces the amount of attitude change. This finding is contrary to what would be expected on the basis of Festinger's hypothesis and is in disagreement with several other experimental studies which have been interpreted as confirming predictions from dissonance theory (Brehm & Cohen, 1962). Currently under way are a number of systematic investigations on the amount of attitude change that occurs when people are induced to engage in role playing by the use of positive (consonant) incentives rather than by negative (dissonant) ones. The results can be expected to help settle theoretical questions about how attitude changes are produced, and, at the same time, to indicate the special conditions needed for the successful use of role playing.

One application of the role-playing hypothesis not dissimilar to the confessional essays required of participants in Chinese Communist "thought reform" is the assignment of essay writing when school children are being persuaded to engage in some desired activity or are being inculcated with the norms of honesty, cleanliness, and tolerance (see Kelman, 1953). Essay contests, which have been sponsored by commercial and civic groups on similar rationale, may also prove to be effective in reducing resistances to new

points of view. Sociodrama has, of course, frequently been used to increase insight and to modify interpersonal attitudes in human-relations education (see Jennings, 1950; Maier, 1952).

The suggestion has been offered that role playing could be adapted for the training of key groups participating in international negotiations—a proposal that perhaps runs afoul the old problem of "who is going to bell the cat?" Whether or not such deliberate applications prove feasible, it should be recognized that the hypothesis predicts important attitudinal effects when representatives of a country—or a party, a union, a business—must as a matter of course speak for their constituency rather than for their private views. The self-convincing aspects of role performance may be a contributing factor to the freezing of positions that block effective negotiation. At international conferences, the *prevention* of spontaneous role playing, by adopting procedures that discourage provocative challenges and extended debates, might contribute to maintaining the atmosphere of a mutual thaw, which could be much more conducive to resolving internation conflicts.

Preparatory Communications and the Impact of Subsequent Events

Since resistances are difficult to overcome, attempts to induce changes in national and international images will often fail, despite all efforts to pinpoint potential waverers, to select the appropriate factual arguments, and to concentrate on appropriate issues. There is, however, another indirect use of communications relevant to public response to international issues that does not encounter the same problems of resistance: *influencing the impact of events by means of preparatory communications* either to *sensitize* the audience to the implications of an expected event, or to *dampen* its emotional and cognitive impact (see Janis, 1959, pp. 219–229).

Clear-cut successes or failures in launching space vehicles, in executing "cease-fire" orders, and in arriving at arms control agreements are typical of the major news events that can induce gross shifts in images of individual nations and of the international order. (See Chapter 5 in this volume.) Often, when an important event is anticipated, policy makers attempt to control its effects through communications designed to "prepare" the audience in advance. The following propositions are derived from the few existing studies that have systematically investigated the conditions under which preparatory communications diminish or augment the psychological impact of subsequent events.

1. *The level of fear evoked by a threatening news event will tend to be reduced if the audience has been previously exposed to preparatory communications that discuss and predict it in advance.*

The element of *surprise* is a major factor that determines the degree of emotional arousal that will be produced by an incontrovertible announcement of "bad news" (see Janis, 1958, 1962). By "bad news" is meant events that are commonly interpreted as portending imminent danger, loss of protective support, or severe impending deprivation ("a rival nation has the capability of destroying all our cities"; "a major source of our food supply is about to be cut off"). Extreme and disruptive fear reactions are most likely to occur if "bad news" comes to the focus of public attention unexpectedly, with no opportunity for prior psychological preparation.

The maximal fear-arousing effect of "bad news" concerning a new threat of war or an official announcement about the failure of a peace mission would be expected, therefore, if nothing at all were said in advance. Conversely, by issuing preparatory communications that discuss and predict beforehand the impending "bad news," it should be possible to moderate the intensity of emotional reactions, and to reduce the magnitude of public pressures toward impulsive or drastic decisions, when a major setback occurs.

2. *When a major news event would normally induce pessimistic expectations, the amount of such change will tend to be reduced if people have been previously exposed to preparatory communications that present grounds for maintaining optimistic expectations.*

This proposition applies to the impact of political, economic, military, or other adverse events that constitute setbacks from the standpoint of the audience's goals and aspirations. The available evidence indicates that communications that discount *in advance* the importance of an impending adverse event and present arguments supporting an optimistic view of the future will tend to reduce the incidence of pessimism when the event actually does materialize. For example, Janis, Lumsdaine, and Gladstone (1951) found that the amount of pessimism induced in American adolescents by President Truman's announcement that the Soviet Union had exploded its first A-bomb was substantially reduced by prior exposure to a radio talk that had predicted and discussed the event beforehand. This type of dampening effect seems to obtain even when the preparatory communication is given many weeks before the adverse news event occurs. Moreover, the blow seems to be softened even when the event falsifies some of the optimistic predictions contained in the prepartory communication. In general, it seems that once people have been influenced by optimistic communications, they will tend to show some degree of resistance to the impact of a corresponding pessimism-inducing event.

The proposition has direct implications for the problem of preventing widespread defeatist expectations about the chances of averting war and of developing effective international control during periods of military crisis. It would also apply to operations by pro-democratic communications that are designed to build up and maintain the morale of anti-totalitarian sectors of the population in totalitarian countries. Appropriate preparatory communications that emphasize realistic grounds for maintaining long-run optimistic expectations should reduce the vulnerability of such groups to demoralization by totalitarian communications about major setbacks to the anti-totalitarian cause.

3. *In the case of communications that present means–consequence predictions for the purpose of inducing conformity to specific recommendations for action, subsequent experiences of failure (which temporarily falsify the communicator's predictions) will be less likely to reduce the sustained effectiveness of the communication if it includes assertions that create a frame of reference for discounting failures.*

This proposition applies primarily to communications that are intended to induce the audience to cope with recurrent problems in some "best" way (such as advice to minority groups or to pro-peace groups as to how to recruit more supporters and how to use them effectively; orientation materials for prospective overseas personnel advising them on how to comport themselves vis-à-vis foreign nationals). The long-run effectiveness of such recommendations depends not only on the power of the arguments presented in their favor but also on the confirmatory or unfavorable experiences encountered by the recipients when they actually attempt to carry out the recommendations. One or two experiences of failure can often incline a person to reject a sound recommendation, even though it would prove successful in the long run.

For prescriptive communications of this type, initial experiences are apt to be a source of interference if some degree of skill must gradually be developed before a successful outcome can be counted on, or if the long-run successful outcome consists of increasing the relative frequency of successes rather than the complete elimination of failures. Under such circumstances, the audience may be more likely to "stick to" the recommendations if they have been prepared to resist the frustrating impact of failures. There is evidence that such an effect is promoted if recommendations are accompanied by explicit predictions that *some* occasional failures will occur, and by explanations that provide a basis for rationalizing or discounting them (see Hovland, Janis, & Kelley, 1953, pp. 273–275).

Insufficient research evidence is available at present for us to know very much about how successfully various publics can be "inoculated" against the effects of major setbacks and bad news. Communications of a preparatory nature may themselves encounter resistances, of course, especially if they emanate from sources that are regarded as untrustworthy or as having manipulative intentions. Nevertheless, if attended to at all, they may still be effective in "structuring" events for the audience in such a way that the significance of subsequent "news" is subtly altered.

Recent research has also suggested other ways in which preparatory communications can be used to modify the subsequent responsiveness of audiences in directions sought by communicators. McGuire and his colleagues, for example, have done extensive experimentation to clarify the processes by which such communications may "immunize" people against being affected by subsequent communications that challenge beliefs and attitudes whose validity had been previously taken for granted (see McGuire, in press; also, McGuire & Papageorgis, 1962). His findings may be relevant in such connections as the preparation of troops to withstand ideological assault on their democratic values if they are captured. There are also some indications that preparatory communications can create increased confidence in one's own judgments or decreased reliance on majority opinion, and thus immunize the individual to some extent from the powerful conformity pressures that he is likely to encounter from in-groups (Samelson, 1957).

A related immunizing effect is linked with the phenomena of role playing discussed in the preceding section:

4. *If, after being exposed to an impressive persuasive communication, the recipients are required to make an overt response that publicly indicates their position on the issue, the effectiveness of subsequent counteracting communications will tend to be reduced.*

Public commitment tends to reinforce and stabilize newly formed images and attitudes (see Hovland, Campbell, & Brock, 1957). Moreover, when a person is encouraged to feel that he has actively chosen a recommended course of action that includes unwelcome aspects, he appears to become predisposed to minimize the unattractive features thereafter, and to resist communications that would magnify them (Brehm, 1960; Hovland & Rosenberg, 1960, pp. 211–213). Once he has been induced to make an overt decision or public commitment to pursue a given course of action, the person will tend to minimize the attractiveness and positive values of the alternative courses of action that were open to him, and to be more resistant to subsequent communications that attempt to influence him to alter his decision (see Festinger, 1957, pp. 32–83; Brehm & Cohen, 1962, pp. 7–10, 299–302).

FACTORS AUGMENTING THE CHANCES OF MODIFYING IMAGES

The chapter up to this point has been oriented primarily around resistances. We have looked into some of their main sources, and also called attention to some of the ways in which they may be overcome or circumvented. We now turn to the following question: When a persuasive campaign reaches potential changers under conditions in which resistances can be overcome to some extent, *what factors will augment the amount of change?* The main types of factors that have been investigated are those specified by Lasswell's classic formula for communications research: *Who* says *what* to *whom* with what *effect?*

One set of factors ("to whom") has already been discussed in our summary of research findings on individual differences in authoritarianism and in other predispositional attributes that enter into a person's motivation to accept or reject communications designed to induce tolerance toward rival outgroups (see pages 208–210). Individual differences are to be expected not only in responsiveness to particular content themes but also in response to each major type of motivating appeal, including those based on fear arousal (see Janis & Feshbach, 1954) and those based on group pressures induced by information about the consensus of judgment among one's peers (see Crutchfield, 1955).

In addition to specific personality needs that predispose certain persons to be highly responsive to one or another limited type of persuasive communication, there are also certain personality attributes that predispose people to have high, moderate, or low resistance to *any* persuasive message, irrespective of what is said, how it is said, or who says it. This *general persuasibility* factor has been inferred from research on individual differences, indicating that when a large audience is exposed to many different types of persuasive communications on many different types of issues, some persons are consistently unaffected, whereas others are moderately persuasible and still others are highly influenced (see Abelson & Lesser, 1959; Hovland & Janis, 1959; Janis & Field, 1959). One personality characteristic that has been found to be predictive of low resistance to all forms of persuasive influences is low self-esteem. Other characteristics that appear to be related to high persuasibility are: (a) inhibition of overt aggressive behavior; (b) high fantasy imagery and strong empathic responses to symbolic representations; and (c) other-directed rather than inner-directed orientation, that is, a value system stressing adaptation to the social environment rather than inner-directed standards for regulating one's conduct. These relationships have been found only in samples of men; the absence of any such relationships in samples of women has been attributed to differences in the social roles prescribed for women and men in our society, which

may also account for the repeated finding that women are more persuasible than men on social and political issues (see Hovland & Janis, 1959, pp. 238–240).

The most thoroughly investigated propositions bearing on the processes of persuasion are those that specify factors involved in the identity of the communicator ("*who* says it") and in the content of the message ("*what* is said"). What follows is a brief summary of the major propositions that, in our judgment, seem most relevant to the problems of international communication and that also appear to be warranted by the existing evidence. The tentative status of these formulations has already been stressed. We offer them not as a Machiavellian handbook to guide the manipulation of opinion, but rather as a checklist of variables that warrant consideration by students and practitioners of mass communication concerning international matters. In this section we shall only occasionally point to specific potential implications in the realm of international affairs, leaving it to the reader to think over the implications for himself. The references cited either are illustrative or direct the reader who wishes to assess the evidence to general sources that will provide him with ready access to listings of the relevant studies.

Image of the Source[3]

1. *Sources regarded by the audience as prestigeful and trustworthy tend to facilitate persuasion; whereas a disesteemed source is at least temporarily a source of interference.*

---

[3] In the present review of factors contributing to the effectiveness of persuasive communication, we omit those pertaining to the channels or media of communication per se. But such factors may function in ways similar to those associated with the image of the source. Different media or channels may carry different degrees of prestige, which in turn can spread to the communicators whose messages they carry. The relevant literature is reviewed by Hovland (1954, pp. 1080–1084) and by Klapper (1960, pp. 104–112).

When a communication is attributed to a highly credible source, it is more likely to be considered a "fair" presentation than when it is attributed to one that is low in credibility. Parallel differences occur with respect to amount of opinion change (cf. Hovland, Janis, & Kelley, 1953, pp. 19–55; Klapper, 1960, pp. 99–105). For example, in one experimental study (Hovland & Weiss, 1951), the net change induced by a set of persuasive communications dealing with national economic developments proved to be *three and one-half times as great* when the communications were attributed to sources high in credibility than when the same communications were attributed to low credibility sources. This effect, however, manifested itself only immediately after the communication and disappeared with time (see proposition 4 below).

2. *When a communicator is attempting to induce the acceptance of unpopular or counter-norm images, more success will be achieved if material highly desirable to the audience is given first, before the less desirable material, in order to build up a more favorable image of the source.*

Acceptable material tends to increase positive attitudes toward the communicator and therefore evokes a more receptive response to his subsequent statements. Conversely, if unacceptable material is presented early in the sequence, the audience is likely to become negativistic toward the communicator and to lose interest in what he is saying (see Hovland, 1957, pp. 136–137; McGuire, 1957).

Some specialists in political warfare have tried to create favorable attitudes toward the source, in clandestine propaganda, by presenting communications that conspicuously pretend to adopt a position that is in accord with that of the audience. While a persuasive communication from an unknown source may improve its chances of being judged as unbiased, logical, and authoritative by explicitly stating at the outset that its purpose is to present a position in accord with the audience's existing images, its main purport cannot deviate markedly from the communicator's stated acceptable position without losing the intended advantage. Unless the critical propaganda theme continues to be "sandwiched in" along with other themes genuinely in accord with the audience's preexisting attitudes, the attempt to conceal the position of the sources is likely to have a boomerang effect, even if the true source is not subsequently exposed by rival groups (see Hovland, Janis, & Kelley, 1953, pp. 21–27, 295–297).

3. *Under conditions where the audience is already motivated to pay attention, learning and remembering the news or informational content of a persuasive message tends to be greater if the communicator explicitly states and consistently represents his position as "neutral" rather than as a proponent or opponent of the audience's point of view.*

When a favorable attitude toward the communicator is elicited, the audience is likely to become more highly motivated to attend to what he says and to accept his conclusions. But when the audience is initially interested in the topic (for example, if the message deals with an important disarmament proposal about which further communication is strongly desired by a political elite), the value of eliciting a favorable attitude toward the source depends upon the goal of the communication.

If the goal is to induce attitude change, Propositions 1 and 2 would apply, and the more the source is esteemed and perceived to be in essential agreement with the audience on other relevant issues, the greater the likelihood that the communication will be effective. But if the purpose is to inform the audience about factual matters in which they are already interested, the content may have a better chance of being learned, remembered, and transmitted to others when the communicator can be represented as a (well-informed) neutral rather than as a proponent or an opponent of the audience's goals and values (cf. Hovland, Janis, & Kelley, 1953, pp. 37–39). Elicitation of a positive or negative affective response toward the communicator tends to focus attention and interest upon him (his affiliation, his manner of speaking, his real intentions, and so forth) to the detriment of learning the specific information that is being presented. In this one respect, a moderately respected neutral source may sometimes be more effective than a highly prestigeful source who is perceived as being "one of us."

4. *Both positive and negative prestige effects tend to be lost over time: the degree to which an audience accepts persuasive statements that are attributed to a prestigeful ("respected" or "trustworthy") source tends to be comparatively high at first but gradually declines; the degree to which an audience accepts the conclusions put forth by a nonprestigeful source tends to be comparatively low at first but gradually increases.*

Many communication specialists operate on the assumption that the influence of any given persuasive message is always maximal immediately after exposure and that, as time goes on, people "forget" the impressive arguments or appeals presented and tend to revert to their original images. But this tendency to regress to former opinions, although of frequent occurrence, is by no means ubiquitous. The reverse tendency is likely to occur in the case of persuasive communications from a distrusted, suspect source (see Hovland,

Janis, & Kelley, 1953, pp. 254–259). Over a period of time, acceptance of the originally discounted statements tends to *increase*—a phenomenon that has been called the "sleeper" effect. This appears to be due to the fact that with the passage of time, the *content* of a statement is less likely to be spontaneously associated with the *source* (people often remember what was said without thinking about who said it).

It follows that when the goal of a persuasive message is to induce *immediate* action, it is especially important for the arguments—and perhaps the entire communication—to be attributed to a source who is regarded by the audience as trustworthy and prestigeful; but this requirement is less important when the goal is to induce delayed actions or to create long-range changes in images. With a "captive" or "captivated" audience, cumulative persuasive effects could presumably be achieved even when the series of persuasive messages consists mainly of statements attributed to a suspect or hostile source (such as a foreign country regarded as "the enemy"). In such instances, communicators might be able to take advantage of the "sleeper effect" if, in subsequent messages issued from seemingly neutral sources, they referred to the alleged "facts" without mentioning anything that would reinstate awareness of their original source.

The proposition that reinstating the connection between source and message tends to counteract the "sleeper effect" has other implications that might also be turned to advantage, when unwanted images originating from discreditable sources are gaining public acceptance. In such instances, countercommunications that make the link between original source and alleged "fact" as conspicuous as possible should prove to be effective.

Content Factors

We turn, finally, to the content of the message. It is generally recognized that attention, comprehension, and acceptance of any controversial topic depend to a great extent not only on what arguments and appeals are used but also on how they are presented. Within certain limits, the effectiveness of a given message can be augmented by the use of devices that involve structural factors such as the order in which key arguments are presented, the degree of emphasis given to opposing arguments, and the way in which the new and old material is introduced. In this section, we shall present a number of propositions having to do with alternative ways of presenting the same persuasive message. These deal with only a small number of the relevant factors, however, that are likely to be taken into account by experienced symbol specialists who are skilled in the art of preparing effective communications. Nevertheless, the development of sound communication strategies can be facilitated by taking cognizance of the few propositions concerning structural factors that have been at least tentatively substantiated by systematic research. On this basis, three major types of variables are singled out as most promising with respect to making a significant difference in the degree to which a communication will successfully induce changes in images: (a) explicit vs. implicit conclusions; (b) one-sided vs. two-sided presentations of arguments; and (c) order of arguments or appeals.

After examining these three structural factors, we shall conclude with a discussion of the effects of using certain types of content themes, particularly those involving threat appeals and related "emotional shock" devices, which are especially relevant for communications dealing with international issues

bearing on the dangers of nuclear armaments and the outbreak of war. (A more general review of studies related to the effects of content characteristics can be found in Hovland, Janis, & Kelley, 1953, pp. 56–165, 241–253; and Klapper, 1960, pp. 112–125.)

1. *In communications that present a series of arguments on complicated political or social issues, it is generally more effective to state the conclusions explicitly than to allow the audience to draw its own conclusions, provided that the message does not directly conflict with important norms of the audience.*

Many speculative discussions have claimed that it is generally more effective to let the audience draw its own conclusions from a presentation of facts and arguments, on the grounds that indirect suggestion is more effective than direct, or that active participation —as in role playing—is advantageous. But the effectiveness of a nondirective approach appears to be limited to highly personal matters of the sort involved in psychotherapy, or to special conditions of insurmountable resistance to direct suggestions, as when the conclusion being supported runs sharply counter to important group norms adhered to by the audience. (See our earlier discussion of instances where an indirect approach appears to be the only hope for exerting any influence whatsoever and our comments about the possibility of achieving some degree of cumulative impact from factual, nonargumentative communications [page 212].)

In the case of communications that discuss relatively impersonal issues for the benefit of receptive audiences, the available evidence indicates that it is generally more effective to state the conclusions or recommendations *explicitly,* even when the communicator is regarded as biased or untrustworthy (see Hovland, Janis, & Kelley, 1953, pp. 100–105; Klapper, 1960, pp. 84–91, 116–117). The omission of an explicit conclusion is sometimes regarded as a sign that the propagandist is trying to conceal his purpose. Moreover, it is often necessary to state the conclusion explicitly in order to prevent the audience from missing the essential point of the arguments—especially when the arguments are complicated.

We cannot feel much certainty, until more research evidence becomes available, about the general effectiveness of conclusion-drawing for various types of persuasive messages designed to influence international attitudes.[4] Nevertheless, most educational or publicity campaigns dealing with current international questions will probably do well to present their conclusions explicitly, with the expectation of maximizing the effects on those people who are already susceptible to influence on the issue, rather than trying to gain the risky benefits of converting opponents by the use of indirect suggestion. The indirect approach is probably useful mainly in those rare instances where opportunities for repeated personal contact with key personnel makes it worthwhile to attempt to change images very gradually, allowing the person to "work through" for himself the implications of every new insight, with a view to bringing about fundamental changes in the individual's personal values and affiliations.

2. *When the audience is strongly opposed to the position advocated by the communicator, it is generally more effective to discuss the opposing arguments than to present only the arguments in favor of one side of the issue.*

The question has often been raised as to whether propaganda is more effective when it concentrates exclusively on the arguments supporting the propagandist's position, than when it includes discussion and/or refutation of the opposing arguments. Hitler and other Nazi propaganda strategists have put forth the claim that in appealing for a specific line of action, no rival or opposing ideas should be discussed because they invite comparisons, hesitation, and doubt. But the available evidence indicates that this principle holds true only under limited conditions, notably when the audience is unaware of or unlikely to think of the arguments on the other side of the issue (see Hovland, Janis, & Kelley, 1953, pp. 105–110; Hovland, Lumsdaine, & Sheffield, 1949, pp. 201–227; Klapper, 1960, pp. 113–116).

With average audiences, a one-sided discussion that either ignores the op-

---

[4] There is some conflicting evidence that raises questions with respect to the limiting conditions under which conclusion-drawing will have differential effects. Thistlethwaite, de Haan, and Kamenetzky (1955) conducted a study specifically focused on the relative effectiveness of "directive" and "nondirective" communications, with Air Force recruits as subjects. The arguments, presented by a single tape recording, pointed to the conclusion that the United States was justified in fighting a limited war in Korea. Relevant attitudes were measured immediately after the communication and after a three-week delay. While explicit statement of the conclusion resulted in greater comprehension, all versions of the communication were equally effective in producing attitude change. There are also suggestions in the work of McGuire (1960) that when a person is exposed to logically related assertions presented in a manner that leaves the logical relationship among them implicit, a trend toward logical consistency is set in motion that later inclines him to shift his opinion to bring it more in line with the premises he believes to be true. McGuire calls this consistency phenomenon the "Socratic effect," since it can be stimulated by posing cogent questions to a person about the grounds for his beliefs.

posing position or presents what is seen as an unfair or distorted picture of it tends to have adverse effects among those who are initially unfavorable to the position being advocated. They are likely to start thinking spontaneously about the relatively sound opposing arguments and to become strongly aware of the biased way in which the issue is being treated. Conversely, they are likely to be more receptive to new considerations if the most impressive opposing arguments, with which they are already familiar, are openly recognized and explicitly discussed. The beneficial effects of a two-sided presentation are probably maximized when the communicator does not attempt to answer every one of the opposing arguments, but limits his critique to those that are weakest and most easily refuted.

In attempting to convince an audience to accept an antithetical position, it is probably effective to discuss the arguments that are in line with the audience's view at the very beginning of the communication, so as to prevent inattentiveness and sustained opposition.

3. *Even when the audience is not initially opposed to the communicator's position, a two-sided presentation will be more effective in creating sustained changes in images than a one-sided presentation, if the communication is given under conditions where the audience will subsequently be exposed to counter-communications (which present the opposing arguments).*

When an audience has already become familiar with the opposing arguments—and has been exposed to some refutations—subsequent counter-propaganda is likely to be much less impressive and more readily resisted (Lumsdaine & Janis, 1953). Since most communication about international issues occurs in a competitive arena in which exposure to counter-communications

can be expected, the proposition will be quite generally applicable. It should hold with especial force for most instances in which education or propaganda concerning vital international issues is disseminated by foreign sources to audiences under totalitarian control. Both Propositions 2 and 3 suggest that two-sided presentations should be more effective in such communications.

4. *If a communicator purports to take account of the arguments on both sides of a controversial issue, the omission or distortion of any important argument (of which the audience is initially aware) will have a more adverse effect than if the communicator makes it clear from the beginning that he is presenting only his own side of the issue.*

From Propositions 2 and 3, it might be expected that foreign propaganda directed to an unfriendly population would ordinarily be maximally effective if it were to create an atmosphere of impartiality and objectivity (as by issuing the propaganda from an apparently neutral source and by deliberately taking account of both sides of the issue). But this type of approach would be likely to have adverse effects whenever the message failed to include *all* the relevant arguments that bolster the audience's initial position. When the communicator explicitly or implicitly conveys the idea that he is presenting both sides of the issue, the omission or "soft-pedalling" of any given argument is likely to become highly noticeable and will tend to augment suspiciousness, even among relatively sympathetic audiences.

Proposition 4 is especially likely to be applicable when government policy prevents mentioning certain critical topics in mass communications to other countries. For instance, during the last few months of World War II, U.S. government agencies were directed to avoid discussing Russia's possible participation in the war against Japan. The omission of this important consideration in recorded programs designed to counteract overoptimism concerning the defeat of Japan among men in the U.S. armed forces was found to have a more adverse effect when the program used a seemingly objective two-sided presentation than when the presentation was one-sided. This adverse effect, however, occurred primarily among the men who would be expected to be especially sensitive to the omission—such as the better educated men and those who had indicated prior to the communication that their optimism was partly based on the expectation that Russia would help the United States to defeat Japan. It did not prevent the two-sided version from being more effective with the majority of the audience (Hovland, Lumsdaine, & Sheffield, 1949, pp. 215–221). Whenever situations of this kind arise, the communicator faces the problem of weighing the advantages of a two-sided presentation (as specified by Propositions 2 and 3) against the disadvantages that have just been discussed. If the channel that is to be used has built up a sustained following and if it seems highly probable that the omission of a crucial unmentionable argument will be noticed by a large proportion of the audience, a one-sided presentation may be more effective.

5. *When the audience has a relatively low degree of interest in the persuasive message, an anticlimax arrangement of the content will be more effective than a climax arrangement.*

The question of how to order the arguments or appeals arises whenever a communication contains more than one essential assertion. Even when a communication is limited to a single idea or theme, a similar problem will arise insofar as the communicator attempts to avoid monotony from mere mechanical repetition and thus uses *varied* repetitions, with different illustrations, formulations, and stylistic devices.

In order to apply Proposition 5, one must be able to rate the various arguments, appeals, illustrations, and varied repetitions of the dominant theme according to their impressiveness or interest-arousing value. When the audience has relatively little initial interest in the topic, it is probably advantageous to place the most impressive and interesting material at the beginning of the communication, so as to arouse the audience's motivation to pay attention to what is being said (see Hovland, Janis, & Kelley, 1953, pp. 112–120). When the most convincing arguments are presented first, the audience is likely to become more receptive to somewhat weaker arguments that occur in later portions of the communication. The climax order, on the other hand, may have some advantages among audiences who are already highly interested in the communication, but generally runs the risk of losing the audience long before the most impressive material is presented. Proposition 5 would be especially applicable in the case of any persuasive campaign dealing with political, social, or ideological issues that are not "burning" questions of the moment.

6. *When contradictory items of information or opposing viewpoints are presented in a single communication, by a single communicator, the side presented first tends to exert more influence than the side presented second.*

This "primacy" effect, when tested with communications designed to induce contradictory images of the same person or organization, proved to be extremely pronounced when contradictory material was not spontaneously salient and when no time interval was allowed for interpolated activities between the first set of information and the second (contradictory) set of information (Asch, 1946; Luchins, 1957; Janis & Feierabend, 1957). The proposition applies directly when, on the basis of Proposition 3 above, a communicator decides to give a two-sided presentation in order to produce more stable changes in the face of *anticipated* counterpropaganda from the opposition. If the audience does *not* spontaneously think about the opposing arguments, a communication from an authoritative source is likely to be more effective if the *con* arguments are presented after, rather than before, the *pro* arguments that support the communicator's conclusion. If the con arguments are made salient at the beginning of the communication, the recipients' motivation to reject the communicator's conclusion will become strongly aroused at the outset and this tendency is likely to weaken the impact of the positive incentives when they are subsequently presented; if the pro arguments are given first, however, the audience's motivation to accept the communicator's conclusion will increase and the negative material, when it subsequently occurs, will tend to be tolerated or ignored. Moreover, if a strong case is made for the communicator's position right from the start, the recipient may make a clear-cut decision to accept it at the outset; thereafter, while attending to the rest of the communication, he would tend to minimize conflict or dissonance by ignoring the opposing ideas (Janis, 1957, 1959).

Threat Appeals

A matter of presentational tactics, involving content variables that have special relevance to communications about international issues, arises in connection with the use of threat appeals. By a "threat appeal" is meant any statement asserting or predicting that the audience will be (or may be) subjected to some source of danger or deprivation. In general, a threat appeal will produce fear reactions if the audience perceives important goals or values as being endangered and anticipates some form of *personal* loss. Political propaganda and other types of mass communications frequently contain threat appeals designed to motivate people to accept specific recommendations as to what one should do in order to avert potential dangers (for example, appeals that play up radiation hazards in order to elicit acceptance of an H-bomb test ban). For maximal effectiveness, this persuasive device requires not only that the communications succeed in arousing fear, but also that the recommendations function as effective *reassurances*. The latter term refers to verbal statements—plans, resolutions, judgments, evaluations—that alleviate or reduce emotional tension. The following propositions deal with the conditions under which threat appeals are most successful in producing acceptance of reassuring recommendations.

1. *The relationship between the degree of fear aroused by a threat appeal and the degree to which the communicator's recommendations elicit sustained acceptance is generally curvilinear: as the level of fear is increased, motivation to accept reassuring recommendations about ways to cope with the danger will be increased; but, as the level of fear mounts higher and higher, resistances are mobilized that can interfere with long-run effectiveness. Tolerance for a strong dosage of fear will be relatively high if the message contains specific recommendations that offer an apparently good solution to the problems posed by the threat, with no obvious loopholes. When these conditions are not met, as is often the case in "scare propaganda," the use of a strong threat appeal will produce less accept-*

ance of the recommendations than a milder appeal.

Communicators often assume that the protective actions or international solutions they advocate will be more readily accepted the more they succeed in frightening the audience about the dangerous consequences of failing to adhere to their recommendations. This assumption may sometimes be correct, especially for emergency warnings and recommendations concerning *immediate* escape actions that can readily be carried out, such as evacuation of a danger area within a few minutes after the warning is issued (see Janis, in press). But the assumption often appears to be incorrect in the case of recommendations that involve *delayed* actions or *sustained* attitudes: for example, evacuating at some future date if the threat materializes; supporting a disarmament movement; favoring prodemocratic policies (see Hovland, Janis, & Kelley, 1953, pp. 56–98; Janis, in press). Particularly in the case of persuasive communications concerning wartime dangers, the *optimal dosage* of fear-arousal might generally be far below the level of the strongest threat appeals that a communicator could use if he chose to do so.[5]

Although powerful threat appeals that arouse intense fear may occasionally prove to be spectacularly successful, it is difficult to predict such an outcome in advance. In order to achieve long-run attitude changes from a threat appeal, it would undoubtedly be advantageous to carry out preliminary "program-assessment" research to select a dosage of fear that will not exceed the optimal level.

In response to any threat appeal that succeeds in evoking fear or anxiety, the audience is likely to develop interfer-

ing resistances while the communication is in progress (Janis & Terwilliger, 1962). Members of the audience experience some degree of residual emotional tension after the communication is over, if the reassurances offered by the communicator are not 100 percent effective in producing expectations of escaping from the threat. This residual emotional tension will motivate *defensive avoidances*—attempts to ward off subsequent exposures to the anxiety-arousing ideas presented in the communication. In other words, the experience of being severely frightened by a discussion of a potential threat—and of being temporarily unable to stop worrying about it—can give rise to a powerful desire to avoid thinking or hearing about it again. This may ultimately result in losing interest in the topic, or minimizing the importance of the threat. When the fear is extreme, even comprehension and learning of the message might sometimes be impaired (Janis, in press).

Defensive avoidance reactions are especially likely to occur if, after arousing a high degree of fear, the communication presents no specific reassurances, or offers reassurances that are regarded by the audience as inadequate to cope with the threat. Accordingly, a campaign that attempts to induce a foreign population to adopt unfavorable attitudes toward their leaders' nationalistic policies by pointing up the dangerous consequences of an outbreak of war is likely to have boomerang effects if strong fear appeals are used without convincing reassurances as to how the danger can be prevented. If the communicator's reassurances are regarded as irrelevant to the threat, impossible to carry out, or only *partially* successful in averting the threat, the use of a strong threat appeal will give rise to

---

[5] Haeffner (1956) has shown this relationship for the subject matter of atomic threat, in persuasive communications that influence people to support a bomb-test ban.

residual emotional tension. Thus, the audience will become motivated to seek other means to alleviate their fears. In this way, a threat appeal that is intended to motivate the audience to take account of a realistic threat of danger can have the paradoxical effect of motivating the audience to adopt wishful beliefs that are antithetical to the communicator's intentions.

The stronger the threat appeal, the greater the chances seem to be that the audience will experience some degree of residual emotional tension after the communication is over, even when specific reassurances are given. When this happens, the audience will become motivated to avoid hearing about or thinking about the potential threat. For example, the use of strong threat appeals in one program among a series of radio broadcasts is likely to diminish the size of the audience on the following programs because many listeners will be left with a strong desire to avoid exposing themselves to similar disturbing communications. When a strong threat appeal is to be used to achieve some tactical political goal, it might therefore be more effective to present it via some unique, isolated channel of communication rather than as part of a standard sustained program, so as to avoid reducing the subsequent effectiveness of the sustained channel.

2. *Inserting reassuring recommendations immediately after fear has been aroused by a threat appeal is a more effective order of presentation than the reverse sequence, in which the reassurances are presented before the threat appeal.*

This proposition, which is in accord with the assumptions of learning theory about fear as an acquired drive (Hovland, Janis, & Kelley, 1953, pp. 60–66) has received some preliminary support from communication experiments (cf.

Cohen, 1957; Hovland, 1957, pp. 135–136). In Cohen's study, which is the main one that supports the principle, the effect was essentially confined to persons who measured low on an index of desire for understanding. Since the possibility is open that the reverse sequence was ineffective with them simply because of its awkwardness and lesser familiarity, we offer the proposition as a tentative suggestion that warrants subsequent appraisal.

Experimental sessions in social-psychological research often end with a "de-briefing" in which the experimenter tells his cooperative subject what the "manipulations" of the study were really about, and sends him on his way, supposedly reassured and friendly to psychological experimentation. On our part, the manipulative cast of our propositional inventory seems so pronounced that we feel the need for some final remarks in a similar vein.

We have been guided in our inventory by the selection of topics—among the many conceivably relevant ones—on which some systematic evidence is available from recent research. Research in this field has, in turn, been guided at least in part by the choice of variables that cut across diverse types of communications and situations, so as to permit generalizations. In the realm of communication content, the most readily generalizable variables, like those we have just been examining, are ones that pertain to formal properties of the communication or to incidental appeals that are relatively extrinsic to the core message. It is useful to focus on these externals, for the way that a message is "mounted" may have much to do with whether it is accepted or rejected by domestic or foreign audiences. All the same, this focused concentration of research should not obscure the importance, in effective communication, of the *cogency, reasonableness,* and, in the long run, *truth* of the message. If the function of "object appraisal" and reality-testing is to be advanced by communications on international affairs (and much pacifically inclined communication has this aim), research on communication has yet to find ways of clarifying the role of such obvious but experimentally elusive ingredients in the process.

REFERENCES

Abelson, R. P. Modes of resolution of belief dilemmas. *J. Confl. Resol.,* 1959, 3, 343–352.

Abelson, R. P., & Lesser, G. S. The measurement of persuasibility in children. In C. I. Hovland & I. L. Janis (Eds.), *Personality and persuasibility.* New Haven: Yale Univer. Press, 1959. Pp. 141–166.

Adorno, T. W., Frenkel-Brunswik, Else, Levinson, D. J., & Sanford, N. *The authoritarian personality.* New York: Harper, 1950.

Albig, W. *Public opinion.* New York: McGraw-Hill, 1939.

Allport, F. H., & Simpson, M. M. Broadcasting to an enemy country: What appeals are effective, and why. *J. soc. Psychol.,* 1946, 23, 217–224.

Allport, G. W. *The nature of prejudice.* Reading, Mass.: Addison-Wesley, 1954.

Allport, G. W., & Postman, L. J. The basic psychology of rumor. *Trans. N.Y. Acad. Sciences, Series II,* 1945, 8, 61–81. (Reprinted in Maccoby, Newcomb, & Hartley, 1958, pp. 54–65; also in Katz, Cartwright, Eldersveld, & Lee, 1954, pp. 394–404.)

Annis, A. D., & Meier, N. C. The induction of opinion through suggestions by means of planted content. *J. soc. Psychol.,* 1934, 5, 65–81.

Asch, S. E. Forming impressions of personality. *J. abnorm. soc. Psychol.,* 1946, 41, 258–290.

Asch, S. E. *Social psychology.* Englewood Cliffs, N.J.: Prentice-Hall, 1952.

Asch, S. E. Effects of group pressure upon the modification and distortion of judgments. In Eleanor E. Maccoby, T. M. Newcomb, & E. L. Hartley (Eds.), *Readings in social psychology* (ed. 3). New York: Holt, Rinehart and Winston, 1958. Pp. 174–183.

Bennett, Edith B. Discussion, decision, commitment and consensus in "group decision." *Hum. Rel.,* 1955, 8, 251–273.

Berelson, B., Lazarsfeld, P. F., & McPhee, W. N. *Voting.* Chicago: Univer. Chicago Press, 1954.

Bernstorff, J. *My three years in America.* New York: Scribner, 1920.

Biderman, A. D. *March to calumny: The story of American POW's in the Korean War.* New York: Macmillan, 1963.

Brehm, J. W. A dissonance analysis of attitude-discrepant behavior. In C. I. Hovland & M. J. Rosenberg (Eds.), *Attitude organization and change.* New Haven: Yale Univer. Press, 1960. Pp. 164–197.

Brehm, J. W., & Cohen, A. R. *Explorations in cognitive dissonance.* New York: Wiley, 1962.

Brodbeck, May The role of small groups in mediating the effects of propaganda. *J. abnorm. soc. Psychol.,* 1956, 52, 166–170.

Cannell, C. F., & MacDonald, J. C. The impact of health news on attitudes and behavior. *Journalism Quart.,* 1956, 33, 315–323.

Cantril, H. *The politics of despair.* New York: Basic Books, 1958.

Cartwright, D., & Zander, A. (Eds.) *Group dynamics: Research and theory* (ed. 2). New York: Harper, 1960.

Charters, W. W., Jr., & Newcomb, T. M. Some attitudinal effects of experimentally increased salience of a membership group. In Eleanor E. Maccoby,

T. M. Newcomb, & E. L. Hartley (Eds.), *Readings in social psychology* (ed. 3). New York: Holt, Rinehart and Winston, 1958. Pp. 276–281.

Christiansen, B. *Attitudes toward foreign affairs as a function of personality.* Oslo: Univer. Oslo Press, 1959.

Christie, R., & Jahoda, Marie (Eds.) *Studies in the scope and method of the authoritarian personality.* New York: Free Press, 1954.

Cohen, A. R. Need for cognition and order of communication as determinants of opinion change. In C. I. Hovland (Ed.), *The order of presentation in persuasion.* New Haven: Yale Univer. Press, 1957. Pp. 79–97.

Converse, P., & Campbell, A. Political standards in secondary groups. In D. Cartwright & A. Zander (Eds.), *Group dynamics: Research and theory* (ed. 2). New York: Harper, 1960. Pp. 300–318.

Cooper, Eunice, & Dinerman, Helen Analysis of the film "Don't be a sucker": A study in communication. *Publ. Opin. Quart.*, 1951, *15*, 243–264.

Cooper, Eunice, & Jahoda, Marie The evasion of propaganda. *J. Psychol.*, 1947, *23*, 15–25. (Reprinted in Katz, Cartwright, Eldersveld, & Lee, 1954, pp. 313–319.)

Crutchfield, R. S. Conformity and character. *Amer. Psychologist*, 1955, *10*, 191–198. (Reprinted in Hollander & Hunt, 1963, pp. 398–408.)

Culbertson, Frances M. Modification of an emotionally held attitude through role playing. *J. abnorm. soc. Psychol.*, 1957, *54*, 230–233.

Duijker, H. C. J., & Frijda, N. H. *National character and national stereotypes* (*Confluence*, Vol. 1). Amsterdam: North Holland Publishing Company, 1960.

Festinger, L. Informal social communication. *Psychol. Rev.*, 1950, 57, 271–282. (Reprinted in Cartwright & Zander, 1960, pp. 286–299; also in Hollander

Festinger, L. *A theory of cognitive dissonance.* New York: Harper, 1957.

Festinger, L., & Carlsmith, J. M. Cognitive consequences of forced compliance. *J. abnorm. soc. Psychol.*, 1959, *58*, 203–210.

Gladstone, A. I., & Taylor, Martha A. Threat-related attitudes and reactions to communications about international events. *J. Confl. Resol.*, 1958, *2*, 17–28.

Haeffner, D. Some effects of guilt-arousing and fear-arousing persuasive communications on opinion change. Unpublished Technical Report, August 15, 1956, Office of Naval Research, Contract Number N6onr-241. (Abridgement of unpublished doctoral dissertation, University of Rochester, 1956.)

Harvey, O. J., & Beverly, G. D. Some personality correlates of concept change through role playing. *J. abnorm. soc. Psychol.*, 1961, *63*, 125–130.

Heider, F. *The psychology of interpersonal relations.* New York: Wiley, 1958.

Himmelweit, Hilde T., Oppenheim, A. N., & Vince, P. *Television and the child.* New York: Oxford Univer. Press, 1958.

Hollander, E. P. Conformity, status, and idiosyncrasy credit. *Psychol. Rev.*, 1958, 65, 117–127. (Reprinted in Hollander & Hunt, 1963, pp. 425–435.)

Hollander, E. P., & Hunt, R. G. (Eds.) *Current perspectives in social psychology: Readings with commentary.* New York: Oxford Univer. Press, 1963.

Hovland, C. I. Effects of the mass media of communication. In G. Lindzey (Ed.), *Handbook of social psychology*, Vol. II. Reading, Mass.: Addison-Wesley, 1954. Pp. 1062–1103.

Hovland, C. I. Summary and implications. In C. I. Hovland (Ed.), *The order of presentation in persuasion.* New Haven: Yale Univer. Press, 1957. Pp. 129–157.

Hovland, C. I. Reconciling conflicting results derived from experimental and survey studies of attitude change. *Amer* in Hollander & Hunt, 1963, pp. 378–389.)

Hovland, C. I., Campbell, Enid H., & Brock, T. The effects of "commitment" on opinion change following communication. In C. I. Hovland (Ed.), *The order of presentation in persuasion.* New Haven: Yale Univer. Press, 1957. Pp. 23–32.

Hovland, C. I., & Janis, I. L. Summary and implications for future research. In C. I. Hovland & I. L. Janis (Eds.), *Personality and persuasibility.* New Haven: Yale Univer. Press, 1959. Pp. 225–254.

Hovland, C. I., Janis, I. L., & Kelley, H. H. *Communication and persuasion.* New Haven: Yale Univer. Press, 1953.

Hovland, C. I., Lumsdaine, A. A., & Sheffield, F. D. *Experiments on mass communication.* Princeton: Princeton Univer. Press, 1949.

Hovland, C. I., & Rosenberg, M. J. Summary and further theoretical issues. In C. I. Hovland & M. J. Rosenberg (Eds.), *Attitude organization and change.* New Haven: Yale Univer. Press, 1960. Pp. 198–232.

Hovland, C. I., & Weiss, W. The influence of source credibility on communication effectiveness. *Publ. Opin. Quart.*, 1951, *15*, 635–650. (Reprinted in Katz, Cartwright, Eldersveld, & Lee, 1954, pp. 337–347.)

Hyman, H. H., & Sheatsley, P. B. Some reasons why information campaigns fail. *Publ. Opin. Quart.*, 1947, *11*, 412–423. (Reprinted in Katz, Cartwright, Eldersveld, & Lee, 1954, pp. 522–531; also in Maccoby, Newcomb, & Hartley, 1958, pp. 164–173.)

International Research Associates, Inc. *Media of communication and the free world as seen by Czechoslovak, Hungarian, and Polish refugees: A report prepared for the Division of Radio Program Evaluation of the Department of State.* New York: International Research Associates, 1953.

Janis, I. L. Motivational effects of differ-ent sequential arrangements of conflicting arguments. In C. I. Hovland (Ed.), *The order of presentation in persuasion.* New Haven: Yale Univer. Press, 1957. Pp. 170–186.

Janis, I. L. *Psychological stress: Psychoanalytic and behavioral studies of surgical patients.* New York: Wiley, 1958.

Janis, I. L. Motivational factors in the resolution of decisional conflicts. In M. R. Jones (Ed.), *Nebraska symposium on motivation, 1959.* Lincoln: Univer. Nebraska Press, 1959. Pp. 198–231.

Janis, I. L. Psychological effects of warnings. In G. W. Baker & D. W. Chapman (Eds.), *Man and society in disaster.* New York: Basic Books, 1962. Pp. 55–92.

Janis, I. L. Personality as a factor in susceptibility to persuasion. In W. Schramm (Ed.), *The science of human communication.* New York: Basic Books, 1963. Pp. 54–64.

Janis, I. L. *Contours of fear: The psychological impact of war, disaster, illness, and stress experiments.* New York: Wiley (in press).

Janis, I. L., & Feierabend, Rosalind L. Effects of alternative ways of ordering pro and con arguments in persuasive communications. In C. I. Hovland (Ed.), *The order of presentation in persuasion.* New Haven: Yale Univer. Press, 1957. Pp. 115–128.

Janis, I. L., & Feshbach, S. Personality differences associated with responsiveness to fear-arousing communications. *J. Pers.*, 1954, *23*, 154–166.

Janis, I. L., & Field, P. B. A behavioral assessment of persuasability: Consistency of individual differences. In C. I. Hovland & I. L. Janis (Eds.), *Personality and persuasability.* New Haven: Yale Univer. Press, 1959. Pp. 29–54.

Janis, I. L., & Gilmore, J. B. The influence of incentive conditions on the success of role playing in modifying attitudes. *J. Pers. soc. Psychol.*, 1965, *1*, 17–27.

Janis, I. L., Hovland, C. I., Field, P. B.,

Linton, Harriet, Graham, Elaine, Cohen, A. R., Rife, D., Abelson, R. P., Lesser, G. S., & King, B. T. *Personality and persuasibility.* New Haven: Yale Univer. Press, 1959.

Janis, I. L., & King, B. T. The influence of role playing on opinion change. *J. abnorm. soc. Psychol.*, 1954, *49*, 211–218.

Janis, I. L., Lumsdaine, A. A., & Gladstone, A. I. Effects of preparatory communications on reactions to a subsequent news event. *Publ. Opin. Quart.*, 1951, *15*, 487–518. (Reprinted in Katz, Cartwright, Eldersveld, & Lee, 1954, pp. 347–362.)

Janis, I. L., & Terwilliger, R. F. An experimental study of psychological resistances to fear arousing communications. *J. abnorm. soc. Psychol.*, 1962, *65*, 403–410.

Jennings, Helen H. Sociodrama as educative process. In Caroline Tryon (Ed.), *Fostering mental health in our schools.* Washington: Assoc. for Supervision and Curriculum Development, Nat. Educ. Assoc., 1950. Pp. 260–285.

Katz, D. The functional approach to the study of attitudes. *Publ. Opin. Quart.*, 1960, *24*, 163–204. (Excerpted in Hollander & Hunt, 1963, pp. 340–350.)

Katz, D., Cartwright, D., Eldersveld, S., & Lee, A. M. (Eds.) *Public opinion and propaganda: A book of readings.* New York: Holt, Rinehart and Winston, 1954.

Katz, D., & Schanck, R. L. *Social psychology.* New York: Wiley, 1938.

Katz, D., & Stotland, E. A preliminary statement to a theory of attitude structure and change. In S. Koch (Ed.), *Psychology: A study of a science,* Vol. 3. New York: McGraw-Hill, 1959. Pp. 423–475.

Katz, E. The diffusion of new ideas and practices. In W. Schramm (Ed.), *The science of human communication.* New York: Basic Books, 1963. Pp. 77–93.

Katz, E., & Lazarsfeld, P. F. *Personal influence: The part played by people in the flow of mass communication.* New York: Free Press, 1955.

Kelley, H. H. Salience of membership and resistance to change of group-anchored attitudes. *Hum. Relat.,* 1955, *8*, 275–289.

Kelley, H. H., & Thibaut, J. W. Experimental studies of group problem solving and process. In G. Lindzey (Ed.), *Handbook of social psychology,* Vol. II. Reading, Mass.: Addison-Wesley, 1954. Pp. 735–785.

Kelman, H. C. Attitude change as a function of response restriction. *Hum. Relat.,* 1953, *6*, 185–214.

Kelman, H. C. Processes of opinion change. *Publ. Opin. Quart.,* 1961, *25*, 57–78. (Excerpted in Hollander & Hunt, 1963, pp. 454–462.)

Kendall, Patricia L., & Wolf, Katherine M. The analysis of deviant cases in communications research. In P. F. Lazarsfeld & F. N. Stanton (Eds.), *Communications research, 1948–1949.* New York: Harper, 1949. Pp. 152–179.

King, B. T., & Janis, I. L. Comparison of the effectiveness of improvised versus non-improvised role playing in producing opinion changes. *Hum. Relat.,* 1956, *9*, 177–186.

Klapper, J. T. *The effects of mass communication.* New York: Free Press, 1960.

Lazarsfeld, P. F. The effects of radio on public opinion. In D. Waples (Ed.), *Print, radio, and film in a democracy.* Chicago: Univer. Chicago Press, 1942.

Lazarsfeld, P. F., Berelson, B., & Gaudet, Hazel *The people's choice* (ed. 2). New York: Columbia Univer. Press, 1948.

Lesser, S. O., & Peter, H. W. Training foreign nationals in the United States. In R. Likert & S. P. Hayes, Jr. (Eds.), *Some applications of behavioral research.* UNESCO, 1957. Pp. 160–206.

Levine, J. M., & Murphy, G. The learning and forgetting of controversial material. *J. abnorm. soc. Psychol.*, 1943, *38*, 507–517. (Reprinted in Maccoby, Newcomb, & Hartley, 1958, pp. 94–101.)

Levinson, D. J. Authoritarian personality and foreign policy. *J. Confl. Resol.*, 1957, *1*, 37–47.

Lifton, R. J. *Thought reform and the psychology of totalism: A study of "brainwashing" in China.* New York: Norton, 1961.

London, I., & Anisimov, O. Nonthematic, nontechnical factors influencing the effectiveness of plausible appeals directed to a Soviet audience. *Psychol. Repts.*, 1956, *2*, 325–330.

Luchins, A. S. Primacy-recency in impression formation. In C. I. Hovland (Ed.), *The order of presentation in persuasion.* New Haven: Yale Univer. Press, 1957. Pp. 33–61.

Lumsdaine, A. A., & Janis, I. L. Resistance to "counter-propaganda" produced by one-sided and two-sided "propaganda" presentations. *Publ. Opin. Quart.*, 1953, *17*, 311–318. (Reprinted in Maccoby, Newcomb, & Hartley, 1958, pp. 131–137.)

Maccoby, Eleanor E., Newcomb, T. M., & Hartley, E. L. (Eds.) *Readings in social psychology* (ed. 3). New York: Holt, Rinehart and Winston, 1958.

Maccoby, N. The new "scientific" rhetoric. In W. Schramm (Ed.), *The science of human communication.* New York: Basic Books, 1963. Pp. 41–53.

MacKinnon, W. J., & Centers, R. Authoritarianism and internationalism. *Publ. Opin. Quart.*, 1956, *20*, 621–630.

Maier, N. R. F. *Principles of human relations.* New York: Wiley, 1952.

McGuire, W. J. *Immunization against persuasion.* New Haven: Yale Univer. Press (in press).

McGuire, W. J. Order of presentation as a factor in "conditioning" persuasiveness. In C. I. Hovland (Ed.), *The order of presentation in persuasion.* New

Haven: Yale Univer. Press, 1957. Pp. 98–114.

McGuire, W. J. A syllogistic analysis of cognitive relationships. In C. I. Hovland & M. J. Rosenberg (Eds.), *Attitude organization and change.* New Haven: Yale Univer. Press, 1960. Pp. 65–111.

McGuire, W. J., & Papageorgis, D. Effectiveness of forewarning in developing resistance to persuasion. *Publ. Opin. Quart.*, 1962, *26*, 24–34.

Mussen, P. H. Some personality and social factors related to changes in children's attitudes toward Negroes. *J. abnorm. soc. Psychol.*, 1950, *45*, 423–441.

Newcomb, T. M. *Social psychology.* New York: Holt, Rinehart and Winston, 1950.

Pettigrew, T. F. Personality and sociocultural factors in intergroup attitudes: A cross-national comparison. *J. Confl. Resol.*, 1958, *2*, 29–42.

Riecken, H. W., & Homans, G. C. Psychological aspects of social structure. In G. Lindzey (Ed.), *Handbook of social psychology*, Vol. II. Reading, Mass.: Addison-Wesley, 1954. Pp. 786–832.

Rosenberg, M. J., & Abelson, R. P. An analysis of cognitive balancing. In C. I. Hovland & M. J. Rosenberg (Eds.), *Attitude organization and change.* New Haven: Yale Univer. Press, 1960. Pp. 112–163.

Samelson, F. Conforming behavior under two conditions of conflict in the cognitive field. *J. abnorm. soc. Psychol.*, 1957, *55*, 181–187.

Sarnoff, I., & Katz, D. The motivational bases of attitude change. *J. abnorm. soc. Psychol.*, 1954, *49*, 115–124.

Schachter, S. Deviation, rejection, and communication. *J. abnorm. soc. Psychol.*, 1951, *46*, 190–207. (Reprinted in Cartwright & Zander, 1960, pp. 260–285.)

Schachter, S., Nuttin, J., DeMonchaux, Cecily, Maucorps, P. H., Osmer, D., Duijker, H., Rommetveit, R., & Israel, J. Cross-cultural experiments on threat and rejection. *Hum. Relat.*, 1954, 7, 403–439.

Schein, E. H. The Chinese indoctrination program for prisoners of war: A study of attempted "brainwashing." In Eleanor E. Maccoby, T. M. Newcomb, & E. L. Hartley (Eds.), *Readings in social psychology* (ed. 3). New York: Holt, Rinehart and Winston, 1958. Pp. 311–334.

Schein, E. H. *Coercive persuasion: A socio-psychological analysis of the "brainwashing" of American civilian prisoners by the Chinese Communists.* New York: Norton, 1961.

Schramm, W., & Carter, R. F. Effectiveness of a political telethon. *Publ. Opin. Quart.*, 1959, 23, 121–126.

Scott, W. A. Attitude change through reward of verbal behavior. *J. abnorm. soc. Psychol.*, 1957, 55, 72–75.

Scott, W. A. Rationality and non-rationality of international attitudes. *J. Confl. Resol.*, 1958, 2, 8–16.

Seeleman, Virginia The influence of attitude upon the remembering of pictorial material. *Arch. Psychol.*, 1941, no. 258.

Smith, H. P., & Rosen, Ellen W. Some psychological correlates of world-mindedness and authoritarianism. *J. Pers.*, 1958, 26, 170–183.

Smith, M. B. The personal setting of public opinions: A study of attitudes toward Russia. *Publ. Opin. Quart.*, 1947, 11, 507–523.

Smith, M. B. Personal values as determinants of a political attitude. *J. Psychol.*, 1949, 28, 477–486.

Smith, M. B. Opinions, personality and political behavior. *Amer. pol. Sci. Rev.*, 1958, 52, 1–17.

Smith, M. B., Bruner, J. S., & White, R. W. *Opinions and personality.* New York: Wiley, 1956.

Star, Shirley A., & Hughes, Helen McG. Report of an educational campaign: The Cincinnati Plan for the United Nations. *Amer. J. Sociol.*, 1950, 55, 389–400.

Tannenbaum, P. H. Initial attitudes toward source and concept as factors in attitude change through communication. *Publ. Opin. Quart.*, 1956, 20, 413–425.

Thistlethwaite, D. L., deHaan, H., & Kamenetzky, J. The effects of "directive" and "non-directive" communication procedures on attitudes. *J. abnorm. soc. Psychol.*, 1955, 51, 103–113.

Tuchman, Barbara W. *The Zimmerman telegram.* New York: Viking, 1958.

Watson, Jeanne, & Lippitt, R. Cross-cultural experience as a source of attitude change. *J. Confl. Resol.*, 1958, 2, 61–66.

7

In the final two chapters of Part One we shall explore national and international images in the context of international conflict. Specifically, we shall look at Soviet and American images that seem to characterize the Cold War, and link these to the nature of the interaction between the two nations and of the foreign policy process within them. These two chapters illustrate the possible implications of research on images and attitudes for vital policy questions, and examine some of the complex methodological issues that arise when one attempts to draw policy implications from such research.

Chapter 7 delineates some of the images of their own country and of the United States held by Soviet citizens, on the basis of a systematic review of available public opinion data. Some of the determinants of these images are spelled out, with special emphasis on the ways in which perceptual distortions grow out of the dynamics of intergroup conflict in general, and out of the conditions of Soviet society in particular. Mutual images of conflicting groups are based on contradictory interpretations of reality and tend, at least to some degree, to mirror each other. Chapter 7 grapples with some of the sticky methodological issues that arise from this circumstance, by attempting to develop criteria for distinguishing distortion from reality and by examining the limitations of the concept of *mirror image*. An attempt is also made to draw the implications that an understanding of Soviet public images has for United States policy vis-à-vis the Soviet Union.

The author of Chapter 7, Ralph K. White, is Professor in the Department of Psychology and the Institute of Sino-Soviet Studies at George Washington University. For a number of years he was associated with the United States Information Agency, carrying out research on public opinion and reactions to USIA output in various parts of the world. He is author of *Value analysis* (1951), and co-author of *Autocracy and democracy: An experimental inquiry* (1960). He was a member of the original Society for the Psychological Study of Social Issues

Committee on the Psychology of War and Peace, and is a member of the Society's current Committee on International Relations. His research interests focus on Soviet public opinion; the psychology of Soviet leaders; and the semantics of socialism and capitalism.

H. C. K.

Images in the Context
of International Conflict

SOVIET PERCEPTIONS OF THE U.S.
AND THE U.S.S.R.

Ralph K. White

Now that the thermonuclear weapon has given to two countries, the United States and the Soviet Union, the power of mutual destruction, it behooves each of them to try to understand the other. This chapter explores a part of that problem: the psychology of the Soviet public.[1]

Since we are primarily concerned with the distortions in the image-systems of Soviet citizens and the reasons for those distortions, we must first undertake a simple description of their assumptions about the world and then try to distinguish, chiefly on the basis of historical evidence, between what may be valid in their assumptions and what seems clearly distorted.

In embarking on an enterprise such as this, it is appropriate to indicate at the outset something of the point of view from which the analysis is approached.

One underlying supposition is that the available evidence should be followed wherever it leads, regardless of what this may do to our Western black-and-white picture of the East-West conflict.

The kind of open-mindedness that such an analysis requires probably does conflict, to some degree, with the all-black enemy image and with the all-white self image that are sometimes considered essential to conflict morale in a group-conflict situation. While an admission that the enemy *feels* right is not an admission that he *is* right in any respect, it does conflict with the simplicity of the black-and-white picture in which the enemy is necessarily seen as wholly diabolical. If one goes further and ascribes any element of validity to what the enemy believes, this conflicts with the simple assumption that all of the truth is on

---

[1] The psychology of the leaders is considered briefly at the end of the chapter, but only to point up certain probable resemblances and differences between them and the general public.

one's own side. In either case there is impairment of the kind of single-minded conflict morale that requires a black-and-white picture to sustain it.

On the other hand, we are living in a thermonuclear age, and it can be reasonably argued that in such an age the black-and-white basis for conflict morale has become obsolete. It could kill us. It sustains the vicious circles of mutual antagonism and of struggle for unlimited power, with increasing suspicion and dedication to the struggle on both sides, that could end in a nuclear catastrophe even though both sides were desperately anxious to avoid it. Probably there was a time, before wars became so destructive, when black-and-white thinking had survival value for a group. Now it is more likely to have counter-survival value. It is time to look for a different basis of morale.

It is suggested here that such a basis exists in the form of a mature, realistic understanding of how the Communists see the world. It is possible to have such an understanding and at the same time to be fully prepared to do whatever is deemed necessary to restrain the aggressive actions to which the Communists' world view may give rise. It is possible to combine it with a policy of military strength and a policy of consistent readiness to resist clearcut Communist aggression if and when it occurs. But it is also a basis for creative forms of tension-reduction and conflict-resolution that would be completely ruled out by the blind hostility and the mental rigidity of the black-and-white picture. It is an essential basis for realism, and realism is essential if we are to escape catastrophe.

If the result of the historical analysis were that "both sides are probably equally right and equally wrong," the increase in realism that would result from an open-minded study of the evidence might have to be paid for by a loss in the courage and determination needed to remain strong and resist Communist encroachments. But, as will become apparent (see especially pp. 249–254), the analysis does not lead to that result.

Such a statement, however, raises immediately the problem of cultural and ideological relativism. If it is true that the entire social background of the Soviet people has created in their minds a "point of view" (a "reality world" or set of ingrained assumptions about the world) of such a nature that "they feel as right from their point of view as we do from ours," how can we avoid going a step further and suspecting that perhaps we feel as right as we do because of cultural conditioning rather than because of the facts? How do we know that our Western "reality world" is any more realistic than theirs? How can we escape from the impasse of relativism and earn the right to speak, with an intact philosophical and anthropological conscience, about "Communist delusions"?

It is here suggested that the only escape from the impasse of relativism lies in a sustained, never-ending appeal to the evidence.

This much can be conceded immediately to the relativist position, even in advance of any study of the specific evidence on the issues of the East–West conflict: "there is probably *some* truth on both sides." A large amount of psychological research[2] and abundant evidence from history, anthropology, and everyday human experience point to the usual strength of the forces of group consensus and conformity. In a situation of intergroup conflict, these

---

[2] See especially Asch (1952). Other relevant psychological research has been on prejudice (for example, Allport, 1954), the "authoritarian personality" (for example, Adorno, Frenkel-Brunswik, Levinson, & Sanford, 1950), dogmatism (Rokeach, 1960), and perceptual distortion (for example, Festinger, 1957).

forces typically result in a distortion of the facts by both sides in the direction of an ethnocentric black-and-white picture. The ingrained, partly unconscious, usually unchallenged assumptions that constitute an individual's "reality world"[3] are built into him from early childhood, largely by the group in which he happens to be; the group can therefore influence the basic premises of his thinking even when he makes a conscious effort to wrench himself loose from its control and to look at the world with fresh eyes.

On the other hand, the proposition that "there is probably some truth on both sides" should be distinguished from the quite different proposition that "there is probably an equal amount of truth on both sides." The word "some" tells nothing about how much, or about what specific elements in the picture are valid and what the nature of the distortion is. It is possible to acknowledge "some" validity in the other's viewpoint without really challenging some of the fundamentals of one's own group's thought. But it is also entirely possible to attribute too much validity to the other's viewpoint, leaning over backward in an effort to avoid ethnocentrism and settling prematurely, before examining the evidence, for the seemingly "objective" conclusion that "probably both sides are equally right and equally wrong." In this morass of conflicting unconscious biases the only hope of even diminishing one's own perceptual distortions, and getting somewhat closer to reality, lies in a stubborn focus on whatever evidence is already available, a stubborn adherence both to the canons of social science and to those of common sense in evaluating the evidence, and a continual, never-satisfied search for new evidence that may be relevant to the points at issue.

Insofar as it can be done within the limits of space and of our knowledge, that is what the first half of this chapter tries to do. It is first simply an exercise in empathy—a summary of what the evidence suggests as to how the East–West conflict looks to most of the ordinary Russian citizens. This is followed by a brief comparison of their reality world with the available evidence, in order to distinguish at least tentatively between what is valid and what is distorted in their image-system. Both of these steps, empathy and dissection, are a necessary preliminary to the main business of the chapter, which is an effort to explain how and why the world-picture of the Soviet people came to be as it is.

THE REALITY WORLD OF THE SOVIET CITIZEN

Perception of the Soviet Union as Peaceful

While few competent Western specialists in Soviet affairs would call the Soviet leaders genuinely "peaceful" (except in the sense that they have an urge to self-preservation and now recognize the danger of nuclear war), there is fairly general agreement that the Soviet people *think* their country (including its government) is peaceful. Although specialists disagree as to the extent and quality of the people's general support of the present regime, on the people's image of their government's foreign policy there is little doubt: they *see* it as a policy of peace. This conclusion is derived both from innumerable conversations inside the U.S.S.R. (where there is always some question about whether the Soviet citizen is being frank or merely conforming to the official line) and also from interviews with former

---

[3] For the term "reality world" and a discussion of its meaning, see Cantril (1958, pp. 11–61).

Soviet citizens outside the U.S.S.R. (where this particular question does not arise).

One of the more startling experiences of a Western visitor to the U.S.S.R. is, often, his discovery of the extent to which the Soviet people he meets appear to assume that their own country and its government have been wholly peaceful. As they often put it, "After what we went through in World War II, how could we be anything but peaceful?"

To the typical Western visitor—who has had more access to the relevant evidence—the opposite seems self-evident. While he may grant immediately that both the Soviet people and their government probably want to avoid a big nuclear war, it seems clear to him that the Soviet and Chinese Communist governments have used force or the threat of force many times in the intermittent, calculating process of extending their own power. Concrete examples of Communist aggression and threats of aggression throng into his mind: the cynical Nazi-Soviet Pact and subsequent partition of Poland, the attack on Finland, the absorption of the Baltic states, the take-over of almost all of Eastern Europe after World War II, the Berlin blockade, the Korean war, Hungary, Tibet, Laos, Vietnam, Quemoy, again Berlin, the Indian border, the stationing of offensive missiles in Cuba. But, amazingly, none of these things seems to come into the ordinary Soviet citizen's mind, or if any do come into his mind he interprets them in a way that preserves his image of Soviet peacefulness.[4] What does come into his mind, so vividly and powerfully that it sweeps everything else aside, is his memory of the horrors of World War II, and of the innocent, suffering, heroic role his country played at that time. To him it seems that everyone in the world must realize that after such an experience the Soviet Union *must* be one of the most peace-loving countries in the world.

The report of an American visitor is typical: "They are not allowed to forget *their* war for a day. Their suffering was terrible. Perhaps they could not forget it even if allowed, but officially it is enforced so much that even the young, who didn't know it [at the time], are tremendously and emotionally aware of it. . . . Often it is strict party-line propaganda even to the words used, but very often it is fervently believed. There were many, many tearful eyes when this subject came up."

Against this background, a statement by a Western visitor that the West is defending itself against Soviet aggression has a strange sound in the ears of the typical Soviet man-in-the-street. "What Soviet aggression?" he asks, and when the Western visitor gives examples the Soviet citizen tends to be incredulous, wounded, and resentful of what he apparently regards as hostile misinterpretations of innocent Soviet actions.

It should be noticed that, as far as the man-in-the-street is concerned (as distinguished from the leaders), this is not a form of ideological Communist fanaticism. It is not that these ordinary Soviet people justify forcible Communist expansion by the greatness of the ideal of a Communist world in which each will be provided for "according to his needs," or by the lasting peace

---

[4] Hungary is a partial exception. Many of the people apparently still feel uneasy about their government's role in crushing the Hungarian uprising, but it is not nearly as salient in their minds as in ours, and, curiously, most of them do not seem to think of it as a warlike act. Those who disapprove of it think of it as reassertion of Soviet domination in Eastern Europe, apparently, but not as "aggression" in the usual sense of that word.

which, according to official Communist doctrine, such a world will bring about. The ordinary Russian citizens are seldom crusaders in this sense; most of them are like the average American in being willing to settle for a live-and-let-live philosophy in international relations. It is, rather, that these men-in-the-street literally do not think there has been any forcible Communist expansion (or, at least, not by the U.S.S.R.). Their conception of their country's peacefulness appears to be qualitatively similar to the conception Americans have of America's peacefulness.

The evidence on these points is now extensive and rather consistent. During the recent period of greatly increased contact between the Soviet people and the outside world (roughly since 1956) there have been innumerable conversations between Westerners and Soviet citizens. There are gaps in the record (little is known about the peasants, for instance); there are differences within the U.S.S.R. (the people in the Baltic states, for instance, being much more anti-Soviet than the Great Russians); and on the degree of general support of the regime there is still controversy among experts.[5] On the points mentioned above, however, there now appears to be a rather high degree of consensus among competent Western observers, including those who have

had the most contact with former Soviet citizens *outside* the U.S.S.R., where the question of keeping up a good Communist front does not arise.[6]

As to the validity of all this evidence there is one serious critical question: how do we know that, when Soviet citizens say such things, it is what they really think? Granting that this is what all or nearly all of them say, how do we know they mean it? After all, theirs is an authoritarian society in which every citizen feels a pressure to say what is officially acceptable whether he means it or not. Why, then, should we take it seriously when they are saying just what the authorities would approve?

There are several reasons to believe that a large majority of them do mean what they say on this point—that their country's foreign policy is peaceful.

One reason, which is very persuasive to those who have directly experienced it, is the emotion that frequently shows in their voice and manner when they are discussing this subject. One often hears reports such as "There were many, many tearful eyes when this subject came up." This does not sound like prudent conformity to an official line.

To be sure, signs of emotion are in general no guarantee of sincerity. When individuals are being compared, the more overtly emotional ones are not at all likely to be the most honest or sincere. The point here is, rather, that

[5] For interpretations stressing the prevalence of tension and discontent, see Pipes (1961) and Burg (1961). For an eloquent and detailed (but now dated) presentation of the thesis that there is widespread latent disaffection, see Lyons (1954).

[6] The chief single published body of evidence on the subject is still that of Bauer, Inkeles, and Kluckhohn (1956) and Inkeles and Bauer (1959). Their work was based largely on the extensive Harvard project for interviewing former Soviet citizens. In addition there are an American Committee for Liberation study based on interviews with 107 especially qualified Western visitors to the U.S.S.R. (1959), a number of reports by American students who have attended Soviet universities, and reports by individuals whose contribution has been unusual in one way or another—for example, Crankshaw (1956; see especially p. 94), Novak (1960), Bronfenbrenner (1960), and Adler (1960). The methodological problems of drawing inferences from conversations inside the U.S.S.R. do not seem to have been systematically discussed as yet by anyone, but the problems of drawing inferences from interviews with escapees have been well covered by Inkeles and Bauer (1959, Chapter 2).

when a given person or group shows more outward emotion on some subjects than on others—when, for instance, the Russian people show more emotion on the question of war and peace than on race relations in the United States—the chances of their having real feeling on the first subject seem higher than the chances of their having it on the second.

Another reason consists of the reports of American visitors that when they have been drawn into discussion of this subject it has usually become an uphill and unrewarding argument. They have usually found more open minds when they have talked about the Negro problem in America, or about American living standards and social security measures, than when, in answering questions, they have tried to make American defensive motives seem plausible in Soviet eyes. Discussion of this subject, unlike the others, usually does not meet with courteous silence and occasional slight nods, but evokes instead vigorous counterargument. Sometimes a hard edge of anger is detectable in their voices, and if by chance the American tries to defend the rearming of West Germany or our alliance with West Germany in NATO the anger sometimes becomes intense.

Overt signs of emotion, then, are one indication that Soviet citizens are relatively honest on this subject, and another is that on this subject they are more vocal, more emphatic, and more resistant to argument than on a number of other subjects. Still another indication is that, according to numerous reports, what they say in private on this subject is usually in line with what they say in public, in front of other Soviet citizens who might be taking mental notes. The qualitative cues that normally indicate sincerity seem to be present. On this point also (though not on the general amount of popular sup-

port of the regime) the testimony of competent Russian-speaking Western observers appears to be close to unanimous. For instance, Bauer, Inkeles, and Kluckhohn (1956) say that "in the majority of instances they [Soviet citizens talking to Western visitors inside the U.S.S.R.] indicated a complete acceptance of official propaganda with regard to foreign affairs" (p. 124). Frederick Barghoorn reported as long ago as 1950 (when the Stalin regime was still in power, and was much more hated than the successors of Stalin, and when memories of wartime collaboration with America were much fresher than they are now): "Unfortunately, particularly among the party and armed forces, it is possible that the Soviet government's monopoly of the instruments of communications may have enabled it to persuade the majority of the Soviet people that if there is war between Russia and America, America must inevitably be the aggressor" (p. 250). With regard to the direction of change since Stalin's time the testimony of Philip Mosely (1963) is significant: "One obvious result of the improvement has been to raise Khrushchev's popularity to a peak Stalin never knew. His eagerness to go out among the people, his willingness to explain his policies frequently and at length, his 'folksy' manner, are all valuable assets. A further consequence has been to increase enormously the credibility of Soviet propaganda among the people generally" (p. 435). It may also be noted that, among respected students of Soviet affairs, even those who are most inclined to see evidence of antiregime attitudes among the people usually grant that most of the people regard the regime as peaceful. Richard Pipes is a case in point, and his psychological explanation of the phenomenon is of special interest:

Despite Russia's obvious advances in aviation and rocketry and the growth of her whole military establishment, many Russians are firmly convinced that the power of the West greatly exceeds that of the Communist bloc. From this idea they deduce that the Soviet government is inherently more peaceful ("strength equals aggressiveness, weakness equals docility"). They interpret the construction of a chain of American bases around the Soviet Union as well as the arming of West Germany as unnecessary provocations on the part of a country which, by virtue of its superior power, has no need for special military safeguards (1961, p. 110).

Finally, it should be noted that this conclusion is agreed upon by most of those (e.g., Bauer, Inkeles, & Kluckhohn, 1956) who are most familiar with the data on interviewing of former residents of the U.S.S.R. *outside* the U.S.S.R., where the bias based on prudent conformity to the official Communist line is no longer a problem.

Perception of the United States as Threatening

While there is a strong underlying feeling of friendliness toward America and Americans (see pp. 256–257), most of the Soviet people also seem to have been persuaded that the "rulers" of the United States are "threatening" them.

The word in their minds is "threatening," not "committing aggression against." While Communist propaganda has often accused America of outright aggression, the basic friendliness of the Soviet people toward America has apparently kept most of them from inwardly accepting such an extreme term. They evidently do not think of any long list of American aggressive actions in the literal sense of a physical attack, as most Americans do in thinking of the aggressive actions of the Soviet government. To be sure, many of them do

think of America's intervention in their civil war in 1918–1920 (with a version of what happened that is very different from the version presented, for example, by Kennan, 1960a, pp. 64–119), and some refer in similar terms to our more recent actions in China, Korea, Guatemala, Lebanon, Cuba, and elsewhere, but these do not seem especially important to them emotionally.

The things that really disturb them— the themes in Communist propaganda that seem to have had a real reverberation in the people's minds—appear to be, rather, America's bases around their border, its nuclear arms, its U-2 flights (to a lesser degree), and, above all, its alliance with the West Germans. These are the chief concrete issues they seem to have in mind when they talk about American "threats."

This is probably the point at which a certain deliberate effort of empathy is most necessary if Americans are to understand the feelings as well as the thoughts of an ordinary Russian man-in-the-street, looking at an image that he believes to be America. Basically he is friendly to the American people, yet he thinks American actions are threatening because he judges those actions on the basis of a set of assumptions that Communist propaganda and other factors have built into his mind, and his ingrained assumptions differ greatly from those of a typical citizen of the West. As Cantril might put it, the Russian "reality world" differs from the American in ways that are difficult for Americans to appreciate fully; or as Lewin might put it, the Russian's "life space" has to be considered as a whole if any part of it is to be seen in the right context. And when Americans try to do that, their own "reality world" (which they may have much reason to regard as more realistic than his, but which is not his) continually tends to obtrude and to interfere with empathic understanding.

The chief difference between the assumptions he brings to bear in judging American actions and the assumptions Americans bring to bear in judging the same actions seems to lie in differing views of Soviet peacefulness. The Russian sees American actions against a background of assumed Soviet peacefulness, while Americans do not. To Americans, since many examples of what they regard as Soviet aggression are fresh in their minds, it seems obvious that actions such as the Western arms program and the alliance with West Germany are needed in order to deter further Soviet aggression. Americans naturally assume that the same examples exist to some degree in the mind of the ordinary Soviet citizen, but, in the light of the evidence that has just been reviewed, this does not seem to be true. There are apparently no examples of Soviet aggression even in the back of his mind (with the partial exception of the Soviet intervention in Hungary). Instead there is World War II, and on that basis he assumes that "the whole world knows" how peaceful the Soviet Union is.

The question for a citizen of the West to ask in his effort to empathize with a typical citizen of the U.S.S.R. (that is, his effort to understand, without necessarily agreeing) is, then, this: if he were a Soviet citizen *and if he literally had complete faith in Soviet peacefulness,* how would he be likely to interpret America's bases on his borders, its nuclear arms overshadowing his own country's, its U-2 flights over his head, and its alliance with the Germans who had attacked his country in 1941?

First let us consider, from the Soviet point of view, the ring of air and missile bases encircling the U.S.S.R., now supplemented by Polaris submarines equipped with atomic missiles. The Soviet government (and Soviet citizens in conversations with Western visitors) have continually asserted that they were not doing anything comparable to America and that America's bases on their borders constituted a one-sided "threat."

To be sure, the Soviet situation is actually quite different from that of America in some ways. For many years America has had a decisive superiority in nuclear weapons and bases, and has not used them since Hiroshima. Even in the early post-Hiroshima years when the United States had an atomic monopoly and did not need to fear Soviet atomic retaliation, the United States did not use them to attack the U.S.S.R. as it could have. A failure to remember this is one of the more glaring omissions in the typical Soviet citizen's version of recent history. From America's point of view its consistent self-restraint should give the Russians sufficient reason to be sure they never will be subject to a sudden atomic attack, especially now when fear of retaliation has entered the picture. This is, however, from the American point of view, and it assumes that Soviet minds work as Americans think they ought to work. If for any reasons, however mistaken, the Soviet people do not have full confidence in America's nuclear self-restraint in the future, their feeling about its missiles on their border could be one of real anxiety.

In any event, there is much evidence of a strong emotional response on the issue of bases. Of course, as always, the propaganda factor should be given due weight. The most obvious reason for the fact that the people are disturbed by the bases is that their leaders have often expressed indignation about them. As Khrushchev put it to Nixon: "The one who is putting an end to bases is for peace. The other is for war." But propaganda can hardly be the only reason for it, because on certain other points propaganda has been relatively ineffective, while on this one the reverberation in the minds of the people has been great. For instance, one American visitor said that "our military bases abroad seem to arouse the greatest natural concern—personal concern—of any of the issues involved," and another reported: "On the question of bases— it is true that Soviet citizens feel encircled, and cannot understand why the United States does not wish them to live in peace."

Next, let us consider from the ordinary Soviet citizen's point of view the nuclear armament of the West. Americans have tended to see their own nuclear build-up very much as they have seen their bases—not as a threat but as a realistic *response* to a Communist threat. Also, they have observed that the Russians themselves have been strenuously competing in the missile-and-nuclear race, and it has been hard to see how they could think participation in this race, as such, was particularly heinous. They were doing it—in fact, they started the whole conflict— so why should they think America was wicked just because it took part in the same race?

This line of thought, however, leaves out of account two factors that, from the ordinary Russian's point of view, have appeared in a different light. In the first place, the West has been ahead in the nuclear race. To be sure, the Russians have had a strength in land armies and conventional arms that has made many in the West feel that the military balance was equal or even that it tipped toward the Communist side. But from a Russian standpoint a basic fact has been that nuclear weapons were decisive in modern war if either side was reckless enough to be the first to use them. America's primary reliance on such weapons, therefore, could have

led Russians to think that America might indeed be reckless enough to be the first to use them.

The second imbalance in the arms race, as the Soviet people apparently interpret it, is more fundamental; it is that the West does not need to arm to defend itself against the Soviet Union because "after what we suffered in World War II, how could we be anything but peaceful!" Assuming, as they evidently do, that their peacefulness is obvious to Americans, they cannot believe that American bases or arms are really defensive in purpose. The only other explanation that comes into their minds, apparently, is that the purpose of these bases and arms is aggressive.

It is not surprising, therefore, that Soviet citizens in talking to an American often take what the American regards as a naively simple view of the problem of disarmament. As they apparently see it, the only thing needed is for America to take the path of disarmament, since obviously the U.S.S.R. would follow suit, and then the clouds of war would disappear. An American visitor in 1961 reports, "I was repeatedly asked why the American government refused to accept Khrushchev's proposals for disarmament. 'We have to disarm,' one of them earnestly said. 'You must go home and tell your people to disarm.'"

The U-2 flights across the Soviet Union are not so often mentioned and now appear to be emotionally the least important of the four major types of American "threat" as perceived by the Russian public. Yet they do stand out in Soviet memories as a dramatic episode punctuating the grim sameness of the East–West conflict, and it is worth while again to try to look at a concrete situation from a Soviet as well as from an American point of view.

From the standpoint of those Americans who decided that they should occur, the U-2 flights were necessary in view of the threat presented by Soviet missile bases, inside the U.S.S.R., to the whole of the free world; and they were additionally justified by the closed character of a totalitarian society, which gave "the Communist aggressors" a one-sided advantage in terms of secrecy. The Communists had rejected the open-skies inspection plan which would have permitted the same kind of procedure on both sides; in a way, therefore, they had forced America's hand. Probably most Americans felt that this was an adequate justification, since most of the criticism in the United States centered on the timing of the flights that occurred just before the Summit meeting, or on the way in which the news was handled, rather than on the idea of the flights themselves. Most Americans probably think of them as simply a form of spying, and since both sides in any power struggle necessarily engage in spying (and since the Communists started this particular power struggle) Americans tend to feel that they should be realistic enough to accept spying on their own side and take it in stride.

From the standpoint of a Soviet citizen the U-2 flights had a different look. They were not ordinary spying, but airplanes flying over their heads as German planes had flown over their heads in the unforgettable Second World War. And, unlike the German planes, these could at any time carry thermonuclear bombs.

Bronfenbrenner has given an account (1960) of one such reaction not long after the U-2 incident occurred. He sat down at a table in a Leningrad restaurant with a young man who asked him "to explain how it could happen that we would send a plane over another nation's soil." He tried to explain it in terms of Soviet rejection of the open-skies policy, saying:

". . . we concluded that the Soviets must have something to hide. Otherwise they wouldn't have any reason for objecting to letting somebody else look. And so we sent a plane to see for ourselves."

"To see for ourselves," my dinner companion repeated. And then, in a much louder voice as he lost control, "I see, for you an airplane is just something to take pretty pictures out of, and do you know what it means to me when I look up and see an airplane? It means the death of my mother, the death of my father, the death of my brothers and sisters and all those that were dear to me. That's what it means to me, and that's what it means to all of us who live in the Soviet Union . . ." (p. 14).

Another Russian elaborated on the theme:

"Today you do not carry nuclear warheads in your planes, but tomorrow you may. And even if you don't fire them, an accident may happen. We cannot allow your planes to fly uninvited over our native land. And once we bomb your bases you may bomb ours, and then there is the horror of war. . . . Oh yes, we spy—but there are sensible spying activities and mad ones that can lead to war. Our spies can find out what they want to without precipitating a situation which leaves us no recourse but to shoot at planes and bases. Our spies do not threaten your land with planes that could carry a bomb" (p. 5).

Emotionally, though, the most important reason for Soviet perception of America as threatening is, quite clearly, our alliance with West Germany.

From the standpoint of most Americans this alliance, in NATO, is natural enough. It is another case of obvious self-defense. Most Americans feel that it was Hitler and the other Nazi rulers of Germany, not the German people as a whole, who attacked the West, attacked Russia, and put millions of

Jews in gas-chambers. Since the war democracy in West Germany has made great strides, and there is good reason to think that the people have turned their attention from war and aggression to the economic development of their country. So, if they can be persuaded to do their share in the defense of Western Europe, why not?

It would be difficult to exaggerate how different the U.S.-German alliance looks to the Soviet people. They see it in the context of their overwhelming emotional preoccupation with World War II, the most significant experience of their lives. The importance of the war in creating their own sense of innocence has already been discussed. It was equally important in creating a sense of the utterly diabolical character of the Germans. As they experienced it, or heard about it, the Germans fell upon them without any provocation and, if it had not been for their heroic defense, would surely have destroyed their country. Only after bitter, bloody years of struggle were they able to throw back the invaders. Since even capitalist America had seen the Nazi danger and given them some help in the struggle, they had hopes that after the war the American people would ally themselves with the Soviet people in making sure that such aggression could never occur again. But no. Inexplicably in their eyes (except on the Marxist theory of evil capitalists wielding great power in America and duping the people with a legend of a Soviet "danger"), America sided with the murderer against the murderer's intended victim, is still doing so, and now has again put a knife into the murderer's hand.

The evidence that a great many Russians see it in this way is abundant. To cite only two from a large number of examples: Bronfenbrenner (1960) quotes a Soviet citizen as saying: "We know the Germans better than you.

Twice in the life of our country we have had to defend ourselves against German aggression. We can't allow this again. And the West German Government is letting Nazis come back to power" (p. 6). And a Western visitor reports: "On German rearmament my discussion was constantly interrupted by emotional outbursts that relived the horrors and sufferings of World War II."

Let us return now to the question asked on p. 245: If a Russian citizen really had this faith in Russian peacefulness, how would he be likely to interpret America's bases on his borders, its nuclear weapons overshadowing those of the U.S.S.R., its U-2 flights over his head, and its alliance with the Germans who attacked his country? Would he believe that these actions were for defense—against *him* and his country? It now seems likely that (especially as influenced by propaganda) he would not. His perception of at least these four of America's actions, in the context of his perception of his own country as wholly and obviously peaceful, would in his mind probably add up to a perception of America, not as an "aggressor" necessarily, but as definitely "threatening."

It should be especially noticed that in all four cases an essential reason for his perception of America as threatening would be his perception of his own country, the U.S.S.R., as wholly and obviously peaceful. And if he assumed that Americans perceive the U.S.S.R. as he does, this would keep him from perceiving or imagining that the Americans might really fear an attack by his own country. Assuming that they are not really afraid, he would hardly suppose that their bases, arms, and so forth were actually defensive in purpose, and he would hardly be likely to reach any other conclusion than that all these things are aggressive.

In other words, the chief factor determining the Soviet people's enemy-image (or rather, their receptivity to official propaganda about that enemy) is their own self-image.

It also works the other way: their self-image depends on their enemy-image. Their picture of their own country as wholly peaceful is preserved—even though the U.S.S.R. too engages in the arms race and other power-oriented policies—by the thought that these policies are only defensive reactions to the enemy's "threats." For instance, when a Soviet citizen looks at his government's policy of bombs instead of butter he can tell himself that it is essential to be strong in order to deter the Western attack that would otherwise be all too possible, and thereby prevent a repetition, perhaps on a larger scale, of the horrors of World War II.

There is, then, a circular cause-and-effect relationship. Given an image of the self as wholly peaceful, the power-oriented actions of the opponent cannot be perceived as anything but aggressive, and given an image of the opponent as aggressive, the power-oriented actions of the self are perceived as defensive and entirely consistent with peacefulness. The two images, peaceful self and aggressive enemy, are mutually complementary and thoroughly interdependent.

It should be noted, finally, that the aggressive enemy in their eyes is not the American people but the "ruling class" in America. For many years we have been familiar with this as a characteristic of Communist propaganda, which ordinarily makes a sharp distinction between the good, peace-loving American "people" and the "ruling circles" in Wall Street and the Pentagon, which are accused of profiting from the arms race and deliberately fomenting it, if not actually wanting

war. What many Americans have failed to realize is that, in this respect too, most of the Soviet people have apparently accepted the official line without much critical thought. As one Western visitor put it, "Most Russians are convinced that there is a wide gulf separating the capitalist ruling class and the masses in America." Another reports: "The dog-eared proposition, 'In England and America there are two classes; one loves the Russian people and the other wants war,' was actually repeated on several occasions." And an American visitor recalls, "Most all of them are convinced that the American people want peace while Wall Street imperialists and war profiteers want war." In the Soviet citizen's mind there is not an all-black image but a *black-top* image of America.

THE VALIDITY OF SOVIET PERCEPTIONS

When the world-picture of the Soviet people is compared with the much larger amount of evidence available to us, what seems to be valid in it and what seems distorted? In order to talk with any confidence about their distortions it is necessary first to make an honest effort to recognize the parts of their image-system that correspond to reality and to distinguish the distortions from these comparatively realistic elements. This is of course a path full of pitfalls (see above, p. 239), one being the danger of accepting uncritically one's own group's ethnocentric black-and-white picture as a criterion of "truth," and another being the danger of leaning over backward in an effort to avoid ethnocentrism. It is nevertheless a path that must be entered upon if we are to escape even partially from the impasse of relativism by focusing on the best available evidence.

The evidence lies chiefly in the field of recent history[7] and an adequate study of it would go far beyond the scope of this chapter. It is possible, though, to examine briefly the two central questions of fact: to what extent are the Soviet people right in seeing their government as nonaggressive, and to what extent are they right in seeing America's "rulers" as engaging in "threats"?

Perception of the Soviet Union as Peaceful

The first question, "To what extent are they right in seeing their government as nonaggressive?" may sound incongruous to most Americans. Even if we define "aggression" in its strictest sense as the use of force or the threat of force to conquer new territory, it seems clear that the Soviet government *has* committed aggression, in this sense, time after time: in attacking Finland, for example, in taking over the Baltic states, in taking over most of Eastern Europe after World War II, in the Berlin blockade, in supporting the North Korean attack on South Korea, in its intervention against the uprising in Hungary, and in its more recent pressures against Berlin.[8] In fact it seems fair to put this down immediately as the first and greatest distortion in Soviet minds: to the extent that they forget or deny or rationalize this cumulative record of outright aggression, they are engaging (with much help from Communist propaganda and cen-

sorship) in an extraordinary feat of self-delusion.

There are nevertheless certain related factors that should be considered in order to get a realistic understanding of what has gone on in the minds of the Soviet people. Taken all together they do not change the objective story of Soviet aggression substantially, but they do make a substantial difference in interpreting how that aggression has been perceived by the Soviet people themselves.

In the case of the attack on Finland the chief mitigating factor in present-day Soviet minds is, probably, the Nazi danger that materialized in terrible form a year and a half later, and the association in their minds between the Finns and the Nazis. It is hard to know how seriously to take the claim of some Soviet citizens today (in agreement with Stalin's official line at the time) that they really believed the Finns started the war. However, even those who saw through this transparent falsehood might now tell themselves that the Soviet attack was a piece of hardheaded *Realpolitik*, pushing outward the defenses of Leningrad while there was still time to do so, in anticipation of the Nazi attack (in alliance with the Finns) that was still to come.[9]

Similarly, they were able to interpret the absorption of the Baltic states as a realistic move in anticipation of a possible Nazi attack. (To be sure, this would not explain why the U.S.S.R. kept those territories after the war was over.)

The take-over of most of Eastern Europe after the war is in Western

---

[7] For some aspects of the requisite historical analysis, see Kennan (1960a, pp. 314–398), Dallin (1960), Beloff (1949). For an official Soviet interpretation of the same events, see Airapetian & Deborin (1961, pp. 246–249, 250–251, 329–330, 370–371, 429–430).

[8] The stationing of offensive missiles in Cuba would seem to belong in a somewhat different category.

[9] For evidence that Finland was not actually an ally of the Nazis at the time of the Soviet attack, but that the Soviet government did suspect this, see Beloff (1949, vol. 2, pp. 305–307). Beloff does not doubt that the Soviet Union was the aggressor.

eyes perhaps the most flagrant, and certainly the largest in scale, of all the Soviet aggressions. But Communist propaganda has partially masked the character of Soviet rule in this area from the Soviet people by talk about "liquidating fascist and reactionary elements" and setting up independent "people's democracies." And here too those Soviet citizens who can read between the lines of Communist propaganda, and who have been led by the events of 1953 and 1956 to recognize that the peoples of the area are *not* independent, may still tell themselves that this is a harsh but necessary way of protecting the U.S.S.R. against any possible repetition of the attack from the West that almost destroyed it in 1941–1943.

The Berlin blockade (which seems to have hardly entered the consciousness of the Soviet people at all) and the more recent pressures on Berlin are also apparently seen primarily in the context of a German danger, and the fear that a German-American alliance may in the future subvert the stability of the present situation in Eastern Europe, if not actually attack the U.S.S.R. Against the background of the Soviet people's experience in World War II it is relatively easy for the government to strike a responsive chord by talking about "liquidating the remnants of World War II," since Berlin can be easily pictured as an outpost of a dangerous enemy, a center for dangerous espionage, and a source of dangerous propaganda.

The Korean war was perhaps the least easily rationalized of the entire list of Soviet aggressions, since it was so far away from the European core of the Soviet Union and could not be easily interpreted in the context of the German danger or any other danger that was real to the Soviet people, and since (as a United Nations group on the spot reported within days after the event) it was unequivocally an unprovoked and well-prepared attack. The one explanation of it that large numbers of Soviet citizens seem to accept is their government's claim that South Korea started the war. We with our better sources of information have ample reason to think that Stalin's government lied to its people in spreading the story of a South Korean attack. But, partly because the whole thing was so far away and they had little or no direct knowledge to serve as a basis for challenging the official line, most of the Soviet public seem to have believed the lie.

As for the Hungarian uprising, we have already seen that there are doubts about it in the minds of the Soviet people, probably more than about any other item on the list. The official line, which insisted that the uprising was the work of a fascist-led minority and that "the" government of Hungary asked the Soviet troops to intervene, is regarded with some skepticism. Here too, however, even those who doubt the official rationalizations can fall back upon *Realpolitik* as a justification; they can tell themselves that a successful uprising would have meant the end of Soviet power in the entire East European area, which would have exposed the Soviet Union, sooner or later, to a greatly heightened danger of Western attack.

In each of these instances, then, there has been a defensive rationale that has been insisted upon by Communist propaganda; none of them has been justified officially as a step toward conquering the world for Communism. In each case this defensive rationale (or one of their own devising) could have been seized upon and uncritically accepted by all of those in the Soviet population who had a psychological need to do so.

One may ask: what about the avowed aim of Communism to expand until the whole world is Communist, and its avowed disregard of "petit bourgeois" scruples against the use of force in achieving this great aim? What about Khrushchev's open boast, "We will bury you"? How can a Soviet citizen fail to see the many Soviet aggressions as steps on this path?

It is true that a basically expansionist philosophy is a part of these citizens' Communist indoctrination, but the slogan of "peaceful coexistence" is also part of their Communist indoctrination. They are continually told that "socialism" will prevail throughout the world not by military conquest but by the example of the Soviet Union's success in creating a better life for its people, by vigorous prosecution of the ideological struggle, and by a series of revolutions in which the "peoples" of the world will choose socialism for themselves unless the military force of the "imperialists" keeps them from doing so. When Khrushchev says "We will bury you" they can easily interpret this not as a threat of military conquest but as equivalent to saying "Our system is stronger than yours and will outlast it; when your system dies a natural death we will be present at its funeral."[10] An image of their present leaders as peaceful is made easier for them also by the possibility of drawing a contrast between Stalin and Khrushchev (the acquiring of domination in Eastern Europe and the Korean war, for instance, can be blamed on Stalin rather than on Khrushchev by those who see them as blameworthy), and by interpreting the conflict with Communist China as primarily due to Khrushchev's commitment to "peaceful coexistence."

It seems likely, then, that the essential distortion in the Soviet citizens' image of their present leaders as peaceful lies in a failure to give due weight to the expansionist element in their leaders' basic philosophy, and to the willingness of their leaders to use force to achieve that expansion whenever the risks of force do not seem too great. Responsible Western students of Communism usually give much weight to this factor; most of the Soviet public seem to give it practically no weight at all. If we postulate two major components in the motivation of all the power-oriented actions of the Soviet leaders, an aggressive motive and a defensive motive, it is psychologically easy for the Soviet public to focus attention only on the defensive motive and to take at face value the insistence of present-day Communist propaganda that the aggressive motive does not exist. In brief, then, it is suggested here that they are right in seeing a defensive component in their leaders' motivation, and wrong in not seeing its aggressive component. (The *extent* of this distortion-by-omission in their minds must be judged by the reader in the light of his own estimate of how important the aggressive component is in the Soviet leaders' minds.)

Perception of the United States as Threatening

How much truth is there in their other basic assumption—that America's arms, bases, U-2 flights, and German alliance imply a danger of an unprovoked American attack? Here the element of truth seems much smaller, and the distortion correspondingly larger. While there have been preventive-war

---

[10] There is a semantic distinction here that many in the West have not recognized. The Russian word that Khrushchev used, *khoronit'*, actually has for Russians the meaning "to be present at the funeral of" more than "to kill and then bury." For a fuller statement of the official line on war and peace, see *Fundamentals of Marxism-Leninism*, pp. 565–584.

advocates in the United States, the vast majority of the American people regard their "positions of strength" policy as forced upon them by the aggressive actions and aggressive philosophy of the Communists. In this respect "Wall Street" and the "military-industrial complex" do not seem very different from the rest of the country. Americans are to a high degree united in distrusting the Communists and in thinking that strength is needed, not to attack the Communists but to deter an attack by them.

Here too, it should be noted, the distortion in the minds of the Soviet public is distortion of a psychological fact, in that they misjudge the thinking of a group other than their own; and here too the basic distortion occurs more by omission than by commission. They misjudge the motives of their own leaders by not seeing an aggressive motive alongside the defensive motives that they perceive quite adequately (or even exaggerate), and they misjudge the psychology of America's leaders, and that of the American public, by not seeing that both leaders and public genuinely fear military aggression by the U.S.S.R. (They do often attribute to our "ruling circles" a great fear of "socialism," but this is a distortion in three ways: it implies that the American people do not fear Soviet aggression; it implies that there are "circles" in America that "rule"—a half-truth at best; and it attributes to these "circles" only a fear of "socialism" and not also a genuine fear of Communist dictatorship, Communist subversion of democratic governments, and Communist military aggression.)

It seems clear, too, that their failure to empathize with and to perceive the genuine fear of Communist aggression on every level of American society is related to their failure to perceive that, in the literal meaning of "aggression,"

their government has repeatedly been aggressive; it has given Americans reason to be afraid. They fail to see that their government has done much (in addition to seeking "positions of strength") that might create apprehension in the West, while America has done little (except to seek "positions of strength") that might create apprehension in the U.S.S.R. It should be especially noted that among the four elements in American behavior that seem to have made the Russian people most anxious—nuclear arms, bases, U-2 flights, and German alliance—not one is aggression in the literal sense of using force to conquer new territory. And when the record of America's behavior in the twentieth century is critically examined it is difficult—even with a sustained effort to avoid a pro-American bias—to find instances of American aggression, in the sense of conquering new territory, that can be compared with any one of half a dozen instances of Soviet aggression.

Again it is really a job for the historian, but we can attempt here a simple layman's analysis of it. For the sake of simplicity and relevance to the current scene let us focus only on what has happened since 1938, and, to be fair, let us try to include at the outset every instance of aggression that has been alleged by either side.

We then find that the list of accusations against America contains perhaps seven significant items: China, Korea, Guatemala, Lebanon, Laos, Vietnam, and Cuba. The list of accusations against the Soviet Union contains at least twenty significant items. Ten have been mentioned in this chapter: the partition of Poland (following the Nazi-Soviet Pact), Finland, the Baltic states, Eastern Europe in 1944–1945, the Berlin blockade, Korea, Hungary, Laos, recent threats to Berlin, Cuba. But if items as doubtful as Korea, Lebanon, and Laos are to be mentioned among the accusations against America, then a considerable number of additional items should be mentioned among the accusations against the Soviet Union, such as threats against Turkey, the temporary occupation of northwestern Iran, guerrilla warfare in Greece, the Philippines, Laos, and Vietnam, the attempted overthrow of the Indonesian republic just after its birth, support of Mao in China, military aid to Arbenz in Guatemala, support of Gizenga in the Congo, and rocket-threats in connection with Suez.

If all of these items were carefully weighted according to their seriousness (for example, the numbers of people involved, and the severity of the political control imposed upon them), and according to their freedom from ambiguity as instances of "aggression," which list would then be more weighty? Although parts of the picture may be controversial, the general upshot seems clear: the Soviet list of aggressions is much more weighty (if, indeed, America can be regarded as having committed "aggression" at all).

In summary, then, some elements of validity in the Soviet public's image of the East–West conflict can be tentatively described as:

1. Seeing the defensive motives that have probably played a major part in the aggressive actions of their government.

2. Seeing that the "capitalists" of the West are opposed to "socialism" and oppose the U.S.S.R. partly for that reason.

3. Seeing that the United States is "threatening" them (though from the American standpoint the "threats" are intended only as deterrence).

And some elements of distortion appear to be:

1. Not seeing that several Soviet actions (Finland, East Europe, Korea, Hungary) have been literally acts of aggression, whatever might be said about their motivation. In the cases of Finland and Korea many actually seem to believe that the other side attacked first. In the case of the Baltic states and other outlying parts of the Soviet empire there has been a tendency to ignore the fact that it *is* an empire in which a number of peoples are being kept under Soviet control by force, against their will.

2. Not seeing the aggressive motives, along with the defensive ones, in these actions by their government.

3. Seeing certain actions by the West (arms, bases, U-2, German alliance) as aggressive when in fact they are not aggression in the literal sense of conquering new territory—as a number of Soviet actions have been—and are overwhelmingly defensive in motivation. The Soviet people are blind to the genuine fear of Soviet aggression that exists in the West.

4. Seeing capitalist "circles" as "ruling" the West, to a much greater extent than is actually the case.

5. Seeing these capitalist "circles" as feeling threatened only by "socialism" when in fact they also feel threatened by Communist dictatorship and aggression.

6. Not seeing that the "peoples" of the West, like the capitalists, fear Soviet aggression and support a policy of armed defense.

7. Perhaps most fundamentally, seeing capitalism as essentially the system Karl Marx described in the nineteenth century, with ruling circles, exploited masses, little or no effort to help the unfortunate, and no important mitigating features.[11]

---

[11] For the thesis that there is a "modal philosophy" which is rendering obsolete the dichotomy of socialism and capitalism as conceived by the Communists, see White (1958).

THE MIRROR IMAGE AND ITS LIMITATIONS

A student of the many historical examples of group self-delusion can hardly fail to be struck by a certain predictability in the ways in which belief-systems tend to depart from what the historian would regard as reality. The predictability is especially marked in the many cases in which two groups are in conflict: Christians and Moslems, Catholics and Protestants, North and South in the American Civil War. Basically the tendency seems always to be toward a black-and-white picture, with one's own group seen as white and the opposing group as black.

Recently this familiar fact has been called the "mirror-image phenomenon." The analogy lies in the fact that a mirror creates much the same kind of similarity-in-reverse; what is black-and-white in one group's image-system becomes white-and-black in the other group's imagery, just as, when any object is held up to a mirror, what originally appeared as left-and-right appears in the mirror as right-and-left. There are also likely to be other similarities, more detailed than simply a reversal of the black-and-white picture.[12] It is true that, along with the similarity, there are usually some marked differences; the self-image of the North in the Civil War, for instance, was quite different in some ways from the self-image of the South. The North knew that it was fighting for national union and, in a sense, against slavery, while the South knew that it was not. Reality is one source of all group imagery, and the real issues in that war were reflected in the nature of the self-

images and enemy-images on both sides. Nevertheless the mirror-image tendency resulting from the conflict itself (interacting with some psychological factors that presumably exist in most if not all human groups) was apparent here as in other human conflicts. Always there seems to be a tendency to exaggerate the virtues on one's own side and the diabolical character of the opposite side, and especially of the leaders on the opposite side. Distortion in these directions may be great on one side and small on the other, but it appears to be always present.

It would be surprising if the Soviet-American conflict were an exception, and in fact the evidence suggests that it is not. Naturally, since the United States and the Soviet Union are very different countries in some ways (one being, for instance, much more wealthy than the other, and a representative of the Western tradition of democracy and individual freedom), there are some marked differences between them in national self-images and enemy-images. But, superimposed on these differences, there are a number of similarities that have a good deal of psychological interest. Leaving aside the question of how much perceptual distortion may be involved in the two sets of images, and looking simply at the descriptive picture of what the two groups tend to believe, we find these similarities:

—The Soviet people tend to see their country as wholly peaceful. Americans tend to see theirs as wholly peaceful.

—The vast majority of the *ordinary* Soviet citizens are not crusaders. They would not knowingly and willingly risk war for one moment in order to force their own ideology or way of life on others. Neither would Americans.

---

12 The mirror analogy has apparently occurred independently to a number of different people; it has been discussed especially by Bronfenbrenner (1960), but also by Osgood (1962) and White (1961).

—They are afraid. As they see it there is an enemy threatening them with a war that could become nuclear. Americans too see a threatening enemy.

—They see not the common people but the rulers of the enemy nation threatening them with war. So do Americans.

—Because they are afraid, they endorse (at least to some extent) the power-seeking actions of their government. They arm, as they see it, in self-defense. So do Americans.

—In their minds there is at least one great blind-spot: they cannot see that the West fears aggression by them. They cannot believe that Americans too (the American people as well as their leaders) are arming in self-defense. Similarly, many Americans cannot believe that the Soviet people really fear the West, or that defensive motives could exist along with aggressive ones in the minds of the Soviet leaders.

The analysis in the previous section suggested that perceptual distortion on the Soviet side may be much greater than on the American side. In addition, there are some general reasons to think that this is what should be expected. Anthropological approaches to the question of the Russian culture or "national character" are by no means wholly unflattering in character (cf. Kluckhohn, 1961; and the chapter by Hanfmann and Beier in Bauer et al., 1956), but they do encourage the generalization that the Russian tradition is less evidence-oriented than the American tradition. More important, there is much reason to think that the pervasiveness of propaganda and censorship in the Soviet Union, and the fact that Soviet children are trained to an ideal of "right" thinking while American children are more encouraged to check beliefs against evidence, should make the possibilities of group self-delusion considerably greater in the Soviet Union than they are here.

In any case, it should be emphasized that the mirror-image concept implies nothing whatever as to the relative amount of truth on either side. Logically, the American image-system could be 100 percent true and the Soviet public's image-system could be 100 percent false, while one was a perfect mirror-image of the other. (In that case, however, one would have to assume a simply enormous amount of distortion on the Soviet side and none at all on the American side, which seems psychologically improbable.)

Even on the descriptive level, the following are some of the differences that should be noticed:

Perhaps the most important single difference is that in the U.S.S.R. there is a basic feeling of warmth and friendliness toward the American people that has only a feeble counterpart in the American feeling of friendliness toward the Russians. There is also a longing for that friendliness to be reciprocated— a wish that we were willing to be their friends. Both are testified to by all or nearly all of the Americans who have visited the U.S.S.R. As Kennan (1960a) puts it: "The fact is that throughout all these years of anti-capitalist and anti-American propaganda in the Soviet Union, the Soviet peoples have remained touchingly well-inclined toward the United States, touchingly unwilling to accept the endless efforts of their government to persuade them that Americans meant them harm" (p. 390). Mosely (1960, p. 464) speaks of a sense of "unrequited love" toward America.

There is even a feeling of similarity or kinship that quite startles some American visitors. According to one recent visitor: "When I asked people why they liked the Americans, they usually indicated that they felt Americans were closest in spirit to Russians. 'You are hospitable and friendly like us,' 'You are made of many nationalities like us,' 'You have created a great land out of the wilderness, just as we are doing.'"

This feeling of friendliness coexists, uneasily and paradoxically, with a suspicion of America's intentions that, as we have seen, is also real and widespread. The ordinary Soviet citizen is ambivalent and perplexed; he wonders "Why are those *good* guys, the Americans, threatening *us*, when all we want is to be friends?"

To a large extent the strain of the ambivalence is relieved by the convenient device of separating the American "people" from their "rulers," which permits the Soviet citizen to continue his feeling of friendliness, concentrating it mainly on the American "people," and also his feeling of suspicion and fear, concentrating it mainly on the American "ruling class." But there are elements of friendliness (often latent) even in their attitude toward the American Government, illustrated by their very great admiration for Roosevelt and some phases of their response to both President Eisenhower and President Kennedy.

Related to their friendliness, probably, is their admiration for America as a rich and wonderful country, which is by no means a replica of the American picture of the U.S.S.R. as poor and drab. The historical roots of this image probably go back well into the nineteenth century. According to Barghoorn (1950): "Virtually every Soviet person among the several hundred with whom I talked during my war years in Russia was impressed by what they had learned of American material prosperity; perhaps the most striking manifestation of this fact was the frequency with which Soviet people would ask Americans the question, 'Things are better in America, aren't they?'" (p. 241).

Since material things are of enormous importance to Russians in the present stage of their development, the fascination of America's wealth is correspondingly great. Life in America is a kind of magic crystal in which they hope to catch glimpses of their own future and their children's future. They do not seem to resent this image as much as they revel in it and draw vicarious satisfaction from it. Copies of the magazine *Amerika*, depicting life in the United States, are in the U.S.S.R. a coveted luxury. This admiration too coexists uneasily with their fear and suspicion of America itself and especially of its "rulers," and with a feeling of moral superiority to America and Americans. The conflict here has been vividly expressed by Werner Knop (quoted by Barghoorn, 1950, p. 257). He was struck by what he called the "half wistful, half frightened way" in which Russians talked about America. According to him, "even when they castigated it you saw how, to them, America was out of this world—a mixture of monster and fairy prince. Something greedy, cruel, decadent and voluptuous, but also something so rich and efficient, so inventive, glittering and daedalian."

This in turn brings up the question of the extent to which Soviet citizens accept the Communist propaganda image of the U.S.S.R. as the vanguard and citadel of the "camp of socialism," leading the world toward justice, peace, and a good life for all, and the correlative image of the United States as the citadel of an evil and decadent "capitalism." To what extent do they identify with the cause of "socialism" in a way that has some psychological similarity to American identification with the cause of freedom and democracy vs. Communist totalitarianism? How important is ideology as an aspect of their self-image and their enemy-image?

The evidence suggests that there is in fact a sizable kernel of truth in the mirror-image idea even here. The Russian people, at least in the cities, do appear to accept rather fully the basic essentials of the system they have now, which they call "socialism" ("communism" has not arrived yet). While they often want changes within the system, they seldom ask for a basic change in the system itself (cf. especially American Committee for Liberation, 1959; Bauer *et al.*, 1956, pp. 114–122; and Crankshaw, 1956, p. 50). This is perhaps similar to the American attitude toward our kind of democracy; we curse its inefficiencies while never dreaming of deliberately departing from its essentials. Most of the Russians (in the cities) seem sure of the moral superiority of "socialism," which they tend to interpret as (among other things) social solidarity and group loyalty in contrast with the rampant individual selfishness that they tend to regard as typical of the capitalist West (Crankshaw, 1956, pp. 50–57). To some extent, too, they seem proud of their country in its role on the international stage as the vanguard of socialism, in a way that resembles the pride that Americans have in their country as the leading power in the struggle for democracy against communism. In both cases there is an absence of crusading spirit, in the minds of the vast majority, but a real pride in seeing one's own country as the firm champion of a cause that seems right.

Nevertheless there is much reason to suspect that there are "buts" in many Soviet minds where there are no corresponding "buts" in the minds of most Americans. This likelihood seems greatest in the case of intellectuals, peasants, and certain minority nationalities. Among the intellectuals, including students, there is a real desire for greater cultural freedom, for greater freedom to read what they like, to travel where they like, and to write and paint as they like, often with conscious envy of their Western counterparts on this score

(Burg, 1961). Among the peasants there has been in the past, and probably still is to a considerable extent, an abiding hatred of the collective farm as an inefficient and oppressive institution. Among certain minority nationalities there are nationalistic reasons to oppose the Russians and the system that the Russians have imposed upon them. Among all elements there is probably a lurking awareness of the inefficiencies of their own system and of the tendency to corruption that pervades it, and, growing out of the general assumption that "things are better in America," a lurking suspicion that the political and economic system of the West may have much to be said for it. This is not to say that these people are not, in their own eyes, "loyal" Soviet citizens. The great majority of them probably are. Their Russian and Soviet nationalism may even be more intense and more chauvinistic because of their psychological need to deny and renounce these lurking doubts. But it is to say that we should be on guard against assuming that in these respects their national self-image is close to an exact replica of our own.

DETERMINANTS OF DISTORTION IN IMAGES OF ENEMY AND SELF

Up to this point we have been considering the *what* of Soviet beliefs, and the element of distortion in those beliefs. We turn now to the *why*. Why does this distortion occur? If we can make some headway in answering this question, treating the Soviet people as a case study in processes and causes of distortion that probably occur whenever any large human group finds itself in conflict with any other large human group, we may succeed in clarifying some basic factors in human conflict in general.

Naturally, the same kind of psychological scrutiny should be given to any elements in our own American belief-system that may be regarded as distortions. For instance, how can one account for the typical American failure to see the genuine fear of American or German-American attack in Soviet minds, or the defensive component in the motivation of Soviet leaders? There is value, however, in focusing first upon the processes of cognitive distortion in another group. Once they have been seen clearly in others they may be more detectable in ourselves.

The Process of Distortion: Selective Attention and Slanted Interpretation

The problem of "why" has two main aspects: the *processes* by which the distortion is brought about (a relatively superficial question, to which the answer seems fairly clear) and the *causes* of distortion—the conscious or unconscious motivating forces that determine in what direction the processes of distortion will operate (a far more fundamental and difficult problem). There seem to be two major processes of distortion, each of which appears both in the propaganda to which Soviet citizens are exposed and spontaneously within their own minds. One is selective attention and the other is slanted interpretation. There are innumerable examples of each.

For example, it is selective attention (as well as a difference in exposure to the facts) when the many Soviet actions that Americans interpret as aggression—Finland, Hungary, Korea, and so on—come freely and often into the mind of an ordinary American citizen, and hardly come into the mind of an ordinary Soviet citizen at all. It is selective attention (on one side or on both) when a Soviet mind is filled with the horrors and heroism of World War II, and with the mystery of why America has allied herself with the aggressor in that war, while these matters now come only occasionally into American minds.[13] It is selective attention (on one side or both) when a Soviet citizen thinks often of American missile bases around his country's border and seldom of his country's attempt to establish a similar base near the United States, while in an American mind it is the other way around.

In all these cases certain facts are fully perceived and often remembered on one side, while on the other side they are only partly perceived and seldom remembered. Selective attention is given to certain kinds of facts and ideas, while selective *inattention* —some would call it "repression"—is given to other kinds. (A distinction is made here between selective inattention, conceived as an active force tending to exclude certain ideas from the conscious field, and ordinary inattention, which occurs merely because other things are more interesting or more relevant to an immediate purpose.)

Examples of slanted interpretation can also be found wherever we look. It is slanted interpretation, for instance (on one side or both), when an American sees the Soviet take-over of Eastern Europe only as a major stride toward Communist conquest of the world, while some Russians see it only as the building of a bulwark of friendly countries against a recurrence of the

---

[13] The prominence of World War II in their thinking is of course largely due to the fact that their actual suffering in it was far greater than ours. But in addition, it is suggested here, the real heroism and innocence of the Russian people in that war are remembered and dwelt upon partly because the thought of them satisfies psychological needs.

kind of capitalist attack that had just devastated the socialist U.S.S.R. It is slanted interpretation (on one side or both) when an American sees German membership in NATO only as getting the reluctant Germans to do their share in building Western defensive strength, while a Russian sees it as a baffling alliance between the essentially good Americans and the unspeakable German aggressors who almost destroyed his country in World War II.

In each of these cases of slanted interpretation a situation is psychologically ambiguous—that is, it is psychologically possible for two persons or groups of persons to attach different interpretations to it—however unambiguous it might be "objectively," or in the eyes of a relatively objective historian. In each case (with a few important exceptions) the raw material of incoming evidence, from which the perceptual process takes its start, is fairly similar on the two sides. Both sides agree that the Soviet Union has been in some sense dominant in Eastern Europe since 1945; both agreed, after certain photographs were published, that the U.S.S.R. had placed in Cuba missiles that could reach and destroy American cities; both agree that West Germany is now a member of NATO and is to some extent rearmed.[14] But as the perceptual process goes on from raw incoming evidence to interpretation of evidence, the two versions of reality diverge far more radically. The Soviet role in Eastern Europe becomes "leadership" in some Soviet eyes and "subjugation" in American eyes; the placing of missiles in Cuba becomes "deterrence" in some Soviet eyes and "aggression" in some American

eyes; the alliance of Americans and Germans in NATO becomes "rearming the aggressor" as seen from the Soviet side and "sharing the burdens of defense" as seen from the American side. Let it be repeated: this description of the facts is not concerned with the amount of slanting on the two sides. We are free to believe that it is much greater on one side than on the other. Our present interest is solely in trying to understand the slanting process itself.

Presumably the process of slanted interpretation described above is partly dependent on differently selected sets of facts, and on selective attention and inattention to those facts.[15] Americans, for instance, have interpreted what happened in Eastern Europe in the years immediately after the war with full awareness of the Iron Curtain that descended around that area, protecting from foreign scrutiny the liquidation of "fascists and reactionaries" which was an essential part of the imposition of Soviet rule. Few of the Soviet people have been in a position to know so much about what happened there. Similarly, Khrushchev was vividly aware, when he placed powerful missiles in Cuba, of the powerful American missiles already placed around the U.S.S.R. Probably few of the American people at that moment were vividly aware of the same fact, and, not seeing his action in the context in which he saw it, they necessarily gave it a different interpretation.

Selective attention and inattention may also play a part in the selection that is made between alternative interpretations of the same raw fact. The alliance between America and West

[14] Finland and Korea are exceptions in that many Russians assert, with seeming conviction, that the other side literally attacked first in both the Finnish and the Korean wars.

[15] Although Soviet censorship is clearly more potent than any similar official action in the West, a question can be raised as to the extent of a more spontaneous selectivity in the press and other purveyors of fact in the West.

Germany in NATO, for instance, is a raw fact. It is psychologically ambiguous in that different groups can interpret it in different ways: as a drawing together of friendly nations for common defense against the Communist danger that threatens both of them, or as an incongruous collusion between essentially good Americans and the brutal aggressors of World War II, the purpose of which must be that their "rulers" are preparing for renewed aggression against the U.S.S.R. An individual on either side can make his selection between these interpretations simply by concentrating all his attention on one and blotting the other out of his mind.

Leaving aside the question of which interpretation is more "true," let us consider, for instance, what might happen in the mind of a Soviet citizen as he reacts to the idea of the German-American alliance. Presumably the second interpretation of it, as an alliance with an unspeakable aggressor, is continually suggested to him by all the newspapers he reads, by nearly all the radio broadcasts he hears, and by most if not all of the individuals with whom he comes in contact. There is already a screening, then, a stacking of the cards, in the ideas coming to him from outside. His own thoughts may conceivably suggest to him that another interpretation, an interpretation of the alliance as defensive in purpose, is possible. In that case, he may, if he is a particularly evidence-oriented individual, do some further thinking—privately—about this other interpretation. He may make some real effort to empathize with Americans and to consider how the alliance might look from an American point of view. But if a rudiment of the Western interpretation comes into his mind and he simply dismisses it without thought, turning his attention away from it and clinging instead—for reasons that deserve more careful psychological examination—to the interpretation prevailing in his own society, it can be said that crude selective attention has dominated his perceptual process and has determined what then appears as a "slanted interpretation."

The potency of selective attention and inattention as described here is not a hopeful augury for communication between countries that are in conflict. The mass media of one country are comparatively powerless in the face of unconsciously motivated inattention in the other country (see Chapter 6). If, for instance, the Voice of America attempts to present to the Soviet people a factual and reasoned statement of the American point of view, a listener whose Soviet pride is hurt by that statement can defend himself against hurt by the simplest of devices: he can stop listening. He may or may not justify his nonlistening by telling himself that the Voice is "a pack of lies" or "just propaganda." The essential fact is simply his nonlistening. The same applies to Americans. How many Americans have ever listened to one of the English-language shortwave broadcasts of Radio Moscow, or read a book or an article written from the Soviet point of view? If the channels of two-way communication are to be cleared, we would do well to understand more about the forces that underlie the process of selective inattention and give it direction.

The Momentum of Distortion: Consonance, Conformity, Propaganda, and the Image of the Loyal Citizen

The conscious and unconscious psychological forces that underlie selective attention and slanted interpretation can be divided into two types: those that sustain a group belief once it is well established (with all the omissions and distortions that the group belief may contain), and those that give an impetus to new forms of distortion. Let us consider first the components of the blind momentum that sustains a group belief once it is established in the minds of the majority.

First, though, if we are going to use the word "unconscious," we had better define it. A wish that is respectable in a given society and quite conscious (the wish that one's own country should be peaceful, or the wish to be a loyal citizen of one's country) may nevertheless have an influence on the thought process that is "unconscious" in the sense that the person himself could not tell us what that influence is. He might readily agree that the wish was in his mind, but not realize that it had influenced his view of reality—since to him his view of reality *is* reality, and he could hardly be expected to agree that any motive within himself (other than a desire to see reality as it is) had influenced him. He could hardly be expected to agree that he is "a wishful thinker."

Then there are other, less respectable wishes, consciously rejected by the individual or not even suspected by him (such as a wish to hurt others, or to see an enemy as wholly evil). They too can influence thinking, and when they do so the process is unconscious in a double sense: not only the effect of the wish on thinking, but also the wish itself is unconscious. If we asked the person about it the chances are that he would angrily deny that any such wish existed in his mind, or simply look at us in bewilderment and wonder about our sanity.

Suppose, now, a Soviet citizen is trying to interpret a psychologically ambiguous situation, such as the Cuban missile crisis. Let us say he has just learned, with dismay, that Soviet missiles capable of destroying American cities have been placed in Cuba by his government, and that the American President regards this as a crisis that could lead to nuclear war. This makes him acutely anxious, because he has vivid memories of World War II; he knows what war means. He feels a need to blame the imminent danger on someone. Someone has been guilty of aggressive action, either his own government (as the President has said), or the "ruling circles" in America. The question is, which? We know the answer: in all probability he will decide that his own government is innocent and the "ruling circles" are guilty. The question for us, then, is how and why he reaches this decision. Of course we cannot really know, but some speculations are more plausible than others.

One major factor, in all probability, is the "consonance" of this interpretation with his established conviction that the U.S.S.R. is peaceful and that a peaceful country does only peaceful things. A country as peaceful as this, he probably feels, simply could not take a needless risk of war; there must be some other good reason for what it has just done. Anything else would be incongruous, "dissonant" with his basic image of the U.S.S.R. It would be a "cognitive" dissonance in that it would seem to him to do violence to the very structure of reality for such a peaceful country to do a nonpeaceful thing. The only explanation "consonant" with his well-established image-system is that the U.S.S.R. is innocent and the blame lies elsewhere.[16]

It may even be that in this situation his established belief in the peacefulness of the U.S.S.R. is more potent in

---

[16] For the theory of consonance and dissonance, and experimental evidence related to it, see Festinger (1957), Heider (1958), Osgood (1962), Cooper and Jahoda (1947).

influencing his next thoughts than his wish that his own country might escape all guilt. And yet, it should be noted, an emphasis on the consonance factor only pushes the problem one step back. The question remains: how did he build up his belief that the U.S.S.R. is inherently peaceful and "could not" take a needless risk of war? Consonance is clearly a "momentum" factor only, explaining nothing about how these powerful perception-determining beliefs were established in the first place.

Much the same can be said of the tendency to conform to the beliefs of one's own group. Suppose our Soviet friend does at some point doubt that his country has done the right and peaceful thing, and suppose the next thought in his mind is how unpopular —or how subject to punishment— he would make himself if he admitted this disloyal thought to his friends or to his "collective." Suppose, too, that this has a conscious or unconscious effect on his subsequent thoughts, steering them in a socially safer direction.[17] The question remains: how did his group build up its established conviction that the U.S.S.R. is peaceful, and that this is so plain that only a disloyal person could doubt it?

At this point an obviously important part of the answer is "propaganda." Propaganda is not only a momentum factor; it is also an impetus factor, a belief-changing factor, insofar as the political leader who is also a propagandist (Lenin, Khrushchev), or who hires and pays propagandists, often attempts to change what the people have previously believed. Communist propagandists have attempted to do this on a particularly large scale. But it should not be forgotten that the propagandist

himself may believe much of what he says, and in believing it he may share a belief that already pervades both the elite and the rank-and-file in the group he is try to influence. In these cases propaganda is a conservative rather than an innovative force.

A good case in point, probably, is the Soviet people's belief that their country is wholly peaceful. The belief in Russian peacefulness was firmly established in Russia long before the Communist revolution of 1917,[18] and in a somewhat different sense the Communists merely continued it. In their own curious way Lenin and his Party maintained the tradition that they yielded to no one in their love of peace. When a Communist propagandist says the same thing today, then, he is being in this sense conservative.

Finally, some attention should be given to a fourth conservative factor that is not often noticed or discussed: the tendency for an individual to become a watchdog over his own thoughts in his desire to be a good, loyal citizen, "in thought as well as deed." Presumably this self-monitoring is something more than conformity, and more than credulous acceptance of propaganda. Insofar as the ideal of "a loyal citizen, in thought as well as deed" has become internalized as part of the individual's own conscience or ego-ideal, he himself takes over the functions of propagandist and censor, and does his best to exclude and disavow "disloyal" thoughts. With a kind of Orwellian double-think, he may then consciously reject at one moment an interpretation which, in the previous moment, had seemed to him to be probably true. Yet he presumably can do this with a good conscience and little or no loss of

---

[17] For evidence on how the need to conform influences thinking, see Asch (1952).

[18] For a critique of the widespread impression that pre-Communist Russia had an especially strong urge to expansion, see Karpovich (1951). The point, though, is not that Russians were peaceful, but only that they believed themselves to be.

pride, since the name he would give to this process would not be "wishful thinking" or "distortion," but "loyal thinking" or perhaps simply "right thinking." This too is clearly a momentum factor, since it would tend to perpetuate especially what the individual feels that "all decent, right-thinking people" believe.

These four separate forces add up to a formidable, even a frightening combination. Like the momentum of an inanimate mass, it is blind. It actively resists the intrusion of new evidence. In a complex and changing world it represents the past more than the present, and its representation of the past has been influenced not only by the reality of the past (for example, the kernels of truth in Karl Marx's indictment of nineteenth-century "capitalism") but also by all the cumulative effect of consciously distorted propaganda and the unconscious mechanisms of distortion, in both leaders and followers, that have given impetus to it in the past.

Let us look, then, at the mechanisms of distortion that may have had a cumulative effect upon it.

The Impetus to Distortion: The Context Hypothesis and Paranoid Suspicion

Coming back to our example of the Soviet citizen wondering how to interpret what had just happened when the Cuban crisis was at its height, it seems likely that his conscious wish to see his own country as wholly peaceful has a real, though unconscious, effect on his thinking. It must be painful to him even to consider the thought that his own country, his expanded self, could be so evil or so mad as to take, knowingly, a serious risk of nuclear war. He must therefore (over and above all the "momentum" forces outlined in the previous section) feel a personal emotional need to discover good reasons that would justify, "rationalize," what his country has just done, and pin all the blame—"project" it—on the rulers of America. It is fortunate for his peace of mind if, at this point, official propaganda comes to his aid and provides these "good" reasons. He can then, without any original thought on his own part, seize on these reasons, give selective attention to them, and accept with real if unconscious gratitude the slanted interpretation they offer.

These are the classical mechanisms of rationalization and projection; in cases such as this one they would probably be recognized and labeled as such even by the least psychoanalytically oriented Western psychologists. While the content of the "good" reasons discovered may be very complex, the two underlying themes can be represented by the very simple formula: "We are not to blame; *they* are." In this formula "we are not to blame" is the rationalization and "they are" is the projection. The rationalization is primary (stemming from the strong and quite conscious wish that one's own country should not be guilty of warmaking) and the projection is secondary (a result of the fact that blame has to be shifted onto someone else, if it is not to rest upon the self). There is here no implied unconscious "need to hate" or "need to see others as evil" except as a by-product of a situation in which there is a need to attach blame to someone and resistance to any attaching of it to the self.

Few can doubt that, in this form, the rationalization-and-projection mechanism plays a significant role in forming the ethnocentric black-and-white picture (the "mirror image") on both sides of every acute group conflict. Rationalization helps to account for the white side of the picture, and projection helps to account for the black side. But what can be doubted is that the rationalization-and-projection mechanism is the only unconscious mechanism operating or even, necessarily, the main one. Two others call for at least some consideration: what is here called the "context hypothesis," and projection of unconscious hostility (the mechanism which, according to the prevailing psychiatric view, is the chief source of paranoid delusions of persecution).

We have already described and illustrated the context hypothesis at several points in this chapter, without naming it. It has two parts: (a) that the power-oriented actions of an opposing group, seen in the context of one's own group's assumed peacefulness, necessarily appear as aggressive, and (b) that the power-oriented actions of one's own group, seen in the context of the other group's assumed aggressiveness, necessarily appear as realistic self-defense. The self-image and the enemy-image are interdependent, each providing a decisive part of the context in which the other is perceived.

It should now be added that when this kind of perception occurs there is not necessarily any strong guilt feeling that needs to be rationalized or projected. Let us consider again the Soviet citizen who is wondering how to interpret the Cuban missile crisis. The context hypothesis implies that, from the very first moment that he learns that his government has actually been placing powerful missiles in Cuba, he sees this primarily in the context of an over-all continuing Western threat that has to be met and deterred "in the only language the aggressor understands— the language of force." He would not necessarily feel any more guilty about his government's action—even unconsciously—than Americans felt when our government stationed missiles in Tur-

key. Assuming that his own country would never use this new military strength aggressively, he might think of it only in the context of its probable deterrent effect on the "aggressor," and in that context it would appear, not as "peaceful" exactly, but as a realistic, hard-headed coping with danger. Therefore there would be little guilt and little need to rationalize guilt or project it onto others. (There might be, as events turned out, criticism of Premier Khrushchev for taking a needless risk or for bungling and having to beat an embarrassing retreat, but not for the stationing of missiles as in itself an aggressive or warlike act.)

At the same time, the defense motives behind America's role in the Bay of Pigs episode, and behind America's willingness to risk war in order to get the powerful Soviet missiles out of Cuba, would probably not be seen by this Soviet citizen at all, because he would not put those actions (as Americans habitually put them) in the context of an over-all Communist threat that had just advanced to within ninety miles of the American border. Not seeing America's fear of Soviet aggression in this broad world context, the Soviet citizen would instead be likely to see American behavior only in the narrow context of "big America and little Cuba." In that context he would consider ridiculous the notion that America is frightened by Cuba, and he would therefore almost inevitably interpret America's actions in terms of a big bad guy bullying a little good guy. (Similarly, many Americans have been unable to conceive of the Soviet attack on Finland, or the Soviet intervention in Hungary, as anything but a simple case of a big bad guy bullying a little good guy. Perhaps they were exactly that and nothing more. The point is that in all of these cases there has been little or no serious consideration of the *possibility* that the power-oriented actions of the leaders on the other side, seen in the context in which they were seen by those leaders, may have been more defensive than offensive.)

As these examples illustrate, the context hypothesis implies a typical blindness to the genuineness of fear and suspicion in the opposing group, which in turn implies a rather extreme failure of empathy. Not empathizing with the other group, one often fails to see the psychological context of that group's actions as seen by its own members.

In addition it should be noted that the Soviet citizens' failure of empathy is related to their apparent tendency to transfer their own frame of reference (their own belief-system) into the minds of Americans. They seem to feel sure that their peacefulness is as obvious to us as it is to them. They make the naive assumption that *"the* world," as they perceive it, is the world as we perceive it, and that we are acting within the same frame of reference. In short, they universalize their own frame of reference. What their great blindspot eliminates from their minds is, at bottom, the difference between their "reality world" and ours.

It has perhaps become clear by now that the context hypothesis involves a circular relationship which poses a chicken-and-egg problem. There is a circularity in the process by which a person's own perceived peacefulness is the context that makes him see another as warlike, and the other's perceived warlikeness is the context that makes the person see his own actions as peaceful, or at least as defensive. Which comes first, the peaceful self-image or the warlike enemy-image —the black or the white part of the black-and-white picture? What factors impinge on this circular system from the outside, in order to get it started in the first place?

One answer seems obvious: the white part of the picture has a direct source of its own in the strong, obvious, conscious desire of nearly all human beings to think well of their own group. As we have seen in the case of the classical mechanism of rationalization-and-projection, the justifying and idealizing of one's own group is an end in itself, quite apart from whether an opposed group is seen as evil or not. Here, then, is one clear input into the system. For instance, the Soviet people's active pleasure at the thought of their own country's peacefulness, in a war-mad world, is probably one of the major initiating forces giving rise to their black-and-white picture. It directly and continually gives fresh impetus to their peaceful self-image, which then maintains itself through all the momentum factors described above, and which also continually sustains the warlike enemy-image by preventing empathy with the enemy's actual fear and suspicion.

Is there also a fresh input on the black side—the belief that the rulers of the opposing group are diabolical? Does it derive reinforcement from forces other than those already discussed (the projection of blame and out-of-context perception of the enemy's power-oriented behavior)? Is there perhaps something like an unconscious "need to hate" or a "need to see others as evil"?

There is little doubt that most psychiatrists, if presented with this question, would say "yes," since they would immediately think of the analogy of paranoid suspicion, or delusions of persecution, both in the true paranoid psychotic and within the range of normal and neurotic personalities. They would use the term "paranoid" (as we do here) without any implication of psychosis, simply as a convenient name for the tendency to hostile misperception or exaggerated suspicion that perhaps exists in some degree in the majority of the human race. According to the prevailing psychiatric interpretation, exaggerated or paranoid suspicion is chiefly caused by projection of unconscious, internally generated hostility.

One reason for bringing in the paranoid analogy is that *exaggerated suspicion,* rather than "fear," seems the most accurate term to characterize the political attitude that calls for explanation. Because of the convenience of the word "fear" it has been used at certain points in this chapter, for instance when speaking of the inability of many Americans to see that the Soviet people genuinely fear an American attack, or when speaking of the Soviet people's fear as the chief reason for their more or less willing acceptance of a bombs-instead-of-butter policy. But the little word "fear," simple as it appears to be, has a rather surprising ambiguity that becomes apparent if its practical consequences are considered.

If exaggerated fear is seen as the core of Soviet misperception of the United States, then the cure for it—some have argued—lies in a drastic reduction or elimination of American military strength, so that the Russians would no longer have any reason for fear. But whenever this possibility is suggested there are many in the West who say in effect, "No, we don't want to eliminate Soviet fear of us; we want to increase it, since it is only their fear of our military strength that keeps them from taking over the whole world by force of arms."

Whether either of these arguments is valid or not, comparing one with the other brings out the fact that the word "fear" is used in two quite different senses. In one context it means a belief that another country *is able* to inflict great harm on one's own country and is certain to do so if attacked (this is the kind of wholesome fear that many

in the West want to maintain in Soviet minds); in the other context it means a belief that another country *wants* to inflict great harm on one's own country and will therefore attack it unless deterred by one's own strength (this is the "paranoid" kind of fear that makes the grim pursuit of national power seem imperative to the Soviet leaders, and leads to power-oriented policies, going beyond the real requirements of self-defense, that basically endanger peace). In one context it means the attribution of strength to another; in the other context it means the attribution of hostility to another. It is only the latter that we are now concerned with, and the word "suspicion" is a much less ambiguous term for it than "fear."

A distinction should be made, also, between realistic suspicion and exaggerated or paranoid suspicion. Churchill was right, in the years 1933–1939, to suspect the motives of Hitler, and to attribute to him a kind of obsessive hostility and a kind of audaciously destructive power-seeking that many others in the West found it hard to believe possible. Hitler *was* diabolical, and so was Stalin. Surely a clear-eyed recognition of this kind of evil, when there is strong evidence that it exists, should not be confused with paranoid thinking, or interpreted in terms of psychoanalytic mechanisms such as "projection of unconscious hostility." In the case of the Soviet leaders and people, therefore, it is only the element of exaggeration or distortion in their suspicion of the "rulers" of the West (however large or small we may think that element is) that now calls for psychological or psychoanalytic interpretation in terms of conscious or unconscious wishes.

There is no clear conscious wish here that could be compared with the conscious wish to think well of one's own group. To see an opposing group as wholly evil is not "wishful thinking" in the same obvious way that seeing one's own group as wholly good is wishful thinking. Fear of nuclear war is not consciously a pleasant emotion at all; the tears in the eyes of Soviet citizens, when they ask an American to tell other Americans how much the Soviet people want peace, are real tears. And yet there are many phenomena in many human cultures, past and present, which suggest that in some perverse way the human animal does often actively (if unconsciously) enjoy frightening himself. The evil spirits that are omnipresent in many primitive societies, the witches and devils of medieval Europe, the gruesome crimes committed in murder mysteries, the devils in the political mythologies of innumerable nations and groups within nations, the martyr complex of many "normal" individuals, the delusions of persecution in the paranoid psychotic—all of these may have something in common, and all of them present a puzzle for the psychologist that is by no means fully or demonstrably solved. In most of them, for example, it would be incongruous to bring in as a major explanation either of the mechanisms we have considered at some length in this chapter: the projection of blame and the context mechanism. Clearly there are forces at work here that we have not yet captured and pinned down.

The psychiatrists may have one good clue, though, in their notion of the projection of unconscious hostility. According to them the formula is "I don't hate him; he hates me," or (if some of the hate is conscious) "Since I hate him I must have a good reason to do so; he must hate me." If one accepts the idea

that maladjusted or semi-maladjusted individuals (which includes most of us) are likely to generate within themselves a kind of diffuse hostility that somehow seeks a hate-object on which to focus itself, and if one accepts also the idea of projection as one of the more frequent devices by which unconscious needs influence the content of conscious thought, then this is at least a respectable hypothesis that calls for further study and research.

A variation on the theme is the view held by many students of Soviet behavior, especially Leites, that the most basic image in the minds of the Communist leaders who cling to the Leninist tradition is an image of a life-and-death struggle in which each of the contending parties is continually seeking to destroy the other.

This is in line with our hypothesis that the core of Soviet misperception of the West is a deadly-earnest suspicion; to them a continuing of the power struggle is imperative because if they let down their guard they would surely be destroyed. It resembles the projection-of-unconscious-hostility hypothesis in that a certain kind of hostility in the self leads to an attributing of the same kind of hostility to the opponent. But it differs from the projection-of-unconscious-hostility hypothesis in that the hostility that is projected is not unconscious. The Communists who are imbued with the Leninist tradition (in the U.S.S.R., China, and elsewhere) know quite well that they would like to destroy the rulers of the capitalist world, along with the capitalist system. They merely take it for granted that their opponent is as inherently, inevitably hostile and power-oriented as they are.[19] They assume that their oppo-

---

[19] See Leites (1954, pp. 27–30, 38–39, 379–416). Similarly, Wolfe (1962) describes Marxism-Leninism as "a combative ideology. At the core of things it finds conflict" (p. 161). And he speaks of "what can only be described as a paranoiac vision of self and 'enemy' and reality that is not subject to rational refutation" (p. 166).

nent's basic world-picture is, like their own, a life-and-death struggle in which weakness on either side will lead to destruction. To them this world-picture is not a world-picture but simply "the world" in which both they and their opponents live and struggle. In other words, this is another case in which it might be more accurate to say that they "universalize" their own frame of reference than to say that they project it into the mind of another.

TO WHAT EXTENT DO THE SOVIET LEADERS RESEMBLE THE PUBLIC?

The question of how the world looks to the leaders of the Soviet Union lies beyond the scope of this chapter.[20] However, a discussion of what the Soviet public thinks can hardly be complete without some consideration of how it may differ from, or resemble, the thinking of the leaders.

The distinction between leaders and public is essential in the U.S.S.R., which is a revolutionary authoritarian society in which a small group at the top has used propaganda and coercion on a vast scale to achieve basic social changes. While the base of grassroots political participation on local matters has broadened considerably in recent years, real power, especially on matters of foreign policy, still appears to be highly concentrated in a not very large group at the top of the pyramid.[21]

Like the public, the leaders continually talk as if the peacefulness of their country and the warlikeness of its enemies were self-evident. There have been innumerable public statements

like that of Khrushchev when he said, "Let it be known to those who want to continue the cold war, so as to turn it sooner or later into a shooting war, that in our time only a madman can start a war, and he himself will perish in its flames" (1960, p. XXX). We have seen reasons to believe that, when the ordinary Soviet citizens say this sort of thing, they mean it. The question now is: Are they in this respect very different from their leaders?

There are at least three ways in which the psychology of the leaders may differ significantly from that of the general public:

1. They are apparently more cynical about truthfulness and more practiced in the art of deception. From the early days of the conspiratorial Party, and at least throughout the entire Stalin era, truthfulness as such has been belittled as a petit-bourgeois virtue in the "esoteric" doctrine of the Party. Premier Khrushchev, during the many years in which (it now seems clear) he must have been continually pretending to be an ardent disciple of Stalin when he was not, proved that he himself was a consummate actor and a past master in the art of concealing his true feelings. Therefore, the double fact that this group puts out a certain type of statement and that the general public believes it does not necessarily mean that the leaders themselves believe it.

2. They have had access to certain types of information that they have not shared with the general public. For instance they may realize, more clearly than the public does, that many of the "fascists and reactionaries" liquidated by the Communists in East Europe in 1945 and 1946 were actually anti-Com-

---

[20] Scholarly discussions of it have been published by such writers as Mosely (1960), Lowenthal (1958), Tucker (1963), Brzezinski (1962), Kennan (1960a), and Wolfe (1962).

[21] For discussion of the present distribution of power in the U.S.S.R., see especially Fainsod (1963).

munist democrats and democratic socialists, that anti-Soviet feeling still rises high in East Europe, that a majority of the Hungarian people supported the uprising of 1956, that the North Koreans started the Korean war, and that the West Germany of today is neither militaristic nor dominated by Nazis. They may quite consciously conceal such facts from the general public, justifying their concealment on the basis of a need for national unity, and yet take them into account in their own thinking about themselves and the West. This would mean that in these ways they would have a less diabolical enemy-image than the public has, and a less innocent self-image. The "context hypothesis" should therefore apply less to them than to the public. They should realize, better than the public does, that the West could have genuine defensive reasons for its power-oriented policies.

Supporting this conjecture, too, is the probability that their minds have been kept sharp by continual use. Unlike the general public they are not subject to the apathy, and the primitive tendency to think only in terms of general images and clichés, that prolonged political nonparticipation tends to produce.[22]

3. On the other hand, the leaders are apparently much more deeply imbued with Marxism-Leninism than the general public is. As the lineal descendants of the original band of Leninist fanatics, they probably share to a considerable degree Lenin's quasi-religious faith in the evilness of the "rulers" of the capitalist world, in the assumption that capitalists *are* the "rulers" of the West, in the warlike character of decaying capitalism, in the idea that capitalism is doomed to decay, and (though the years may have modified this one) in

the desirability and necessity of a world revolution "guided" by themselves. In the past, at least, this ideology has been intimately connected with an extraordinary concentration on the calculating pursuit of power. As Gabriel Almond (1954) put it: "Such a pure and unequivocal power orientation leaves most of us with feelings of disbelief and wonder" (p. 376).

Although most of the public appear to accept this ideology of world revolution (in its present "peaceful coexistence" guise) without conscious disagreement, there are few signs that they really care about it, and many signs that their hearts are elsewhere —in the material progress of their own society, and in the maintaining of peace. Unlike their leaders, they do not seem preoccupied with the goal of power. According to Barghoorn (1950): "I never met any Soviet people who seemed to take pride in Soviet political and territorial expansion, in pan-Slavism or in the extension of Communist power" (p. 250).

This difference in goals supports the conjecture that the leaders' images also may be different. While, as we have seen, their better access to information may make them less paranoid in their outlook upon the West than the general public is, their ideology probably makes them more so. The diabolical character of Wall Street is for them an article of faith, on which a great part of their own lives has been built. Also, if they still take very seriously the goal of world revolution, they may also take seriously the idea that the "rulers" of the West are afraid of this revolution and are likely to lash out at it in desperation. Aware of their own dynamic, expansionist philosophy and their own hostility to the ruling classes of the

---

[22] Crankshaw (1956) says that "for the ordinary Russian citizen politics means next to nothing" (p. 20).

West, they may genuinely see "struggle" as the basic law of life (at least until world revolution occurs) and find it hard to believe that their enemies are not similarly ready to seize upon, and take advantage of, any "weakness" on the other side. Through this kind of projection mechanism they may have developed an enemy image considerably more diabolical than that of the Soviet people, who are tired of perpetual struggle and would like nothing better than to settle down to a live-and-let-live relationship with the West.

These are three good reasons for not identifying the thinking of the Soviet leaders with that of the public. On the other hand, there are several reasons for thinking that the difference between their world-view and that of the public is less than some Americans have supposed:

1. They have shared many of the same experiences—above all, the searing experience of World War II. There is no reason to doubt the sincerity of the ordinary Soviet citizen when he says "After what we suffered in the Second World War, how could we possibly want another?" Similarly, the leaders may have a vivid anxiety about a potential future German danger (even if not an immediate one in terms of Nazis being now in control), and may be genuinely disturbed by American bases close to their borders, by American superiority in nuclear weapons, and by the U-2 flights.

Their areas of nonexperience and of ignorance also probably have much in common. For instance, both leaders and public are out of touch with the actual thinking of ordinary Americans, and may therefore find it easy not to perceive the genuineness of the American "people's" lack of trust in Soviet intentions. Premier Khrushchev may have come to the United States with a genuine belief that the ordinary American is friendly to and trusting of the USSR; at least he seemed to have this belief when he reported back to his people that "from the very first steps on American soil I was so closely guarded that it was absolutely impossible to contact the ordinary Americans. . . . But the people waved and shouted, though very often they could not see me" (1960, p. XIX). Both leaders and people, too, have had little opportunity to learn that the capitalist "ruling circles" in America do not actually "rule," and that they are largely composed of ordinary human beings, similar to the rest of the country in their abhorrence of war. In the vacuum that this ignorance creates in their minds they can, like their own people, easily imagine demons.

2. They probably share many of the same mechanisms of self-deception. If an ordinary Soviet citizen has an unconscious need to forget about the Nazi-Soviet pact, the Finnish war, the Korean war, and other embarrassing subjects, so do the members of the Presidium. If this leads the ordinary citizen to be blind to the defensive motives behind the power-oriented actions of the West, it could tend to create in Presidium minds the same blindness. If an ordinary citizen has a need to see only the self-defensive reasons for the Soviet intervention in Hungary, so, probably, do those who ordered the intervention. If an ordinary citizen has an obscure psychological need (perhaps involving projection of internally generated hostility) to accept the Marxian picture of the "rulers" of the West as diabolical, so, presumably, do the successors of Nikita Khrushchev.

3. The top decision-making leaders, being by any calculation less than 1 percent of the people, may be influenced in some degree by the remaining 99+ percent. While this was much less true in Stalin's day it does appear to be

true to a significant extent now. At least since Stalin's death there seems to have been a significant seeping upward of the live-and-let-live value system of the general public, even into the Presidium. Khrushchev himself, originally a peasant and then a manual worker, obviously took pride in what he regarded as his continuing closeness to the mentality of workers and peasants, and his continuing contact with them. If there has been since Lenin's death a fading of the revolutionary fervor of the members of the ruling group (manifested, among other things, by Stalin's doctrine of "socialism in one country" and by Khrushchev's readiness to break with the Chinese on the possibility of peaceful coexistence) the change can perhaps be attributed in large part to this seeping upward of the value-system and the assumptions of the less ideologically oriented 99+ percent of the Soviet people.

4. A propagandist often has a tendency to be persuaded by his own propaganda. This has been well established by experiments (Kelman, 1953; Janis & King, 1954; Scott, 1957, 1959) and by everyday observation. Self-deception is probably a good deal commoner than consciously cynical lying, at least in our own society, and the same may well be true of the U.S.S.R. The leaders and propagandists may have started out with a belief in most of what they were saying, and as they talked and talked they probably came to believe more and more of it. (It should be noted that this is not at all inconsistent with a willingness to engage in outright lying whenever there seems to be a good reason to do so—the Korean war is probably a case in point—and a continual willingness to engage in conscious exaggeration of some things and softpedaling of others. It is quite possible psychologically for a person to indulge in both conscious lying and unconscious self-deception.)

5. Much of the evidence on what has been called here the Soviet "public" actually comes from the upper-middle strata of Soviet society, and on general grounds it seems unlikely that there are radical differences—sharp discontinuities—between them and the top group that is just above them in the power pyramid. Since the top group is recruited chiefly from the strata just below it, and remains in relatively close social contact with those strata, a considerable degree of psychological similarity, with only moderate differences of emphasis, seems probable.

Up to this point the terms "leaders" and "public" have been used as if there were a sharp distinction between them. While it is important to make the distinction it is actually not as sharp as is often assumed; there are a number of intermediate levels between the decision-making leaders at the top of the power pyramid and the relatively apathetic, nonpolitical masses who perhaps constitute the majority in every society and almost certainly do so in the U.S.S.R. It is in these intermediate levels, and not in the masses, that one might hope for the development of some analogue of the "pressure of public opinion" that exists in the relatively democratic countries of the West. The high-intermediate levels have some importance, since the leaders' tenure of power depends on keeping their loyalty. What they want and what they assume therefore makes a difference, indirectly if not directly.

The question of the amount of difference in viewpoint between leaders and public is still one of the most controversial questions in this field. Our analysis cannot settle that controversy, but it does suggest that there may be psychological factors, in the minds of Western observers, making for an exaggeration of the contrast between the values and assumptions of this "public" and those of the men at the top. As we have seen, the Soviet public has an image of the United States that draws entirely too sharp a contrast between "rulers" and "people." Perhaps Western observers of the U.S.S.R. need to be on guard against a similar tendency in themselves.

What does seem likely is that there are very significant differences of emphasis *within* each stratum between the more militantly Communist elements, largely concentrated in the higher echelons of the Party, and the less militant, more open-minded elements, especially among the non-Party intelligentsia and the upper-middle strata of the general population.[23] These differences of emphasis probably include a much greater concern with world Communism in the more militant group and a more live-and-let-live attitude toward world affairs in the less militant group and in the great majority of the public. Probably on the whole the leaders' self-image is less innocently peaceful, and much more resolutely dedicated to the expansion of national power, than the self-image of the public. On the other hand, the leaders' enemy-image is probably at least as diabolical as that of the general public. It could well be more so, since the factors of greater information and more active thinking in the minds of the leaders, which might make them less "paranoid," are probably more than balanced by their greater acceptance of the Marxian demonology and their greater basic commitment to a picture of the present-day world as a life-and-death struggle. Their suspicion of what our rulers may want to do to them (their "fear" of us in this sense of the

word "fear") is therefore, in all probability, quite genuine.

This is also, it may be added, the judgment of most of those Western scholars who have studied most thoroughly the direct evidence as to the words and actions of the Soviet leaders. For instance, Leites (1953) says that, in the Bolshevik view, "between all-out attacks on the Party, the enemy—who 'never lays down his arms'—constantly calculates the possibilities of intensifying hostile acts against it. Hence another total attack may come at any time" (p. 404). And Kennan (1960b) speaks of their being convinced of "the inalterable hostility of the capitalist world" (p. 30).[24] As we have seen, this kind of exaggerated suspicion does not by any means preclude preoccupation with power as the primary goal of their foreign policy; in fact, "aggressive" motivation based on preoccupation with power and "defensive" motivation based on an urge to self-preservation (combined with paranoid misperception of the enemy) can be psychologically complementary. In all probability both are important in the thinking of the Soviet leaders. It would appear, then, that the Soviet people differ from their leaders in one important respect— a much lesser concern with the goal of power as such; but they resemble them in another important respect—a desire for power as a way of being safe in a world that is assumed to be essentially hostile.

Obviously there are problems here in plenty. We will therefore attempt no estimate of *how much* resemblance there may be between the images in the minds of the Soviet leaders and

[23] For an elaboration of the differences in viewpoint within the Communist elite, see especially Tucker (1963, pp. 201–213).

[24] For the pre-revolutionary historical background of present-day Russian suspicion of the West, see Byrnes (1962). He says, for example, "While the Soviet leaders are almost as suspicious and fearful of the West as was Pobedonostsev. . . ." (p. 139).

those in the minds of the people. It is hoped only that the considerations advanced in this section may be of some help to the reader in arriving at his own estimate.

RELEVANCE TO THE EAST–WEST CONFLICT

Since the Soviet leaders rather than the public have the missiles and make the decisions, this analysis of the psychology of the public can have only an indirect bearing on policies relating to the double task of conducting the East–West conflict and preventing nuclear war. It may have an indirect bearing, however, in three ways:

1. It suggests some ways in which any group conflict may generate processes of group self-delusion that cloud the judgment of the participants. To whatever extent the West is subject to these same processes, the analysis may help Westerners to guard against similar self-delusion in their own perceptions of reality.

2. While the direct influence of the Soviet public on the decisions of their leaders is probably small, especially in the foreign-policy field, their indirect influence may be considerable since they constitute a large part of the psychological climate in which the leaders live. The values and assumptions of the great majority of the people are likely to influence those of their leaders, in the long run, even if the people have little or no direct effect on particular decisions.

3. While, as we have seen, the psychology of the leaders clearly differs from that of the general public in some ways, there are other ways in which there is reason to believe that they are similar. To whatever extent this is true, a study of the thinking of the public may help us to understand that of the decision-making leaders themselves.

In one way in particular such a study may help us to empathize realistically with those leaders: it may help us to recognize adequately the element of real fear and real suspicion—however mistaken it may be—in their image of our "ruling circles." Since that image has nonrational roots and great momentum, nothing we can do or say is likely to effect a large and sudden change in it. Nevertheless, the post-Stalin leaders have shown rationality in many ways. There is therefore some reason to hope that, if we consciously make the changing of their image of us a major objective, we may be able over a period of years to achieve a substantial measure of success.

While the analysis provides no simple formula as to how this can be done, it does suggest the importance of distinguishing clearly between friendliness and weakness. A policy of being strong enough to deter Communist aggression and of resisting Communist aggression—*if*, as in the Korean war, it has unambiguously occurred—does not necessarily require us to refrain from sensible acts of cooperation at other times because they could be mistaken for appeasement. The analysis suggests, too, how easily we may perceive as unequivocal aggression an action of the Communist leaders which, from their point of view, is primarily defensive in purpose. We would be wise, then, to cultivate empathy in ourselves as well as courage, and businesslike cooperation as well as strength. We would be wise to consider every contemplated American or Western action from the point of view of the Communist leaders as well as our own, and to keep in mind not only the dangers of a Munich-like policy that rewards aggression but also the need to stop the

wheels of mutual fear and suspicion—
and if possible to make them turn the
other way.

REFERENCES

Adler, H. *How to talk with Russians.*
Privately mimeographed, 1960.

Adorno, T. W., Frenkel-Brunswik, Else,
Levinson, D., & Sanford, N. *The authoritarian personality.* New York: Harper, 1950.

Airapetian, M. E., & Deborin, G. A.
Etapy vnieshnei politiki SSSR (Stages
in the foreign policy of the USSR). Moscow: Sotsekgiz, 1961.

Allport, G. W. *The nature of prejudice.*
Reading, Mass.: Addison-Wesley, 1954.

Almond, G. *The appeals of Communism.*
Princeton: Princeton Univer. Press,
1954.

American Committee for Liberation
*Soviet attitudes as reported by recent
visitors to the USSR.* New York: Author,
1959.

Asch, S. E. Effects of group pressure
upon the modification and distortion of
judgments. In G. E. Swanson, T. M.
Newcomb, & E. L. Hartley (Eds.),
Readings in social psychology. New
York: Holt, Rinehart and Winston, 1952.
Pp. 2–11.

Barghoorn, F. *The Soviet image of the
United States.* New York: Harcourt,
Brace, 1950.

Bauer, R., Inkeles, A., & Kluckhohn, C.
How the Soviet system works. Cambridge, Mass.: Harvard Univer. Press,
1956.

Beloff, M. *The foreign policy of Soviet
Russia, 1929–1941.* New York: Oxford
Univer. Press, 1949. 2 vols.

Bronfenbrenner, U. *A social psychologist
looks at the Soviet Union.* Mimeographed, 1960.

Brzezinski, Z. K. *Ideology and power in
Soviet politics.* New York: Praeger,
1962.

Burg, D. Life in Soviet universities.
Daedalus, April 1961, 38–46.

Byrnes, R. F. Attitudes toward the West.
In I. Lederer (Ed.), *Russian foreign
policy.* New Haven: Yale Univer. Press,
1962. Pp. 109–141.

Cantril, H. *The politics of despair.* New
York: Basic Books, 1958.

Cooper, Eunice, & Jahoda, Marie The
evasion of propaganda: How prejudiced
people respond to anti-prejudice propaganda. *J. Psychol.,* 1947, *23,* 15–25.

Crankshaw, E. *Russia without Stalin:
The emerging pattern.* New York:
Viking, 1956.

Dallin, A. (Ed.) *Soviet conduct in world
affairs: A selection of readings.* New
York: Columbia Univer. Press, 1960.

Fainsod, M. *How Russia is ruled* (Rev.
ed.). Cambridge, Mass.: Harvard Univer. Press, 1963.

Festinger, L. *A theory of cognitive dissonance.* New York: Harper, 1957.

Fundamentals of Marxism-Leninism. Moscow: Foreign Languages Publishing
House, 1959.

Heider, F. *The psychology of interpersonal relations.* New York: Wiley, 1958.

Inkeles, A., & Bauer, R. *The Soviet citizen.* Cambridge, Mass.: Harvard Univer.
Press, 1959.

Janis, I., & King, B. T. The influence of
role-playing on opinion-change. *J.
abnorm. soc. Psychol.,* 1954, *49,* 211–
218.

Karpovich, M. Russian imperialism or
communist aggression? *New Leader,*
June 4, 11, 1951. (Reprinted in R. A.
Goldwin, Ed., *Readings in Russian for-
eign policy.* New York: Oxford Univer.
Press, 1959. Pp. 657–666.)

Kelman, H. C. Attitude change as a function of response restriction. *Hum. Relat.,*
1953, *6,* 185–214.

Kennan, G. F. *Russia and the West under Lenin and Stalin.* Boston: Little,
Brown, 1960. (a)

Kennan, G. F. *Soviet foreign policy,*

1917–1941. Princeton: Van Nostrand, 1960. (b)

Khrushchev, N. S. *For victory in peaceful competition with Capitalism*. New York: Dutton, 1960.

Kluckhohn, C. Studies of the Russian national character. In A. Inkeles & K. Geiger (Eds.), *Soviet society: A book of readings*. Boston: Houghton-Mifflin, 1961. Pp. 607–619.

Leites, N. *A study of Bolshevism*. New York: Free Press, 1953.

Lowenthal, R. The logic of one-party rule. *Problems of Communism*, March–April 1958.

Lyons, E. *Our secret allies*. New York: Duell, Sloan & Pearce, 1954.

Mosely, P. E. *The Kremlin and world politics*. New York: Vintage, 1960.

Mosely, P. E. Soviet myths and realities. In P. E. Mosely (Ed.), *The Soviet Union, 1922–1962*. New York: Praeger, 1963.

Novak, J. *The future is ours, comrade*. Garden City: Doubleday, 1960.

Pipes, R. The public mood. *Harper's Magazine*, May 1961, *222*, 107–112.

Osgood, C. E. *An alternative to war or surrender*. Urbana: Univer. Illinois Press, 1962.

Rokeach, M. *The open and closed mind*. New York: Basic Books, 1960.

Scott, W. A. Attitude change through reward of verbal behavior. *J. abnorm. soc. Psychol.*, 1957, *55*, 72–75.

Scott, W. A. Attitude change by response reinforcement: Replication and extension. *Sociometry*, 1959, *22*, 328–335.

Tucker, R. C. *The Soviet political mind*. New York: Praeger, 1963.

White, R. K. The Cold War and the modal philosophy. *J. Confl. Resol.*, 1958, *2*, 43–50.

White, R. K. Misconceptions in Soviet and American images. Paper read at meeting of American Psychological Association, New York, Sept. 1961.

Wolfe, B. D. Communist ideology and Soviet foreign policy. *Foreign Affairs*, 1962, *41*, 152–170.

8

In Chapter 8 we turn to data on American images—specifically, on the ways in which American public opinion formulates the issues of the Cold War. The chapter describes the consensus on Cold-War issues that public opinion data seem to reveal, examines some of the psychological and social processes that might produce this consensus, and discusses the reasons why it may be more apparent than real. These reasons include the typical methodology of opinion polling which, it is pointed out, encourages a deflection of stated opinions in the direction of perceived consensus. The chapter then proceeds to examine the processes of opinion formation on policy issues, drawing on studies of demographic and personality correlates of different approaches to the Cold War. In doing so, the chapter returns to some of the conceptual approaches and some of the sources of data that we have already encountered in Chapters 3 and 6. In Chapter 8, however, the primary emphasis is on relating these materials to the foreign policy process. Specifically, the attempt is made to draw implications from this analysis for the possibilities of policy innovation, which is often unduly constrained by an image of a firm and immovable public opinion.

Milton J. Rosenberg, the author of Chapter 8, is Professor of Psychology at Dartmouth College. He is senior author of *Attitude organization and change* (1960). As a member of the Committee on International Relations of the Society for the Psychological Study of Social Issues he is organizing a new research effort on the dynamics of public opinion on foreign policy issues. His other research interests currently focus on attitude change from the point of view of consistency theory; social and personality correlates of reactions to public issues; and the social psychology of the psychological experiment and of the interview.

H. C. K.

Images in Relation to the Policy Process

AMERICAN PUBLIC OPINION ON COLD-WAR ISSUES

Milton J. Rosenberg

The Cold War approaches its twen-tieth anniversary. Policy makers on both sides, inhibited from as free a recourse to the threat of conclusive military action as was once available, have of necessity sought to avoid ul-timate confrontation. Indeed they seem to have tacitly agreed that the issue of final hegemony must be put aside, except for its occasional evocation in propagandistic rhetoric. Instead they have pursued the conflict in terms of a set of particular and limited issues. Though these have varied over time (from Azerbaijan and the United Nations effort in Korea in the mid and late '40s to Berlin, Viet Nam, and arms inspection issues in the early '60s) the structure and style of the continuing competition have shown a certain note-worthy regularity.

One problematic aspect of this settled pattern of international competition has been the role in it of "public opinion."

In the two great power centers of Washington and Moscow, and in sub-sidiary ones such as Peking and Paris, the opinions of the public, or rather of numerous and discriminable publics, seem to matter a great deal; they en-gage the interest not only of those who control the making of policy but also of those who advise them, those who re-ceive their decisions for implementation and those, in the West at least, who hold the power of legislative assent or veto.

The purpose of this chapter is to clarify certain important aspects of the general relationship between public opinion and the policy process and to do this in a way that is pointed both toward the recent history of the Cold War and toward the prospects for it resolution. The first section examine some ways in which public opinion enters into policy formulation and ex-ecution. This will include, among othe things, the effects on policy of the "images" of public opinion held by those who are involved in policy development. Succeeding sections will deal with ways of improving the validity of those images and with recent theory and research that help to deepen and extend their content. Throughout the chapter, the discussion of these matters is guided by the conviction that their clarification will contribute to the more effective design and utilization of policy in pursuit of the goal of international stability.

PUBLIC OPINION AND THE FOREIGN POLICY PROCESS

The general relevance of public opinion for the policy process may be reduced to at least four relationships. The first of these is the desire of national leaders to influence the opinions of publics that lie beyond the reach of their own direct power. Most commonly these are composed of the residents of "uncommitted" nations. It is a matter of continuing controversy whether it is really possible, through propaganda or action, to persuade such publics that one or the other of the leading nations is pacific in its intentions, altruistic in its purposes, or admirable for its achievements. However, it is now generally understood that, at least in the short run, a "neutral" nation will move toward or away from one or the other of the great powers not on the basis of public opinion but because those who lead it perceive that in so doing they are gaining economic, territorial, defensive, or other kinds of advantage for their nation. Thus the ruling elites of the contesting major powers are probably not as deeply interested in public opinion in the uncommitted areas of the world as they are sometimes thought to be. Usually, and particularly in the Western nations, they are more directly and more constantly concerned with the policy-related opinions that are held within their own spheres of influence; that is, they are more dependably attentive to the opinions of the publics that make up their own nations. This is the kind of public opinion upon which this chapter will focus.

The three remaining types of relationships between the policy process and public opinion that are to be discussed here are then *intranational* in locus, though they often have quite direct significance for international strategies and competitive encounters. We shall briefly consider public opinion as a *resource* in policy execution and as a *source* of policy innovation. In somewhat greater compass, because it helps define the pertinence of the empirical studies to be reviewed in later sections of this chapter, we shall then consider public opinion as a *constraint* upon policy innovation.

Broad approval by the majority of a national public of the visible policies of its leaders, or at least assent to these policies, would seem to be a *sine qua non* for the successful execution of policy and for the maintenance of governing power itself. When "morale" fails fully and unequivocally, wars are lost, governments collapse, economies flounder. In this sense public opinion is a *sustaining* resource. But it may also be used as an *active* and *manipulable* resource, as a way of increasing the prominence and credibility of initiatives and responses in international competition. Thus it seems likely that civil defense programs, and particularly campaigns to create a pattern of national opinion favorable to the financing and building of fall-out shelters, have at times had the effect of increasing the credibility of America's announced willingness to employ "massive retaliation," to "go to the brink"—and beyond if necessary—in defense of its interests. The positive correlation between recurrent emphases on shelter-building and variations in the level of American-Soviet tension suggests some conscious effort to use the mass media to mobilize and shape visible national opinion in ways that will convey national militancy; though an even simpler relationship is probably also involved— that between international tension and threat and the reactive search for magical symbolizations of security. The continuing controversy between government spokesmen and editors over "news management" in the United States may be read as reflecting, among other things, an awareness of the fact that disingenuous attempts to manipulate public opinion for tactical gain have become more common in recent years.

Can public opinion also operate as a *source* of policy? Can it, when strongly mobilized and effectively expressed, actually drive leaders to undertake changes that they would not otherwise have considered? Publicists engaged in organizing protest movements and in mounting legislative lobbies frequently claim that this is so. Indeed the sounding of this claim not only justifies the publicist's role, but is prescribed by it.

But a close examination of such campaigns suggests that rarely can they exert enough pressure, enough directed mass indignation, to force even the most democratic of governments into previously unconsidered or rejected paths of action. What they do sometimes accomplish is to change the image of public opinion held by persons capable of affecting policy decisions; indeed they may often alter the image of public opinion held by the public itself. And on occasion the consequence will be to free policy-makers and legislative "watchdogs" from inhibiting apprehen-

sions about the domestic consequences of significant shifts on matters of international policy.

As policy-makers have become more aware of this sort of process, they have sometimes tended to utilize it. A possible recent example was the apparent indirect encouragement by the Kennedy administration, in the months before the negotiation of the nuclear test-ban, of the efforts of various peace organizations that had been pressuring it in just that direction. One instance was a broadly distributed letter from an *ad hoc* committee of academics that urged professors to lend their names and financial support to the pro-test-ban effort; the letter went on to imply, guardedly but unambiguously, that assurances had been received that such action would be welcomed by an administration that was convinced that a test-ban was in the national interest but was at the same time unsanguine about the prospects for senatorial ratification.

In examining and rejecting the idea that public opinion (at intensities less than those that generate revolutions) can operate as an important *source* of policy innovation, I have touched upon another notion that is generally given somewhat greater credence: namely that public opinion, or the perception of it, sets limits to the possibility of policy changes and innovations. We arrive then at the question of whether public opinion is indeed a major *constraint* upon the process of policy formulation itself.

The nearly consensual answer since de Tocqueville (who is, indeed, also the canonical source of the question) has been affirmative. For some commentators and ideologists this assumed ultimate "sovereignty of the public" has been the confirming glory of Western, and particularly American, democratic achievement. De Tocqueville himself was ambivalent about this aspect of American mass democracy, though some modern readings stress his troubled concern that inherent in it were the debasement of political intelligence and the loss of governmental flexibility.

Whether or not "mass society" has come to its full development, we have had since Ortega (1932) an abundance of social observers (among current writers one thinks immediately of Fromm, 1941; Kahler, 1957; Riesman, 1950; Mills, 1956; Arendt, 1951) who diagnose modern man as socially disoriented, estranged from any authentic comprehension of pressing public issues, essentially depoliticized; and yet in spite of this (or because of it) usually rigid and unyielding in his uninformed political judgments, or else prone to occasional arousals of excessive and ill-considered political enthusiasm and indignation. It is some such vision of the essential political incompetence of the mass in modern democratic states that has troubled and energized the thought of those who, like Walter Lippmann, have sought to integrate the perspectives of political philosophy with the practical necessity for governments to act wisely and creatively.

Much of Lippmann's argument in his influential book *Essays in the public philosophy* (1955) flows from his characterization of mass democratic government as hemmed in, particularly in the management of its foreign relations, by a public opinion that is always some years behind the times. The generative source of this outdated public opinion is discovered in earlier efforts, often initiated by the government itself, to mobilize public support for previous policies. The paradox thus suggested can be summarized in the terms of this chapter: Efforts to affect public opinion so that it will have utility as a *resource* have the consequence over time (and because of the sheer sluggishness and

rigidity of the ordinary man's political mentality) of generating *constraints* upon the flexibility and freedom for rationality that policy-makers must enjoy.

This hypothesis is an intriguing one, not only because of practical implications and the way in which it highlights a basic dilemma in political philosophy, but also because it is founded on two assumptions that have been much discussed, and not infrequently studied, in recent years. The first of these assumptions is that those who are engaged in policy-formulating activities are in fact persuaded that their continuation in power *depends* upon their making some visible effort to serve the public will; and that they do in actuality often undertake to meet the policy specifications implicit in the perceived content of majority public opinion. The second assumption is that the opinions of publics on policy issues are stable enough and detailed enough in their content for the members of those publics to be capable of feeling directly served or violated by governmental action.

Certain social scientists have questioned these asumptions. In so doing they have not necessarily shown them to be unfounded, but they have demonstrated that they require qualification and more detailed examination. The emergence in political science of the behavioral approach is nowhere more visible than in the many investigations into how, in reality rather than in idealized formal definitions, legislative and other governmental roles are acted out. Miller and Stokes (1963; see also Miller, 1962) in one of the most detailed and well-designed empirical studies so far reported in this area, seem to have demonstrated a number of important things about the relationship between congressmen and their constituencies. They examine the degree of congruence between the congressman's roll-call performance, his privately expressed policy views, and the sampled opinions of voters in his home-district; and on this basis they identify a number of factors that seem to increase or diminish the extent to which a congressman's voting record is affected by his perceptions of constituency opinion. One of these is the variable of issue content. Presently the area of civil rights is the one in which legislative performance seems to be most attuned to home district majority opinion. A similar relationship, of smaller but significant magnitude, is found in the area of "social welfare" issues. However, in the domain of foreign policy or, more specifically, on the dimension of "foreign involvement versus isolationism" no such relationship is visible in the data developed by Miller and Stokes.

Their interpretation, based upon interviews with voters conducted in 1958, is that these voters show a comparatively low awareness of, or interest in, the particulars of "involvement versus isolation" issues. This in turn they ascribe to the fact that something like a bipartisan consensus has prevailed on matters of foreign policy:

Understanding of the distant mysteries of foreign policy has not been promoted through the partisan specifications of alternatives. Mr. Eisenhower's great contribution to American political life was to obliterate the isolationist-internationalist dichotomy which had characterized postwar party allegiances. But in making internationalists out of many Republican voters and reviving the possibility of flexibility in America's foreign policy posture, the cues by which policy alternatives are given political implications for the voter were destroyed. In 1958 foreign policy stood as an emerging question for public discussion, so poorly meshed with the existing operations of the representative system as to limit the creation of the links which bind the acts of the representatives into the desires of the represented (Miller, 1962, p. 28).

Other writers, impressed by these and similar findings, have tended to discount the pertinence of public opinion as a source of constraint upon the development of international policy decisions. Thus Converse (1963), speaking both as a public opinion specialist and as one interested in the peace movement, draws this conclusion from the work of Miller and Stokes and from his own years of "close contact with political opinions in the mass public":

Clearly, in foreign affairs, decision-makers are not convinced that the mass public has sufficient information to pass worthwhile judgment, and few of us who have had contact with opinion surveys would dare say them nay (p. 41).

On these grounds he advises peace movement workers to direct their persuasive efforts not "downward" (that is to the mass public) but rather "upward" (to policy-makers) and "sideways" (to other well-educated, politically active citizens).

The note of realism struck in such studies and commentaries is of course welcome, as realism always is. One main consequence of the development and widespread use of survey techniques has been the discovery, dismaying to many who have made it, that "the public" is extremely uninformed about the very facts of international relations. The proportions of respondents who cannot identify the world's leading political figures, who cannot even recognize such terms as NATO, Common Market, or OAS, is, in most surveys, distressingly large.

From this fact, however, or from the fact that American congressmen seem uninfluenced by constituency opinion on certain dimensions of foreign policy, it does not follow that only more specialized, more politically literate, and more organized minority publics are capable of imposing constraints upon the formulation and execution of foreign policy. There seem to be some other important considerations from which it can be argued that mass opinion (or rather the way in which it is perceived) does constrain policy processes to a greater extent than Miller and Stokes, Converse, and others have estimated.

Let us first submit the Miller-Stokes findings to somewhat closer examination. The only dimension of foreign policy represented in their data is that of internationalism versus isolationism; but, as they themselves suggest, this issue has disappeared from the realm of partisan controversy. However, other foreign policy issues, most of them concerned with *how* international relations should be conducted, have replaced it. Most notably, foreign policy debate in America and other Western countries (and indeed debate in and between certain Communist nations as well) has for some years been focused on the choice between a guarded approach to increasing international conciliation or a continued reliance upon an unyielding "hard-line" pattern of armed deterrence and mutual distrust. One wonders if congressmen's votes on the test ban, on cultural exchange programs, and on military budgets might not yield higher correlations with back-home opinions than their votes on the issues examined by Miller and Stokes.

It is also worth noting that Miller and Stokes find *stronger* correlations between home-district opinions and the voting records of congressmen who come from "safe districts" than in the case of congressmen who live with the threat of biannual electoral recall. This might suggest that a congressman who serves a district in which public opinion is fairly uniform will find it easier to represent back-home views in his legislative voting, and further that his performance in the model of an "instructed delegate" will indeed facilitate his retention of office. Incidentally, the widespread use of polling procedures by congressmen themselves, methodologically inadequate as these surveys usually are (see Alpert *et al.,* 1954), suggests the extent to which many congressmen are overtly concerned with keeping up with the content of back-home opinion. However, it may be that some congressmen use these mail surveys not to find out what they need to do to please their constituents but rather what they need to do to "educate" them. Others, as Hawver (1954) suggests, may simply be engaging in public relations.

But beyond such cavils there lies a more obvious and more important consideration. It is that in the nations of the Western alliance generally, and in the Eastern nations certainly, the planning and execution of foreign policy is in the hands of the executive branch of government and its specialized agencies (cf. Chapter 12 in this volume for further discussion of this point). In the democracies the men who hold national governmental power, and those who govern the *party* in national power, will of necessity be more responsive than the average individual legislator to the injury they may do themselves by grossly violating "national opinion." Thus in the United States, for example, evidence of the constraining influence of mass public opinion upon foreign policy might best be sought in the choices made by the President and the group of policy advisors and court-initiates (some of whom, to be sure, may be legislative figures) that surrounds him. It is in the positions *they* endorse or avoid, in the proposed innovations *they* risk, discard, or delay, that one may discover the ultimate power over policy of the consensual pattern of mass opinion as they perceive it.[1]

The suggestion that those who control policy formulation are inhibited by apprehensions over public opinion requires some qualification. For one thing, this inhibition does not necessarily take the form of feeling bound by the specific percentages of pro and con reactions to particular issues as yielded by the respondents in "last week's poll." Instead, policy-makers usually recognize the validity of the specialist's claim that mass opinion is short on detail, sometimes rather unspecific, and often sluggishly unresponsive to exact issues of policy choice, except as these have direct and obvious bearing upon the individual's continuing, conscious concern for his immediate welfare. Indeed many practical politicians seem to have known this for some time before social scientists discovered it. But what the policy-controlling members of governmental and party elites *do* usually credit is that, at any given time, there is some generalized and established frame of reference against which the mass public may be most readily brought to interpret and evaluate policy changes. Thus, at least until recently, it seemed that large sectors of the American public were rather accepting of attempts to get them to examine almost any departures in foreign policy in terms of whether these indicated that the government was being "hard or soft on Communism."[2]

Whether a given policy innovation can be so structured that the public will locate it at the negative pole of such a generalized scale of evaluation (and thus how it will affect the electoral prospects and legislative successes of the group in power) depend in large part upon what the political opposition tries to make of the contemplated policy innovation and how successful it is in its attempts. Thus innovative departures in foreign policy will often be tested out in "trial balloon" form. If the opposition elects to try to shoot the balloon down (or if individual oppositionists attempt to advance their political careers by directing their fire at it), it may hastily be pulled down. Party colleagues of the balloonist will disagree with him; he himself will insist that he spoke not officially but only for himself and only to stimulate discussion. If such a tactical withdrawal is not made, those behind the launching of the balloon will watch closely to gauge whether important publics can possibly be brought to dangerous levels of mobilized indignation, to levels that threaten electoral losses and legislative or financial abandonments.

In some basic sense, then, the mobilization of apparent public opposition or indignation comprises an attempt on the part of partisan opposition groups or individuals to use public opinion as a *resource*. Where such attempts are, or seem, successful, public opinion will achieve the status of an effective *constraint* upon policy innovation. Of course constraints merely constrain; they do not necessarily defeat and ob-

---

[1] However, lest the importance of the average legislator in the shaping of policy be slighted, it is necessary to add that he can affect that process in various ways; most obviously, by what he conveys about how he is likely to vote on those policy decisions that will be available for legislative review; but also in other ways, such as reporting how "the folks back home" will react to particular policy undertakings.

[2] A possible indication of an ongoing shift in present American public opinion on Cold-War issues is that for some sectors of the public (though probably not for the majority) this frame of reference is now less salient than one defined in terms of "reducing or increasing the danger of nuclear war."

literate policy changes. If a contemplated innovation is withdrawn, this is often only so that it may be *redrawn*—changed in its form of statement and in its supporting arguments and once again put forward.

Perhaps the most significant effect of public opinion on policy undertakings is in fostering anticipations of the process that has been described here. Such anticipations will often determine the way in which a policy change is initially presented to the public or the way in which it is defended after it has been launched. Whether the constraining power of public opinion is anticipated or directly encountered, it may contribute significantly to altering the meaning, the potential efficacy, the very original purpose of the contemplated policy change. Thus, while public opinion operating as a constraint upon policy rarely stops innovations in their tracks, it may often *transform* them. And the authors of the original policy plan, having become caught up in "seeing it through the mill," may sometimes be less than completely cognizant that some such transformation, some such deflection away from their original purposes, has in fact occurred.

In sum, I have suggested that, in the area of foreign relations, elitist perceptions of the opinions of publics (whether these be specialized and articulate pressure groups or the "mass public" itself) tend to have some effect upon policy processes, and particularly that at times they do *constrain* and limit the shaping and execution of policy innovations. The extent to which policy processes are controlled by such perceptions has hardly been assessed in any systematic studies. Nor are we in a position to say anything definite about the comparative importance of role, personality, situation, and issue variables as they might heighten or reduce the magnitude of this relationship. Clearly what

is needed is research in which those who contribute to the policy process are interviewed and observed as they develop their own perceptions of public opinion and as they adapt to these perceptions. It should be quite possible to pursue questions of the following sorts empirically: What kinds of elitists worry about what kinds of opinions as held by what kinds of publics? How are their perceptions of the content and strength of public opinion shaped? What mechanisms do they employ, and under what conditions, in yielding to, or in avoiding, the constraints upon policy that are associated with such perceptions?

At the same time, if we are to develop a more systematic and detailed knowledge of the role of public opinion in the policy process, we must also address ourselves to the other side of the transaction between the individual in power and the individual in the public. We need, then, to deepen and extend our understanding of the *psychology* of public opinion. Among the questions that require examination are these: How do members of publics develop, or fail to develop, sustained and detailed orientations toward policy issues? What relations obtain between these orientations as privately held and as overtly expressed? Considering their content and organization, how are such orientations related to aspects of the person's social identity? How are they related to the personality systems in which they are imbedded?

From recent research and theoretical writing, we can draw some fairly reliable answers to some of these questions and some more tentative, but provocative, answers to others. The main purpose of this chapter is to review and integrate such answers in a way that will demonstrate their relevance for policy-making and execution. At the same time I shall try to examine this material for its bearing on some methodological and theoretical issues in social psychology. A forecast of the remainder of this chapter will suggest the scope and limits of the approach that I propose to take.

The immediately succeeding section attempts a sort of applied epistemology. Polls and surveys comprise the main source of information about the distribution of public opinion on policy issues. However, analysis of various aspects of the public opinion interview suggests that respondents may often give a kind of invalid self-report in which opinion expression is deflected from private indifference toward endorsement of perceived consensus. A major consequence is that the views held by policy-makers about relevant public opinion are often inaccurate and unnecessarily inhibiting in their influence upon policy formulation and execution. One corrective to this kind of distortion in public opinion data is the comprehensive analysis of its possible sources; another is the development of new approaches to the assessment of attitudes on public issues. Governing the discussion of these matters is the proposition that closer analysis and better measurement of public opinion will reveal that, at least as far as this source of constraint is concerned, the policy process may often be pursued with much more flexibility and openness than policy specialists concerned with Cold-War problems have heretofore allowed themselves.

However, an adequate response to the constraining power of public opinion requires, also, a clearer understanding of how those who are not indifferent to policy issues acquire their interest in these issues and their evaluative orientations toward them. A separate section addressed to this question is guided by the sort of "functionalist" orientation that has been described in Chapter 6 by Janis and Smith. This section in turn provides the groundwork for the major task to which I have addressed myself: to report and analyze a number of studies, including some of my own, that have sought to disclose the correlates and sources of attitudes on those policy issues that figure importantly in the present debate about whether, and how, the Cold War is to be prosecuted or resolved. In its bearing upon problems of policy, the import of this last major section is that the attitudes of different portions of the public can, in some degree, be altered or reinforced in ways that will reduce still further the constraints that existing public opinion tends to impose upon policy innovation.

In the main, the point of view that I have here forecasted, and whose validity and applicability I shall now attempt to establish, approaches public opinion as an obstacle (though a somewhat surmountable one) to the achievement of required national and international goals. If public opinion does presently play this role more than any other, this is not a truly acceptable or inevitable state of affairs. In some concluding comments I shall presume to go beyond the limited questions of how to interpret and alter present public opinion constraints upon policy innovation, and offer some suggestions about why large sections of the public are incompetent in matters of foreign policy and what, in the light of a commitment to the democratic model of social order, ought to be done about it.

THE SOURCES AND DETECTION OF INVALID CONSENSUS ON POLICY ISSUES

How do persons involved in the policy process derive their ideas about the content and intensity of public opinion on policy issues? The question is a variant of a broader and more philosophical one: How does a person come to know the mind of another? Most directly such knowledge of the other begins with what we are *told* about him, either by himself or by others who have elicited such reports from him. As the size and geographic dispersion of constituencies and publics have increased, and as the demands on policymakers have multiplied, those who fill such roles have found themselves less capable of gauging public opinion through direct contact. Nor have they been willing to depend solely upon impressions conveyed from various sections of the country by political allies, local officials, and journalists. Instead they have turned increasingly to the product of an industry that arose, in part, in response to their need—to the reports of the pollsters and social surveyors.

If it is true that public opinion as apprehended by leaders does play some role at least in their perceptual organization of policy issues and in the shaping of their responses to those issues, then a critical examination of this major source of their knowledge about public opinion becomes essential. Specifically it should be asked: How trustworthy, how free from error, is the information conveyed by professional surveyors of public opinion? If error is present, does it have a random quality or is it likely to show systematic bias in a particular direction?

Through the writings of Percy Bridgman (1927), social scientists were first confronted with the idea that the very act and technique of scientific observation may transform the appearance or even the substance of that which is being observed. Recently Orne (1962), Riecken (1962), Rosenthal (1963), and others have examined the ways in which experimental procedures in the laboratory may contaminate and distort

the phenomena they presume to study. In similar fashion, it is highly probable that the study of public opinion through interviews and questionnaires often affects and transforms (and perhaps even creates) its object. To disclose the analysis that lies behind this assertion, and to evaluate the procedures upon which knowledge about public opinion is typically based, will require a commentary upon certain usually unexamined aspects of the public opinion interview.

Attitude Expression in the Interview Situation

It is in the nature of the situation in which one person asks another to reveal himself that the latter is unlikely to respond spontaneously. He is far more likely to draw from the range of things he might say, and from the set of ways he might say them, some selection that suits the occasion, that helps him to reduce the apprehensions aroused by the situation as well as to approach the fulfillments it promises. In this the typical respondent in a public opinion interview (or, for that matter, the patient responding to a clinician, the applicant to a personnel manager, and even the public personage to a journalist) is usually not attempting to deceive. Rather, he is involved in yet another round of the never-ending search for a coherent, socially acceptable and yet personally believable identity.

In recent years a number of social researchers have become sensitive to this dilemma. Some, like Kahn and Cannell (1957), have encountered it in the form of a set of response-distorting effects that they trace to inadequate interviewing and question-phrasing procedures. Others, like David Riesman (1964), have gone on to analyze the interview as a ritualized exchange, governed by a set of implicit norms that encourage ego-enhancing self-revelation in a setting that, by virtue of its isolation and impermanence, can have no lasting consequences.

Still another and related approach to the psychology of the interview, particularly the kind of interview in which the respondent is asked to report his evaluative position on current policy issues and alternatives, will be suggested here. It is based upon the reflections of the author and various colleagues whom he has questioned about their experiences as interviewers. It is offered without any substantial, direct test of its propositions, though much of what is asserted is consistent with incidental findings in a variety of methodological studies as well as experimental studies on attitude dynamics.

From Thomas and Znaniecki (1918) to Lewin (1935) and beyond, numerous writers have stressed that behavior is guided by, and is expressive of, the individual's "definition of the situation." Yet it is remarkable that, until recently, there has been so little investigation or even systematic speculation concerning the respondent's-eye view of the public opinion interview. This is a matter for considerable concern, because the definitions that guide the interviewer and respondent are not likely to be completely or even largely identical.

To understand why this should be so we must note, first of all, that the actual nature, purpose, and rationale of the transaction that the respondent has agreed to are often not at all clear to him. Even when such matters are *explained,* these explanations may not be fully understood or, if understood, fully credited. In the midst of this ambiguity, certain other meanings and challenges will be perceived, misperceived, or projectively elaborated by the respondent and these will in turn tend to affect the style and substance of his responding.

One type of subjective interpretation that is likely to influence the respondent's self-report of his attitudes is particularly common when, in comparison to the interviewer, the respondent is of lesser apparent status, education, or sophistication. Under such circumstances he often feels that his competence is being tested; and thus his guiding concern is that he not show himself to be totally uninformed on, or uninvolved in, the public issues that the interviewer puts before him. A basic consequence of such concern is that the respondent may, with some private sense of urgency, seek to recall and repeat as his own, those positions that he has already heard expressed and defended. These of course will tend to be the ones that prevail in the mass media and which reach him through those media or through "opinion leaders" (see Lazarsfeld & Menzel, 1963) who are more closely attuned to them.

Another subjective feature of the interview situation is that many respondents, even those who *do* feel themselves the interviewer's social equals, may doubt whether the guarantee of anonymity can be trusted. Where this is the case, the respondent may be concerned that the opinions he expresses might ultimately be used to judge his "loyalty," "patriotism," or "right thinking," and that such judgments of him will have some bearing upon his continued welfare. So near-paranoid a set of suspicions is perhaps less likely to arise these days than was the case a few years ago when loyalty tests were a more directly sanctioned kind of undertaking. But to the extent that the prevalence of Cold-War tensions has affected the differential distribution of social reinforcement for political opinions, and thus has made the avowal of certain opinions more anxiety-provoking than others, a concern for the respectability of one's interview responses may continue to influence opinion statements even when the expectation that one is actually risking danger has faded.

This pattern of apprehension is hardly one that we would expect to be restricted to interviews conducted in democratic nations. Surely similar feelings are aroused when opinion interviews are undertaken, as is in fact more frequently being done, in some of the Eastern bloc and neutral countries. Indeed one might expect that the strength, scope, and influence of such apprehensions would vary directly with the extent to which overt deviance from societally-sanctioned positions has in the past led to private suffering or to anxiety-laden concern over incalculable consequences.

From the foregoing considerations we begin to glimpse a paradox. One area of decision in which elitist perceptions of public opinion have probably influenced the policy process is that involving the prosecution or resolution of the Cold War. Yet "public opinion" on Cold-War issues may well be less than frankly expressed in all instances; often its expression may be polarized in directions that confirm the continuation of the pattern of international conflict that has exerted that polarizing influence. Perhaps this has had some part in the very maintenance of the Cold-War pattern, though surely many other factors have played as important, or more important, roles.

At the time of writing the tide of tension in the Cold War has ostensibly been ebbing for better than a year. Could it then be argued that, if this trend continues as far as ultimate East–West settlement and the achievement of international trust, the data gathered in interviews on international issues will become sufficiently valid so that we may take them at face value? I am convinced that such an expectation would be quite unjustified. The tendency to avoid anxiety or overt difficulty by resonating what one perceives to be conventional and sanctioned opinion is merely a heightened form of a far more pervasive and unavoidable psychological process, which manifests itself even in the absence of significant threat for deviance. This more "normal" underlying process is grounded in the elementary fact that humans are motivated to please each other, to win from each other respect and admiration. Such needs are of particular pertinence when one has agreed to submit oneself to study and evaluation by an "expert." But how, in the brief compass of an hour or less spent together, is the respondent to find a way of unlocking the interviewer's approval? The more naive he is, the more he will tend to assume that those views and opinions that he takes to be generally held are also congenial to the interviewer. Thus, through this dynamic as well, reference to available consensual standards may guide a good deal of what the respondent has to say about his own attitudes on issues of policy.

So far I have dealt with motivations that impel the respondent to shape his attitude-expressions to his perception of consensual standards because "judgment by the other" is of importance to him. Less immediately apparent, but no less significant, is the respondent's capacity to stand in judgment upon himself. The members of most literate, mass societies are taught, or at least regularly told, that a measure of one's worth is the extent to which one attends to public issues and feels responsibly involved in them. Whether this is conveyed in the content of a democratic ideology of "responsible citizenship" or in the context of an ideology of "socialist construction" or in yet other terms, the consequence is that many men come to judge their human value by the evidence of social involvement that they manage to put before themselves.

Persons so oriented will tend to maintain self-esteem by striving to view themselves as attitudinally involved in the world of issues around them. Yet the extent and detail of that involvement, its very reality, are tested only upon special occasions. One of these is, of course, the public opinion interview. Thus problems of *self-judgment* may drive at least some respondents toward the avowal of positions that they have not truly internalized, or toward an intensity of avowal that exceeds actual conviction; and again such avowals are more likely to be directed toward, rather than away from, what the individual takes to be the prevailing consensus.

Another variant of the process in which the need for positive self-judgment may influence how the individual reports upon his attitudes is displayed by a type of person with whom many social theorists are now obsessively concerned. He is the one whose relationship to the social order is marked by a sense of deep confusion and isolation, who feels himself powerless and disoriented in the face of the great issues and public processes that for him seem to occur "out there," far beyond the reach of his own competence or knowledge. His "alienation" is not so much a chosen stance of estrangement as an imposed and humiliating sense of his social irrelevance. For some of these individuals the burden of imposed alienation is transformed by elaborating the fiction that they themselves have willed their estrangement; but for others it remains an aching problem, one that can be diminished only by the achievement of some kind of *engagement,* some form of investment in public issues. The latter kind of person will welcome the provision of cues to attitu-

dinal commitment; and, again, it is the consensual cues that are most likely to guide him and to be reflected in what he has to say if fate, in the form of a pollster drawing a sample, sends an interviewer to his door.

In summary, I have proposed that a number of different psychological processes and human dilemmas converge to exert a certain kind of influence upon public opinion data: To the extent that the policy issue in question is perceived as evoking a general consensual response (that is, to the extent that a particular position on the issue is widely represented as endorsed by prestigeful figures and institutions and by "the people" generally) the expression of public opinion, as evidenced in opinion surveys, will be deflected toward that perceived consensus.

This is not to suggest that such data are thereby rendered meaningless; on the contrary, it is useful to know just what are the areas and issues in which the public allows itself little or no overt deviance. But, where the influence of consensual pressures and standards has grossly affected the collection of public opinion data, certain important discriminations as between individual respondents, or between sectors of the sampled population, become extremely difficult. Most significantly, we then lack criteria by which to discriminate three different types of respondents and thus we cannot estimate their comparative proportions. The first type are those who actually do hold the attitudes they profess—those from whom the interview or questionnaire procedure has thus elicited valid self-reports. A second group is composed of those who have been subject to the kinds of processes that have been described here—those who avow the apparently consensual position not so much out of inner conviction as out of a need to win some kind of approval from the interviewer or from the self. From such respondents the procedure of inquiry has elicited invalid self-reports in the sense that they have claimed an attitudinal fixity that they do not in fact possess. Still a third group of respondents is conceivable for whom a more dramatic type of invalidity might obtain. These would be persons who actually hold attitudes opposite to the consensual standard but who have, either with direct knowledge of duplicity or with more intricate techniques of self-deception, represented themselves as committed to the perceived consensus.[3]

An illustration may help both to demonstrate the applicability of this classification and to point toward some relevant further considerations. Should the People's Republic of China (significantly, poll questions often refer to "Red China") be admitted to the United Nations? The question has been asked many times in public opinion surveys in the United States and with all national samples the vast majority express clear opposition.

At the same time the public treatment of this issue by governmental figures, commentators, editorialists, and spokesmen for major organizations has been quite unequivocally congruent with "public opinion." That small proportion of the national public who closely follow foreign relations problems through the accounts of specialized publications may have some awareness that present policy on this issue is not likely to remain forever as intractable and unvarying as it now appears; but such predictive information simply has not reached the "average man." To the contrary, for him this is one of the issues most clearly incorporated within the category of "opposition to Communism," a category that in itself is perhaps still the most salient and general item of national consensus as presently perceived.

Of course the very force of that consensus, and its influence over the issue-relevant communications that reach the public, will have an attitude-shaping effect upon many persons, in this instance probably upon a large majority. We can therefore assume that the *modal* group is the first of the three suggested above: That is, we can assume that the larger number of respondents are essentially describing themselves accurately, that they do oppose the admission of China to the United Nations (at least when they are asked to think about it) and that in the absence of strong counter-pressures they will continue to do so. Still, it seems quite conceivable that some significant portion of the sampled population is essentially apathetic to the issue but finds it easier, more appropriate to the needs that are aroused in the interview situation, to parrot what it conceives to be the acceptable position. And there may indeed be some smaller number of respondents who have privately entertained positive thoughts about United Nations membership for Communist China but are simply too apprehensive or intimidated to acknowledge this.

The interpretation that public opinion data overestimate, to a significant degree, the consensus on this particular issue may or may not be correct. But what is crucially important is that the very kind of question raised here cannot be *empirically* resolved in most instances in which standard opinion polling techniques have been employed.

---

[3] A similar classification in terms of varying degrees of validity is likely to be applicable when, after influence has been attempted, individuals report themselves as having undergone attitude change (see Kelman, 1961).

For those techniques rely primarily upon the datum of self-placement. The respondent either selects a position from a prepared list of alternatives or else his "open-ended" response is tabulated into one or another category of a coding scheme of such alternatives. Additional data that might be used to assess the validity of the respondent's self-placement are usually not collected or, if collected, are not usually analyzed in ways that permit such assessment.

As a consequence of this failing, yet another difficulty compounds the dilemma described by Lippmann. Not only is flexibility for rational policy development and revision hampered because public opinion lingers over a consensual view that was fostered to facilitate the execution of earlier policy decisions; but the extent of private deviation from that consensus, or of withdrawal of interest from its object, will tend for some time to escape clear notice. Thus the judgment that certain policy revisions or innovations that are deemed desirable are politically inadvisable for the present, though based upon predictions from public opinion data, may often be incorrect. The usually unquestioned assumption that such data are isomorphic to the distribution and intensity of the public's real attitudes may then inhibit participants in the policy process from utilizing the degree of freedom that is actually available to them.

A somewhat subtler error of interpretation also deserves mention. Though by "attitudes" we mean comparatively stable evaluative orientations toward social objects, and though this is what we attempt to gauge in attitude measurement, it is obvious that attitudes do change; or, more accurately, that some attitudes are more readily modifiable than others. But too often confrontation with a strongly skewed distribution of public opinion data, by suggesting the prevalence of a consensual view in the reference population, suggests also that "they shall not be moved." This equation is simply not correct. Even if we were to assume that all the self-characterizations gathered from a sampled population were accurate, they are only characterizations of how the respondents felt at the time they were questioned. Thus at least some of those in the sampled population who have given valid self-reports (for example, of their opposition to admitting Communist China into the United Nations) will be capable of reorganizing their attitudes if governmental endorsement and justifications of a policy change are persuasively presented to them. Furthermore, as Janis and Smith show in Chapter 6 in this volume, it is now possible to specify many ways of increasing the efficacy of communications intended to explain and justify policy choices. It is also possible to gather information about the detailed structure and content of the relevant attitudes, about their significance in the lives of the individuals who hold them and about many other related matters, and such knowledge helps to identify the kinds of persons who are most likely to be influenced and the kinds of persuasive techniques most likely to produce such influence.

The judgment that public opinion can often be rather readily influenced might seem quite routine to those specialists in persuasion who aspire to such goals as influencing the public's preferences for competing toothpastes or automobiles. The possibility of affecting mass attitudes through persuasive communication is, after all, the basic proposition upon which is founded the work of professional advertisers, public relations specialists, and other propagandists. But as regards the possibility of influencing the evaluations of policy issues that are held by various publics, an unnecessary pessimism often prevails. Not only is this due to the uncritical acceptance of apparently consensual public opinion distributions, but also to the mistaken equation of consensus with attitudinal rigidity.

The major implication of the discussion so far is that public opinion reports, even when they seem to reflect a gross public consensus, need not inhibit policy flexibility or delay policy revision as much as they often seem to have done. It has been argued that such consensus is often more apparent than real, and that even when real it does not necessarily forecast the failure of attempts to foster its reorganization through lucid communication of relevant arguments, information, and endorsements.

If this were more fully recognized it would in turn tend to diminish a major dysfunction associated with the otherwise valuable use of public opinion data in the guidance of policy planning. That dysfunction is the interpretation of opinion reports in ways that render policy development less flexible than it should be, and less adaptive than it can be, in the face of problems that must be directly confronted in the pursuit of national and international welfare.

Increasing the Validity of Attitude Measurement

So far my argument has been largely hortatory. However the present concern with how extremely skewed opinion data on policy questions ought to be interpreted leads us on to certain more specific recommendations about available methodological aids, some of which are grounded in recent theoretical analyses of the structure and dynamics of attitudes on foreign policy and other issues.

Of the various conceivable devices for getting around the kind of ambiguity in "consensual" public opinion data that has been stressed here, the most immediately apparent is the use of respondent *panels*. If a person is interviewed on two or more separate occasions and his expressed views hold constant over time, this might well be taken as partial evidence that some stable evaluative orientation *is* being reflected in his interview responses. On the other hand, the tendency to deflect interview responses toward conformity with the perceived consensus, which is the very contaminant we are seeking to uncover, could well operate on *all* such interview occasions. In fact that tendency is likely to be bolstered by some desire to maintain "test-retest" consistency.

More useful would be the collection of data on variables that are correlated with attitudinal stability. This would involve investigation of such matters as: the extent to which the stated attitude is congruent with normative pressures directed at the respondent from those who stand close to him in group life; the degree and kind of "functional utility" that the holding of the attitude has for the respondent's ego-defensive systems; the centrality of the attitude's location in the respondent's "attitudinal space"; the quality of openness or rigidity that characterizes his cognitive processes. Such information would help us to estimate the extent to which the expressed attitudes do or do not rest upon really stable and internalized evaluative orientations. Unfortunately, trustworthy measurement on these dimensions is not quite as readily achieved as some experimenters in the areas of social and personality psychology have suggested. Still, it is probably not excessively optimistic to look to such academically based survey organizations as the National Opinion Research Center and the Survey Research Center for the continuing development of more effective procedures for eliciting such information and for utilizing it in interpreting the meaning of opinion data on "consensual" and other policy issues.[4]

We can only take brief notice of some other useful developments, most of which have arisen in the context of basic experimental research in social psychology. The development of the concept of "social desirability" motivation and of various questionnaire devices for its measurement (for example, Crowne & Marlowe, 1960; Edwards, 1957) offers considerable promise. The person with a strong need to win approval by representing himself in ways that he thinks socially desirable has been shown more likely to yield to consensual pressure in numerous laboratory situations (Strickland & Crowne, 1962; Crowne & Liverant, 1963). The further refinement of scales assessing this variable and their employment with survey respondents as part of a preliminary battery of personality measures could be a great aid in locating those whose responses on ostensibly consensual issues ought to be closely scrutinized.

Another expedient that might readily be employed would be to expose the respondent, after his attitudinal self-characterizations have been elicited, to communications (printed on a card or played on a portable tape recorder) that are opposite to his attitude and that have already been pretested for their persuasive potency. Those respondents who then report themselves influenced might be viewed as having had less real attitudinal fixity to begin with. The proportion of such induced

"attitude change" in the sampled population might be taken as an index of the extent to which an apparently consensual attitude distribution is in fact contaminated by trends toward mere external conformity. There is, however, one immediately obvious defect in such a scheme. Yielding in the direction of the change-inducing communications might in itself be due to a need to placate demands or pressures that are perceived as coming from the interviewer, and thus for some respondents this might be just as undetectable a form of invalid self-characterization as that which it seeks to disclose.

There is yet another approach that needs to be considered. In the author's opinion it is the best grounded in recent theoretical and experimental work in the study of attitudes; and it seems to be rather directly applicable to the basic problem of determining the extent to which the reactions of individual respondents or subgroups of a sampled population reflect, or are guided by, reference to an apparent consensus of national opinion. The background for this approach is the set of consistency models already mentioned by Scott in Chapter 3 in this volume. Some aspects of these models and their implications for the conceptualization of attitudes will be discussed before we turn to their particular significance in developing a methodology to cope with the problem of invalid self-characterizations.

Despite certain important differences in focus and mode of statement, all of these models converge upon a number of basic points. The first of these concerns the very way in which they define attitudes. Conventionally, social psychologists have used the word "at-

---

[4] There appears to be a difference in the inventiveness with which typical "commercial" and "academic" survey organizations have approached methodological and interpretive issues. The latter have tended to be more regularly concerned with criticizing, revising, and enlarging their procedures.

titude" to designate an "affective set." In practice the range of possible affects toward whose arousal our attitudes might dispose us has been reduced to simple bipolar dimensions keyed to terms like "good–bad," "like–dislike," or "pro–con." However, a number of studies (Campbell, 1947; Cartwright, 1949; M. J. Rosenberg, 1956; Smith, 1949; Woodruff & DiVesta, 1948) have demonstrated that there is a close relationship between such stable dispositional habits of evaluation and the individual's percepts, beliefs, or opinions about the object being evaluated. In simplest terms, it has been shown that feelings and beliefs toward social and other objects tend to fit together in rather consistent patterns. The findings from these studies returned attention to the relevance of the earlier recommendation by Krech and Crutchfield (1948) that an attitude is best conceived as "an enduring organization of motivational, emotional, perceptual, and cognitive processes with respect to some aspect of the individual's world."

Resident in this view of attitudes is the implication that intra-attitudinal consistency will be sought after and that its disruption will generate attempts at rectification, at reestablishment of consistency. This is another item of agreement between a number of recent theories of attitude dynamics. In fact it is the major similarity between such consistency models as those of Heider (1946, 1958), Osgood and Tannenbaum (1955), Cartwright and Harary (1956), Newcomb (1953), M. J. Rosenberg (1956, 1960a), and Abelson and Rosenberg (1958). The well-known dissonance theory developed by Festinger (1957) and heavily researched by him and by Brehm and Cohen (1962) takes a somewhat more unique propositional approach, but it is still closely related to these other models in assuming a basic intolerance for inconsistency ("dissonance") between attitudinal and other cognitions, particularly cognitions about how one has *acted* toward the attitude object.

It is important to note that none of the models goes so far as to predict that *any* degree of inconsistency will be intolerable; all that is implied, as I have suggested elsewhere (Rosenberg, 1960b), is that the generation of inconsistency, if it proceeds to a magnitude that transcends an assumed intolerance threshold (whose height is a function of "person" variables, situational ones, and attitude-specific ones), will be followed by symbolic activity; and that that activity will continue until inconsistency is reduced either through restoration of the original attitude or through attitude change. Numerous experimental confirmations of this sort of prediction have been reported in the volumes by Heider (1958), Festinger (1957), Brehm and Cohen (1962), and Rosenberg, Hovland *et al.* (1960).

The immediate present import of these propositions and confirming studies is their clear suggestion that true attitudes (in the sense of relatively *stable* patterns of evaluative-cognitive response to particular objects) will show internal consistency; or at least will not be marked by gross inconsistency. It would be expected that a person who gives a valid self-characterization when, for example, he reports opposition to United Nations admission of Communist China, will also have available a set of beliefs about the consequences of Chinese admission that are more consistent with his expressed affective evaluation (and probably also more detailed in content) than the set of attitude-relevant beliefs available to a person whose reported opposition represents an invalid self-characterization. Thus, the person who reports himself as adhering to a highly consensual position but who has not internalized it or who actually has some private commitment to the opposite position, might be more easily identified if we undertook to map the content and structure of his attitude more fully than is usually done.

One way in which such mapping may be undertaken will be described here. Having given a characterization of his affective position on a given issue (say, again, admission of Communist China to the United Nations) the respondent is asked to rate a number of "values" or "goals" or "ends" for their worth or importance to him. Then he is asked to rate each of these goals for the extent to which it would be "attained or blocked" through the agency of the attitude object (for example, "To what extent would each of these goals be attained or blocked if Communist China were admitted to the United Nations?") More detailed description of this sort of procedure is given in some earlier publications (M. J. Rosenberg, 1956, 1960b; Scott, 1959).

Three replicated findings have been obtained when this form of measurement has been used. The first is that an index expressing the over-all direction and strength of the measured attitudinal cognitions is found to correlate rather closely with the direct measure of attitudinal affect (for example, a person who opposes United Nations admission of Communist China will see it as defeating desirable goals and facilitating undesirable ones; the number of such beliefs and the certainty with which they are held will tend to be in proportion with the *extremity* of his affective opposition to admission of Communist China). A second finding is that the relationship between the affective and cognitive components when estimated by this method is closer for some subjects than for

others. Most important for our present concern is yet another finding: When the same attitudes are measured again, at a later date, those subjects who showed less original affective-cognitive consistency now show greater attitude change. This will be the case both when there has been some intervening attempt to produce such change (Scott, 1959) and also when all that has intervened is the elapse of a week or two (Rosenberg, 1961).

It appears then that comparatively *stable* attitudes (*real* attitudes in the definitional sense of the concept) show greater internal consistency than *unstable* attitudes. Putting this another way it might be argued that when an evaluative judgment on some policy issue is backed by some set of justifying percepts and arguments, it will remain anchored in the face of new pressures or new counter-information. This is not to say that it cannot be altered, but merely that the effects of attempts to alter it will be slowed by the fact that the attitude is anchored. Thus, knowledge of the degree of initial affective-cognitive consistency will help to discriminate between potentially stable and unstable evaluative orientations, between those orientations that *are* in fact in use and those that tend to be merely momentary approximations or imitations of such orientations.

The technique of cognitive mapping advocated here allows us to estimate not only affective-cognitive consistency but also a number of other attributes of the intra-attitudinal structure: the richness and detail of the pattern of attitudinal cognitions; the presence or absence of some few inconsistent cognitions in contrast to a larger number of consistent ones; the singularity of, or overlap between, the meanings of these cognitive elements of the attitude. These attributes may also help to predict how stable over time and in the face of pressure toward change the attitude structure actually is.

In occasional opinion surveys (usually those undertaken by the academically based survey research groups) the respondent's self-characterization is followed by an open-ended inquiry ("Would you explain the reasons or arguments for your saying this?" or "Why do you feel this way about it?" etc.). Answers to such questions largely represent the cognitive elements of the attitude. Thus, this is extremely valuable material to have, but usually not enough is done with it. If it were even loosely analyzed for what it reveals about the internal consistency and detail of the attitude, this would help to determine just how much an apparently consensual pattern in the data should be accepted for what it appears to be. One way to render such data more readily available for analysis is to ask the respondent to rate his own spontaneously produced attitudinal cognitions for both the importance to him of the "goals" they highlight and the direction and strength of the relationships that he believes to obtain between the attitude object and those goals. In other words, it is possible to graft onto the standard form of open-ended inquiry the technique already described for mapping and quantifying the cognitive content of an attitude. A recent paper (Rosenberg and Oltman, 1962) describes this procedure in greater detail and reports a strong relationship between the separate indices of the affective and cognitive components.

The possibility of closer measurement of the cognitive component of attitudes and pseudo-attitudes does, in my view, appear to promise some gain in pursuit of the problem of differentiating them from one another. Yet it is necessary to note that even this corrective procedure might be subject to the basic problem of deflection of

response toward attitudes that are perceived as consensual, but not privately held by the respondent. It is possible that, having given a disingenuous self-characterization of his affective position, a respondent would then offer up some similarly disingenuous supporting arguments. However, this is probably less likely than might at first appear, particularly if the data are obtained in the form of the respondent's ratings of his own open-ended assertions. If privately he is either apathetic on the issue or holds a position opposite to the consensual one, he will usually not be *aware* of the best arguments, the more complex cognitive considerations, in support of the position he is overtly endorsing. Nor will he necessarily be able, or motivated, to suppress such counter-considerations as do *actually* seem to him admissible. This suggests that of the two ways of attempting measurement of the cognitive aspects of the attitude (through the standard use of "value" terms or through the respondent's ratings of his own cognitive assertions) the latter would be more likely to diminish the amount of dissimulation that gets into the data.

Starting from a particular dysfunction in the relation between policy-formulating activities and the content of public opinion data, we have examined certain methodological innovations in attitude measurement. The prospect in general appears to be fairly hopeful. Opinion surveyors can do a fair amount by way of gathering data that will help them to judge grossly skewed distributions in ways that will not lead to overestimation of the likely amount of public resistance or indignation toward policy changes. At the same time investigation of attitudes in these more detailed terms could provide much useful information to guide policy specialists in communicating to the public about the necessity for re-examination and rectification of earlier policy choices.

THE SHAPING OF ATTITUDES ON POLICY ISSUES

The need to maintain some degree of consistency within and between our attitudes is in some part a product of social learning. Its strength is affected by the degree to which the person has been rewarded for his cognitive elaborations in support of affective preferences or aversions. Thus we might expect lower thresholds of response to inconsistency from those who have been reared by articulate, highly educated parents. Similarly it is clear that in certain social settings the demand for consistency is a stronger requirement than in others.

However, beyond such individual and situational variations in the strength of this demand lies the fact that it is apparently experienced by at least all nonpsychotic persons. This, in turn, bespeaks a more basic psychological principle: that the very maintenance of the human level of behavioral complexity requires that, wherever possible, decisions be routinized and pre-patterned. Unless one held stable habits of evaluation and response toward one's wife, child and work associates, and toward traffic lights, postal regulations, calls from friends, and so on, the various other and more unexpected challenges to decision that arise, even during a normal day, could barely be acknowledged; one's adaptive efficiency would be grossly hampered and ultimately psychological self-maintenance would prove impossible.

From these considerations we would expect that man's capacity to use symbolic activity for the reduction or elimi-

nation of inner conflict (and thus his capacity for developing internally consistent and stable attitudes) will be clearly in evidence with those persons, issues, institutions, dilemmas, and needs that are regularly and frequently encountered in response-demanding contexts. Both daily observation and research data confirm this expectation.

But man's attitudinal life seems also to extend beyond such routine foci as spouse, children, job, neighborhood, and preferences for "lighter" Scotch or heavier reading. How are we to explain the fact that some care deeply, and many more care at least moderately about rather distant matters—about persons, institutions, issues, and policy choices that lie beyond the immediate scope of their own lives and thus do not seem to require direct response? How do ordinary persons, the kind who compose the publics that are the occasional objects of elitist concern, come to have attitudes favoring or opposing such things as disarmament, trade negotiations with East European nations, neutralization of Southeast Asia, atomic testing, the multilateral force, invasion of Cuba, and shelter programs?

Many people, to be sure, do *not* develop attitudes on such matters, though they may of course perceive what the prevailing and widely acceptable attitudes are and may guide their overt behavior accordingly. These are the persons most prone to the kind of invalid self-characterization on consensual issues that we have viewed as a major, and too often unsuspected, contaminant of public opinion data. Many others, particularly in those societies in which modes of mass communication have been established and have made it possible for matters of policy to be "noised abroad," do develop attitudinal investment in general issues. But often the intensity of such attitudes, the extent of their internal consistency (and thus of their over-all stability) are of smaller scope than is the case with attitudes toward objects of more immediate and direct importance.

Still, it is apparent that there are many individuals whose attitudes on issues of policy show as much intensity and internal consistency as do their attitudes in more personal realms. And certainly it is even more apparent that there is a still larger number of persons who are capable of such interest on at least certain issues, or who can, under special circumstances, be brought to that level.

For persons capable of developing and holding attitudes toward policy issues or other distant matters (be those attitudes large or small in number, broad or narrow in range, and more or less intense) we must ask: Where does such involvement come from? In what needs of the person, as these interact with what aspects of his phenomenal world, are its sources to be discovered? Part of the answer would seem to lie in the fact that, with the application of intelligence, distant matters can be perceived as affecting personal needs and welfare. Another important factor may be man's penchant for using his curiosity as a way of getting beyond the dulling constrictions of familiar routines, problems, and involvements.

Yet another part of the answer, and one that is more directly pertinent to the main concern of this chapter, has already been touched upon. It involves the desires for social acceptance, for meaningful social identity, and for the maintenance of the sense that one is engaged in true and effective social intercourse with one's fellows. All of these (and not merely the need for acceptance) are served by adherence to group "norms." The broad collectivities that are organized around commonalities of economic interest, religious affiliation, ethnic source, racial origin, re-

gional location, or social-educational level, and the face-to-face social units that compose them, have attitude-prescribing power. Their "members" are bound to one another by the real interests they share, and also by the symbolic usages that define and extend those interests. This is true for established collectivities into which the individual enters by birth or by his own seeking; and it is equally true of new collectivities (ranging from friendship cliques to social movements) in whose very development the individual may assist.

Thus it is that a Catholic coal miner named Krakowicz, who has never been out of his slag-laden Pennsylvania valley, may have strong and predictable feelings not only about mine safety, the local church, and John L. Lewis, but also about the beauty of the Polish countryside, about Wladislaw Gomulka, about Jews, and about "rolling back the Iron Curtain."

Nor are his stable affects toward such objects acquired and maintained merely by rote conditioning, in which social reward automatically follows the expression of normative judgments and social punishment is unwaveringly imposed for counter-normative judgments. Those attitudes that he and his fellows have "inherited" they have examined together; doubts have been voiced, inconsistencies noted, and even rebellion has been essayed by some. But the main consequence has been to train the participants in finding old rationales acceptable or in developing new ones to redress doubt and confusion. Those other shared attitudes that have arisen in response to new objects (such as Gomulka both before and after 1956) have developed not merely through the prescriptions, interpretations, and arguments that have been drawn for them by their priests, union officials, and local political leaders, but also, in considerable part, through argumentative discourse (one of the great and universal pleasures) among themselves.

If their final attitudinal product at some given time is quite similar to what one would find in a comparable group five valleys away, this does not signify that they have not probed, have not contributed their originality and personal force to the task of "figuring things out." It merely means that, in their struggle to remain competent in the face of distant matters that yet seem to engage the interests and symbols by which they anchor their social identity, the members of both groups have worked with the same psychological equipment. They have been guided toward the shaping of comparable normative patterns by many already established similarities: their long-standing loyalties; their routinized denotations of what "out there" is worth attention and what is not; the culturally filtered facts available to them; the culturally styled modes of argumentation and verification that they employ; the transregional, general authorities and leaders to whom they defer.

To convey that group standards and norm-formation processes govern the arousal of interest in distant issues and guide the choice of position on such issues, I have used an example of a rather isolated and homogeneous group. There are still many such intact groups, even in the major industrialized and urbanized nations, but they are statistically atypical. It is by now commonplace to characterize the United States as a nation in which social and physical mobility, and urban anonymity, tend to disrupt and reorganize social identity. This can be overstated, since urban studies show that some ethnic groups remain impressively intact across generations. At the same time it is true that many Americans,

though less than "alienated," are becoming somewhat detached from compelling group traditions. Also, many others find themselves identified with collectivities whose normative prescriptions are at variance with, or even in opposition to, one another.

However, even when they are subject to such processes, most Americans still remain located within organized group life; and for any particular area of public concern their attitudes, to the extent that they hold real attitudes, will still tend to be directly influenced by the normative standards of one or another of their reference groups. But in this sort of modern situation, those who need to maintain strong attitudinal orientations toward public issues may also become receptive to still other kinds of influences. Usually these will only play a secondary role. But occasionally such other influences may take over and preempt the importance formerly held by reference group standards. Probably this will happen only when virtually all of the individual's original and relevant reference group identifications have undergone gross decay.

A limited case in point is the aspiration on the part of many intellectuals (including those engaged in the policy process) to develop their attitudes toward Cold-War issues on a "rational" basis. Their holding of this aspiration, and perhaps also their occasional fulfillment of it, is facilitated by their sense of removal from compelling reference group involvements that would force unwavering loyalties to one or another unexamined position. (This is not to say that those who attempt to extend the "claims of reason" to the limit of their admissibility are thereby able to avoid the indirect influence upon their cognitive processes of their actual social histories or, for that matter, of their ego-defensive styles.)

A contrasting, but equally pertinent, example is found in the search for attitudinal certainty through some new kind of collective experience. This search often leads persons for whom prevailing reference group traditions have become largely inauthentic into the ranks of new social movements—movements whose leaders have developed a special rhetoric or ideology through which intense, but previously inchoate, dissatisfactions can be dramatically voiced.[5] (For a related analysis, see Chapter 5 in this volume, especially Figure 5.2.)

However, I have already suggested that in most cases the weakening of the power of social groupings to exert control over attitudes toward public issues is only partial. It is not of sufficient magnitude to leave typical individuals uninfluenced by group norms; nor is it sufficient to move them toward a seriously attempted reliance upon independent rationality or into a search for new collectivities that offer new certainties. Instead its most widespread consequence (apart from fostering indifference) has been that, on certain kinds of issues, it has afforded to many the gift (or burden) of greater freedom for idiosyncratically influenced response. Thus, as group control of attitudes grows more complex and correspondingly less potent, a second major source of such control, namely the personality of the individual, takes on greater actual significance. In consequence, the repressed hostility or conflicted passivity of a New Yorker, or of a resident of Paris or Moscow,

will play a larger role in determining his attitudes toward many of the social issues he perceives than will comparable characteristics in a Saudi Arabian tribesman, a Masai herdsman, or even a member of an Israeli Kibbutz.

An interesting implication of this point is that the study of emotional correlates of social attitudes is becoming more relevant, more capable of locating relationships of large significance, as the transformation of nations into mass societies continues. For example, the well-known studies by Adorno, Frenkel-Brunswik, *et al.* (1950) have demonstrated that ethnic hostility is, in a certain sense, "chosen" as an attitudinal orientation by those who thereby gain some discharge of repressed hostility and some relief, through projective disavowal, from the guilt associated with sensual and aggressive needs that they cannot directly acknowledge. But, as Pettigrew (1961) has suggested and as Stephen Potter might have said, "not in the South"; nor for that matter in South Africa.

When group pressures summate toward a highly normative prescription of distaste for a minority, prejudice will be less expressive of personality. However, when such normative standards weaken or when they are countered by competing standards, the individual is closer to "freedom" in choosing and elaborating his own orientation in line with his deeper values and conflicts. Thus his affective commitments on such issues as civil rights and his cognitive elaborations of them are regulated by, and are in the service of, the

---

[5] An extremely interesting analysis of the Birch Society, and of "radical right" movements generally, will be found in a recent volume edited by Bell (1963). Available data are interpreted as showing that rapid economic and social mobility have, for the typical member, engendered "status anxiety" about the sources, the acceptability, and the permanence of his rise; and that these in turn have rendered conventional middle class conservatism inadequately reassuring. It is contended that in this situation the recruit to the organized radical right finds anxiety reduction in the normative celebration of themes of indignation, of vigilance against conspiracy, and of dedicated opposition to central governmental power.

passions and mechanisms and very modes of psychic organization that lie at the core of his individuality.

In these last comments I have been delineating, if only broadly and imprecisely, the idea upon which the "functional approach" to social attitudes has been developed. That idea in its simplest form is that social attitudes can have ego-defensive significance and utility. But such functionalists as Katz, Sarnoff, and McClintock (1956) and Smith, Bruner, and White (1956) have described still other functions that attitudes may serve.

For example, it is important to note, as Katz and his colleagues have done, that attitudes are a variety of knowledge. The ambiguity of the issues that reach us from "out there"; the fact that the authoritative communicators of the mass media invest those issues with a significance so great as to suggest that human fate hangs upon them; the fact that still one does not quite know just how or why relevance is to be found in de Gaulle's intransigence, the Dalai Lama's exile, the threats of the Arab League or the Italian government's "opening to the left": all of these work to drive at least the more imaginative and responsive of men toward attitudinal involvement.

Thus the problem that I have already raised, of how distant matters of no immediate personal import become objects of attitudes, can be further clarified in terms of the very functionalist concepts that have been explicated here. Even when issues, events, and personages are *not* within the scope of the normative forces that act upon them, many men reach out toward such objects and strive to elaborate stable and consistent affective-cognitive structures around them. In doing so, they are groping toward a stilling of internal and perhaps uncomprehended psychic imperatives and at the same time to-

ward an expansion of "knowledge" that may help them to find a place to stand on the shifting terrain of "a world they never made" but in which they must live.

Returning to the problems of the policy specialist we are now in a position to make a second major recommendation. If public opinion is deemed pertinent in the determination of policy itself and in the design of policy presentations, it is not only important to know how valid and stable a "consensual" poll distribution actually is; it is of equal or greater importance to know how particular attitudes, and the complex structures into which they are integrated, are shaped through the interaction of normative prescriptions and the needs, conflicts, and adaptive mechanisms of individual personalities. For where policy innovation is deemed both necessary and politically dangerous, such knowledge could suggest ways of meeting and surmounting the dangers and thus could foster effective pursuit of the basic intent of the chosen policy.

Fully adequate studies that provide the kind of complex analysis I am recommending to the policy specialist's attention are barely available; and this is because it is both extremely difficult and expensive to carry them out. Smith, Bruner, and White (1956) conducted one such study. It took them a few years of intensive investigation with virtually every conceivable technique of measurement and interviewing to come to the point at which they felt that they clearly understood the attitudes toward the Soviet Union of ten men! The ultimate product was a fully detailed and masterful demonstration of how the social experience and personality dynamics of each of these men had shaped the complex inner content of his attitudes and how these worked in turn to express and confirm the social and psychic forces that had generated them.

Investigations of this sort, however, are not only difficult to carry out; their richness and intricacy also make them difficult to digest and the possibility of generalizing from them is thereby limited. But there is another sort of study, of which we have a number of examples, that can be of great value in tracking the policy attitudes of publics and persons to their normative and personality sources. I am referring to studies that attempt to assess the correlation between patterns of attitudinal orientation toward policy issues and the social and personality characteristics of the attitude holders. These studies have the additional value of indirectly illuminating the ways in which such normative and individual factors are activated by, and work to mediate the influence of, the presentation of policy problems and positions by the empowered elite and its competitors.

From a critical and speculative examination of some recent work of this type it may be possible to clarify still further the basic problems of how the policy and public attitude processes are related to each other and how dysfunctions in that relationship might be rectified or reduced. This sort of review and speculative analysis is attempted in the next section.

CORRELATES OF COLD-WAR ATTITUDES

Two types of studies on Cold-War attitudes are available. In one group are surveys conducted by the major poll-ing organizations. Though they usually do obtain data about certain simple demographic and social variables such as sex, age, region and educational level, it is not easy to clarify the meaning of the correlations turned up by such surveys; nor do they offer any real aid in uncovering the underlying dynamics of attitudes in the Cold-War policy area. This is so for two reasons: typically such surveys are multipurpose undertakings and they contain only a few isolated questions on some currently salient aspect of Cold-War policy; also they usually feature no correctives for the possibility that respondents will shift their answers toward the perceived consensus. However, a few national sample surveys in this area, such as one conducted by the Michigan Survey Research Center and another by the Canadian Peace Research Institute, have had much broader scope and some of their findings will be discussed here.

In the main I shall consider the findings of a second group of studies. These have been conducted with more limited, nonrandom, samples. At the same time they have attempted far more detailed measurement of patterns of attitudes on Cold-War issues and have also attempted more detailed examination of the extent and meaning of their correlation with social and personality variables.[6]

In terms of our present concern, the main value of national sample surveys is the information they give us about the apparently prevailing consensus. Taken together, they suggest that for well over a decade the majority of Americans have, when interviewed, voiced endorsement of that quasi-offi-

---

[6] In comparison to typical national surveys, these "nonrandom" studies may be less contaminated by disguised indifference masquerading as commitment. This is not only because they have usually employed more detailed attitude measurement, but also because some of these studies have concentrated on better educated samples and others have provided true anonymity to respondents by way of the use of self-administering questionnaires. Thus the fact that the

cial view of the Cold War that has been conveyed by the mass media and that has been elaborated as normative when the content of group life touches upon the great, but distant, issues of foreign policy.

As Withey (1962) has noted in reporting upon the majority opinion pattern uncovered in the detailed and comparatively intricate sample survey that he conducted for the Survey Research Center late in 1961:

Russia is seen either as simply making a power play for extended and perhaps global control or she is seen as trying to spread Communism. In "opposition" to this, the United States is seen, most broadly as trying to keep the peace (p. 7) . . . Our problems with the USSR are thus frequently seen as a black-and-white affair, especially in terms of US sincerity, rightness, and focal interest on peace (p. 11).

From this study it is also clear that the national public accepts (or at least accepted in the fall of 1961) the strategic style to which American leadership had been committed since the late 1940s:

The US is clearly exonerated of blame in the cold war though it is not clearly regarded as effective, nor are people clear on what policies would be better. . . . Aspects of policies of containment and deterrence would appear to have widespread

support as do policies weakening the Communist expansion-potential . . . (p. 19).

However, the general American public should not be judged, from these data, to be militant beyond all sense of self-interest or humanitarian concern; for, to summarize one other main finding, there was evidence of approval for "policies that provide any possibility of tension reduction without a loss of security" (p. 19).

An extensive survey conducted in Canada (see Paul and Laulicht, 1963), and certain others of more limited scope that have been carried out in Western Europe, seem to suggest that the same pattern of public opinion prevails in other nations of the Western alliance, but with certain important differences: the Soviet Union is viewed somewhat more moderately, and apprehensions about ultimately disastrous consequences of the policy of nuclear deterrence are somewhat more widespread; at the same time one notes a related interest, greater than appears in comparable data from the United States, in the negotiation of conciliatory arrangements and in the strengthening of international agencies.

In short, these studies confirm the impression that Western publics generally, and the American public even more clearly, have kept their stated policy preferences at least loosely coordinated with the policies that they have perceived their elites as pursuing.

---

samples used have not been randomly drawn from the national public is compensated by other advantages. At any rate, a few of the studies in this group *have* employed probability sampling within the locales in which they have been carried out. In general, then, though the sampling limitations of these studies should be kept in mind, this need not impose a gross inhibition upon attempts to generalize from them about the Cold-War attitudes of Americans and the correlates of those attitudes. Some evidence supporting this point is available in the pattern of findings that seems to emerge when the various more limited, but more adequately sampled, national polls on specific Cold-War issues are combined. Thus, despite their presumed distortion in the consensual direction, and especially as regards those findings that concern such simple matters as sexual, religious, and regional differences on particular issues, these poll studies are rather congruent with data obtained in the more detailed, "nonrandom" studies described in this chapter.

The general view that has already been elaborated concerning public opinion on distant issues suggests, however, that probably many of these persons are, despite their nonneutral responding in opinion interviews, rather detached, withdrawn, or even apathetic toward the main policy and strategic questions of the Cold War. It is clearly possible, therefore, that such persons are capable of being persuaded to accept, or at least tacitly to allow, policy innovation in previously undeveloped directions.

But what of those others whose knowledgeability, attitudinal consistency, and intensity all testify to their having invested many policy issues with personal, "cathected" significance? Such persons, whenever they come to perceive new policy perspectives as threatening their cherished convictions and commitments, are more prone to "fight for what they believe," to mount protests and to accept the guidance and leadership of specialists in the mobilization of public indignation.

Surely, from the standpoint of the practical interest of an elite in retaining its power, it must remain concerned with the probable reactions of individuals of this type when they become aware that policy re-examination and innovation are being undertaken. But that concern can be realistically tempered, and perhaps more effectively turned toward serving the pursuit of national and international welfare, if it is infused with knowledge about the nature of such potentially reactive publics, if it is informed by some understanding of *how* and *why* members of such publics have come to feel and think as they do on Cold-War policy issues.

The importance of this orientation becomes all the more apparent when one bears in mind that, though "consensual," the pattern of pro-Cold-War attitudes is not shown by any study to be totally uniform either' across a national random sample or in those special nonrandom populations that have been chosen for closer study. Indeed it seems likely that the tentative approach toward *détente* that began with the resolution of the Cuban missile crisis and was further implemented by the negotiation of the atmospheric test-ban treaty, has begun to influence public opinion. The general pattern of overt preference for negotiation toward tension-reduction and settlement of East–West differences that has recently been receiving partial endorsement by Western leadership, may now be fostering the emergence of a socially acceptable, anti-Cold-War orientation among sectors of the general public. It then becomes all the more desirable that factors related to a preference for one or the other general orientation be investigated and examined.

Recent empirical work in the social sciences seems to have made some contribution in this direction. Despite its limitations, this work and critical analysis of it have progressed far enough for an attempt to draw some generalizations, or at least to delineate some emerging and uncertain ones. To this end we shall now turn to a number of those studies that have endeavored, by way of comparatively complex measurement, both to determine where people stand on certain issues relevant to Cold-War policy and to relate these data to aspects of the person's social identity and his individual pattern of character organization.

Sex Differences

Perhaps the simplest among many findings, as well as one of the most commonly replicated, is that men are less prone to acknowledge apprehension over the risk of war than are women. Similarly it has been found that they are more prone to accept the strategic use of the threat of war and are more ready to credit the idea that under extreme circumstances actual recourse to war is acceptable or even desirable.

A study by Putney and Middleton (1962) suggests these, as well as many other, interesting findings. With a sample of 1200 college students, and using scales intended to measure the basic acceptability of war and also the degree of provocation deemed necessary to justify the use of nuclear weapons by the United States, they find that only about 25 percent of this sample could in any sense be described as rejecting war. But when the sex groups are compared they find clear differences. For example: 50 percent of the males view "pacifist demonstrations" as "harmful to the interests of the American people" as compared to 37 percent of the females; 33 percent of the males as compared to 16 percent of the females say that they would favor nuclear retaliation in response to nonnuclear attack by the U.S.S.R. upon one of our allies; the modal category of "acceptable" American casualties in a nuclear war is 25 to 50 percent for males and 10 to 25 percent for females.

Summarizing their data in this area Putney and Middleton comment that not only "are males far more likely to accept war, quite independently of the scale used," but also that they

. . . differ markedly in their image of war. They are more certain nuclear weapons should be used. On the other hand, they expect lighter casualties, and are more likely to believe that the United States could achieve a meaningful victory in a nuclear war. They are more confident that they personally would survive the war, and that they would want to survive it; the males are also more likely to have a knowl-

edge of nuclear weapons. In general, the males are better informed on nuclear war and more likely to accept it as a possible national policy. They are also more optimistic about its outcome in both a personal and a social sense. They seem, in short, more closely attuned to the viewpoints expressed by American leaders than are the females (p. 665).

Subsidiary findings of similar import have been reported by Berlo (1962) who, in a national sample survey with 2000 Americans, found that females worriedly viewed atomic attack as more likely than did males; by Withey (1962), who observed a similar difference in the national survey carried out by the Michigan Survey Research Center; and by Waxler (1961), who found that, among a sample of 200 middle-class Bostonians, men were more optimistic than women about the possibility of avoiding war.

In one study that I have conducted, responses to various aspects of the "Cold-War consensus" were assessed in a sample of college students from a Midwestern area in which "hard-line" militancy was a strongly normative position. In this study too, similar sex differences, though of somewhat smaller magnitude, were obtained. Illustrative findings are that only 10 percent of the males agreed that it had been "wrong for the U.S. to resume nuclear testing" whereas 24 percent of the females agreed; and 15 percent of the males, as compared to 29 percent of the females, endorsed the view that "neutralist critics are justified in fearing that we are a 'war mongering' nation."

The source and meaning of this often replicated sex difference may lie in the fact that males are usually more fully involved in the larger general society and thus are both more subject to, and more responsive to, normative pressures and agencies of ideological training. However, an even more basic factor may be responsible: namely, our culturally standardized definitions of the sex roles, and the influence of these definitions upon the actual value choices that contribute to the development and stabilization of personality. Thus there is certainly the merit of plausibility in the explanation suggested by Putney and Middleton (1962):

This difference in orientation toward war may be the result of more general differences in sex roles in American society. Many subsequent studies have supported the early findings of Terman and Miles that American males manifest ". . . greater self-assertion and aggressiveness; they express more hardihood and fearlessness, and more roughness of manners, language and sentiments. The females express themselves as more compassionate and sympathetic, more timid, more fastidious and esthetically sensitive, more emotional in general . . ." It may be that males are disposed to accept war as a part of their general "aggressiveness" and "fearlessness," and their "roughness of . . . language and sentiments" may make them more ready to acknowledge acceptance of war (p. 665).

It is worth considering the related possibility that the sex difference may be more a function of differences in how men and women feel they *should* represent and characterize themselves; beyond the influence of such stylistic preferences, a completely valid type of attitude measurement (which is probably not achieved even in such ambitious and careful studies as that of Putney and Middleton) might reveal considerably less difference between the sexes.

At any rate, the available data suggest one clear recommendation that would be of use if and when policy specialists in the Western nations, and for that matter in the Soviet world, undertake to move more rapidly toward disarmament and mutual cooperation: They will probably find greater initial receptivity from women than from men, and explanations stressing the values of greatest concern to women (but shared, in the familial context, by their husbands) may well be the ones that should be most fully developed during the initial stages of a supporting program of mass communication.[7]

Ethnic, Race, and Regional Differences

In view of the importance that the behavioral sciences attach to group life as a source of attitudes, it is surprising how little research has addressed itself to the effects of membership in certain ethnic, racial, and regional collectivities upon the individual's general response to problems of Cold-War policy. Particularly surprising is the absence of any analysis of the attitude patterns of ethnic groups whose origins are in those nations of Eastern Europe that have now been incorporated into the Soviet bloc.

From the work of Gleitman and Greenbaum (1960) we know something of the scope and severity of the anti-Communist passion of Hungarian refugees who came to the United States in the wake of the 1956 revolt. According to these investigators "the hostility often has generalized, so that even non-Hungarian issues are judged exclusively from a Hungarian, anti-Communist viewpoint" (p. 76). But what

[7] Yet another basis from which the same recommendation might be drawn lies in the fact (certainly consistent with the research data on sex-differences) that women have been far more active than men as participants in the Peace Movement. Indeed, one of the most insistent and effective of these groups has been Women for Peace.

of the established Hungarian (and for that matter Polish, Rumanian, Czech, Bulgarian, and German) communities in the United States? The support given by many of the leaders of these communities to such organizations as The Assembly of Captive Nations, the editorial content of their newspapers, the voting records of legislators with large Slavic or German blocs within their constituencies, all suggest that these groups are strongly committed to the "hard-line" goal, once articulated by Secretary Dulles but now perhaps tacitly abandoned, of "rolling back the Iron Curtain." If such an impression were confirmed by further survey studies, or by reanalysis of available data, it would be important to ask whether second and third generation members of those ethnic groups hold to such expectations and demands with an intensity equal to that of their immigrant parents and grandparents.

In general, the popular "melting pot" image has been a guiding, but unactualized, American myth. In reality, ethnic identification and community organization have persisted, even in the case of north-European groups and certainly for south-European, east-European and Asiatic ones. Perhaps it is the celebration of this very myth of a unified and uniform America that has limited inquiry into the influence of ethnic differences upon attitudes toward foreign policy and other Cold-War issues.

It is of incidental interest to note that the one ethnic group about whose Cold-War orientations we do have some information, is the Jewish one. This would seem to be due to the fact that, while ethnic identity is rarely examined as an attitude correlate in either national or local studies, religion often is. Thus the double classification of Jews as both a trans-national ethnic community and as a religious group

fosters their visibility in available studies. However, since American Jews are by no means randomly distributed across the dimensions of educational level, economic level, political preference, or regional location it is difficult to interpret the final meaning of data on their attitudes toward Cold-War issues. But whatever interpretation one might put upon it, it does seem clear that, compared to others, Jewish respondents are somewhat more rejecting of hard-line positions on various issues.

Perhaps the most impressive available evidence to this effect is in a series of studies on reactions to the efforts of the Civil Defense Agency to encourage the building of fallout shelters. In a study conducted by Barton (1963) in Bergen County, New Jersey, only 4 percent of his Jewish sample, as compared to 10 percent of the Christian sample, spontaneously mentioned building a shelter as "the best thing you yourself could do to protect yourself and your family from the danger of war." On the other hand, 40 percent of the Jewish portion of the sample spontaneously mentioned some form of political action ("trying to elect people who will avoid war," "joining peace groups," "working for peace," and so on) as compared to only 6 percent of the Catholics and 17 percent of the Protestants. Similarly, the Jewish respondents more frequently endorsed the desirability of negotiations with the Soviet Union (78 percent) when compared with the Catholics (60 percent) and the Protestants (57 percent).

Ekman (1963), in a study comparing a shelter-oriented organization and a competing anti-shelter, peace group in the San Francisco area, found that no Jews belonged to the former group while one fourth of the membership of the latter group were Jews. Similarly, Rose (1963), in a survey conducted in Northampton, Massachusetts, found that his Jewish respondents were more prone to reject the idea of building fallout shelters than either Catholics or Protestants.

While of considerable interest, these data might be viewed as only highlighting further the desirability of gathering (or drawing from available data files) information about ethnic identity as a correlate of orientation toward Cold-War issues.

Regional differences, in contrast to ethnic ones, have received occasional attention in a few detailed studies of Cold-War attitudes. Until recently general political surveys (and voting statistics) have shown the American Midwest, particularly its heavily agricultural sections, to be the "national stronghold of conservatism" (though lately the mountain states of the West have seemed on the verge of claiming the title). When one turns to the few available studies that attempt to compare Cold-War attitudes in different regions of the country a parallel pattern is noted.

Thus, in the data collected by Putney and Middleton (1962) from college groups in the four main national regions, the far-Western respondents are lower on "acceptance of war" on all three of the scale measures that were employed. Their difference from the rest of the sample is significant at the .05 probability level. The Midwestern students are clearly highest in "acceptance of war" while the Northeastern and Southern samples occupy an intermediate position.

In my own studies on attitudes toward issues that serve to differentiate the general "hard-line" orientation from the "conciliation" orientation I have tested attitudes of this sort with samples from four different educational institutions and also in one community survey. Most relevant to the question of regional differences are the data

from 136 male undergraduates at Dartmouth College and 121 male undergraduates at Ohio State University. The former group are predominantly from the Northeastern states, though some 32 percent are from other regions of the country. Only 5 percent of the Ohio State sample are from outside the Midwest while about 85 percent are from Ohio and the remaining 10 percent are from other Midwestern states. (Social class is a possible contaminating factor, there being in the Ohio group a larger number of students whose fathers are in working-class occupations; however, within the Ohio group there are no general Cold-War attitude differences between the two broad social classes.)

Despite the limits of this kind of non-random sampling, I have been impressed by the fact that on ten of the twelve issues tested, statistically significant differences were obtained. All of these were at the .05 level or better, and all indicated that the Ohio group deviates less than the Dartmouth group from the hard-line pattern that at the time of testing (in the spring and fall of 1963) was still the dominantly consensual one on a national basis. Some examples of these differences, given in terms of the percentages disagreeing with the prevailing hard-line position, are the following: While 28 percent of the Dartmouth group agreed that "it was wrong for the U.S. to resume nuclear testing" only 10 percent of the Ohio students agreed; the statement that "the American way of life is better than any other in this history of the human race" was rejected by 30 percent of the Dartmouth group and only 15 percent of the Ohio group; 54 percent of the Dartmouth group, compared to 26 percent of the Ohio group, agreed that Americans should "put aside their hostility and distrust toward the Soviet Union and begin to appreciate some of the good points about that country"; 49 percent of the Dartmouth group and 33 percent of the Ohio group rejected the view that "the U.S. was completely within its political and moral rights when it supported and helped to organize the invasion of Cuba"; 46 percent of the Dartmouth group rejected the view that "we would be foolish ever to trust the Communist powers," while the comparable figure for the Ohio group was 27 percent.

The reasons for the apparently greater popularity of hard-line views in the Midwest are by no means clearly understood, though many speculative interpretations have been advanced. Probably all of the following factors have played some role: the comparatively high proportions in that region of persons of Slavic and German background; its lingering, populist-like, anti-Eastern orientation; the role of fundamentalist religion (see the next section); and perhaps even a tendency to view war as less unacceptable when one is about a thousand miles from either coast. But wherever the full historical and functional explanations may lie, it should be remembered that such regional traditions, once established, do tend to maintain and reinforce themselves; that is, they have considerable normative power over individuals.[8]

One other group factor that may exert influence upon how Americans respond to Cold-War issues is that of race. We have entered an era of national life in which the single most salient fact is that over one tenth of all Americans are becoming militantly enraged by the disadvantages they suffer as Negroes. Are they on this basis tending, as some Negro leaders have suggested they will, toward increasing detachment from nationally normative attitudes? Or are they, in their hunger for real membership in America, "overconforming" to those norms? Or might they not, because of their increasingly ramified awareness of the complexity of their present struggle, tend to lack any real interest in questions of Cold-War policy and prospects?

Again it is rather surprising that virtually no data from which an answer might be drawn are available. Berlo (1962) has reported what appears to be just about the only finding in this area: better than one half of the Negroes in his national sample thought it likely that the United States would suffer nuclear attack, as compared to less than one third of the white portion of his sample.

What can be drawn from the foregoing discussion that might be pertinent for those specialists whose role, or private inclination, it is to worry about public response to the alteration of policy perspectives? One important point is that there are many congressional districts in which the balance (sometimes even the majority) of electoral power is held by some particular ethnic group. Representatives from such districts are usually attuned to the interests of such groups, whether or not they themselves belong to them. By serving those interests they often become long-term members of Congress and in turn often rise to prominent seniority. Their apprehensions about "back-home" response to certain kinds of policy change (such as in-

---

[8] In the Midwest a major agency in the mediation of that normative power may be the local and regional news media. It is my impression, though I do not know of any confirming studies, that the newspapers of that region are more uniformly and compulsively hard-line in their treatment of Cold-War issues, and particularly in their celebration of anti-Communist militancy, than those that are published on the East or West Coasts.

creased trade or cultural contact with some Balkan nation) may, therefore, lead them to directing their power against these changes. If more data on the actual opinions of such ethnic groups were available they might be used to decrease such apprehensions on the part of legislators or else to guide the design of more effective explanatory communications to their aroused constituents.

Studies probing more thoroughly, and more deeply, into the opinion patterns characteristic of the populations of major geographic regions would have similar value. For example, at present "radical right" organizations of the sort that consistently oppose any progress toward international conciliation are well organized and highly vocal in certain Western states. Their efforts in stimulating letter-writing campaigns and petitions and other forms of pressure are intended to convey to senators, congressmen, and to others who must also reckon with the dangers of electoral recall, that a hardline consensus is prevalent and must be obeyed. Again data, particularly the kind that presume to get beyond the elicitation of a few routine answers to routine questions, will be of use in helping to assess and resist the claims and threats of those political "indignants" whose aspiration it is to fix American policy in a permanent com-

mitment to "winning," rather than resolving, the Cold War.[9]

The small amount of data on Midwestern attitudes (if confirmed in further investigations) also suggests that in that region campaigns of explanation and justification will be particularly required if American policy moves toward guarded resolution and settlement of outstanding issues between it and the Soviet Union.

Religious Differences

Somewhat more information is available on religious differences than on other group-membership characteristics. A number of studies do seem to establish that differences in religion are related to differences in stated orientation on such issues as how to deal with the Communist nations, the acceptability of war as a policy alternative, or the desirability of civil defense programs.

Data from the studies by Barton (1963), Rose (1963), and Ekman (1963) showing that, in general, Jews were somewhat more resistant than Protestants and Catholics to civil defense programs and correspondingly were more oriented toward "political action for peace," have already been mentioned.

In the Northampton data reported by Rose another religious difference stands out. The Catholic respondents

---

[9] As the final draft of this chapter was being checked, the Republican Convention of 1964 had just been completed. Its choice of a hard-line candidate, its endorsement of a strongly anticonciliatory platform, and the new dominance of extreme rightists in the party, all promised a considerable increase in the force with which Cold-War militancy would be publicly advocated and supported. Though it seemed likely that the Democratic candidate would be returned to the Presidency, the question remains whether the opposition's vigorous avowal of the hard line will have a persisting effect in increasing the anticonciliatory pressures that will be brought to bear upon the government in the next few years. In part this will probably depend upon the actual size of the Republican vote; in part it will depend upon how much propagandistic skill is used to coordinate hard-line claims with the ethnic and regional factors already discussed, and with other factors treated below. At any rate, for a while at least, the need will be all the greater for policy-makers to be able to distinguish the extent to which assent to the hard line by some portion of the public is something less than a deeply anchored commitment, and is capable of alteration through the use of appropriate counterarguments and appeals.

are clearly more pro-shelter than the Protestant ones. Thirty percent of the former group and only 17 percent of the latter say that they "would build" shelters. Still more impressive is the fact that 52 percent of the Protestants are clearly opposed to the idea of providing shelters for themselves but only 29 percent of the Catholics are in the same category. Inevitably the religious data, in most studies using local samples, are confounded with the ethnic factor. Thus, the Catholics of the Northampton area are virtually all Irish, French Canadian, and Polish in background and the latter two groups are considerably overrepresented compared to their proportions in the national population of Catholics.

However, Barton in his study (1963) conducted in Bergen County, where the percentage of French Canadian and Polish residents is clearly lower, reports rather similar findings. Only 5 percent of his Catholic respondents spontaneously mention "political action for peace" as an expedient available to them, as compared to 17 percent among the Protestants and 40 percent among the Jews. Of considerable interest is the interaction between the factors of Catholicism and educational level. For example, the proportion of Protestants who "favor negotiation" (as one among a number of responses to the danger of war) remains constant across educational levels, varying between 55 to 58 percent; but among the Catholics about 70 percent of those who did not get beyond high school "favor negotiation" as compared to only 41 percent of those who attended college. On a number of other issues the college-educated Catholics are the group highest in the total sample in the expression of hardline attitudes.

Though this may be a phenomenon that is due to undetected local factors,

it seems consistent with certain general observations. The college-educated American Catholic is usually a person who has experienced comparatively rapid social mobility. As various writers have suggested (see Bell, 1963), status anxieties associated with movement into middle class life, particularly in those who come from minority groups that perceive themselves as having suffered some social rejection, tend to dispose individuals to "super-Americanism"; that is, they come to seek ways of identifying themselves with what they take to be the national ideology and the patriotic cause of its vigilant defense. This, combined with the kind of strong anti-Communist indoctrination that has been fostered in most Catholic colleges, may well dispose college-educated Catholics to an insistent identification with the militant implications of what has been the consensual orientation toward Cold-War issues.

Recognizing that many religionists are only nominally so, that their describing themselves as Catholic, Methodist, Presbyterian, or Jewish is not a trustworthy index of the extent and content of their religious involvement, some investigators have tried to assess the degree of religiosity, regardless of denomination. Such indices have also been found to predict some of the variance in orientation toward Cold-War issues.

It might well be expected that the direction of such a relationship would be for the most religious to be most pacific; it might be assumed that their ostensibly deep commitment to the Judeo-Christian ethic would dispose them to reject war as an instrument of policy, heavy armament as a strategic approach, and fallout shelters as a measure of survival, while it would also lead them to endorse efforts toward negotiation and conciliation of international tensions. The available data make it rather clear that such predictions are opposite to reality.

Evidence on this matter was gathered in the Canadian survey first reported by Paul and Laulicht (1963). In a recent and more complex analysis of these data (Laulicht & Paul, in press), all respondents were classified on a "religious dogmatism" scale which ranged from "agnostics on one end to fundamentalist Protestants and Catholics at the other end." Jews and "moderate Protestants," such as Anglicans and members of the United Church, were classified in between these extremes "according to their degree of participation in their churches."

One might want to question the apparent fact that a participation index was used in determining where Jews and "moderate Protestants," but not fundamentalists or Catholics, were to be assigned on the scale of religious dogmatism. Nevertheless, the main finding with this measure was that

. . . religious dogmatism is associated [significantly] with an acceptance of bigger military forces, being favorable to (or at least not being afraid of) the spread of nuclear weapons, and being distrustful of, if not actually hostile to, a co-existence policy. . . . The striking fact is that there is no indication that people who are high on religious dogmatism are more in favor of disarmament than agnostics and nominal church members. In fact the reverse is true, in varying but significant degrees for business and labor leaders, for contributors [to the Canadian Peace Research Institute], for the total national sample and the informed subsample.

The authors also report that those who consider themselves "good Christians" have a lower sense of "personal responsibility" (for "being active in efforts to prevent war") than those who, because they are agnostics or nonparticipating church members, consider themselves "poor Christians."

Additional evidence substantiating these Canadian data is available from the study by Rose (1963) that has already been described. For his 437 respondents in the Northampton area he computed an index of "religiosity," based upon a series of questions about the respondents' belief in God, their church attendance, and how religious they considered themselves to be. Of those classified as highest in religiosity 32 percent saw the possibility of war as "very great" or "great," as compared to 11 percent of those low on religiosity. Another related finding concerns the proportions of respondents agreeing with the statement that "Communism is an evil in the world; it must be stamped out." Of those high on religiosity 62 percent agreed with this statement, as compared to 26 percent of those low on religiosity. Similarly, the less religious the individual reported himself to be the more likely he was "to hold that Communism is simply a different system which should not be condemned (27 percent of those lowest in religiosity, 8 percent of those highest)" (p. 33). Moreover, among the high religiosity respondents 7 percent (as compared with 2 percent in the low religiosity group) reported that they had built or planned to build fallout shelters; 29 percent (compared with 6 percent in the low group) agreed they "would build a shelter if I could afford it."

In my own studies on Cold-War attitudes, mentioned above, it was also possible to check this factor. In these studies a version of Nettler's (1957) scale of "alienation" was administered. This included three questions that reflect the same constellation that Rose has designated by the term "religiosity." These questions asked the person to indicate the extent to which he "liked to participate in church activities"; believed that "religion is either mostly myth or mostly true"; and believed that "human life is either an expression of divine purpose or is only the result of chance and evolution."

In all of the college and community groups that were investigated, the relation between total score on the Cold-War Consensus Scale and each of the three respective religiosity items was highly significant. Thus, persons who report themselves as enjoying church participation, as thinking religion "mostly true" and life "an expression of divine purpose" (these items are, of course, strongly intercorrelated) are considerably higher than those who show low religious interest or conviction, in their acceptance of the various hard-line attitude positions that were presented for their evaluation.

The data that have been summarized here suggest many possible explanations, all of considerable interest and all generating equal frustration because they cannot be further tested through presently available data.

The most immediately apparent possibility is simply that the campaign against "Godless Communism" has indeed been waged from many pulpits for over a decade. Thus many devoted churchgoers have been exposed to exhortations of a sort that might have made the Cold War seem more desirable, perhaps even more inevitable.

Furthermore, in Protestant fundamentalism, chiliastic themes persist, and an eschatology that predicts an imminent "second coming," and the approaching cataclysmic "end of historical time," is often the doctrinal base of certain major sects and denominations. Such views explain the Cold War more dramatically, and perhaps less ambiguously, than any others that are available; and in a sense they *justify* and *legitimate* it. Training and belief

in such doctrines may readily dispose individuals to a fuller, perhaps even to a less anxious, acceptance of the hard-line view. On the other hand, Catholic theology does not pursue as simple a course as that found in some forms of Protestantism; nor, for that matter, are devout Catholics given as much exposure to theology. If they find the hard-line orientation more acceptable this may simply be due to the anti-Communist militancy that their church stood for during the post-war years under Pius XII. Assuming this to be correct we might well expect that the Church's shift toward an endorsement of coexistence, as marked by Pope John's encyclical *Pacem in terris,* may soon be reflected in changes in the stated views of typical lay Catholics; though certainly this will depend upon the extent to which Catholic periodicals and clergy undertake to communicate and support this alteration in Vatican policy.

Beyond such explanations lie the possible influence of various other factors that are correlated with religiosity or with membership in either the Catholic church or in fundamentalist Protestant groups. Thus it might be asked whether the ethnic factor (for example, the anti-Soviet interests of American Slavic and South German groups; the American Irish community's history, on the basis of its anglophobia and other subtler factors, of entrapment in indignant but inconsistent rightism) may not account for the available findings on Catholics. As for the fundamentalists, they are in large part drawn from lower educational levels and probably are markedly less informed on the very facts that define modern international problems; on this basis they might be much less capable of resisting the kinds of mass communication that have for so many years urged Americans toward acceptance of the hard-line view.

Yet another possibility is that both religiosity and submission to the authoritarian claims of fundamentalism or Catholicism may be fostered by authoritarian trends in individual character. As we shall shortly see, there is considerable evidence suggesting that such character patterns are *strongly* correlated with acceptance of severe versions of the Cold-War orientation.

Finally, one other interpretation comes to mind. We know now from the work of Asch (1956), Edwards (1957), Crowne and Marlowe (1960), Couch and Keniston (1961), and others that some persons show a rather consistent and pervasive need to win approval by conforming to perceived social demands and expectations. In an earlier section of this chapter I have already argued that such proclivities may often foster systematic deflection of opinion statement toward what is perceived as the consensual view on matters of Cold-War policy. Might not persons prone to this kind of approval-seeking be just as likely to report themselves as religious in excess of their actual private convictions? This in itself might account for the findings on religiosity, though it would have less pertinence for explaining actual denominational differences in Cold-War orientation.

It should be clear by now that the kinds of data we are examining in this chapter are by nature incapable of unequivocal interpretation. To the distressing fact that respondents do not always "report themselves aright" must be added the fact that, even when they do, many of the things they report about their attitudes and about their social identities and personalities are linked in patterns of covariation and determination that we cannot readily disentangle. Thus, causal explanation

remains beyond our firm grasp unless we turn to other kinds of investigative approaches. The major value of questionnaire and interview studies such as are being examined here lies in their orienting the investigator and theorist to a range of possible interpretations of "overdetermined" phenomena. More intricate methods of data treatment such as factor analysis, analysis of variance, or partial and multiple correlation are of considerable use in further deciphering the meaning of such phenomena. But ultimately the best way to uncover the causal patterns that lie behind attitudinal orientations (on Cold-War issues or any other kinds of social issues) is through detailed longitudinal, developmental studies in which the shaping of those orientations is observed as it occurs.

However, these strictures do not diminish the interest and hypothesis-generating value of the available research studies on correlates of Cold-War attitudes. Returning to our consideration of the religious factor we may ask, as we have done earlier, whether there are any useful recommendations that might be offered to the policy specialist. The church as an institution would seem, not only from the data reviewed here but also from its recent history, to be capable of considerable influence over its members. The risks of policy innovation in seemingly anticonsensual directions might well be reduced if this fact were kept in mind. Appeal to some of the values urged by religious institutions will often be possible if the policies requiring explanation are ones that are directed toward "peace on earth and good will toward men." Furthermore, clergymen seem to compose an opinion-leader public and it would be useful, therefore, to consider ways of fostering increased sophistication on policy issues among them. Many possibilities along these lines are conceivable, including efforts to expand the curricula of divinity schools so that they will encompass policy concerns. Another possibility is closer contact, on the part of policy specialists, with the church press and with the social affairs departments maintained by most of the liberal denominations.

Perhaps too it will become more apparent that branding our international competitors as "Godless" is not only somewhat disingenuous (since, despite the boom in our public religiosity, our culture too has become extremely secularized) but is also dysfunctional: for probably the celebration of this propaganda theme has worked to bind many conservative churchmen and their congregations to a vision of an inflexible anti-Soviet crusade. If, as now seems to be the case, Western policy-makers are coming to believe that that crusade ought to be transformed into a *quest* for a workable pattern of guarded coexistence in which international competition may be pursued without blundering into war, then the reduction of religious themes in propaganda may contribute to restoring the kind of opinion climate that will facilitate that quest.

Differences in Social Class and Educational Level

Students of American political life have often tested the quasi-Marxian prediction that the working class will be more "revolutionary" (or at least more liberal) than the middle class; and that prediction has in the main been found to be mistaken (see Lipset, 1960). Despite the fact that comparatively low income is associated with self-reported and electoral preference for the Democratic party, American workers, except on occasional "bread and butter" issues, have seemed to some observers to be more nationalistic and sometimes even more conservative than those in the more advantaged socio-economic strata. In studies of Cold-War attitudes a similar relationship to social class might be discerned, though the evidence for it is far weaker than for some of the other variables that we have already examined.

From Barton's data (1963) we learn that in the Bergen County sample, among those who did not graduate from high school only 3 percent (as compared to 27 percent among the college educated) mention personal political action as a solution to the threat of war. The relationship remains substantially the same when only the Protestant portion of the sample is examined. On the other hand, Barton finds little difference between social class groups, as indexed by educational level, in the proportions favoring "negotiation" or "strength" in our relations with the Soviet Union.

On the basis of the Northampton data, Rose (1963) reports that on the fallout shelter question the "would build" and "won't build" proportions are 30 and 27 percent respectively for those who did not complete high school, and 17 and 50 percent respectively for those who attended college. A finding of similar scope and direction is obtained when annual family income is used as an index of social class.

In contrast, Modigliani (1963) has reported a study with a sample of 121 residents of Watertown, Massachusetts, in which the percentages "favoring more conciliatory policies" are higher at low educational levels than among the college-educated. One suspects that this college-educated group has a large Irish Catholic component and thus that we have here another instance of the relationship that Barton noted with his New Jersey sample.

My own research on acceptance and partial rejection of the Cold-War consensus has permitted an analysis in terms of social class for some 500 undergraduates tested at Ohio State University. Controlling for sex, there is no difference on the Cold-War Consensus Scale between students of working-class background and those of middle-class background, as classified on the basis of their fathers' occupations. However, *within* the middle-class group certain differences do appear. After controlling for religion and "authoritarianism," we find that among the Protestant males who are in the higher half of the F Scale distribution (see below), those whose fathers are in business occupations are significantly ($p < .06$) more accepting of the general hard-line approach than those whose fathers are professionals. In the comparable female group there is a somewhat weaker trend ($p < .09$) in the same direction.

Laulicht and Paul (in press) report that they find no major social-class differences in stated attitudes on the wide range of Cold-War issues investigated in their Canadian survey. Similarly, Putney and Middleton (1962) report that "social class, estimated on the basis of father's occupation, shows no marked or consistent relationship to acceptance of war." However, they suggest that the class factor cannot be properly investigated with college students since they are comparatively "homogeneous with regard to social class—if not in social class background, then in social class reference group" (p. 661).

Compared to the data on sex and religion and the clues bearing upon the inadequately investigated ethnic factor, the social class variable seems to be less clearly and less strongly related to attitudes on Cold-War issues. Furthermore, where such relationships are ob-

served, there is sometimes evidence that they may be expressive of other, more direct, relationships between Cold-War orientation and some general or local *correlates* of social class level.

One is forced to the tentative conclusion that the groupings in terms of income, educational level, and type of employment, by which the class concept is indexed, do not provide the relevant reference standards to which individuals look for normative guidance on Cold-War problems. It may well be that on issues involving the uses of nuclear threat, civil defense programs, conciliatory negotiation, and so forth, persons within both the working- and middle-class groups are guided much less by a sense of shared economic interest than by their diverse religious and ethnic memberships, by sex-based patterns of valuing, and by still other determinants that are located closer to the core of individual character structure.

This is not to deny, however, that a narrower kind of economic subclass variable may influence Cold-War orientation. For example, it may be that the suggestion in the Ohio State data of greater hard-line militancy in the business, as opposed to the professional sector of the middle class, is a function of a near-normative conviction that the business community will prosper only if the international successes of Communism are checked and ultimately reversed. Nor can it be denied that class-based ideology may well exert a far larger control over attitudes toward numerous domestic issues whose connection to matters of foreign policy is not usually clear to typical Americans.

One further point should be noted in regard to social class. Many opinion surveys have made clear that the working class is in the main less informed than the middle class, not only on the details of a wide range of public issues, but also as regards the meaning or even the occurrence of significant events, and the very identity of issue-relevant personages and institutions. The consequences of such ignorance for the issue positions one might take have not been fully investigated. But it has often been speculated that lack of sophistication in any policy area will dispose an individual either to easy manipulability or, conversely, to an unyielding rigidity by which he defends himself against acknowledgment of his general disorientation. However, the extent and content of a person's information on public issues is closely correlated with many other factors that are related to social class and educational level; and this makes it particularly difficult to interpret available data for what they might reveal about the influence of higher and lower levels of relevant information upon the shaping of Cold-War attitudes.[10]

Turning again to the question of how to give an effective public account of policy revisions and innovations, we may draw at least one recommendation from our discussion of the social class variable. If, on the basis of available studies, Americans appear not to be deeply concerned about the relations between their economic interests and the pattern of future East–West relationships, this may be because research defines classes too broadly and in-

clusively. However, the possibility that a portion of the middle class, namely the business sector, may perceive its welfare to depend upon the continuation of the Cold War is paralleled by the hard-line urgings that have often come from particular managerial and labor groups. In part such anticonciliatory advocacy is due, as is often honestly acknowledged, to concern about the injurious economic consequences that are expected to follow from arms cutbacks and disarmament agreements. If the presently discernible policy shift toward a search for settlement and tension reduction is to be effectively pursued, it would be advisable to take steps to clarify the likelihood that the ultimate economic effects of disarmament would actually be beneficial. Increased governmental commitment, both to the detailed study of the conversion problem and to the dissemination of the resultant findings, may then be of considerable value; for the perception that economic welfare may be advanced by proposed policy changes will certainly make for fuller public consideration of the other possible consequences of those changes.

Differences in Political Party and Ideology

A close examination of recent studies on Cold-War attitudes reveals only a few differences between Demo-

---

[10] From a few of the studies conducted with middle-class college students, at least one interpretation does seem possible. Since the mass media have in the main presented information on Cold-War matters in a context of support for hard-line policies, those individuals who are better informed, in the limited sense of knowing more about arms technology or about the external events associated with particular international crises, may also show more support for hard-line positions. Yet, as Putney and Middleton (1962) have shown in a separate experimental study, exposing people to information that is presented in a pro-conciliation context increases both their knowledge of Cold-War-related facts and their acceptance of the conciliatory orientation. Thus it appears that on Cold-War matters, as on other public issues, the typical person is capable of being considerably influenced, both in his knowledge and his views, by mass media content. A further implication is that it would be possible to achieve some reduction in the extent of public demand for hard-line policies if the scope of the "information" conveyed by the mass media were to be broadened.

crats and Republicans and these are of a rather limited and unimpressive order. Rose (1963) reports that the self-identified Republicans in his sample are more opposed than the Democrats to providing themselves with fallout shelters. But this may well be a reflection of the comparatively pro-shelter attitudes of the Catholic and low-education portions of his sample.

Archibald, Ekman, and Stone (1963) report a questionnaire study, carried out in the San Francisco area, with members of the county and state central committees of the Democratic and Republican parties. Conducted shortly after the Cuban missile crisis, the study dealt largely with evaluations of the Kennedy administration's handling of that crisis. It is a matter of no great surprise that the degree of satisfaction with the administration's performance and with its continuing policy toward Cuba as it appeared at that time, was largely a matter of whether one was a Democratic or Republican spokesman.

In studies in which political preference between the two major parties has been related to the general predilection toward hard-line or conciliatory approaches, however, the results have been much more inconclusive. In the college samples that I have investigated, the respondents' party preferences were usually unrelated to their scores on the Cold-War Consensus Scale. Incidental findings from a few other studies are of similar import.

This paucity of party-based differences can in part be accounted for by the prevalence—until recently, and despite inevitable cross-party attacks —of a gross interparty consensus on Cold-War policy (largely a shared commitment to containment, deterrence, peripheral "brush fire wars," and "negotiation from strength"). Thus, merely being a Democrat or Republican has not provided individuals with distinctive orientations toward Cold-War issues.

Still, it might be expected that, because the Democratic and Republican parties are groupings of "liberals" and "conservatives" respectively, persons identified with the former party would be prone to a more conciliatory orientation than those identified with the latter. However, it becomes constantly more clear that the liberal–conservative difference between the parties at the present time is far from a simple matter. Both parties contain "left" and "right" elements so that, for example, the liberal segment within Congress includes many Republicans and the conservative one many Democrats.

Studies by McClosky (1958) seem to confirm that the stated political preferences of individuals have less to do with their basic conservatism or liberalism than with other matters. McClosky developed a Conservatism Scale with items reflecting the kinds of social and political beliefs traditionally stressed by philosophical and other ideologists of conservatism. The items are all highly intercorrelated, they are correctly identified by judges as "conservative," and scores on this scale correlate well with various other scales —yet this scale does not predict the party preferences or voting choices of individuals.

At present, then, the two major American political parties are, as many political scientists have argued, loose confederations; and people join or identify with one or the other of them largely because of normative influences based on religious, ethnic, social class, and regional group traditions. That they are usually able to persuade themselves that their liberal or conservative views are represented by the chosen party is no great feat of self-deception; there are spokesmen enough for both value approaches, and enough party leaders who specialize in synthesizing or avoiding ideological dilemmas, for any man to reassure himself that he is in the party to which he truly belongs.

This may well be an unstable pattern. At the time of writing, the ascendance of extreme conservatives to control of the Republican power structure seems to have been consolidated. If this control is maintained, a long-range consequence could be the political regrouping that some observers think necessary.

A clear derivation from the foregoing discussion is that political ideology correlates of orientations toward Cold-War issues may be found more readily by comparing self-avowed liberals and conservatives of either party preference.

I have already noted that analysis of the college samples in my own studies showed no clear relation between the Cold-War Consensus Scale and self-designation as a Democrat or Republican. However, the actual alternatives between which respondents chose in describing themselves politically were: liberal Democrat, conservative Democrat, liberal Republican, conservative Republican, other. With each of the samples, combining "liberal Democrats" and "liberal Republicans" into one group and "conservative Democrats" and "conservative Republicans" into another yields significant differences in the degree to which most hard-line items are accepted or rejected. In all these comparisons the self-designated liberals are more questioning and rejecting of the Cold-War consensus.

Chesler and Schmuck (1964), in a study conducted during the Cuban crisis of 1962, assessed the attitudes of 69 University of Michigan students toward the administration's general policy, toward the imposition of a naval quarantine around Cuba, and toward a local demonstration protesting the quarantine and a second demonstration protesting the first one. A number of scales "measuring several dimensions of personality and socio-political orientations" were also administered, including the Politico-Economic Conservatism Scale (Form 60) developed by Adorno et al. (1950). For our present purposes, the most relevant finding was the positive and significant relationship between high general conservatism scores and the view that the United States should have invaded Cuba "long ago" or that "we and OAS should invade now"; low conservatism scores were related to the view that the blockade should be dropped and the problem turned over to the United Nations, or that the United States should strive to establish friendly relations with Cuba.

Also, significant correlations were obtained between the Conservatism Scale and two other scales: a scale designed to measure attitudes toward disarmament ($r = .25$, $p < .05$); and the Patriotism Scale developed by Adorno et al. ($r = .42$, $p < .05$). While the Conservatism Scale did not predict significantly to an attitude measure testing intolerance for open dissent by "people who disagree with public policy," the Patriotism Scale did.

Additional evidence that general political conservatism is related to the hard-line attitude pattern is available in the data collected by Putney and Middleton (1962). On all three of their major Guttman-type scales assessing aspects of the Cold-War orientation they find differences between "highly liberal" and "highly conservative" respondents. (These latter designations appear to have been based upon self-characterizations by the respondents.) The conservatives are significantly more accepting of war as an instrument of policy, and favor nuclear retaliation at lower levels of provocation than do the liberals.

In the Laulicht and Paul (in press) Canadian study a finding consistent with those that have been reviewed here is that "fear of socialism" and of "government expansion" (which it would seem reasonable to take as representative of conservative ideology) are "important and key variables in predicting cold war attitudes."

Certainly, then, the liberalism–conservatism dimension is more closely related to variations in Cold-War attitudes than is the mere designation of persons as Democrats or Republicans. But in what does the source of the relationship lie? It may be a simple and direct derivative from conservative ideological insistence upon the sanctity of private property and of entrepreneurial capitalism and individual political freedom. Conservatives are certainly correct in seeing Communism as antithetical to those institutions, even if they are often undiscriminating in viewing the liberal, mixed-economy systems of some of our Western allies as posing similar threats.

McClosky (1958) suggests another possibility when he interprets his detailed data as showing that conservatism is often associated with certain other nonpolitical, psychological qualities; for example, with aggressiveness and cognitive rigidity. This could dispose the individual to a fuller acceptance of the hard-line pattern, for in the light of such personality attributes that pattern might be more "functional," that is, more personally rewarding, for the conservative person.

In sketching this possibility one is aware of the questionable penchant of liberal social scientists for that special form of the genetic fallacy in which one discredits disfavored political attitudes by somehow reducing them to the status of ego-defenses or worse.

Yet, the functionalist theoretical perspective does argue persuasively that many of our attitudes are "expressive" of deeper modes of psychological orientation; and that the acquisition of still other attitudes has been facilitated because their avowal helps to discharge repressed impulses or to impose order upon chaotic inner conflicts. It is not likely that there is a conservative personality; but there may be certain separate personality bases (though hardly "causes") for conservatism, as there may be others for liberalism. More cautiously, it might at least be reasoned that the choice between competing perspectives on Cold-War issues is influenced not only by the kinds of determinants so far reviewed but by personality factors as well. It is to some investigations concerning this possibility that we shall turn in the next section.

But first let us ask whether there are any advisory implications in the foregoing discussion of political correlates of Cold-War attitudes. The fact that conservatism seems to be so strongly related to attitudes favoring the maintenance of Cold-War militancy is congruent with the role that the organized far right has achieved for itself in the policy process in recent years. That role has been one of a highly vocal, activist minority that has exerted pressure at crucial points on what it has taken to be crucial issues.

The resulting apprehensions aroused in legislators, party leaders, and members of the executive branch of government have often been sufficient to force modification or withdrawal of particular policy initiatives (as in our attempts to render aid to some of the Balkan nations and thus "detach" them from their full dependence upon the Soviet Union). These apprehensions have also caused a general muting of the concern for achieving a more stable international settlement through which national interests might thus be more safely pursued. Indeed, the predictability of rightist protest and attempts at mobilizing indignation has had the general effect of increasing the disingenuousness of governmental discussions on matters of basic policy; and where clarity is sacrificed efficacy will inevitably be reduced.

In the face of this situation two things might well be recognized. One is that some of the basic values shown by research to be implicit in conservative criticism of foreign policy are not fully shared by many members of the public who are ordinarily influenced by such criticism. More effective and direct argument over the aggressive and xenophobic implications of that criticism will probably help to reduce its influence. The second point is simply that "honesty is the best policy" in the advocacy and examination of foreign policy. Direct confrontation of the difference in the kinds of worlds actually envisioned by the liberal and conservative mentalities may do a great deal toward clearing the air in policy areas. Cutting down the haze generated by the smoke-screen defenses that recent administrations have used to cover their retreats from rightist criticism can only have the effect of increasing the visibility of the actual problems and prospects that require rational policy response.

Personality Differences

The functionalist view that attitudes on public issues may reflect, express, and help to resolve "deeper" needs and conflicts is, at least in a loose sense, derived from psychoanalytic theory. Early studies (for a review see Murphy, Murphy, & Newcomb, 1937) on the relationship between personality and political orientation seem to have erred both in formulating hypotheses that were too rigidly psychoanalytic and in often using inapplicable or poorly developed measures of personality and attitude variables. Perhaps another defect was that there was too great a conceptual distance between the kinds of personality variables and attitude variables that were delineated.

The work of Fromm (1941, 1947), Maslow (1943), and the Adorno, Frenkel-Brunswik group (1950) contributed to a conceptual clarification that reoriented study in this area in more profitable directions. It shifted attention from underlying character dynamics conceived in strictly intrapsychic terms to patterns of general ideology or orientation that were assumed to mediate between personality and adult social-political experience.

In operational terms this shift was evidenced in the development of a set of scales designed to assess "authoritarian" and "equalitarian" trends in character, as these were expressed in particular kinds of social values and perspectives. Thus, the assumption seems to have been that the authoritarian's preference for strong leadership, his intolerance for institutions facilitating impulse release, and his predilection for severe rejection of "alien views" and their defenders, would provide the immediate framework for the development of his social, political, and economic attitudes, and would therefore be better predictors of these attitudes than the deeper psychodynamic constellations that lay behind the whole process.

The actual approach by which the California group of researchers (Adorno et al., 1950) developed the well-known F Scale measure of authoritarianism involved various kinds of validation against clinical material, and against other scales; but guiding the whole intricate process was their conceptualization of a character pattern whose dynamic core lay in the primary repression of potent and overwhelming hostility originally aimed against parents and other severe, but close, authority figures. Anxiety associated with this central problem was presumed to be reduced by secondary defenses that include displaced aggression toward other, safer, targets; suppression of basic sensual impulses; disavowal of those impulses through their projection onto targets of aggression; a view of life in which the underlying aggressiveness energizes an exaggeration of the importance of power, force, domination, and submission in human affairs; and (defending the whole syndrome from its intrinsic inconsistencies) a type of cognitive rigidity and dogmatism that admits of little subtlety in self-understanding or in the appreciation of the intricacies of public issues.

The California group did not attempt a full account of the social and historical sources of this pattern, or of the opposite "equalitarian" pattern. Nevertheless, their theorizing essentially elaborates the individual, psychological implications of that approach in social theory that interprets modern life as isolating man, as depriving him of the possibility of achieving autonomy within social involvements and also of the sense that life can be guided by cooperative arrangements and ultimately altruistic values. In this view, modern man, despite his conformity to normative requirements, is seen as suffering a private estrangement from true "community," an estrangement whose pain and ambiguity can best be reduced by his turning his indignation toward a search for the enemy and whose loneliness can best be diminished by enlisting, or joining, others in that search. In focusing upon the etiological importance of parental

severity and irrational use of authority, the California investigators were perhaps voicing this same interpretation, but "writ small" in the language of the domestic, rather than the societal, drama.

As I have already noted, a particular virtue of the empirical approach of these investigators was their attempt to assess the presence of the authoritarian character pattern by way of scale items that were meant to reflect its expression through more manifest themes of social orientation, value, and prejudice. Thus the F Scale, which has gone through many revisions, asks subjects to report the extent of their agreement or disagreement with such "opinions" as: the most important thing to teach children is absolute obedience to their parents; the businessman and the manufacturer are much more important to society than the artist and professor; most people don't realize how much our lives are controlled by plots hatched in secret places; an insult to our honor should always be punished; there are two kinds of people in the world, the weak and the strong; prison is too good for sex criminals, they should be publicly whipped or worse.

The main prediction in their original research was that authoritarians would show greater racial prejudice and general ethnocentric hostility than nonauthoritarians. Despite the vast literature of argument and reinterpretation that this work stimulated we can, I think, take that hypothesis as verified; though we would have to note the pertinence of the frequent criticism (see Christie & Jahoda, 1954) that normative sources of prejudice can often play as large a role as characterological sources.

From this brief history and interpretation of some major aspects of the study of authoritarianism it should be clear why many researchers have predicted that the hard-line approach to Cold-War problems will be favored by authoritarian persons. The high aggressiveness, projectivity, cognitive rigidity, and ethnocentrism of the authoritarian are assumed to dispose him to find meaning and validity in severe versions of the Cold-War orientation. By enthusing over the policy of "winning the Cold War," by accepting the uses of military threat and excitedly contemplating the possibility that a showdown may soon be necessary, by crediting the claim that "there are traitors in our midst" and that they should be suppressed, by adding his assent to hostile or condescending views of the peoples of other nations, the authoritarian person may achieve a needed confirmation of the very assumptions upon which he has anchored his own identity. More simply, he derives cathartic release of the sort that helps to keep that identity viable.

This general hypothesis, at least in many of its crucial aspects, has been rather strongly confirmed by a number of recent studies. We shall begin our review of this research with some studies employing measures that, though somewhat less ambitious than the F Scale, have been guided by the same general view and are addressed to particular aspects of the authoritarian pattern.

A group of such studies has been reported by Morris Rosenberg. In one of these (1956) he employed a Misanthropy Scale designed to assess the extent to which an individual has or lacks "faith in people." Scores on this scale were found to be significantly related to attitudes about "the nature of government." Those with high "faith in people" were found to be more likely to hold "democratic attitudes." A later study (1957) elicited college students' reactions to a few straightforward questions bearing upon problems in international affairs ("Which is the best deterrent against war, the U.N. or the atom bomb?"). Those scoring high on misanthropy were found, to a statistically significant extent, to express views conveying mistrust, and reliance upon force and power in international relations. Thus the person who is incapable of faith in people seems incapable also of faith in the possibility that nations may yet come to order their relationships equitably and with a shared concern for restricting the dangers of recourse to force.

Farber (1955), attempting to place individuals upon a basic dimension of psychoanalytic character-typology, developed a scale of "Anality" whose items allow respondents to indicate whether they are given to "orderliness, frugality, and obstinacy." The psychoanalytic hypothesis is that this sort of character pattern is founded upon a dynamic in which repressed aggressiveness plays a major role. This ties it closely to the theory of authoritarianism and yields a similar prediction: that "anal" persons would be disposed to accept hard-line themes of toughness toward nations perceived as threatening their own. This prediction was tested by relating the anality scores of 132 college students to their scores on a Political Aggression Scale which consisted of four items, each voicing the basic theme of "getting tough with the Communists." The relationship observed was clearly in the predicted direction. Of those high on anality 66 percent were also high in endorsing a "tough" approach to the Communist powers, as compared to only 32 percent of those low on anality.

The valuable study by Putney and Middleton (1962), much of whose content has already been reported, included some items drawn from a Guttman-type scale of "status concern" that had been developed by Kaufman

(1957). The general theory of authoritarian character predicts that authoritarians will have higher concern with "pecking order" relationships and higher investment in attaining superordinate positions in the social hierarchy. The correlations in the Putney and Middleton study between status concern and two of the three scales indexing acceptance or rejection of the hard-line approach, were significant at the .05 level. As expected, high status concern was found to be associated with a general acceptance of forceful military response to provocations from the Communist nations and to a rejection of a policy favoring disarmament arrangements.

A frequently voiced hypothesis about authoritarianism is that, by virtue of the cognitive rigidity through which its underlying conflicts are sealed over, it will be associated with a general "intolerance for ambiguity." Thus the authoritarian is found to view intellectualism (which to him seems a perverse courting of unnecessary complexity) with impatient disdain. In their study with Michigan undergraduates, Chesler and Schmuck (1964) administered an Intellectualism Scale that called for evaluative response to such items as "Ideas are all right but it's getting the job done that counts" and "Too few college students are intellectually inclined." This scale was more closely related than any other to scores on their Armament–Disarmament Scale ($r = -.35$, $p < .05$). Students who favored intellectualism rejected a policy of heavy armament; students who rejected intellectualism favored that policy.

Levinson, who was one of the participants in the original work on authoritarianism and ethnic hostility, has developed an Internationalism-Nationalism Scale, most of whose twelve items sound such themes as anti-Soviet

militancy, trust in armed deterrence, and intolerance for conciliatory approaches. The scale has high reliability and the strong relationships between individual item scores and total score suggest that an organized cluster of attitudes is being assessed. In a study with 84 Harvard students (1957) he obtained a wide distribution of scores on this scale and found that it was significantly correlated with the Ethnocentrism Scale, the Traditional Family Ideology Scale (reflecting "autocratic orientation toward child-rearing, husband-wife relations and other aspects of family life") and also with a scale of Religious Conventionalism.

Christiansen (1959) carried out a rather eclectic investigation in which a number of different projective and questionnaire measures were employed. This work is of particular interest in that it was conducted in Norway with military and naval cadets and appears to be the only close study so far reported on the personality correlates of the attitudes of non-Americans toward problems of international competition and aggression. The findings seem, in general, to be consistent with the other studies that have been reviewed here, though the data do not permit a simple classification of the respondents into authoritarian and nonauthoritarian groups.

We turn now to studies that have used versions of the F Scale itself, rather than derivatives or correlates of it as in most of the research described above. MacKinnon and Centers (1957) report a survey study in which respondents took a short version of the F Scale and also answered attitude questions on two issues concerning the reduction of Soviet-American tensions: trade with the Soviet Union and "teachers talking to their students about the Russian system or way of life." Authoritarian and equalitarian halves of the sample were obtained through a median split on the F Scale distribution. These groups differed strongly from each other on both these issues and in the predicted directions.

Of particular value in this study is the fact that reasons given by the respondents for their attitudes were subjected to a coding analysis. Thus, even for the minority of authoritarians who do approve of teaching about Russia, the cognitive aspects of their attitudes are notably different from those in the nonauthoritarian portion of the sample. It is reported that

. . . they less often refer to the mental processes such knowledge can implement, the intergroup tensions it can reduce, or the importance of holding a general liberal outlook. Other analyses confirm the lesser appreciation of authoritarians for the functional aspects of knowledge about Russia, and particularly for its tension-easing potentialities (p. 628).

Farris (1960), working with a random sample of some 500 whites in a southern city, found a clear relationship between their F Scale scores and their scores on a scale measuring "jingoism," which is defined as "an exaggerated patriotism and an endorsement of a relatively aggressive or bellicose policy in foreign affairs" (p. 52). High authoritarianism was also found to be related, though in complex interaction with educational level, to a belief in the likelihood of war.

In my own studies I have employed either a version of the original F Scale or one in which the statement of half of the items is reversed in the nonauthoritarian direction. With either scale, those scoring as high authoritarians have usually been found to show significantly greater acceptance of the hard-line approach to Cold-War issues than those obtaining lower F Scale scores.

Occasionally F Scale items have been included in national sample surveys. The lack of depth or range in the testing of foreign policy attitudes in such surveys reduces their value for the present inquiry. But at least two such studies deserve mention here. Lane (1955) reports that, in a Survey Research Center study conducted in 1952, high and low authoritarians showed significant differences in the policies they favored for resolving the Korean War. The high authoritarians favored either "pulling out of Korea" or bombing Manchuria and China. The low authoritarians preferred negotiation looking toward a compromise settlement.

Working from similar data collected in 1949 and 1950, and using the same analytic approach, Janowitz and Marvick (1953) found high authoritarians more disposed toward "isolationism" than low authoritarians. This, and the evidence from Lane that some authoritarians favored "pulling out of Korea," might seem to conflict with our summary of more recent studies that show high authoritarians to be committed to action against the Communist nations rather than to a withdrawal from the world in which those nations exist. But this discrepancy is reduced when we recall that in the decade following the collection of these data Cold-War activism and commitment to the continuing struggle became increasingly central themes of our bipartisan foreign policy and of mass communication on international issues. As rationalization and endorsement of the Cold War flourished, the authoritarians' attitude orientations were probably affected in a related way.

A second and somewhat subtler point is that the older authoritarian isolationist style was hardly a detached statesmanlike concern that "foreign entanglements" be avoided. Rather it was rich with contempt for "lesser breeds" and, as Fensterwald (1958) has pointed out, it was isolationist only when looking westward toward Europe; its eastward orientation seems to have had a rather imperialistic cast.

At any rate, from more recent studies there can be little question that ten to fifteen years of exposure to containment and deterrence ideology have provided the authoritarian with a presently stable channelling of his character-based needs toward the goal of victory in the Cold War and toward a stance that disdains conciliation and disarmament as a kind of cowardly yielding. If "isolationism" persists at all in the context of the authoritarian's decidedly interventionist orientation, this is probably only through the subsidiary hard-line theme of disdain for some of our allies, and for the United Nations, as untrustworthy and as lacking in sufficient anti-Soviet militancy. The study by Fensterwald (1958) presents some data suggestive of this difference between respondents scoring high and low on the F Scale. But even more clearly visible in Fensterwald's data is the common finding that those high on authoritarianism (assessed by a short form of the F Scale) are decidedly more supporting of the aggressive, hard-line orientation to international problems than those low on authoritarianism.

By comparing the Janowitz and Marvick (1953) study with the various more recent ones that have been reviewed here, it is possible to recommend a partial antidote to the despair over seemingly intractable, rightist public opinion that has been felt by some who urge basic foreign policy revision. It would appear that the authoritarian mentality can be redirected toward different policy views under sufficient tutelage by the mass media. I am inclined to believe that the typical authoritarian may be considerably more

capable of shifting targets (though not of doing without targets) than some writers have suggested.

Implicit in the original theorizing about authoritarianism, and in much of the foregoing research, is the idea that authoritarian persons are, necessarily, more rigidly conforming to normative controls than are nonauthoritarians. This has seemed to me too simple an interpretation and thus in my own research I have attempted to subject it to direct examination in the context of attitudes on Cold-War issues.

Theories about the way modern society disrupts human identity and fosters apathy and detachment from the general social order have widely employed the concepts of *anomie* and *alienation*. Attempts to determine how far such transformation has proceeded in different social groups have led, therefore, to the development of scales designed to measure these variables. Srole's (1951) Anomie Scale was one such effort and numerous scales of "alienation" (see Seeman, 1959, for a useful commentary and review) are in the same category.

It is interesting that clear and stable relationships between such measures and measures of authoritarian trends in character have not been regularly obtained. In my own research with college groups I have found that Nettler's (1957) Alienation Scale (which assesses the extent to which the person accepts or rejects the consumer preferences, leisure-time tastes, and guiding platitudes that define American mass life) is either weakly correlated or not at all correlated with the F Scale.

Superficially this appears odd, for theory might suggest that the authoritarian, with his penchant for submission to power, will inevitably submit to society. But, at least in the college groups with which most of my own research on Cold-War attitudes has been conducted, this is not the case. Certain authoritarians seem quite capable of directing their aggressiveness into distaste for what is standard and routine in the banal and often visibly hypocritical patterning of mass life and mass myth. (Liberal social scientists with partisan axes to grind probably err widely in assuming the authoritarian person to be incapable of any real sensibility in responding to the world about him.)

Perhaps we would do better to conceive of the authoritarianism syndrome as fitting equally well into a number of different patterns of total ego-organization. Thus, as regards alienation and distance from society, we might take the view that authoritarians (like equalitarians) may range (even if not in identical frequency distributions) all the way from nonconforming inward-émigrés to totally conforming slaves of sanction.

The main finding from my own studies that is pertinent to this discussion is that both the F and Alienation Scales predict quite significantly to the Cold-War Consensus Scale. As I have indicated, the results with the F Scale are the same as in other studies on authoritarianism and Cold-War attitudes. With the Alienation scale, the finding is that those who score high tend to reject hard-line items significantly more than those who score low. What is more striking is that with most of the college samples, and also with one noncollege sample, a clear ordering of degree of deviance from the Cold-War consensus is obtained. The most accepting group are those high on authoritarianism and low on alienation; the most rejecting group are those low on authoritarianism and high on alienation. The two other groups (high authoritarianism–high alienation and low authoritarianism–low alienation) are not only intermediate in acceptance

of the hard-line pattern but are usually not significantly different from one another. Thus, to the extent that an authoritarian person is removed from mass society and is capable of rejecting important aspects of its normative system, he will tend to be less clearly pro-Cold-War; in fact, in these particular studies his acceptance of the hard-line approach is no greater than that of equalitarian persons who are involved in mass society and who adhere to major features of its normative system.

Apart from the meaning I have attempted to put upon these findings they suggest at least one other point: though the authoritarian syndrome has been persuasively shown to be closely related to the Cold-War orientation, there has perhaps been less attention than is warranted to other factors that may mediate or modify that relationship. What yet remains particularly unclear is whether authoritarianism and certain partial correlates of it that are also predictive of the hard-line orientation (particularly religiosity and conservatism) play separate roles in the internalization and stabilization of this attitude pattern. I view it as likely, but undemonstrated, that they are at least somewhat independent of one another. Conservatism and religiosity (even if their acquisition has been guided by authoritarian needs) are belief and value structures whose very content enjoins an acceptance of the major items in the hard-line ideology; on the other hand, authoritarianism is a kind of character organization and, as such, it probably makes for a more direct, emotional resonance to the hard-line ideology. As I have already suggested in another context, the only way out of the interpretive dilemmas posed by overdetermined phenomena is through developmental, psychogenetic study. Short of that we must rely upon more complex types of data analysis and upon our capacities to think about data both critically and creatively.[11]

As in previous sections, we may ask what advice can be derived for the policy specialist and for those who communicate to the public for him. The most salient of the points noted above is simply that, while the authoritarian character pattern is, like others, not readily transformable, the aims and policy orientations toward which it is directed are not immune to influence. Furthermore, the kinds of persuasive arguments used to win the assent of authoritarian persons to policy revisions that we expect them to find uncongenial, can sometimes be shaped in ways that engage their character-based values. An example of this possible strategy is provided by MacKinnon and Centers (1957):

> When the issue is trade with the Soviet, the argument that trade would promote American economic benefits should appeal to authoritarians. Among reasons for trading with Russia . . . prosperity as the benefit and the ingroup as the benefactor predominate among authoritarians. "Good for jobs" and "good for business" should appeal to the authoritarian element of the working and middle classes respectively (p. 629).

To whom such appeals and arguments should be directed is, of course, a difficult question. But available findings about the comparative scope of the au-

thoritarian orientation in different sectors of the population could provide a loose guide if one were desired.

SUMMARY AND FURTHER RECOMMENDATIONS

The skeletal structure of this chapter can be reviewed in a series of points.

1. It was suggested that public opinion as perceived by policy-makers often works to constrain or even to block policy changes that seem to promise advancement toward major national and international goals.

2. It was suggested that dependence upon poll data often leads administrators, legislators, party officials, and others who join with technical specialists in the shaping of policy, into certain major errors. Particularly these errors take the form of overestimating both the extent of public involvement in policy issues and the likelihood of public rejection of policy innovations.

3. It was suggested that the foregoing characterization is especially applicable to those aspects of present foreign policy that bear upon the choice between effective conciliation or expansion of the Cold War. Thus, a close examination of social-psychological research on public opinion in this area was attempted in this chapter.

4. Along these lines, the nature of the opinion interview was closely examined and an attempt was made to

---

[11] Little has been said in this section about "response set," "acquiescence," and other methodological problems that were first closely examined in connection with the F Scale and its derivatives. Such problems are involved in *all* attempts to use questionnaire procedures for the assessment of personality and personality-based social orientations. Analyses guided by an awareness of these problems have been very useful in developing improved versions of authoritarianism scales. When these have been used (as in some of the studies reviewed here) correlative results quite similar to those reported earlier have usually been obtained. Thus the literature of criticism of the F Scale does not seem to me to discredit the present conclusion that, at least among middle-class persons (with whom the larger part of this research has been done), authoritarianism disposes not only to ethnic and religious prejudice, but also to a preference for the hard-line approach on Cold-War issues.

clarify various ways in which opinion statement is deflected away from private conviction or apathy and toward the perceived Cold-War consensus. Some possible methodological correctives whose application might enable more valid assessment of public opinion were presented. In general it was suggested that on matters of foreign policy there is, if only because of the extent of partial public apathy, considerable possibility of "freedom for rationality."

5. Research on various factors that are correlated with preference or distaste for the hard-line orientation toward Cold-War issues was reviewed. Some main correlates of the opinion pattern favoring continued military and diplomatic severity toward all Communist nations were delineated. These include religiosity, conservatism, authoritarian character structure, and possibly ethnic and regional factors as well. Also, men were found to be more pro-Cold-War than women.

6. Throughout the review of studies on these matters it was suggested that the available findings could help in guiding attempts to win public acceptance of further policy changes or to forestall politically expressed public indignation toward such changes. Most of the illustrations of this possibility dealt with the advancement of policies fostering disarmament and settlement of East–West differences. The use of these examples was based not only upon the conviction that such policies are in the interest of national and general human goals, but also upon the impression, now held by many competent observers, that the American and West European governments, and probably also the Soviet government, have elected to proceed, however warily, toward guarded conciliation.

The immediate import of this chapter, then, has been somewhat optimistic in recommending that public opinion

can, within limits, be "handled"; and this despite the ignorance, apathy, narrow group interest, and individual character disorder that affect much of its content and rigidity.

But in a more considered sense there is reason for troubled concern over the fact that public opinion is more to be handled than consulted. The view of the democratic mass as essentially incompetent on issues that affect its ultimate welfare seems, as Lippmann has argued, to be applicable to our present national situation. But whereas Lippmann, and others who also draw upon the Burkean tradition, see this as the inevitable and tragic defect of political democracy, there is an alternative view that seems just as admissible. I am persuaded that public opinion has not always been, and need not continue to be, so great a burden and so poor a resource.

The development of mass education and mass communication have brought modern democratic states closer to the possibility of achieving mass political literacy. Also men are now freer, and will become still more so, from the brutalizing effects of dulling labor, from enslavement to the bitterness generated by poverty, from the narrowing of understanding bred by regional and cultural isolation.

If, as these liberating changes develop, men are also given more direct access to relevant information and to the real meaning of policy controversies, we might well look forward to the ultimate emergence of a more responsible kind of public opinion. We might then reduce the number of those who alternate between apathy and indignation and increase the number of those who attempt to think judiciously about how the basic goals of peace and polity are to be achieved.

What I am suggesting is that the potential threat that public opinion poses for the pursuit of rational policy is in part due to the fact that governmental and communication elites have been so ready to hide the facts, and to misrepresent or oversimplify the actual justifications for policy choices. In consequence, public opinion has remained far more uninformed and rigid than it need have been.

The best possible example of this may be in the problem at hand. If the mobilization of public support for the Cold War had, from its initiation in the late 1940s, stressed the view that containment was a necessary but limited strategy that looked toward its own obsolescence, present public response to conciliatory undertakings might be far less hostile. But, instead, the account the public received regressed rapidly to the rhetoric of a crusade against consummate, unmodifiable evil.

Perhaps there is a kind of Gresham's law of mass communication in which deceptive and evasive communications, appealing to narrow interests and prejudice, inevitably drive out communications that combine candor with an appeal to intelligence and higher values. But it is just as likely that the opposite is the case: that given a chance to know what is really happening "out there" and given an opportunity to consider policy alternatives in their true complexity, much of the public would be able to achieve deeper interest in policy problems and a fuller appreciation of the necessity that policy decisions be guided by ultimately humane purposes.

Thus, an important recommendation must be added to my argument that public opinion can be handled; namely, that in attempting to do this, every effort should be made to give the public the facts relevant to policy decisions and to foster a realistic understanding both of the necessity for tension reduction and of the limits that must be heeded if that goal is to be effectively sought. If this is not undertaken some of the constraints imposed by public opinion may, as I have argued, nevertheless be overcome; but those in the elite who would use their influence upon policy for the pursuit of the ultimate pacification of an extremely dangerous international situation, would find little sustaining encouragement or understanding in the national temper; and without this they cannot act openly and effectively in the directions that wisdom recommends.

If such an improvement of communication on policy matters is not undertaken, there will be no way of stemming the influence of those factors of narrow interest and emotional difficulty that appear to control what many Americans think and feel about Cold-War issues; and thus the passions of this portion of the public will remain available for manipulation by those elitist authoritarians who are eager to lead the nation into adventures on the brink of cataclysm.

REFERENCES

Abelson, R. P., & Rosenberg, M. J. Symbolic psycho-logic: A model of attitudinal cognition. *Behav. Sci.*, 1958, *3*, 1–13.

Adorno, T. W., Frenkel-Brunswik, Else, Levinson, D. J., & Sanford, R. N. *The authoritarian personality.* New York: Harper, 1950.

Alpert, H., Hawver, C., Cantwell, F. V., DeVany, P. M., & Kriesberg, M. Congressional use of polls: A symposium. *Publ. Opin. Quart.*, 1954, *18*, 121–142.

Archibald, Kathleen, Ekman, P., & Stone, G. *Reactions of political leaders to a crisis situation: Cuba and American policy.* Paper read at annual meeting of American Psychological Association, 1963.

Arendt, Hannah *The origins of totalitarianism*. New York: Harcourt, Brace, 1951.

Asch, S. E. Studies of independence and conformity: I. A minority of one against a unanimous majority. *Psychol. Monogr.*, 1956, 70(9), 1–70.

Barton, A. A survey of suburban residents on what to do about the danger of war. *Council for Correspondence Newsl.*, 1963, No. 24, 3–11.

Bell, D. (Ed.) *The radical right*. Garden City, N.Y.: Doubleday, 1963.

Berlo, D. K. *The public's opinions on existing or potential fallout shelter programs*. Michigan State University, 1962.

Brehm, J. W., & Cohen, A. R. *Explorations in cognitive dissonance*. New York: Wiley, 1962.

Bridgman, P. W. *The logic of modern physics*. New York: Macmillan, 1927.

Campbell, D. T. *The generality of a social attitude*. Unpublished doctoral dissertation, University of California, Berkeley, 1947.

Cartwright, D. Some principles of mass persuasion. *Hum. Relat.*, 1949, 2, 253–268.

Cartwright, D., & Harary, F. Structural balance: A generalization of Heider's theory. *Psychol. Rev.*, 1956, 63, 277–293.

Chesler, M., & Schmuck, R. Student reactions to the Cuban crisis and public dissent. *Publ. Opin. Quart.*, 1964, 28, 467–482.

Christiansen, B. *Attitudes towards foreign affairs as a function of personality*. Oslo: Oslo Univer. Press, 1959.

Christie, R., & Jahoda, Marie (Eds.) *Studies in the scope and method of "the authoritarian personality."* New York: Free Press, 1954.

Converse, P. E. Comments on the three studies. *Council for Correspondence Newsl.*, 1963, No. 24, 37–42.

Couch, A., & Keniston, K. Agreeing response set and social desirability. *J. abnorm. soc. Psychol.*, 1961, 62, 175–179.

Crowne, D. P., & Liverant, S. Conformity under varying conditions of personal commitment. *J. abnorm. soc. Psychol.*, 1963, 66, 547–555.

Crowne, D. P., & Marlowe, D. A new scale of social desirability independent of psychopathology. *J. consult. Psychol.*, 1960, 24, 349–354.

Edwards, A. L. *The social desirability variable in personality assessment and research*. New York: Holt, Rinehart and Winston, 1957.

Ekman, P. Divergent reactions to the threat of war. *Council for Correspondence Newsl.*, 1963, No. 24, 11–25.

Farber, M. L. The anal character and political aggression. *J. abnorm. soc. Psychol.*, 1955, 51, 486–489.

Farris, C. D. Selected attitudes on foreign affairs as correlates of authoritarianism and political anomie. *J. Politics*, 1960, 22, 50–67.

Fensterwald, B. The anatomy of American isolationism and expansionism (Parts 1 and 2). *J. Confl. Resol.*, 1958, 2, 111–139, 280–309.

Festinger, L. *A theory of cognitive dissonance*. New York: Harper, 1957.

Fromm, E. *Escape from freedom*. New York: Holt, Rinehart and Winston, 1941.

Fromm, E. *Man for himself*. New York: Holt, Rinehart and Winston, 1947.

Gleitman, H., & Greenbaum, J. J. Hungarian socio-political attitudes and revolutionary action. *Publ. Opin. Quart.*, 1960, 24, 62–76.

Hawver, C. The congressman and his public opinion poll. *Publ. Opin. Quart.*, 1954, 18, 123–129.

Heider, F. Attitudes and cognitive organization. *J. Psychol.*, 1946, 21, 107–112.

Heider, F. *The psychology of interpersonal relations*. New York: Wiley, 1958.

Janowitz, M., & Marvick, D. Authoritarianism and political behavior. *Publ. Opin. Quart.*, 1953, 17, 185–202.

Kahler, E. *The tower and the abyss*. New York: Braziller, 1957.

Kahn, R., & Cannell, C. F. *The dynamics*

of interviewing: Theory, technique and cases. New York: Wiley, 1957.

Katz, D., Sarnoff, I., & McClintock, C. Ego defense and attitude change. *Hum. Relat.,* 1956, *9,* 27–46.

Kaufman, W. C. Status, authoritarianism, and anti-semitism. *Amer. J. Sociol.,* 1957, *62,* 379–382.

Kelman, H. C. Processes of opinion change. *Publ. Opin. Quart.,* 1961, *25,* 57–78.

Krech, D., & Crutchfield, R. *Theory and problems of social psychology.* New York: McGraw-Hill, 1948.

Lane, R. E. Political personality and electoral choice. *Amer. polit. Sci. Rev.,* 1955, *49,* 173–190.

Laulicht, J., & Paul, J. Some major findings of the C.P.R.I. Attitude Study. *Int. soc. Sci. J.* (in press).

Lazarsfeld, P., & Menzel, H. Mass media and personal influence. In W. Schramm (Ed.), *The science of human communication.* New York: Basic Books, 1963. Pp. 94–115.

Levinson, D. J. Authoritarian personality and foreign policy. *J. Confl. Resol.,* 1957, *1,* 37–47.

Lewin, K. *Dynamic theory of personality.* New York: McGraw-Hill, 1935.

Lippmann, W. *Essays in the public philosophy.* Boston: Little, Brown, 1955.

Lipset, S. M. *Political man: The social bases of politics.* Garden City, N.Y.: Doubleday, 1960.

MacKinnon, W. J., & Centers, R. Authoritarianism and internationalism. *Publ. Opin. Quart.,* 1957, *20,* 621–630.

McClosky, H. Conservatism and personality. *Amer. pol. Sci. Rev.,* 1958, *52,* 27–45.

Maslow, A. H. The authoritarian character structure. *J. soc. Psychol.,* 1943, *18,* 401–411.

Miller, W. E. *Majority rule and the representative system.* Paper read at annual meeting of American Political Science Association, 1962.

Miller, W. E., & Stokes, D. E. Constitu-

ency influence in Congress. *Amer. pol. Sci. Rev.,* 1963, *57,* 45–56.

Mills, C. W. *The power elite.* New York: Oxford Univer. Press, 1956.

Modigliani, A. Facts, beliefs and baloney about the cold war public. *Council for Correspondence Newsl.,* 1963, No. 24, 50–56.

Murphy, G., Murphy, Lois B., & Newcomb, T. M. *Experimental social psychology.* New York: Harper, 1937.

Nettler, G. A measure of alienation. *Amer. sociol. Rev.,* 1957, *22,* 670–677.

Newcomb, T. M. An approach to the study of communicative acts. *Psychol. Rev.,* 1953, *60,* 393–404.

Orne, M. T. On the social psychology of the psychological experiment: With particular reference to demand characteristics and their implications. *Amer. Psychologist,* 1962, *17,* 776–783.

Ortega y Gasset, J. *The revolt of the masses.* New York: Norton, 1932.

Osgood, C. E., & Tannenbaum, P. H. The principle of congruity in the prediction of attitude change. *Psychol. Rev.,* 1955, *62,* 42–55.

Paul, J., & Laulicht, J. *In your opinion: Leaders' and voters' attitudes on defence and disarmament* (Vol. I). Clarkson, Ontario: Canadian Peace Research Institute, 1963.

Pettigrew, T. F. Social psychology and desegregation research. *Amer. Psychologist,* 1961, *16,* 105–112.

Putney, S., & Middleton, R. Some factors associated with student acceptance or rejection of war. *Amer. sociol. Rev.,* 1962, *27,* 655–667.

Riecken, H. W. A program for research on experiments in social psychology. In *Decisions, values and groups* (Vol. II). New York: Pergamon Press, 1962.

Riesman, D. *The lonely crowd.* New Haven: Yale Univer. Press, 1950.

Riesman, D. *Abundance for what? And other essays.* Garden City, N.Y.: Doubleday, 1964.

Rose, P. I. Citizens' opinions on civil

defense. *Council for Correspondence Newsl.*, 1963, No. 24, 25–37.

Rosenberg, M.   Misanthropy and political ideology. *Amer. sociol. Rev.*, 1956, *21*, 690–695.

Rosenberg, M.   Misanthropy and attitudes toward international affairs. *J. Confl. Resol.*, 1957, *1*, 340–345.

Rosenberg, M. J.   Cognitive structure and attitudinal affect. *J. abnorm. soc. Psychol.*, 1956, *53*, 367–372.

Rosenberg, M. J.   Cognitive reorganization in response to the hypnotic reversal of attitudinal affect. *J. Pers.*, 1960, *28*, 39–63. (a)

Rosenberg, M. J.   A structural theory of attitude dynamics. *Publ. Opin. Quart.*, 1960, *24*, 319–340. (b)

Rosenberg, M. J.   *A research program on consistency and change in social attitudes.* Mimeographed paper, 1961.

Rosenberg, M. J., Hovland, C. I., McGuire, W. J., Abelson, R. P., & Brehm, J. W. *Attitude organization and change.* New Haven: Yale Univer. Press, 1960.

Rosenberg, M. J., & Oltman, P. K.   Consistency between attitudinal affect and spontaneous cognitions. *J. Psychol.*, 1962, *54*, 485–490.

Rosenthal, R.   On the social psychology of the psychological experiment: The experimenter's hypothesis as unintended determinant of experimental results. *Amer. Scientist*, 1963, *51*, 268–283.

Scott, W. A.   Cognitive consistency, response reinforcement, and attitude change. *Sociometry*, 1959, *22*, 219–229.

Seeman, M.   On the meaning of alienation. *Amer. sociol. Rev.*, 1959, *24*, 783–791.

Smith, M. B.   Personal values as determinants of a political attitude. *J. Psychol.*, 1949, *28*, 477–486.

Smith, M. B., Bruner, J. S., & White, R. W. *Opinions and personality.* New York: Wiley, 1956.

Srole, L.   *Social dysfunction, personality and social distance attitudes.* Paper read at annual meeting of American Sociological Society, 1951.

Strickland, Bonnie R., & Crowne, D. P.   Conformity under conditions of simulated group pressure as a function of the need for social approval. *J. soc. Psychol.*, 1962, *58*, 171–181.

Thomas, W. I., & Znaniecki, F.   *The Polish peasant in Europe and America* (5 vols.) Boston: Badger, 1918.

Waxler, Nancy E.   *Response to threat: A survey of attitudes toward nuclear war.* Unpublished paper, 1961.

Withey, S. B.   Public opinion on war and shelters. *New University Thought*, 1962, *2*(3), 6–19.

Woodruff, A. D., & DiVesta, F. J.   The relationship between values, concepts and attitudes. *Educ. psychol. Measmt.*, 1948, *8*, 645–660.

Part Two

Processes of Interaction
in International Relations

9

In exploring processes of interaction in international relations we take as our primary object of study the social interaction of individuals in an international relations context. At the same time, however, these interactions between individuals and the situations within which they occur can be seen—to varying degrees—as manifestations of the interaction between nation-states. Thus, while the empirical anchoring-points of the chapters that follow are always the actions and interactions of individuals, the outcome variables with which a number of the chapters are largely concerned involve the actions and interactions of states.

Our exploration begins with two chapters that focus on some of the processes of interaction that are widely distributed across the elites and publics of a national population and serve to create a state of readiness for certain kinds of international action. The main interest is in the total product that emerges from these interactions—in the societal processes formed by the aggregation of social interactions occurring among many individuals and groups throughout the population. The products of these interactions—and hence the data to which the next two chapters refer—are widely held feelings, expectations, and beliefs, which add up to national moods and national ideologies. Some of the methodological problems involved, in determining how firm, stable, and even "real" these consensual products are, were discussed in Chapter 8.

Several of the chapters in Part Two are concerned with the role of subjective factors in the determination of policy and action. Chapter 9 dwells on subjective factors in their most general form: the underlying "climate" within which international action and reaction take place. The climate for international action and the public moods that constitute it are indeed elusive phenomena. Yet, we must come to grips with them and, as is pointed out in Chapter 9, they are increasingly becoming accessible to systematic study—for example, through methods of content analysis, such as those developed by Robert North and his associates. Subsequent chapters in Part Two—and particularly Chapter 11—will attempt to deal with these phenomena by focusing on more specific aspects of the general underlying climate.

Very appropriately, the author of the lead chapter in Part Two is one of the true pioneers in the social-psychological study of political behavior. Harold D. Lasswell is now Edward J. Phelps Professor of Law and Political Science at Yale University. He is past president of the American Political Science Association; and recipient of the American Council of Learned Societies Prize. His numerous books, which have been appearing regularly for several decades, include *Psychopathology and politics; World politics and personal insecurity; Power and personality; Power and society* (with Abraham Kaplan); and *The future of political science*. His current research interests focus on the sociology and psychology of authority and control.

H. C. K.

The Climate of
International Action

Harold D. Lasswell

A word may be said about the carrying over of the term *climate*—a term in
excellent standing among meteorolo-
gists—into the analysis of international
behavior. As a rule the growth of the
modern social and psychological sciences has been accompanied by the
dropping out of words that were originally borrowed from philosophy and
the physical sciences. Purism has its
limits, however, and the connotations
of otherwise dubious terms are sometimes remarkably felicitous. The more
sensitive we have become to the moods,
affects, sentiments, and ideas of men in
the aggregate the more frequent has
been the use of "climate" to designate a
middle configuration between sharply
defined images on the one hand and
clear-cut terminations or decision outcomes on the other. In nature the climate is not to be confused with drift-
ing clouds in a particular quarter of the
sky or with a tremendous downpour.
Rather, the conception of climate is of
a generalized model of relatively stable
occurrences among all the components
of weather that are found in a given
habitat during a season or a longer
cycle of events.

To refer to the climate of international action is to borrow an expression
well endowed with the connotations
required to characterize some generalized features of a collective process at
a given cross-section in time. The time-
slice in question is the sequence of
interaction during a given period in
the arena of world politics. The length
of time can be varied to fit the problem
with which the scientific observer is
concerned. Hence one may speak with
Toynbee and other comparative historians of the climate of civilizations or
epochs;[1] or one may collapse the interval accordion-like until it deals with

---

[1] It would be a rewarding exercise to collect all the terms for "climate" that Toynbee
employed in his monumental account of the "civilizations" that he conceived to be the significant entities of history. A systematic mode of dealing with such terms is outlined later in the
present chapter.

"Europe in the summer of 1914" or, as in the present inquiry, with phases in any context of international action.

THE WORLD POLITICAL PROCESS

We shall assess the usefulness of the conception of climate by considering it in the framework of a general theory of politics where emphasis is put on the interaction between the political process and the social process of which it is part.[2] A social process is briefly characterized as "people" pursuing "valued outcomes (values)" through "institutions" in a "resource environment." The valued outcomes are classified into such culminating interactions as winning or losing wars, giving or receiving information, exchanging goods and services, giving or receiving physical care, affording or taking opportunities to perform with excellence, giving or receiving affection, tendering or withholding respect, living up to or deviating from standards of responsible conduct. Suitably generalized, these eight valued outcomes are referred to as power, enlightenment, wealth, wellbeing, skill, affection, respect, rectitude. As students of world politics we are most directly concerned with power outcomes or decisions, which are commitments that are expected to be enforced or are being enforced against challengers. Participants in the social process are conceived as seeking to maximize their value position (or at least to improve their net control of values). During any given period they manage the values available to them as bases for influencing outcomes, thus treating them as scope values. Hence

power or "decision influence" figures in varying degree at different times as base or scope for the accumulation of power, wealth, or other values.

Political institutions are practices that are relatively specialized to the shaping and sharing of power. A "practice" is defined as a pattern of relatively stable subjective events ("perspectives") and behaviors ("operations"). The political "myth" is the pattern of perspectives; the "technique" is the operational pattern.

Focusing upon world politics, it is most convenient to regard the most important "participants" as individuals and organized groups, and to classify the latter as nation states, intergovernmental international organizations, international political parties, pressure associations, and other private organizations.

The "perspectives" of each participant include the symbols of identification employed in characterizing the Self and Other; general and specific value demands; expectations about past, present, and future occurrences. Participants share perspectives in varying degree, incorporating as part of the Self those who are fellow communists, capitalists, former colonial powers, Europeans, and so on; including common demands for "security," "unity," "economic growth," and the like; and emphasizing former historical ties and future prospects. The most significant shared perspective, however, is doubtless the expectation of violence, that is, the expectation that, regardless of formal acquiescence in a common international order, the probability of large-scale resort to extreme coercion is high.

---

[2] For expositions of the theoretical system and preliminary applications in various fields see, for example, Lasswell and Kaplan (1950); McDougal, Lasswell, and Vlasic (1963); Arens and Lasswell (1961); and Rogow and Lasswell (1963).

By "arena" we designate the effective context of interaction in world politics. Included are the many organized sub-arenas that correlate the activities of two or more nation states. It is fundamental to take note of the fact that the arena as a whole remains incompletely organized, falling short of the requirements for minimum public order.

The "base values" at the disposal of each participant vary enormously from one another. However, every nation state has at its disposal a modicum of power that is expressed in, and results from, the authoritative doctrine of "equality" of states.

The "strategies" employed in managing base values include diplomatic, informational, economic, and military components; and strategy may call for isolated or concerted action. "Outcomes" have been mentioned above; and "effects" are post-outcome consequences for values and institutions.

How do we locate the climate of international action in the map that has been sketched in the foregoing paragraphs? How can climate be described and explained? How can we formulate a strategy of inquiry appropriate to the challenge of understanding and controlling climatic change?

CLIMATE AND COLLECTIVE MOOD

Since the term "climate" carries the connotation of subjective events it is closely related to the category "perspectives" set forth above. It is proposed to give prominence to two features: (a) the degree of intensity, or stress toward action; and (b) the value orientation of the most generalized, hence least referential, content. If we examine statements in which responsible authors use the conception of climate we find that it is often employed to speak of the intensities involved; thus, a situation is "explosive," not "quiet." The accent is also upon highly generalized content, as when an epoch is called an "age of anxiety" (cf. Auden, 1947) or "insecurity," or a period of "self-confidence" or "distrust." We equate the notion of climate in international affairs with the conception of mood, recognizing that moods can be distinguished by degrees of intensity and by generalized value orientation of content.

Since we describe the entire social and political process in terms of sequences of interaction, it is evident that mood must be understood to be a phase of action. In seeking to clarify the generalized content of mood we distinguish among subjective events according to explicitness of reference. In a fundamental sense all subjective events "refer"; indeed, referentiality may be taken as the critical distinction between subjective and nonsubjective events in the universal event manifold. Subjective events differ greatly, however, in specificity of reference. If we use the term "image" to designate patterns of relatively specific reference, it leaves the term "mood" free to designate highly generalized reference. Although collective moods may overlap political ideologies, policies, and perceptions and interact with them, it is possible to identify the mood component of the sequence.

By classifying international moods according to value outcome, we can make the relationship between mood and action rather explicit, and explicitness facilitates the formulation and exploration of hypotheses regarding international climate. We speak of generalized content in terms such as assertiveness (power), curiosity (enlightenment), acquisitiveness (wealth), anxiety (well-being), love (affection), humiliation (respect), recrimination (rectitude). The images with which moods may be associated differ from time to time: assertiveness is directed against Germany at one moment and France at another; curiosity may be oriented toward sea or land or outer space; acquisitiveness may be aimed at the polar regions or celestial bodies, or at particular instruments of production; anxiety may flit confusedly among perceived sources in the external or the domestic arena; inspiration may be elicited by the arts and crafts of native or foreign cultures; love, even adoration, may greet visiting warriors or statesmen; a national sense of humiliation or of guilt may be interlaced with many different symbolic contents.

THE DESCRIPTION OF INTERNATIONAL MOODS

When historians, novelists, or even social scientists attempt to describe the presence or absence of intensity, or the dominant subjective content of a period, they find themselves almost irresistibly drawn to the use of "evocative" vocabulary. The "literary" impulse takes over to some extent since the challenge is to describe the contours of a whole in the same way that one seeks to communicate about a Navajo sand painting by some other device than counting the number of grains of sand used by the medicine man in arranging it. One explanation of why recent psychologists have had comparatively little to say about international climates is that they have been embarrassed by the seeming necessity of adopting "literary" language to do it.

As a sample of the type of evocative writing that finds an answering resonance among historians as well as novelists and political analysts we may cite the following passage by a distinguished Yugoslavian novelist (Andrič, 1960):

. . . The year 1914 will always remain unique. So at least it seemed to those who lived through it. . . . How could they explain and express those collective shudders which suddenly ran through all men and which from living beings were transmitted to inert objects, to districts and to buildings? How could they describe that swirling current among men which passed from dumb animal fear to suicidal enthusiasm, from the lowest impulses of bloodlust to the greatest and most noble of sacrifices, wherein man for a moment touches the sphere of greater worlds with other laws?

That was a time on the limits of two epochs in human history whence one could more easily see the end of that epoch which was closing than the beginning of that new one which was opening. Then one sought for a justification for violence and found some name borrowed from the spiritual treasury of the past century for savagery and bloodlust. All that took place still had the outer semblance of dignity and the attraction of novelty, a terrible, short-lived and inexpressible charm which later disappeared so completely that even those who then felt it so strongly could no longer evoke its memory (pp. 360–361).

Characterizations of the climate of international affairs may single out for emphasis distinctive features of the perspectives that prevail in the context. This applies, for example, to the treatment of "expectations." At times the atmosphere of foreboding comes to dominate the life of the whole community, as it did when Christendom approached the first millennium after Christ, a year that was widely believed to mark the End of the World and the Last Judgment. We are aware of sanguine expectations that sweep through the peoples of vast areas and find expression in movements of translocal scope. Modern historians try to recapture the "spirit of the Crusades" in the years when every stratum of European society was fired with confidence in the imminent success of the mission to redeem the Holy Sepulchre from the Infidel. (For hints of the literature, see Cohn, 1957.)

In many cases the predominating theme of a period is overwhelming determination, a "demand" to achieve a valued outcome, even though the prospects are compromised by obstacles of the most formidable character. The middle years of many wars have displayed these features—at least in retrospect. The enthusiasm, the shock, even the panic of the opening year is over. Dreams of quick victory or nightmares of impending defeat have faded into a settled determination to endure, to stick it out to the end, perhaps to victory, or at least to an honorable peace. In World War I there were months in 1916 when many leaders and led among the members of the Entente or the Central Powers approximated the same image of resigned tenacity (Tuchman, 1962).

In some circumstances the significant fact is the rejection of ancient "identities" and the emergence of a redefined conception of self, a redefinition of the boundaries of the primary ego that occurs among hundreds of thousands or even millions of people. The long history of the diffusion of the Christian religion is marked by chapters in which whole peoples have been seized by the Holy Spirit—as the phrase sometimes was—and in a fever of conversion rejected all parochial faiths and sought baptism and communion. In more recent times European and trans-European history has been profoundly affected by the rise of secular symbols of universal claim and aspiration, especially by the emergence of political

nationalism, proletarianism, or racism (cf. Deutsch, 1953).

Given the tools now at the disposal of the social and behavioral sciences it is unnecessary to assume that the "literary" approach to the study of international moods cannot be supplemented and to some extent superseded. Interviewing procedures can be adapted to contemporary, hence emerging, events in the world arena. Content analysis, on the other hand, can be applied to both contemporary and historical events. At present the available instruments of research have been sparingly applied; hence the principal objective of the present discussion is to point to possibilities. (On content analysis in general, see Pool, 1959; and North *et al.*, 1963.)

Granted that the techniques of content analysis can be adapted to the task of establishing quantitative measures of mood among international elites, what of the mid-elite and the rank and file of the world community? It is not too difficult to obtain the recorded public and many private statements of heads of states and other conspicuous members of the official or the active elites of the globe. Where elite newspapers and other printed media can be found we are able to summarize the news and commentary that are directed to influential audiences by channels subject to elite control. But what of the other participants in the total context?

Karen Dovring has strikingly demonstrated how skill in content analysis can often penetrate the screen that shuts off our view of the lower strata. The reference is to her study of the Swedish hymnals used in the eighteenth century.[3] The hymnal of the state church was revised and to the amazement of top ecclesiastical authorities

---

[3] Her study of the hymnbook revision episode was published in Lund, Sweden, in 1951 (in two volumes with a summary of the first volume in English), and is described in Dovring (1959).

the common people flooded the local chapels and sang enthusiastically. When the hymns are analyzed it turns out that there is a sharp increase in hymns that refer to the "Blood of the Lamb." The lower classes saw in this a democratic emphasis upon the point that Christ died for *all* people. The authorities were so appalled that they accused the hymn revisors of being subversively influenced by the dangerous doctrines circulating among the French philosophers.

The scientific analyst feels professionally called upon to testify to his familiarity with the point that statements by A regarding B's subjective events are inferences from B's behavior, which may be classified as relatively specialized to communication or not. Communications are sequences of "signs," which are either movements (spoken words and gestures) or parts of the resource environment (printed texts, for instance) employed to mediate between subjective events. The historian's characterization of the climate of an epoch is based upon an enormous volume of inferences from recorded communications, recorded deeds, and surviving culture materials. The latter are artifacts—processed raw materials of the resource environment—such as dwellings, public edifices, objects of art. Each source of inferences is amenable to quantitative investigation by appropriate methods.[4]

THEORY OF COLLECTIVE MOOD

Having characterized the climate of international relations in terms of collective mood, and suggested some of the procedures that can be applied to the description of mood, we must turn next to the problem of explanation. What hypotheses can be proposed that are in harmony with such investigations as have been reported, and are likely to yield promising results?

It is evident that stable moods of any two participants in the international arena can be symmetrical or asymmetrical in direction, evaluative orientation, or level of intensity. The directions may be reciprocal or not; in the former case the sharers of the mood take one another as targets. The orientation can be indulgent or deprivational, as when there is reciprocal friendliness or antagonism. The level may be highly intense (as in belligerency) or not (as in a popular alliance).

The maximization postulate suggests the fundamental point that mood events depend upon net value expectations. What gains or losses sustain stable or unstable moods?

A promising clue seems to be that *a mood in international relations is stabilized when it fosters both intra-elite cooperation and cooperation between elites, mid-elites, and rank and file.* When members of an elite can take it for granted that other elite members share a common mood perspective, they can be more sure of the consequences of what they do and say. If officials of a coalition perceive that they are genuinely united in the will to resist an enemy coalition, the anxieties of uncertainty are reduced or forestalled. It is clear that other officials will in all probability respond favorably to communications or to collaborative activities that confirm or enhance

[4] Art historians are especially involved with characterizations of mood, although historians of all modes of communication must pay some deference to the mediating role of mood in mobilizing responses to the environing world. The following statement, which appears in the Paine-Soper volume on *The art and architecture of Japan* (1955) is representative: "The terrible

the common mood.[5] Hence in the reporting of intelligence information and estimates it is tempting to slant the communication to sustain the coalition. The same point applies to promotional operations: the advocacy of new policies or of the continuation of established policies is likely to prove more successful if formulated in terms compatible with the joint militancy of the elites. Similarly, whatever prescriptions are crystallized by treaty or executive agreement have a better prospect of enforcement if they are couched in phrases that sustain the common mood. Likewise, when it is necessary to invoke a prescription and to complain of an alleged violation, the chances of success are improved by adopting a mode of expression that echoes the common theme. In applying agreements to concrete cases the likelihood of compliance is increased by the same tactic. If an adverse report must be given in appraising the implementation of official policy, the prospects of objective consideration are brightened by reaffirmation of the common perspective. If old prescriptions and established expectations must be terminated or frustrated, the process can go forward more expeditiously and with fewer resentments if the dominant mood is evoked.

The analysis indicates that much more is involved than absence of anxiety in expectations regarding the fundamental orientation of other elite members. Anxiety reduction or avoidance is an indulgence in terms of well-being; but indulgences of all kinds occur. Personal relations are enormously facilitated by the congeniality and mutual respect forthcoming when a common perspective is emphasized. Mutual felicitations in terms of devotion to duty and service of the cause constitute indulgences in terms of rectitude. The tendering of support in decisions allegedly compatible with the common perspective is a power indulgence; and we have alluded above to the possibility of favorable consequences in terms of information (enlightenment), wealth, or skill opportunities.

We have been enumerating some of the gains (or avoided losses) that foster a common international climate among cooperating elites. The role of an inclusive mood is further illuminated if we call attention to the deprivations that are inflicted formally and informally when an intra-elite statement or deed is perceived as out of harmony with the dominant mood. Many intelligence reports are filed and many reporters looked upon askance because of their "undue pessimism."[6] Policies that are advocated in the vernacular of crass ego-assertion court defeat during a period of intense devotion to the larger interests of the community. The same point applies to initiatives at every other phase of the decision process (prescription, invocation, application, appraisal, termination).

---

danger of the great force of Kublai Khan was averted . . . the war and the long period of anxiety were politically disruptive and artistically deadening, which may account for the curious phenomenon in the fourteenth century of strong Chinese influence immediately succeeding the nationalist tendency of the Kamakura period" (p. 53).

[5] See the graph depicting "National" and "Universal-Revolutionary" symbols in May-Day slogans of the Communist Party of the Soviet Union (1918–1943). The former rose and the latter dropped off in the war years (Lasswell, 1945, p. 78). For general background, see North (1962).

[6] For a detailed study of the perspectives at all levels that led up to the great surprise of Pearl Harbor, see Barbara Wohlstetter (1962).

What has been said about intra-elite relations is no less applicable to the relations between elite and mid-elite or rank and file. In approaching a powerful official the person of lesser status is relieved of much trepidation if he can rely upon the expectation that a common mood, such as determination to win the war, provides a common tie. Hence positive advantages accrue to individuals who talk and comport themselves in ways that resonate in key with the mood of elites. Similarly, deprivations are in store for anyone who speaks out of turn or engages in a course of discordant conduct.

Under what circumstances are the factors weakened that preserve an international climate? The reply is, in part, that *elite or non-elite experience that flagrantly contradicts the expectations that sustain the mood tends to undermine its continuation.* The preceding analysis has underlined the point that mood stability is a self-perpetuating and self-extending process to the extent that it screens perceptions to harmonize with it.

It is not probable that acquired expectations will be firmly enough embedded to exclude forever the recognition of incompatible events. In international politics it is impossible to keep secret for long such battles as Waterloo or many more humble enengagements. When events are less obviously decisive many direct observer-participants may continue to perceive them according to established mood-screens ("a local rebuff," "a strategic withdrawal," "a rectification of the line"). The messages sent through channels may reach officials whose perspectives remain unrevised; or who, if no longer sharing the former mood, are unsure of the consequences of

allowing any intimations of defeat to appear in their reports.

Little systematic investigation in world politics has been addressed to the task of discovering the circumstances in which events of various kinds modify established expectations and hence weaken prevailing moods. Similarly, few explorations have been devoted to another set of factors that influence the preservation of mood, namely, value demands. The relevant hypothesis is that *the rise of elite or non-elite demands other than the demands that sustain the mood tend to undermine its continuation.*

On many occasions the climate of politics seems to undergo remarkably rapid transformation, and to give way to collective absorption in the pursuit of other than political outcomes. At the end of wars, for example, it is not unusual to see "apolitical" or "anti-political" moods and to find that collective activities are mainly directed toward religion, or "having a good time."[7] Typically the "facts of life" have falsified the expectations that sustained the political mood; but other factors must be taken into account if we are to explain the rising mood. Why religion? Why "a good time"? Why "money"?

Questions of this kind call for a fully contextual examination to be made of the cultural predispositions of the nations involved. Such a project must consider the predispositions held by all members of a culture; and give weight to subcultural predispositions according to class, interest, and personality.

Culture

In his analysis of the folktales of Africa, Radin (1952) calls attention to the fact that the tales of all African

---

[7] Phenomena are comparable under the stress of great environmental deprivation. See Festinger, Riecken, and Schachter (1956).

folk societies are remarkably similar in theme and style (with the significant exception of the oldest, most isolated, and least stratified societies such as the Bushmen). The outstanding picture of these folktales is that they rarely deal with cosmic origins or the life of the Gods. They are man-centered. Not only that, "wishfulfillment" stories are pushed into the background. We learn that "human heroes with plots taken from purely human situations" are predominant; and that "with uncompromising realism" man is pitted against man. Even traditional animal-tales have been, or are in process of being, "transformed into a human hero" who has authentically human adventures. Radin's explanation of African tales is that African cultures are remarkably mixed and recent, and unintegrated. "Assuredly we have the right to infer that it is largely because the people are living in an insecure and semi-chaotic world, with its loss of values and inward demoralization, that cruelty and wanton murder loom so large in many of their tales" (p. 9).

Class

The climate of every historical period is substantially affected by the social origins and the class subculture of the elites of the time. We are becoming aware of the hitherto muted impact upon modern diplomatic style of the landlord-officer-bureaucrat-theologian-jurist of ancient Byzantium (Bozeman, 1960). In our time the rise of the scientist and engineer is modifying the weight of many factors in the approach to public policy. Preoccupied for the most part with physical events, the scientist trained in physics, chemistry, and astronomy is presumably accustomed to employ quite different scales in the measurement of time-space manifolds than laymen, or even other scientists, such as plant or animal ecologists, or students of comparative culture, whose observational field is closer to the layman's perspectives. Is the significance of science for mood in world affairs that states of intense commitment to parochial loyalties are undermined, resulting in creeping indifference or contempt for activities other than science itself? Does this mean withdrawal of concern for the outcome of the bipolar struggle between the Soviet and non-Soviet powers, and willingness to acquiesce in whatever elite policies provide base values for the cultivation of science?[8]

Interest

An interest group is defined as less inclusive than a culture or class; it may indeed cut across these boundaries in pursuit of specific strategies expected to yield particular advantages. The many specialties in science and scholarship constitute interest groups. In the preceding paragraph we were calling attention to the possible consequences of exposure to the subculture of scientific interests for the perspectives of power elites who begin to recruit more members of the decision class from persons with scientific backgrounds. A common recommendation for world unity is the encouragement of transnational pluralization of interest groups. During any short time period the political result may be the opposite of that intended, partly because of the mood of distrust with which power elites look upon these activities. The *transnational role players who evoke confidence in the members of political elite B are*

---

[8] See Barber and Hirsch (1962), and the growing literature on the role of scientists in nuclear policy.

likely to forfeit the confidence of members of political elite A in their own country. The world arena, organized as it is in terms of the expectation of violence, favors the success of elites who cultivate suspicion of individuals and groups possessing a diverse pattern of foreign acceptances. To some extent, of course, these individuals are useful pawns in power strategy. For instance, the German Ambassador in London in 1914 was kept uninformed by his superiors of the decision to fight. He was a well-known lover of England and the English and would be more effective in reassuring the British government if he did not know the truth (see Lichnowski, 1928). Well-meaning scientists, scholars, pacifists, humanists, commercial middlemen, and the like, spontaneously contribute to such deceptions, not by exaggerating "peaceful intentions" but by playing down the likelihood of "critical contingencies." The moods of universal brotherhood often contribute to specific tactics of surprise, confusion, and betrayal. "Timing" is the critical dimension. Can it be located more definitely by contemporaries? (See Barghoorn, 1964.)

Personality

The most dramatic instances of mood change in world affairs are expressed in individuals who have come to top elite positions as agitational and organizing leaders in countries whose recent humiliations in world politics appear to be disproportionate to the value assets actually available or potential. The defeat of Russia, Italy, and Ger-

many in World War I created such an extraordinary discrepancy; and the Bolshevik, Fascist, and Nazi movements were the restorative phase of collective action. The personalities who came to the top aided in transforming the mood of the interwar years in Europe and the world. Is public role-playing by top elite figures the most dependable guide to the mood configuration of a time period? Or is it predictively most significant to take a sample of the newest active elite members?[9]

Crisis Level

Strictly speaking "crisis level" calls for reclassification of the preceding four factors according to level of high, middle, or low crisis. The call is for systematic investigation of *rapid, moderate,* or *slow* changes in *great, medium,* or *low* value indulgence or deprivation (first in terms of power; ultimately of all values).

Many societies seem to exhibit predispositions to cyclical changes of a drastic kind.[10] The long history of peasant-landlord societies is a case in point. During many years—even generations—the countryside may seem stolid, obedient, unchanging. Then suddenly an epidemic of peasant (or slave) rebellions surges against the manor or the agent in residence, burning, pillaging, and destroying. Startled landlords and urbanites listen in shocked disbelief to the outrages perpetrated by the "childlike" peasants whom they "know so well," and whom they have often been able to "bring to their senses" with the aid of foreign or

---

[9] For data on elite changes consult Marvick (1961); Kautsky (1962); and Johnson (1962). Beginning in 1965 the elite studies originally published at Stanford will be republished and augmented by the M.I.T. Press (edited by H. D. Lasswell, D. Lerner, and I. de S. Pool).

[10] A cyclical model requires a "ceiling" and a "floor." Some models of armament and war crises assign an unlimited role to cumulative moods. See the remarks on mood in the theoretical models proposed by L. F. Richardson, A. Rapoport, and K. Boulding in Schelling (1963), footnote, p. 472.

urban armies. "Tranquillity punctuated by desperation" would appear to be the formula that suggests the mood profile built into the social context of social systems of this kind, save that the "tranquillity" refers to quite different subjectivities when the participant is landlord or serf.

It will be convenient to classify the predispositions relating to mood according to *repertory* and *agenda*. The mood repertory includes the range of mood patterns that have been exhibited in the past history of a participating body politic. The repertory can be sorted out according to dominant value, which, for example, may show that some participants are almost entirely lacking in predispositions to become seized by concern for economic or religious outcomes. The repertory can be subclassified to bring out the range of moods that have been crystallized in past politics. Some societies have no significant war pattern; others have experience in imperialism, colonial subjection, national emancipation, civil war, or international cooperation.

The expression *mood agenda* is intended to designate the detailed practices that are part of the predispositions that relate to a particular item in the mood repertory. The national myth is differentiated dynasty by dynasty, regime by regime, generation by generation. Key anecdotes, legal formulas, and doctrinal propositions constitute the agenda of each mood. Under various contingencies the agenda may be reinvoked and revalidated in the lives of the current generation. Frederick Barbarossa rides again. A new dynasty has succeeded to the mandate of Heaven and after subduing the rebels at home must restore order among the barbarians at the border. The mood agenda is a legacy of scripts and masks for the never-ending drama in the arena of power.[11]

A STRATEGY OF INQUIRY

If the analysis of climate outlined in this chapter is tenable, collective as well as individual moods are important components of the international political process. Every initiative to act has some impact, however slight, upon the flow of mood; it is at the phase of mood formation that conflicting, facilitating, and nonrelevant initiatives are consolidated and focused toward narrower objectives in time and place. Hence the climate of an international arena is performing a selective role among dispositions to act and thus exercising a selective influence upon detailed perspectives, communications, and collaborations. The dominant mood or moods that come to the fore are stabilizers of the tempo and content of collective action.

We have stressed the advantages to cooperating elites of a common mood: intra-elite communication, hence joint policy coordination, is accelerated since uncertainties of mutuality are reduced or forestalled. If elites are unified the chances are increased that non-elite elements of the arena will go along with their elites, since deviations are subject to deprivation, while conformities are indulged.

If we treat propositions regarding the international climate as hypotheses for the guidance of inquiry, several possible lines of research are suggested. It is feasible to use and improve existing institutions that are responsible for

---

[11] A method of establishing the loci and timing of historical sequences is exhibited in Chao-Ting Chi (1936). On the periodization problem—with reference to China—see the commentary of Toynbee on his critics (1961).

surveying contemporary trends.[12] Properly designed analysis of the content of elite-to-elite and elite-to-non-elite media of communication can disclose (a) the distribution of common moods, (b) the distribution of deviations. Research upon samples of (a) and (b) can throw light upon the pattern of conditioning factors that account for these responses.

Many important hypotheses—inspired by the maximization postulate—can be investigated by analyzing the changing content of the media. For instance, the proposition that *moods are self-sustaining* can be explored in international politics by taking note of the frequency and speed with which deviations are overcome. If nations A and B are on mutually friendly terms, and the elite press of A suddenly criticizes B adversely, the probability is that this deviation will not last long. The former balance of positive references to B is likely to be restored at once. Even without official directives the "misunderstanding" will be counterbalanced by reaffirmations of "confidence." Very likely official measures are taken to resolve a burgeoning dispute through ordinary diplomatic channels. The same self-correcting sequence typically appears when nations A and B are symmetrical in mood content but asymmetrical as to target, taking one another as targets. If the elite press of A takes a friendly line toward B, this deviation is not likely to last. It will be omitted or dismissed as an exception, and the prevailing balance of adverse references will recur. Official action by A may be taken to maintain distrust of B (perhaps to prevent A's coalition mate C from taking alarm).

Research can be directed to discovering mood flexibility in relation to its communication environment in the world arena. In discussing A and B above we were assuming that a common mood could be described and that any deviation on the part of media in either country is presently corrected. A more fundamental way to approach the situation is to examine the sequence of interaction between utterances. Where mood is stabilized among coalitions of allies, opponents, and uncommitted powers, deviations are presumably noted more promptly than conformities. Deviations are provocations to reaffirm or even to reconsider one's previous outlook. In the first example of the preceding paragraph, if we examine A's original criticism of B and in turn investigate the content of B's elite press, we may see that B reacts sharply; hence A's prompt reassurance indicates prompt awareness of B (an indicator of high reactivity to the environment). If C's elite press editorializes, it may or may not be noted by A or B.

It will be useful to focus upon the shifts, since they provide clues to the dynamism of politics. The evidence yielded by the study of content can be supplemented by examining reactivities to all other features of the environment that are likely to influence politics.

A means of pinpointing useful research is to compare deviations among media that are controlled by, or that cater to, known components of the nations involved. In open societies where popular governments are functioning it is relevant to follow deviations according to political party, elite and general circulation press (includ-

---

[12] In order to keep abreast of the changing context of world politics, it is essential to improve the coverage provided by surveys of trends that use relatively "extensive" methods of continuous observation. More "intensive" studies need to be made periodically in order to disclose changing "predispositions" in depth. For a research design of the kind required, though adapted to another field, see Brodbeck and Jones (1963).

ing radio-TV), regions, and pressure organizations. Useful comparisons can be made among professional organs, such as the journals of legal, political, and social science associations, and speeches and statements of top officials.[13]

An important question concerns the interplay of affect, ideology, and policy. The term "ideology," of course, refers to general doctrines, formulas, and statements of folklore relating to the body politic. Since international arenas are incompletely integrated the ideologies relating to them are far less elaborate than those relating to national systems. (See Chapter 10 in this volume.) In fact one of the most interesting problems connected with the climate of international action is to what extent it modifies the interpretations given to national ideologies.

In this connection we take note of a technical issue that rises when ideologies are looked into. What indices shall be selected of the minimum frequencies before a given key symbol or statement is to be recognized as part of an ideology? A single occurrence is not enough to establish that a statement is well enough accepted to justify inclusion. Some indication is needed of acceptance, of the intensity with which the item is included in the system of belief, faith, and loyalty.

There are grounds for the hypothesis that changes of mood prefigure changes of ideology and policy. The proposition that "ideology becomes phraseology" can be supported by comparative studies of the waning of support for newly introduced ideologies at centers of world revolutionary (or lesser) movements. The weakening of faith, loyalty, and belief is indicated by the decline of dogmatic and instantaneous reaffirmations of the revolutionary system. It can be shown that various elite and non-elite groups lose ardor for many of the specific doctrines and policies initially propagated. However, these influences are checked by the mood-conserving tendencies, outlined above.

There are many situations worthy of research in which the crumbling of support for the established ideology has been greatly underestimated by most contemporary political leaders and analysts. For instance, they have been taken by surprise to discover that young people have failed of indoctrination. At the other extreme are miscalculations that are presumably based upon the failure of metropolitan leaders to keep in touch with the more conservative perspectives of small town and rural communities (see Vali, 1961; and Cantril, 1958). Research can throw light on two closely related problems: the differential rate of political change, and the faulty intelligence estimates accepted by elites.

We have been discussing investigations that rely for the most part upon content analysis of media of communication, or upon available data of social change reported by responsible agencies. Research can be made more refined by employing more intensive methods, adding data obtained by brief sample interviews, and by prolonged depth interviews. Case studies of historical figures can exhaust the biographical sources; and studies of historical incidents can draw on all forms of evidence.

Part of the manipulative strategy of politics calls for mood control by the use of both communication and non-communication instruments. Research can be directed to the examination of campaigns which, though launched

---

[13] Differential responsiveness among media and audiences is examined in Almond (1954) and Burks (1961).

under broadly comparable conditions, have had different results. Programs of investigation can proceed by matching the scope of the objectives sought (for example, victory, defeat; revolution, counter-revolution; reform, counter-reform), the base values at the disposal of participants (national or local, large or small assets), the strategies employed (persuasion or coercion, for instance), and outcome (success, failure).

Studies of the recent or remote past, which depend upon correlation and case methods, call for supplementation by experiments, prototypes, and active intervention. The latter can only be conducted in the turmoil of actual politics.

It is probable that when the climate of international action is made the object of more extended investigation by the full armory of methods appropriate to the task, the results will greatly illuminate the pace and goals of world history. For the mood phase of action is the stream bed where all tributary initiatives and messages meet and fuse in a dominant channel leading toward activities that conform to or modify the previous requirements of ideology and policy.

REFERENCES

Almond, G. A. *The appeals of Communism*. Princeton: Princeton Univer. Press, 1954.

Andrič, I. *The bridge on the Drina*. Translated from the Serbo-Croat by L. F. Edwards. New York: New American Library, 1960.

Arens, R., & Lasswell, H. D. *In defense of public order: The emerging field of sanction law*. New York: Columbia Univer. Press, 1961.

Auden, W. H. *The age of anxiety*. New York: Random House, 1947.

Barber, B., & Hirsch, W. (Eds.) *The sociology of science*. New York: Free Press, 1962.

Barghoorn, F. C. *Soviet foreign propaganda*. Princeton: Princeton Univer. Press, 1964.

Bozeman, Adda B. *Politics and culture in international history*. Princeton: Princeton Univer. Press, 1960.

Brodbeck, A. J., & Jones, Dorothy B. Television viewing and norm-violating practices and perspectives of adolescents: A synchronized depth and scope program of policy research. In L. Arons & M. A. May, *Television and human behavior*. New York: Appleton-Century-Crofts, 1963.

Burks, R. V. *The dynamics of Communism in Eastern Europe*. Princeton: Princeton Univer. Press, 1961.

Cantril, H. *The politics of despair*. New York: Basic Books, 1958.

Chi, Chao-Ting *Key economic areas in Chinese history as revealed in the development of public works for water control*. London: Allen and Unwin, 1936.

Cohn, N. *The pursuit of the millennium*. New York: Oxford Univer. Press, 1957.

Deutsch, K. W. *Nationalism and social communication: An inquiry into the foundations of nationality*. New York: M.I.T. and Wiley, 1953.

Dovring, Karen *Road of propaganda: The semantics of communication*. New York: Philosophical Library, 1959.

Festinger, L., Riecken, H. W., & Schachter, S. *When prophecy fails*. Minneapolis: Univer. Minnesota Press, 1956.

Johnson, J. J. (Ed.) *The role of the military in underdeveloped countries*. Princeton: Princeton Univer. Press, 1962.

Kautsky, J. H. (Ed.) *Political change in underdeveloped countries*. New York: Wiley, 1962.

Lasswell, H. D. *World politics faces economics*. New York: McGraw-Hill, 1945.

Lasswell, H. D., & Kaplan, A. *Power and society: A framework for political in-*

quiry. New Haven: Yale Univer. Press, 1950.

Lichnowski, K. M., Fürst von *Heading for the abyss: Reminiscences by Prince Lichnowski.* London: Constable, 1928.

Marvick, D. (Ed.) *Political decision makers.* New York: Free Press, 1961.

McDougal, M. S., Lasswell, H. D., & Vlasic, I. A. *The public order of space.* New Haven: Yale Univer. Press, 1963.

North, R. C. (Ed.) Case studies in conflict. *J. Confl. Resol.,* 1962, *6*(3).

North, R. C., Holsti, O. R., Zaninovich, M. G., & Zinnes, Dina A. *Content analysis: A handbook with applications for the study of international crisis.* Evanston, Illinois: Northwestern Univer. Press, 1963.

Paine, R. T., & Soper, A. *The art and architecture of Japan.* Baltimore: Penguin Books, 1955.

Pool, I. de S. (Ed.) *Trends in content analysis.* Urbana: Univer. Illinois Press, 1959.

Radin, P. Introduction. In P. Radin (Ed.), *African folktales and sculpture.* Bollingen Series XXXII. New York: Pantheon Books, 1952.

Rogow, A., & Lasswell, H. D. *Power, corruption, and rectitude.* New York: Prentice-Hall, 1963.

Schelling, T. C. War without pain, and other models. *World Politics,* 1963, *15,* 465–487.

Toynbee, A. J. *A study of history.* New York: Oxford Univer. Press, 1961.

Tuchman, Barbara W. *The guns of August.* New York: Macmillan, 1962.

Vali, F. A. *Rift and revolution in Hungary.* Cambridge, Mass.: Harvard Univer. Press, 1961.

Wohlstetter, Barbara *Pearl Harbor: Learning and decision.* Stanford: Stanford Univer. Press, 1962.

10

The next chapter continues our exploration of societal processes formed by the aggregation of social interactions that are widely distributed across a national population. The interaction products with which Chapter 10 is concerned are the shared beliefs and sentiments that constitute national ideologies. What types of nationalism are likely to develop in different kinds of national systems, and what are the conditions under which they tend to be aroused? How does the nationalist ideology prevailing in a society affect the orientation toward international relations that this society typically takes? Specifically, what is the relationship between type of nationalist ideology and the strategies of conflict resolution that a state is likely to adopt? And what is the relationship between type of ideology and the strategies of conflict resolution to which a state is likely to be responsive? These are the questions to which the next chapter is addressed.

The starting-point of this chapter is at the macroscopic or system level—that is, at the level of the nation-state itself. Social-psychological concepts are used, however, in order to hypothesize about the effects of system variables on international behavior: Given a national system at a particular stage of development and with a particular set of functions, what values and beliefs is its ideology likely to stress? And, given a particular ideology, what goals and assumptions are likely to govern action in the international arena? These concepts help to bridge system characteristics and the behavior of national decision-makers; and at the same time they facilitate empirical study of the effects of system characteristics by making them accessible to social-psychological measurement techniques.

The author of Chapter 10, Daniel Katz, is Professor of Psychology at the University of Michigan, and Program Director in its Survey Research Center. He is also on the Executive Committee of the University's Center for Research on Conflict Resolution. In 1946–1947 he was president of the Society for the Psychological Study of Social Issues; and currently he is Editor of the *Journal of Personality and*

Social Psychology. He is co-author of *Students' attitudes* (1931), and *Social psychology* (1938); and co-editor of *Research methods in the behavioral sciences* (1953), and *Public opinion and propaganda* (1954). His current research interests include the psychology of nationalism; the motivation of underprivileged groups; and the social psychology of organizations.

H. C. K.

Nationalism and Strategies of International Conflict Resolution*

Daniel Katz

The major concern of this chapter is an analysis of the strategies for dealing with international conflict. In this analysis we shall examine how conflicts arise, the forms they assume, and the methods by which they are resolved. The background for approaching these problems is to be found in a study of the functions of the national state and its integrating ideology of nationalism. Nation states and their nationalistic ideologies are not of a piece, and different forms of nationalism have different consequences for international conflict. One type of nation state will behave differently from another both as an active agent in the international scene and as the reactive recipient of external influences.

Our approach will be social-psychological in that we will consider both the nature of the social systems, national and international, and the nature of the psychological variables involved. Thus we are interested both in the people, whose many partial, parallel, and interdependent acts comprise national behavior, and in the social settings in which these actions take place. We are not so much concerned with the national leader as a personality but as a person operating in the role of decision-maker with all the constraints and pressures this implies. In contrast, the individual-psychological, or personality, approach attempts to explain the events at the macroscopic level by postulating a

* The author is heavily indebted to his colleagues Herbert C. Kelman and Richard Flacks for the discussion of nationalism in this chapter. His collaboration with them on a research project on nationalism is the source of much of the present discussion. Neither Dr. Kelman nor Dr. Flacks, however, is responsible for any errors or misconceptions that may appear in this formulation.

parallel process at the microscopic level. For example, nations take belligerent actions and it is assumed that this is a function of the aggressive warlike character of their peoples, as if social processes consisted of the summation of individuals acting in parallel rather than of complex patterns of interaction. The facts are, however, that a declaration of war by a national state is the outcome of many interdependent cycles and subcycles of behavior within which personal aggressiveness may be an inconsequential variable.

A social-psychological approach differs not only from the individual or personality approach but also from the conventional point of view of social science. Political science and history, for example, are more concerned with the global description of social structures, products, or outcomes and the interactions of complex systems. Collective structures are seen as independent of people. These structures comprise the walls of the human maze and so determine behavior rather than being determined by human beings. The approach of social psychology, however, is to inquire into the walls of the human maze, since after all these walls are made up of people playing their roles in predictable fashion. In other words, the social system does not consist of a physical structure like an automobile, which exists even when it is not functioning. A social system ceases to exist the moment it stops functioning, because its systemic character consists in the relationships between acts of people.

The personality theorist, in looking at belligerent national action, would see people showing aggression; the political scientist would see nations at war; and the social psychologist would see people playing their various roles in the national structure in relation to their needs and the social constraints of the situation. Each approach would seek different causal variables: the personality theorist would look to the frustrations in the child-rearing practices of the society; the political scientist might seek for the informational input of a threatening nature coming from another nation; and the social psychologist would search for the reasons why citizens can be mobilized into military roles in playing their parts in the system, and why national leaders behave as they do in their capacities as decision-makers.

An example of the basic thesis to be developed in these pages is the observation that the tactics and strategies employed by national decision-makers are a function of the forces and constraints affecting them as the incumbents of positions in a given structure. Though ideal models of rational decision-making can be urged upon these leaders by mathematicians, the fact remains that the models they will employ in practice will be limited by the system constraints in which they operate. Organizational variables impose limits on leadership behavior in that (a) they set the range of choices outside of which no decision can be made and (b) they present a hierarchy of alternatives or a priority of choices. Thus March and Simon (1958) have pointed out in their analysis of the cognitive limits of rationality in organization decision-making that the approach to problem-solving is through a limited and simplified model of the real situation. The way in which the situation is simplified and defined is partly in terms of *givens* of the organizational structure and its immediately preceding history. Typically, there will not be a thorough search to find all the alternative possible answers to a problem, nor will there be an adequate assessment of the risk and certainty of consequences attached to each alternative, nor will there be a complete utility ordering of the consequences of all possible alternatives. For each of these processes there will be a short-circuiting, simplification, and distortion based upon existing organizational variables.

Our general procedure will be to start at the system level to find the relevant variables that affect people as members of their nation. The major systems to be considered are the nation state and the international system. We shall then turn to the ways in which people become involved in national roles and the conditions for arousing their behavior as nationals. Finally, we shall use these considerations in discussing the strategies employed by nations for dealing with international conflict.

THE NATION STATE AND ITS IDEOLOGY

In viewing the nation state as the critical unit at the social system level, we shall first call attention to its major functions and then to the part played by nationalism or the ideology of the nation state in its functioning.

Functions of the Nation State

Three major functions of the political state can be identified:

1. *Internal Integration.* The state as the source of political decisions is the final arbiter of the allocation of resources, the final arbiter of conflicts within the society, and an important mechanism for providing common services to the society. In most of the societies with which we are familiar the state has a monopoly on the use of organized physical force for the implementation of its decisions. When organized force is employed by any subgroup we have a society in rebellion. Even conservative Southerners in the United States will not countenance organized force in opposition to desegregation. Intrasystem conflict within the nation is generally resolved, compromised, or muted by the hierarchical authority structure of the political state.

2. *The Maximization of a Favorable Input—Output Ratio for the Society.* The state, like other systems, functions to provide effective utilization of resources both within its borders and in its dealings with the outside world. Thus, there are moves to acquire territory, resources, and markets. There are also moves to control such resources when they cannot be directly acquired. The primitive method is conquest and confiscation. We tend to neglect this aspect of the development of national states though much of history is the story of one group moving in on another and subjugating it (Oppenheimer, 1914). The United States too had this origin but it is neglected because the native inhabitants were too weak and too sparse a population to put up much of a fight. The resort to force in the American Revolution led to the creation of the American state. Though this primitive means for maximizing systemic resources has been replaced in part by economic forms of domination, the basic point is that social systems do move toward a favorable input—output ratio of resources.

This maximizing dynamic generally pushes in the direction of growth and expansion. It is, moreover, accelerated or decelerated by the type of dominant institutions of the society. The mode of its expression is similarly determined by these major subsystems of the society. The Marxians saw the socio-economic institutions, the ownership of the means of production, or the social relations of production, as the key institution. To-day we give greater emphasis to technology and to bureaucratic structure. While there are those like Kardiner (1945) who regard the socializing process of the family as the key institution, we would argue that, at the very least, technology and bureaucracy contribute heavily to the maximizing dynamic of modern, industrialized nations. It is this dynamic that has the heaviest implications for international conflict and cooperation. Maximization of the operations of the system does not necessarily benefit all members of the system or even a majority of them. It is the system that is being advanced, not its individual members.

3. *Survival and Protection against External Enemies.* This function is the counterpart of the expanding dynamic in that a nation not only moves to extend its control and influence internationally but in turn is the object of influences and sometimes aggression from other nations. Self-preservation and survival can be as strong forces at the group as at the individual level. National security is a central value reflecting the emphasis upon survival. Its potency is such that it can be invoked even in the absence of realistic threats to the nation.

Since the state is the guardian of the national interest, and since it represents the organization of the forces of the society for this purpose, it moves to acquire power in relation to other states. Any danger to its survival or any threat from without leads to attempts to increase the power of the national state.

The problem of peace is one of identifying those forces and institutions within interrelated societies that are expansionist or overly defensive in nature and of determining the ways in which their dynamics can be handled

without military conflict. Nationalism is part of this problem in that, as a system ideology, it not only reflects the functions of the system but also contributes to systemic functioning.

Nationalism, the Ideology of the Nation State

Nationalism as a property of the nation state is the ideology that both reflects and sustains the major functions of the state. As a value system it not only justifies and glorifies the major activities of the state, but it also helps to give direction to them. It is both an effect and a cause of the functions of the state. In speaking of nationalism as a system ideology we refer to the integrated set of values and beliefs that represent a coherent pattern for the collectivity. Individual members of the system may show varying degrees of acceptance of these beliefs and values; the leaders will have a more articulated belief pattern, and official pronouncements and documents may contain specific elaborations. There is no simple one-to-one relationship between system ideology and the sum of the attitudes of individual members. Individuals will show, however, modal acceptance of certain selected beliefs.

Three types of nationalistic ideology can be distinguished. All three of these value systems are generally represented in the ideology of the nation state.

1. *Statism.* One type of nationalistic ideology centers around the political state itself; we shall refer to it as statism, for want of a better term. It includes the doctrine of national sovereignty, the doctrine that the authority of the state is absolute and supreme, that the state is the legitimate source for decisions affecting the political system as a whole, that allegiance to the state and its legitimately made deci-

sions is the duty of all citizens. It also includes the belief that the state functions to protect national security and to advance national interests that are valued in themselves. Related to this ideology of the national state are the symbols that reify its existence, the offices of its titular head, the King, President, and so on.

Value systems about the nation state can vary in terms of reification of the state as opposed to a realistic differentiated conception of it. Reified belief systems, for example, would center values around an entity standing above the people. More realistic beliefs would see the state as the collective instrument for compromising and solving common problems.

2. *Institutional Nationalism.* Another type of nationalistic ideology would center around certain societal institutions as the embodiment of national purpose and national goals. Thus, American nationalism may consist in part of belief systems about the political institution of democracy, and the economic institution of free enterprise and the related institution of technology as expressions of American national purpose. Value systems centering around these institutions can exist independently of values about the national state itself, but they are often linked to one another or even fused. Thus, nationalism has an input from the dominant institutions of the society. Advancing national interests means extending these institutions.

The interaction of value systems about the state and about the dominant institutions of a society has interesting implications for international behavior. On the one hand this linkage may result in policies of aggressive nationalistic expansion. On the other hand, the institutional values may outweigh the values of the political state for some

subgroupings of society and make for international cooperation. For some of the owning and privileged groups in Europe during the Hitler era the values of the socio-economic institutions were more important than values of the political state. In this case national values were deserted in favor of institutional values. It may also happen, however, that two or more nations with similar institutions have a basis for cooperation because their nationalisms embrace common value systems based upon similar social structures. Conflict, of course, can still result when similarly structured societies are competing for the same common objects, in other words, when there is a realistic basis for conflict. John Paul's example (1963) of twelve men stranded on a desert island with Elizabeth Taylor may be relevant here. They have the same common values, the same goal, and hence plenty of conflict. Where there is little to be gained from conflict, however, cooperation is a real possibility between systems sharing common institutions, as we have seen in the development of the European community.

3. *Cultural Identity.* A third type of national ideology consists of the values centering around the character of a people, the common cultural heritage, the language, the way of life of a people, in short the *cultural identity* supposedly shared by the members of the nation state. At the individual level we speak of consciousness of kind of fellow nationals. In extreme form this is often called ethnocentrism or racism. These values can exist without linkage to a national state, as with the Jewish group in the United States. When a nation state does exist, however, it quickly links together the ideology of the state with the cultural identity of the people.

Generic Dimensions of Nationalism: Affective Symbolic Codes vs. Pragmatic Reality Codes

We have distinguished among three components of nationalism with respect to substantive belief areas. Another fundamental distinction concerns the generic psychological basis of nationalistic values. Two dimensions are of relevance to the role of these values in national and international problems. The first is the symbolic or reality-oriented character of the value or belief. By symbolic we do not mean that the value stands for something it is not, as in language symbols, but rather that the symbol is accepted as the essential reality. The beliefs are reified and have little in the way of an objective referent. They are what Thurman Arnold (1935) referred to when he spoke of symbols of government, or what some of the semanticists have in mind when they speak of polarized concepts. The doctrine of national sovereignty has much of this character. In contrast to such symbolic codes are the empirically oriented belief systems, which have objective referents. The symbolic codes are closed to everyday experience, the reality codes are not. Thus, when people believe in the majesty of the law as if it were a supernatural force, they will accept the idea that the law must take its course even if in a given case the accused are not guilty. Others, however, may see the law as a set of rules for accomplishing human objectives that can be changed to accord with new problems. In the former case we are dealing with a symbolic belief, in the latter with a reality-oriented belief.

A second dimension is the amount of emotional investment in the belief. Some beliefs have a heavy affective loading. Others are held with little emotional feeling. Though there is not a perfect correlation between the symbolic–reality dimension and the amount of affective loading, the symbolic values in general tend to have much more emotional loading than do the reality beliefs.

The integration of people into a group, organization, or larger system can occur at two levels. At the one level they are tied into the structure through their emotional investment in system symbols. These sacred values are accepted without question and generally have to do with the nobility of the system and its mission. Leaders can invoke these symbols to hold people in the system, to excommunicate deviants, to mobilize followers for emergency action. At another level people are integrated into the system through their functional interdependence in their everyday activities and their empirically oriented beliefs about these interdependent activities. Durkheim's profound analysis (1933) of the nature of societal solidarity called attention to these two types of integration. In societies characterized by a slight division of labor, with people performing the same types of tasks, the integrating factor was a collective moral conscience. Deviations from moral norms led to an outraged public feeling that was the basis of criminal law. In societies characterized by a great deal of division of labor the integrating factor became the functional interdependence of people and their acceptance of civil codes governing their relations with one another. Though our use of affective symbolic codes as against empirical belief systems is not an exact reiteration of the Durkheim analysis, it is similar in pointing to two different bases of social integration. Our contention is that either or both methods can be operating in any given social structure and, further, that the strategies for dealing with conflict must take account of the differences between these two kinds of integration and the two kinds of values systems they reflect. We shall return to this problem, but for the present purpose of exposition let us merely call attention to an example of the operation of these two belief codes. The experienced leader will often avoid conflict within a structure by introducing change in such a way that none of the symbolic values of the system is made salient. The change will be presented as dealing with practical problems in terms of empirical belief systems. The less experienced leader will unwittingly touch off some of the sacred symbols and be in difficulty.

Dynamics of National Systems

Nations are not only integrated by the various types of national value systems but also by more objective factors: specifically, the functional interdependence of the substructures within the nation, and the common fate and common rewards accruing to its members. Nations will differ with respect to internal structure and institutions. Where there is a high degree of commonality of reward and of functional interdependence there is also a high degree of objective integration and hence less need for a heavy emphasis upon national ideology of a symbolic affective kind. National leaders can use symbolic integration to achieve more objective integration, as did Hitler and his fellow Nazi leaders. Though the Nazis succeeded in destroying most of the organized substructures within Germany that were relatively independent of the state, they never achieved as much economic integration as the totalitarian state implies.

In addition to the differences in social structure it is also important to take into account the inputs into the national system, both from its own internal resources and from its relations with other nations. The United States, as a developing nation with a continent of natural resources available to it, presents a pattern different from that of Germany, arriving as a latecomer to the international scene with the world resources already staked out by other nations. If we take into account both the social structure of the nation and its available inputs we can distinguish among four patterns: (1) the revolutionary society, characterized by the development of a nation as the expression of new institutions replacing or overthrowing old institutions, (2) the empire-building society, characterized by the extension of national power on an exploitive basis, (3) the bureaucratic technological society, either of a capitalistic or of a socialist type, and (4) the declining society, in which the state or its subsystems are blocked, threatened, or losing power. This is not intended as a comprehensive typology of national states but as an illustration of how differing social structures with differing inputs will move toward different patterns of nationalism.

1. The revolutionary society would be illustrated by the development of national states in overthrowing feudal institutions. This is the classic picture of nationalism in the writings of Carleton Hayes (1926). There are some similarities here with the growing nationalism in underdeveloped countries that have successfully revolted against colonialism. The older institutions in both of these instances were exploitive in character and the revolt is fostered by groups who seek a more advantageous position. These groups develop national ideology as a weapon in the struggle and in so doing they broaden the ideological base of the conflict to include all the people of the society. The hypothesis here is that there is a close linkage and even an integration be-

tween all three types of national ideology: the political doctrines about the new state, the values centering about new institutions, and the ethnocentrism of the people. The new nation state is the people's state—that is, people of that nationality; it stands for new institutions and a new and better way of life. Such an integrated ideology has real advantages in mobilizing people on a mass basis behind national leaders. And it has some reality basis in that most of the people have a common fate in throwing out the oppressors, especially if they are foreigners.

The fusion of these elements may make for more potential conflict with other nations. Not only are other nations seen as rivals, if there is competition for scarce resources, but they are also seen as threats, if they represent either different institutions or different cultural values.

2. The empire-building period is one of direct power moves to maximize the input–output ratio for the dominant institutions of the society. Expansionist power is accompanied by an ideology that attempts a continued integration of the three components of nationalism. Integration becomes more difficult, however, in that the commonality of interests of all subgroups in the nation and of all nationals against other nations and other nationals is less clear. Certain privileged subgroups benefit much more from expansionist power moves than do others. To maintain the integration of the society, the ethnocentrism doctrine moves toward the extreme of racism—for example, toward the doctrine of the white man's burden (now reversed among some African nationals) as a type of extreme aggressive ethnocentrism. At the psychological level, some of the motivational basis of nationalism shifts from identification based upon consciousness of kind to compensatory mechanisms of identification with power symbols.

3. With the rise of such economic institutions as the market place and with the accumulation of investment capital and the increasing division of labor, nations move toward becoming technological bureaucratic societies. This form of social organization has certain characteristics that have implications for nationalism. Some of these characteristics are: (a) the divorce of organizational forms from traditional, personal, and nonfunctional elements, thus permitting flexibility and rapid growth; (b) the development of role readiness as part of childhood socialization (the ability of people to move into any role so long as it is legitimized); (c) a value orientation that is geared to pragmatic outcomes rather than absolute, sacred symbols (hence the development of technology is favored—in fact technology is often the leading subsystem of the total society); (d) an increase in the standard of living for all people because of the efficiencies of the system; and (e) the development of a maximization or growth dynamic.

The maximization dynamic of the technological bureaucratic system derives from many sources. Bureaucratic technological structures call for a high degree of specialization of labor and of function. To operate effectively the system requires great chunks of physical and social space, as well as large numbers of mobile people to allow for specialization of function. Thus, in the United States, with all our anti-trust laws, there is a continuing problem of holding down the size of organizations. Another source of maximization is the tendency to acquire control over the inputs into the system, either by direct acquisition of input sources or indirect mechanisms for tying them into the system. An industrial firm, for example, may acquire title to its sources of supply or may develop control over satellite companies that furnish it raw or semi-processed materials. Moreover, anticipatory mechanisms develop, such as research and development departments in industrial organizations, for more complete exploitation of the system's potential in dealing with its environment. Growth, then, becomes inevitable until checked by powerful forces external to the system.

In bureaucratic society the linkage between the political aspects of nationalism and the cultural identification with nationality becomes further weakened. As the nation state becomes more bureaucratized the ethnocentrist element is no longer closely tied to statism. The national identity of people is now more a matter of their bureaucratic roles and less a matter of the distinctive culture of the nation. What ties the citizen to the nation state is less the affective symbol codes than the ideology of the state as the source of bureaucratic authority.

If this analysis is correct, then it would follow that ethnocentrism or identification with cultural identity is a minor factor in promoting or otherwise affecting international conflict between bureaucratic states. Attempts to minimize conflict by intercultural contact, by trying to develop tolerance and understanding of other nationals, are exaggerated as a means of preventing war. Differentiated cultural identities of peoples can facilitate militant propaganda once a conflict is under way, but the fact of cultural differences does not in itself generate international conflict. We do not engage in war against another nation because they possess a different culture or a different set of customs. Otherwise the United States would have fought France rather than Germany in 1916 and in 1941. In fact American soldiers in both wars had something of this naive conception and wondered why they were fighting the Germans rather than the French. The facts are, however, that they were fighting against Germany since wars are clashes between political states, not between peoples of different cultures. It may help the cause of peace if we can get individuals from one culture to understand individuals from another culture, but this is not the major means for bringing about a peaceful world.

4. When the state or its subsystems become blocked in expansion and threatened with loss of power, a retreatist or revivalist nationalism is fostered. The power expansion may be blocked by the superior power of other nations or by other constraints in the external environment. This may lead to a redefinition of nationalism, which narrows the nationality definition with respect to the types of people and the kinds of values considered truly patriotic. There is a restriction in what is considered genuinely national and in those who qualify as true nationals. More attention may be given to internal enemies than to external. The state no longer receives unquestioning allegiance, but it, too, is redefined in terms of old traditions.

Often this type of nationalism is represented by groups within the population who are losing power or are threatened with the loss of power. Hence they narrow the concept of the national to include only those like themselves. The radical right in the United States may reflect some of this psychology.

THE AROUSAL OF NATIONALISM AND THE ASSUMPTION OF NATIONAL ROLES

In spite of the state's priority over other social structures, the role systems comprising the national state are often latent rather than active in the national population. The life of the ordinary citizen is devoted to his roles as a member of his occupation, of his family, his church, his union, and so forth. His national roles may make few demands in times of peace. He does vote on occasion and may even take part in the political process more actively. He pays his taxes and obeys national laws. He gives customary compliance to national rituals, such as standing when the national anthem is played. Yet his national involvement does not occupy much of his psychological life space. When the nation is at war, however, the situation changes radically. More national roles are specified for him and many of his peace time roles become national roles, for example, his peace time role as a worker in a plant now becomes that of a defense worker for the nation.

Forces and Conditions Basic to the Arousal of Nationalism

What, then, are the latent forces in the individual that can be aroused for his assumption of national roles and what are the conditions for the arousal of these forces? Four types of forces can be distinguished: (1) emotional and behavioral conditioning to national symbols, (2) the sense of personal identity as a national, (3) compensatory and defensive identification with militant nationalism, and (4) instrumental involvement in the national structure.

1. *Emotional and Behavioral Conditioning to National Symbols.* Part of the socialization process in many countries includes the conditioning of the behavior of children in the observance of national rituals. In the United States, for example, school children pledge allegiance to the flag in unison, rise together in singing the national anthem, and at a more complex level are encouraged to worship national heroes and detest traitors. This

conditioning includes an acceptance of national authorities such as the President or the Supreme Court speaking in their appropriate legitimate roles. The depth of the emotional affect that becomes tied to national symbols in this fashion will vary depending upon the intensity of the experience and the amount of repetition. The depth of the affective conditioning is not always great because of the mechanical nature of the process, akin in some instances to a class repeating aloud the German prepositions governing the accusative case. National states vary in the intensity of this type of training. What is always potent, however, is the social reinforcement in the process. The ritual is observed by everyone and no deviations are tolerated. Not many learning experiences of the child have this unanimity of social reinforcement.

The emotional and social conditioning in itself does not provide an adequate basis for the generalization of responses to many of the complex situations in which the individual is expected to play a national role. The basic arousal condition is the appearance of the old stimulus of the flag or some other symbol to which the individual shows respect. Another arousal condition is the perceived unanimity of others following a supposedly patriotic course of action. This is consistent with early training in which no deviations were permitted in the observance of national rituals. This respect and compliance can generalize to the acceptance of a specific directive from national authority, as in the case of the presidential letter asking the person to join the armed forces. But it provides little basis for the citizen in peacetime engaging in activities supportive of a national policy supposedly representing national interests. In other words, emotional conditioning does lay the foundation for the belief in patriotism as a positive value, but it does not specify how patriotism can be expressed beyond respecting national symbols, complying with orders from national authorities, and conforming to the patriotic practices of the overwhelming majority.

2. *The Formation of the Self Concept as Inclusive of National Identity.* A significant aspect of the socialization process is the development of the individual's perception of himself as a national, as an Englishman, a Frenchman, an Algerian, and so on. The growing child establishes his self identity not only as a unique personality but as an individual belonging to an in-group showing the same values and orientations in contrast to foreign out-groups. This group identification develops readily around immediate local groupings, but extends to people embraced by the national structure with a common fate, history, and culture. National identity, thus, is an anchoring frame for the individual's conception of himself. Many Englishmen living in the United States will not change their citizenship and cannot understand how any Englishman could make such a change. It would be tantamount to rejecting his self image.

The factors conducive to the development of a sense of national identity also have implications for the arousal conditions in adult life that lead to national role taking. They have to do with the simplicity of cognitive structuring in terms of in-group vs. out-group under circumstances of competition and conflict. Thus, a people possessing a homogeneous culture with a perceived common fate in competitive contact with other nations can readily internalize a sense of national identification. We called attention earlier to the possible fusion of statism, institutional ideology, and cultural identity. Where it occurs we generally find a high incidence of people whose self concepts include a feeling of national identity.

Even though an individual includes his national identity as part of his self concept it is latent in most situations. It becomes manifest under conditions of confrontation at two levels. At the level of personal experience it is aroused by direct contact with other nationals either through travel abroad or through the presence of foreigners in one's own country. Its arousal is further facilitated and the feeling maintained if the confrontation with other nationals entails some degree of conflict, competition, or even comparison. Thus, programs of cultural exchange designed to improve international understanding are not necessarily successful in changing attitudes toward other nationals in a favorable direction. (See, for example, Selltiz and Cook, 1962.) The visiting foreigner is made aware of his foreignness and is stimulated to compare his nation with the host nation. This may have a variety of consequences. Much depends upon the type of experience, the expectations of the person, and his personality characteristics. (See Chapters 4 and 15 in this volume.)

At the secondary level of the world created by the mass media and communications from leaders, the sense of national identity is aroused by perceived matters of *national interest* and *national security* in relation to other nations. Again the closeness of the problem to the citizens is an important variable. The Cuban situation was more potent in arousing American nationalism than the situation in Viet Nam.

3. *Compensatory Identification.* We have been describing a positive extension of the individual's self image to include people like himself with the same values and interests. In addition there is a type of national identification

that is based not so much on the individual's attraction by the advantages of group belongingness as on his attempts to solve his own internal conflicts and insecurities. In general this is referred to as defensive or compensatory identification. Here the motivation stems from the individual's own inadequacy and his attempts to be part of a powerful group from which he can derive a vicarious sense of power. This is basically the authoritarian syndrome as described by Adorno, Frenkel-Brunswik, Levinson, and Sanford (1950). It has been demonstrated that individuals who have met their childhood conflicts through repression of their hostilities can readily project their hatreds on the out-group. Thus ethnocentrism, anti-Semitism, and chauvinism have been found to have some degree of relationship with personality insecurity. Moreover, attitudes of emotional rejection of minority out-groups are correlated with attitudes highly critical of international cooperation (Levinson, 1957). Similarly, a study of Norwegian nationalism reports that power-oriented nationalism is related to the authoritarianism syndrome, whereas a people-oriented nationalism is not (Bay, Gullväg, Ofstad, & Tønnessen, 1950). We are postulating, then, a defense mechanism of compensatory identification with the nation as an intervening variable which links the person's initial mode of handling conflict with certain types of nationalism.

Germany after World War I presents an example of the conditions making for the development of this type of defensive identification. Young people reared in fairly authoritarian families, made even more insecure by conditions of economic deprivation, readily sought psychic compensation in identifying with the power of their nation. The situation was aggravated by the fact that the nation had been defeated in a war and that its signs of power such as a large military force had been stripped away. The needs of the people were such, however, that they refused to face their military defeat in World War I and instead accepted the notion that the army had been betrayed by traitors at home (Fried, 1942). The Nazis, by providing a rationale for their needs and by furnishing through their marching storm troops, their uniforms, and their military slogans a visible indication of German strength, built something of a mass basis for their final coming to power.

The basis, then, for compensatory identification is the repressed hostility of a people stemming from early frustrations. The conditions for its arousal are similar frustrations and threats to security in the present. Since we are dealing here primarily with problems internal to individuals, it is not so much the actual threat from outside forces that triggers them off. Any event can be seized upon by leaders, as an insult to national honor and a threat to national power, to exploit this type of identification and arouse people to assume national roles. Even if the duly constituted national leadership takes a responsible position in minimizing possible external threats, the danger is that leaders seeking power will seize upon incidents to rally people to the defense of the nation and to indict the present leaders. Whereas national interest is the more common means for arousing the positive types of national identification, appeals about national honor and national power are more effective for eliciting defensive identification.

4. *Instrumental Involvement in the National Structure.* National involvement also has a firm basis in all the instrumental rewards that accrue to the loyal citizen in playing his part in society. People often assume their na-

tional roles in large measure because their way of life and their means of livelihood are tied into the national structure. To refuse to accept the legitimate demands of the nation is to reject the system. There is an all-or-none quality about the matter (Allport, 1962). One is either a loyal citizen or he is not. The realistic alternatives to rejecting the system are forbidding and vary from imprisonment and exile to virtual ostracism. Hence people will pay their taxes, testify before the House Committee on Un-American Activities, and support their national leaders because they want to remain in the system. And the greater the rewards accruing from system membership, the less will individuals consider the prospects of deserting the system.

In describing the forces of emotional conditioning and of positive and of compensatory identification we were calling attention to the internalized factors that make the expression of nationalism rewarding in and of itself. But we are now recognizing the fact that for many people and at many times the assumption of a national role may be an instrumental act which is motivated by its consequences rather than by the intrinsic satisfactions from performing it. And it has been our general thesis that in large bureaucratic societies such instrumental involvement may be relatively more important than in newly emerging national states. There is a common belief that the conduct of modern total war requires that the masses of people be stirred to action by a hate propaganda against the enemy. The facts are, however, that the war effort of the United States in World War II was accomplished with no concerted governmental campaign of an emotional or ideological character. The domestic propaganda efforts were limited to specific practical programs, such as buying bonds, saving scarce materials, observing the ration rules, and following suggestions with respect to security of information. There was a marked absence of parades, of beating of drums, and of emotional arousal. Whatever emotional dynamics existed arose largely from the conflict itself and not from a planned program of indoctrination.

The arousal condition for instrumental national involvement is the appearance of the legitimate symbols of national authority. This can be at the specific level, where either the symbol or legal directive calls for some particular act of compliance; or at the general level, where a national leader attempts to secure support for a program of action. At the specific level the critical issue is the legitimacy and appropriateness of the demand, in other words, whether it comes from duly constituted authority speaking in their realms of jurisdiction. For example, some of the Southern states in the United States attempted to create a conflict over symbols by asserting the supremacy of state rather than federal laws in areas of civil rights. Where actual resistance to national authority was threatened the federal government nationalized the state militia and made clear the priority of legal symbols, so that governors had to step aside and acknowledge federal authority. At the general level the national leader must speak as a national figure and not as the representative of a specific party or group. At the general level, moreover, national symbols such as the Constitution or polarized concepts such as national security may be employed to encourage a course of action through appeals to national involvement. Such appeals, which are directed at the basic membership character of belonging to the national structure, are most effective in emergency situations or circumstances in which people see their way of life being threatened by internal or external enemies.

For purposes of exposition we have presented these four sources of motivational support for the assumption of national roles as if they were alternative and independent bases for action. In practice, however, the general finding would be that a number of these motive patterns reinforce one another. The conditioning to national symbols, even if not accompanied by intense affective experience, does make clear to the individual the things he must observe to protect his instrumental national involvement. And the fusion of a sense of personal identity as a national with the instrumental involvement in the structure provides a combination of motive forces that may operate in a multiplicative rather than a simple additive manner. The great energizing fire of nationalism in the newly emerging nation states in the seventeenth and eighteenth centuries was a fusion of such motives. The rising middle classes found increasing instrumental returns from the expansion of their nations and at the same time derived psychic satisfactions from their new national identities.

The Relationship between Psychological Sources of National Role-Taking and the Nature of the Nation State

Though there is some combination of the forces basic to national role-taking in all nations, the relative emphasis upon a given factor will vary according to the nature of the nation state. We have already indicated that the revolutionary and newly emerging nation tends to integrate both instrumental rewards and satisfactions from personal identification as a national for key groups in the society; and that the nation preserving some of its basic institutions through counter-revolution relies heavily upon compensatory identification with power symbols. Many nation states today, however, are well-developed bureaucratic structures representative of an advanced technological society. There are certain elements that are common to such large technological bureaucratic societies with respect to nationalistic ideology and the taking of national roles by leaders and citizens. Specifically, in these types of nations (1) there is some tendency toward divorcing the cultural identity of the people and doctrines of statism, (2) people are tied into the national state more through their functional involvement in the structure of the society than through their ideological commitment to its symbols and (3) bureaucratic functioning creates a task orientation in which leaders learn to deal with problems at the reality rather than the symbol level.

1. The divorce between the cultural identity and doctrines of statism means that the people of a country can still identify with one another and with their way of life without a concurrent commitment to the symbols of government. Americans can derive major satisfactions from being Americans without loving their government. There is even a question as to whether the English crown symbolizes the British political state as much as it does the cultural identity of the English people. Certainly since Winston Churchill there has been no British political leader who has integrated in his own personality the cultural as well as the political ideals of the British.

This shift away from the marriage of political and cultural symbols has profound implications for international conflict and cooperation. It means in effect that there is a popular basis in certain nations for political cooperation and for the peaceful settlement of international disputes, providing people can retain their cultural identity.

2. The affective conditioning to national symbols still takes place in the socialization process but it has become more of a routine matter in the bureaucratic state. In the smaller and newer states, and in an earlier day in the older states, this conditioning was accompanied by the development of personalized beliefs about the symbols. But these symbols have lost some of their potency in arousing deep feelings in a bureaucratic society. A reported insult to the American flag is not as widely perceived as a sense of personal outrage as was once the case. People still assume their national roles but more on the basis of their functional involvement in the national structure.

This change from emotional commitment to national symbols to involvement in functional roles also has important consequences for international conflict. Warlike sentiment is not so easily aroused throughout the population of the nation by the news of international incidents or insults to national honor. The mass media have carried stories about scores of American soldiers being killed in Viet Nam without an outburst of patriotic emotion in the nation. National leadership now has an increased scope in defining international situations for the people and perhaps a more difficult task in justifying an actual declaration of war.

3. National leaders in a bureaucratic society cannot escape the influence of the organizational training of the society. To be an effective organizational leader the individual has to acquire skills in building and maintaining a structure and in increasing its effectiveness and productivity. All this requires a heavy task orientation and an assessment of objective and social realities. The leader who spends his time

in flying flags, getting embroiled in symbolic fights, is often left behind in the competition for higher positions.

INTERNATIONAL SYSTEMS AND TYPES OF CONFLICT

Nation states are not self-contained as the proponents of isolation assume. Systems of economic exchange and other forms of cooperative activity are more common than is generally recognized. In addition to formal organizations such as the United Nations, UNESCO, the World Court, the World Health Organization, international scientific, professional, religious, and business organizations, there are many other international systems. These range from cooperative arrangements for communication, news, travel, copyrights, the control of criminal activity, and the exchange of students and specialized personnel to international cartels. Some of the clearest forms of such international systems are regional in nature, such as the European Common Market, or the Scandinavian Union in which the passport from one Scandinavian country is recognized by any other Scandinavian country as the equivalent of its own passport for many purposes. Every nation is involved with many other nations through treaty arrangements covering a wide range of problems. In September 1963, for example, the United States had 622 treaties in force governing its relations with other nations.

A number of these international arrangements may actually increase the potential for conflict in that they organize the world into opposing camps such as NATO, the Comintern, SEATO, or the European Community. The effect of these arrangements, however, is probably to increase the magnitude of the disaster if it should come rather than to make its occurrence more likely. A major alliance can exert a controlling influence on its more belligerent members.

In his theory of internation relations, Guetzkow (1957) maintains that regional associations of nations will tend to delay a world organization to the extent that such regional groupings successfully meet the needs of members. If the needs can be satisfied within the regional structure there is less motivation toward broader international collaboration and more turning inward to the regional structure. Though Guetzkow does acknowledge that regional isolation could be breached by needs not provided for by the regional organization, he does not believe that successful collaboration will generalize beyond the nation states collaborating. From the short-run point of view this theory has much merit but it may overlook the long-range consequences of the impairment of national sovereignty, and the undermining of the linkage of cultural identity to statism. Nationalistic doctrines of this type constitute a major barrier to the acceptance of a World Court and an enforceable system of international law. The fact of regional association will not in itself produce a world order and is thus not a *positive* force in this direction, but it will help to undermine such *negative* forces against world cooperation as national sovereignty.

Another weakness in international systems that Guetzkow describes is the singleness of function in many cooperative arrangements. An international labor association has the one objective of cooperation with respect to workers' interests. When that goal is met or recedes in importance relative to other needs the international organization loses significance. On the other hand, international associations that could fulfill multiple needs would be a potent factor in producing generalized support for world cooperation. Hence some writers have stressed the fact that the hope for the United Nations is to assume more functions and thus develop a greater amount of interconnection among nations in many fields of endeavor.

The growth of international systems has been accompanied by a tremendous increase in cross-national communication, travel, and contact. The number of days of American tourist stay in Europe in 1957, for example, was 33 million, or triple the volume of that before the war. This shrinking of the physical and psychological universe and the breakdown of national barriers has fostered the development of world opinion as a factor in international relations. In fact the prestige of America abroad became one of the campaign issues in the 1960 election.

The problem is, however, that the involvement of people in the international system is not as wide or as deep as involvement in the national system. In the first place only a small minority of nationals are directly involved in international systems. The growth of tourism and of international exchange of students does not necessarily mean an increase in the number of people who actually play an international role. Many political and industrial leaders do become members of international systems but the primary membership of the political leader is in his own nation state. It is possible, of course, that the exchange of students and of specialized personnel has some effect in that these people may be more supportive of their own national leaders when these officials assume a cooperative international position. It is doubtful that the same effect holds for the tourist group.

Implications of National System Analysis for Strategies in Dealing with International Conflict

It is our contention that national decision-making is neither a rational process in the objective, mathematical sense nor dominantly the expression of the personalities of a few national leaders. Rather it represents the subjective rationality of the national system. The economic and social structure of the nation, the current valence of different types of national ideology, and the inputs from internal and external sources define the limits within which leaders formulate policy and take action. Not all alternatives for action are explored, and the weights assigned to possible consequences are heavily affected by system forces. The different patterns of national systems we have described not only have historical reference but they have contemporary relevance: not all nation states are of a piece and hence each will follow its own subjective patterns of rationality in taking actions that increase or decrease international tension.

Political leaders are the centers of networks of decision-making about national policy. Although they are just one link in the total chain and although their degrees of freedom in making choices are very limited, they are *key* links and they are commonly perceived as playing the role of advancing national interest and protecting national security. They can be challenged by competitors for their leadership roles on the basis of their actions, their pronouncements, and their stance with respect to national prestige, national advantage or disadvantage, and national security. The challenge will be open and public in a democracy and covert and implicit in a totalitarian state. They cannot be seen as less patriotic, less protective of national interest than their competitors.

In a sense national officials also play roles as members of international systems. Here they must be responsive to the demands of the international system if they are to negotiate successfully for their own country, and thus they are impelled toward a longer-range point of view of national interest and of the common goals of many countries than would be true of the rank-and-file of their own nation. These dual roles often place them in a position of conflict in that the agreement that makes sense for the international system may not be one they can defend as patriotic representatives of their country. Part of the art of diplomacy is to evolve formulas for the settlement of a dispute that will be palatable to the people of the contending nations. Where the leader gives primary consideration to his international role he is likely to experience rejection of his efforts from his own people, as was the case with Woodrow Wilson in his contributions toward the development of the League of Nations. The dominant forces playing upon the national leader, save perhaps for small powerless nations, are the internal subgroups of his own country, especially the rival political factions, which interpret his moves from the point of view of a narrow nationalism. Exceptions do occur; for example, domestic business interests will sometimes push for agreements with foreign business interests. In general, however, the forces from within the nation are more immediate and more potent and more shortsighted concerning national interests than are the forces in the international system. Domestic organizations that theoretically could counter these national pressures, such as the Friends of the United Nations or the Foreign Policy Association, are too weak to be of much help. And the chances of such organizations gaining real power are remote because they are built around men of good will and of intellectual understanding and have little functional basis.

Sources of International Conflict

The international system reflects not only the cooperative interconnectedness of nation states and their subgroupings, but also the competitive and conflictual strivings of their subsystems. The types of conflict are not capricious in character but are rooted in the type of nation state involved and the dominant functions it is carrying out.

In discussing the nature of national systems we have already described the dynamic sources of conflict between nations. The maximization dynamic according to which systems push toward completion—toward realizing more of their basic character—often results in expansionistic moves. The nation may attempt to extend its title or control over resources, territory, and markets. It may attempt to extend its institutions and ideology beyond its borders. Conflict results either from encroachment on another nation or its preserves, or from competition with a similar expanding system. The sources for expansion may be of two types: the first is a genuine push toward maximizing the return to the system and the second is a compensatory move to cover over the failure of internal integration. In this second case the internal conflicts of the nation state may not have been resolved by the political system. These unresolved conflicts are then projected outward upon other nations. Since the symbols of the state can be used to rally the nation against external threat, elite groups may maximize the external conflicts to create internal unity. In so doing they may link their own enemies within the nation to the enemies with-

out—a technique utilized effectively by Hitler but not unique to him. Externalization of internal conflict is an ancient but not anachronistic cause of tension and war.

A more indirect form of the external solution of internal problems occurs in the building up of an industrial-military complex to maintain the economy of a nation. In the United States some of the motivation behind the fifty billion dollars spent on defense, comprising over half the national budget, is to meet domestic problems of full employment and economic growth.

These generic causes of struggle take different forms of expression depending on the type of nationalism and nation state, as we have already suggested. Economic conflicts arise over competition for scarce resources and markets. But even in the economic sphere different objectives may be sought at different developmental stages. At one period colonization and the subjugation of other peoples was the answer, at another point ownership of their essential resources backed up by military force was sufficient, and more recently control through bureaucratic devices has been effective.

In addition to the economic manifestation of the maximization dynamic we need to take account of its *ideological expression*. In the newly emerging state or in the expanding national system the justification of the way of life and the institutions of the society in a nationalistic ideology create conditions of conflict. The struggle between the East and the West in its ideological form is between value systems centering not merely around social institutions but around nationalistically conceived social institutions. Ideological conflict is not limited, however, to the confrontation of different national value systems of expanding structures. The doctrine of statism and national sovereignty of any country is always a potential source of incompatibility with that of other countries, as are value systems about the essential rightness of its institutions and the superiority of its culture. These ideologies make possible the mobilization of the people around concepts of national honor, national purpose, or national security. In general the ideological basis for conflict is greatest when all three types of nationalism (statism, cultural identity, and beliefs in national institutions) are tightly integrated and when these belief systems are more symbolically than empirically oriented.

Since nation states are in good part systems for dealing with power relationships, the most general form that conflicts between nations assume is one of a *power* struggle. Political power is utilized to support both economic and ideological interests. But power is not only a means for securing economic advantage or ideological maximization, it is also a source of conflict in its own right. It is a measure of the strength of a national system in general and, since this measure is relative to the power of other nations, it constitutes a continuing potential for conflict. Werner Levi (1960) expresses this as follows:

The quest for power becomes a major occupation of the state and a standard by which most aspects of its life and activities are measured, no matter how relative the magnitude of the desired power may be. It can be granted that, as states usually assert for the diplomatic record, they do not seek power for its own sake; they do so merely as a means to the end of satisfying their needs. . . . But whatever the end of the search for power and whatever the qualifications and limitations, the possibility remains that it can itself lead to violent conflict. States may become rivals in vying for elements of power or in one at-

tempting to become more powerful than the other. The paradox here is that the search for power, even if only to have it available for a future conflict of interests, may itself become a source of violent conflict (pp. 411–420).

As Singer (1965) has pointed out, the international system of two nations in potential conflict has a built-in mechanism for intensifying the conflict. The political elite of country A may assume a hostile stance toward country B. This elite group receives positive feedback from its own citizens in moving toward a position of strength. In country B, however, the political elite responds with similar hostile moves. This gives added justification to country A for its actions and for increasing the severity of those actions. A similar process is, however, going on in the antagonist nation, B. There is thus reinforcement for the political elites in both countries, both from their own citizenry and from the behavior of the other nation. Hence the interaction between the states makes it difficult to reverse the self-perpetuating and self-enhancing cycles of militant preparations within the nation state.

Though many international conflicts are rooted in more than a single source, there are disputes that are basically economic, others that are in good part ideological, and still others that are dominantly power-oriented. Different types of struggles will show some differences with respect to the strategies appropriate to their causal basis. For example, labor-management conflicts in the United States have sometimes represented economic disputes and sometimes ideological differences. The American Federation of Labor assumed that the basic conflict was one of immediate economic interest and accordingly followed bread-and-butter unionism in which they accepted the business ethic of the culture. Though their leaders might drive a hard bargain, the disagreements were negotiable at the conference table. In contrast, radical unions like the I.W.W., committed to a certain type of Marxism, assumed that the differences were ideological. Hence these matters were not amenable to the same type of bargaining process.

Many conflicts of course are mixtures of economic, ideological, and power differences, and their resulting strategies and modes of resolution may shift as one or the other basic source becomes salient. Hence the following analysis of conflict strategies will make reference to their relevance to given sources of conflict.

METHODS AND STRATEGIES FOR DEALING WITH CONFLICT

Though parties to a conflict may utilize a wide range of specific methods for advancing their cause, for living with tensions, or for bringing an end to the conflict, these techniques can be subsumed under six broad classes. At the one extreme, to utilize H. Shepard's (1961) analysis, would be the primitive methods of force and violence and destruction that imply the annihilation of the opponent, and at the other extreme would be the methods of integrative solution involving problem-solving. Intermediate between these extremes would be the recognition of an involuntary interdependence with bargaining and limited warfare as its expression. More specifically, we shall use the following categories for our analysis: (1) the use of force, threats, counterthreats, and deterrence, (2) conflict denial, (3) conflict restriction and containment, (4) nonviolence and ideological conversion, (5) bargaining and compromise, and (6) problem-solving

and creative integration. A number of these methods may of course appear in progression or combination. Thus, attempts to negotiate a compromise settlement may follow the use of threats so that a nation tries to bargain from a position of assumed strength. These methods and their combinations need to be considered with respect to their outcomes, that is, to whether they produce an intensification of conflict, a continuation, a reduction, or a genuine solution.

The Use of Force, Threats, and Deterrence

Traditionally, nations have relied upon force or threats of force as the ultimate means of securing their objectives or of resisting aggressor nations. The logic is that there is no answer to force but superior force. The nations that have not built up their armaments have been those either too weak or too well protected geographically to need armies. The United States, in a fortunate strategic position, did little to build up its armed might until its international involvement in an atomic age. It is to be expected that fascist nations with their glorification of physical force would give the highest priority to military armament. But communist nations, accepting socialistic doctrines of the common humanity of mankind, have also proceeded to develop their military might. Democracies have proved no exception. Even India, despite its greater acceptance of an ideology of nonviolence than the Western nations, reacted to the Chinese attacks upon its northern border by dismissing its defense minister and by seriously moving to build up its armed forces. It must be remembered that the very nature of the state makes this type of development logical. The state as the organization that holds a monopoly of organized force within the nation is so constituted as to turn to military means when threatened from without.

The threatened nation generally reacts to threats and a show of force by counter-measures of the same type. Very weak and powerless nations may capitulate and attempt to appease the superior power, although in 1939 Poland, despite its relative weakness, mobilized its strength against Hitler's threats. In the main, when a nation has some prospect of power parity, its response to threat is reactive in nature—it counters by mobilizing its strength and presenting counter-threats. In such a situation the armaments race proceeds apace. Russia and the United States have both developed their atomic arsenals with the objective of attaining an overkill capability.

The argument for counter-threat and deterrence is to make the prospect of successful outcome of aggression by the other side unlikely or at least so costly that it will not be attempted. Though the ability to muster force against threats has on occasion discouraged aggression, it is no guarantee of security or peace. The opposing side may perceive a point of advantage in striking at a particular time whether or not it has correctly assessed the situation. And the logic of utilizing force as the means of handling conflict would justify a preventive war by one's own side based on the assessment of a favorable set of circumstances. In addition to these hard-headed considerations, account must be taken of the psychologic of the reliance upon force. A psychology of threat and deterrence leads to a situation in both nations in which there is a perceived magnification of the belligerence and intransigence of the other side and to resulting actions of a belligerent character. A spiraling process develops that limits the role of national leaders to their specific function as protectors of national security. In this situation the perceptions of the actions of the other side are subjected to a coding process in the mass media that makes for simplification and distortion. The temporal dimension of the spiraling process becomes all important, for if it proceeds too rapidly there is no opportunity for other system forces to cut through the cycle before war breaks out. R. North, R. A. Brody, and O. Holsti (1964) have shown that such a cycle developed rapidly in 1914 after the assassination of the Austrian Archduke. The rapid spiral of events precipitated a war that many of the important leaders on both sides did not want.

Resort to force creates four specific dynamics within a national system making for war. (1) It builds up an elite group of military specialists who think in terms of overkill capacity, preventive war, and a gaming psychology in which millions of human lives are weighted in terms of tactical costs rather than in human terms. (2) It fosters a military-economic complex, to use Eisenhower's term, the power of which is geared to ever-increasing armament. The facts are that this complex is aided and abetted by local groups throughout the country who fight vigorously for their share of defense contracts. (3) It creates mechanisms for international destruction that can be triggered into action by events other than the warlike moves of an enemy. (4) It leads to a climate of opinion that equates national security and strength with the relative nuclear striking power of the country. Within this climate, national leaders are under constraints not to appear to do anything that could be interpreted as appeasement of the other side.

Though reliance upon force and deterrence does not ordinarily create specific system forces making for peace, the prospect of nuclear warfare does present a special case. The use of force at the level of nuclear weapons is no solution of the power struggle. Both sides are decimated if not destroyed by the nature of the conflict. Hence there are forces within the national system, both East and West, that are pushing against nuclear conflict. The elites of the West are not eager to have the economic empires in which they are involved blown to bits. The Russian leaders, who have developed their institutions through a long, difficult period, do not wish to see their chance for further development destroyed by a nuclear holocaust. In the strategy of military planning there is no percentage in a war in which both sides will lose.

The Hegelian dialectic which postulates antithesis or reaction formation at the social level may find a curious confirmation in that the development of organized force creates a dynamic for peace. Pacifists have long cherished the belief that armed weapons will become so terrible that no nation will dare to go to war. The military-minded share some of this belief, and their strategy of deterrence is based upon it. In the past this type of belief has proved to be wishful thinking on the part of the pacifists and militarists alike. We have reached the point, however, where it is increasingly clear that the nations involved in the Cold War have more in common in maintaining peace than in destroying it. Such a perception of common fate was extremely difficult before the development of nuclear weapons. And of course even this perception today will not guarantee peace. The perception does not extend to all groups. Certain types of military specialists do not share it. Nor do extremist groups who may come to power if the responsible authorities are not seen as coping adequately with national problems. Moreover, the functioning social system of a nation is a complex matter and is not governed primarily by a common perception of the means for survival. Nevertheless, the recognition of mutual dependence in controlling a nuclear disaster is growing and is a force to be reckoned with in assessing the chances for peace.

Limitations of Threat in Dealing with Revolutionary States. Threats of force against the newly emerging revolutionary state by older nations often do not have the desired effects. The national leaders of the young government, representing as they do the new institutions, would jeopardize their positions of leadership if they appeared to betray the revolution. Hence they will risk destruction by the external enemy rather than play a submissive role. The common belief that these revolutionary leaders only understand toughness and force overlooks the roles they play in their own system and the dynamics of that system. Hence these leaders are more likely to recognize a show of force if this technique is accompanied by offers of negotiation that make their own internal position tenable.

Diplomatic recognition is critical for the new government in its early stages. Recognition is first of all the necessary condition for any attempts to negotiate with the new state. Failure to recognize its existence means that important channels of communication are closed, that other nations are not prepared to accept it in the family of nations. It is not only a blow to the psychological pride of the country but is also interpreted as an action bordering on war. The older nations, however, are sometimes reluctant to grant recognition because they do not want to give their moral support to a regime inimical to their own interests and ideological principles. Withholding of recognition is part of a campaign to undermine the new government and is often accompanied by economic sanctions and tariff embargoes and even by support to counter-revolutionary forces. The major problem with these attempts at overthrowing the new government is that they do not necessarily work. The philosophy of punishment, threat, and force is used, but generally in a fairly feeble manner. The older countries believe that the new regime will not last and that minor support to its enemies and moral chastisement will bring about its downfall. This is in part due to the fact that the information sources utilized generally represent the older power structure rather than the forces of change. Hence the assessment of new governments by the established powers has been repeatedly in error, whether the new regime was in Russia, China, Africa, or Cuba. It is not so much that diplomats and legislators are incapable of learning from experience in the international field as that they are captives of their own closed informational system.

A critical determinant of the outcome of a policy of nonrecognition, threats, and sanctions toward a new government is the extent to which the new regime represents a newly developing set of institutions within the society. If a revolution is a palace revolution or a coup d'état in which the only change is the replacement of one set of rulers by another, then a hostile international climate may be enough to overthrow it. If, however, the revolutionary government reflects changed internal institutions, it is not likely to be changed from without save by crushing sanctions and organized force. Historically the error has often been made, as we have just noted, of regarding a new revolutionary regime as a new group of adventurous leaders without the support of changed institutions within their own borders.

Finally it should be noted that the use of force, of threats, and of deterrence is no solution for ideological conflicts. Religious and political ideologies have withstood military might throughout history. The Nazi conquest of Europe did not insure the success of Nazi doctrines nor did the Nazi defeat guarantee the success of democratic beliefs. It is true that a military triumph and subsequent totalitarian control over generations can produce ideological changes. Even in this case, however, it is more the teaching of the new generation in a different context that leads to change than the imposition of the ideology through force.

Conflict Denial

At the individual level we recognize the doctrine that it takes two to make a fight. If a person ignores the insults and belligerent attitude of an aggressor he may avert a struggle. Within an organized group the top leadership will sometimes refuse to recognize intragroup feuding in the hope that it will go away or at least remain below threshold. At the national level the same policy is on occasion followed toward the actions of other nations. There is a large area of national and international incidents that can be perceived as threatening or aggressive actions on the one hand or as innocuous or trivial behavior on the other.

Denial of conflict at the national level is not so much a matter of blocked perceptions, as is the case at the individual level, but a matter of interpretation of the actions of other nations. Four conditions make for conflict denial. In the first place, the nationalism of the well-established bureaucratic state is not as sensitive to insults to its symbols as is the revolutionary nationalism of the newly developing state or the regressive nationalism of the counter-revolutionary state.

In the second place, the national state that is functioning satisfactorily and has few internal problems will minimize the potentially aggressive actions of other nations. Both leaders and masses are not eager to jeopardize the satisfactory state of affairs.

In the third place, some degree of involvement in international systems can lead to interpretation of national policies and practices as non-warlike in character. Some elements in the upper classes in Britain and France were involved in the preservation of conservative social structure in Germany to such an extent that they refused to credit Hitler's regime with warlike intentions. They thought they could do business with Hitler. Similarly, the identification of some of the ruling group in India with Communist China's struggle against white colonialism blinded them to China's aggressive policies until India was actually invaded.

In the fourth place, the weak, powerless nation may refuse to acknowledge the true meaning of hostile acts against itself by a powerful neighbor in the hope of avoiding a disastrous conflict.

Relation of Denial to Types of Nationalism. The interaction of the two conditions of symbol sensitivity and internal conflict has implications for international relations. The belligerence and flexing of muscles of a newly emerging national state can be ignored for a period in the hope that its development and expansionism will not assume a military form. The newly developing nation need not resort to force against other countries if it can make progress through internal growth and external economic expansion. But the regressive type of nationalism, if it captures the state, can rarely succeed without the resort to military aggressiveness or war. The very reason for the revival of the patriotism of the past is the failure of internal institutions to meet the problems of the present. Instead of the development of new institutions there is an attempt to anticipate revolutionary change by a reactionary counter-revolution. This is accomplished by internal repression and the use of the machinery of the state to resurrect old institutions utilizing emotional chauvinism. There is a narrowing of national norms and any form of deviation is labeled as treasonable. The nation is thus on a military footing to combat internal evil and external threat. The dynamic is one of war. To maintain power the elite groups, moreover, must make societal institutions work better than they did before the counter-revolution took over and one method is that of external conquest and confiscation. The internal stresses and strains are projected outward. This externalization of internal conflict occurs in other types of nation states but regressive nationalism is the example par excellence of this process.

Thus conflict denial is not a satisfactory technique for dealing with a nation whose outward belligerence is determined not so much by its relations with other powers as by its own internal conflictual dynamics.

Consequences of Denial. The outcome of the denial method of dealing with conflict can lead either to its minimization or its aggravation. We have suggested some of the factors that will predispose toward one or the other of these types of outcome. At the level of tactics the problem becomes one of the realistic assessment of the nature of conflictual tendencies in the other party. If an action by another nation appears aggressive or can be interpreted as belligerent, there are criteria for evaluating its underlying meaning. We have already noted that the most important assessment relates to an understanding of the internal institutions and the character of the nationalism of the state in question. In addition, the following practical criteria are often employed. If the incident is the outcome of a deliberate official policy of the nation it can be interpreted in terms of that official policy. The actions of individuals, even though they hold official positions, such as American congressmen, are not necessarily representative of national policy. A second criterion is the purpose of the course of action that may have aggressive implications. Its objective may be for internal consumption rather than to serve as a blueprint for foreign policy. It may be a move by the moderate group in power to undercut the extremist group and so can be discounted in part by the other nation. Sometimes the party in power may espouse a belligerent nationalism during an election campaign, which is intended to affect the election outcome and not to affect international relations. Such a line of conduct may get out of hand and take on a logic of its own. Often, however, the professional diplomats are sufficiently informed about the meaning of national actions to be able to discount the sabre-rattling that is intended for domestic rather than foreign consumption. A third criterion is the consistent and cumulative character of aggressive or potentially aggressive actions. As the pattern of *Mein Kampf* (rearmament, militant nationalism and racism, and aggression to secure German domination) became translated into action it became increasingly clear that other nations could not negotiate with Hitler. The strategy of nations seeking peace thus may follow a pattern of not imputing belligerent intentions to other nations on the basis of one or two incidents but of waiting and testing the objectives of the other side.

Conflict Restriction and Control: Limited War

Another strategy of conflict reduction, not necessarily coordinate with or independent of negotiation and deterrence, is the localization and containment of overt conflict. The Cold War has been marked by armed clashes that have been successfully confined to the locality in which they occurred. Geographical restriction and psychological definition have been employed for this purpose so that even the Korean struggle was viewed as a police action rather than a war. The containment of conflict is an interesting aspect of national policy in that it reflects the reluctance of the major powers to follow through on the logical consequences of force and deterrence to an all-out war. Thus it often reflects the difficulties described by T. C. Schelling (1957) with respect to the coordination of the mutual expectancies of each side toward the anticipations of the other. On the one hand the use of force in itself logically implies a breakdown in negotiation, but on the other hand restriction on the force to be employed calls for some degree of agreement. Thus, for limited war there must be agreement or acquiescence about the limits in situations where communication is greatly restricted. In his analysis Schelling argues that implicit agreements can be reached to restrict the conduct of a war but they must be about *qualitatively* distinctive courses of action and not about *matters of degree.* Both sides refrained from using poison gas in World War II, but such an agreement on the basis of tacit understanding could not have occurred with respect to some *limited degree* of the use of poison gas. With incomplete communication the situation itself defines the accepted practice and hence must provide a *clear anchoring point*. In Korea both sides refrained from atomic weapons of all sorts, tactical and strategic, clean and unclean. In fact the Chinese did not use conventional bombs against the major American supply base of Pusan with the tacit understanding that the United States would not use atomic weapons, according to subsequent press reports. A Soviet diplomat was reported to have leaked information to the West that atomic bombing of Manchurian bases would result in Chinese bombing of South Korean supply centers and even of Japan. Whatever the factual details, both sides followed the line of not violating mutual expectations based upon limited communication.

Prior announcement of intentions by one side in advance of conflict (Schelling suggests), even though not formally agreed to by the other, can help to set up limitations in the struggle if the proposal is qualitatively clear and of an all-or-none character. In an actual emergency the prior announcement could serve to crystallize expectations and guide courses of action. For example, the statement by a nuclear power that it will not resort to atomic weapons in the protection of its interests in the Near East might help to confine the conflict to the use of conventional weapons by both sides even if war broke out.

Nonviolence and Ideological Conversion

The pacifist doctrines of nonviolence are sometimes seen as techniques of denial and appeasement. The nonviolent Gandhian philosophy, however, is not of this character. It is pacifist only in method. In a sense it is militant in its moral objectives and permits no departure from its ethical principles. The central norm of the system, according to A. Naess (1958), is "act in a group struggle and act, moreover, in a way conducive to long term reduction of violence." The emphasis is upon action and not passivity, and not only upon refraining from violence oneself but on behaving so that violence in others will be reduced. To attain that objective the person must avoid actions that would have the effect of humiliating the rival group, attempt to achieve a high degree of empathy with respect to the values of members of the opposing group, adopt a consistent attitude of trust toward the rival group, including an open statement of one's own plans and intentions, and initiate friendly interactions with opponents. In addition one must make visible sacrifices for one's cause and maintain a consistent set of positive activities which are an attempt at the explicit realization of the goals of the group.

Janis and Katz (1959) have called attention to some of the psychological mechanisms that are called into play with the use of violence and that distort its good objectives. The guilt associated with the use of violence leads to justification through the attribution of evil to the target. Participating in violent action may lead to a weakening of superego controls. The social sanctioning of violence, which is normally seen as antisocial, can lead to all types of excesses in its use, for now primitive impulses receive social approval.

Mutual Understanding and Nonviolence. The logic of the pacifist methods is that threat, force, and violence are evil and that they can not be used to secure good outcomes. There is a rejection of the separation of means from ends and a repudiation of the notion that the end justifies the means. The assumption is that unethical means will corrupt a good objective. The pacifist argument is that arming to the teeth will not necessarily deter an opponent but will change the nation resorting to armament and threats into the same evil warlike character as the opponent. The logic of handling conflicts through force readily countenances a preventive war even by the side originally seeking to protect itself rather than to aggress against others. The nonviolent rationale, on the other hand, assumes that the readiness to use force, violence, and preventive war is self-defeating. The possible success of force against an opponent is only temporary, for the opponent or other opponents will rise again. Moreover, the nation enjoying temporary success is corrupted in its way of life because it has taken on the character of an executioner.

Not all methods or all advocates of peaceful policy reflect this philosophy in complete or ideal form. Nonetheless, it was the major tactic in winning the independence of India from British rule. It was moreover, employed by the early Christians in establishing the Church within the Roman empire. Nonviolence, though not always approximating the Gandhian ideal, has been a major weapon of the Negroes in fighting the battle of civil rights in the United States. Where this tactic has been employed it creates real problems for the opposition. Since it is tied to moral principles or humanitarian goals, and since it pleads for the oppressor as well as for the oppressed, it defies the traditional coping behavior of force and authority. Organized force is rationalized as necessary in dealing with illegality but the use of nonviolence creates a reversal of norms in which the legal authorities appear brutal and immoral.

The tactic of nonviolent moral persuasion has seen little use at the international level. It has been primarily a strategy for revolutionary movements within a national structure. Nonetheless, some of its precepts, such as empathy and understanding and positive nonviolent actions toward moral goals, have application for the behavior of nations. The mutual trust emphasized in this doctrine is one basis of treaties and international agreements. Though many treaties have been broken or maintained by force, many have also resided on trust. Moreover, the nonviolence philosophy cuts through the reactive cumulative character of suspicion, threat, and counter-threat and its ascending cycle of tension.

Pacifist and religious groups embracing the doctrine of nonviolence tend to remain outside the national system with respect to decision-making. The philosophy is important, not because these splinter groups are likely to become critical actors within the national system, but because their ideas may have some impact over time on decision-makers. We shall turn, then, to consider methods of negotiation and compromise which assume that some degree of conflict resolution is possible without the exertion of force.

Bargaining and Compromise

A common complement of the use of threat is the resort to negotiation to reach a compromise settlement. After the threat of a strike by organized labor, or during a strike, the representatives of the union and of management will sit down at the bargaining table to attempt to reach some agreement about the dispute. Negotiations are possible only if each side is prepared to give up something in order to gain some of its objectives. In other words, the contending parties must be ready to accept a compromise rather than to seek for a final solution of all their differences.

The logic of bargaining and compromise is well suited for reaching agreement about economic and power differences, but it is scarcely appropriate for the settlement of ideological differences of a symbolic character. Workers can settle their dispute with management over wages and fringe benefits by accepting a compromise, such as half the wage increase they wanted, without compromising their ethical standards. They cannot, however, bargain an ideological principle without compromising their moral position. For example, they cannot allow the company to appoint the union stewards in the foundry in return for fringe benefits without sacrificing the ideological principle of having their own independent union, any more than the company can allow the union to name the manager who is to run the foundry.

There is an all-or-none quality to moral principles. We consider the mother of a single illegitimate child as immoral as the mother of illegitimate twins or triplets. Hence ethical standards as such are not the proper subject matter of bargaining and compromise, though the means for achieving them may be. This simple principle has not been grasped by the majority of the white people in the United States with respect to the civil rights of Negroes. The majority position has been one of gradualism, of delay, and of compromise. The intensity of the Negro reaction has come as a surprise. But to the Negroes a moral issue is at stake, which is not subject to bargaining. If their children are entitled to equality of opportunity in public education as the Supreme Court has ruled, then a compromise which would permit integrated schooling up to fifth grade only is unacceptable.

In controversies, then, there should be clarity about the points of difference and the methods for dealing with them. To prevent the two types of difference from getting confused both sides may send to the bargaining table task-oriented representatives, rather than ideologues. One function of the umpire or arbiter in labor disputes is to keep the negotiations centered around bread-and-butter issues rather than around ideological principles.

In international relations the same logic applies. Trade agreements can be negotiated between Communist and capitalist countries if the discussions are about trade and not about ideology. The major difficulty in the use of bargaining at the international level is that the countries involved have a nationalistic ideology to uphold which can exacerbate their differences and make a compromise impossible. Much as Berlin has been a source of controversy, the United States cannot offer to trade it to the Soviet Union for some other city, because of moral commitments and ideological considerations.

The problem at the international level is one of the needless contamination of economic and power differences with nationalistic ideology. Such confusion hampers the negotiation process in areas where it might prove useful. A major criticism of former Secretary of State John Foster Dulles was his use of moralistic symbols in describing American and Russian policies. He saw controversies between the East and West as differences in basic morality. By moving to the plane of ideological symbols, he contributed to placing issues on a level where bargaining and compromise were impossible.

In general, however, there seems to be an increasing tendency for large bureaucratic nations to select leaders who are pragmatic, task-oriented men with some system perspective and understanding of the nature of national and international structure. The ideologues like Churchill were products of an older order. Hence we may find greater willingness and ability at negotiation and compromise among the younger leaders of the large bureaucratic societies.

Another confusion of moral principles and pragmatic issues can be seen in the United States policy with respect to the diplomatic recognition of other nations. Diplomatic recognition can be used pragmatically in two ways. It can be withheld in the hope of undermining a new government, or it can be bestowed to encourage it and maintain channels of communication. But it can also be used as a moral weapon; that is, the refusal to recognize the new government is supported by the rationale that the new regime is illegitimate and evil. This was the American rationale for not recognizing Soviet Russia for the first fifteen years of its existence. The difficulty with this policy was that the United States finally had to recognize the Soviet Union even though its character had not changed. The long period of diplomatic and other forms of boycott may have contributed to the Stalin era of international distrust and irresponsibility. Moreover, the confusion of moral and practical issues inherent in American policy is apparent when the United States recognizes dictatorial and reactionary regimes, so that among some groups outside the United States the American government is seen as endorsing undemocratic governments. The recent agreement about a "hot line" of direct telephonic communication between the Kremlin and Washington to avert an accidental war shows how far the United States has moved from its earlier moral position of not communicating with an opponent regarded as unclean. Nevertheless, the old ideological principle is still invoked against the government of Communist China and against its admission to the United Nations and the family of nations. The United States is one of the few nations that still refuse to grant recognition to the government of some 600,000,000 Chinese people. And this tough policy toward China does not seem to have made it less militant.

Often it is difficult to achieve successful negotiation of differences because disagreements about present problems of conflicting interests have taken on a moral cast and a win-lose character. Nations have committed themselves to a position from which it is difficult to withdraw. J. D. Singer (1958) points out, therefore, that negotiations should start on procedures for handling future events, rather than on immediately pressing issues. Success in such areas may prepare the way for other types of negotiations.

The outcome of the process of negotiation over pragmatic matters is not necessarily successful in achieving compromise even if ideological issues do not confuse the bargaining. There is a tendency to move toward a deadlock in that each side wants to drive as hard a bargain as possible and thus starts with as high a level of demands as possible. Hence there is the problem of knowing what the other side will really settle for and the reluctance to yield on any essential before the antagonist does. Real movement in negotiation may therefore never get very far and may sometimes not even get started. The intensity of the need, by either or both of the parties, for some settlement is one factor facilitating movement. Another factor is the ingenuity in finding a concession valued by the other side, but not of much value to one's own group.

Where an umpire or arbiter is utilized in labor-management conflict, part of his role is to ascertain the realistic as against the stated positions of both contending parties. He can then suggest proposals in the intermediate area of the realistic demands of the two groups or leak information to each side about what the other group will settle for. He can assess the reality basis of the threats of either side to leave the negotiation table and resort to force. He can then communicate his assessment to the other side.

In international disputes similar devices of arbitration are employed to help in the negotiation process. The services of the larger nations are often employed in disputes between smaller powers. International commissions are accepted even by the more powerful nations in some areas of disagreement. The symbolic principle of national sovereignty serves as a serious obstacle for the big powers in accepting the services of an international arbiter for issues deemed important. Neither Russia nor the United States is willing to utilize either the United Nations or the World Court for the arbitration of their basic differences.

As modern nation states take on more and more of the form of large technological bureaucratic structures, they are likely to depart from adherence to absolutistic dogmas of national sovereignty. A major function of leadership in such structures is negotiation, compromise, and adjudication to maintain the balance of the component subsystems. Hence more carry-over to the international system of the negotiation principle is possible and even probable.

Negotiation and bargaining are not necessarily used in isolation as the only method for conflict reduction. They often follow the use of threats and the mobilization of force so that one or both sides are negotiating from a position of strength. One area of empirical research that has not been exploited is the examination of the validity of the argument that negotiation from a position of strength is the most effective basis for bargaining. Case studies of international conferences resulting in agreement or deadlock could explore the types of conditions leading to given outcomes.

The difficulty with the compromise outcome, however, is that the basic problem may not be solved and may continue to be a source of tension. Fundamental political settlements, it is often contended, must come before bargaining about specific issues. On the other hand, a genuine solution of differences in interests and ideology may be impossible of accomplishment and in fact may not be necessary for the preservation of the peace. Getting down to basic issues often means the invoking of affective ideological symbols, whereas more may be attained by negotiations in which emphasis is upon securing procedural agreements.

Shifting from a Strategy of Deterrence to One of Negotiation. We have already commented on the common notion that if negotiations are to be effective for a given party it must bargain from a position of strength. This point of view generally is a one-sided appraisal of the struggle and overlooks the two-sided nature of conflict, which could logically result in deadlock and even war if both sides accepted this philosophy. A radically different strategy has been enunciated by Charles Osgood (1959) in his doctrine of graduated unilateral disengagement. Osgood argues that the way to reverse the tensions–arms-race spiral would be to take a unilateral step towards disarmament. Such a unilateral act, to be effective in inducing the enemy to reciprocate, "(1) should, in terms of *military aggression,* be clearly disadvantageous to the side making it, yet not cripplingly so; (2) should be such as to be clearly perceived by the enemy as reducing his external threat; (3) should not increase the enemy's threat to *our* heartland; (4) should be such that reciprocal action by the enemy is available and clearly indicated; (5) should be announced in advance and widely publicized to ally, neutral and enemy countries—as regards the nature of the act, its purpose as part of a consistent policy, and the expected reciprocation; (6) but should not demand prior commitment to reciprocation by the enemy as a condition for its commission" (p. 316).

The major problem in Osgood's proposal is not the probable effectiveness of the unilateral act but the difficulty of any nation taking the first step. The graduated unilateral disengagement has the advantage, however, of pointing to the key problem of cutting the cycle of the arms race, in which tension leads to more armament and more armament to more tension. A negotiated mutual move toward slowing this race could have some of the effects of the Osgood proposal. At least this has been the hope in the treaty between the United States and Russia banning nuclear testing in the atmosphere. In fact, President Kennedy's 1963 speech at American University suggested that he appreciated the merit of the Osgood analysis.

The test-ban agreement was preceded by moves that also reduced the threat–arms spiral. Specifically there has been a shift away from intensifying the perception of threat by both sides in changing the emphasis from first-strike capability to second-strike retaliatory power. The first-strike capability aimed at the military demolition of the opponent is interpreted as more threatening than a retaliatory second strike because it is more offensive than defensive in nature. It is predicated upon the success of beating the enemy to the punch and its build-up implies

aggression. Its weapons and their disposition could not survive a retaliatory strike if it failed in the initial round. Hence a well-developed first-strike capability may create some feeling of security to the side possessing it, but resulting insecurity to the other side in that it is geared to going first, to aggression and offense. Thus, Soviet Russia regarded United States weapons in Turkey and at other points close to its borders as part of our first-strike capability, useful to the United States for aggressive purposes only. In the same fashion the United States regarded atomic weapons in Cuba as part of a first-strike capability and hence as offensive weapons. Both sides have moved in the direction of giving greater emphasis to retaliatory strikes with some lessening of the tension between them. To reduce the tension still further there would have to be more pulling back of atomic bases and less concern with a weapons system geared to a first-strike capability.

Problem Solving and Creative Integration

Mary P. Follett in her *Creative experience* (1924) applied to social disputes the distinction between compromise and genuine solution, which Edwin B. Holt (1915) conceptualized at the level of individual conflict. Holt pointed out that the individual can meet his internal conflicts by alternate concessions to both sets of conflicting impulses or he can, through discriminating analysis, discover an integration or solution. Follett used the term "creative experience" to describe the same problem-solving process in social disagreements in which a discriminating course of conduct could permit each individual to achieve his central purpose. More recently Anatol Rapoport (1961) has called attention to the same need for deeper analysis of problems with which Holt and Follett were concerned. Many problems are not capable of solution with the usual approach and take on the character of dilemmas. To solve them requires a new frame of reference. They are like puzzles that continue to baffle us as long as we remain in the usual set and apply the usual techniques. It is only when we shift our approach and utilize a radically different set of assumptions that the dilemma can be solved.

In a recent volume entitled *Preventing World War III* (Wright, Evan, & Deutsch, 1962) scholars and scientists from many disciplines have discarded the conventional assumptions of policy makers and have set forth imaginative proposals for more integrative solutions of the conflict between the East and West. They include, for example, the following suggestions:

1. An extension of the United Nations to include a forum of supranational communities (the unit of membership would not be a nation state but a regional entity) and a forum of infranational entities where the membership consists of nongovernmental or private organizations (Evan, 1962).

2. The development of a community of international interest through cooperation among nations to employ world-wide technology for improving the climate by transporting great masses of water, by directing ocean currents, and by modifying the reflective properties of the earth's surface (C. Pokrovsky, 1962).

3. The diversification of the areas of international competition for prestige. If there are many different types of repeated contests, from the exploration of outer space to the conquest of diseases in underdeveloped areas, a defeat by one nation in the prestige competition is not total or necessarily irreversible (Etzioni, 1962).

4. Unilateral moves in areas other than those of immediate obvious tension. The proposal of C. Osgood for a graduated program of tension reduction through a unilateral step toward disarmament has already been discussed. D. Riesman (1962) points out that similar unilateral moves could be made in other ways and has illustrated his point by the "Nylon War"—a satirical example in which American consumer goods are dumped throughout Russia without charge.

5. Internationalizing military force. The problem of national security is now met by national military forces and generally by alliances between nations for the cooperative use of their armies and weapons. This cooperative arrangement could be extended by setting up a new international institution to which nations would contribute their armaments and armed forces. Countries would maintain their national identities in every other respect, but would turn to this international force for protection against attack. The essence of this proposal is that it means a change in commitment to means rather than to goals. Thus it emphasizes a pragmatic solution through a new institutional arrangement rather than a restructuring of value systems concerning national identity and nonviolence (Kelman, 1962).

6. Economic steps toward peace. The industrial-military complex with its pressures toward maintaining and increasing the armament build-up is not an inevitable development. It is socially determined and hence can be changed through social planning. E. Benoit (1962) gives specifications for how the economic consequences of disarmament can be handled without major disruption of the economy. They include (a) allocating some stated proportion of the cut in the national military budget to nonmilitary pro-

grams, (b) encouraging defense contractors to budget as a deductible cost some percentage of their contracts to programs for handling their reconversion problems, (c) tax reductions for companies engaged in innovation and risk-taking, and (d) across the board tax cuts on personal income.

The many proposals offered by social scientists who have approached the dilemma of international tension from a problem-solving point of view differ in theoretical merit and practical utility. They can be dismissed as too academic and too remote from the practical operations of the national system. Such a blanket rejection, however, is in itself unrealistic in that the national system is not without adaptive features. These adaptive features of the modern technological bureaucracy, which is empirically oriented, make possible the acceptance of innovative ideas under given system conditions. For example, the Kennedy administration, confronted with the dilemma of the survival of our national system in its present form, showed interest in the Osgood proposals for reducing international tensions and made progress in its treaties banning atmospheric testing and prohibiting atomic weapons in space. The Benoit proposals for economic steps toward peace are sufficiently close to current measures to cut taxes and to guide the national economy in given directions so that they are not outside the system. In summary, creative ideas of a problem-solving type can gain acceptance if they are adaptable to the functioning of the national system in which they are made.

Finally, the development of the European community is an interesting case sudy of a creative solution to some of the age-old conflicts among European nations. The bitter memories of past wars and the deep antagonisms between some of the countries would have prevented the most optimistic internationalists of a preceding generation from predicting a unified Europe. But the economic and technological forces of the competing bureaucratic systems pushed toward integration. Haas (1958) has written about this development as follows: "The 'good' Europeans are not the main creators of the regional community that is growing up; the process of community formation is dominated by nationally constituted groups with specific interests and aims, willing and able to adjust their aspirations by turning to supranational means when the course appears profitable" (p. xiv). Trade union members and businessmen both saw the advantages of a more rational organization of industrial and political life. Haas names four conditions as critical to European integration: (a) industrialized nations already heavily involved in international trade and finance, (b) the organization of the masses in these countries in interest groups and political parties, (c) the leadership of these groups by elites competing for influence, and (d) the influence of traditions and assumptions of political democracy upon these elites.

The European integrative process can, moreover, be described within the framework of our social-psychological analysis of nation states. We had specified that the assumption of national roles depended upon the arousal of one or more of four types of factors: emotional conditioning to national symbols, sense of national identity, compensatory identification, and instrumental rewards. Moreover, we had assumed that with the growth of technological bureaucracy the instrumental involvement becomes more important than emotional conditioning to symbols and that the sense of national identity no longer has to be tied to national symbols. In the European nations the interest groups pushing for regional unity were more concerned with instrumental rewards than with symbols and they saw clearly that their way of life could be enriched by extending the subsystems to which they belonged across national boundaries. At the same time they could maintain their national identity in noneconomic sectors of life. In short, the nation state, in spite of its dominant role during the past two centuries, is not the final organizational arrangement of human lives. The increasing interdependence of all parts of the world in the space age may be productive of the further growth of international systems.

The European development has interesting implications for the sociological position that a peaceful world order is dependent upon consensus with respect to a common set of values. Thus Talcott Parsons (1962) argues that "every effort be made to promulgate carefully considered statements of value commitments which may provide a basis for consensus among both have and have-not nations" (p. 318). There is, however, a grave danger in an emphasis upon ideological agreement. Once discussion begins at this level the symbolic character of values involving absolutistic, finalistic, affective, and moral qualities may precipitate conflict rather than debate. It would seem wiser to emphasize common practical interests, as in European integration, and to seek agreement on ideological values as a later step in the process. Parsons himself recognizes this problem in part when he speaks of downgrading some issues that formerly have been treated as fundamental moral issues. Such downgrading, however, can occur more readily in a context of task solution of empirical problems than in a discussion of values per se. Finally Parsons does note the significance of establishing consensus at the procedural level.

Again, it seems wiser to attempt to gain acceptance of procedures for solving problems and for institutionalizing specific norms than of general value codes. Both Communist and capitalist societies already have some common norms about specific practices, and integration can be achieved at this procedural normative level more readily than at the level of ideological goals. Bureaucratic expansion as in the developing European community has proceeded in this fashion. The surplus meanings and the irrelevant emotions associated with the ideological symbols of a system are more functional for mobilizing that system against a competing system than for reaching consensus across systems.

REFERENCES

Adorno, T. W., Frenkel-Brunswik, Else, Levinson, D. J., & Sanford, N. *The authoritarian personality.* New York: Harper, 1950.

Allport, F. H. A structuronomic conception of behavior. *J. abnorm. soc. Psychol.,* 1962, *64,* 3–30.

Arnold, T. *Symbols of government.* New Haven: Yale Univer. Press, 1935.

Bay, C., Gullväg, I., Ofstad, H., & Tønnessen, H. *Nationalism: A study of identification with people and power.* Oslo: Institute of Social Research, 1950. (Mimeographed)

Benoit, E. Economic steps towards peace. In Q. Wright, W. M. Evan, & M. Deutsch (Eds.), *Preventing World War III.* New York: Simon & Schuster, 1962. Pp. 136–154.

Durkheim, E. *The division of labor.* Translated by G. Simpson. New York: Macmillan, 1933.

Etzioni, A. International prestige and peaceful competition. In Q. Wright, W. M. Evan, & M. Deutsch (Eds.). *Pre-*

venting *World War III*. New York: Simon & Schuster, 1962. Pp. 226–245.

Evan, W. M. Transnational forums for peace. In Q. Wright, W. M. Evan, & M. Deutsch (Eds.), *Preventing World War III*. New York: Simon & Schuster, 1962. Pp. 393–409.

Follett, Mary *Creative experience*. New York: Longmans, Green, 1924.

Fried, H. E. *The guilt of the German army*. New York: Macmillan, 1942.

Guetzkow, H. Isolation and collaboration: A partial theory of international relations. *J. Confl. Resol.*, 1957, *1*, 48–68.

Haas, E. B. *The uniting of Europe*. Stanford: Stanford Univer. Press, 1958.

Hayes, C. J. H. *Essays on nationalism*. New York: Macmillan, 1926.

Holt, E. B. *The Freudian wish*. New York: Holt, Rinehart and Winston, 1915.

Janis, I. L., & Katz, D. The reduction of intergroup hostility. *J. Confl. Resol.*, 1959, *3*, 85–100.

Kardiner, A., *et al*. *The psychological frontiers of society*. New York: Columbia Univer. Press, 1945.

Kelman, H. C. Internationalizing military force. In Q. Wright, W. M. Evan, & M. Deutsch (Eds.), *Preventing World War III*. New York: Simon & Schuster, 1962. Pp. 106–122.

Levi, W. On the causes of war and the conditions of peace. *J. Confl. Resol.*, 1960, *4*, 411–420.

Levinson, D. J. Authoritarian personality and foreign policy. *J. Confl. Resol.*, 1957, *1*, 37–47.

March, J. G., & Simon, H. A. *Organizations*. New York: Wiley, 1958.

Naess, A. A systematization of Gandhian ethics of conflict resolution. *J. Confl. Resol.*, 1958, *2*, 140–155.

North, R. C., Brody, R. A., and Holsti, O. R. Some empirical data on the conflict spiral. *Peace Research Society (International) Papers*, 1964, *1*, 1–14.

Oppenheimer, F. *The state*. Indianapolis: Bobbs-Merrill, 1914.

Osgood, C. E. Suggestions for winning the real war with communism. *J. Confl. Resol.*, 1959, *3*, 295–325.

Parsons, T. Polarization of the world and international order. In Q. Wright, W. M. Evan, & M. Deutsch (Eds.), *Preventing World War III*. New York: Simon & Schuster, 1962. Pp. 310–331.

Paul, J. *Research for peace*. Canadian Peace Research Institute, 1963. (Mimeographed)

Pokrovsky, G. I. Improving the world. In Q. Wright, W. M. Evan, & M. Deutsch (Eds.), *Preventing World War III*. New York: Simon & Schuster, 1962. Pp. 278–288.

Rapoport, A. A new logic for the test ban. *The Nation*, April 1, 1961.

Riesman, D. The nylon war. In Q. Wright, W. M. Evan, & M. Deutsch (Eds.), *Preventing World War III*. New York: Simon & Schuster, 1962. Pp. 213–225.

Schelling, T. C. Bargaining, communication and limited war. *J. Confl. Resol.*, 1957, *1*, 19–36.

Selltiz, Claire, & Cook, S. W. Factors influencing attitudes of foreign students toward the host country. *J. soc. Issues*, 1962, *18*(1), 7–23.

Shepard, H. A. Responses to situations of competition and conflict. In Elise Boulding (Ed.), *Conflict management in organizations*. Ann Arbor, Mich.: Foundation for Research on Human Behavior, 1961. Pp. 33–41.

Singer, J. D. Threat-perception and the armament-tension dilemma. *J. Confl. Resol.*, 1958, *2*, 90–105.

Singer, J. D. The political science of human conflict. In E. B. McNeil (Ed.), *The nature of human conflict*. Englewood Cliffs, N.J.: Prentice-Hall, 1965. Pp. 139–154.

Wright, Q., Evan, W. M., & Deutsch, M. (Eds.) *Preventing World War III*. New York: Simon & Schuster, 1962.

11

In the last two chapters we examined some of the underlying societal processes within a nation—reflected in public moods and ideologies—that create a predisposition or a state of readiness for one or another kind of international action. In the next two chapters we turn to an examination of processes involved in the actual interaction of two or more nations, given a particular international situation and a particular pattern of relations between the interacting nations. Specifically, these chapters focus on individual actors—typically, though not exclusively, those who are responsible for state action—and explore the psychological and social processes that encompass their definition of the situation and their choice of action. These processes, in turn, determine the actions and reactions of the interacting states toward each other, and hence the ultimate outcome of the interaction.

Chapter 11 is concerned with the processes of perception and orientation, occurring within two interacting nations, as each observes the actions of the other and in turn reacts to them. These processes constitute the definition of the international situation on the part of individual actors, and determine the course that national action is likely to take. What are the conditions under which another nation will be perceived as threatening or nonthreatening? What are some of the sources of misunderstanding and inability to correct preconceptions? What is the process whereby trust or distrust between two nations develops? What are the conditions under which such attitudes become built-in assumptions and inflexible patterns, and the conditions under which they remain open and amenable to change? What determines the level of responsiveness that marks the general orientation of two nations to each other? Under what conditions do action and reaction mutually reinforce each other, leading to a vicious circle—as in an armaments race? How can such a circle be broken? And how can a benevolent circle be initiated? These are the kinds of questions to which the next chapter is addressed.

Chapter 11 continues, in a sense, the exploration of the climate of international action, started in Chapter 9. But, whereas Chapter 9 was concerned with general underlying moods that predispose a nation to act in certain ways, Chapter 11 focuses on the more specific atmosphere within which the relationship between two nations is carried out. Chapter 11 can also be seen as a bridge between Parts One and Two of this volume. It is primarily concerned with mutual images of interacting nations and the determinants of these images, but its emphasis is on the role of these images in the determination of international action. It takes the process of image formation and change, essentially, as a step in the sequence of interaction between nations—the step that marks the definition of the situation, preparatory to the choice of action.

Dean G. Pruitt, the author of Chapter 11, is Associate Professor in the Department of Psychology and the Center for Research on Social Behavior at the University of Delaware. At the same time he is Research Associate in the International Relations Program, Northwestern University. He is a member of the Committee on International Relations of the Society for the Psychological Study of Social Issues. He has published articles on decision-making and on psychological approaches to international relations. His current research interests focus on interpersonal and intergroup interaction; and on negotiation and bargaining.

H. C. K.

Definition of the Situation as a Determinant of International Action*

Dean G. Pruitt

INTRODUCTION

Meaningful propositions about international relations can be derived from a variety of frameworks. The nations of the world can be viewed as a single system with characteristics transcending those of the individual nations that comprise it.[1] Or one can focus on individual nations and explain their for-eign policies in terms of national attributes such as goals and capabilities.[2] Alternatively, national decision-makers can be viewed as a problem-solving group and their decisions explained in terms of patterns of communication and power.[3] Finally, some meaningful insights can be derived from a reduction of national behavior to the actions and predilections of individual citi-

* Preparation of this manuscript was supported by the Office of Naval Research, Contract Nonr–2285(02).

[1] The systems approach to theory in international relations has been taken by writers on the balance of power (for example, Haas, 1953; and Claude, 1962), by Organski (1958) in his theory of the power transition, by Kaplan (1957) in his typology of international systems, by Brody (1963) in his experimental study of the nth-nation problem, and by a number of writers whose work is included in Rosenau (1961, Parts II and IV).

[2] Most textbooks of international relations (for example, Organski, 1958, and Van Dyke, 1957) discuss national goals and capabilities. (See also Knorr, 1956.) In recent years, a variety of other national attributes have been cited as determinants of foreign policy (see Rummel, 1963; Sprout & Sprout, 1957; Wright, 1955).

[3] The decision-making approach to national behavior is discussed in Chapter 12 of this volume. The most prominent publication in this area is a monograph by Snyder, Bruck, and Sapin (1962).

zens.[4] All of these approaches have something to offer, but only the last will be utilized in this chapter.

In tracing the behavior of the state to the behavior of individual citizens, we do not mean to imply that all citizens are equally involved. Some, who can be called decision-makers, are centrally involved, taking an active role in the formulation and execution of foreign policy. Others, more peripherally located, provide guidance to the decision-makers by stating goals, limits, and proposals for action. Still others play no active part but, through their potential for action, force decision-makers to move in certain directions and avoid others.

By reducing international behavior to the behavior of individuals, it is possible to draw on the principles of psychology to derive new hypotheses. In doing so we need not be restricted to the narrow models of the 1930s and early 1940s, when psychologists often attributed international behavior to the irrational expression of strong emotions. Psychology as a whole has progressed since that time, and human behavior is now viewed as a complex combination of many factors: motives, emotions, perceptions, predictions about the future, and the like. Today, there is no need to choose between the view that man is rational and the view that he is irrational. Both can be encompassed within the same conceptual framework.

One way to account for an individual's social behavior is to describe his definition of the social situation.[5] By this is meant his image of the people around him—their capabilities, intentions, and traits—and his view of how these people relate to his goals and codes of behavior. Likewise, the decisions made by a policy-maker or the

proposals, goals, and limits communicated to him by another citizen may be derived from a *definition of the international situation*. By this is meant a set of images possessed by an individual, representing his view of what other nations are like, what relevance they have to the goals of his own nation, and what behavior toward them would be appropriate for his own nation. Taking this approach, it is possible to distinguish three broad classes of images that influence action toward another nation:

1. *Predictions about the future behavior of the other nation.* Policy makers and interested citizens are constantly trying to predict the future behavior of other nations. Such predictions are useful for detecting new problems and new opportunities to pursue established goals. In addition, when proposals for new policies are being discussed, it is often useful to try to predict how other nations will react.

2. *Perceptions of the basic characteristics of the other nation.* Most people are not content with simply observing and predicting another person's actions. They usually want to go deeper and assess his basic characteristics, the springs from which his behavior flows. The same is true in the perception of nations. Whole nations are classified into categories such as friendly, hostile, weak, or trustworthy. People rely on such characterizations to explain the behavior of another nation and to predict what it will do in the future. They are also used as a guide to the choice of appropriate policies for dealing with the nation.

3. *Conceptions of appropriate ways for dealing with the other nation.* When two nations interact over a period of time, certain patterns often

---

[4] Examples of the individual approach to theory will be presented throughout this chapter.

[5] This concept was first introduced, in a slightly different form, by Thomas and Znaniecki (1927).

emerge, that is, certain kinds of action that are repeated over and over. The United States regularly consults the British in matters regarding Hong Kong. The Egyptians take every opportunity to make tough remarks concerning Israel. To some extent, each individual action is determined by the events of the moment. But the fact that certain patterns are repeated suggests, in addition, the existence of policies or rules of thumb concerning the actions that are deemed appropriate to take toward another nation under most circumstances.

This chapter will deal primarily with three rather specific kinds of image, corresponding to the three broad classes just described. The three images are: (a) *threat perception,* the belief that the future behavior of another nation is likely to frustrate the attainment of a specific goal; (b) *trust* or *distrust,* the perception of the basic characteristics of another nation as generally trustworthy or untrustworthy; and (c) *responsiveness,* the conception of how helpful one's nation should be in dealing with another nation—a general orientation that underlies many more specific action patterns. After a brief discussion of the impact of these three types of images on national behavior, we shall examine in detail the ways in which they develop and change in the course of the interaction between two nations. The shape that these images take constitutes the definition of the international situation on which national action is based.

Most of the ideas presented will be grounded in psychological theory and research but speculative with regard to international relations.

Threat Perception and Its Consequences

National behavior can often be traced to the perception that another nation is threatening a basic goal. In some cases, military security seems threatened. In other cases, economic or political goals seem in jeopardy.

A variety of tactics is available for coping with perceived threat. It may be possible to improve the capability of one's own nation, as in the military sphere, by equipping an army or courting allies. Or an attempt may be made to reduce the other nation's capability, as by interrupting its supply lines or by preventive attack. It may also be possible to alter the intentions of the other nation's leaders by arguing persuasively, making contingent threats and promises, or altering conditions that they see as frustrating. If none of these tactics succeeds, the only way to escape a sense of threat may be to give up the goal that is threatened. Most of the tactics just described are among the basic elements of what is commonly called "international politics."

Besides eliciting behavior designed to cope with the problem, the perception of threat is likely to produce psychological tension in the observer. Several lines of evidence reveal that psychological stress is intimately related to the efficiency of problem-solving. The relationship is probably curvilinear (Driver, 1962), some stress being necessary to motivate activity but too much stress causing a reduction in efficiency. People differ in the levels of stress at which they are optimally efficient, and the optimal level of stress differs from problem to problem (Sarason & Palola, 1960).

A few studies have gone more deeply into the problem and identified some of the psychological processes that are impaired by high stress. Various experiments (for example, Cowen, 1952; Katchmar, Ross, & Andrews, 1958; and others reviewed by Osgood, 1962) have shown that people tend to become rigid and repetitive under stress. They think up fewer new alternatives and are, therefore, more likely to persist in old, maladaptive approaches. Experimenters (for example, Driver, 1962) have also found that the dimensionality of thinking reduces under stress, in other words, that individual objects (in Driver's thesis, other nations) seem less complicated the greater the stress. In addition, some authors have speculated that stress causes a reduction in the number of consequences considered in evaluating a potential course of action. In part, this may be due to foreshortened perspective, that is, to increased difficulty in thinking ahead (Osgood, 1962). It may also derive in part from a reduction in the number of goals considered worthy of pursuit (Milburn, 1961).

The findings and hypotheses just described have relevance to national decision-making. They suggest that in times of "national stress," when national aspirations seem threatened, decision-makers are likely (a) to be less aware of the complexity of their environment, (b) to consider fewer alternatives, and (c) to choose among alternatives more impulsively with less adequate review of their consequences.

Threat perception is often a prominent feature of the progression of events that lead to war. Actions taken by one nation to defend itself against threat are often seen as evidence of threat by the citizens of another. This may lead to defensive preparations by the other nation, which, in turn, are seen as further evidence of threat by citizens of the first. Thus international tension may develop through a "circular process" (see pp. 420 ff.) that produces a deepening sense of threat on both sides. Such circular processes have often culminated in war, the actual outbreak taking place in a time of crisis when the sense of threat became so great on one or both sides that decision-makers lost their capacity to think clearly about the problems at hand.

Evidence of unclear thinking in a time of crisis can be found in a series of emotional statements made by the German Kaiser just prior to the German invasion of Belgium and France in 1914, as cited by Zinnes, North, and Koch (1961).

Trust, Distrust, and Their Consequences

Distrust and threat perception are not synonymous. While threat perception is the expectation that another nation will be harmful *in a specific way*, distrust is the expectation that another nation will usually be harmful. One can exist without the other. For example, an American businessman may feel quite threatened by Japanese advances in the manufacturing of electronic equipment and yet feel relatively trusting toward the Japanese in general. The same American may be profoundly distrustful of Communist China and yet perceive little military threat from that quarter.

Though not the same thing, distrust and threat perception are often causally related. The more they distrust another nation, the more likely are people to perceive it as a threat to some or all of the interests of their own nation. Conversely, continued perception of threat from another nation produces an increased level of distrust.

When a nation is distrusted, another curious phenomenon is sometimes found. People tend to blame a lot of their misfortunes on the nation, including many for which it is not clearly responsible (Osgood, 1962). The resulting misconceptions may reduce their capacity for coping with reality. An example can be seen in the official American government position about the causes of the riots in Japan that prevented President Eisenhower's visit in 1959. At the time they occurred, these riots were blamed on the Soviet

Union, in accordance with the usual stereotype. Today, it is commonly recognized that the causes of the riots lay primarily in Japanese society rather than in Moscow.

The less trusted another nation, the less effort is made to understand the motives of its leaders. Everything they do seems part of a basic, evil scheme that is unaffected by such things as struggles between competing political factions or threats from the outside. It is particularly hard to believe that these leaders are reacting defensively to actions taken by one's own nation. An example of the latter point may be seen in Churchill's failure in 1940 to anticipate that the Germans would occupy Norway if the British attempted to stop German shipping on the Norwegian coast. According to Fox (1959), Churchill went ahead with the blockade because he believed that the Nazis would invade Norway if they wanted to, regardless of British actions.

Trust can be defined as the expectation that another nation will usually be helpful. The more trusted another nation, the less likely it is to be perceived as a threat, for two reasons: (a) Trust acts as a "shock-absorbing cushion" (Osgood, 1962) against evidence of threat. The more trusted another nation, the greater the tendency to discount or reinterpret evidence of threat from that nation. (b) Mutual trust also makes it easier for two nations to negotiate agreements, since the citizens of each can anticipate that the citizens of the other will uphold their end of the bargain. As a consequence, international cooperation increases and with it communication. Increased communication, in turn, reduces the chance that people in either nation will reach a false conclusion about the extent to which the other nation threatens their interests.

Responsiveness and Its Consequences

Regularities can often be found in the extent to which *one nation is helpful or harmful toward another*. A variety of possible explanations can be given for such regularities. In this chapter, they are attributed to orientations of responsiveness,[6] that is, to conceptions in the minds of individuals of the degree to which their nation should be helpful toward another nation.

The existence and importance of such orientations are suggested by the results of an interview study conducted by the author (Pruitt, 1964). Interviews were taken from fourteen members of the XYZ Office in one of the geographic bureaus of the Department of State, an office that handles relations with a group of *friendly* nations. In the interviews, each officer was asked to describe the procedure employed in solving two policy problems on which he had recently worked.

Members of the XYZ Office seemed to see their role largely as one of persuading other parts of the government to take the interests of certain friendly nations into consideration when formulating American policy. In other words, they consciously adopted and implemented responsive orientations toward the needs of certain other nations. To paraphrase the remarks of one of the top men in the office, "One of the basic policies of the XYZ Office is to prevent other agencies from irritating too much the countries under our wing, as for instance to stop the Agriculture Department from undercutting a commodity market in _____."

---

[6] The term "responsiveness" is borrowed from the writings of K. W. Deutsch (1957), who uses it in a closely related sense. It is equally applicable to international and interpersonal relations.

Carrying out this role often led XYZ officers into conflict with members of other agencies over the extent to which the government should make concessions to the other nations, with the XYZ Office usually favoring more concessions. Such conflicts were often won by members of the XYZ Office, which suggests that these officers had a good deal of support throughout the government for the definition of their roles. Thus the ultimate roots of their responsiveness appeared to run deeply into the political structure of the nation.

Before turning to specific applications of the concept to international relations, a few general comments need to be made about the way responsiveness affects behavior. Responsiveness can be thought of as a variable, ranging from very weak to very strong. Two relationships can be postulated between responsiveness and willingness to help another party:

1. The greater one's responsiveness, the greater one's willingness to sacrifice his own welfare to be helpful to the other.

2. If one is at all responsive, one's willingness to adopt a course of action is contingent on the degree to which it helps the other.[7]

The author's State Department interviews yielded support for the second of these two propositions. According to a highly placed informant, when a friendly nation makes a request of the United States, an XYZ officer will attempt to evaluate the importance of this request to the nation that made it. If the people who made it do not consider it important, the XYZ Office will simply bring it to the attention of other parts of the government. But if there appear to be strong feelings in the other nation, members of the XYZ Office are likely to "go to bat" for the request. In short, XYZ officers tend to push more vigorously for the adoption of a policy the more important it seems to people in the other nation.

Responsiveness affects the choice of tactics during controversies. The more responsive a person feels toward another nation, the more likely is he to want his nation to use *mild tactics* in dealing with the other nation, such as discussion, compromise, contingent promise, and the like; and the less likely is he to allow the use of *harsh tactics* such as subversion, propaganda, contingent threats, shows of force, and the like.

It follows that when responsiveness is strong in one nation and especially when it is strong in both, controversies tend to be short-lived. Vicious circles of punishment and counter-punishment are unlikely to persist because at least one side is unwilling to return in punishment what it has received from the other.

Furthermore, like trust, responsiveness on one or both sides facilitates the negotiation of agreements. This is so because responsiveness makes people more willing to accept an unequal proposal, one that seems to benefit the

---

[7] The two points just made are summarized in a mathematical formulation devised by the author (Pruitt, 1962); within the context of decision theory:

$$U_1(X) = A_1(X) + \beta_{12}A_2(X)$$

where $U_1(X)$ is the utility to Party 1 of alternative X

$A_1(X)$ is the "selfish advantage" of alternative X to Party 1

$A_2(X)$ is the "selfish advantage" of alternative X to Party 2

β_{12} is Party 1's level of responsiveness to Party 2.

This formulation suggests the possibility of finding negative responsiveness, which will cause an alternative to have lower utility the more valuable it is to the other side. Such an attitude is often found toward nations that are labeled "enemies."

other nation more than their own. The stronger the responsiveness, the less the insistence on exact tit for tat. As a result, a wider range of proposals is available, and a proposal acceptable to both sides is more likely to be found.

Responsiveness is closely related to trust. People who trust another nation are likely to be responsive to it and vice versa. In addition, over the long run, responsiveness on one side tends to elicit trust on the other, because people on the other side come to see that the first side is interested in their welfare. A discussion of the relationship between trust and responsiveness in the formation of alliances and unions between states can be found in the work of K. W. Deutsch (1957).

Though closely related, trust and responsiveness cannot be treated simply as two versions of the same variable because the correlation between them is not perfect. Examples can be found in which people in one nation exhibit great trust but little responsiveness toward another nation—for example, the traditional view held by citizens of many colonial nations toward their colonies. Likewise, great responsiveness can sometimes be found associated with little trust, as in the outlook of the citizens of a small nation that is trying to appease a powerful aggressor.

As a concept, responsiveness is closely related to the traditional notion of "power" used by many political scientists. The two concepts are really opposite sides of a coin, since power can be defined as the capacity to influence and responsiveness as the willingness to be influenced. However, responsiveness is a more analytic concept, in the sense of describing a link in the causal chain that is closer to observable behavior. As such, it conforms more closely to the criteria recently enunciated by Katz and Stotland (1959) for the development of useful concepts in the behavioral sciences. It is also more closely allied to concepts in the fields of sociology and psychology, where rich bodies of theory already exist that can be "mined" for new insights into international behavior.

Summary

Certain aspects of international behavior can be attributed to the images of other nations held by individual people. Three kinds of image are particularly important: threat perception, distrust (together with its opposite, trust), and responsiveness. Threat perception leads to the adoption of defensive tactics and also produces psychological tensions that may impair the quality of national problem-solving. Distrust is a more basic perception of another nation and may underlie threat perception in addition to producing such phenomena as a tendency to blame the other nation for all misfortunes and to fail to analyze the motives of its leaders. Level of responsiveness is negatively correlated with the harshness of tactics recommended for dealing with another nation and positively related to the likelihood of seeing middle ground in negotiations with that nation.

THE DEVELOPMENT OF THREAT PERCEPTION

Threat perception has been defined as the anticipation of frustration from another nation. It is not a perception of something tangible but rather an *inference*, involving a more or less intuitive "piecing together" of evidence. In this section, the psychology of inference will be used as a basis for building a model of threat perception.

A Model of Threat Perception

Threats are inferred from two kinds of evidence: evidence of *capability* to do harm and evidence of *intent* to do it. Both must be present before another nation is viewed as a threat.

Singer (1958) illustrates this point. "The British today maintain a relatively formidable military establishment, capable of rendering extensive damage to . . . the United States" (p. 94). But Washington does not feel threatened because there is no perceived intent. "Conversely, the extreme hostility of the Egyptian government, because it is not coupled with significant military capability, has not produced any important level of threat-perception in Washington" (p. 94). Threat is perceived, as in American-Soviet relations, when there is evidence of both capability and intent. Singer has proposed a quasi-mathematical formulation that summarizes his position: "Threat-Perception = Estimated Capability × Estimated Intent" (p. 94).

Estimates of capability and intent, in turn, are also inferred and need to be explained in psychological terms.

Hypotheses about the process of inference can be drawn from the Directive-State Theory of Perception (Allport, 1955). Most inferences are based in part on evidence and in part on *predispositions* that affect the interpretation of evidence. Predispositions, in turn, originate in motivational and emotional states, attitudes and past experience. Two generalizations can be made about the interplay of predispositions and evidence in determining inference: (a) The stronger a predisposition, the more influence it will have on what is inferred. (b) The weaker or more ambiguous the evidence, the greater the influence of predispositions.

Predispositions have their effect by altering the perception of evidence. Sometimes a piece of evidence is distorted to conform with a predisposition (Stagner, 1961). But more often the alteration consists of *perceptual emphasis,* in which evidence supporting a predisposition is given greater weight than it deserves, or *perceptual defense,* in which evidence contrary to a predisposition is discounted or ignored. Perceptual emphasis and defense together produce a phenomenon called *possibilistic thinking* (Fromm, 1961), in which something is seen as "probable" that would only be seen as "possible" if the evidence were objectively appraised. Osgood (1962) describes an extreme form of possibilistic thinking in the behavior of the paranoid patient: "If the paranoid knows it is possible that his doctor belongs to a secret society persecuting him, he is likely to leap to the conclusion that his doctor does belong, and then the paranoid acts accordingly" (p. 30).

Determinants of the Predisposition to Perceive Threat

Predispositions to perceive threat can be traced to a variety of sources.

As mentioned earlier, they may derive from an attitude of *distrust,* in which another nation is seen as basically hostile to the interests of one's own nation. The greater the level of distrust, the more attention is given to any piece of evidence that suggests the existence of a threat. An example of possibilistic thinking resulting from distrust is given by Zinnes, North, and Koch (1961) in their analysis of the events leading up to World War I. In 1914, when Russia mobilized as a deterrent to Austrian aggression against Serbia, the German Kaiser concluded that his old adversary in the race for colonies, *England,* was about to attack. The words of the Kaiser illustrate the process through which distrust of England was converted into the perception of threat: "The net has been suddenly thrown over our head and England sneeringly reaps the brilliant success of her persistently prosecuted purely anti-German world policy." The causes of distrust itself will be analyzed in the next section.

Predispositions to perceive threat can also arise from *past experience*. Psychological research (for example, Bruner & Postman, 1949) shows that people interpret ambiguous visual stimuli in terms of things they have seen in the past. It follows that past experience with an unpleasant event can make people especially alert to evidence suggesting that this event is about to recur. For example, the citizens of a nation that has experienced a surprise attack are likely to be especially impressed with any evidence that such an attack is again in the making. "This time we won't be caught napping." Some observers of the American scene (for example, U Thant) have suggested that experience with the surprise attack on Pearl Harbor has made Americans overly alert to the danger of another surprise attack. Such a predisposition does not lead to the perception of threat from a specific nation, but rather to the perception of a specific kind of threat.

Predispositions may also originate in the natural and supposed healthy practice of *contingency planning*, planning for the worst possible contingency. Although much can be said in favor of contingency planning, the danger that it may lead to possibilistic thinking should be recognized. To do his job, the contingency planner must pay a lot of attention to evidence that his nation is threatened and little to evidence that it is safe. From such one-sided perusal of the evidence, it is only a short psychological step to the conclusion that one's nation is really in danger.

Another source of threat perception comes into being when contingency planning and actual threat perception lead to the building of *institutions for coping with threat*. There are two reasons for this:

1. Institutions provide many services to people associated with them, including such things as financial support, education, status, and a sense of personal identity. As a result, people come to have a "vested" interest in their continuation. People associated with an institution that is designed to cope with a threat have a vested interest in the continuation of the threat, which may result in a predisposition to perceive threat.

2. On a "psycho-logical" basis (Abelson & Rosenberg, 1958), people are likely to find it inconsistent to prepare for a threat that may not exist. As a result, when an institution is built to cope with a threat, people are rather easily convinced of the existence of the threat. The men who have planned and developed the institution are probably most predisposed to such a belief and least able to adjust to a new situation of diminished threat. It follows that a new generation of statesmen may be needed to develop an adequate orientation toward another nation that once was a formidable threat but now has become relatively harmless.

Anxiety may also create a predisposition to perceive threat. Anxiety can be thought of as a general feeling of apprehension without a specific object. Fear, on the other hand, has a specific object. Anxiety is usually more distressing than fear; and some writers have suggested that people defend themselves against it by transforming it into fear, that is, by identifying and becoming obsessed about a supposedly threatening object in their environment.

Freud (1949, p. 345) called this transformation "expectant dread."

There is an obvious relationship between expectant dread and threat perception. When people are anxious, they cast about for some concrete object to fear; they become predisposed to perceive threat. Milburn (in a private communication) has suggested that this process may underlie some cases of international threat perception. In times of national dislocation, when anxieties rise, an entire population may begin to overinterpret minimal evidence of threat from another nation.

Evidence of Threatening Intent

Two broad classes of evidence have been mentioned that contribute to the perception of threat: evidence of capability and evidence of intent. Only the latter will be discussed in this section, since it is more obviously a matter of inference. What are the bases for inferring threatening intent?

Capability. In addition to the direct part that it plays in threat perception, capability is often regarded as a clue to intent. There are two reasons for so regarding it:

1. Having a capability sometimes encourages the development of a goal. A nation that has, let us say, a capability for making war will be more likely to solve its problems by war and the threat of war than a nation that does not have such a capability. Knowing this, the neighbors of a well-armed nation will often be suspicious of its intentions.

2. Capability is often developed in the pursuit of goals. If a nation wants to invade its neighbors, it is likely to build a war machine. Knowing this, the neighbors of a nation that is arming will often be suspicious of its intentions.

The *extent* to which the second line of reasoning produces a sense of threat depends, in part, on the type of capability involved. In the modern world, military security derives in good measure from the invulnerability of retaliatory (deterrent) forces. If another nation seems to be developing the capability to destroy our retaliatory forces, we are likely to feel extremely threatened (Schelling, 1960). On the other hand, if they are simply making progress in protecting their own armaments, we are not so likely to become alarmed (Milburn, 1961) and may even welcome their progress as a step toward a more stable military environment. In addition, isolated weapon systems that are highly vulnerable may be seen as evidence of the intention to launch a surprise attack because they can only be used for a first strike (M. Deutsch, 1961).

The extent to which the second line of reasoning leads to a sense of threat depends, in addition, on other evidence. Sometimes a nation's reasons for arming are apparent and legitimate. For example, one of its enemies may be arming against it. When this happens, people in other nations may become uneasy for the first reason cited (because of the stockpile that is being built) but are not likely to feel greatly threatened. The point can be illustrated by American assessment of Communist Chinese motives for building up troops across from Quemoy and Matsu in 1962. Had this mobilization come at another time, American officials might have been very worried about the security of these islands. But it was remembered that earlier in the year the *Nationalist* Chinese had made many remarks about the necessity of attacking the mainland that year. This offered a good defensive reason for the Communist buildup; and after the initial shock, Washington was not especially alarmed.

Unfortunately, it is very hard for people to accept the view that another nation is arming in defense against *their nation*. Such preparations are more often perceived as evidence of threat than as understandable measures to avoid an attack. We see this today in both the United States and the Soviet Union (Bronfenbrenner, 1961, and Chapter 7 in this volume). On both sides, people refuse to believe that the other side arms, at least in part, out of fear—despite the abundant evidence of a classical arms race.

Why do people have such blindspots? One reason may lie in the prevalent assumption that other people see us the way we see ourselves. If we see our country as peace-loving, it is difficult to believe that others fear us. Another may lie in the difficulty people have in empathizing with the citizens of an "enemy" nation. Enemies are a breed apart, not quite human. We cannot easily put ourselves in their shoes. American reaction to the U-2 incident is a case in point. Few Americans were able to picture themselves in the place of a Russian learning that an American plane had been shot down over his territory. Consequently, most Americans did not seem to realize that the Russians could genuinely regard this incident as a provocation. Other reasons for such blindspots are developed in Chapter 7 in this volume.

Actions. The actions of another nation are a major source of information about its intentions. Some actions are unambiguous. Others are more obscure, and must be interpreted through roundabout reasoning. When intentions are inferred from actions, the actions are being used as *signs*. Little is known about the relationship between signs and what they signify, but it is possible to speculate.

One approach to this problem is implied in a model of tacit bargaining in limited war proposed by Schelling (1957, 1960) but not as yet empirically tested. The sign from which an intention is inferred consists of *stepping over* a "boundary" on a conceptual dimension. An example, derived from Schelling, is shown in Figure 11.1. The continuum in this figure represents a conceptual dimension on which the decison-makers of Nation X locate the choice of weapon systems by Nation Y, a nation with which they are at war. The vertical lines on the continuum represent boundaries between weapon systems *as perceived by the leaders of Nation X*. In Case 1, there is only one such boundary, between conventional and nuclear weapons. In Case 2 such a boundary is also found between tactical and strategic nuclear weapons.

So long as Nation Y stays on the low yield (left hand) side of a boundary, the leaders of Nation X will believe that it intends to go no further than the boundary. But if Nation Y steps over such a boundary and chooses a weapon system with higher yield, the leaders of Nation X will expect it to go on to the next boundary or, if there is no next boundary, to the end of the dimension. More specifically, in Case 1, if Y employs tanks (Y at point Y_1), X will expect Y to go no further than the use of TNT bombs in its choice of weapon systems. But if Y employs tactical A bombs (Y at point Y_2), X will conclude that Y is probably going to use strategic H bombs at some time in the future. In Case 2, where there is a perceptual boundary between tactical and strategic A bombs, Y's use of tactical A bombs will not lead X to conclude that Y intends to employ a full range of nuclear weapons. The potential for limiting the war is, of course, greater in

Case 2 than in Case 1; and in general it can be said that there is less chance that a war will escalate the more perceptual boundaries there are on such a dimension. The boundary model underlying this example is assumed to have broader application than the limitation of war.

Besides examining the relationship between signs and what they signify, it is also necessary to ask how sign-significate relationships develop. Learning theory (especially Tolman, 1932) provides one answer: past experience. For example, past experience reveals that troops which cross a border (sign) usually try to keep going until they have taken control of the country (sig-

the Japanese wished to fight only a limited war.

Schelling (1957, 1960), in the analysis of tacit bargaining from which Figure 11.1 was derived, provides no systematic explanation of how signs gain meaning; but some ideas can be gleaned from his discussion. Boundaries, such as those shown in Figure 11.1, gain their meaning in part through being *perceptually distinct* to the observer. For example, rivers constitute a perceptually distinct geographic line and are, therefore, often a workable cease-fire line beyond which each side is confident that the other will not advance. It is not enough, however, for a boundary to be perceptually distinct

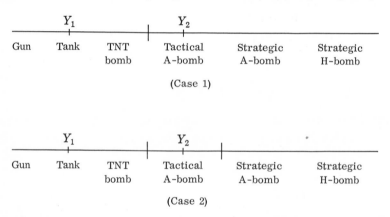

Fig. 11.1. Dimensions employed by the leaders of Nation X in classifying the level of armament systems currently used by Nation Y. Perceptual boundaries are indicated by the longer vertical lines on these dimensions.

nified intention). When such a sign is encountered, most people expect the usual historical result to follow. This kind of reasoning can lead to error. For example, on the basis of past experience, many Americans interpreted the Japanese surprise attack on Pearl Harbor as part of a plan to invade the continental United States. Recent perusal of Japanese documents (Morton, 1960) suggests, on the contrary, that

to the observer; he must also believe that it is perceptually distinct to his opponents before he will use it to interpret their behavior.

One further point needs to be made about the interpretation of actions. As in the case of capabilities, the more that is known about the motives underlying an action, the smaller the likelihood of misinterpretation. If the leaders of one nation can explain why they are attacking a second nation, they can sometimes keep third nations from feeling threatened.

Statements. Statements made by people in one nation are often interpreted as evidence of threat by people in another. Declarations of war are an obvious example. When predispositions are strong, even minor statements by low officials or newsmen may look like evidence of threat. Statements of the intention not to do something harmful are less often believed than statements of the intention to do something harmful, because the former are more likely to be seen as propaganda aimed at making a good impression.

A question arises about *contingent threats.* A contingent threat is a commitment to retaliate; for example, a statement by the President of the United States that an attack on Western Europe will lead to nuclear retaliation. M. Deutsch (1961) has suggested that contingent threats produce a sense of insecurity (that is, a feeling of threat), even when the recipient of the threat intends to comply. He writes: "The (contingent) threat of using force is perceived to be an expression of an underlying intent to injure, rather than of self defense" (p. 63). Unfortunately, there seems to be no empirical evidence on this point.

Conditions Faced by the Other Nation. In judging the motives of other people, we often draw on what is known about the problems they face and the incentives they perceive. For example, the more benefit another person can derive from harming our interests, the more threatened we are

likely to feel (Solomon, 1960). The same is probably true of international relations. The more benefit a nation can derive from harming our interests, the more threatened we are likely to feel.

Sources of Ambiguity in the Evidence of Threat

It was pointed out earlier that predispositions to perceive threat have a greater effect the more ambiguous the evidence concerning capability and intent. This section will review some of the sources of ambiguity in evidence.[8]

Some kinds of evidence are *inherently* more ambiguous than others. For example, evidence about intent is usually more ambiguous than evidence about capability. Capability as evidence of intent is especially ambiguous, since a nation may be arming for various reasons. Some statements are highly ambiguous and, therefore, highly susceptible to misinterpretation as evidence of threat; for example, President Kennedy's classic remark, "Under some conditions the United States might use nuclear weapons first."

In addition, certain *conditions* impair a nation's capacity to get clear-cut evidence about another nation and thus heighten the likelihood that predispositions will influence perception. Ambiguity is more likely (a) the smaller the number of highly placed people who know the other nation well, (b) the poorer the capacity to empathize with citizens of the other nation, and (c) the fewer the channels of communication with the other nation. These points will be illustrated by comparing American-British with American-Soviet relations. Americans feel more threatened by the

---

[8] The implication should not be drawn from this discussion that ambiguity is always undesirable. A certain amount of ambiguity in *contingent* threats may be beneficial, in the sense that a nation may be able to guard itself against a broader range of injustices if there is some ambiguity about the circumstances under which it will retaliate.

Soviet Union than by Britain in part for realistic reasons, but also, we conjecture, in part because of the greater level of ambiguity that exists in evidence concerning the Soviet Union, coupled, of course, with a general predisposition to distrust the Soviets.

American-British Relations. To begin with, there are many highly placed people in the United States who know a lot about the government and people of Britain and the conditions that prevail in that country. This knowledge permits them to interpret quite accurately the reasons for statements and actions from the other nation. Potential misunderstandings are thereby avoided. Secondly, many Americans can empathize with the British, which also reduces the likelihood of misinterpreting statements and actions. Finally, and probably most important, there are many channels of communication between the two countries. One kind of channel is based on private citizens, who often converse with one another. Another is based on diplomats, who frequently develop informal working relationships that permit ready access to one another. A third connects the people on each side with the leaders on the other.

Channels of communication can reduce the likelihood of threat perception in a number of ways. They can be used to transmit information about capabilities and *intentions,* so that there is less guesswork for the other side. They can also be used to explain the reasons behind certain actions or statements that might otherwise be misinterpreted. Furthermore, they can be used to communicate *expectations* about how the other side should behave, that is, information about conceptual boundaries. Without such information, the other side may inadvertently cross a critical boundary and

be seen as a threat. Finally, such channels can be used to talk about methods of handling violations of expectations. Each side can make information available about the *penalties* it will invoke if the other harms its interests, and the *techniques of absolution* the other can use to rid itself of these penalties if they are invoked.

Laboratory research on interpersonal interaction confirms the points just made. In a bargaining game, M. Deutsch (1958) discovered that communication increases the expectation that the other side will cooperate (provided each side is initially oriented toward improving its own welfare rather than harming the welfare of the other). One of Deutsch's associates, Loomis (1959), established that communication about each of the four topics italicized in the previous paragraph (intentions, expectations, penalties, and techniques of absolution) adds to the expectation that the other side will cooperate—in the minds of both the sender of the message and its receiver.

Not only do channels of communication exist between the United States and Britain, but also there is a good deal of trust in these channels; people on both sides tend to believe the messages that come over them. This further reduces the likelihood of misunderstanding. Trust in these channels derives, in part, from the broader trust that is found in most aspects of Anglo-American relations. But in part, it has been built up separately for each channel. Information relevant to the latter point was given by a respondent in the author's study of the State Department. He suggested that trust between diplomats builds up slowly, even when they come from nations that are basically friendly. Each must learn the other's "code"—learn to distinguish between the occasions when he is speaking officially, as a representative of his gov ernment, and the occasions when he is speaking informally. Each must spend a period of time testing the credibility of what the other has said informally. If a trusting relationship finally develops, it must be guarded carefully, because it can easily be destroyed by telling a few lies in an informal manner. Once destroyed, it is hard to rebuild. To the extent that a nation wishes to keep credible channels open, it must scrupulously refrain from using them to transmit lies.

American-Soviet Relations. American-Soviet relations present a contrast to Anglo-American relations. For one thing, few Americans know much about the Soviet Union, and the ones who do are not always highly placed.[9] Furthermore, travel is restricted so that it is hard to learn much about the Soviet Union. In addition, Americans are not good at empathizing with Russians. Finally, there are only a few communication channels between the two nations, and most of them are not considered very trustworthy.[10] Instead of establishing working relationships, diplomats tend to be icy and to exhibit a competitive outlook toward one another that precludes trust. Few American citizens are able to keep up sustained contact with Soviet citizens. Both sides conduct campaigns to discredit the leadership of the other side, so that people do not listen when these leaders speak.

In short, conditions in Soviet-American relations are such that clear-cut perception is at a minimum and the chances for misinterpretation at a maximum. Misinterpretations are not the only, and probably not even the major, source of threat perception in Soviet-American relations; but they play an important part and are, therefore, worthy of study.

Summary

Threats are inferred from two kinds of evidence: evidence of capability and evidence of intent. Evidence of intent can take a variety of forms, including capability, actions, statements, and conditions faced by the other nation. "Predispositions" to perceive threat create systematic distortions in the perception of evidence, leading to "possibilistic thinking" in which future events are seen as probable that should only be seen as possible. Predispositions to perceive threat result from distrust, past experience, contingency planning, anxiety, and the existence of institutions to cope with threat. Possibilistic thinking is more likely the more ambiguous the evidence. The ambiguity of evidence about another nation is partially dependent on the nature of the evidence and partially on the nature of the relationship with that nation.

THE DEVELOPMENT OF TRUST AND DISTRUST

Trust has been defined as the perception that another nation will usually be helpful and avoid being harmful; distrust, as the perception that another

---

[9] The latter point is even more true in Chinese-American relations where, on both sides, the people who knew most about the other side were systematically eliminated from the government during the Korean War.

[10] Antagonism between two nations does not preclude the existence of a few communication channels that are trusted by both sides. Communication channels develop on an individual-to-individual level and follow somewhat different laws than those that govern nation-to-nation relations. There may even be considerable trust in some Soviet-American channels.

nation will usually be harmful.[11] Both are images of basic characteristics of the other nation. Essentially, they are the two ends of a single dimension.

Determinants of the Level of Trust or Distrust

Incentives Affecting the Other Nation. One reason for trusting another nation is the awareness that this nation has incentives for behaving in a trustworthy fashion and that its leaders recognize these incentives.[12] To understand the origins of trust, therefore, it may be useful to examine the incentives underlying trustworthiness. Why is one nation highly reliable and helpful, another moderately reliable and helpful, and a third unreliable and vicious?

As used in this chapter, the concepts "trustworthiness" and "responsiveness" are identical, so that all of the material in the next section will be relevant to the sources of trustworthiness. One of the points to be made in that section concerns the positive relationship between our responsiveness toward another nation and the extent to which that nation is seen as capable of manipulating our welfare without incurring costs ("effective fate-control"). The more control they seem to have over our welfare, the more reason we have to be responsive (the greater our incentive to be trustworthy). It follows that people in another nation are more likely to place trust in our nation the more control they think they have over our welfare. Solomon (1960) has demonstrated this proposition on the interpersonal level.

Past Experience with the Other Nation. In some cases, trust or distrust is based on what is known about another nation's past behavior, particularly that part of its past behavior that has directly affected our own welfare. Trust is likely to develop if the other nation has engaged in helpful behavior, distrust if it has engaged in harmful behavior.

Whether an action is seen as helpful or harmful depends on the goals of the perceiver. Actions are seen as helpful if they move the perceiver's nation toward goals he considers appropriate, and harmful if they set it back.

To some extent, goals are similar from person to person and nation to nation. Most people are concerned with the integrity of their nation's frontiers and consider a breach of these frontiers as harmful. Other obvious examples of universal national goals (and attempts to order them in importance) can be found in most textbooks on international relations (for example, Organski, 1958; and Van Dyke, 1957).

There are also differences between nations and between individuals within nations regarding national goals. Some of them reflect differences in "level of aspiration." Whenever goal objects can be ordered on a dimension from less to more desirable and an individual's goal located on this dimension we speak of this goal as his level of aspiration on that dimension. It may also be possible to characterize an entire nation in terms of the dominant level of aspiration among its more influential citizens. For example, we might assert that the Guatemalan level of aspiration for aid from America is $10,000,000.

---

[11] Most of the psychological literature on trust and distrust (for example, M. Deutsch, 1958, 1960a, 1960b; Loomis, 1959; and Solomon, 1960) employs these terms to describe the expectation that another party will be helpful or harmful in a specific way. In this literature, the term "distrust" is identical with the term "threat perception" as used in this chapter.

[12] The idea that trust can arise from knowledge of the incentives affecting another party has also been postulated by Lieberman (1964) in the form of a concept called "i-trust."

Experimental research (Lewin *et al.*, 1944) suggests that past attainment is a major determinant of level of aspiration. The more has been achieved in the past, the higher the level of aspiration. Thus, for example, if $5,000,000 in foreign aid is offered to a given country, its reaction would depend on its past attainments. If, in the past, no aid has been given, such an offer will be seen as helpful, since the level of aspiration is low. On the other hand, if $10,000,000 was given last year and only $5,000,000 this year, the level of aid will seem disappointingly small.

The *attainment of others* is also an important determinant of level of aspiration. If some nations are treated generously and others not, the latter are likely to be unhappy about the level of aid given to them.

Homans (1961) has suggested the importance of another variable, which he calls *investment*. The greater a person's investment in something, the higher his level of aspiration with regard to it. Thus, a person whose "investments" include a college education will aspire to a better job than one whose "investments" include only an eighth-grade education. The notion of investment may be useful for analyzing international affairs. For example, looking now at the donor of foreign aid, many people see such aid as an investment and expect a lot of cooperation from the nations to whom it has been given. For these people, the same action may seem harmful if it comes from a nation that has received a lot of aid and helpful if it comes from a nation that has received little.

Finally, a study by Jones and deCharms (1957) has shown that level of aspiration rises as a function of the other person's *perceived capability*. Dissatisfaction with the help given by another person was greater if he had the ability to be helpful but chose not to be than if he did not have the ability.

This finding may help explain the occasional statements of dissatisfaction voiced by citizens of smaller nations at the amount of aid given them by larger nations. From their vantage point, the larger nations seem to have much more to give away.

In interpersonal relations, the impact of another person's helpful or harmful actions on our level of trust also depends on our knowledge of *why* the other person acted as he did. If his actions seem freely taken, they will make a bigger impression on our level of trust than if they seem forced on him by circumstances beyond his control. Evidence for this last point can be found in a study by Strickland (1958) in which styles of supervision were compared. An inverse relationship was found between the amount of supervision and the amount of trust later shown in the subordinate. Closer supervision seemed to make a supervisor feel that *his* actions had produced the good performance of his subordinates. Since he did not see his subordinates as free agents, he had no basis for evaluating their trustworthiness. Another interpretation of Strickland's findings would be that helpful behavior from another person will have less influence on the degree to which we trust him the more control we think we have over him. If two people have been equally helpful, we will be more impressed by the behavior of the one who seems less under our control.

Similar hypotheses can be stated for international relations. Another nation's actions will have more effect on our level of trust or distrust the more voluntary these actions seem to have been. The latter point has interesting strategic implications: If a nation wants to be trusted, it should try to demonstrate that its helpful actions are freely taken and that it adopts policies that harm the interests of another nation only when compelled to do so by forces beyond its control. Evidence of the use of such a strategy was found by the author in his study of the State Department. When a request from another nation had to be turned down, an elaborate attempt was often made to persuade its diplomats that the State Department had no other choice, that, for example, the decision had been dictated by budgetary limitations, statutory restrictions, or other supposedly unalterable conditions.

Tests of Trustworthiness. In making judgments about another person, men do not rely exclusively on unsolicited data. Sometimes they actively manipulate the other person to elicit reactions and then make judgments about his character on the basis of these reactions. If the degree to which the other person can be trusted is at issue, such a manipulation can be called a "test of trustworthiness."

Tests of trustworthiness also appear in international relations. For example, a Washington correspondent, William J. Jorden, reported that a test of the Russians was being developed by the early Kennedy Administration:

In dealing with Moscow, the President and his policy advisers want to find out whether the Soviet leadership is really interested in meaningful agreements, whether "peaceful coexistence" is a slogan or a serious policy. They expect to find out in Laos and in Vietnam, in Cuba, in a variety of trouble spots in Africa, particularly in the Congo, and in the nuclear test ban talks at Geneva. The *test* will be in whether peaceful settlements are possible and whether agreements once achieved are lived up to (*New York Times,* April 9, 1961, Section E3; italics added).

In the same vein, one of the arguments for Senate ratification of the Test-ban Treaty was the test that it provided, in the eyes of the world, of America's peaceful intentions.

General Evaluation of the Other Nation. Social psychologists (for example, Krech, Crutchfield, & Ballachey, 1962) have often noted a phenomenon called the "halo effect," in which judgments about specific characteristics of another person are based on the overall evaluation of that person. Judgments about another person's trustworthiness clearly are subject to the halo effect. A similar phenomenon is probably found in the perception of nations. This means that we can look for the antecedents of trust and distrust in the determinants of the way a nation is generally evaluated.

Past experience is one such determinant, which has already been discussed. Another is similarity of culture: "good" nations have political and economic systems that are similar to our own; "bad" nations have divergent values and viewpoints. In addition, ideologies sometimes give guidance concerning how to evaluate another nation. For example, communism teaches its adherents that capitalist nations are bad, and vice versa.

A nation's relationship with a third party may determine how it is evaluated. In the theory of *cognitive balance* (Heider, 1946, 1958; Cartwright & Harary, 1956) it is hypothesized that a man who favors person A and notes that persons A and B are friends will tend to become favorable toward person B. If he favors person A and notes that persons A and B are enemies, he will tend to become unfavorable toward person B. There are six other similar principles of cognitive balance. Harary (1961) has extended these principles to international relations, using them to explain changes in the way certain nations evaluated one another during the 1956 crises over Suez and

Hungary. Recent improvements in American images of the Soviet Union may reflect the same principles. For Americans who feel very unfavorable toward Communist China and perceive the growing antagonism between China and the Soviet Union, it is "psychologically" consistent to become more favorable toward the Soviet Union.

Finally, the defense mechanism of *projection* may account for some cases in which other nations are evaluated unfavorably and, therefore, distrusted. Projection is a psychological technique, which enables a man to remain unaware of his own motives by attributing the same motives to other people. Gladstone (1959) has suggested that projection may be involved when other nations are negatively evaluated and labeled "enemies." Gladstone's theory is only partially developed, since it does not specify the conditions under which projection will take place or the factors that determine the identity of the nation that is seen as the "enemy."

The extent to which a person's overall evaluation of another nation determines his level of trust may be dependent on his personality. Steiner (1954) has evidence that people with authoritarian outlooks on life are more susceptible to the halo effect than people with egalitarian outlooks. Scott (1962), on the other hand, has questioned the importance of personality as a determinant of international perception. He stresses, instead, the level of information about other countries and argues essentially that the halo effect characterizes the thinking of the poorly informed.

Determinants of the Flexibility of Trust or Distrust

So far, we have only discussed the level of trust or distrust. But there are other important features of such an image, in particular its flexibility and complexity. By *flexibility* is meant the ease with which an image can be changed. By *complexity* is meant its degree of differentiation.

Some of the determinants of flexibility and inflexibility can be found *in the image itself*. Certain kinds of image are easy to change; others have become built-in assumptions.

One feature of an image is the *number* of cognitive elements supporting it, that is, the number of past experiences, beliefs, other images, and the like, from which the individual can deduce his image. The more supporting cognitive elements, the harder it is to change the image.

Also important is the consistency of the supporting elements, the extent to which they agree in supporting trust vs. distrust. The more consistent the elements supporting an image, the less flexible the image (Krech, Crutchfield, & Ballachey, 1962). Images that are based on the evaluative dimension are likely to be relatively inflexible, since the elements supporting them are likely to be fairly consistent. In addition, the flexibility of an image seems to be an inverse function of the extremity of its level (Tannenbaum, 1956). The higher the level of trust or distrust, the lower its flexibility.

From the discussion so far, one might gain the impression that images are passive structures, responding automatically to the weight of cognitive elements generated by outside influences. However, recent research suggests that this is not the case. Images tend to be *self-reinforcing*. Once established, they often have a dynamic of their own, enabling them to generate more and more supporting cognitive elements. A number of *circular feedback processes* can be described that account for the self-reinforcement often found in images of trust or distrust.

Some have their locus within the individual, others in the relationship between the individual and society, and still others in the relations between nations.

Two of the psychological mechanisms described earlier jointly define a vicious circle within the individual: (a) distrust of another nation produces a predisposition to perceive that nation as a threat, and (b) perceiving another nation as a threat leads to distrust. In other words, distrust produces threat perception which produces more distrust. Similarly, it is possible to describe a benevolent circle in which trust reinforces itself by making a person alert to evidence of helpful behavior from the other nation.

In addition, circular processes can be found in the relationship between the individual and society. For one thing, people often talk publicly about their images. Given such public commitment, the flexibility of these images is likely to be diminished because of social pressures to maintain consistency and honesty (Hovland, 1958). Furthermore, if enough people publicly express an image, others will begin to perceive it as a group norm. As a result of this perception more people will adopt it and still others will hesitate to voice opposition. In either case, the impression that there is group consensus regarding this image will receive further support.

Trust and distrust are also perpetuated through their effect on communication with the nation toward which they are directed. As was mentioned earlier, trust encourages and distrust discourages the development of channels through which credible messages can be transmitted. When channels are open, there is little opportunity for the kind of misunderstandings that contribute to distrust. When channels are clogged, it is not so easy to explain why seemingly harmful and threatening actions have to be taken. Misunderstandings may arise that reinforce distrust. Newcomb (1947) calls the reinforcement of distrust by this mechanism "autistic hostility."

One other international circular process has already been partially described in the Introduction (p. 396). Preparations for dealing with perceived threat from another nation are sometimes, paradoxically, seen as evidence of threat by people in the other nation. Since distrust contributes to threat perception and threat perception to distrust we have here another example of a vicious circle through which distrust is reinforced: A's distrust produces A's perception of threat, produces A's defensive preparations, produces B's perception of threat, produces B's defensive preparations, reinforces A's perception of threat, reinforces A's distrust. A similar but benevolent circle, through which trust is perpetuated, can also be described. Both are varieties of what Merton (1957) has called the "self-fulfilling prophecy."

What relationship exists between these circular processes and the flexibility of trust and distrust? As they operate, such circular processes produce more and more cognitive elements to support the images from which they originate. It follows that the more actively they operate, the more extreme and less flexible the image becomes. The nature of the factors that determine the activity level of these processes is not clear.

The self-reinforcing feature of images has an important implication for international politics; namely, that certain kinds of national action can produce results that are wholly or partially *irrevocable*, by generating images that become self-perpetuating. The Berlin Blockade of 1948 may be a case in point. Once the blockade had been instituted and a resulting high level of distrust engendered in American minds, there was no way back. Removing the blockade and settling political issues could not reestablish the former level of trust. The distrust seemed to have taken on a dynamic of its own.

Further discussion of circular processes will be encountered in the final section of this chapter.

Determinants of the Complexity of Trust and Distrust

The notion of complexity may need further explanation. We have spoken of trust as if it were a single, unitary dimension, and in many people's thinking it is. However, there are people with a more sophisticated view, who recognize that a nation is more trustworthy under some circumstances than under others. Such people can be said to have a complex (as opposed to a simplex) image. An example of a complex image can be seen in a carefully worded statement by James J. Wadsworth, former United States Ambassador to the United Nations. He says:

I think generally, by and large, that the Russian Government has every intention of living up to any agreement they make from the standpoint of nuclear tests or the larger areas of disarmament. Nobody in the world, including ourselves, can guarantee what a successor government might do (*New York Times*, January 18, 1961).

Wadsworth's statement reflects a complex image because it specifies the *conditions* under which the other nation can be more or less trusted. Unfortunately, few people see this much complexity in other nations. Most images of trust are much simpler. An example is the familiar, overgeneralized admonition, "You can't trust the Russians."

The complexity of trust or distrust depends in part on the nature of the cognitive elements that give it support. Trust that is based on knowledge of the incentives governing the behavior of the other party is likely to be fairly complex. We expect a colleague to be more honest about his work than about his personal life, because we know that he anticipates greater penalties for lying about his professional activities. On the other hand, when trust or distrust is derived from a global evaluation of the other side as "good" or "bad," the image is likely to be rather simple in structure. If the other party is seen as "good" it will be generally trusted; if "bad" it will be generally distrusted.

The picture is more complicated where trust is based on past experience with the other party. Complexity depends, in large part, on how extensively past experiences have "generalized." For example, suppose I have been cheated at cards by a Turk. If I conclude only that this Turk is dishonest at cards, I may still have a very complex image of Turks in general. If I generalize further and conclude that all Turks are dishonest at cards, my image of Turks is somewhat simpler. If I generalize completely and conclude that all Turks are dishonest, my image is very simple indeed.

Some principles of "stimulus generalization" from learning theory may be applicable here (see Hilgard, 1956; Kimble, 1961), although little is known about the implications of learning theory for the theory of attitudes and images. Learning theorists describe a habit as more generalized the greater the range of stimuli that evoke it. Analogously, the "habit" of trust or distrust can be thought of as more generalized the less its complexity, that is, the greater the range of objects or circumstances to which it seems appropriate. Students of learning have found that a habit generalizes more widely (a) the more frequently it has been rehearsed (at least up to a point in the number of rehearsals) and (b) the stronger the level of drive at the time of performance. Analogously, we can postulate that a person who has been mistreated by the national of another country or seen the interests of his nation hurt by another country will have a simpler, more generalized image of distrust (a) the more often he has had this experience and (b) the greater his current level of emotional arousal.

Learning theorists have also described a principle of "discrimination." The greater the discrimination between two stimuli, the less generalization occurs between them. Discrimination is partly a function of variety of experience. The more varied a man's experience, the more distinctions he will learn and the less broadly will his habits generalize. Thus, people who have had a variety of experiences with another nation will develop a complex view of that nation's trustworthiness, while people who have had just a few experiences will tend to overgeneralize them. Support for these conclusions may be drawn indirectly from an experimental study by Scott (1962 and Chapter 3 in this volume), in which he discovered that people who know less about international relations have simpler images, involving fewer dimensions.

Discriminations can also be established through the learning of labels (Dollard & Miller, 1950). When two situations have different names, a discrimination is made between them and habits learned in one do not generalize readily to the other. Conversely, when two situations have the same name, behavior learned in one generalizes easily to the other.

Some propagandists seem to be trying to prevent the generalization of trust or distrust in the minds of their audiences by giving different labels to different things. For example, Premier Khrushchev often stressed the difference between military and nonmilitary competition. He emphasized that the Soviet Union would engage in the second but not in the first. By stressing this distinction, he may have been trying to prevent Westerners from overgeneralizing the implications of Soviet provocation in the economic and political spheres and concluding that Russia was untrustworthy in the military sphere as well. Conversely, some propagandists seem to be trying to eliminate discriminations in the minds of their audiences, so that trust or distrust will generalize freely from one situation to another. Such an attempt is evident in the doctrine of "collective security," which holds that an attack against one country is a threat to all. This doctrine tries to eliminate the natural distinction between the fate of other countries and the fate of your own country, and thereby make it appear that you cannot trust a nation which has been untrustworthy toward another nation.

Summary

Images of trust or distrust have three dimensions: level, flexibility, and complexity. Level of trust or distrust is a function of what is known about the incentives affecting the other nation, past experience with the other nation, and the way the other nation is generally evaluated. Flexibility is dependent on the number of cognitive elements supporting an image of trust, the consistency of these elements and the vigor of certain circular processes through which images reinforce themselves. Complexity depends on the kinds of cognitive elements supporting an image and the extent to which past experience with the object of an image has generalized.

THE DEVELOPMENT OF RESPONSIVENESS

Responsiveness has been defined as the conception of how helpful one's nation should be toward another nation. It can also be thought of as an orientation, or "conation," in the traditional language of psychology. The term is not used to describe behavior, but rather the psychological events antecedent to behavior.

Though responsiveness is certainly a property of the individual it may be possible to speak of a national level of responsiveness if some kind of weighted average of the responsiveness of individual citizens can be devised.

Determinants of Level of Responsiveness

Responsiveness has a number of antecedents, including images of the other nation, past experience with the other nation, and various strategic considerations. Some of these antecedents are nonrational, but many are rational. Rational and nonrational factors often operate side by side in producing an individual's level of responsiveness toward another nation.

Images of the Other Nation. Some of the images discussed in earlier sections undoubtedly have an impact on responsiveness. Responsiveness toward another nation declines when that nation is seen as a threat. Since distrust engenders threat perception, it follows that responsiveness is an inverse function of distrust. Responsiveness is also determined by the way another nation is evaluated. These points are relatively obvious.

Hostility or anger can also produce a reduction in responsiveness. At one time, many psychologists attributed the outbreak of war to hostility toward other nations. Most of them (for example, Durbin & Bowlby, 1939; Tolman, 1942) also believed that international hostility derives unconsciously from the anger that originates in frustrations faced by ordinary citizens in their daily lives. Today it is clear that both points are oversimplifications, for two reasons:

1. The traditional hostility theory of war implied that emotions erupt into war as they sometimes erupt into fist fights. A more sophisticated view would hold that hostility contributes to war, along with other factors, by reducing responsiviness toward another nation. Reduced responsiveness leads to a choice of harsher tactics for dealing with the nation, which may in turn produce a vicious circle of provocation and counterprovocation, at the end of which each side perceives the other as a major threat. War may then arise as a preventive measure or to overcome what looks like intolerable frustration.

2. Recent research evidence (for example, Berkowitz, 1962) clearly supports the assumption that *some* international hostility results from the frustrations experienced by ordinary citizens. But this assumption cannot carry the full burden of explanation. *Most* of the hostility felt toward other nations can more easily be explained as a reaction to unpleasant past experiences with these nations.

Past Experience with the Other Nation. Nations, like persons, tend to follow a matching rule, that is, to increase responsiveness when another nation becomes more helpful and decrease responsiveness when another nation becomes more harmful, or threatening. Another name for observance of the matching rule is "reciprocity." Use of the matching rule can be explained in at least three ways:

1. *As moral behavior.* Gouldner

(1960) has described a "norm of reciprocity" in interpersonal relations which, in its most universal form, can be described as a belief that people should help and not injure those who have helped them. Though this norm has considerable weight in interpersonal relations, its importance in international relations is not too clear. It seems unreasonable to believe that the average nation will follow such a social norm as selflessly as the average individual. Individuals are more capable of sacrificing their interests for moral considerations than are collectivities. Yet it also seems unreasonable to believe that such considerations play no part in international relations. Else why should the "realist" philosophers (for example, Morgenthau, 1960) inveigh so stridently against them? Perhaps the importance of such a norm depends on the sense of community between two nations. A "negative" norm of reciprocity, in which a moral obligation is felt to repay evil with evil, is also found in interpersonal relations. There seems little question that it is also a prominent feature of international relations.

2. *As a reaction to changed images.* When one nation becomes more helpful to another, people in the other nation are likely to see it as more "friendly" or "trustworthy." This, in turn, may lead them to become more responsive. On the other hand, if the first nation becomes more harmful, unfavorable images are likely to develop, which destroy responsiveness.

3. *As a strategy.* It is often expedient to reciprocate, to reward another party for cooperation and to punish it, within limits, for injury. If cooperation is not repaid, the other party may be less helpful in the future (Gouldner, 1960). If an injury goes unpunished, its perpetrator has no incentive for limiting his behavior in the future and may

not even be aware of the trouble he is causing. Recognizing all of this, national decision-makers are likely to use the matching rule as a strategy for molding the other nation's future behavior.

This last explanation for reciprocity implies the further proposition, that the matching rule will be employed more vigorously the greater one's future dependence on the other nation (the greater the other nation's "fate-control"). This suggests that a nation will repay its debts to the extent that it is dependent on the other. Cases of "ingratitude" in international affairs (such as the frequent failure after a war to repay the favors of nations that were helpful during the war) can be explained by the reduced dependence on the other nation. The proposition just stated also implies that a nation will be more prone to retaliate for injuries the more dependent it is on another nation. Though certainly a logical derivation, this implication is hard to reconcile with the dictates of prudence. More thinking and evidence are clearly needed on this topic.

Another way of describing the matching rule is to say that responsiveness increases as a function of cooperation and decreases as a function of conflict. It follows that conditions leading to cooperation are antecedent to increases in responsiveness, such as a common problem, a mutual enemy, or a desire for peace. Conditions leading to conflict are antecedent to reductions in responsiveness, such as doctrinal incompatibilities or uneven distribution of resources or privileges.

Although the matching rule is followed in most situations, there are exceptions. Some findings by Solomon (1960) on interpersonal relations suggest that when another person is seen as weak, increases in his level of cooperation beyond a certain point may lead to *decreases* in responsiveness toward him. It would be unwarranted to generalize these findings, since they are based on observations in a highly restricted situation. But they illustrate the need for careful research in this area.

Strategies for Dealing with the Other Nation. Use of the matching rule has already been mentioned as a rational strategy. In addition, several other kinds of rational strategy can be described that lead to *noncontingent* increases in responsiveness toward another nation. In this context, changes in responsiveness are due to conscious policy decisions.

1. *Building and maintaining good will.* To the extent that another nation is following the matching rule, it should be possible to manipulate its level of responsiveness by adjusting our own level of responsiveness. If we want the other nation's level of responsiveness to increase, we should increase our own; if we want it maintained at its present level, we should maintain our own. Such strategies are sometimes termed "building and maintaining good will." The responsiveness exhibited by the XYZ officers who participated in the author's State Department study (Pruitt, 1962, 1964) seemed to derive primarily from this kind of strategy. Statements such as the following were frequently made in defense of cooperation with other nations: "If 'no' had been flatly said, there would have been a danger of deterioration of relations." "We have to get permission for whatever we're going to do in _____ so we're interested in keeping the _____ happy." "If the relations with _____

were to deteriorate, we might have to withdraw from our bases there."

2. *Making the other nation more dependent.* By helping another nation in concrete ways, we demonstrate to the people of that nation how helpful we can be in the future. This may cause them to feel more dependent on us and thereby increase our ability to command favors from them in the future. In adopting a policy of increased responsiveness, which will produce a larger number of concrete acts of helpfulness to another nation, a nation's leaders may be trying to increase their influence over the other nation. This kind of strategy is closely related to one described by Thibaut and Kelley (1959, p. 121).

3. *Signaling a willingness to negotiate.* Sometimes helpful actions are used as a signal to the other nation, indicating a willingness to "do business." The adoption of a policy of increased responsiveness, which means an across-the-board increase in the number of helpful actions, may serve as a massive signal of this kind. Such signals have repeatedly been used by the leaders of the Soviet Union when they want to negotiate an agreement with the West. Responsiveness is first increased ("tensions" are reduced), and then a proposal is made for negotiations. The increase in responsiveness is meant to signal a resolve to negotiate in good faith. Such a strategy can be used effectively when there is sentiment for negotiation on the other side.[13]

Conditions Affecting the Use of Responsiveness as a Strategy. In all three of the strategies just described, responsiveness is maintained or increased in

---

[13] This kind of strategy is sometimes coupled with an effort to increase the sentiment for negotiation on the other side. Such an effort may take the form of *decreased* responsiveness, which produces a crisis just prior to the increase in responsiveness that signals willingness to negotiate an end to the crisis. Again, the Soviet Union has often used this combination of strategies to persuade the West to negotiate.

an effort to persuade the other nation to act benevolently. It follows that responsiveness will be greater toward another nation the greater that nation's apparent capacity for benevolence.

A nation's capacity for benevolence toward another can be called its *fate-control* over the other (Thibaut & Kelley, 1959). Since benevolent action can take either of two forms, engaging in helpful behavior or refraining from harmful behavior, it follows that fate-control includes both the capacity to help (such as possession of needed resources) and the capacity to harm (such as ability to shift allegiance to a rival of the other nation). The former can be called positive fate-control; the latter, negative fate-control.

Thibaut and Kelley (1959) define fate-control more precisely as the range of utilities through which one party can move another. Fate-control and *dependence* are opposite sides of the same coin. To the extent that A has fate-control over B, B can be said to be dependent on A.

Both positive and negative fate-control are antecedent to responsiveness; but responsiveness based on positive fate-control is more stable because positive fate-control itself is more stable. Since positive fate-control is the ability to reward, its possession by one party is likely to be welcomed by the other. Negative fate-control, or the ability to punish, is likely to be resented by the other party, whose responsiveness will be accompanied by *attempts to find an avenue of escape*. Hence the instability of negative fate-control.

In addition to being a function of the other nation's apparent *level* of fate-control, responsiveness is also a function of the other nation's apparent *flexibility* in using its fate-control. The more rigidly helpful or harmful the other nation, the less benefit can be gained from responsiveness toward it.

Responsiveness will be adopted for strategic reasons only to the extent that there seems to be some chance of influencing the other nation to act more benevolently than it otherwise would.

An example of inflexible fate-control can be seen in United States relations with many other nations today. Though possessed of extraordinary capacity to help or harm most nations, America has low flexibility. It cannot easily withdraw its economic aid or use its military forces to seize power. As a result, the leaders of a small nation such as South Vietnam can maintain an extremely low level of responsiveness toward the United States despite the fact that their economy is dependent on American aid and that American troops are dispersed throughout their countryside.

Most of America's inflexibility derives from the existence of two formidable rivals, the Soviet Union and Communist China. It can be said in general that a nation is less flexible in using its fate-control the less acceptable to it are the consequences of such use. America cannot withdraw aid from South Vietnam because of the danger of a Soviet or Chinese takeover. France cannot be effectively disciplined because of the danger that the NATO alliance will disintegrate. It is not even possible to command responsiveness from Cuba, because that island is protected by Soviet military power.

In summary, it has been asserted that one nation's responsiveness toward another is a joint function of the other nation's apparent level of fate-control and its apparent flexibility in the use of this fate-control. A single concept, *level of effective fate-control*, will henceforth be used to refer to the combination of these two antecedents of responsiveness, although little is known about the way they combine to determine this level. Effective fate-control is a psychological entity, existing in the mind of the perceiver.

The responsiveness strategies described in the last section are oriented toward future outcomes and will, therefore, only be adopted by people who can look ahead and weigh the future. In times of psychological stress, when perspectives tend to become limited, the use of such strategies may be curtailed. At such times, images and emotions are likely to gain more weight in determining levels of responsiveness, while rational considerations take more of a back seat. This sometimes happens in international crises. People begin to insist that "friends" be treated as friends and "enemies" as enemies, forgetting that it may be expedient to remain responsive toward "enemies" who have high fate-control. Such a reaction to crisis is especially characteristic of individuals who need to perceive the world in a highly structured way (Driver, 1962).

Mutual Responsiveness

As we have already seen, levels of responsiveness in the interaction of two nations tend to be reciprocal. When responsiveness is high on one side, it is likely to be high on the other, and vice versa. Some reasons for this phenomenon will be discussed in the next section. This reciprocal nature of responsiveness makes it possible in many cases to speak of a unitary level of mutual responsiveness in the relations between two nations.

It may be possible, to some extent, to predict the level of mutual responsiveness between two nations on the basis of the level of fate-control each has over the other and the type of fate-control involved, whether positive (the capacity to be helpful) or negative (the capacity to be harmful).

Mutual responsiveness is likely to be high when two nations have strong, positive fate-control over one another, that is, when they have much to give one another. Effective fate-control is high on both sides in the sense that each side knows that it must be helpful in order to gain cooperation from the other. In addition, to the extent that an exchange of favors actually develops, positive images will be produced that further enhance responsiveness on both sides. An example can be seen in the relationship between the United States and Great Britain since the war.

When two nations have strong negative fate-control over one another, responsiveness is likely to be low on both sides. A situation of mutual deterrence exists, in which each side's fate-control at least partially balances the other's, thus reducing the flexibility of its use. As a result, neither side has much effective fate-control. Furthermore, each is likely to see the other as something of a threat and (especially if fate-control has ever been utilized) to have a negative evaluation of the other, both of which lead to reduced responsiveness. Still, the picture is not quite so dismal as it might seem. Negative fate-control never *completely* balances negative fate-control. Each side recognizes the danger inherent in pushing the other *too far*. At some point the other side may find the risk of using its fate-control less onerous than the continued endurance of frustration. Out of respect to the harm which the other can perpetrate if sufficiently provoked, each must retain a certain level of responsiveness toward the other. Such a situation seems to obtain in Soviet-American relations today.

The lowest level of mutual responsiveness in peacetime seems to derive from a peculiar yet common condition in which one nation has little fate-control of any kind and the other has high negative, but ineffective fate-control. Examples can be seen in the relations between the United States, on the one hand, and China or Cuba, on the other. In both cases, the United States has overwhelming military strength but is incapable of using it because of world public opinion and Soviet guarantees of defense. In both cases the other nation is too weak on its own to harm the United States and seems to have little to offer the United States. This pattern has two implications: (a) an uncompromising hostility on the part of the powerful nation, whose citizens see no reason to be responsive, and (b) a sense of frustration and threat among the citizens of the small nation, which produces a similar low level of responsiveness.

This peculiar situation was also evident in Soviet-American relations in the first few years of the Cold War. But then, with Soviet advances in weaponry, the situation changed to one involving mutual negative fate-control, and responsiveness improved somewhat on both sides.

Summary

An individual's level of responsiveness toward another nation is partially a function of past experience with that nation and partially a function of other images. In this respect, responsiveness is similar to trust. Unlike trust, responsiveness is also frequently a matter of government policy, representing an element of strategic planning. Such a policy may be adopted for the purpose of repaying debts, building good will, making the other party dependent, or signaling a willingness to negotiate. The greater the other nation's effective fate-control, the more need will be seen for such a policy and the more responsiveness will be shown toward the other nation. Responsiveness based on positive fate-control is theoretically more stable than responsiveness based on negative fate-control.

It is usually possible to speak of a level of mutual responsiveness in the relations between two nations. Mutual responsiveness will usually be high when two nations have strong, positive fate-control over one another, moderately low when both have strong negative fate-control, and very low when one has little fate-control of any kind and the other has strong negative but ineffective fate-control.

STABILITY AND CHANGE IN IMAGES

Most of the ideas presented so far in this chapter can be characterized as *one-step* statements of causation. One variable (sometimes in conjunction with others) is said to be causally related to another; for example, contingency planning is said to be antecedent to threat perception. Not many *two-step* or *multi-step* processes have been described, in which one event produces another that then produces a third, and so on. Yet many of the most interesting and characteristic patterns of international relations take this form. In particular, it is essential to mention again the ubiquitous *international circular processes* in which images in one nation produce actions that affect images in another, which in turn produce actions that modify images in the first. In addition to contributing to the inflexibility of trust and distrust, international circular processes are found in almost all periods when international images are changing.

An example was given in the Introduction (p. 396) of the kind of vicious circle that appears during preparedness races: alternating increases in military preparedness in response to the perception of threat produce a progressively deepening sense of threat in the two opposing nations. It is also possible to conceive of a benevolent circle in which a reduction in the degree to which people in nation A see nation B as a threat produces behavior in A that causes B in turn to act less threatening, thereby reinforcing the trend in A toward seeing B as less of a threat.

A similar sort of circular process occurs during periods in which trust and responsiveness are changing. In the case of responsiveness, a benevolent circle of the following kind is sometimes found: increased responsiveness on one side makes that side more helpful, which makes the other side more responsive and therefore more helpful, which in turn reinforces the first side's responsiveness. A vicious circle is also found in which a reduction in responsiveness on one side makes the other more punitive, which leads to further deterioration of the first side's responsiveness. Again, such circles may go through several generations.

An example of a vicious circle that went through several generations can be seen in the recent series of actions and reactions on the part of the United States and Cuba, which led to a complete deterioration of responsiveness on both sides. This example also illustrates another important point about circular processes that has not yet been explicitly stated, that images usually change *in the same direction on both sides*. Perceived threat, trust, and responsiveness increase or decrease simultaneously on both sides.

Although images are sometimes in flux, as was recently the case in Cuban-American relations, they more often stay relatively *stable* over a period of time. As a matter of fact, current (early 1964) Cuban-American relations can be so described; by and large, the same

high levels of perceived threat and distrust and the same low level of responsiveness are retained month after month.

To understand stable images, we need to answer two questions: why do images stabilize—that is, why do circular processes slow down and stop? and what determines the level at which an image stabilizes?

To answer the first question, it is necessary to take a close look at the nature of a stable image. Under the microscope, images that are basically stable are seen to exhibit minor *fluctuations*. Rather than standing perfectly still, they oscillate around a stable reference point, first deteriorating and then improving or first improving and then deteriorating. Images on both sides of an international relationship are often involved simultaneously in such fluctuations. As the images in one nation begin to deteriorate or improve, a comparable movement is often observed in the other nation, exactly as if a circular process were beginning. But then, somehow, the process is reversed and the images on both sides return to their previous state. An example may help the reader picture such fluctuations. During the Suez Crisis, both the United States and Great Britain greatly antagonized one another. First Britain failed to notify the United States of its intention to use arms; then the United States put pressure on the British to halt their invasion. A vicious circle seemed to have begun and, for some time thereafter, trust and responsiveness were at a low ebb. But then the system returned to its earlier level, and trust and responsiveness were fully reconstituted.

If stable images exhibit the features just described, it may be profitable to rephrase the first question. Instead of asking why some images stabilize, it may make more sense to ask why incipient vicious and benevolent circles are abortive in some image systems and not in others. Or more specifically, why did the vicious circle that seemed to begin in British-American relations peter out while a superficially similar vicious circle in Cuban-American relations spiraled to a grim conclusion?

To answer this and the second question, we need to examine circular processes more closely.

Richardson Equilibrium Models

The most extensive treatment of a circular process has been presented by Lewis F. Richardson in his mathematical analysis of the arms race (Richardson, 1939). Richardson's ideas have recently been revived by Rapoport (1957, 1960), and his original papers have been reprinted (Richardson, 1960).

A Model of the Arms Race. Richardson presents his model in the form of differential equations, but the same material can be presented more simply in graphical form.

Richardson assumes that arms races are driven by alternating perceptions of threat. One nation arms to protect itself from another, which causes the other to arm further, and so on. In Figure 11.2, dimension x represents Nation X's expenditure on arms, and dimension y represents Nation Y's expenditure. Every point in the space defined by these coordinates represents a possible combination of expenditures for the two nations. Line $L2$ shows the level of expenditure that the leaders of Nation Y would consider appropriate for every level of expenditure that Nation X might make. If their actual level of expenditure is below this line, the leaders of Y will spend more on arms; if above this line, existing armaments will be destroyed. Line $L1$ shows the level of expenditure considered appropriate by the leaders of Nation X for every level of expenditure made by Nation Y.

The equations for these two lines are as follows:

$L1: x = ay + g$ (X's expenditure as a function of Y's)

$L2: y = bx + h$ (Y's expenditure as a function of X's)

Where a (the slope of line $L1$ with respect to the y axis) is the "reaction potential" of Nation X, in other words, the amount by which the leaders of Nation X feel it necessary to increase their expenditure for every unit increase in the expenditure of Nation Y.

b (the slope of line $L2$ with respect to x axis) is the reaction potential of Nation Y.

g (the intercept of line $L1$ on the x axis) is the level of expenditure that X would make if Y were disarmed. It is proportional to the "permanent grievances" felt by X against Y.

h (the intercept of line $L2$ on the y axis) is the level of expenditure that Y would make if X were disarmed, and is proportional to Y's grievances against X.

At the point where the two lines intersect, both nations are satisfied with their expenditure on arms. This point is comparable to an equilibrium in physics. Like a physical equilibrium, it can be either stable or unstable. If it is stable, expenditures on both sides will always move to this point, no matter where they begin. A deviation from the equilibrium point, in whatever direction, will be corrected. A stable equilibrium is shown in Figure 11.2. If the equilibrium is unstable, as in Figure 11.3, expenditures will either increase or decrease indefinitely, depending on where they start. Whether the equilibrium is stable or not depends on the

diction. Nevertheless it incorporates enough features of the arms race to have considerable theoretical interest.

Extension of the Arms Race Model to Other Circular Processes. Several

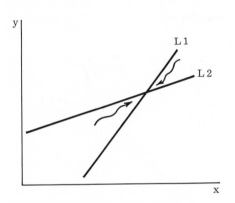

Fig. 11.2. Graphical representation of Richardson's model of the armaments race. The arrows illustrate the approach of armament expenditures toward a stable equilibrium point.

slopes of lines *L1* and *L2* and thus on the reaction potentials: if the product *ab* is less than 1, the system will be stable; if equal to or greater than 1, it will be unstable.

Richardson attempted to verify his system by applying it to the arms races of 1908–1914 and 1929–1939. He assumed that both races involved unstable equilibria, of the type shown in Figure 11.3, where each side feels militarily secure only if it has more arms than the other. The first application was fairly successful; the second, a good deal less so. The problems involved in measuring reaction potential and permanent grievances have never been adequately solved, so that the model is limited in usefulness for practical pre-

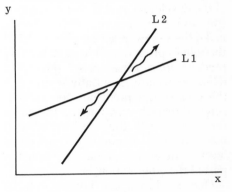

Fig. 11.3. The movement of armament expenditures away from the equilibrium point in the unstable case.

writers (for example, Abelson, 1963; Boulding, 1962) have suggested the possibility of extending Richardson's models to circular processes other than the arms race. Some tentative "Richardson equilibrium models" applied to military threat perception and responsiveness will be presented here. All are based on the stable equilibrium paradigm illustrated in Figure 11.2, although one includes features of the unstable paradigm as well.

1. *Military threat perception.* Let us relabel the axes in Figure 11.2, making the *x* axis stand for the degree to which people in Nation X see Nation Y as a military threat and the *y* axis stand for the degree to which people in Y see X as a threat. It should be possible to construct lines *L1* and *L2* in this space, since threat perception in each nation depends, at least in part, on defensive

424

PROCESSES OF INTERACTION

preparations in the other, which in turn depend on threat perception in the other. The lines need not be straight, but let us assume at first that they are.

On the basis of the earlier analysis of the development of threat perception (pp. 399–407), it seems reasonable to make the slopes (reaction potentials) of these lines proportional to each nation's *predisposition to perceive threat.* In doing so, we are essentially saying that the greater the predisposition to perceive threat in any nation, the more threatened will the citizens of that nation feel in response to any given level of defensive preparations on the part of the other nation.

One conclusion can immediately be drawn from this analysis: that the actual level of threat perception in *both* nations at equilibrium will be greater, the stronger the predisposition to perceive threat in *either* nation.

Now let us relax the assumption that L1 and L2 should be drawn as straight lines. We have said (p. 408) that distrust increases as a function of the perceived harmfulness of the other nation's behavior. We have also said (p. 400) that distrust predisposes people to perceive threat. It follows that the predisposition to perceive threat is a function of the perceived harmfulness of the other nation's behavior. The more trouble they make, the more predisposed we become to find new evidence of troublemaking. We have also said that another nation's defensive preparations are often seen as harmful behavior and that defensive preparations result from the perception of threat. From all of this, it can be deduced that one nation's predisposition to perceive threat is a direct function of the other's actual level of threat perception. This deduction is expressed by the curved lines shown in Figure 11.4. When one nation perceives little

threat, the other's reaction potential is small (the slope is relatively flat), because the first has shown little cause for distrust. But when the first nation perceives a great deal of threat, its preparations are likely to cause the other's reaction potential to become very great (the slope becomes relatively steep).

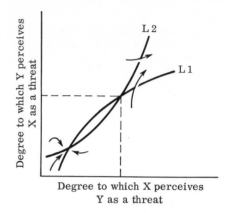

Fig. 11.4. Model of reciprocal threat perception, in which the slopes of the lines are determined by trust, which in turn is an inverse function of the other nation's level of threat perception.

The model shown in Figure 11.4 has some interesting properties. It contains two equilibrium points, the lower one stable and the upper one unstable. If movement starts anywhere to the left of or below the broken line, it will go to the stable point. But if it starts anywhere to the right of or above the broken line, it will continue indefinitely toward greater and greater perception of threat on both sides. There is a discontinuity at the broken line, akin to the "critical mass" in nuclear physics. So long as momentary fluctuations in either nation's perception of threat stay within bounds, there will be no basic change in threat perception. But if the level of threat perception *in either nation* crosses this threshold, there is no way back to stability. Trust is shattered, and a vicious circle involving threat perception and defensive preparation engulfs both sides.

This kind of model may prove useful as a way of accounting for the "points of no return" that were discussed in connection with the stability of trust. The speculative nature of the model and its application must, however, be frankly admitted.

2. *Responsiveness.* It may also be possible to apply the Richardson model to circular processes involving responsiveness (Pruitt, 1962). The x axis can stand for the general level of responsiveness in Nation X toward Nation Y, and the y axis for the general level of responsiveness in Y toward X. The discussion of the matching rule in the preceding section suggests that Nation X's and Nation Y's responsiveness are interdependent. It should, therefore, be possible to draw lines $L1$ and $L2$ in this space. A possible diagram is shown in Figure 11.5. (It should be noted in this figure that movement upward and outward implies that images are improving rather than deteriorating as in earlier figures.)

Following our earlier analysis of responsiveness, we can postulate that a nation's *reaction potential* (the slope of the line relating its level of responsiveness to the level of responsiveness in the other nation) will be a function of the other nation's level of *effective fate-control.* This derives from the assumption that a nation will make more concerted use of the matching rule the more there is to be gained by "teaching" the other nation to cooperate. In addition, to the extent that a nation utilizes the three rational strategies described earlier (p. 417), its *basic level* of responsiveness (the intercept of its reaction line on its axis) should also be a function of the other nation's level of effective fate-control.

The relationship just postulated between responsiveness and effective fate-control is illustrated in Figure 11.5. If Nation X's effective fate-control increases while Y's remains the same, line $L2$ will move to position $L2'$. It is interesting to note that the result of such a movement is an increase in responsiveness for *both* nations, with Nation Y's responsiveness showing the larger increase.

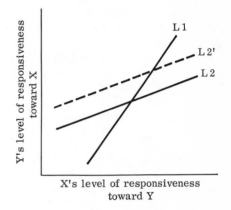

Fig. 11.5. Model of reciprocal responsiveness. The equilibrium points are stable.

Implications of the Extended Richardson Models. The Richardson equilibrium models just described have a number of features that are similar to aspects of real-life international relations.

Assuming a time delay between changes in one nation's images and changes in the other's, all movement in a Richardson system takes a zig-zag course; first images change in one nation, then in the other, then again in the first, and so on. This zig-zag motion resembles that found in the real-life international circular processes and incipient processes described earlier.

Within the zig-zag pattern, there are two distinguishable kinds of movement in a Richardson system that resemble the two kinds of movement found in real-life images. *Temporary movement* resembles the fluctuations that are usually found in essentially stable real-life images. This kind of movement occurs in a Richardson system when a *momentary force* causes images in one nation to deviate from a stable equilibrium point. By the nature of the system, images in the other nation must follow suit. But when the momentary force has dissipated, images on both sides will return to the original point of equilibrium.

Fundamental movement in a Richardson system resembles true changes in real-life images. This kind of movement is found under two conditions: (a) when a *persistent force* produces changes in the functions relating images in one nation to images in the other (lines *L1* and *L2*) and thereby alters the location of a stable equilibrium point, or (b) when a *momentary force* displaces an image from an unstable equilibrium point. Where there is a single stable equilibrium point, momentary forces never produce lasting changes in images.

Assuming that most real-life situations are best described by a Richardson equilibrium model containing a single stable equilibrium point (as in Figures 11.2 and 11.5), the answer to the first question raised above, as modified on page 421, reduces to a distinction between momentary and persistent forces, that is, between forces that affect images but dissipate over time and forces that affect images and endure over time. An example of a momentary force would be an international incident challenging the sovereignty of a nation. Examples of persistent forces would include changes in many of the parameters discussed earlier, such as changes in the predisposition to perceive threat or changes in effective fate-control. Momentary forces produce fluctuations around an equilibrium point; persistent forces produce basic changes in images by changing the functions that define the location of the equilibrium point.

The distinction between momentary and basic forces may help us understand why British-American relations returned to normal after the Suez crisis while Cuban-American relations after the revolution spiraled to mutual hostility. In both cases, the downward motion began with the incidents that produced anger on both sides. Anger can be considered a momentary force since it tends to dissipate over time. In British-American relations there were no other changes and the system rapidly returned to its old equilibrium point. A basic force developed in the other case in the form of fundamental changes in the effective fate-control of the United States over Cuba. As time went on, the Cubans became increasingly dependent on the Soviet Union and thereby increasingly independent of the United States. United States markets were no longer so needed, and United States military capability no longer so feared. The Cubans could afford to reduce their responsiveness permanently, since United States good will was no longer so critical. Concomitant permanent changes in American responsiveness were inevitable.

The answer just given to the first question may not initially look like a theoretical advance. To explain permanent change in terms of enduring forces and temporary change in terms of momentary forces may seem tautological. However, we contend that there is theoretical power in the notion that certain kinds of forces, though having an effect on images, cannot produce circular processes leading to permanent change. This is a step beyond the naive observation that any kind of change in an image can trigger a benevolent or vicious circle. The ultimate test of this approach hinges, of course, on the development of a roster of momentary and persistent forces buttressed by clear-cut operational definitions.

The answer to the second question on page 421 depends on the shape and location of lines *L1* and *L2*, which await greater sophistication of measurement.

An Alternative Approach. It is possible to suggest at least one other way of explaining why vicious circles are not always initiated by negative changes in images—the view that vicious circles are regulated by the *fear of conflict*. In this view, momentary changes in images leading to harmful behavior on one side will always be met by a *desire* to retaliate on the other. But people on the other side may also take an *overview of the situation* and recognize that retaliation will probably lead to a vicious circle that is not in the national interest. The more important it seems to avoid conflict, the more likely are they to inhibit the impulse to retaliate. In essence, this view argues that insight into the danger of starting a vicious circle can cause national leaders to avoid steps that might lead to such a circle.

An explanation for the failure of a vicious circle to materialize in the Suez crisis can be derived from this viewpoint, which is somewhat different from the one given above. Taking an overview, leaders in the United States and Britain may have recognized that retaliation would produce counter-retaliation until there was a full-blown conflict between their nations. Such an outcome was undesirable because of the effective fate-control possessed by each nation. So the impulse to retaliate was held in check and replaced by attempts to resolve existing conflict. By assigning a prominent role to effective fate-control, this explanation resembles the one derived from the Richardson-type responsiveness model, but a different intervening mechanism is postulated.

Graduated Reciprocation in Tension-Reduction

No discussion of changes in international images would be complete without mentioning Charles Osgood's proposals for alleviating Cold-War tensions. Osgood (1959, 1962) describes an arms race as a series of reciprocal initiatives in which each side alternately contributes to international "tension" (presumably threat perception) and distrust. He suggests the possibility of producing an "arms race in reverse" with each side alternately taking tension-reducing initiatives. To produce such a reversal, it is necessary for one nation (Osgood talks in terms of the United States) to adopt a policy called Graduated Reciprocation in Tension-Reduction or GRIT. This policy involves a series of unilateral initiatives designed to reduce tension and increase trust on the other side. Examples of such initiatives for the United States might include deactivating overseas military bases, recognizing Communist China, or making the DEW-line (early warning system) bidirectional so that the Russians could be warned of an attack from the United States. If the policy were successful, it would elicit reciprocal action from the other nation, which should more than repay the sacrifices involved in the early initiatives. In other words, it would start a benevolent circle toward improved images on both sides.

Osgood (1962) further suggests a series of guidelines to follow in implementing GRIT. Among them are the following:

(a) Unilateral initiatives must not reduce our capacity to inflict unacceptable nuclear retaliation on an opponent should we be attacked. . . . (c) Unilateral initiatives must be graduated in risk according to the degree of reciprocation obtained from opponents. . . . (g) Unilateral initiatives must be announced publicly at some reasonable interval prior to their execution and identified as part of a deliberate policy of reducing and controlling tensions. (h) In their announcement, unilateral initiatives should include explicit invitation to reciprocation in some form. . . . (j) Unilateral initiatives must be continued over a considerable period, regardless of immediate reciprocation or events of a tension-increasing nature elsewhere. . . .(l) Unilateral initiatives must be as unambiguous and as susceptible to verification as possible (pp. 89–107).

In addition, Osgood implies that a nation adopting GRIT should try to make its actions seem as voluntary as possible, to avoid their being attributed to internal or external pressures.

If we grant the efficiency of unilateral moves in producing a benevolent circle, some of the guidelines proposed by Osgood are consonant with the theoretical ideas presented in this chapter. For example, guidelines (j) and (l) must be followed in order to overcome the predisposition to discount evidence of reduced threat that is sure to be found in the other nation. The recommendation that initiatives be made to appear voluntary is consonant with Strickland's finding (1958), cited earlier, that freely taken helpful actions are the most productive of trust.[14] Osgood's suggestion in guidelines (g) and (h) that intentions and expectations be clearly communicated to the other nation is consonant with the findings of Loomis (1959) cited earlier. Loomis' study also indicates that an adequate communication should include statements about what will be done if the other side fails to comply and about ways in which the other side can gain "absolution" if it first fails to comply and later changes its mind.

Several other guidelines might be added to Osgood's list: (a) Choose initiatives that dramatize ways in which our nation can be helpful in the future to our opponents. This will cause our opponents to feel more dependent on us and, therefore, to be more likely to reciprocate. (b) Take advantage of periods of improved international relations generated by GRIT to negotiate agreements that provide a foundation for lasting friendship—for example, agreements that make both nations more dependent on one another. (c) Endeavor to bring our opponents into some of the planning of GRIT. One of GRIT's goals is to elicit reciprocation from the other nation. We are asking them to cooperate. Yet Osgood does not suggest that they participate in the planning. Social psychologists (for example, Coch & French, 1948) have frequently found that people are more likely to adopt innovations when they think they have participated in planning them. This does not imply letting the Russians "write our ticket" for GRIT, but does suggest the value of exploring ways to involve them in the planning

---

[14] One might almost deduce from this that GRIT will be more effective the stronger the nation adopting it, which implies that the familiar recipe "arm to negotiate" should be replaced with the guideline "arm to make concessions." However, the issue is more complicated, since arming prior to making concessions may increase the other side's distrust more than concessions can reduce it.

and thereby cause them to become more identified with the project.

Granting all the points about guidelines, a basic question still remains whether a series of initiatives from one side in a controversy can produce a benevolent circle. Some help in answering this question can be obtained from the Richardson equilibrium models described earlier in this section, though these models admittedly have their weaknesses. Some of the moves in a GRIT program involve reducing military capability and can, therefore, be diagrammed in the space shown in Figures 11.2 and 11.3 or, with suitable modifications, the space shown in Figure 11.4. Others can be thought of as reflecting increased responsiveness and can, therefore, be diagrammed in the space shown in Figure 11.5.

One implication of this analogy is that GRIT *will be more effective under some circumstances than under others*, that is, under circumstances in which basic forces have already caused a stable equilibrium to move in the direction of improved images. As a matter of fact, the Richardson equilibrium models almost *predict* that GRIT will be adopted under such circumstances. For example, consider a case in which one or both nations have increased their level of effective fate-control (as when a mutual enemy appears) or in which predispositions to perceive threat have diminished (as when one or both sides recognize that the other fears war).

But what of the case in which basic forces have not already created a setting favorable to basic changes in images? Suppose images are at equilibrium and one nation just decides to become less threatening or more responsive?

Taking a pessimistic view of the determinants of fundamental changes in images, we can predict some move-

ment in the other nation's orientation *but not an equal movement.* For example, in Figure 11.5, Nation Y's adoption of GRIT might simply imply that line L2 moves to position L2'. As can be seen from the new equilibrium point, Nation X will reciprocate to some extent, but not equally. A similar prediction can be developed in the realm of threat perception. In the face of unequal response from the other nation, how long will people in the nation that originally adopted GRIT be willing to maintain their program?

More optimistically, it is possible to argue that unilateral initiatives have a more basic effect on other nations, such as by altering what we have called "reaction potentials." This argument has been incorporated into the curved lines shown in Figure 11.4. It is difficult to go further with this argument, however, because of the primitive nature of our theory. Clearly there is need for the massive effort at theory building strongly recommended by Osgood.

Summary

When images change, they take a stepwise course, changing first in one nation, then in the other, and then again in the first. This mode of change can be called an "international circular process." When images stabilize, they do not stand perfectly still but fluctuate around a stable reference point. To understand stability and change in images, it may be useful to analyze circular processes as a class. Richardson's mathematical analysis of the arms race seems to offer a possible model for this class of phenomena. It can easily be extended to circular movements in the perception of military threat, trust, and responsiveness. Such an extension forces us to distinguish between persistent forces, that permanently alter the functions relating one nation's actions to another's reactions, and momentary forces. Changes in some of the variables discussed in earlier sections, such as effective fate-control, can be tentatively identified as persistent forces. But little can be said with certainty, since there is no real evidence concerning changes of images in systems involving two parties. Osgood has described a strategy, known as GRIT, involving a series of unilateral, tension-reducing moves and designed to produce a reversal in the arms race. The Richardson equilibrium models described in this section may be useful for posing questions about Osgood's recommendations.

REFERENCES

Abelson, R. P. A "derivation" of Richardson's equations. *J. Confl. Resol.*, 1963, 7, 13–15.

Abelson, R. P., & Rosenberg, M. J. Symbolic psycho-logic: A model of attitudinal cognition. *Behav. Sci.*, 1958, 3, 1–13.

Allport, F. H. *Theories of perception and the concept of structure.* New York: Wiley, 1955.

Berkowitz, L. *Aggression: A social psychological analysis.* New York: McGraw-Hill, 1962.

Boulding, K. E. *Conflict and defense.* New York: Harper, 1962.

Brody, R. A. Some systematic effects of the spread of nuclear weapons technology: A study through simulation of a multi-nuclear future. *J. Confl. Resol.*, 1963, 7, 663–753.

Bronfenbrenner, U. The mirror image in Soviet-American relations: A social psychologist's report. *J. soc. Issues*, 1961, 17, 45–56.

Bruner, J. S., & Postman, L. J. On the perception of incongruity: A paradigm. *J. Pers.*, 1949, 18, 206–223.

Cartwright, D., & Harary, F. Structural balance: A generalization of Heider's theory. *Psychol. Rev.*, 1956, 63, 277–293.

Claude, I. L., Jr. *Power and international relations.* New York: Random House, 1962.

Coch, L., & French, J. R. P., Jr. Overcoming resistance to change. *Hum. Relat.*, 1948, 1, 512–532.

Cowen, E. L. Influence of varying degrees of psychological stress on problem-solving rigidity. *J. abnorm. soc. Psychol.*, 1952, 47, 512–519.

Deutsch, K. W., *et al. Political community and the North Atlantic area.* Princeton, N.J.: Princeton Univer. Press, 1957.

Deutsch, M. Trust and suspicion. *J. Confl. Resol.*, 1958, 2, 265–279.

Deutsch, M. The effect of motivational orientation upon trust and suspicion. *Hum. Relat.*, 1960, 13, 123–140. (a)

Deutsch, M. Trust, trustworthiness and the F Scale. *J. abnorm. soc. Psychol.*, 1960, 61, 138–140. (b)

Deutsch, M. Some considerations relevant to national policy. *J. soc. Issues*, 1961, 17, 57–68.

Dollard, J., & Miller, N. E. *Personality and psychotherapy.* New York: McGraw-Hill, 1950.

Driver, M. J. *Conceptual structure and group processes in an inter-nation simulation. Part I: The perception of simulated nations.* Princeton, N. J.: Educational Testing Service, 1962.

Durbin, E. F. M., & Bowlby, J. *Personal aggressiveness and war.* New York: Columbia Univer. Press, 1939.

Fox, A. B. *The power of small states: Diplomacy in World War II.* Chicago: Univer. Chicago Press, 1959.

Freud, S. *A general introduction to psychoanalysis.* New York: Perma Giants, 1949.

Fromm, E. Sane thinking in foreign policy. Advertisement in the *New York Times*, January 22, 1961, 4E.

Gladstone, A. I. The conception of the enemy. *J. Confl. Resol.*, 1959, 3, 132–137.

Gouldner, A. W. The norm of reciprocity: A preliminary statement. *Amer. sociol. Rev.*, 1960, *25*, 161–178.

Haas, E. B. The balance of power: Prescription, concept, or propaganda? *World Politics*, 1953, 5, 442–477.

Harary, F. A structural analysis of the situation in the Middle East. *J. Confl. Resol.*, 1961, *5*, 167–178.

Heider, F. Attitudes and cognitive organization. *J. Psychol.*, 1946, *21*, 107–112.

Heider, F. *The psychology of interpersonal relations.* New York: Wiley, 1958.

Hilgard, E. R. *Theories of learning* (ed. 2). New York: Appleton-Century-Crofts, 1956.

Homans, G. C. *Social behavior: Its elementary forms.* New York: Harcourt, Brace, 1961.

Hovland, C. I. The role of primacy and recency in persuasive communication. In Eleanor E. Maccoby, T. M. Newcomb, & E. L. Hartley (Eds.), *Readings in social psychology.* New York: Holt, Rinehart and Winston, 1958.

Jones, E. E., & de Charms, R. Changes in social perception as a function of the personal relevance of behavior. *Sociometry*, 1957, *20*, 75–85.

Kaplan, M. *System and process in international politics.* New York: Wiley, 1957.

Katchmar, L. T., Ross, S., & Andrews, T. G. Effects of stress and anxiety on performance of a complex verbal-coding task. *J. exp. Psychol.*, 1958, *55*, 559–564.

Katz, D., & Stotland, E. A preliminary statement to a theory of attitude structure and change. In S. Koch (Ed.), *Psychology: A study of a science.* Vol. 3. New York: McGraw-Hill, 1959. Pp. 423–475.

Kimble, G. A. *Hilgard and Marquis' Conditioning and learning.* New York: Appleton-Century-Crofts, 1961.

Knorr, K. *The war potential of nations.*

Princeton, N. J.: Princeton Univer. Press, 1956.

Krech, D., Crutchfield, R. S., & Ballachey, E. L. *Individual in society.* New York: McGraw-Hill, 1962.

Lewin, K., *et al.* Level of aspiration. In J. McV. Hunt (Ed.), *Personality and the behavior disorders.* Vol. I. New York: Ronald, 1944. Pp. 333–378.

Lieberman, B. *i*-Trust: A notion of trust in three-person games and international affairs. *J. Confl. Resol.*, 1964, *8*, 271–280.

Loomis, J. L. Communication, the development of trust and cooperative behavior. *Hum. Relat.*, 1959, *12*, 305–315.

Merton, R. K. The self-fulfilling prophecy. In *Social theory and social structure* (rev. ed.). New York: Free Press, 1957.

Milburn, T. W. The concept of deterrence: Some logical and psychological considerations. *J. soc. Issues*, 1961, *17*, 3–11.

Morgenthau, H. J. *Politics among nations* (ed. 3). New York: Random House, 1959.

Morton, L. Historia mentem armet: Lessons of the past. *World Politics*, 1960, *12*, 155–164.

Newcomb, T. M. Autistic hostility and social reality. *Hum. Relat.*, 1947, *1*, 69–86.

Organski, A. F. K. *World politics.* New York: Knopf, 1958.

Osgood, C. E. Suggestions for winning the real war with communism. *J. Confl. Resol.*, 1959, *3*, 295–325.

Osgood, C. E. *An alternative to war or surrender.* Urbana: Univer. Illinois Press, 1962.

Pruitt, D. G. An analysis of responsiveness between nations. *J. Confl. Resol.*, 1962, *6*, 5–18.

Pruitt, D. G. *Problem solving in the Department of State* (The Social Science Foundation and Department of International Relations Monograph Series in World Affairs). Denver: University of Denver, 1964.

Rapoport, A. L. F. Richardson's mathematical theory of war. *J. Confl. Resol.*, 1957, *1*, 249–304.

Rapoport, A. *Fights, games, and debates.* Ann Arbor, Mich.: Univer. Michigan Press, 1960.

Richardson, L. F. Generalization foreign politics. *British J. Psychol. Monogr. Suppls.*, 1939, 23.

Richardson, L. F. *Arms and insecurity.* Chicago: Quadrangle Books, 1960.

Rosenau, J. N. (Ed.) *International politics and foreign policy: A reader in research and theory.* New York: Free Press, 1961.

Rummel, R. J. *Dimensions of conflict behavior within and between nations.* Technical report of research on National Science Foundation Contract NSF-G24827, Northwestern University, 1963.

Sarason, I. G., & Palola, E. G. The relationship of test and general anxiety, difficulty of task, and experimental instructions to performance. *J. exp. Psychol.*, 1960, 59, 185–191.

Schelling, T. C. Bargaining, communication and limited war. *J. Confl. Resol.*, 1957, *1*, 19–36.

Schelling, T. C. *The strategy of conflict.* Cambridge, Mass.: Harvard Univer. Press, 1960.

Scott, W. A. Cognitive complexity and cognitive flexibility. *Sociometry*, 1962, 25, 405–414.

Singer, J. D. Threat-perception and the armament-tension dilemma. *J. Confl. Resol.*, 1958, 2, 90–105.

Snyder, R. C., Bruck, H. W., and Sapin, B. (Eds.) *Foreign policy decision making: An approach to the study of international politics.* New York: Free Press, 1962.

Solomon, L. The influence of some types of power relationships and game strategies upon the development of interpersonal trust. *J. abnorm. soc. Psychol.*, 1960, *61*, 223–230.

Sprout, H., & Sprout, Margaret Environmental factors in the study of international politics. *J. Confl. Resol.*, 1957, *1*, 309–328.

Stagner, R. Personality dynamics and social conflict. *J. soc. Issues*, 1961, *17*, 28–44.

Steiner, I. D. Ethnocentrism and tolerance of trait inconsistency. *J. abnorm. soc. Psychol.*, 1954, *49*, 349–354.

Strickland, L. H. Surveillance and trust. *J. Pers.*, 1958, *28*, 200–215.

Tannenbaum, P. H. Initial attitude toward source and concept as factors in attitude change through communication. *Publ. Opin. Quart.*, 1956, *20*, 413–425.

Thibaut, J., & Kelley, H. H. *The social psychology of groups.* New York: Wiley, 1959.

Thomas, W. I., & Znaniecki, F. *The Polish peasant in Europe and America.* New York: Knopf, 1927.

Tolman, E. C. *Drives toward war.* New York: Appleton-Century-Crofts, 1942.

Tolman, E. C. *Purposive behavior in animals and men.* New York: Appleton-Century-Crofts, 1932.

Van Dyke, V. *International politics.* New York: Appleton-Century-Crofts, 1957.

Wright, Q. *The study of international relations.* New York: Appleton-Century-Crofts, 1955.

Zinnes, Dina A., North, R. C., and Koch, H. E. Capability, threat, and the outbreak of war. In J. N. Rosenau (Ed.), *International politics and foreign policy.* New York: Free Press, 1961.

12

The next chapter continues our exploration of the interaction between nations, as manifested in the psychological and social processes in which responsible individual actors engage in a particular international situation. Specifically, Chapter 12 is concerned with the processes of deliberation and the organizational processes involved when national officials develop and execute foreign policy decisions. How does the occasion for decision affect the process and outcome? In particular, what form does the process take when decisions have to be made under crisis conditions? What effects do the personality characteristics, the social backgrounds and experiences, and the personal values of decision-makers have on the process? How does the organizational context in which the decision is made—particularly the patterns of communication and influence that characterize this context—determine the course of the decision? These are some of the questions that the chapter attempts to answer.

In addressing these questions, Chapter 12 also touches on some of the general issues that confront the decision-making approach: What constitutes an appropriate theoretical model? What is the relationship between psychological and sociological variables? What are the limits within which the personality of the decision-maker can influence the process? And what contributions by what elements in the society enter into the decision-making process? The emphasis of this chapter is largely on decision-making *within* a national government, although some comparisons between national and international decision-making organizations are presented. A more detailed analysis of the characteristics of intergovernmental organizations will be found in Chapter 14.

The two authors of Chapter 12 were associated with each other, for a number of years, in the International Relations Program of Northwestern University. One earlier product of their collaboration was the monograph on *National and international decision-making*, published by the Institute for International Order (1961).

James A. Robinson is now Professor of Political Science at Ohio State University. He is author of *Congress and foreign policy-making* (1962), and *The House Rules Committee* (1963). His current research interests focus on crisis decision-making; the simulation of decision processes; and the relationship between decision process and decision outcomes. In 1957–1958 he was a Congressional Fellow of the American Political Science Association.

Richard C. Snyder is Benjamin Franklin Professor of Decision-Making, and Chairman of the Department of Political Science at Northwestern University. He is author and co-author of a number of books, including *The most favored nation clause* (1948); *Roots of political behavior* (1949); *American foreign policy* (1954); and *Foreign policy decision-making* (1962). His current research interests include the study of intersocietal influence processes and cross-cultural comparisons of foreign policy-making; the integration of decision theories in the social sciences; and the application of learning theory and experimental techniques to the teaching of political science and to political education.

H. C. K.

Decision-Making in

International Politics *

James A. Robinson and Richard C. Snyder

THE STATE OF RESEARCH

If one dates the beginnings of the international political system of nation-states from the Treaty of Westphalia, something called international political activity or behavior has existed for more than three hundred years. During this period as many "decisions" must have been made as there are stars in the heavens. Whatever the number, the universe of decisions is extraordinarily large. Yet these rich and abundant data have been analyzed little. Often they have not even been accurately observed; they have less often been recorded reliably. Not until Abel (1941) compared 25 decisions to go to war had systematic analysis been made of international decision-making. Even now, in spite of the appearance of new theories of decision in several academic disciplines, the number of theoretically

oriented, empirically executed studies of international decisions is small. To discuss decision-making in international politics is to engage in an essentially prescientific exercise, one that involves analogy, extrapolation, projection, and reduction from decisional studies of other units and levels of analysis to the international political system. Much of what follows is a review of concepts and propositions, derived from a disparate literature, that are potentially relevant to understanding international decision-making. This review is arranged according to a generalized conception of the way in which organizations make decisions. This has been set forth in somewhat different form elsewhere (Snyder, Bruck, & Sapin, 1954, 1962; Snyder & Paige, 1958; Snyder & Robinson, 1961; Robinson, 1962b); like all conceptual schemes, it has been modified through research, that of many others as well as our own. We

* The authors are grateful to Lucia Walton, who made innumerable suggestions for revising an early draft of this chapter.

shall cite and categorize a number of studies that bear on the theoretical issues and refer to several studies of single decisions, decision-makers, and decisional units.

Boundaries of Decision Theories and International Relations Theories

Before proceeding further, we wish to comment on two recurring questions that are put to decision theorists concerned with international relations. One is the question whether decision-making studies are equivalent to the whole field of international relations. A listing of only some of the conventional topics of the field should help answer this:

Resources of nations
    Economic resources
    Military resources
    Area, geography, and environment
    Technical and scientific skills
    Population
Systems analysis
    Theories of balance of power and
        its consequences for war
    Types of international systems
    Types of international organizations
    Patterns of nation formation and
        integration
Diplomatic history
International law
Functions of international conflict

To be sure, decisions are often made about some of these topics—for example, decisions about the use of resources by states, or choices among theories of international adjudication by courts. Many of these factors, however, are "given" to decision-makers; the decision theorist may be interested in the way in which these "givens" are used or deployed by decision-makers, but he is unlikely to inquire into their origins, except to the extent that they may have been subject to someone's choice. Sim-

ilarly, the decision theorist may use diplomatic history or international law as source material, as, for example, in reconstructing the intellectual process by which certain decisions are taken; but these subjects have their own *raison d'être*.

Thus, we hold that international decision-making, broad as it is as an object of study, is not equivalent to the whole of international relations. Our conception of decision-making, which is the core of this essay, will itself be evidence of this.

Whether international decision-making is the same as, or more than, foreign policy-making, or perhaps comparative foreign policy-making, is another recurring question. Put another way, the question is part of a larger issue: whether international relations is (or should be) the study of relations *between* and *among* nations or whether it is essentially the study of decisions *within* nations about relations with other nations. It is accurate to say that many, perhaps most, international decision-making studies are concerned with national foreign policy-making; they are *intra*national rather than *inter*national. Yet, no one would pretend that intranational policy-making studies in one or two or *n* countries would adequately explain a sample of international decisions. Not even a comparative study of foreign offices would equal all of international relations if it did not deal with *interactions* among foreign offices and if it were confined to comparisons of aspects of the decision process within national offices. The same could be said for a study of decision-making within the United Nations. If one asks how the international system makes decisions, he is asking about something more than national foreign policy-making. Yet, as our earlier discussion noted, even this would not embrace the whole field of international relations.

We have said that international decision-making is not all of international relations but that it is more than foreign policy-making. Can we, without being definitive, be more precise in identifying the core of our concern, the overlap between decision-making and international politics? It is useful to think of international systems, not merely of an international system. These systems consist of actors (individuals, roles, nations, and multinational organizations) interacting with each other in ways that affect or have some influence on each other.

Decisions refer to choices between or among alternative courses of action by a decisional unit. Narrowly conceived, decision theory might refer to choice of alternatives, but we prefer to include the search for alternatives, and even the decision as to what problems will be dealt with (Simon, 1963), as well as choice and execution. Although some problems are thrust upon a decision unit, as when Britain withdrew support of Greece and Turkey in 1947 and the United States intervened (Jones, 1955), not all problems are given to decision-makers. Selections must be made. Even when decision-makers have no choice about dealing with problems (as they could not avoid some response to the Korean invasion of South Korea in 1950), problems must be interpreted, categorized, and defined. For example, United States policy-makers could have interpreted the invasion as Russian-inspired (Paige, 1959) and could have read the intentions of the Peiping government in several ways (Whiting, 1960). Similarly, alternatives often are not given but must be formulated. Such construction of alternatives is illustrated in presidential efforts to resolve differences among contending groups in formulating foreign-aid policies toward such countries as Spain and Yugoslavia (Koenig, 1962).

Thus, international decision-making embraces the ways in which national and international actors select problems to be considered for choices of alternative courses of action and make these choices. Strictly speaking, international decision-making would often be more accurately designated as international policy-making, in that the international system lacks sanctions for enforcing compliance with its policies. The international system cannot make decisions authoritatively for all nations and bind subunits to comply. In this sense, the globe is analogous to a large metropolitan area of interacting municipalities, each of which can speak—that is, decide—for itself, but no one of which can decide for the area, which may consist of as many as 1,400 governments, as a whole (Wood, with Almendinger, 1961). Thus, global policy consists of the collection, accumulation, and intersection of decisions taken by subunits.

Alternative Conceptions of Decision Processes

Several "conceptions" have evolved concerning ways in which individuals, groups, organizations, nations, and international systems make decisions. We use the ambiguous term "conceptions" instead of the technical terms, "models" or "theories," because many such formulations are loose, suggestive approaches that identify variables or categories for data collection rather than specify predictive relations among variables. We will select and characterize several of these conceptions as a preface to a more detailed presentation of our own.

The classic conception of decision-making has its origins in economic theory and was influential in business and public administration for fifty years. It assumed as decision-maker a rational man who knew all possible alternatives, understood the possible consequences of each of these alternatives, and had arrived at a clear hierarchy of preferences among them. This eighteenth- and nineteenth-century formulation has undergone a thorough and severe critique from twentieth-century social science. Among students of politics, Simon (1957a, pp. xxvii–xxix; 1957b, pp. 196–206, 241–273; 1961) has been foremost in challenging these asumptions. The issues are reviewed explicitly and summarily in March and Simon (1958, pp. 136–171) and in March (1962, pp. 196–198). The rational-man model has been criticized on both logical and psychological grounds: logically, the possibile creation or discovery of an additional alternative cannot be excluded; psychologically, a decision-maker is incapable of performing the immense mental activity required by the assumptions of economic man. In Herbert Simon's apt description, "Our world is a world of limited, serial information processors dealing with complexity that, for all practical purposes, is infinite in comparison with their information gathering and computing powers. It is a world peopled by creatures of bounded rationality" (1963). To substitute for *maximizing* behavior, Simon proposed *satisficing* behavior: activity that considers alternatives sequentially until one that seems "good enough" to meet one's requirements is found and then adopted. The satisficing conception is illustrated in a case study of the adoption of new data-processing equipment in a business firm (Cyert, Simon, & Trow, 1956).

In contrast to the psychological character of the rational-man model and that of its alternative, the satisficing model, Bentley (1935) introduced to the modern world the notion that interest or pressure groups are the decisive factors in governmental policies. Individual behavior accounts for less of the variance in governmental policies than group activity does. The pioneer work, originally published in 1908, was neglected for two decades or more, and its most influential reformulation did not appear until Truman (1951) published *The govermental process*. Hilsman (1958, 1959) applies this point of view to studying conflict and consensus in United States foreign policy. Related concepts include veto groups (Riesman, 1950; Birnbaum, 1961), countervailing forces, influence as credit (Banfield, 1961), overlapping games (Long, 1958), access, and communication. These theoretical perspectives are refined and extended in a monumental case study of the adoption of a new trade agreement program by the United States in 1955 (Bauer, Pool, & Dexter, 1963). This case emphasizes foreign policy decision-making as a social process rather than an intellectual process and identifies mechanisms of group and intergroup activity that tend toward decision.

Boulding (1956) defined "the political process" as "the mutual modification of images through the processes of feedback and communication" (p. 102). Different types of organizations are available for performing "the political function" in a social system. These range along a continuum that measures the degree to which "feedback" mechanisms report nonleader responses to leader stimuli, which may then be altered in light of the new messages.

Lasswell (1956) set forth seven functional categories for the analysis of any decision. The categories correspond to chronological stages through which decision-makers proceed in making and executing a choice. The functions (or categories or stages) are those of information (problem identification and search), recommendation (proposed alternatives), prescription (sanctional selection of alternatives), invocation (general enforcement), application (specific enforcement), appraisal (review), and termination (conclusion of decision). This conception was developed from extensive work in jurisprudence and has had its decisive influence in judicial decision-making, including international law (McDougal et al., 1960; Arens & Lasswell, 1961; McDougal & Feliciano, 1961; Donnelly et al., 1962; McDougal, Lasswell, & Vlasic, 1963), although it has been used in other policy contexts (Robinson, 1962a, pp. 1–22; 1963, pp. 10–21).

Each of these conceptions suggests considerable application: it is *the* theory of rational man; *the* process of government; *the* governmental process; *the* decision process; *the* political process. An implication is that all men, all governments, all decisions have the characteristics of the particular conception. Such willful generalization, in our view, has been a wholesome stimulus to a search for patterns amidst apparent dissimilarities. Indeed, an early statement of our approach to decision-making promised to be applicable to all kinds of organizations, private as well as public, legislative as well as executive (Snyder, 1958, p. 24).

An alternative way of conceiving of policy-making is in terms of a typology of decision or policy processes. A universal process is not postulated; rather numerous processes are proposed to encompass a wide and, we would hope, eventually inclusive range of phenomena. One of the virtues of a typology is that it readily suggests hypothetical links between each of the types and such other factors as the conditions under which this particular type of process will be employed, the relation of process to system, and the consequences for policy outcomes if the particular process is employed (Robinson, 1962c). A typology consists not so much of definitions as of elements or factors or variables for building hypotheses; it is a step closer to theory.

Among typologies of policy processes we mention one that has been influential. Dahl and Lindblom (1953) identified four basic social control processes for deciding questions of value. *Hierarchy* is control of nonleaders by leaders; *bargaining* is control of leaders by other leaders; *polyarchy* is control of leaders by nonleaders; and the *price mechanism* is a quantitative but decentralized combination of control of leaders by leaders and nonleaders. Dahl's subsequent empirical study of community decisions, however, departed from both the language and substance of this typology (1961). Indeed, one of the difficulties with pure types such as these is their admixture in empirical situations, whether in laboratory or in field research. For example, the same organization may exhibit signs of both hierarchy and bargaining.

Our conception of explanations for decisions encompasses characteristics of both "the decision process" and "types of decision process." We suggest a set of categories, each of which contains subtypes or dimensions, that seems applicable to a diverse number of decisions and decisional units (Snyder & Paige, 1958; Paige, 1959; Young & Robinson, 1962; Robinson, 1963). The initial formulation (Snyder, Bruck, & Sapin, 1954, 1962; Snyder, 1958) has undergone change (Snyder & Paige, 1958; Snyder & Robinson, 1961). The effort is to make it at once suggestive of hypotheses and inclusive of propositions from other theories, not necessarily decision theories.

We conceive of three major factors or clusters of factors in explaining a decisional outcome: the occasion for decision; the individual decision-maker;

and the organizational context in which he decides. In the interaction of situational, individual, and organizational variables as they ultimately affect decision outcomes, we see one of the main themes of social-psychological approaches to international behavior. Before outlining this three-fold conception of decision-making, we wish to stress that it combines psychological and sociological levels of analysis. Moreover, it incorporates both "intellectual" factors and "organizational" factors. The conceptions introduced above usually contain one or the other but not both. Simon's "satisficing man" and Lasswell's functional conception of decision-making emphasize the intellectual process of decision. Problem-solving style, information, definitions of the situation, values, and similar factors are part of intellectual process. Bentley and Bauer, Pool, and Dexter, for example, stress social or organizational processes, including how groups relate to each other, communication patterns and procedures, organizational rules, and the like.

THE CONCEPT OF OCCASION FOR DECISION

The origins of every decision are, strictly speaking, different, and decision-makers' interpretations of each decisional situation may vary considerably. However, comparison and generalization require a search for some basic and recurring categories or characteristics of decisions. Decision-makers classify cases as more or less like previous ones; whether observers can develop discriminating categories and dimensions is one of the current challenges to decision theory. As an elementary set of criteria for categorizing or comparing cases the following three characteristics are proposed: the extent

of anticipation and prior programing of the decision; the ratio of time available for making a decision to demands of the task; and the scope and domain of values at stake.

Anticipated or Unanticipated Situations

Occasions for decision may be distinguished as follows: either they came as a surprise to the decision-makers or some prior planning identified the possibility of their occurrence. The North Korean invasion of South Korea apparently was unanticipated by the decision unit that responded to the attack. Although a policy-planning paper predicting a Soviet probe somewhere on the perimeter of the United States' sphere of influence was circulating through lower echelons of the American government early in 1950, it had not reached the President and his most intimate advisers. Likewise, the presence of Soviet missiles in Cuba in 1962 seems to have been unanticipated by American foreign policy-makers; several previous allegations of a Soviet build-up, accurate or inaccurate, were not confirmed by reconnaisance, and the American decision-makers did not develop policies until after confirmation was obtained (Larson, 1963).

Even if a situation is anticipated or counted as possible, programed actions may not be developed. Whether a situation of surprise differs from a situation of anticipation without prepared response cannot be determined without empirical investigation, although it seems reasonable to expect differences in reaction, in use of decision time, and perhaps in decision outcomes also.

Decision Time and Task Demands

A second characteristic of any decision occasion is the time available for response. Time affects the number of alternatives that may be considered. Although the relation between time and number of alternatives is not necessarily a linear one, still, in the absence of programed decisions, short decision time reduces the opportunities to scan for different courses of action. The Korean decision (Paige, 1959) was one in which the United States committed land and air forces in a matter of days, and the Cuban missile situation of 1962 was similar in decision time. The Cuban invasion of 1961 required important decisions within a matter of hours (Alsop, 1961; Murphy, 1961; Szulc & Meyer, 1962), and reaction time was hardly longer at certain stages of the U-2 episode of 1960 (Wise & Ross, 1962). As is well known, many have worried about the few moments of decision time given a President in the event of apparent nuclear attack; President Eisenhower ordered an atomic alert before entering four hours of anesthesia, and the United States nuclear defenses were alerted within minutes after the assassination of President Kennedy, in the interim before Lyndon Johnson took the oath of office.

Decision time is not necessarily as simple a matter to operationalize as clock time would suggest. Time may mean different things to different decision-makers; one may require five minutes for a task for which another may need an hour. Our way of dealing with this problem is by proposing that decision theory include individual psychological variables such as intelligence, mental agility, and creativity; propositions may eventually be formulated and tested in which such individual capacities are related to time and their interactions are related to decision outcome.

A more difficult problem arises from combining time with task complexity. Even when clock time seems extended, the decision situation may be so complicated that many tasks must be performed in reaching a policy. The series of British decisions to join the Common Market from 1960 through 1962 bore some characteristics of long time mixed with numerous and complex tasks (Young & Robinson, 1962).

In terms of sheer length of time, the United Kingdom had approximately two and one half years from the spring of 1960 until late 1962 to make and implement the decisions to negotiate and to join. When one considers the detailed and technical negotiations required to facilitate membership and the delicate political consultations required to obtain the consent of the parties affected by Britain's decision, two years is not a long period for decision. Moreover, to these considerations must be added a third: Britain was simultaneously concerned with a number of other critical foreign-policy decisions. In the summer of 1960 occurred a Summit Conference that ended without ever really beginning. Throughout 1961 and 1962 Britain was reconsidering her defense policy, including her use of independent nuclear weapons, and also was trying to find some solution to her last remaining colonial problem, that in Central Africa. These difficult and time-consuming occasions for decision also crowded the agenda of an already busy and preoccupied Cabinet and set of ministries.

In addition to the fact that the intricacies of the subject matter constituted a limit on the usual advantages of two years of decision time, there was the large number of parties to the decision. These were not necessarily participants in the decision in the sense that they had a constitutional function. Some were "advisory" rather than "representational" parties or participants (Snyder, Bruck, & Sapin, 1962, pp. 122–124). Although they did not have a veto or even a vote, their advice was sought and they were regularly informed of the stages of the decision. Those who did not have a direct vote included the Commonwealth and European Free Trade Association governments and the United States. Domestic interest groups did not have a vote, but the long-standing traditions of British politics whereby interests have a close consultative part in decisions affecting them were respected. Periodically during the negotiations preparing for the decision to join, the Lord Privy Seal met with these groups and briefed them on the progress of his talks with the European Economic Community and the representatives of the Six. At one time, the London *Times* reported that "for every six hours Mr. [Edward] Heath spends in negotiations with the European Economic Community, he later spends eight hours consulting the Commonwealth and the EFTA representatives in Brussels and with the High Commissioners in London" (February 20, 1962).

In short, while the time for decision was long in months, it was relatively crowded in terms of demands upon it. Intricate and detailed technical work was involved; extensive consultations with domestic and foreign parties were expected or necessary; and the Government's foreign policy agenda was already a long one. Decision time, then, is not to be regarded as absolute; it is relative to the intricacies of the decision itself and to the number of parties to the decision. Finding operational measures that fit a time-to-task ratio concept of decision time remains a foremost task on the agenda of decision theory.

Scope and Domain of Values at Stake

The scope and domain of values affected obviously varies from decision to decision, with high-level policy-makers ordinarily confronted with only the most vital ones. Contemporary international decisions of the greatest value consequence are those involving the choice of violent or nonviolent alternatives, the development of economic and political institutions in new states, and the construction of rules and procedures for the conduct of international relations. These three are intimately related to almost all the basic values in any list or typology of values (for example, Lasswell & Kaplan, 1950).

The Concept of Crisis. Decisions that arise without prior planning, allow short time for response, and have high value consequences, we have designated as "most crisis-like" decisions (C. F. Hermann, 1963, pp. 63–65; Robinson, 1962b). At the other end of the continuum of decisional situations would be one in which the problem was anticipated by the unit of decision, some advance contingency plan was perhaps adopted, considerable time for deciding is available, and relatively slight consequences would result. The Korean decision (Paige, 1959) and the Monroney Resolution in which the Senate prodded the Eisenhower Administration to support an International Development Association (Robinson, 1960) are stark contrasts.

No definitive brief should or could be held for this simple classification. Further research will undoubtedly refine it if not substitute another for it. We can report that an extensive simulation of crisis decision-making based on this conception of decision occasion has been completed and that the data generated from eleven individual simulations are being analyzed (Hermann et al., 1964a). This project should contribute to the refinement of the concept of decision situation.

Our efforts to find a workable definition of crisis, as one kind of decision occasion, were not arbitrary. Initial formulations were based on case studies of foreign-policy decisions (for example, McClelland, 1962; Paige, 1959) and made with reference to relevant social-psychological studies of stress, disaster, and related concepts (Robinson, 1962b; Snyder, 1962). Subsequent modifications were made following an inventory of propositions about organizational decision-making (C. F. Hermann, 1963, pp. 63–65). Our conception bears striking similarities to dimensions of the concept as used in such dissimilar studies as Hill's inquiry into adjustment to crises of war separation and reunion (1949, pp. 8–21) and Davis' study of the reaction of fourteen families to polio (1963, pp. 15–44).

INDIVIDUAL CHARACTERICTICS OF DECISION-MAKERS

Although psychology is one of the more advanced of the social and behavioral sciences and common sense abounds with regard to the importance of personality in politics, applications of psychology to political and especially to international decision-making are relatively few. The technical instruments and the formal theories have rarely been employed in the study of political phenomena. Lasswell's (1930) early initiative in interviewing public officials for the purpose of relating their personalities to their political behavior has not been extended on anything like the scale it deserves. Lane's (1959) inventory of social-psychological studies of politics is almost exclusively devoted to political recruitment and participation and to the functions of political activity for the individual psyche. The applications to the political system that have been most considered have been those concerned with the extent and nature of electoral involvement.

The influence of personality on decision outcome is largely unexplored. From the beginning of the "behavioral" influence on political science, students of "political psychology" have dwelt more on recruitment of different "types" of personalities or persons with varying personal characteristics into different roles, such as political, bureaucratic, or agitational, than on the impact of personality types on decision outcomes. When the case or clinical method was followed by survey methods, the trend continued, as in the studies by McConaughy (1950) of legislators and by Hennessy (1959) of political activists. This approach has received renewed emphasis by Rogow and Lasswell (1963, pp. 44–54), who refine and extend earlier theories of the effects of psychological deprivation on role recruitment. However, role occupants, even when they share similar characteristics accounting for their selection, may differ in their decision-making behavior. Lasswell and Almond (1935) conducted a pioneering and neglected field experiment which demonstrated that welfare agents differed in their claim-granting according to differences in their personality characteristics as these interacted with characteristics of their clients.

We attribute the paucity of psychological research on decision-makers in general and international decision-makers in particular to "sociology of knowledge" factors rather than to any absence of intrinsic relevance of personality to decisional behavior. The relevance of personality is demonstrated, for example, by Scodel, Ratoosh, and Minas (1959), who conducted experiments on the relation of personal characteristics to risk-taking. They found that a group of military personnel selected more high-payoff–low-probability bets than a control group of college students. Within the college group, those who selected high-payoff alternatives were higher on the theoretical and esthetic values and lower on the economic and political values of the Allport-Vernon-Lindzey Study of Values than the low-payoff group. The low-payoff group was higher on need achievement than the high-payoff group. Intelligence was not significantly related to degree of risk-taking, but was inversely related to consistency or variability in risk-taking.

The authors of the best book on voting are scholars whose previous political studies show a strong psychological orientation; however, they incline to a pessimistic view of the relevance of personality (Campbell *et al.*, 1960, pp. 499–519). Most political scientists have not had the necessary technical skills to enter this thorny field and were right, in our view, not to undertake basic psychological research. Hence, they have had to await the development of some reasonably well validated psychological instruments that they could borrow for their own purposes. Moreover, until recently those who possessed requisite psychological theory and sophistication in test construction were removed from the substantive interests of politics and international relations. The increasingly frequent conferences, seminars, and symposia jointly involving psychologists and international relations specialists provide opportunities for constructive collaboration without increasing the risks of inexperience, irrelevant and misconceived borrowings, and neglect of disciplinary obligations.

We have elected to categorize individual attributes of decision-makers into *personality characteristics, social backgrounds and experiences,* and *personal values.* Here we shall cite some of the relevant research, including case studies of particular decisions and of individual decision-makers. It will be noted that when we refer to individual characteristics of decision-makers, we do not mean only personality characteristics of the idiosyncratic type. We are not necessarily referring only to the effects on decision of the particular individual who happened to be placed in a decision-making position and of the nature of his particular needs and complexes. We are referring also to such factors as social backgrounds, previous experience, and personal values that may characterize the elites from which decision-makers are recruited. Looking at individual characteristics does not imply looking exclusively at the personal idiosyncrasies of decision-makers (Snyder, Bruck, & Sapin, 1962, pp. 155–171).

Personality Characteristics

Personality includes a wide range of factors potentially and hypothetically related to decisional performance. Variables such as propensity to assume high risks, tolerance of ambiguity and uncertainty, intelligence, creativity, self-esteem, dominance, submissiveness, need for power, need for achievement, and need for affiliation appear to have some possible connections with decision-making styles and outcomes. The need for power has long interested political science. Lasswell's hypotheses of the 1930s have been applied clinically to the cases of Woodrow Wilson and Colonel House. George and George (1956) explain certain of Wilson's decisions that had consequences for United States foreign policy and international relations of Europe, in terms of his childhood deprivation of affection and esteem for which he compensated through a craving for power and dominance over others. Although not a psychological study, C. P. Snow's dramatic account of the wartime conflict between Sir Henry Tizard and F. A. Lindemann (later Lord Cherwell) over decisions involving highly technical information has overtones of high need for power on both sides (Snow, 1961, pp. 4–53). Rogow's (1963) personality-oriented biography of the late James Forrestal, first Secretary of Defense, places the individual in the context of the organizational and situational demands of high-level foreign policy-making. And although it is not about an international decision-maker, Gottfried's *Boss Cermak of Chicago* (1961, pp. 336–351, 365–378) is unusual in its explicit relating of the psychosomatic condition (colitis) of the subject to his political behavior (power-seeking). Smith (1962), a journalist, probed the background of a contemporary member of the Senate Foreign Relations Committee to account for his political behavior; the biographical data appear consistent with certain of Rogow's and Lasswell's hypotheses.

Charles and Margaret Hermann (1962) "matched" personality characteristics of leading figures in European diplomacy on the eve of World War I, as revealed by the Stanford Conflict Studies' extensive reconstruction of that history (Koch, 1959), with participants in two simulated "reruns" of the six weeks prior to the outbreak of that war. Their ingenious effort to find for the simulation subjects who possessed some of the same personal characteristics as those of the Kaiser, Lord Grey, and others comprised several steps. First, speeches and autobiographical materials were content-analyzed for traits listed in standard psychological inventories. Second, the California Psychological Inventory and a semantic differential instrument consisting of thirteen concepts were administered to candidate-subjects, from whom participants matching profiles of the his-

torical figures were finally chosen. Particular attention was given to dominance, self-acceptance, and self-control. In neither run did war occur, although in at least one of the runs war appeared imminent during 'the final decision period. Certain actions of simulation participants seemed similar to 1914 personalities, such as the dominance of particular leaders over others and the calling of conferences in vain efforts to resolve conflicts.

Margaret Hermann (1963) content-analyzed legislative speeches for personality characteristics related to the legislator's nationalism or internationalism as revealed both in attitudinal statements and in roll-call votes. She reported significant relationships between sense of security or insecurity, tolerance or intolerance of ambiguity, and positive or negative people-orientation, on the one hand, and the congressman's voting record on nationalism or internationalism on the other. The following propositions were supported:

1.a. The greater a congressman's sense of insecurity, the more nationalistic his voting record.

1.b. The greater a congressman's sense of security, the more internationalistic his voting record.

2.a. The greater a congressman's intolerance of ambiguity, the more nationalistic his voting record.

2.b. The greater a congressman's tolerance of ambiguity, the more internationalistic his voting record.

3.a. The more negative a congressman's orientation to or value of people, the more nationalistic his voting record.

3.b. The more positive a congressman's orientation to or value of people, the more internationalistic his voting record.

Social Backgrounds and Experiences

William S. White (1959) reported that when Robert B. Anderson was appointed Secretary of the Navy, he sent for the biographies of all high-ranking naval officers. Past experience, including education, travel, religion, occupation, and profession, has long been thought to affect future performance, including political behavior. Matthews has reviewed the classical theories (1954, pp. 6–19) and tested hypotheses relating constituency, status, and prior political experience to senatorial influence (1960, pp. 92–117). Influence varies with the legislator's observance of certain Senate folkways; senators from safe states, who have had prior political experience and who come to the Senate at an early age, are more likely to observe the folkways and hence, are more likely to be influential. Pool, Keller, and Bauer (1956) have shown that foreign travel alters the *bases* and *rationale* of businessmen's views of foreign trade policy although it may not alter the direction of their attitudes. Acheson (1960, pp. 27–35), in an insightful historical lesson, admonishes Presidents to consider the status and public reputation of candidates for Secretary of State in addition to the usual qualifications of competence and to avoid appointing one whose political or other background characteristics make it difficult for him to be subordinate to the President. Cole (1960) traced the constituent and organizational influences on the neutrality policies of a former chairman of the Senate Foreign Relations Committee. Gilbert (1955) traced the early senatorial experience of a modern senator and member of that Committee and showed that by learning and adhering to the norms of the Senate, he catapulted from the status of "bad boy" to one of considerable influence.

Robinson (1963, pp. 89–109) identified some of the special and rare conditions under which a legislator's constituency-values will be unambiguously related to his committee decisions, as when the issue has low salience within the House of Representatives. Froman (1963, pp. 85–121) connects constituency differences to variations in congressional voting (including voting on foreign policy and on reciprocal trade agreement legislation initiated by the President) while holding party and incumbency variables constant. Rieselbach (1963) investigated the relations between congressmen's "isolationism" or "internationalism" and their party affiliation, ethnicity, religion, education, urbanism, occupation, margin of election, prior political experience, and other variables. He found that, between 1939 and 1958, party affiliation became less predictive of the foreign policy votes of congressmen, while constituency characteristics increased in their predictive strength. Alger (1963) described some of the effects of experience in the General Assembly on temporary delegates to the United Nations. He summarizes these elsewhere in this volume (see Chapter 14). In general, temporary delegates to the United Nations acquire new information, perspectives, and orientations that are likely to enter into their contribution to international decisions when they resume their national roles at home.

Much research on social backgrounds and career patterns has been conducted for theoretical reasons other than decision-making (for example, Buck's [1963] study of the recruitment of British political leaders). Hence, it is often difficult to relate differences in background and experience to variations in decisional performance. For students of decision theory, an extension of the work summarized above to a number of foreign offices and international organizations would be appropriate. Key questions are what, if any, policy positions are systematically favored or disadvantaged by variations in recruitment and socialization, and what kinds of experience are associated with what kinds of styles of decisional performance?

Values of Decision-Makers

We conceive of values, ideology, or philosophy as relatively enduring orientations toward goal objects of a social system or subsystem as distinguished from relatively transitory postures, such as attitudes or opinions (Green, 1954; Kluckhohn & Strodtbeck, 1961, pp. 1–48; Minar, 1961). We are interested in the ways in which these are related to, or mediated in their relation to, decisions or policy outcomes.

Policy-makers have need to distinguish basic value orientations from ephemeral shifting attitudes. During the 1930s, profound public and congressional opposition to Bolshevism abounded in the United States, and this contributed to the delay in United States recognition of the U.S.S.R. In spite of opposition to Communism, as Dawson (1959) shows, the public were, contrary to the Administration's expectations, able to distinguish between their values opposing Communism and their attitudes or opinions toward aid to Russia in 1941. While remaining opposed to Communism, the public changed from negative attitudes toward including Russia in the lend-lease program to positive approval of such aid as a tactical device. Similarly, Kempton (1955, p. 303) recalls that in 1937 half a million American college students swore not to fight in any war. But, when the Selective Service Act was adopted three and a half years later, fewer than one hundred men refused to register, and by 1943 only

1,400 had gone to prison for ideological or ethical defiance of the draft.

Among elites there may be a similar slippage between values and attitudes and between attitudes and behavior. Charles de Gaulle's "shift" of French policy toward Algeria might not have been predicted from his earlier values about overseas territories. Harold Macmillan's leading the British retreat from Suez might not have been expected, given his apparent early advocacy of intervention. The "moderate" leadership of several Southern governors to accept some of the implications of the federal courts' decisions on school integration might not have been obvious from their prior attitude statements. But in situations in which one set of values conflicts with another (loss of Algeria vs. domestic political stability and continental leadership, or retreat vs. national bankruptcy, or some desegregation vs. violence and constitutional disorder), we realize the perils of one-dimensional value analysis.

Robinson (1962a, p. 180) found a .41 product moment correlation between congressmen's foreign policy attitudes, as revealed in interviews, and their roll-call behavior. Miller and Stokes (1963) found a tau beta correlation of .42 between foreign policy attitudes and votes on a sample drawn from the same universe. Tau beta is usually regarded as a more conservative measure and hence suggests a stronger relationship in the Miller and Stokes study. The difference is most probably attributable to the more discriminating interview questions in the latter study. Still, the relationship of values and attitudes to behavior is not perfect. Knowledge of the ways in which situational factors and organizational processes intervene to mediate this relationship is, therefore, high on the agenda of the needs of decision theory and research. We have already identified a number of characteristics of decision situations that seem important. Now we must ask what kinds of organizational rules, constraints, and procedures might be expected to mediate the effects of personal values in international decision-making. Such questions point to organizational context as a third important cluster of variables in decision processes.

ORGANIZATION OF DECISION-MAKERS

Typologies vs. Dimensions

Foreign policy within nations and international relations among nations are conducted in and by organizations. That is to say, the decision-makers do not act only in their individual capacities but also operate within a set of rules, constraints, and expectations.[1] Much of their interaction with other decision-makers is mediated by an elaborate communication network rather than conducted face to face. Major concepts and propositions about organizations are systematically inventoried in Blau and Scott (1962), Etzioni (1961), and March and Simon (1958). Some categories or types of organizations might usefully be postulated so that organization can be treated as a variable rather than as a constant and so that decision theory can relate variations in types of organization to differences in decisions.

Typologies have been suggested by Dahl and Lindblom (1953) and Etzioni (1961), among others. As noted earlier, Dahl and Lindblom compare organizations in terms of control relations between leaders and nonleaders. Hier-

archical organizations are characterized by control of leaders over nonleaders; bargaining organizations are those in which leaders control leaders; and polyarchical organizations are ones in which leaders are controlled by nonleaders. Etzioni classified organizations in terms of whether control is exercised by *coercion* or *remuneration* and whether the source of control is *normative* (single) or *dual*. Both typologies refine older conceptions of organizations in terms of a continuum of centralization and decentralization. Formerly, centralization was thought of as the hierarchical monopoly of authority, while decentralization was defined as the sharing of decisions and the diffusion or democratizing of authority. In the language of information theory, the difference between these polar types of organizations is in the extent to which they contain mechanisms for reporting nonleader reactions to the leadership's potential or actual decisions so that the next decisions may be modified in the light of the nonleader preferences (Boulding, 1956; Deutsch, 1963).

Although we have expressed our sympathy for the development and use of typologies of organizations (or of decision situations or individual decision-maker characteristics), there is no gainsaying that a priori typologies are often full of disappointments in empirical research. Earlier we referred to the failure of Dahl and Lindblom's four impressive a priori types of policy processes to be empirically useful in Dahl's New Haven study. Other examples no doubt can be added. Is the search for types a blind alley? What alternatives are there?

We cannot do without some criteria of variation. In order to formulate state-

---

[1] In American foreign policy this is often illustrated by comparing statements and actions of Presidents with their pre- and/or post-presidential attitudes and behavior. Both Harry Truman and Dwight Eisenhower have taken positions that seem "inconsistent" with their presidential positions and may be explained by their having freed themselves of official roles, constraints, and expectations.

ments such as "Changes in X will be followed by changes in Y," we need some way of talking about changes in X. So far, typologies have involved simultaneous variations along too many dimensions, and variables have been dichotomous. This is understandably typical of early stages of empirical work. However, we now may be in need of less gross characteristics for distinguishing organizations. If all organizations exhibit bureaucracy or bargaining, then we need more specific dimensions than dichotomies suggest; it is not the presence or absence of bureaucratization that will intrigue us, but ways of converting bureaucratization from a dichotomy to a continuum.

Fortunately, efforts in precisely this direction have recently been made, and with promising results. Hall (1961, 1962, 1963) developed a questionnaire to measure variations in six dimensions of bureaucratization: division of labor based on functional specialization; hierarchical authority; rules covering rights and duties of incumbents; procedures for dealing with work situations; impersonality of interpersonal relations; appointment and promotion on the basis of technical competence. These characteristics are classic Weberian elements of bureaucracy, but Hall's instrument, so far used in five governmental and five nongovernmental organizations, makes it possible to compare organizations by placing them in relative positions on each dimension. Moreover, in this method of measurement an organization's position on one dimension does not necessarily correlate with its position on another. The implication for decision theory is that the prospects for treating organization as a variable, and a measurable one at that, are much improved. We may be able to move into more subtle differentiations than legislative vs. bureaucratic, decentralized vs. centralized, and the like.

Recent perspectives on communication suggest other ways of differentiating organizational structures and processes that might be relevant to decision theory. For example, Bauer, Pool, and Dexter (1963), in refining the pressure group model of policy-making, make important advances in applying rather specific communications hypotheses to the passage of foreign trade legislation in 1955. They suggest that communication acts as a "trigger" rather than a "force" in influencing policy-makers, that is, it opens or activates latent predispositions or images but rarely alters or converts the listener, as vector models suggest. Moreover, congressmen have considerable discretion in deciding what information they will receive and attend to by the way they define their job or role.

We are, to be sure, a long way from having a list of documented and measurable dimensions of organizational process. Classic bureaucratic and communication models, and recent empirical research on them, however, suggest we may have a key to finding characteristic variations in organizations that may be hypothetically related to variations in decision situation and individual decision-makers. Some description of the organizational context, while hardly exhaustive, may provide clues to the identification of a cluster of variables that are not always self-evident and to the way these might enter into our theorizing. One of the possible advantages of such a description is that it would highlight the potential contributions of the vast literature on organizational behavior.

Characteristics of Foreign Policy Organizations

The foreign policy organization within the typical national government of a complex society consists of a relatively large number of agencies and individuals linked by a network of lines of authority and channels of communication. A rather elaborate division of labor—allocation of power and responsibility—results from the sheer magnitude of size and the many complex tasks to be performed. Differentiation of roles and functions creates diverse subunits whose activities have mutual impact. Some degree of articulation and coordination is necessary. Regardless of how centralized the total governmental system is, delegation of authority to act, plus informal bases of power or influence, will produce semi-autonomous subunits and, often, blurred jurisdictional boundaries. The formal allocation of power and responsibility may or may not coincide with operating realities. There will be a set of explicit or implicit, written and unwritten rules and expectations that guide role performance, rewards and punishments, and the supply of resources needed by the organization for the fulfillment of its mission. Agencies within the organization will compete for scarce resources, and the foreign policy organization itself will usually have to compete with other governmental functions. The rate of personnel turnover will vary, as will the mode of recruitment, but the organization retains its structure regardless of what happens to individual members, and some members will be permanently assigned to the organization. Changes in specific assignments may be frequent even for career officials. The conduct of individual members in their prescribed roles may be guided by more than a single motive, and it cannot be presumed that the national interest or a specific assignment is the predominant motive. However, there is a sense in which the organization *qua* organization is more of a "constant" than the other factors that enter into foreign policy formation. If this thumb-nail sketch is brief and abstract, its elements are familiar enough.

What are some of the more obvious implications of the organizational context? *Conflict* is pervasive and arises from the different values, experiences, viewpoints, and objectives associated with different agencies, roles, and functions. It is rare that one fails to find in the daily paper evidence of strains and tensions between units of power and responsibility, of concern for positional influence and prestige of individuals and agencies, of vested interests in particular programs for their own sake, and of two or more opposed interpretations of a major problem confronting the nation. Less publicized, but of equal potential importance, are differences of perspectives between officers "back home" in various bureaus and divisions and diplomats "in the field" who are closer to events, between staff and line officers, between area experts and substantive experts, between political appointees and career officers, and so on. Often, choices of great portent must be made between alternative intelligence estimates of critical situations. Jurisdictional conflicts arise because the delegation of authority is ambiguous or because problems do not fit neatly the division of labor.

It is not that these conflicts are "bad." Our language immediately above is intended to be descriptive, not evaluative. Whatever the merits of certain kinds of conflict, or their "dysfunctional" consequences by some standard, our point is that they must be (and usually are) *resolved*. Resolution may be achieved by persuasion, by "clearance" procedures, by voting, by bargaining, and by high authority. These modes of liquidating disagreement or obtaining agreement are operative within as well as between agencies. Politics and diplomacy accurately describe many of the processes through which consensus is reached and influences are brought to bear on outcomes. It is not uncommon for lawyers to represent two intra-organizational units in a negotiation.

Side by side with conflict are, of course, coordination and cooperation. Division of labor means that specialized roles and task forces make different contributions to foreign policy and have different locations in the total web of external contacts and relations. Depending on the substance and complexity of various problems, some degree of *mobilization* of skills, time, resources, and power to act is required. The many faces of foreign policy must be fitted into a mosaic before authoritative, coherent action is possible. Leadership, communication, assignment of specific responsibilities, and evaluation of information all enter into the *activation* of relevant organizational components and the formation of strategies. Mobilization and problem-solving activities imply subdecisions—what shall be decided when and by whom? Availability of resources and personnel, as well as money and equipment in the broadest sense, will necessitate further choices and planning.

Foreign policy-making, then, transpires in an organizational context having its own political forces, its own rules of the game, and even its own sets of subgoals. Decision-makers must work for each other, with each other, and sometimes against each other. The very processes of conflict resolution, consensus building, and mobilization for action will affect what can be done and how long it will take.

Organizational Differences between National and International Policy-Making

In the absence of more research on dimensions of organization, we may think of two more or less typical patterns of international decision-making. Foreign office decision-making is predominantly hierarchical, whether in the United States, Great Britain, the Soviet Union, Japan, or Norway (Black and Thompson, 1963; Macridis, 1959). Variations exist within this pattern, with Great Britain probably more centralized and hierarchical than the United States, but *intranational* policies are, on the whole, close to the familiar bureaucratic model. *International* policy-making, on the other hand, is based on decentralized interaction among a number of relatively independent hierarchies of leaders. Leaders control leaders in what has been labeled a bargaining situation. The United Nations and various regional organizations have formalized in a permanent way what traditionally occurred only occasionally and temporarily in multilateral conferences and congresses. The organizations function more in the decentralized fashion of legislatures than in the hierarchical manner of bureaucracies; votes are taken under a majority or a unanimity rule; minorities may sometimes defeat a near unanimous vote by casting a veto, or they may avoid a vote by threat of a veto; and enforcement of decisions depends on bargaining and "remuneration" rather than on expected observance backed by coercion.

National Policy-Making. Much more research has been done on the organizational component of international decision-making than on the individual factor. However, most of the organizational studies are of *intranational*, foreign office policy-making, and usually they are single country studies rather than comparative (for example, Black & Thompson, 1963). Studies of organizational structure and case studies of decisions are the major types of research done on foreign offices.

Foreign policy-making in Great Britain is probably more hierarchical than in the United States, although Bishop (1961, pp. 375–376) and Beloff (1961) emphasize the multiplicity of interests that participate in British decisions. Extensive consultation and bargaining with opposition, party, constituency, and organized interests also occur in Britain. This characteristic of British foreign policy-making is illustrated by a journalist's reconstruction of the British decision to join Israel and France in a war against Egypt (Childers, 1962). Epstein (1960) reviewed the postdecisional bargaining, between and within the parties in the House of Commons, that contributed to a reversal of policy on Suez and that set the background for the next round of policy decisions. Harold and Margaret Sprout (1958) delineated some of the factors that enter into an organization's decision to change a major policy, as indicated by the Sandys White Paper on defense policy of 1957. Young and Robinson (1962) took a gross view of a set of related decisions culminating in Britain's decision to seek membership in the Common Market and noted the extensive bargaining among many interests within the essentially hierarchical British system. These several foreign policy decisions reveal characteristics similar to a number of British domestic decisions of recent years, including the adoption of national health services (Eckstein, 1960), the licensing of commercial television (Wilson, 1961), and the restriction of capital punishment (Christoph, 1962).

The literature on American foreign policy-making is considerably greater than that for any other country. This reflects the greater amount of social science effort in America and the culture-bias of social scientists. Excluding the extensive work in diplomatic history, studies of United States foreign policy fall into two main categories, those that describe and analyze the organizations and institutions that contribute to policy and those that present detailed cases of particular decisions or policies.

Among organizational studies, general surveys of the total policy-making structure are to be found in numerous textbooks (for example, Snyder & Furniss, 1954) and in the report of the Brookings Institution (1960) to the Senate Committee on Foreign Relations. The Brookings study combines description (based on more than 150 interviews with high-level policy-makers) and recommendations. The series of studies undertaken by the Senate Foreign Relations Committee in 1959–1960 were primarily "content" or "issue" studies, with the exception of the study done by the Brookings Institution. However, the 1960 hearings and recommendations of the Subcommittee on National Policy Machinery of the Committee on Government Operation were directed at the policy-making process. Its hearings were dominated by former government officials rather than by professional observers and analysts of policy-making. Although the Subcommittee's staff canvassed a wide body of thought, no research was undertaken into the way in which the process of making national security policy was functioning. Many of the Committee's recommendations showed signs of the influence of Richard Neustadt's *Presidential power* (1960) and were especially critical of committees as a policy-making instrument. Several of its recommendations, notably the abolition of a number of committees and the bypassing of the National Security Council and the Cabinet, were adopted by the new Administration in 1961. However, most of the abolished committees had not been meeting for months or years and were, thus, merely taken off the books; there was little behavioral change. Moreover, the Cuban and Soviet difficulties of spring 1961 led to an apparently increased use of the National Security Council and the Cabinet as coordinating if not decision-making bodies.

Numerous case studies illustrating the interaction of the major institutions are available. Dawson (1959) retraced the decision to extend aid to Russia in 1941, with emphasis on the influence of public opinion; Price (1955) and Jones (1955) reviewed the development of the Marshall Plan and focused primarily on executive agencies; Haviland (1958) followed the 1957 foreign aid bill through the basic steps from drafting to adoption and highlighted the bargaining between Congress and the executive; Cohen (1957) detailed the making of the treaty with Japan with special reference to the Senate, informal advisers, interest groups, public opinion, and the press; and Paige (1959) reconstructed the decision to resist aggression in Korea with emphasis on the *ad hoc* group formed to respond to the crisis.

The major institutions in foreign policy-making are clearly within the executive branch—the Office of the President, the Department of State, and the Department of Defense. Neustadt's book is the most recent major study of the Presidency and is based to a considerable extent on his personal experience in the Truman Administration and is illustrated by three case studies: the recall of MacArthur, the seizure of the steel industries, and the intervention of troops in Little Rock. It should be supplemented by Sorensen's (1963) insightful formulation of his personal experience as a close adviser to and observer of President Kennedy and by Neustadt's subsequent comparison of F. D. Roosevelt's and Kennedy's organizational styles (1963).

The cases cited above on general organizational structure are applicable to the Presidency. Others include several older cases reviewed in Chamberlain (1946); May (1960) considers Presidential decisions about war extending from Madison's term to Eisenhower's; Simon (1953) recounts the changes in the first organizations to administer European recovery and points out the importance of the President's perspectives and images in staffing such organizations and in setting their goals.

"The Pentagon," that complex of military and civilian planners and makers of defense policy, has taken on a role virtually co-equal to that of the State Department in influencing foreign policy. Sapin and Snyder (1954) have written a general introduction to the role of the military in foreign policy; Hammond (1961) and Huntington (1961) have analyzed and evaluated the Pentagon's performance in the post-World War II years. Policy-making studies now cover a spectrum that includes operations research, management, simulation, procurement, process, and the like. For example, Hitch and McKean (1960) have probed the economics of defense policies and programs for deciding some financial issues. A recent study by the Harvard Business School analyzes the weapons-acquisition process (Peck & Scherer, 1962). And, to add one more example, Kahn reviews ways of *Thinking about the unthinkable* (1962).

The role of Congress in foreign policy is considered in Cheever and Haviland's (1952) analysis of the effects of separation of powers on the policy process. Dahl (1950) is concerned with ways in which the executive could be made responsible to Congress and in which Congress could be made more responsible to the values of the public. Carroll (1958) provides a comprehensive account of the House of Representatives' influence in foreign affairs in a way not matched by any similar study of the Senate. Farnsworth (1961) analyzes several specialized activities of the Senate Foreign Relations Committee. Robinson (1962a) concentrates on the relationships between information, policy initiation, and influence in legislative-executive relations. Dawson (1962) considers legislative innovation in military and defense policy.

More than twenty case studies include material on the role of Congress in foreign policy. Most of these are summarized and compared in Robinson (1962a, pp. 23–69). Others include MacAlister Brown's (1961) illustration of the ways in which Congress can exercise its "oversight function" in reviewing State Department performance, and Howard Swearer's (1961) study of the alternative legislative means to finance annual foreign aid programs.

The role of the legislature in foreign policy is primarily that of legitimator or amender of executive action. To the extent that Congress (or Parliament) takes initiative, its role is in issues of marginal importance, having little influence on basic values. When the occasion for decision is crisis-like or involves any matter of perceived importance to the executive, the executive will take the initiative. Legislative influence will be confined to vetoing or modifying executive action. There are legal and constitutional explanations for this distribution of legislative-executive participation in foreign policy, but other factors operate also. The Constitution has not changed with respect to the executive role, yet in the twentieth century executives everywhere have gained power (participation in decisions) at the expense of legislatures. The increasing need to process large amounts of information about the foreign environment, a need for which bureaucracies are more fit than legislatures, may explain part of the enhanced position of the executive (Robinson, 1962a).

The influence of public opinion on foreign policy is a controversial and unsettled issue. Lippmann's (1955) description is that of executive governments subject to the will of electorates that are represented by parliaments. We have already indicated our conception of the role of legislatures as one of minimal influence on foreign policy. If parliamentary bodies are not the nexus between opinion and executive policy, what is the connection?

If a link exists, it does so as a consequence of executive policy-makers' anticipations of *future* opinion about *not-as-yet salient* issues. Almond (1950) and Key (1961) and a wealth of survey and other data document low information and low involvement among "the publics" on foreign affairs. Cohen (1963) finds this true of the publics' interest in newspaper reporting of international relations. To the extent to which opinion affects policy it does so through the policy-makers' prediction of what public opinion would be if it were aroused. However, politicians vary in the accuracy of their predictions, and as Dawson (1959) has shown, the Roosevelt Administration bound itself to an interpretation of public opinion that was not supported by survey data on how the public actually felt. Bauer, Pool, and Dexter (1963) also argue that policy-makers have considerable decision latitude with relative freedom from control by public opinion.

Still another mechanism for the impact of public opinion is through specialized foreign policy publics. Almond (1950) identified "attentive publics," and Rosenau (1963) has documented how one of them was discovered and/

or created in behalf of foreign aid in 1958. One can think of a list of several foreign issues on which specialized publics have emerged: China policy, the United Nations, the test ban, and German unification. Those who actively participate in one policy issue are not necessarily those who follow and contribute to debate on other issues.

Elite opinion groups are frequently "co-opted" by the executive for *ad hoc* temporary service. Alger (1962) has shown that creation of special study groups, commissions, and similar bodies is a means of providing the executive with new perspectives, as well as of legitimating other viewpoints. One sees evidence of the presence of this "external bureaucracy" especially at the transition from one presidential administration to another.

Generally speaking, we conceive of the impact of public opinion in the decision process as depending on the nature of the problem, especially the amount of decision time available, and the previous discussion of it; the decision-makers' need to have the affiliation and support of others (Wilson's intransigence and Truman's decisiveness are examples of minimal concern for opinion); and the way in which the policy-making structure is designed to report (accurately or not) public sentiment (Elder, 1957; Brown, 1961). Variations in these three major factors in the decision process will affect the influence of public opinion.

International Policy-Making. Regional and international organizations are more typical of decentralized and bargaining-like organizations. Early studies of such organizations were formal and legal, but more recently evidence has accumulated concerning the relations among individual, group, and national actors within these organiza-

tions. Alger (1961) has enumerated some of the major types of "nonresolution" activities of the General Assembly. Hovet has followed the development of blocs within the United Nations (1960) and has considered whether they foreshadow an embryo of political parties (1962). Such organizational studies are supplemented by studies of particular decisions. For example, Matecki (1957) reconstructed the major steps in the creation of the International Finance Corporation, and Hadwen and Kaufman (1960) reported United Nations decisions regarding a special fund for aid to underdeveloped countries.

The growing number of regional organizations—in the North Atlantic, in Latin America, in Southeast Asia, in the Middle East, among the Arab states, in Africa, and in Western Europe—offer a source for "field studies" of organizational decision-making. Haas (1958) has done a massive work on post-World War II organizational developments in Europe, including quasi-parliamentary bodies and specialized organs to decide questions of defense, coal and steel, atomic energy, customs, and tariffs. Merkl (1962) reports on recent harbingers of cross-national political parties forming in specialized organizations.

The numerous new organizations in Western Europe, those that constitute the movement toward European integration, operate on a pattern of decision-making different from that of the polar types of national foreign policy-making or United Nations policy-making. As Haas (1958, pp. 492–511) and Lindberg (1963, pp. 107–295) make clear, the European Economic Community, the Coal and Steel Community, and related agencies have acquired decision-making structures of their own. In the rigorous meaning of decision, they make some choices for which they invoke sanctions to bind compliance. They are more than actors, roles, and institutions participating with other units in a bargaining situation from which a policy will emerge. The European Economic Commission and the High Authority of the Coal and Steel Community have a jurisdiction in which they take decisions that are not dependent on the unanimity of the member states. Judicial organs to which appeals may be taken are available, but parliamentary organs to which the "technocracies" are responsible have yet to be developed.

Depending on the occasion for decision, the European communities employ different organizational processes. Some decisions are taken by the Commissions after consideration of the member governments' interests, but not necessarily with the unanimous agreement of those governments. Others are taken by the Communities on the basis of agreement among member countries. Hence, both the foreign policymaking and the international policymaking characteristics are present. These new decision-making units are of interest, therefore, for the variations on certain organizational dimensions that occur within them.

CONCLUSION: WHOSE IMAGES COUNT, UNDER WHAT CONDITIONS?

The main purpose of inquiries about decision-making processes is to determine whether and how decision process affects the content of decision outcome. Does the process of making a decision make any difference for the substance of the decision? Do different kinds of processes reach different results? Do different combinations of situation, individuals, and organizations produce different policies? Or is de-

cision-making as simple as one of C. P. Snow's characters twice asserts: ". . . whatever rules one has, sensible men usually reach a sensible conclusion" (1960, pp. 221, 374)?

We may specify this general question in terms of one of the recurring themes of this volume, image. The issues are whose images count, under what conditions, and at what points in international policy-making processes.

Whose images count depends, first, on the occasion for decision. Powerholders vary from issue to issue. Those who involve themselves in policies concerning West Germany are not necessarily the same as those who participate in decisions about nuclear testing. Various studies of influence, in communities, in legislatures, and in other settings agree that power varies with the issue. Lyndon Johnson typified the contrary view when in 1960 he rationalized his decision to forego immense senatorial influence for the alleged obscurity of the Vice Presidency: "Power is where power goes." These two opposing points of view are reflected in the controversies engendered by certain nonempirical work on "the power elite" and "the establishment."

Influence varies not only with the value at issue in a decision situation, but with the level of crisis as well. The Korean crisis of 1950 brought together an unusual, virtually unique *ad hoc* decision unit, one that was drawn partly from official role occupants and partly from officials who were available in Washington. Elements of innovation were evident in the selection of participants in the Kennedy Administration's handling of its two Cuban crises. Decision-making personnel in these crises differed from that in more routine decisions.

The situation not only determines, in part, who will participate in a decision, and, thus, whose images count, but also affects the selection and formation of images. North, Brody, and Holsti (1964) and Holsti and North (1963) find that in crisis situations, if decision-makers in one country perceive themselves threatened by decision-makers in another, the probability is high that those who think they are threatened will respond with a threat. This response confirms to the original threatening group that its hostility was justified, and it then responds with further threats. Thus originates the spiral effect of perception, threat, response by threat, confirmation, further threat, and so on.

Crisis also affects the number and the breadth of alternative images that may be available in decision. Current simulations of crisis decision-making (Hermann et al., 1964b) reveal that "in a crisis, as contrasted with a non-crisis, the perception of only one or two available courses of action is more likely than of more numerous alternatives" (p. 9). Moreover, "in a crisis, as contrasted with a non-crisis, there will be less search for alternative courses of action" (p. 8). These hypotheses suggest that aspirations regarding a "good" solution to a problem are reduced in a crisis, particularly if organizational consideration of alternatives is sequential rather than simultaneous, as is typical. In other words, the "satisficing" mechanism may enter into the decision process at an early point, so that a nation's decision-makers will be more willing to accept, in a crisis as compared to a non-crisis situation, one of the first alternatives that occurs to them.

The truth of the proposition that influence varies with the personality of decision-makers seems obvious, but, as our earlier review of the literature indicated, hard evidence has not been collected. Among hypotheses for which data are available is the one that social backgrounds of decision-makers

are increasingly "democratic." In urban politics, in Congress, in Parliament, and in foreign offices, class counts for less than it did a generation or two generations ago. The consequence is that more varied images and perspectives are being considered in foreign and international policy-making.

Whose images count further depends on the organizational arena in which decisions are taken. The placing of many items on the United Nations agenda or before new multilateral organizations involves different participants with different values than would be the case if the decision unit were bilateral.

Within the American foreign policy process, the major base of influence is the executive branch. In this branch lies the initiative for innovation—not in Congress, or in the press, or anywhere else. Legislatures, mass media, and other participating roles may check, limit, thwart, constrain, veto, or delay executive action, but usually they cannot initiate, except at the pleasure of the executive. This is true in the United Kingdom as well as in the United States. It appears to be so in the Soviet Union, in France, and in other world powers.

Furthermore, within the executive agencies of governments, different situations may evoke or activate different organizational patterns or processes. When decision time is short, as it was during the Berlin airlift, the Korean invasion, and the Suez invasion, fewer agencies and fewer factors are likely to be involved than when there is a long time for decision. In the cases just mentioned, decision time ranged from several hours to several weeks. In other decisions, when perhaps four to sixteen months may be available, time allows for more agencies to participate and more factors to be considered. For example, annual foreign aid bills, the original Marshall Plan, the formation of NATO, the creation of the United Nations, and the periodic renewal of Reciprocal Trade Legislation have involved many executive agencies and the legislative process also.

These hypotheses, of course, only serve to illustrate some of the mechanisms and processes by which images enter into decision-making. Fuller and more exact knowledge about the influence of various images on international policies seems to us to depend on the growth and development of research on the interactions of situations, on individual decision-makers, and on organizational settings in international arenas.

REFERENCES

Abel, T.   The element of decision in the pattern of war. *Amer. sociol. Rev.*, 1941, 6, 853–859.

Acheson, D. G.   The President and the Secretary of State. In D. K. Price (Ed.), *The Secretary of State*. Englewood Cliffs, N. J.: Prentice-Hall, 1960. Pp. 27–50.

Alger, C. F.   Non-resolution consequences of the United Nations and their effect on international conflict. *J. Confl. Resol.*, 1961, 5, 128–145.

Alger, C. F.   The external bureaucracy in United States foreign affairs. *Admin. Sci. Quart.*, 1962, 7, 50–78.

Alger, C. F.   United Nations participation as a learning experience. *Publ. Opin. Quart.*, 1963, 27, 411–426.

Almond, G.   *The American people and foreign policy*. New York: Harcourt, Brace, 1950.

Alsop, S.   The lessons of the Cuban disaster. *Sat. Eve. Post*, June 24, 1961, 26–27, 68–70.

Arens, R., & Lasswell, H. D.   *In defense of public order: The emerging field of sanction law*. New York: Columbia Univer. Press, 1961.

Banfield, E. C.   *Political influence*. New York: Free Press, 1961.

Bauer, R., Pool, I. de S., & Dexter, L. A. *American business and public policy: The politics of foreign trade*. New York: Atherton, 1963.

Beloff, M.   *New dimensions in foreign policy, a study in British administrative experience, 1947–1959*. New York: Macmillan, 1961.

Bentley, A. F.   *The process of government: A study of social pressures*. Evanston: The Principia Press of Illinois, 1935.

Birnbaum, N.   David Riesman's image of political process. In S. M. Lipset & L. Lowenthal (Eds.), *Culture and social character: The work of David Riesman reviewed*. New York: Free Press, 1961. Pp. 207–225.

Bishop, D. G.   *The administration of foreign affairs*. Syracuse: Syracuse Univer. Press, 1961.

Black, J. E., & Thompson, K. W.   *Foreign policies in a world of change*. New York: Harper, 1963.

Blau, P. M., & Scott, W. R.   *Formal organizations: A comparative approach*. San Francisco: Chandler Publishing Co., 1962.

Boulding, K.   *The image*. Ann Arbor: Univer. Michigan Press, 1956.

Brookings Institution   *United States foreign policy: The formulation and administration of United States foreign policy*. Washington: Government Printing Office, 1960.

Brown, M.   The demise of State Department public opinion polls: A study in legislative oversight. *Midw. J. pol. Sci.*, 1961, 5, 1–17.

Buck, P. W.   *Amateur and professionals in British politics, 1918–59*. Chicago: Univer. Chicago Press, 1963.

Campbell, A., Converse, P., Miller, W. E., & Stokes, D. E.   *The American voter*. New York: Wiley, 1960.

Carroll, H. N.   *The House of Representatives and foreign affairs*. Pittsburgh: Univer. Pittsburgh Press, 1958.

Chamberlain, L. *The President, Congress, and legislation.* New York: Columbia Univer. Press, 1946.

Cheever, D., & Haviland, H. F., Jr. *American foreign policy and the separation of powers.* Cambridge, Mass.: Harvard Univer. Press, 1952.

Childers, E. B. *The road to Suez.* London: Macgibbon & Kee, 1962.

Christoph, J. *Capital punishment and British politics.* Chicago: Univer. Chicago Press, 1962.

Cohen, B. C. *The political process and foreign policy: The making of the Japanese peace settlement.* Princeton: Princeton Univer. Press, 1957.

Cohen, B. C. *The press and foreign policy.* Princeton: Princeton Univer. Press, 1963.

Cole, W. S. Senator Key Pittman and American neutrality policies, 1933–40. *Miss. Valley hist. Rev.,* 1960, *46,* 644–662.

Cyert, R. B., Simon, H. A., & Trow, D. B. Observation of a business decision. *J. Business,* 1956, *29,* 237–248.

Dahl, R. A. *Congress and foreign policy.* New York: Harcourt, Brace, 1950.

Dahl, R. A. *Who governs? Democracy and power in an American city.* New Haven: Yale Univer. Press, 1961.

Dahl, R. A., & Lindblom, C. E. *Politics, economics and welfare.* New York: Harper, 1953.

Davis, F. *Passage through crisis: Polio victims and their families.* Indianapolis: Bobbs-Merrill, 1963.

Dawson, R. H. *The decision to aid Russia, 1941: Foreign policy and domestic politics.* Chapel Hill: Univer. North Carolina Press, 1959.

Dawson, R. H. Congressional innovation in defense policy: Legislative authorization of weapons systems. *Amer. pol. Sci. Rev.,* 1962, *56,* 42–57.

Deutsch, K. W. *The nerves of government: Models of political communication and control.* New York: Free Press, 1963.

Donnelly, R. C., Goldstein, J., & Schwartz,

R. D. *Criminal law.* New York: Free Press, 1962.

Eckstein, H. *Pressure group politics: The case of the British Medical Association.* London: Allen & Unwin, 1960.

Elder, R. The public studies division of the Department of State: Public opinion analysts in the formulation and conduct of American foreign policy. *West. pol. Quart.,* 1957, *10,* 783–792.

Epstein, L. D. Partisan foreign policy: Britain in the Suez Crisis. *World Politics,* 1960, *12,* 201–214.

Etzioni, A. *A comparative analysis of complex organizations.* New York: Free Press, 1961.

Farnsworth, D. N. *The Senate Committee on Foreign Relations.* Urbana: Univer. Illinois Press, 1961.

Froman, L. A., Jr. *Congressmen and their constituencies.* Chicago: Rand McNally, 1963.

George, A. L., & George, Juliette L. *Woodrow Wilson and Colonel House: A personality study.* New York: John Day, 1956.

Gilbert, C. E. Problems of a senator [Hubert H. Humphrey]. Unpublished doctoral dissertation, Northwestern University, 1955.

Gottfried, A. *Boss Cermak of Chicago.* Seattle: Univer. Washington Press, 1961.

Green, B. F. Attitude measurement. In G. Lindzey (Ed.), *Handbook of social psychology.* Vol. 1. Reading, Mass.: Addison-Wesley, 1954. Pp. 335–369.

Haas, E. *The uniting of Europe: Political, social, and economic forces, 1950–1957.* Stanford: Stanford Univer. Press, 1958.

Hadwen, J. G., & Kaufman, J. *How United Nations decisions are made.* Leyden: Sythoff, 1960.

Hall, R. H. An empirical study of bureaucratic dimensions and their relation to other organizational characteristics. Unpublished doctoral dissertation, Ohio State University, 1961.

Hall, R. H. Intraorganizational structural

variation: Application of the bureaucratic model. *Admin. Sci. Quart.*, 1962, 7, 295–308.

Hall, R. H.   The concept of bureaucracy: An empirical assessment. *Amer. J. Sociol.*, 1963, 69, 32–40.

Hammond, P. Y.   *Organizing for defense: The American military establishment in the twentieth century.* Princeton: Princeton Univer. Press, 1961.

Haviland, H. F., Jr.   Foreign aid and the policy process: 1957. *Amer. pol. Sci. Rev.*, 1958, 52, 689–724.

Hennessy, B. C.   Politicals and apoliticals: Some measurements of personality traits. *Midw. J. pol. Sci.*, 1959, 3, 336–355.

Hermann, C. F.   Some consequences of crisis which limit the viability of organizations. *Admin. Sci. Quart.*, 1963, 8, 61–82.

Hermann, C. F., & Hermann, Margaret G.   The potential use of historical data for validation studies of the Inter-Nation Simulation: The outbreak of World War I as an illustration. Unpublished paper, 1962.

Hermann, C. F., Hermann, Margaret G., & Robinson, J. A.   Studies in crisis decision-making. In progress, 1964.(a)

Hermann, C. F., Hermann, Margaret G., & Robinson, J. A.   Memorandum #1 for Project Michelson: Some relations of crisis to selected decision processes and outcome variables. Unpublished paper, Northwestern University, February, 1964.(b)

Hermann, Margaret G.   Some personal characteristics related to foreign aid voting of Congressmen. M. A. thesis, Northwestern University, 1963. (Mimeographed)

Hill, R.   *Families under stress: Adjustment to the crisis of war separation and reunion.* New York: Harper, 1949.

Hilsman, R.   Congressional-Executive relations and the foreign policy consensus. *Amer. pol. Sci. Rev.*, 1958, 52, 725–744.

Hilsman, R.   The foreign policy consensus: An interim research report. *J. Confl. Resol.*, 1959, 3, 361–382.

Hitch, C., & McKean, R.   *The economics of defense in the nuclear age.* Cambridge, Mass.: Harvard Univer. Press, 1960.

Holsti, O. R., & North, R. C.   Perceptions of hostility and economic variables in the 1914 crisis. Stanford Studies in International Conflict and Integration, November, 1963. (Mimeographed)

Hovet, T., Jr.   *Bloc politics in the United Nations.* Cambridge, Mass.: Harvard Univer. Press, 1960.

Hovet, T., Jr.   Political parties in the U.N.? Paper prepared for the annual meeting of the American Political Science Association, Washington, D.C., September 1962.

Huntington, S. P.   *The common defense.* New York: Columbia Univer. Press, 1961.

Jones, J. M.   *The fifteen weeks.* New York: Viking, 1955.

Kahn, H.   *Thinking about the unthinkable.* New York: Horizon Press, 1962.

Kempton, M.   *Part of our time.* New York: Simon & Schuster, 1955.

Key, V. O., Jr.   *Public opinion and American democracy.* New York: Knopf, 1961.

Kluckhohn, Florence R., & Strodtbeck, F. L.   *Variations in value orientations.* New York: Harper, 1961.

Koch, H. E., Jr., *et al.*   Documentary chronology of events preceding the outbreak of the First World War: 28 June–6 August, 1914. Conflict Studies Project, Stanford University, 1959. (Mimeographed)

Koenig, L. W.   Foreign aid to Spain and Yugoslavia: Harry Truman does his duty. In A. F. Westin (Ed.), *The uses of power: Seven cases in American politics.* New York: Harcourt, Brace, 1962. Pp. 73–116.

Lane, R. E.   *Political life: Why people get involved in politics.* New York: Free Press, 1959.

Larson, D. L.   *The 'Cuban Crisis' of*

1962: Selected documents and chronology. New York: Houghton Mifflin, 1963.

Lasswell, H. D. Psychopathology and politics. Chicago: Univer. Chicago Press, 1930. (A new edition with afterthoughts by the author. New York: Viking, 1960.)

Lasswell, H. D. The decision process: Seven categories of functional analysis. College Park, Md.: Bureau of Government Research, 1956.

Lasswell, H. D., & Almond, G. Twisting relief rules. Personnel J., 1935, 13, 338–343. (Reprinted in H. D. Lasswell, The analysis of political behavior. New York: Oxford Univer. Press, 1949. Pp. 261–267.)

Lasswell, H. D., & Kaplan, A. Power and society: A framework for political inquiry. New Haven: Yale Univer. Press, 1950.

Lindberg, L. N. The political dynamics of European economic integration. Stanford: Stanford Univer. Press, 1963.

Lippmann, W. Essays on the public philosophy. Boston: Little, Brown, 1955.

Long, N. The local community as an ecology of games. Amer. J. Sociol., 1958, 44, 251–261. (Reprinted in The polity. Chicago: Rand McNally, 1962. Pp. 130–155.)

McClelland, C. A. Decisional opportunity and political controversy: The Quemoy case. J. Confl. Resol., 1962, 6, 201–213.

McConaughy, J. B. Certain personality factors of state legislators in South Carolina. Amer. pol. Sci. Rev., 1950, 44, 897–903.

McDougal, M. S., et al. Studies in world public order. New Haven: Yale Univer. Press, 1960.

McDougal, M. S., & Feliciano, F. P. Law and minimum world public order. New Haven: Yale Univer. Press, 1961.

McDougal, M. S., Lasswell, H. D., & Vlasic, I. A. Law and public order in space. New Haven: Yale Univer. Press, 1963.

Macridis, R. C. (Ed.) Foreign policy in world politics. Englewood Cliffs, N.J.: Prentice-Hall, 1959.

March, J. G. Some recent substantive and methodological developments in the theory of organizational decision-making. In A. Ranney (Ed.), Essays on the behavioral study of politics. Urbana: Univer. Illinois Press, 1962. Pp. 191–208.

March, J. G., & Simon, H. A., with Guetzkow, H. Organizations. New York: Wiley, 1958.

Matecki, B. E. Establishment of the International Finance Corporation and United States policy: A case study in international organization. New York: Praeger, 1957.

Matthews, D. R. The social background of political decision-makers. New York: Random House, 1954.

Matthews, D. R. United States senators and their world. Chapel Hill: Univer. North Carolina Press, 1960.

May, E. The ultimate decision. New York: Braziller, 1960.

Merkl, P. H. Supranational parties in some European assemblies. Paper prepared for the annual meeting of the American Political Science Association, Washington, D.C., September 1962.

Miller, W. E., & Stokes, D. E. Constituency influence in Congress. Amer. pol. Sci. Rev., 1963, 57, 45–56.

Minar, D. W. Ideology and political behavior. Midw. J. pol. Sci., 1961, 5, 317–331.

Murphy, C. J. V. Cuba: The record set straight. Fortune, September 1961, 64(3), 92–97, 223–236.

Neustadt, R. Presidential power. New York: Wiley, 1960.

Neustadt, R. Approaches to staffing the presidency: Notes on FDR and JFK. Amer. pol. Sci. Rev., 1963, 57, 855–863.

North, R. C., Brody, R. A., & Holsti, O. R. Some empirical data on the conflict spiral. Peace Research Society (International) Papers, 1964, 1, 1–14.

Paige, G. D. The Korean decision (June

24–30, 1950): A reconstruction of decision-making events. Unpublished doctoral dissertation, Northwestern University, 1959.

Peck, M. J., & Scherer, F. M. *The weapons acquisition process.* Cambridge, Mass.: Harvard Univer. Press, 1962.

Pool, I. de S., Keller, Suzanne, & Bauer, R. A. The influence of foreign travel on political attitudes of American businessmen. *Publ. Opin. Quart.*, 1956, *20*, 165–167.

Price, H. B. *The Marshall Plan and its meaning.* Ithaca, N.Y.: Cornell Univer. Press, 1955.

Rieselbach, L. N. Congressional isolationist behavior, 1939–1958. Unpublished doctoral dissertation, Yale University, 1963.

Riesman, D. *The lonely crowd.* New Haven: Yale Univer. Press, 1950.

Robinson, J. A. *The Monroney resolution: Congressional initiative in foreign policy-making.* New York: McGraw-Hill, 1960.

Robinson, J. A. *Congress and foreign policy-making: A study of legislative influence and initiative.* Homewood, Ill.: Dorsey, 1962. (a)

Robinson, J. A. The concept of crisis in decision-making. In *Series studies in social and economic sciences, No. 11.* Washington, D.C.: National Institute of Social and Behavioral Science, 1962. (b)

Robinson, J. A. The major problems of political science. In L. K. Caldwell (Ed.), *Politics and public affairs.* Bloomington, Ind.: Institute of Training for Public Service, 1962. (c)

Robinson, J. A. *The House Rules Committee.* Indianapolis: Bobbs-Merrill, 1963.

Rogow, A. A. *James Forrestal: A study of personality, politics and policy.* New York: Macmillan, 1963.

Rogow, A. A., & Lasswell, H. D. *Power, corruption, and rectitude.* Englewood Cliffs, N.J.: Prentice-Hall, 1963.

Rosenau, J. N. *National leadership and foreign policy: A case study in the mobilization of public support.* Princeton: Princeton Univer. Press, 1963.

Sapin, B., & Snyder, R. C. *The role of the military in American foreign policy.* Garden City, N.Y.: Doubleday, 1954.

Scodel, A. P., Ratoosh, P., & Minas, J. S. Some personality correlates of decision making under conditions of risk. *Behav. Sci.*, 1959, *4*, 19–28.

Simon, H. A. Birth of an organization: The Economic Cooperation Administration. *Publ. Admin. Rev.*, 1953, *13*, 227–236.

Simon, H. A. *Administrative behavior: A study of decision-making processes in administrative organizations.* New York: Macmillan, 1957. (a)

Simon, H. A. *Models of man: Social and rational.* New York: Wiley, 1957. (b)

Simon, H. A. Political research: The decision-making framework. Paper delivered at the annual meeting of the American Political Science Association, New York, September 1963.

Smith, A. R. *The tiger in the Senate: The biography of Wayne Morse.* Garden City, N.Y.: Doubleday, 1962.

Snow, C. P. *The affair.* New York: Scribner, 1960.

Snow, C. P. *Science and government.* Cambridge, Mass.: Harvard Univer. Press, 1961.

Snyder, R. C. A decision-making approach to the study of political phenomena. In R. Young (Ed.), *Approaches to the study of politics.* Evanston, Ill.: Northwestern Univer. Press, 1958. Pp. 3–38.

Snyder, R. C. The Korean decision (1950) and the analysis of crisis decision-making. Paper presented at the Conference on Decision-Making in Crises, Stanford University, January 12–13, 1962.

Snyder, R. C., Bruck, H. W., & Sapin, B. *Decision-making as an approach to the study of international politics.* Princeton: Foreign Policy Analysis Project, 1954.

Snyder, R. C., Bruck, H. W., & Sapin, B. (Eds.) *Foreign policy decision-making.* New York: Free Press, 1962.

Snyder, R. C., & Furniss, E. S. *American foreign policy.* New York: Holt, Rinehart and Winston, 1954.

Snyder, R. C., & Paige, G. D. The United States decision to resist aggression in Korea. *Admin. Sci. Quart.,* 1958, 3, 341–379.

Snyder, R. C., & Robinson, J. A. *National and international decision-making.* New York: Institute for International Order, 1961.

Sorensen, T. C. *Decision-making in the White House.* New York: Columbia Univer. Press, 1963.

Sprout, H., & Sprout, Margaret Ecological and behavioral models in the analysis of state capabilities—considered with special reference to the British White Paper on defense, April 1957. Paper presented at a symposium on the interrelations of behavioral and ecological models, Northwestern University, June 20–21, 1958.

Swearer, H. R. The controversy over "backdoor" financing in the 86th Congress, first session. Unpublished manuscript, 1961.

Szulc, T., & Meyer, K. E. *The Cuban invasion: The chronicle of a disaster.* New York: Ballantine Books, 1962.

Truman, D. B. *The governmental process: Political interests and public opinion.* New York: Knopf, 1951.

White, W. S. The new power behind Eisenhower's throne. *Harper's,* December 1959, 79–82.

Whiting, A. S. *China crosses the Yalu: The decision to enter the Korean war.* New York: Macmillan, 1960.

Wilson, H. H. *Pressure group: The campaign for commercial television.* London: Secker and Warburg, 1961.

Wise, D., & Ross, T. B. *The U-2 affair.* New York: Random House, 1962.

Wood, R. C., with Almendinger, V. V. *1400 governments: The political economy of the New York metropolitan region.* Cambridge, Mass.: Harvard Univer. Press, 1961.

Young, R., & Robinson, J. A. Parliamentary decision-making in Great Britain: The case of the Common Market. Paper delivered at the annual meeting of the American Political Science Association, Washington, D.C., September 1962.

13

The remaining three chapters of Part Two are devoted to an exploration of three different kinds of situations in which individuals of different nationality engage in direct, face-to-face interaction with one another. The situations to be discussed vary in the degree to which the individual participants act as representatives of their nations or as individuals—a factor of considerable significance for the course of the interaction.

Chapter 13 is concerned with bargaining and negotiation in international relations. The participants in international negotiations clearly act as representatives of their governments rather than as individuals. Their freedom of action may be restricted to varying degrees—depending, for example, on the negotiator's level in the decision-making hierarchy, and on the issue under discussion. Even those negotiators, however, who come with minimal instructions and with maximal opportunities for exploring new directions, operate under powerful constraints. This is certainly one of the major characteristics of the interaction situation in which international negotiations take place, in contrast to other situations in which participants are freer to react spontaneously.

Given this kind of situation, then, what form does the interaction take? How are the process and outcome of negotiation affected by the conditions under which it takes place? How are they altered, for example, if negotiations are conducted under conditions of limited information, or under conditions of stress, or in a multilingual setting? What effects do the preexisting mutual images of the negotiating parties, the personal characteristics of the negotiators, and their domestic reference groups have on the negotiating process and its outcome? What latitude exists even within the constraints of the situation? And what role do interpersonal factors play in determining the course of the interaction? In addressing these and other questions, Chapter 13 draws on the experimental literature on small group interaction and on studies of bargaining and negotiation in other settings, such as labor-management relations. These are juxtaposed to the literature on diplomacy, and consideration is given to the issues involved in generalizing from laboratory situations and from other settings to the special circumstances of negotiation in international relations.

Chapter 13 can also be seen as continuous with Chapter 10. Both are concerned with an analysis of strategies of conflict resolution. But, whereas Chapter 10 examines these on a macroscopic level, and relates choice of strategy to certain broad societal processes, Chapter 13 engages in a microscopic analysis of processes of conflict resolution and of the variables that determine their exact course. In yet another sense, Chapter 13 continues the work of Chapter 12 by focusing on one type of interaction process involved in the conduct of foreign affairs by responsible individual actors.

The chapter is a product of the collaboration of two social psychologists with strong interdisciplinary identifications.

Jack Sawyer is Assistant Professor of Psychology and Sociology at the University of Chicago. He has published articles on interpersonal conflict, game theory, sociometric analysis, psychological aspects of international relations, and methodological problems. His current research interests focus on the experimental study of bargaining, negotiation, and the resolution of interpersonal conflict; and the prediction of interpersonal attraction.

Harold Guetzkow is Professor of Political Science and Psychology, and Director of the Simulated International Processes project in the International Relations Program, Northwestern University. He is author of *Multiple loyalties: Theoretical approach to a problem in international organization* (1955), and co-author of *The Organization of American States* (1959), *Simulation in international relations: Developments for research and teaching* (1963), and *A social psychology of group processes for decision-making* (1964). His current interests include field and laboratory research in international politics.

H. C. K.

Bargaining and Negotiation in International Relations*

Jack Sawyer and Harold Guetzkow

"Let us not be blind to our differences—but let us also direct attention to our common interests and to the means by which those differences can be resolved. And if we cannot now end our differences, at least we can help make the world safe for diversity"—John F. Kennedy, American University, June 10, 1963.

Morgenthau (1956) points out that nations, in resolving their differences, ". . . have always had a choice among three alternatives: diplomacy, war, and renunciation . . . [but] modern technology . . . has destroyed this rational equality . . . there is no longer safety in renunciation or victory in war" (pp. 410–411). To the remaining possibility of diplomatic negotiation, this chapter is devoted.

Negotiation is a process through which two or more parties—be they individuals, groups, or larger social units —interact in developing potential agreements to provide guidance and regula-

tion of their future behavior. Such negotiation is conducted not only between nations, but also between government departments, political factions, labor and management, gangs, neighbors, and spouses.

At the international level, negotiation may be regarded as one of the major functions of diplomacy that together constitute "the conduct of business between states by peaceful means" (Satow, 1957, p. 1). Other major functions include the interchange of political, economic, and military information, including "technical discussions" that do not seek agreement; and the execu-

* The authors are grateful to Peter Allen for his insightful comments and suggestions on the manuscript, to Lawrence A. Eberhardt and Ellen Kay Trimberger for their diligent and highly informed search of the international relations and social-psychological literature, respectively, and to Herbert Kelman for his continued intellectual contributions and personal stimulation throughout the production of the present analysis.

tion of procedures (such as routine consular arrangements for commercial and tourist traffic) reflecting in some cases traditional practice or previous negotiation, and in others trivial or noncontroversial problems that do not require formal negotiation.

Thus, the present analysis is not directly concerned with the whole of diplomacy, let alone of the larger sphere of international relations, though these are both crucial in providing its context. Further, *within* the area of international negotiation, the focus of the present analysis is upon social-psychological aspects. This is not to assert that international conflict arises simply from misperception and misunderstanding; on the contrary, conflict appears to result in large part from objective incompatibility of goals among states. It is the thesis of this analysis, however, that even such genuine conflict of interests may be heightened or mitigated by psychological factors, and that these may influence its eventual outcome. As Snyder (1962) indicates, ". . . development or existence of effective bargaining techniques would seem to be one of the necessary elements in the institutionalization of nonviolent modes of handling clashes of interest among nations" (p. 155).

Such problems of conflict, while possibly stimulating "much of the best thinking in all the social sciences" (Bernard, 1965, p. 442), have yet to result in a substantial body of systematic empirical research on international negotiation. The inferred importance of social-psychological aspects derives from neither the controlled laboratory experiment nor the systematic field investigation which compose the field's principal techniques. The relevance of social psychology is suggested, rather, by the continuing observations and analyses of diplomats and scholars who have devoted their careers to practicing

and studying international relations. Such observations and analyses—of which the most recent and extensive integration is Iklé's *How nations negotiate*—provide the starting-point for the present treatment and indicate points of social-psychological research that should be examined. Because little if any such research deals directly with the situation of international negotiation, the present analysis is intended more as provocative than definitive. Through providing a framework and indicating possible points of relevancy, this chapter hopes to stimulate some of the research it cannot summarize.

For social-psychological analysis, negotiation may be regarded as composed of five aspects: (a) *goals,* motivating the parties to enter and sustain (b) the *process* of negotiation itself, which involves communications and actions leading to (c) certain *outcomes* for each—all occurring within and influenced by (d) preexisting *background* factors of cultural traditions and relations between and within parties, and (e) specific situational *conditions* under which the negotiation is conducted. These five aspects and their relations constitute a preliminary social-psychological model of negotiation, portrayed in Figure 13.1.

This model provides a framework for the present analysis, which devotes a major section to each of the five aspects. Within each, a number of more specific elements are treated, as indicated in Figure 13.1. Attention is thus directed not only to the narrower problem of bargaining over given alternatives, but also to such processes as establishing the domain of initial concern, searching for new alternatives, or arranging for the execution of negotiated agreements. Figure 13.1 also shows the approximate temporal flow of negotiation: *Goals* and *background* factors exist initially, and both influence the on-going *process,* as do the contemporary *conditions;* the resulting *outcome* may at any given time also produce feedback that alters the goals or process.

GOALS OF NEGOTIATION

As Haas and Whiting (1956) point out, the underlying purpose of negotiation may not be agreement at all, but rather suggests, include maintaining contact, substituting for violent action, intelligence, and deception. These important functions of negotiation are not treated in the present analysis since they minimize the relevance of the process of direct exchange which forms the present focus. Rather, this analysis examines those situations in which potential outcomes are sufficiently promising to encourage serious efforts toward agreement.

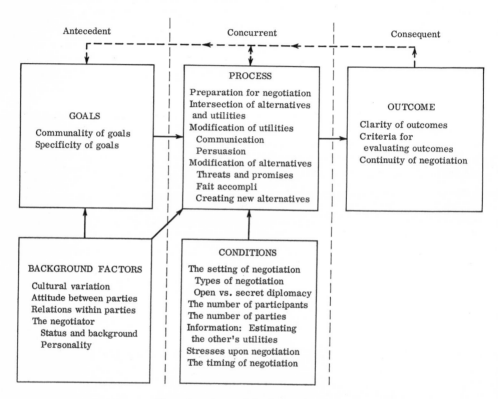

Fig. 13.1. A model of negotiation

delay or propaganda. Delay forestalls action while one awaits more favorable circumstances; propaganda seeks to embarrass the other party, to promote positions world opinion will favor, or simply to avoid the onus of failing to negotiate. Other side effects, Iklé (1964)

In such bargaining in good faith, the goal of each party may be taken as the end-state it desires to achieve. Many outcomes (including lack of agreement) are possible, and each party may establish an order of preference among them. Then the goal of each party may be stated more broadly, and more realistically: to obtain the most favored outcome to which the other party will agree. Favorability of the outcomes the parties are likely to obtain depends in considerable part on the way their interests are related. Considering international relations, Friedrich (1963, p. 486) distinguishes four cases: common interest, complementary interests, conflicting interests, and completely contradictory interests. While little if any social-psychological research deals with the effect of national goals, there is evidence, presented in the following section, on effects associated with perceived or actual communality or conflict of goals.

Communality of Goals

Probably the factor most promotive of the mutual satisfaction of both parties to a negotiation is the extent to which their goals are, or can be made to be, in agreement. As Thucydides observed in ancient Greece, "identity of interests is the surest of bonds, whether between states or individuals."

Sherif and his associates (1961) have explored effects of introducing into a conflict situation superordinate goals—goals that are compelling to both parties but unattainable by either alone. In a summer camp, each of two groups of middle-class eleven-year-old boys quickly developed an in-group solidarity, which was promoted by their athletic and more general competition with, and then antagonism toward, the other group. Conflict was evidenced in such behavior as stereotypic ratings of the other group, raids upon their cabin, and relative overestimation of own group performance. Contact between the groups, even in pleasant situations (such as eating), did not serve to reduce conflict, but rather led them to give more vent to it, on one occasion producing a food-throwing fight. When, however, both groups were hungry and the truck which would bring food was stuck, they pulled together; similarly, when the staff had sabotaged the water supply, the groups concerted to locate and relieve the impediment. Subsequently, their ratings of members of the other group became substantially more favorable.

Superordinate goals appear at other levels of interaction as well. LeVine (1961) notes their use in controlling conflict between primitive societies through the inclusion of other communities in the primary descent group. Recognition of a common ancestor by male members of contiguous communities makes homicide equivalent to fratricide, and "punishable by the ancestor spirits if reparations are not paid" (LeVine, 1961, p. 12). In labor-management relations, there are often goals to which both parties subscribe (procedural rules for negotiation, desire to avoid a strike). Another superordinate goal is the pursuit of science—as Rabinowitch (1964) asserts, ". . . the first common enterprise of mankind" (p. 246). That scientific knowledge cannot long be the province of one nation alone promotes such cooperative explorations as the scientific development of Antarctica, the International Geophysical Year, and the International Year of the Quiet Sun.

Another common goal at the international level is suggested by Riker (1962), who characterizes contemporary international relations as the "age of maneuver," in which the main though perhaps implicit goal for both major powers is simply ". . . the prolongation of the age for the greatest possible duration . . . since the end of the age is likely also to be the end of the leadership of both powers . . ." (p. 238). Thus they illustrate a supranational communality of goals, in their joint desire to avoid nuclear war and to control the price paid in the continuing negotiation for allies.

Another type of objective communality occurs when two parties have complementary goals. Through certain activities, such as international trade, reciprocal benefits may accrue from a meshing of the varying needs and capabilities of different nations. This phenomenon of reciprocal advantage operates at many levels. In analyzing the costs and rewards of interpersonal behavior, Homans (1961) declares, "The open secret of human exchange is to give the other man behavior that is more valuable to him than it is costly to you and to get from him behavior that is more valuable to you than it is costly to him" (p. 62). In dealing with the Soviet Union, Milburn (1964) advocates that the United States employ, ". . . along with the threat of nuclear retaliation . . . a system of rewards or encouragements for actions which are consistent with, or at least certainly not detrimental to, United States goals" (p. 186).

Krauss (1963) experimentally induced interdependence of goals by adding to or subtracting from a subject's reward 20 percent of the other's reward. In a game where subjects' (symbolic) trucks must share a one-way road (which either player could block by closing a gate) or traverse a much longer path, pairs of subjects reached their destinations significantly sooner when each had a positive stake in the other's welfare. Thus Krauss established a *situation* in which a person necessarily has a positive stake in the other's welfare; it is also possible to assess, as an individual *personality* characteristic, the extent to which an individual values the welfare of another in relation to his own. The Altruism Scale (Sawyer, 1964) measures an individual's orientation toward the welfare of another on a dimension ranging from pure co-operation through individualism to pure competition; on this scale, YMCA college students are more cooperative, business students more individualistic, and social science students tend more to reward friends but punish enemies.

Communality of goals, in situations like the preceding ones, is influential in negotiation not only as an actuality, but also in the way it is perceived. Yet perceived and actual communality of goals may differ widely. Parties to a conflict may subjectively define their interests in such a way as to be mutually incompatible. Each party may desire not merely to be strong, but strong*er* than the other, not just rich, but rich*er;* such relative goals are necessarily antagonistic, since they cannot simultaneously be achieved by both parties. The failure of experimental subjects to concert upon choices that would provide them the greatest payoff has been interpreted as due to an interest in obtaining more than the other person, even at a cost in the absolute amount of money received (Scodel, Minas, Ratoosh, & Lipetz, 1959; Minas, Scodel, Marlowe, & Rawson, 1960).

Even when there is actual agreement, it may not be perceived. Such was the case in an experiment involving two groups offering competing solutions to a given problem. After members of each group had indicated that they were completely familiar with the solution proposed by the other, Blake and Mouton (1961b) presented them with statements of four kinds: statements common to both solutions, statements occurring in either one or the other, and statements occurring in neither solution. In ten repetitions of this experiment, eighteen of the twenty groups mistakenly identified statements common to both solutions as solely their own, thus underestimating actual agreement; only two groups misidentified common statements as solely the other's. In international negotiation it seems likely that exact agreement of actual and perceived communality of goals is rare; such discrepancy may have important consequences.

Specificity of Goals

It seems reasonable that negotiation involving broad, loosely defined goals would differ from that involving more specific goals. As then Foreign Minister Pearson of Canada noted, if you are unclear in the definition of your goals, ". . . you are not likely to be clear in their expression" (1959, p. 49).

Generality and long-time perspective appear to contribute to vagueness of goals; it is easier to be precise concerning given situations and times. Yet among a number of reasonably well defined, short-run goals particular to different given situations there may be considerable inconsistencies; this is the situation confronting a major power with global interests. To rationalize such a range of goals requires a highly general statement, such as that of the United States President's Commission on National Goals (1960, pp. 15–20).

In guiding particular negotiations, specific goals may often be more crucial than general principles: Schokking and Anderson (1960) assert that the Coal and Steel Community and the Common Market were achieved less through the high ideals of European integration than by the practical economic gains that motivated continuing negotiation and accommodation on specific points.

Vagueness and generality of goals is sometimes associated with the presence of an all-encompassing ideology. Disagreement may thus be extended from a conflict of interest to a conflict of values, arising not from scarcity but from ". . . dissensus concerning the normative value of a social object" (Aubert, 1963, p. 29). Such is the case in a "struggle for men's minds" in which competing systems each aspire to impose their moral codes universally.

Kaplan and Katzenbach (1961) note that "unlimited objectives" on the part of nations ". . . stir the antagonism or opposition of others . . ." (p. 344). Berkowitz (1962), in reviewing evidence on intergroup hostility, notes further that ". . . whether or not there is any active proselytizing on the part of the ideology, or any desire to press the beliefs onto others, people maintaining opposing beliefs frequently are threatened by the very existence of the rival system" (p. 171). In the first place, universalistic ideology, even if it is not actively expansionist at the moment, is always a potential threat to become so. Moreover, the very existence of an apparently viable opposing ideology may make a person less certain of his own beliefs. When, as with ideology, objective validity is difficult to assess, the dissonance of continued counter-assertion may be highly disconcerting; as Berkowitz concludes, ". . . aggressive tendencies are aroused and directed toward the perceived source of the frustration—the people proclaiming the opposing opinions" (p. 177). Such behavior appears consistent with R. E. Osgood's analysis of the interaction of political ends and military means in Europe since the seventeenth century, in which he concludes that unlimited goals tend to produce unlimited violence—that the diplomacy of negotiation fails ". . . in the absence of a guiding political decision to pursue limited objectives" (1957, p. 62).

THE PROCESS OF NEGOTIATION

The prospect of achieving their interdependent goals through negotiation leads nations to the process itself. The process of negotiation includes all actions or communications, by any party to the negotiation, either made within the negotiating situation or intended to influence its outcome. Steps in this process, as treated in the following sections, include (a) preliminary negotiation concerning procedure and agenda, (b) formulation of alternatives and preferences of each party into a joint decision matrix, (c) communication and persuasion intended to alter the other party's perception of the situation, and (d) threats and promises, *faits accomplis,* and creative problem-solving activity intended to narrow or widen the range of available outcomes and alternatives.

Preparation for Negotiation

Specific motivations to seek negotiation include impending expiration of a previous agreement (such as a lease of a foreign location for a defense base), the development (often through technological advance) of a previously inconsequential or nonexistent area (such as production of fissionable materials), and specific political acts of another nation (such as violation of an existing agreement). Changing circumstances such as these may initiate a sequence of procedural negotiation, agenda development, and finally, a decision to enter upon substantive negotiation.

Procedural Negotiation. At the Peace of Westphalia in 1648, it took six months for delegates to decide in what order they should enter and be seated in the negotiating chamber (Durant & Durant, 1960). Three centuries later, at the Potsdam Conference of 1945, Churchill, Stalin, and Truman were able to agree upon a mode of entering the conference room only by arranging to emerge simultaneously from three separate doors (Morgenthau, 1960). Such continuing concern illustrates and attests to the importance of procedural

matters in negotiation. If granting precedence in entering a room is an acknowledgment of general superiority, then it will be resisted as prejudicial to ensuing negotiation. To obviate such questions by arbitrary procedures (like alphabetical seating) is a major end of formal diplomatic protocol, such as represented in Satow's *Guide to diplomatic practice* (1957).

Other questions of procedure include the number and rank of participants to represent a party, the length and frequency of sessions, the languages to be employed (treated separately later), and the rules by which discussion is to proceed. Any of these arrangements may have an influence upon later negotiation, and consequently, particularly if the stakes in the eventual substantive negotiation are large, much time may be consumed in this stage. When problems of *how* negotiation is to be conducted are settled, however, attention may be concentrated upon the question of specifically *what* is to be negotiated.

Agenda Development. Starting with proposals from each party for issues to be negotiated, the parties must jointly decide which issues shall constitute the agenda. The choice is critical, as it influences the outcome of negotiation itself; Schattschneider (1957), referring to domestic politics, asserts that, "The definition of alternatives is the supreme instrument of power . . . [it] is the choice of conflicts, and the choice of conflict allocates power" (p. 937). For this reason, many higher-level officials will enter negotiation only after the agenda has been specified.

Agenda vary markedly in the number of issues they contain, and advantages can be cited for both the long and the short. Narrow agenda may confine negotiation to that area that has best promise of resolution and prevent jeopardizing it by unduly contentious items. However, upon any single issue, parties are likely to reach alternatives in which their interests are strictly opposed, and relative gain by one implies relative loss by the other. As Rusk (1955, p. 129) observed of debate in the United Nations, the tendency to isolate issues makes them more difficult to adjust. Through widening the agenda to include unrelated items, it may be possible to effect trading, in which, for each party, losses in one area are balanced by gains in another. The large number of contract clauses considered simultaneously in labor-management negotiation serves this function. A wider agenda may also provide room for placing less controversial issues at the beginning, as suggested by Sharp (1953), to permit group procedure to develop more fully before critical matters are treated.

The Decision to Enter Negotiation. Given the prospective agenda, the parties make a decision (perhaps implicit) to go ahead with substantive negotiation at that time, to postpone negotiation, or to call it off altogether. To enter negotiation implies expectation of a better result from participating than from refraining, whether based upon the motivations for delay or propaganda characterized earlier or upon the expected outcome of the negotiation itself. To evaluate the expected benefit from negotiation involves assessment of possible outcomes in relation to original national goals, a task commonly reserved for higher policy officials, though the creation of alternatives is often a function of staff persons at lower levels. The highlighting of alternatives is emphasized by Black (1960) in discussing the role of the World Bank; the prime task, he asserts, of diplomats involved in economic development is ". . . to illumi-

nate the choices . . . and to provide evidence on which the decision-makers can weigh the benefits and costs of alternative courses of action" (pp. 24–25). If the evaluation of prospective outcomes is favorable, negotiation will generally ensue, though even then the rules of procedure, the agenda, and the specific alternatives may continue to evolve.

Intersection of Alternatives and Utilities

At the onset of negotiation, the situation may be conceptualized in terms of four main elements: (a) the negotiating parties, (b) the alternative actions that might be taken by each party, (c) the various outcomes expected to result from their combined actions, and (d) the utility each party ascribes to each of the various outcomes. Such a formulation, derived from the theory of games, has proven highly stimulating of both theory and empirical research dealing with interaction situations, not only in the field of economics (Shubik, 1959), which originally motivated game theory (Von Neumann & Morgenstern, 1944), but in other social sciences as well, including both social psychology (Rapoport, 1960; Thibaut & Kelley, 1959) and international relations (Kaplan, 1957; Schelling, 1960). In the following two sections, game theoretic models are articulated with international negotiation; then empirical evidence of actual choice in such game situations is presented.

The Decision Matrix. The four elements of parties, alternatives, outcomes, and utilities may profitably be placed in matrix form, of which Figure 13.2 provides a highly simplified example. Consider two nations, A and B, negotiating over possible reduction in tariffs.

For purposes of illustration, let Nation A have but two alternative actions that it might eventually take (though game theory can accommodate any number of alternatives): to reduce its tariff on the commodity in question to a lower "compromise" level, or to "hold out" at the present higher level. These two alternatives are represented by the first and second rows of the matrix. Nation

formulation as here illustrated with tariffs may also be applied to a much wider range of interaction situations. The alternatives at stake could just as well involve the number of inspections of suspected nuclear explosions, the terms of a development loan, or the size and extent of cultural exchanges.

In the illustration involving tariffs, if each nation can take either action,

Alternatives for Nation B / *Alternatives for Nation A*	HOLD OUT for present high tariff	Lower tariff to a COMPROMISE level
HOLD OUT for present high tariff	*Outcome* Status quo: both tariffs remain high *Utility* 0 for A 0 for B	*Outcome* A's tariff remains high B's tariff lowered *Utility* +10 for A -5 for B
Lower tariff to a COMPROMISE level	*Outcome* A's tariff lowered B's tariff remains high *Utility* -5 for A +10 for B	*Outcome* Both tariffs are lowered *Utility* +5 for A +5 for B

Fig. 13.2. Illustrative matrix of outcomes and utilities when each of two nations may alternatively lower its tariff to a "compromise" level or "hold out" at the present high level

B has two corresponding alternatives, represented by the two columns.

Designation of the alternatives as "compromise" and "hold out" is intended to suggest that such a matrix

independently of the other, there are four possible outcomes, as indicated in the four cells of the matrix: both tariffs may be lowered, only A's may be lowered, only B's may be lowered, or both may remain high. Let each of these four outcomes have a certain utility for each party, as shown by the numbers in Figure 13.2. The status quo of the existing higher tariffs is taken as a reference point, so that this outcome has zero utility for each party. The utilities of the other outcomes are shown as incremental amounts over the utility of the status quo; the negative utility for a nation when it alone lowers its tariff represents a worsening over the status quo for that nation.

It is important to note that the sum of the utilities to the two parties is higher for some outcomes than for others; in other words, this matrix belongs to the class referred to as non-constant-sum (or non-zero-sum). These are to be distinguished from zero-sum situations, in which one party gains only at the direct expense of the other; in such situations, negotiation is pointless. When some outcomes are better for both parties, however, and some worse, negotiation offers promise; it is these situations with which the present analysis is concerned.

The utilities in a decision matrix represent the over-all value placed upon the particular outcomes. In some cases, it is possible to translate this directly into monetary terms; for example, the values given in Figure 13.2 might represent millions of dollars. More commonly, political and other values for which, unlike money, there is no standard metric, do not permit such ready translation between objective and subjective utility measures. In practice, then, utility of outcomes is generally assessed by the judgmental evaluation of policy officials, as described earlier. In any event, utility is taken, both operationally and conceptually, to correspond directly to preference; outcomes of higher utility are those that are more highly preferred, and vice versa. The correspondence, though, is strictly definitional: Higher utilities do not "cause" higher preferences.

It is the resulting matrix of utility values that makes explicit the "intersecting alternatives and utilities" with which the present section is concerned. This matrix specifies the way in which the utility experienced by each party depends upon the choices of both, thus promoting the ability of a party to understand how it may achieve as good an outcome as possible, given that the other party is trying to do the same.

In the present example, the best outcome for either nation occurs when it retains high tariffs while the other nation reduces its tariffs. Regardless of whether the other nation retains or lowers its tariffs, however, it is better for a nation to retain its own at the high level. (For example, if B retains its tariffs, A prefers 0 to −5; if B has lowered its tariffs, A prefers 10 to 5.) Yet if each nation adopts this orientation and independently chooses to retain its current high tariffs, the result is the status quo, which both prefer less than a mutual reduction. Thus, such a choice situation presents a dilemma, in that two parties, each choosing independently to its own advantage, together produce an outcome neither prefers.[1] The way out of such a dilemma, of course, is for the

---

[1] Some economists argue that unilateral tariff reduction benefits a nation, regardless of the actions of other nations—which says that the utilities in the illustrative matrix misrepresent the actual value that would be derived. Nonetheless, the reluctance of nations to reduce tariffs implies they do not perceive such unconditional gain—and it is their *perception,* right or wrong, that determines their decisions.

When perceived utilities *are* as in Figure 13.2, the situation, given another context, is the "Prisoner's Dilemma" (Luce & Raiffa, 1957), whose peculiarly self-defeating characteristics

choices to be not independent, but rather the result of mutual agreement. For analyzing this more complex but more realistic case of non-independent choices, a graphical representation is particularly illuminating.

The Negotiation Graph. When choices are made jointly rather than

trasted with a *negotiation graph* of jointly selected outcomes. The four outcomes of our example are plotted in the negotiation graph of Figure 13.3 according to the utility each outcome possesses for A and for B. In this formulation the special character of "both holding out" is readily apparent; for this outcome alone, the utility of *both* par-

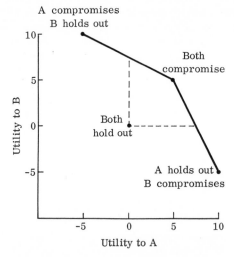

Fig. 13.3. Graph of illustrative utilities for the four possible outcomes when each of two interacting parties has the alternatives of "compromising" and of "holding out"

independently, it is useful to regard them as being made among outcomes (four, in the tariff example) rather than between the (two) alternative actions. Thus a *decision matrix* of independently chosen alternatives may be con-

ties could be increased by choosing another outcome. Among the other three outcomes, however, an increase in the utility for one party necessarily means a decrease in the utility for the other; thus these three points are Pareto

have stimulated much theoretical and empirical investigation, some of which is later analyzed. The context of the original formulation involves two prisoners, whom the district attorney knows to be guilty, though he lacks the evidence to convict. He holds the two prisoners separately and tells each that if he confesses and the other does not, he will be given but a very light sentence for turning state's evidence whereas the other will receive a maximum sentence. If both confess, each will receive heavy sentences, though less than maximum. If neither confesses, the district attorney will press other minor but provable charges which would result in moderately light sentences for each. Thus, choosing independently, each prisoner finds it better to confess, regardless of whether he expects the other to confess or not.

optima, and the parties might be expected to restrict their bargaining to them. Each point represents the best outcome a party can achieve given a particular level of outcome for the other; together they define the "utility frontier" (Bishop, 1963), "social optima" (Pareto, 1909), or "contract curve" (Edgeworth, 1881).

For any point that is not Pareto-optimal, another point can be found providing greater utility for one party without decreasing the utility for the other. Hence, bargaining "solutions" widely assume that parties will settle upon one of these Pareto optima. A further restriction to the outcomes among which negotiation takes place is furnished by the minimum guarantee to each party by acting unilaterally. In the example of Figures 13.2 and 13.3, either party can, by holding out, guarantee himself an outcome no worse than the status quo (whereas if he compromises unilaterally, he may lose 5).

Consequently, it is reasonable to assume that negotiation is further restricted to those outcomes whose utility at least equals that of the status quo resulting from no agreement; such outcomes compose the "negotiation set" (Luce & Raiffa, 1957). In Figure 13.3, the negotiation set includes only the mutual compromise. However, formulation of alternatives in the form of a graph makes obvious the possibility for intermediate actions and outcomes; tariffs could be cut by varying amounts, creating a nearly continuous set of outcomes falling in the area of the line connecting the three points in Figure 13.3. The utility frontier would then probably take the form of a curve, concave toward the origin.

On this essentially continuous utility frontier, the negotiation set would comprise that portion (encompassed by the dotted lines in Figure 13.3) where neither party's outcome is worse than the status quo. Within the negotiation set, however, many outcomes are possible and among these neither practicing negotiators nor game theorists are presently able to specify universally accepted principles of choice, though game theory has developed one more or less plausible solution, presented later in the section on outcome. In the absence of a definitive theoretical solution to negotiation, it is profitable to ascertain empirically what outcomes result in practice. A number of experiments using a game-theory formulation have been conducted, most of them employing the procedure of subjects independently selecting alternative actions in a matrix rather than that of jointly negotiating over outcomes.

Actual Choice in Conflict Situations. Using a Prisoner's Dilemma game matrix where the preferences for outcomes were similar to those in Figure 13.2, Deutsch (1958) found that his subjects, in line with the rationale presented above, tended to hold out: 64 percent of subjects, instructed simply to maximize their own reward, chose this strategy. Similarly competitive results have been found by Scodel, Minas, Ratoosh, and Lipetz (1959), Minas, Scodel, Marlowe, and Rawson (1960), and others.

When choice in conflict situations is repeated over a number of occasions, even though each choice is made in ignorance of the other's immediate choice at that time, it is no longer clearly best to adopt the "hold out" strategy. Even in the absence of formal communication, tacit communication may permit concerting upon the joint compromise that each prefers to lack of agreement. Such a process may take some time. In from ten to fifty repetitions, Scodel *et al.* (1959), Deutsch (1958), Minas *et al.* (1960), and Rapoport (1963) each found stable or declining probabilities of choosing the compromise response; but when Rapoport continued his observations for another 250 to 650 trials, he found the compromise response to rise to substantially above the initial level.

Like repeated sessions, communality of goals also promotes choice of the compromise alternative. Pilisuk and Rapoport (1964) employed seven different Prisoner's Dilemma matrices that varied in the relative utilities resulting from joint compromise, from lack of agreement, and from one party holding out while the other compromised. They found the proportion of persons choosing the compromise solution to increase consistently as the conflict in goals became less pronounced.

Even where there is some communality of goals, however, if there is sufficient negative feeling between the parties, they may redefine the matrix of outcomes as a zero-sum situation by looking, in effect, at the difference in utilities to each, rather than at their absolute level. The prime concern of each party, then, is simply to obtain an outcome relatively better than that of the other, even if neither outcome is particularly desirable. This has frequently been the case at the termination of a war, when the absolute welfare of the winning as well as of the losing party was less than it would have been in the absence of a war, or sometimes even less than in the prewar state.

An increase in a zero-sum or competitive orientation can also arise when the absolute level of the utilities is small. It seems quite possible that "winning"—getting more than the other by trying to force him to compromise while holding out oneself—might be valued more when there is little or no absolute reward. To get 100 points in a parlor game is good or bad only in relation to what others receive. But to get $100 is good, regardless of what others receive.

The relatively high level of non-compromising choice in the preceding experiments has in every case been in a situation in which the monetary reward was nil or negligible. The few experiments using larger rewards find substantially more cooperative results. Using a Prisoner's Dilemma matrix similar to the preceding (though employing many alternatives rather than only two), Messé and Sawyer (1964) found an unexpectedly high degree of cooperation, which they attributed in part to rewards that, particularly to subjects of ages thirteen and seventeen, appeared rather large: from 0 to 75 cents for each of ten trials. Siegel and Fouraker (1960), in an experiment on bilateral monopoly also employing sizeable rewards, likewise found subjects concerting upon the alternatives that maximized their joint reward. Subjects could agree to exchange any number of units between one and thirty; but when each subject knew both his own and the other's reward structure, the average discrepancy from the Pareto-optimal solution of exchanging exactly nine units was less than one-fifth of a unit. Even when neither subject knew the reward structure for the other, the discrepancy from the Pareto optimum was only one and one-quarter units.

Though the findings just referred to all derive from experimental research, at least one large-scale test of a game theory model in actual political decisions has been conducted. In the three-member districts of the Illinois House of Representatives, committees from each party decide to run either one, two, or three candidates, thus creating a situation that can be modeled by a 3×3 matrix, in which the rows and columns indicate the number of candidates nominated by each party, and the cell entries indicate the number elected, presumably representing the utility of that outcome. The model specifying the number of candidates a party should run, given the expected distribution of the vote, predicted the actual decisions in 69 percent of the more than 1300 elections between 1902 and 1954 (Sawyer & MacRae, 1962).

At the level of international relations, Zinnes, North, and Koch (1961) record how "hold-out" strategies were employed during the negotiation of July 1914 between the Allies and the Central Powers in which the world situation was defined essentially as a Prisoner's Dilemma. Feeling grievously ". . . trapped, by a 'hated, lying, conscienceless nation of shopkeepers,' Germany would go down fighting nevertheless. For the Kaiser asserted [in a note jotted in the margin of a diplomatic report of July 30th] '. . . if we are bled to death, England shall at least lose India'" (p. 496).

Dynamic Alternatives and Utilities. In virtually all the analyses of interacting alternatives and utilities just considered—theoretical and empirical alike—both alternatives and utilities for outcomes have been assumed, explicitly or implicitly, to be completely static. In an experiment, for example, this assumption may be reflected by a fixed matrix in which there is no opportunity over the course of interaction for change either in the utilities in the cells of the matrix or in the alternatives represented by the rows and columns. Yet such a static situation, while providing a basic formulation for negotiation, is rare in practice.

Two modifications of the basic situation, more common in practice, are (a) those in which utilities for outcomes may change during the course of negotiation, though alternatives remain fixed, and (b) those in which alternatives themselves may also be added, modified, or eliminated. Thus change results either in the utility entries in the matrix, or in the defining rows and columns themselves, producing in either case a new matrix. These two

important cases provide the foci for the remaining two sections dealing with process; they are, indeed, the core of what is generally taken as the central process of negotiation—reciprocal argument and counterargument, proposal and counterproposal, in an attempt to agree upon actions and outcomes mutually perceived as beneficial. We shall first examine communication and persuasion—processes fundamental to changing utilities, and then turn to processes of a creative or problem-solving nature leading to modified alternatives. (See Chapter 10 for a discussion of some conditions under which these two approaches are selected as strategies of international conflict resolution.)

Modification of Utilities: Communication and Persuasion

To change the utilities certain outcomes hold for the other party is frequently a major interim goal for a negotiator, for if the other party can be made to value more highly the outcomes one prefers himself, the probability of obtaining these is increased. Communication and persuasion, major agents in the process of modifying utilities, concern the way in which the arguments and proposals of each party are understood by the other.

Communication. Communication between parties to an international negotiation is complicated first of all by language. Shades of connotative differences and culturally specific meanings hinder effective translation. The critical concept, "to compromise," is illustrative: Both in English and in French, it has two principal meanings, yet their priority is reversed. Hence an American's request "to adjust and settle a difference by mutual agreement" might be interpreted by a Frenchman as a suggestion "to expose, to endanger, to embarrass (one's character, reputation, and so on)." If the Russian phrase whose literal translation is "We will bury you" and which connotes "We will outlive you" is instead interpreted "We will destroy you," quite different implications are perceived (Klineberg, 1964, p. 153).

The history of diplomatic practice suggests that as the fullness of communication increases, negotiation becomes easier. For example, of diplomatic communication in the nineteenth century, Prime Minister Gladstone observed that, "Personal and domestic relations with the ruling families abroad give openings, in delicate cases, for saying more, and saying it at once more gently and more efficaciously than could be ventured in the more formal correspondence and under contacts of governments" (Nicolson, 1939, p. 67). At the other extreme, Schelling and Halperin (1961) point out how confusing it may be to employ silence as "a mode of communication." They note that, ". . . failure to deny rumors, refusal to answer questions, attempts to take emphasis away from certain issues, all tend to communicate something . . ." (p. 81) which may variously be revealing, deceptive, or confusing.

In laboratory experimentation, the Prisoner's Dilemma matrix has been employed to assess the effects of communication. Deutsch (1958) finds that among pairs of college students motivated to maximize their own reward, the opportunity to communicate is associated with an increase in the proportion choosing cooperatively from 13 to 59 percent. Using a similar situation, Loomis (1959) finds that students having more opportunity for communication not only behave more cooperatively but also express more trust in each other.

But the very conflict that negotiation might resolve may itself make communication more difficult to commence. As the result of another experiment, Deutsch and Krauss (1962) suggest that, "Where barriers to communication exist, a situation in which the parties are compelled to communicate will be more effective than one in which the choice to talk or not is put on a voluntary basis" (p. 75). The increasing activity of international organizations, such as the United Nations, provides considerable opportunity for communication, much of it of an informal nature where specific issues are not at stake or in public view and hence wider exploration of alternatives may be conducted (cf. Chapter 14).

Persuasion. The aim of much communication in negotiation is to persuade the other party that his self-interest is not what he thought, by providing information, interpretation, or implications that cause him to reassess the utility of various outcomes. This purported misevaluation may stem from three sources—the effect of the act itself upon its maker, the effect of consequent behavior by the other, and the effect of consequent behavior by third parties—thus furnishing a persuader three somewhat distinct appeals:

1. Intrinsic interest: You should want to do this, for its direct benefit, which possibly you do not fully perceive. "Lower tariffs will permit your people to buy imported goods more cheaply."

2. Second party effects (for example, threat of force): If you don't do it, I may do something you won't like. "If you do not lower your tariffs, we may raise ours."

3. Third party effects (for example, norms): Others want you to do so, and will give their approval. "Other countries will approve if you lower your tariffs." (This and the preceding case are most applicable in "variable-threat" bargaining [Bishop, 1963] in which, if

no agreement results, parties may take unilateral actions; if nonagreement simply preserves the status quo, persuasion may only appeal, as in case 1, to intrinsic interest.)

Each of these appeals, if successful, would result in the reappraisal of the values of certain outcomes, so that a party's self-interest might dictate different choices than before.

Self-interest, in diplomacy and elsewhere, has been a durable concept. In 1716, Callieres enjoined diplomats to "make each proposition which you put forward appear as a statement of the interests of those with whom you are negotiating, for since diplomacy is the attempt to find a basis for common action or agreement, it is obvious that the more the opposing party can be brought to see your designs in their own light and to accept them thus, the more surely will their cooperation for any action be fruitful alike to themselves and to you" (1919, p. 122–123).

The modification of utilities by the most skillful diplomatic persuasion, however, will seldom result in situations in which the most favored outcome of one party is also the most favored outcome of the other. Rather there will usually remain, not a single Pareto point, but several, and in choosing among these one party gains only at the loss of the other. At this point, bargaining often becomes a matter of trying to establish what is the least the other will take and convincing him that that is the most one will give.

The least favorable terms a party will accept in preference to lack of agreement is thus a crucial concept; it enters into analysis of competition between firms as the "threat point" (Bishop, 1963), of labor-management relations as the "resistance points" (Walton & McKersie, 1965), and of political negotiation as the "minimum disposition" (Iklé & Leites, 1962). A lower limit to the minimum disposition is often formed by the value of the status quo. In Figure 13.2, for example, the minimum disposition for each might be the value of 0 from mutual holding out; each of the unilateral compromises then falls below the minimum disposition of one or the other party.

Thus it is important that each party estimate not only its own "minimum disposition," but also that of the other party. Yet the minimum dispositions of the two parties are clearly related; how much one will take depends in part upon how much the other will give. Consequently, knowing that the other party is making a similar estimate, I may try to modify his minimum disposition ". . . to make him believe or feel that he would prefer an agreement to no agreement on terms more favorable to me than he originally thought. . . . (1) By altering the actual situation on which his Minimum Disposition is based. . . . (2) By pointing out the advantages and minimizing the disadvantages of my proposed terms. . . . (3) By conveying to my opponent (actual or faked) estimates of his Minimum Disposition, and (4) By portraying to my opponent a certain intrinsic development of the negotiations and convincing him that the *Negotiation Mores* require that he follow this development" (Iklé & Leites, 1962, p. 23).

I may also attempt to modify the other's estimate of my own minimum disposition "(1) By altering the actual situation on which my opponent's estimate of my Minimum Disposition is based. . . . (2) By convincing my opponent that it would be disastrous or impossible for me to agree to less than my proposed terms. . . . (3) By exhibiting attitudes consistent with a Minimum Disposition more favorable than my opponent's estimates" (Iklé & Leites, 1962, p. 24).

A related question is whether one should advance a "sham bargaining position" which one thinks the other considers less favorable than his minimum disposition (as with "blue sky" proposals in labor-management negotiation). Advantage may accrue if the other's minimum disposition is initially lower than thought or if simply forwarding the sham position lowers the other's minimum disposition; further, a sham position leaves more room for expected "concessions" and also makes it more difficult for the other to estimate one's own minimum disposition. On the other hand, it may be difficult to obtain public support for extreme positions, and if such support is obtained the other may think agreement is impossible and discontinue negotiation; in any event agreement may be delayed and concessions from a sham position may set precedent for future real concessions. The abundant rationale both for and against sham positions strongly suggests need for systematic empirical test.

Psychological experimentation has explored the related concept of "level of aspiration," which may be a factor in determining initial minimum disposition and rates of concession from the initial position. Siegel and Fouraker (1960) operationalized this concept by telling one member of a bargaining pair that if he achieved $6.10, he could participate in the second part, in which he would have a chance to double his winnings; the other subject was told the same, but the amount specified was $2.10. In an otherwise symmetrical situation, the former group averaged $6.25, the latter $3.25. On the basis of empirical and rational analyses, Siegel and Fouraker suggest that ". . . the bargainer who (1) opens negotiations with a high request, (2) has a small rate of concession, (3) has a high minimum level of expectation, and (4) is very perceptive and quite unyielding, will

fare better than his opponent who provides the base upon which these relative evaluations were made" (p. 93). Some of the same principles are applied to international negotiation by Kissinger (1960), who argues that ". . . effectiveness at the conference table depends on overstating one's demands" and on the other hand, "If we make proposals in which we really believe, we must inevitably be somewhat rigid about them" (p. 205).

A party's communications are more likely to be effective in modifying the utilities of the other if the party is regarded as a credible source (Hovland, Janis, & Kelley, 1953, Ch. 2); this can vary both among nations and among various offices and individuals within a nation. In addition, Aronson, Turner, and Carlsmith (1963) found that for persons reading a communication attributed to a highly credible source, the more discrepant the communication from their own opinion, the more they changed (consonant with Kissinger's assertion). For persons exposed to the same communication attributed, however, to a source of only moderate credibility, increasing discrepancy led to increased change only to a point; as discrepancy became extreme, opinion change decreased.

Thus it appears that the effectiveness of sham bargaining positions, and possibly of other tactics of communication and persuasion, may depend markedly upon the circumstances under which they are employed. One of the most important of these circumstances concerns just what alternatives are available to each party; the following section explores how alternatives themselves may be changed.

Modification of Alternatives

If modifications are considered to be of two kinds—those that only subtract from the available set of alternatives, and those that add as well as possibly subtract—successful threats, promises, and *faits accomplis* are of the first kind, and creative problem-solving approaches are of the second kind. Which may be called for depends, as we shall see, on the initial state of the decision matrix of alternatives and preferences.

Threats and Promises. A threat is a representation that if another party acts in a way one disfavors, one will take an action detrimental to the other. It is important, however, that the other party be convinced that the detrimental action will not also be taken even if he complies. For this reason, as pointed out by Schelling (1960), a threatened action must be detrimental not only to the recipient, but to the initiator as well. The threat of massive retaliation furnishes an example: Its purpose (as that of threats generally) is to deter; but whether it succeeds or fails in deterring, the initiator has no immediate motivation to carry out the threat, since it harms him as well as the other.

The logical structure of promises is essentially similar to that of threats. Promises are representations that if the other behaves in a way one favors, one will then take an action beneficial to the other, even though one would then prefer not to do so. In the Prisoner's Dilemma matrix of Figure 13.2, B, if he is choosing after A, may induce a cooperative solution of 5 to each by making an enforceable promise that he will choose his compromise alternative if A has chosen his, though in fact B would then prefer to choose to hold out, gaining 10.

Thus, in either threats or promises, one represents that given certain action by the other, meant to be deterred or induced, he will choose against his own immediate welfare. For such a representation to be credible, a party must have a way of demonstrating to the other that he would in fact be

bound (by honor, public opinion, or other restraints) to carry out the otherwise undesired action; it will be most convincing, indeed, if he can show the other how the carrying out is an automatic consequence of the other's action, in which no intervention is possible.

Liska (1960) emphasizes, in the area of foreign aid, the importance of the credibility of threatened withdrawal of aid, pointing out that, "The policy of aid and its results will suffer as long as any existing alliance or strategic facility is treated as indispensable"; he concludes that, "To demonstrate American nondependence and alternatives repeatedly, even at great economic and political cost in the individual instance, is the greatest single requirement of an effective policy . . ." (p.33).

If a threat or promise is sufficiently credible for the party who is its target to believe that it would actually be carried out, then it should have the primary effect intended: effectively to reduce the possibilities with which the party is confronted. (The reduction actually occurs directly in outcomes: The target party knows that if he chooses a certain alternative, only an undesired outcome is possible; then effectively that entire alternative is eliminated.) Thus the result is a reduced matrix of alternatives and preferences defining a different interaction situation.

Deutsch and Krauss (1960, 1962) have examined experimentally the effect of threat upon interpersonal bargaining, using the "trucking game" where the optimal solution is for the two persons both to use the main one-way road, alternating as to who goes first. In one experimental condition, each person had a gate that he could close, blocking the main road; in another condition, only one person had such a gate; in the third, neither had a gate. The threat that presumably could be implicitly conveyed to the other is

"If you don't let me use the main one-way road first, I'll close my gate, forcing us both to take our private [longer, less rewarding] roads." Results showed the possession of a gate to be deleterious. Whereas average earnings were positive when neither had a gate, they were negative when one did, and more negative when both did.

It may appear surprising that the party having the sole gate fared more poorly than the two parties in the condition in which neither had a gate, since the person with the sole gate should be able to force the other to choose between going second on the main road or taking his longer alternate road. (Actually, however, the party lacking a gate also blocks, whenever his truck is on the main road.) It seems unlikely, however, that subjects clearly perceived and unequivocally communicated the full potentiality for the use of threat, and hence this experiment does not provide a test of Schelling's (1960) analysis.

It does seem to imply, however, that subjects were not sufficiently "rational" either to employ appropriately or to disregard a potentially detrimental device; rather they used it with substantial frequency and to their considerable loss. Deutsch and Krauss (1960) suggest the detriment arises from ". . . the cultural interpretation of yielding (to a peer or subordinate) under duress . . . perceived as a negatively valued form of behavior with negative implications for the self-image . . . because the locus of causality is perceived to be outside the person's voluntary control" (p. 188). At the international level, yielding may also be valued negatively, as illustrated earlier by the Kaiser's reaction to the Allied powers. And speaking out of his experience with seventeenth- and eighteenth-century diplomacy, Callieres observed "Menaces always do harm to negotiation and they frequently push one party to extremities to which they would not have resorted without provocation. It is well known that injured vanity frequently drives men into courses which a sober estimate of their own interests would lead them to avoid" (1919, p. 125).

Meeker, Shure, and Moore (1964), in a near-replication of Deutsch and Krauss (1960), similarly found that among pairs of persons both having the capability of threat, those in which neither employed it achieved better outcomes. In exploring further for explanations, they found the achievement of good outcomes in these cases to be associated largely with the initial expectation by both subjects of winning exactly 50 percent of the reward (that is, with cooperative pre-game dispositions on the part of both subjects). Among pairs of subjects who failed to reach a cooperative agreement within the first five trials, however, those using the threat *more* during that time were more likely to reach cooperative agreement eventually. The authors suggest that delay by an initially conciliatory subject "in responding to a threat with a counterthreat displays to the aggressive member a weak intention to resist and encourages him to persist in his original demands. These then become increasingly unacceptable to the conciliatory member" (p. 122). Further, among subjects who seek no more than 50 percent of the earnings, those who respond with a counterthreat within two trials of the other's threat are much more likely to achieve cooperative agreement.

Thus these results are somewhat more consistent with the theory of Schelling (1960) than are those of Deutsch and Krauss (1960); the partial incongruity of the results of these two experiments is indicative of the extent of added experimentation required for more complete and more definitive empirical assessment of the effect of threats and promises.

Fait Accompli. Like a successful threat or promise, a *fait accompli* reduces the decision matrix by eliminating as possibilities certain outcomes and alternatives. The result is likewise similar: The party who is the target is left with a situation in which his best outcomes are eliminated and the least undesirable of the remainder are just the ones preferred by the initiating party. If the target party then chooses to his advantage, the initiator benefits. The preemptory nature of the *fait accompli* may to such an extent antagonize its target, however, that punishing the other (even at one's own loss) becomes attractive—if only to discourage repetition.

As an illustration of the *fait accompli*, Lerche (1956) indicates how unilateral action by the United States in establishing SEATO minimized the extent of its compromise in reaching final agreement with Great Britain on the nature of the alliance.

The essential element of the *fait accompli* is the ability of one party to put the choice to the other on a "take it or leave it" basis. This situation has been represented experimentally by Joseph and Willis (1963), who contrasted "simultaneous" choice (where neither person knew the other's choice at the time he made his own) with sequential choice in which the second person could only accept the choice of the first, or reject it and thus cause both to receive nothing. Consistent with the above rationale, sequential choice resulted in greater inequality between the rewards of the two persons.

Creating New Alternatives. Frequently, two parties to negotiation will be confronted by a decision matrix in which there is no single outcome that both prefer to lack of agreement. Nego-

tiation will then necessarily fail unless higher utilities emerge, either through reassessment of existing outcomes or through development of new outcomes. The first possibility has been considered in connection with communication and persuasion. Often, however, the initial evaluations of outcomes have been made after extensive and public review, and consequently these may be little subject to modification, if only for the reason that otherwise the negotiators might be charged with abandoning their constituency.

Through the modification and addition of alternatives, though, it may be possible to create new outcomes on which agreement can be achieved, as did Churchill, Truman, and Stalin when they solved their problem of precedence in entering the Potsdam negotiating chamber by emerging simultaneously through three doors. New outcomes should, then, in comparison with prior outcomes, increase the utility for one party while, at the least, not decreasing that of the other; thus the utility frontier is extended beyond its previous location.

The process of devising more favorable alternatives and outcomes may be characterized as one of "creative problem-solving" since it involves innovation rather than mere selection among given possibilities. As with creative processes more generally, however, relatively little is understood of its operation. Although the characteristics and the development of creative individuals have been extensively investigated (Stein & Heinze, 1960; Taylor, 1964), only recently has much systematic attention been given to questions concerning the situational conditions and organizational processes that foster creativity (Steiner, 1965). To what extent, for example, is the development of new alternatives promoted by the formality or informality of the proceedings, the size and composition of the negotiating teams, or the degree of time pressure under which the negotiation occurs? May informal or unofficial meetings, like the Pugwash and later Conferences on Science and World Affairs, produce an environment in which a "game of ideas" can result in otherwise unexamined alternatives?

Among the few relevant aspects of group creativity in problem-solving that have been extensively studied is the effect of initial solicitation of a wide range of positions. In surveying several studies, Kelley and Thibaut (1954) concluded that ". . . there is good reason to believe that . . . multiplicity of opinion . . . is a very real basis for the formation of accurate and undistorted judgments within the group. . . . [For this reason] special techniques are sometimes used to maximize expressed heterogeneity in a group, such as that of taking a census of opinions or ideas at the beginning of a group discussion" (p. 722). The way in which such a census contributes is suggested by the work of Lorge, Davitz, Fox, and Herrold (1953); they find that the mode by which training in staff procedures improves group decisions is not through enhancing individual performance but simply through lowering the group's tendency to neglect member suggestions. This finding suggests a need to examine just how tightly the agenda should be set, so as to provide sufficient focus while simultaneously minimizing the loss of good alternatives. If, at the stage of agenda development, the chairman proposes many alternative solutions, greater final consensus is found to develop (Guetzkow & Gyr, 1954). In areas where many alternatives are easily available, this process is facilitated; perhaps the success of the periodic meetings on the General Agreement of Trade and Tariffs stems in part from the multiplicity of items that may be considered.

Given the degree of initial diversity of positions and alternatives, the progressive group interaction and climate further influence the group creativity. Fiedler (1962) examines the nature of interaction within 32 four-person groups seeking to produce three original and different stories for an ambiguous picture from the Thematic Apperception Test. Classifying all interaction into five categories and distinguishing groups as "tense" or "relaxed" on the basis of members' criticality of each other, Fiedler finds ". . . (a) that procedural and irrelevant comments tended to aid the creativity of relaxed groups but hindered tense groups; (b) the more task-oriented 'elaboration of ideas' and higher total activity aided the tense groups but not relaxed groups" (p. 315). This suggests the possible importance, for promoting creative solutions, of tailoring the kind of interaction to the degree of tension inherent in the situation. In this and other studies, Fiedler finds that "leaders who perceive their least preferred co-worker favorably tend to be most effective under pleasant and relaxed group conditions, while leaders who perceive . . . [their least preferred co-worker] unfavorably are more effective under unpleasant stressful group climates" (1962, p. 318). It may be, more generally, that broad acceptance is favorable under relaxed circumstances, sharp differentiation in more tense situations.

THE OUTCOME OF NEGOTIATION

Out of the matrix of modified alternatives and utilities resulting from the process of negotiation may eventually come resolution upon a specified outcome. In international negotiation, the form of these outcomes varies widely, from formal and highly explicit treaties to informal and often vague understandings, with the result sometimes being a virtual lack of any agreement at all. The degree of explicitness is one of the most crucial dimensions on which agreements vary, since it affects the influence they have on future conduct. Another important aspect is how "good" an outcome results, and in what senses this may be evaluated. Finally, it is important to note the continuing nature of negotiation. An outcome itself may provide stimulus for future negotiation and in any event has influence upon the larger continuing process of international relations. The following three sections treat these aspects of clarity of outcomes, criteria for outcomes, and their implications for continuity of negotiation.

Clarity of Outcomes

The extent to which outcomes may vary in explicitness is illustrated in the five forms Schelling and Halperin (1961) outline for arms control agreements, which include formal treaties with detailed specifications, executive agreements, explicit but informal understandings, tacit understandings, and mere self-restraint consciously contingent upon the other's behavior. Though these vary widely, even the most formal agreement cannot provide for all contingencies, or necessarily provide exact interpretation in each case. Yet specificity is often crucial; as Davison (1958) notes, the vagueness of the Potsdam agreement in 1945 permitted continuing disagreement among the great powers in interpreting the status of Berlin.

Imperfect clarity of outcomes may stem not from the difficulty of exhaustiveness but from the difficulty of agreement itself. Sometimes an ambiguously worded clause is purposely inserted to permit agreement where otherwise an entire negotiation would fail. The Convocation of Bishops in 1531 acquiesced in acknowledging Henry VIII "the protector and only supreme head of the Church and clergy of England" only after devising the phrase, ". . . so far as the law of Christ allows," thus satisfying themselves in principle and Henry in practice (Durant, 1957, p. 545). Where in effect the minimum dispositions of the parties do not overlap (that is, the least one will take exceeds the most the other will give), premature attempts at closure may create unnecessary acrimony. Rusk (1955) has suggested that the United Nations provide more effectively for the possibility of terminating debate without a resolution.

When there is sufficient consensus to arrive at a fairly definitive agreement, and clarity is desired, it is then important to concert upon an alternative that is eminently clear to all parties. Schelling (1960), in considering the effect of the prominence of an alternative, points out that the largely tacit agreement in World War II upon "*no* poison gas" was, among the many alternatives (limit its use to military personnel, or only with warning, and so on), the only completely unambiguous one.

Even in explicit negotiation, prominence furnishes a strong guide, as illustrated by the prevalence of rivers as territorial boundaries and of round numbers in the settlement of damage suits. In the negotiation of tariffs, an across-the-board reduction of constant percentages on all commodities is a highly prominent alternative; once this principle (often defended as that) is abandoned, it is difficult to justify any particular set of differential percentages.

Agreement over tariffs illustrates an important contrast with most outcomes of international negotiation, in that it involves a metric like money that is both more objective and more easily fractionated than the usual political incommensurables. For political practices, however, another strong source of prominent alternatives is precedent. Russell (1958) documents how frequently practices of the old League of Nations influenced the negotiations at Moscow, Cairo, Teheran, Dumbarton Oaks, and San Francisco that led to the United Nations Charter.

Criteria for Evaluating Outcomes

Whatever the clarity of the outcome, each party may place upon it at least an approximate value, if not a completely determinate one. Then the question may be asked, given the alternatives among which each party had to choose, and the values of their associated outcomes, "Is this a 'good' solution?" In a zero- or constant-sum game, the minimax theorem provides a definitive answer. There, each party has a minimax strategy which makes his minimum outcome as favorable as possible, regardless of the other's strategy, and if one party employs his minimax strategy, the other can do no better than to employ his also; as a result each receives exactly his guaranteed minimum. Though the minimax theorem does not hold generally in non-zero-sum games, its effect is illustrated in the matrix of Figure 13.2, where by holding out either party may guarantee himself no worse than the status quo, whereas to compromise means risking a loss.

No such compelling solution exists in the more realistic case of non-zero-sum negotiating situations. By making four assumptions, however, about the characteristics of a desirable allocation between the two parties, it is possible to derive a general solution. Nash (1950, 1953) proposes four assumptions, which he shows determine a unique solution: (a) Pareto optimality: no solution is acceptable if there is another giving one party a better outcome and the other no worse an outcome; (b) symmetry: if, when utilities are measured as the increment over the value of no agreement, there is for each outcome giving a utility of x to one party and y to the other another outcome giving the reverse utilities, then the solution gives equal utility to each party; (c) transformation invariance: an order-preserving linear transformation of either party's utility scale (such as doubling or adding a constant to the value of each outcome) does not change the solution; and (d) independence of irrelevant alternatives: if a new outcome is added, either the solution is unchanged or it becomes the new outcome. The unique solution determined by these four assumptions is simply that outcome for which the product of the utilities to the two parties is maximized, when each utility is taken as the increment over the value of no agreement.

In the graph of Figure 13.3, the product of the utilities for mutual compromise is 25, larger than the product of any other pair. Further, as rough illustration of Nash's assumptions, it can be observed that (a) this point is on the utility frontier, (b) it is on a 45-degree line from the origin which symmetrically bisects the set of points, (c) the product of the utilities at the mutual compromise would still be greatest were either party's utilities doubled, for example, and (d) no point between the three Pareto points or within their boundary has a higher product. Various criticisms can be made of Nash's last three assumptions; yet as Bishop (1963) points out, "The leading entrant among bargaining theories of the more orthodox game-theoretic type is unquestionably the one proposed by John Nash" (p. 563).

In some bargaining situations, assumption (c) seems particularly vulnerable; it asserts, for example, that there is no difference between a situation in which two parties are dividing one dollar between themselves (assuming linear utility for money) and a situation in which whatever portion one party receives will then be multiplied 100-fold from an outside source. White (in press) finds such assymmetry to make substantial difference when two persons are trying to agree on a choice among seven alternatives providing amounts to the first and second persons on the following scale: (0 to the first, 30 to the second), (1, 25), (2, 20), (3, 15), (4, 10), (5, 5), and (6, 0). Though the Nash solution is (3, 15), in practice the egalitarian solution of (5, 5) is frequently chosen, and occasionally the social-welfare solution of (0, 30) is selected.

In one sense, having formal principles providing generally agreed upon solutions may seem impossible or irrelevant, since, as suggested in considering modes of persuasion, each party may simply desire to convince the other that it will absolutely take no less than the maximum the other can give, and otherwise prefers nonagreement. Yet in the long run, the best solution may not be the one whose outcome provides most immediate utility, for as pointed out by Callieres in 1716 and frequently before and since, ". . . there is no durable treaty which is not founded on reciprocal advantage" (1919, p. 110). A nation should, in its own interest, be concerned that the other's outcome is sufficiently high to motivate him to keep the agreement. If one nation, by hard bargaining, succeeds in getting the other to accept an agreement providing an outcome only slightly above its minimum disposition, a small shift in the relative power of the two nations may cause the agreement to be unacceptable Many labor economists (for example, Hicks, 1948) and negotiators have stressed that the goal of arbitrators and mediators should not be to promote "fair" solutions (exceedingly difficult in any event, because of varying standards of what is "fair") but rather to achieve acceptable solutions that adequately reflect the respective power of each party, and hence are likely to be kept. Nash's analysis may be regarded as one attempt to specify such a solution.

Solutions such as the above provide for negotiated agreement, which is possible when minimum dispositions overlap. When they do not, the outcome is either simply lack of agreement or possibly larger conflict (corresponding to "fixed threat" and "variable threat" situations of bargaining among firms [Bishop, 1963]). Larger, violent conflict virtually always hurts one party more than it helps the other and frequently leaves both parties with outcomes poorer than those they might have achieved through negotiation. Hence, the occurrence of larger conflict rather than a negotiated outcome may be ascribed to the failure of at least one party to predict correctly the outcome of such larger conflict. The continued Arab-Israeli disputes since 1948 furnish illustration (Lenczowski, 1962, Ch. 2). In part because of national and religious ideology, minimum dispositions overlap little if at all; the various negotiated outcomes do not appear sufficiently attractive to both parties to insure their observance; and larger conflict sporadically erupts.

Continuity of Negotiation

When negotiation results in agreement, provision must be made for its execution, the conduct of which frequently though not invariably falls into the classification of nonnegotiative diplomacy distinguished at the very outset of this chapter. But the impossibility of complete explicitness may necessitate later interpretation of unforeseen cases. Many agreements provide procedures for their interpretation, which may take the form of minor negotiation themselves. Agreements may also provide for their extension to related, though as yet unagreed-upon areas, and thus preface further negotiation.

To provide routinely for handling minor adjustments subsequent to a negotiation may imply some institutionalization of the negotiating relation. In labor-management relations, grievance procedures treating specific cases within the framework of a larger agreement function to prevent such cases from precipitating major conflict. At the international level, Schelling and Halperin (1961) suggest that inspection of arms control agreements may facilitate continuing negotiation, by providing opportunity for informal consultation and discussion.

In other ways, too, negotiation perpetuates itself. Agreement, even in a minor area, may provide future expectation of successful negotiation. Further, the act of negotiation itself may, through the necessity of coordination of procedure and related matters, broaden areas of common values. Finally, particular negotiations and their outcomes influence concurrent and subsequent negotiation not only in that area but more generally, providing a constant feedback that modifies the goals, process, and outcome of the larger continuing negotiation among nations.

CONDITIONS INFLUENCING THE PROCESS OF NEGOTIATION

The first three parts of this chapter have followed the natural sequence of goals, process, and outcome as they develop over the course of negotiation. They have treated the essence of what actually occurs during negotiation. Influencing what occurs, however, are two other major aspects: the conditions under which the process of negotiation transpires, and background factors existing at the onset of negotiation. The distinction between background and conditions is temporal, as indicated in Figure 13.1; though some characteristics cannot be unambiguously ordered, in general this distinction is maintained. Thus, the present portion treats concurrent conditions whose values are specific to particular negotiating situations. The next following portion treats more general factors of background, that can usually be assessed prior to the onset of negotiation.

The concurrent conditions influencing the process of negotiation are considered in six general classes: (a) the setting, whether summit, embassy, or other levels, with open or closed proceedings; (b) the number of individual participants; (c) the number of negotiating parties; (d) the amount of information each party possesses about the utilities of the other; (e) the amount of stress impinging upon the negotiation (because of its importance, difficulty, etc.); and (f) the timing, duration, and phasing of negotiation.

The Setting of Negotiation

One of the most crucial factors in a negotiation is the diplomatic level at which it is conducted. This factor, together with the distinction between negotiations arranged for more general or more special purposes, permits distinguishing four situations that constitute principal types of negotiation.

Types of Negotiation. Most common is traditional bilateral diplomacy conducted routinely between the embassy in a foreign country and the corresponding part of that country's foreign office. More recent, embodied in the League of Nations, but represented much more extensively by the United Nations, is parliamentary diplomacy, with a permanent body, regular meetings, general interests, and broad membership (cf. Chapter 14). Conference diplomacy consists of *ad hoc* meetings for particular purposes, though these may be of a long-continuing nature, as in the post-World War II disarmament negotiations. Summit meetings may be considered as a special type of conference diplomacy, in which the negotiators are heads of state. Like all conference diplomacy, these meetings may be bilateral or multilateral. Another important, though somewhat less prominent, type of negotiation, involves the "consultative diplomacy" that transpires within such international organizations as NATO and the Organization of American States.

Conference and parliamentary diplomacy are sometimes called the "new" diplomacy, in contrast with the secret bilateral diplomacy that almost exclusively characterized the international relations of seventeenth-, eighteenth-, and nineteenth-century Europe. Because of their size and publicity, conference and especially parliamentary diplomacy are frequently less negotiation than debate, for which they have been widely and sharply criticized.

At the same time, parliamentary diplomacy through the United Nations performs functions that are useful adjuncts to negotiation. First, it simply provides a meeting place where delegates have the opportunity to see one another without their meeting being an occasion; it bears in this sense some similarity to professional meetings, where business is conducted in the corridors as well as in formal sessions.

Second, an international forum provides an exchange of information through general exposure to widely differing points of view. Further, the pressure these differing viewpoints exert to speak in a language of common interest may, Morgenthau (1960) suggests, likewise exert subtle influences on subsequent actions themselves. Bauer (1958) offers psychological evidence for essentially the same proposition: that ". . . the audience influences the way in which the communicator organizes new information and thereby what he himself may remember and/or believe at a later point in time" (p. 68). He notes also that the communication itself represents an item of behavior with which later behavior must often be reconciled.

Third, the setting of parliamentary diplomacy often provides opportunities for third parties, in the exercise of their own interests, to mediate or otherwise mitigate conflicts. All three of these functions are broadly related to the communication of information concerning possible alternatives and the utilities other parties ascribe to various outcomes; in this way they may precede and facilitate the course of negotiation itself. Many features of the new diplomacy promote this wider distribution of information; the dimension most clearly differentiating it from traditional bilateral diplomacy is that of secrecy vs. publicity, discussed in the following paragraphs.

Open vs. Secret Diplomacy. The call, around the end of World War I, for "open covenants, openly arrived at," by figures as diverse as Wilson and Trotsky, signaled the beginning of an era in which not only the outcome, but also the day-by-day process of international negotiation is frequently known far beyond the small circle of principal negotiators. Increasing ease of transportation and communication have promoted both the desire and the means for making public, as it occurs, the continuing process of negotiation. Widespread publicity for negotiation necessarily makes it more likely that a party, in selecting strategies, will consider not only their likelihood of promoting a beneficial agreement, but also their effect upon interested onlookers. Information officers for each nation typically brief members of the press, before the conference, on their delegation's position; and following each closed session, they report their view of the proceedings. Rusk (1955) decries this "football stadium psychology" in the United Nations, which emphasizes scoring points in a debate, and tends to freeze positions as soon as they are put forward, hindering subsequent accommodation.

Aside from the effects of playing to the audience outside the conference room, the more open the negotiation, the greater the restrictions placed upon the principal negotiator by the presence of numerous experts with interests in various parts of his proposals. A negotiator may be deterred from reaching an agreement, which his government as a whole would accept, by various special pleadings from those who feel that, in their particular area, too much is being bargained away.

Many analysts consider these effects emanating from others inside and outside the conference room to be deleterious to negotiation, and suggest greater secrecy of proceedings. Secrecy of process is to be distinguished, however, from secrecy of outcome: Kirkpatrick (1960), for example, calls for "open covenants—but unopenly arrived at." And Morgenthau (1960) asserts, "Disclosure of the results of diplomatic negotiation is required by the principles of democracy, for without it there can be no democratic control of foreign policy. Yet . . . it takes only common sense derived from daily experience to realize that it is impossible to nego-

tiate in public on anything in which parties other than the negotiators are interested" (p. 553).

Contributing substantially to the decline in secrecy has been a growth in size, reflected both in the number of individual participants and in the number of negotiating parties.

The Number of Individual Participants

Quite apart from the number of parties represented (to be treated in the following section), the sheer number of individual participants has many consequences for the negotiating process; secrecy, for example, becomes most unlikely when scores, or even hundreds occupy the conference room.

Several concomitants of size have been studied among small groups. Bales and Borgatta (1955), in observing differences in the type of interaction in twenty-four groups of sizes two through seven, conclude that "Most of the trends observed appear to be results of two gross factors. The first is that the relative talking time available per member decreases as size increases. The second is that each person is confronted with an absolutely larger number of persons as size increases. Each is under pressure to maintain a more or less adequate relationship with each other. Thus as size increases, each member has more relationships to maintain, and less time to do so" (p. 401).

The limitation of speaking time is such that in fifty-five groups of sizes five to twenty observed by Castore (1962), the average number of persons to whom each individual directed at least one remark during the course of an hour declined from around four to five for smaller groups to around two to three for larger groups. As in most laboratory group reseach, these were single, undifferentiated groups; in international negotiation the number of parties and individuals should be distinguished, as six-man negotiating teams from each of two nations probably form a "smaller" group in some sense than do pairs of representatives from each of six nations.

Although felt tension or antagonism toward others is difficult to assess, its overt expression has been observed to increase with group size; Thomas and Fink (1963), surveying thirty-one studies involving group size, conclude that, "Tentatively it would appear that smaller groups inhibit expression of disagreements and dissatisfactions more than larger groups . . ." (p. 375). The authors also find effects on group organization: ". . . as size increases there will be decreasing group cohesiveness and increasing organization and division of labor in the group . . ." (p. 375).

Because complexity and ensuing procedural formalities tend to transform larger groups into situations of debate rather than negotiation, it has been suggested (for example, Wright, 1954) that negotiation per se be strictly limited to parties whose power positions make their consent indispensable. Hankey (1946), writing from his diplomatic experience, suggests both a source and a cure of overpopulated sessions:

It is always a difficulty in international gatherings that, if an expert of one nation is called in for a particular question, the corresponding experts of all the other nations (whether really required or not) enter the room also. Once they have entered, it is difficult to eject them, even when their subject has been dealt with, particularly if they are Cabinet Ministers or officers or officials of high rank. Curiosity detains them. Meanwhile other subjects are raised and fresh troops come in until the room is overcrowded, and any intimacy in discussion becomes impossible.

This real difficulty in all international work can only be surmounted by very firm handling. [It has been met] . . . by the heads of Governments meeting to deal with all the secret matters in a tiny room to which the indispensable experts were admitted only so long as their presence was required" (p. 25).

Such size limitation was in fact achieved in the meetings of Clemenceau, Orlando, Wilson, and Lloyd George at the Paris Peace Conference of 1919, for which Hankey served as the sole secretary.

The Number of Negotiating Parties

Added parties to a negotiation contribute not only to group size but also to the strategic complexity of the situation. In multilateral diplomacy, the existence of interacting alternatives and utilities of several nations, rather than only two, means that many more outcomes are possible, each of them more complex. Yet it is still possible to represent these multiparty situations within a game theoretic formulation analogous to that employed for two parties in Figures 13.2 and 13.3—simply by extending the dimensionality. Analysis becomes more difficult, though, and "solutions" progressively less definitive. There has been, however, considerable empirical investigation dealing with actual behavior of individuals in multiparty negotiation.

The formation of coalitions among parties has been the focus of most empirical research, as it is basic to most resolutions of multiparty negotiation. In the analysis of coalition formation, there are two major questions: (a) what parties will combine, and (b) how the rewards of coalition membership will be divided. The simplest case—that of three parties—has been treated theoretically by Caplow (1956, 1959) and experimentally by Vinacke and Arkoff (1957). The latter assigned to each of three persons in a group a "power score" (such as 2, 3, or 4) that determined his progress in a winner-take-all game. At their pleasure, any two of the three subjects could join in a coalition, adding their power scores. For many of the groups, the power scores were such that any coalition would win, yet in practice the coalition between the two weaker members formed much more frequently. Although the authors interpret this nonrationally, the result also follows directly from the power scores alone, if anticipated reward split is considered. Without adducing added motives, one may reason that if those with higher power scores may be expected to demand a higher share, they make poor coalition partners. In general, to estimate the value to him of a potential coalition, a negotiator should multiply its expected reward by his expected portion.

If each party takes the orientation of seeking a coalition that maximizes his reward, the tendency may be for the formation of a "minimum winning coalition" (Riker, 1962). Such a result would be consistent with the hypothesis of Mack and Snyder (1957) that "*Social conflict tends toward bipolarization of power relations and to centralize the bases of effective power*" (p. 231). Because the calculation of power is uncertain, however, a coalition may seek somewhat more power than the minimum winning amount. Thus recruitment of borderline members is highly crucial when there are but two major coalitions; those parties having no strong a priori inclination toward one coalition or the other may secure a disproportionately high price for even partial and temporary affiliation. Among contemporary illustrations of this rewarding practice is the success of the United Arab Republic in balancing the Soviet Union and the United States as "alternate donors" (Liska, 1960).

To the extent that the common interest forming the basis for coalition is thus closely circumscribed, coalition is likely to be an ephemeral relation (as shifting alliances of this century alone illustrate), though the process of acting in coalition may in itself extend the area of common interest. The rational difficulty of stable coalition is demonstrated by Rapoport (1960) in the game in which three men decide, by majority vote, how to divide a dollar, so that any two can agree to split it, 50–50, say. One of the partners may then be approached by the third man with an offer of more than 50 cents, but if he accepts, he becomes liable to a coalition between his new and his former partners, since they could both do better with each other. Then the original defector is the odd man, and the cycle may repeat. To avoid becoming the odd man, reason suggests that, "If you are one of the lucky ones who gets 50 cents, do not accept any offers from the player frozen out. For as soon as you get more than 50 cents, you become vulnerable to a conspiracy of the two other players against you" (p. 209).

Thus a crucial problem of coalition is that of maintaining stability—probably best promoted by returning consistent benefit to one's coalition partner, resisting the temptation to desert for temporary gain. Lieberman (1964) found eight triads of Harvard undergraduates to differ markedly in their ability to maintain stable coalitions: With 39 chances to alter coalitions, the actual frequencies of change were 2, 2, 2, 5, 9, 22, 24, and 33. The three possible coalitions differed in value, and among "strictly rational" players in Rapoport's sense, the most profitable should always form. The actual reward received, over all combinations, however, was only one third of the way from that of the minimal coalition to that of the optimal coalition.

Added parties to a negotiation may function not in a symmetrical role, but rather as mediators, arbitrators, or others whose actions are not the object of agreement. Such third parties may perform or aid in any of the previously described processes of negotiation. For example, they may contribute to widening the agenda, bringing the parties to the conflict curve (eliminating non-Pareto outcomes), or selecting specific divisions along the conflict curve. Sometimes the only unacceptable feature of a proposal lies not in its terms but merely in its being forwarded by the other party, making its acceptance appear as a loss of face. The impasse resulting when both parties feel this way may be resolved, Schelling and Halperin (1961) suggest, by a mediator acting as a neutral source for the basically acceptable proposal. Another way in which a mediator may function is in providing information to each party about the strength with which the other holds his position—information shown in the following section to be both crucial and difficult to obtain.

Information: Estimating the Other's Utilities for Various Outcomes

In all of the processes of negotiation that have been considered, information concerning the utilities the other places upon the various possible outcomes has been crucial. Imperfect information about the other's utilities complicates not only the original decision matrix but also the processes of communication and persuasion and of creating new alternatives. Consequently, it is important to examine the sources of such obscurity.

The Difficulty of Knowing Another's Values. To know what is the best outcome one may expect to achieve one

must know the expectations of the other, but these, in turn, depend upon one's own. Lack of such information lends importance to the previously described process of persuasion, in which each party tries to alter the other's utilities for certain outcomes while leaving unchanged or strengthening his own utilities, as the other sees them. Frequently, a principal aspect of the negotiation may be this attempt to establish to the other party the strength of one's values, for if it is known just how much each party desires certain outcomes—exactly how far it would go to achieve them and precisely what it would do if frustrated—the solution is often readily apparent to all.

Morgenthau (1960) suggests that, "To demonstrate to the rest of the world the power one's own nation possesses, revealing neither too much nor too little, is the task of a wisely conceived policy of prestige" (p. 85). A nation whose power is underestimated, such as that of the Soviet Union or the United States in 1940, may suffer attacks that would otherwise be deterred. While there may be at least temporary advantage in having one's power overestimated (as Britain's was by Hitler in 1940), there seems to be, as these examples suggest, little gained in having it underestimated, and a nation needs to be able to demonstrate its true strength.

One problem in demonstration of political power is the lack of a metric, such as money furnishes for economic power. Correspondingly, the amount of negotiation over terms appears relatively smaller in economic transactions than in political relations. Yet economic negotiation was not always as relatively efficient as it is today. The decreasing amount, over the centuries, of protracted negotiation in economic transactions has been associated with development of a medium of exchange, wider markets, and other factors, many of whose functions may be conceived as contributing to more nearly perfect information. Haggling has simply become uneconomic. It may be that increasingly fuller knowledge of political values will similarly facilitate settlement of international negotiations.

Knowledge of the other's values, however, is often difficult to achieve, at any level of negotiation. Blake and Mouton (1961a) established an experimental debate in which representatives of two groups having prepared different solutions to a problem were to convince each other and the representatives of two neutral groups of the worth of their own solutions. Preparatory to the debate, members of both groups received the written solutions prepared by each and spent two hours discussing their relative merits. Although subjects' ". . . subjective experience is one of *certainty of insight* into the proposal of the competing group" (p. 217), in each of twenty groups, the average actual knowledge of the other's solution, as measured by an objective test, was less than that of one's own. In recognition of such difficulty of understanding, Carl Rogers (1952) suggested that in a conflict situation each party should first state the position of the other, to the latter's satisfaction.

In the absence of certain information about the value the other places upon certain outcomes, Harsanyi (1962) suggests that parties may (a) assign the other stereotypic values (based, for example, in individuals, upon such factors as sex, age, and social status); or (b) adjust their estimates of the other's values on the basis of the offers he makes, though this presents the problem of unlimited bluffing. In practice, parties usually combine these, having some a priori notion of the other's values, which is nonetheless

somewhat subject to modification on the basis of his behavior.

The Effect of Information: Good or Bad? Harsanyi (1962), reasoning from an analysis of the negotiation process (Harsanyi, 1956; Zeuthen, 1930) whose result is comparable to that of the previously considered solution of Nash (1950, 1953), concludes that complete information necessarily produces wholly determinate solutions. When each of two rational bargainers knows the other's utility function, ". . . a conflict would never arise because each party would know what his own payoff would be under the solution of the game and would only ask for that particular payoff, so the two parties' bids would never contain incompatible demands" (p. 36). This is strictly true, of course, only if the "rational bargainers" recognize and accept the "solution," implying also their acceptance of its not entirely unquestionable assumptions, previously specified in the consideration of outcome.

Considerable opinion among labor economists supports the value of information in collective bargaining. J. R. Hicks (1948) holds that, "The majority of strikes are doubtless the result of faulty negotiation . . . adequate knowledge will always make a settlement possible. The danger lies in ignorance by one side of the other's dispositions, and in hasty breaking-off of negotiations" (pp. 146–147). Sumner Slichter is quoted by Chamberlain (1958) as saying that, "Perhaps the most frequent mistake which employers make in the field of labor policy is not to tell the union officers and members enough about the business" (p. 155).

Siegel and Fouraker (1960) provide experimental support for the value of information; in their simulated bargaining situations under conditions of bilateral monopoly, "increasing the amount of relevant information available to bargainers increases their tendency to maximize joint payoff" (p. 41) and also ". . . tends to lead to a more equal division of the joint payoff" (p. 70). Pilisuk and Rapoport (1964) found that when neither person knew the Prisoner's Dilemma matrix specifying his and the other's rewards for the four choice combinations, the proportion choosing cooperatively was about 25 percent less than otherwise. Moreover, even though subjects should have eventually been able to infer their own values completely and at least the ordering of the other's, repeated trials increased rather than decreased the differences; after 300 trials, about two thirds of the choices in the known matrix are cooperative and only one third in the unknown matrix. The result suggests that even if the initial information deficit is remedied, a residual effect causes continuing noncooperation.

An apparently contrary view on the value of information comes from Clark Kerr (1954), who holds that ". . . misunderstanding and the misuse of words have probably made a substantial contribution to industrial peace" (p. 233) by disguising from both parties how antagonistic their motives actually were. Morgenstern (1961) asserts that, in international relations, as in poker, one must bluff, and call the other's possible bluffs; otherwise one's strategy is completely known to the other. In both poker and international relations, it may indeed be profitable for a party to pretend more strength than he has— *if* he is able to go unchallenged. Yet in international relations, unlike poker, it is seldom profitable to have a position strongly challenged, even (and perhaps especially) if it is *not* a bluff. (This difference reflects a distinction between non-zero-sum situations and those in which one party wins only at the direct expense of the other.)

Another possible function of lack of information is suggested by Moore and Tumin (1949): to prevent resentment over maldistribution. Yet with greater information, there might not be "maldistribution," but rather distribution in accord with the respective true power positions of the parties, and hence possibly a more stable settlement, along the lines specified by balance-of-power analyses.

These somewhat conflicting views on the value of information may be partially reconciled if we assume that mutually beneficial and lasting agreements are promoted by information not only about the utilities of the other, but also about the certainty with which these are held. This assumption is based on a distinction between two aspects in the estimation of utility: (a) the expected utility a party ascribes to an outcome, and (b) the precision with which his estimate is made (corresponding to the mean and standard deviation of such estimates). For example, the best single estimate a party could make might be that a given outcome were worth 10 units, but he might also realize that its value could well be as low as 5 or as high as 20. Only in the case of perfect certainty as to the outcome's worth would the single value suffice to convey full information. Otherwise, a given expected value of an outcome might have quite different implications depending upon how precisely it is estimated. To assume falsely that the estimates of the other are highly precise may cause a party to overreact; to realize the imprecision of his estimates may temper response. If, as Bauer (1961) suggests, ". . . both Soviet and American observers have over-rationalized notions as to what transpires in the other society" (p. 226), then treating the other's values as entirely fixed may neglect areas of potential agreement and add unnecessarily to the difficulties of negotiation.

Stresses upon Negotiation

"Stress" is taken to incorporate the possible effects upon negotiation of such generally complicating factors as a constraint to reach agreement by a certain time, a high level of antagonism between parties, threatened detrimental unilateral actions in the event of nonagreement, gross incompatibility of bargaining positions, importance of the negotiation, and other conditions usually impeding agreement. To qualify as stressful, however, these conditions must be perceived as such by the participants; a time constraint, for example, may sometimes be found stressful and at other times not. "Stress" here refers also to what is often characterized as "tension" or as "threat" (in a psychological sense, not in the sense of threats and promises as strategies).

Stress is sometimes associated with ambiguity in one's relation to the other party or in other aspects of the situation. Cohen (1959), using employees and their supervisors, verified the hypothesis that, "The more ambiguous a situation [in terms of unclarity of goal and inconsistency of the supervisor] in which power is being exercised over an individual who is highly motivated toward need satisfaction, the more threat he will experience" (p. 38). Lack of ambiguity may sometimes have so much value for nations, Kaplan and Katzenbach (1961) suggest in their analysis of international law, that they will prefer even an outmoded rule to possible uncertainty resulting from its challenge in the course of negotiation.

Threat to the common activity of a group has often been found to increase the degree of integration among members within the group. This tendency, Berkowitz (1962) asserts, in reviewing a number of studies, occurs because ". . . *the individual members become more highly attracted to each other when they believe their fellow members can and will help them satisfy their desires.* The presence of an external threat can make the other group members much more important to the individual; he may need them to overcome the external frustration, and so, these others become more attractive to him" (p. 189). Yet, in some cases, threat may *not* increase group integration. Hamblin (1958) presents evidence tending to imply that, when a crisis situation having no likely solution is imposed upon a group, integration will actually decrease.

Other concomitants of threat often accompany a change in integration. Lanzetta (1954) found that when an experiment was structured as an evaluative test, presumably to become part of subjects' college records, groups had not only less interpersonal tension, but also less motivation to achieve, less leadership behavior, fewer suggestions, and were less forceful and initiating in their attack upon the problem. In general, threat restricted activity and decreased problem-solving effectiveness. It appears possible that stress induced by the polemics of the Cold War may have similar effects upon international negotiation.

Another detrimental effect of stressful stimuli is noted by Janis and Feshbach (1953), who exposed students to one of three persuasive lectures on dental hygiene containing exhortations that varied in their allusion to the dangers of neglect, and so on. The lectures had the intended effect of arousing varying degrees of concern in the listeners. While those who had heard the strong lecture reported themselves to be most worried, however, they actually changed their dental habits least; those hearing the lecture arousing minimal fear changed their habits most.

The relation of stress to performance is generally thought to be curvilinear: Mild stress tends to improve performance, but beyond a certain intensity, added stress is detrimental. One of the ways in which higher levels of stress may operate to decrease performance is through restriction in perception of alternatives, so that in time of stress the ability to add or modify alternatives may be curtailed (see Chapter 12 in this volume). A closely related phenomenon is decreasing complexity of the perceptual space in which objects and persons are located; there may occur an increasing tendency under stress to locate all stimuli on a single dimension ranging from good to bad, and this single dimension may even collapse to two points—simply "which side are you on?"

In an Inter-Nation Simulation (Guetzkow, 1959) in which three-man groups representing each of seven hypothetical nations conducted international relations, Driver (1962) applied multidimensional scaling to the perceptions subjects held of the similarity of the seven nations. In those sessions in which stress was considered moderate (because war did not occur), perceptions of the seven nations required for their representation at least three distinct dimensions, including alliances, power, and leadership. In those sessions in which stress was considered either mild (because they were the first runs at their respective locations and administered more loosely) or intense (because war occurred), only two dimensions (alliances and power) were required.

Though in the Driver experiment no deliberate actions were taken to modify the level of stress, it is possible to introduce experimentally variations intended to affect stress. Crow (1963) conducted one session of the Inter-Nation Simulation in which a confederate, the Central Decision-Maker of one of the two bloc leaders in a five-nation world, first acted in a firm though not harsh fashion, then introduced C. E. Osgood's (1962) plan for "graduated reciprocation in international tension-reduction" (GRIT) by announcing and consistently carrying out small, unilateral acts designed to reduce tension, and inviting their reciprocation. Tension level, measured at each of thirteen periods, showed an increase to the point at which GRIT was applied, then a decrease, achieving its lowest level at the end of the thirteenth period.

Timing in Negotiation

Because stress, information, and other conditions, as well as alternatives and preferences, change during the process of negotiation, the specific timing of communications and actions is often highly critical. Changes in outside factors are also influential and even the fact that negotiations have already been underway for a number of sessions creates an altered situation. Research on interpersonal, industrial, and international behavior analyzed here bears especially upon two aspects of timing in negotiation: (a) the relation between cooperative behavior and the length of negotiation, and (b) the phasing of behavior in negotiation and its relation to effectiveness.

Rapoport's (1963) 300-trial experiments demonstrate the importance of long-continuing observation. Although the proportion of "compromise" choices in a Prisoner's Dilemma fell from an initial level of 50 percent to an average of 40 percent over the first 50 trials, by the last block of 50 trials, the average had risen to 65 percent. By that time, nearly all of the pairs of subjects had essentially stabilized at either a mutual compromise or a mutual hold out.

In another Prisoner's Dilemma situation, Pilisuk and Rapoport (1964) presented two groups of subjects with formally equivalent matrices and situations differing only in that one called for each subject to make twenty interim moves (of which the other was unaware) before reporting his final move, whereas the other called for only a single final move. Whether because of the greater number of opportunities for consideration, the mere added time required, or other factors, the subjects making twenty moves arrived more frequently at situations of mutual compromise. These results correspond somewhat to a rationale that may be offered for lengthy roll-call voting and other essentially unnecessary procedures: The delay provides time for accommodation (even if only of thought rather than through interaction) that would otherwise be prevented.

The order in which more and less cooperative actions are taken may influence the response of the other party. Scodel (1962) and Bixenstine and Wilson (1963) both find, in Prisoner's Dilemma matrices, that a high level of cooperative ("compromise") choices on the part of a confederate is more effective in inducing cooperation on the part of a subject when it is preceded by a period of uncooperative ("hold out") choice. An initially highly cooperative choice may even be regarded with suspicion, whereas to progress "cautiously" toward the more risky, but potentially more beneficial mutual compromise may appear more reasonable.

It so happens that the two patterns— of increasing and of decreasing rates of cooperative acts within a negotiating session—have been strongly char-

acteristic of the behavior of the two super-powers in their post-World War II disarmament negotiations. In seven selected rounds of negotiations, the United States made 82 percent of its concessions in the first third of the round, while the Soviet Union made 75 percent of its concessions in the final third (Jensen, 1963). One may speculate on whether more success might have resulted from some other phasing.

The occurrence of phases has also been observed in labor-management negotiation. Douglas (1957) presents anecdotal evidence for the existence of three phases: (a) "establishing the bargaining range," in which parties make uncompromising demands; (b) "reconnoitering the range," in which parties seriously explore possible agreements; and (c) "precipitating the decision-making crisis," in which each party attempts to put a "final offer" to the other in such a way that he must "take it or leave it" and will be motivated to accept. Behavior in Douglas's first phase may be intended to influence through communication and persuasion the other's estimates of utilities and also to convince the membership of each party that their negotiating team is representing their position strongly. The shift to more conciliatory behavior in the second phase corresponds to the sequence found to be effective in the experiments described above; it allows for the creation of new alternatives providing better outcomes.

The object in the third phase is much like that of Schelling's (1960) "strategic move": ". . . to set up for one's self and communicate persuasively to the other player a mode of behavior . . . that leaves the other a simple maximization problem whose solution for him is the optimum for one's self, and to destroy the other's ability to do the same" (p. 160). While it might appear that a "strategic move" could be taken at the very outset of negotiation, such phases as Douglas describes are highly useful in helping insure that appropriate conditions exist for the successful execution of a "strategic move." However, if the bargaining has remained sufficiently tight so that the minimum dispositions have barely met (rather than overlapping substantially), then it does not matter who makes the final offer, since only a single point is mutually acceptable.

More detailed, empirical analysis of labor-management mediation sessions has been conducted by Landsberger (1955), who examined the extent to which the sequence of interaction corresponds to Bales and Strodtbeck's (1951) hypothesis of "phase movement." This hypothesis specifies that in a problem-solving group, acts of orientation (as categorized by Interaction Process Analysis [Bales, 1950]), reach their highest frequency in the first third of the discussion, those of evaluation in the second third, and those of suggestion and affect (both positive and negative) in the final third.

Landsberger's findings, on the basis of his more specific classification of acts, appear to fill in consistently the broader outlines of Douglas's analysis: Orientation contributes to "establishing the bargaining range," evaluation to "reconnoitering the range," and suggestion and affect to "precipitating the decision-making crisis." In addition, Landsberger found a higher incidence of successful mediation among those cases in which the ordering of interaction corresponded more closely to the phase hypothesis. Though it seems reasonable that international negotiations, too, progress through phases, their particular incidence and effect are yet to be subjected to systematic empirical analysis.

BACKGROUND FACTORS INFLUENCING NEGOTIATION

The conditions discussed in the foregoing sections form a part of the specific negotiating situation itself; in addition, however, there are certain factors providing a more or less set background against which the negotiation occurs. These background factors also influence the course of negotiation, though in general less immediately and directly. In the following sections, they are treated in an order of roughly decreasing scope and increasing specificity. We shall consider the effect upon negotiation, first, of broad cultural traditions of the negotiating nations, next of the particular existing relations between the nations, then of the relations between different units within a single nation (as those of the negotiating team to other parts of its government), and finally, of the characteristics of individual negotiators.

Cultural Variation

As a result of their distinct historical development, nations come to acquire what may be regarded as "national character . . . *relatively enduring personality characteristics and patterns that are modal among the adult members of the society*" (Inkeles & Levinson, 1954, p. 983). National character is related to many other aspects of a society's general socio-cultural system, from child-rearing practices to the type of political system it supports, and consequently influences the types of goals and processes the society pursues in negotiation. Erikson (1963), for example, relates the American family pattern, which unlike many European patterns allows both sexes and all ages to have some say, to the nature of American politics, ". . . a rocking sea of checks and balances in which uncompromising absolutes must drown" (p. 318). More and more, such differences in national character may affect interaction among the elites who conduct international relations, because both the democratization of diplomacy over recent centuries and technological advances in communication and transportation have tied diplomats more closely to the rest of their nation. No longer is it so likely, as in seventeenth- and eighteenth-century Europe, when diplomats were often part of a common aristocracy, that they may have more in common with their counterparts from other nations than with the nation they represent.

Many observations have been made of the way differences between nations in social and cultural characteristics affect both the policies of the nation and the way in which they are pursued. From his visit to the United States in 1835, de Tocqueville concluded that, "Foreign politics demand scarcely any of those qualities which are peculiar to a democracy; they require, on the contrary, the perfect use of almost all those in which it is deficient" (1959, p. 243). Of twentieth-century diplomacy, Hayter (1960) asserts that, "No great power, except perhaps the Soviet Union, suffers or has ever suffered so much as America does from self-imposed limitations on its diplomacy" (p. 9). This he credits to an historical distaste for alliances, unparticular anti-colonialism, separation and division of powers between executive and legislature, and a distrust and disdain for foreigners as a whole.

Other aspects of American character are illustrated in the diplomacy surrounding the U-2 incident. Accused of violating Soviet airspace, the United States first reacted with a self-righteous

denial. Later, confronted by undeniable evidence, it fully confessed, which according to the national myth of George Washington and the cherry tree, should bring forgiveness and approval (Blanchard, 1962). Both kinds of reaction are extreme, and in many circumstances may be inappropriate, however compatible with national character. They are examples of the strength of restraints a nation places upon itself, and even if such restraints be detrimental, ". . . the procedures of diplomacy," as Halle (1960) notes, "must be in harmony with the society which operates them" (p. 140).

The face-to-face conduct of negotiations may be influenced by behavioral discrepancies when persons of different cultural backgrounds are brought together. Klineberg (1964) illustrates the kinds of problems that can arise in international conferences. If Americans and Europeans, all previously unacquainted, are brought together, the Americans may be calling each other by first name while Frenchmen and Germans are still addressing their countrymen by title. Though this may reflect solely cultural differences in formality of address, the American pattern may nonetheless be perceived by the others as representing the formation of a clique and regarded with suspicion. Other attitudes relevant to group process also differ among nations. Using Chinese, American, Near Eastern, and South American students as informants on committee functioning in their cultures, Gyr (1951) found national differences in (a) uncertainty about motives of other committee members, (b) desire to cooperate in reaching a group goal, (c) recognition of the superiority of the leader, and (d) trustfulness. If such cultural differences extend to negotiation, they seem likely to influence its progress, particularly when the disparity in practices is large.

Experience with different organizational structures may influence behavior in a new situation. In an experiment on group problem-solving, Cohen, Bennis, and Wolkon (1962) first created two conditions. In ten of the groups, they permitted communication only between one central person and each of the other group members, but not among these others themselves. In the other ten groups, each person could communicate with two others, in a circular network. In the second part of the experiment, in which all groups had the circular communication network, those having first experienced the more centrally structured network generally developed systems that enabled them to solve problems both faster and more accurately. Moreover, those with the more structured prior experience were more satisfied in the second half. It would thus seem important to examine, in the context of international negotiation, the effect of bringing together, in the same group, individuals whose domestic experiences are with more and less structured situations.

Even in the relatively noncontroversial area of cultural exchange, Wedge (1961) has suggested that different conceptions of the relations between man and state may affect Soviet-American negotiation. The Soviet view that the governments can speak for the students and institutions involved causes them to be impatient with American requests on behalf of students who want to study certain taboo questions, or with American institutions who refuse students as not having the proper background, even though the Soviet government has certified them.

Thus, in many areas of international negotiation, broad cultural differences among nations may influence the way they understand and react to each other. But aside from these general cultural factors, more specific attitudes between particular nations are also relevant.

Attitude between Negotiating Parties

As a result of all the prior relations between a given pair of nations, each may be considered to hold a certain "attitude" or "image" of the other. These attitudes or images are crucial to the process and outcome of international negotiation because—distorted or not—they influence substantially both (a) the actions one party takes toward the other, and (b) the interpretations he places upon the acts of the other.

In contrast with broad cultural characteristics, which presumably influence a nation's relations with all others, these attitudes derive from and in turn influence the history of relations between two particular nations. In integrating the previous history into an attitude at a given moment, varying weights may be given to specific incidents; presumably more weight is given to those crucial to the "national interest," though matters more relevant to pride than power may also be weighted heavily. Past animosities (and friendships, too) are frequently heavily discounted, as in Anglo-American relations, or even in relations involving much more recent colonies, such as the six former French-African colonies that opted for full membership in the French Community.

Attitudes may of course differ from reality, as is illustrated in considering the possible distinctions between national character and its perception. That the perception of national character does not always conform to its reality is suggested in observations long reported by diplomats on what appear to them as characteristic differences between their own behavior and that of their counterparts from other nations.

In 1813, the first Earl of Malmesbury offered the following advice to an entrant to the foreign service: "Englishmen should be most particularly on their guard against such men [those who, upon your first arrival in a foreign country, appear the most eager to make friendly acquaintance and to communicate their ideas], for we have none such on our side the water, and are ourselves so little *coming* towards foreigners, that we are astonished and gratified when we find a different treatment from that which strangers experience here; but our reserve and *ill manners* are infinitely less dangerous to the stranger than these premature and hollow civilities" (Satow, 1957, pp. 96–97).

To another observer, Englishmen also appeared quite unlike other men, though in less preferred ways. From the perspective of his father's ministry in London during the American Civil War, Henry Adams observed that, "Knowledge of human nature is the beginning and end of political education, but several years of arduous study in the neighborhood of Westminster led Henry Adams to think that knowledge of English human nature had little or no value outside of England. In Paris, such a habit stood in one's way; in America, it roused all the instincts of native jealousy. The English mind was one-sided, eccentric, systematically unsystematic, and logically illogical. The less one knew of it, the better" (1931, p. 180).

It seems likely that assumptions about foreigners—like stereotypes in general—are usually partly but not wholly true (Klineberg, 1950). But true or false, if acted upon, they may influence international negotiation, not only through beliefs of negotiators and policy-makers themselves, but also through constraints placed upon them by the beliefs of their publics. Strong

American distaste for revolutionary Bolsheviks may have contributed to the delay from 1917 to 1933 in official United States recognition of the government of the Soviet Union. Stereotypes may even have an effect upon those stereotyped, by justifying or otherwise making more likely the imputed characteristic, as Bronfenbrenner (1961) suggests in his discussion of the Soviet-American "mirror-image phenomenon."

When systematic differences are perceived between one's own group and another, it is usual that those of one's own group are considered superior. Such ethnocentrism—stressing one's own distinguishing values as best—may function to compensate for a relatively low general standing in the international prestige system, particularly for underdeveloped nations (Lagos, 1963). Ethnocentrism, however, is by no means expressed only by countries low in status; the history of colonialism is replete with illustration of the stereotypes the European conquerors held of the conquered, as well as vice versa.

Ethnocentrism may be increased under the conditions of stress that frequently accompany negotiation. Berkowitz (1961) found anti-Semitic (and generally ethnocentric) individuals to make grosser differentiations (as in lumping together all "outsiders") when frustrated by the experimenter than when not frustrated; unprejudiced individuals, on the other hand, made finer discriminations when frustrated than when not, suggesting that they differentiate the source of their difficulty from other factors.

The importance to negotiation of ethnocentrism and stereotypy, like that of attitude in general, lies in their influence upon the way in which the actions of the other party are perceived and responded to. A negative attitude stemming from whatever source is likely to predispose a negative inter-pretation of subsequent actions. As C. E. Osgood notes, "It is cognitively inconsistent for us to think of people we dislike and distrust making honest, conciliatory moves . . ." (1960, p. 341). Heider (1958) and Newcomb (1959) have similarly observed tendencies toward consistency in interpersonal perception. In international negotiation, this may be illustrated by interpretations given to a disarmament proposal made by the other party; whether one decides that it is a genuine proposal or merely for propaganda purposes depends in large part upon his a priori attitude.

If negative attitudes toward the other lead consistently to negative interpretations of his actions, thus further reinforcing one's negative attitude and leading to negative actions on one's own part, then the original attitude is highly critical. Krauss (1963) confirmed this importance in a laboratory experiment in which fictitious negative and positive information about the other influenced bargaining outcome in the corresponding direction. In recognition of the importance of attitude, labor-management mediators frequently act to mitigate the unfavorable view each party has of the other. On the international scene, however, it seems likely that mass media frequently serve to heighten rather than reduce unfavorable attitudes.

Negative attitudes become self-reinforcing through a process of autistic hostility (Newcomb, 1947) which at the international level may contribute to spiraling of conflict. Wright (1963) found Newcomb's formulation predictive of the development of reinforcing cycles of hostility in the inter-country negotiations occurring in an Inter-Nation Simulation. Zinnes (1963) found a similar spiraling of hostility in the diplomatic messages exchanged between members of the Dual Alliance and the Triple Entente during the six weeks prior to the outbreak of World War I. Expressions of hostility from a state in one camp toward a state in the other camp regularly were followed by reciprocal expressions of hostility, though not necessarily between the same two states.

Thus, in game experiments, in experimental simulation of international relations, and in analysis of actual diplomatic correspondence, the images parties hold of each other have been found to be consistently related to the process and outcome of their interaction.

Relations within a Negotiating Party

For negotiating parties as complex as nations, the goals, process, and outcome of negotiation are influenced not only by attitudes reflecting previous relations *between* the parties, but also by the relations *within* each party. Many influences from within the nation impinge upon the negotiator, ranging from broad and diffuse factors of public opinion, through more specific pressures from various offices within his government, even to the highly particular concerns of other members of his negotiating team sitting in the same room. Though these forces may conflict, with each other and with what the negotiator himself might feel is intrinsically the best course, they nonetheless are part of the background that influences his actions. These conflicts arise, according to the present analysis, because of different experiences and interests on the part of the various groups and individuals. In examining the characteristics of these influences, we shall begin with the more general and then proceed to the more specific.

Most general of all is public opinion, whose support is often crucial for given negotiations. Yet as Dahl (1950) points out, the influences of public opinion pose a dilemma: Only if public opinion is fluid and undecided will the full range of theoretical alternatives be open; to the extent that public opinion hardens, alternatives are foreclosed. But because effectiveness in foreign policy depends finally upon the willingness of a nation to indulge in collective sacrifices, to rely on a fluid and indefinite public opinion is to substitute a reed for a sword" (p. 247). Thus if the effect of public opinion upon negotiation is to limit its freedom while increasing its power, it is important to examine the nature of these limitations. Three basic limitations are that public opinion (a) inclines toward simple alternatives, (b) is frequently hard to change, and (c) may well be inconsistent in its various positions. (See Chapter 8 in the present volume.)

The force toward simple solutions is associated with the intrinsic difficulties of a large and amorphous entity such as public opinion in exchanging and processing complex information. It is difficult for public opinion to formulate new alternatives; rather its expression generally consists in favoring or disfavoring certain simply formulated existing alternatives. As Bastert (1960) notes, "In a democracy there must be heavy reliance on translating diplomatic action into principles easily understood and widely held, in line with national tradition and deeply aware of the insistence upon moral responsibility" (p. 521).

In favoring and disfavoring existing alternatives, the effect of public opinion is to narrow the range of alternatives, and thus to reduce the flexibility of the negotiator to propose new alternatives he sees as beneficial. Yet such limitations may sometimes result in strategic advantage, by serving as evidence of commitment to a certain position; leaders may convincingly claim they are not free to accept the proposals of the other party because their constituency would not support such an agreement. Thus, like *faits accomplis* and successful threats and promises, such narrowing of alternatives through the action of public opinion may serve to reduce the choice of the other in a way advantageous to oneself.

Yet because a position strongly held by public opinion is often not easily modified, such a strategy may create difficulties if the demanded alternative is not obtained. When in 1846, two years after Polk was elected President of the United States on the slogan "fifty-four forty or fight," the government did neither but instead settled the Oregon dispute with Britain at the forty-ninth parallel, many expansionists accused Polk of betrayal and deception. Apparently Polk felt sufficiently bound by the expansionistic fervor he had promoted to seek aid in release from it by the unusual step of laying the British proposal for compromise before the Congress for advice, prior to execution of the treaty. As in many cases, public opinion was more easily aroused than quieted.

Another difficulty in the operation of public opinion, elaborated by Scott in Chapter 3 of the present volume, results because, unlike individual attitudes on more proximate matters, public opinion on international relations is subject to few constraints toward either rationality or cognitive consistency. As analyzed by Morgenthau (1960), "Public opinion, while dreading war, demands that its diplomats act as heroes who do not yield in the face of the enemy, even at the risk of war, and condemns as weaklings and traitors those who yield, albeit only halfway, for the sake of peace" (p. 554).

Public opinion frequently operates through pressure groups, the legislature, government agencies, or other organizations, though in all of these public opinion is but one of several forces. These organizations themselves exert influence upon the goals, process, and outcome of international negotiation in some of the same ways as does public opinion. In the United States, the constitutional separation of powers may act to reduce alternatives. Robinson (1962) indicates how the Senate's instructions decreased flexibility but increased bargaining strength of the United States representatives to the World Bank negotiations on establishing the International Development Association.

Finally, influences may derive from the foreign office personnel with whom a negotiator associates and discusses questions of policy and strategy, and to whom he looks for approval of his performance. Such influential individuals by no means need be superiors. Kirkpatrick (1960) suggests that standards of personal loyalty cause negotiators to ". . . dislike letting down the experts who are sitting behind them" and that one ". . . is only human if, anxious to avoid the reproachful glance of men whom he esteems, he tries to put up the best show he can" (p. 109).

Thus within a nation, many and diverse influences, from highly general public opinion to highly specific interpersonal relations, act upon the negotiator. In probing the bases of conflict between these various influences, it is illuminating to consider Pruitt's (1962) study of decision-making in the State Department, in which he contrasted its orientations with those of other government agencies. In nine cases of conflict between an office of the Department of State responsible for continuing relations with a certain group of countries and other governmental agencies, it was invariably the State Department that favored more concessions to the country in question.

Pruitt suggests that while this tendency might result simply from superior knowledge of the other country and the extent to which it will agree, more frequently it reflects an orientation toward sustaining the long-term cooperation of the other nation by being responsive to its desires (see Pruitt's discussion in Chapter 11 of the present volume). For the State Department the values of the other nation are more prominent because, in contrast to many other agencies, it is responsible for continuing relations with that other nation. But, while an agency responsible for relations with a particular nation may be more open to that nation's expectations, it is not entirely free to act correspondingly because other agencies not having this function react differently. The different reactions stem from different organizational experiences, and both may provide inputs to the negotiation process.

Different reactions may be manifested not only by different organizations, but also by the same organizations and individuals as their environment alters. In a small-group experiment, Kelley (1955) found that Catholics who had just received material intended to heighten the salience of their church membership were more likely to express attitudes in accord with the church's position than were subjects receiving unrelated neutral material.

As the European Economic Community has developed, many groups and individuals have found themselves in situations in which the relevance of international as opposed to national considerations is sharply increased. In discussing the "spill-over" effect between integrated economic sectors and as yet unintegrated areas, Haas (1958) indicates that ". . . in the process of reformulating expectations and demands, the interest groups in question [industrialists, dealers, and trade unions] approach one another supranationally while their erstwhile ties with national friends undergo deterioration" (1958, p. 313). Similar phenomena (described by Alger in Chapter 14) of shifting orientations have been noted among the delegates and staff a nation sends to the United Nations, although their original backgrounds are similar to those of their counterparts in the nation's national diplomatic service. As such contact in supranational organizations increases, one may perhaps expect a corresponding increase in the value accorded in specific negotiations to the continuing maintenance of mutually beneficial long-term relations.

The Negotiator

According to Harold Nicolson, British career diplomat, "Nobody who has not actually watched statesmen dealing with each other can have any real idea of the immense part played in human affairs by such unavowable and often unrecognizable causes as lassitude, affability, personal affection or dislike, misunderstanding, deafness or incomplete command of a foreign language, vanity, social engagements, interruptions and momentary health" (1946, p. 19). Characteristics associated with the negotiator are considered in two classes: (a) those involving the role of negotiator, especially the effect of his status level and background, and (b) personality attributes of the individual.

Status and Background of Negotiators. The level of the senior representatives in any particular negotiation varies widely, including heads of state, foreign ministers, professional diplomats, military, and other special representatives. Each of these levels has certain advantages and disadvantages that make it more appropriate to one situation than another (Haas and Whiting, 1956). Heads of state have the unique advantage of being best able

to commit their nations, but often suffer from lack of time, lack of specific experience, and undue pressures to produce results. As Vansittart (1950) points out, ". . . personal diplomacy was much favored by both Churchill and Roosevelt, who loved to carry on negotiation free from 'interference.' This predilection was facilitated, and in part necessitated, by war; but such courses are always apt to go too far and to produce errors which might be avoided, given better opportunities for briefing. When it came to personal diplomacy with Stalin, the results were more unfortunate" (p. 187).

The frequently extreme visibility and consequent pressure when heads of state negotiate may make the desire to avoid loss of face a principal motivation; this may also be used as a bargaining tactic, but if employed by both chiefs, it appears likely to result in stalemate. Foreign ministers usually have more experience with the particular issues, may be less able to commit their nation, and otherwise suffer most of the same disadvantages, to a somewhat lesser degree, as do heads of state.

Typically, the bulk of bilateral negotiation is carried out through diplomats stationed at an embassy in the foreign capital. These include both career diplomats and political appointees. Special representatives are frequently experts whose background is particularly suited for specific negotiations. Special representatives and political appointees are the "amateur diplomats" upon whom the United States, according to some critics, relies unduly. Kennan (1959) has characterized these diplomats as "lawyer-moralists," who inject an excessively legalistic and inflexible attitude into diplomacy. Diplomatic inexperience, however, may have the advantage of promoting new approaches in place of conventional but no longer applicable procedures. Moreover, amateur diplomats who are politicians should, according to the analysis of Dahl and Lindblom (1953), have qualities highly appropriate for negotiators, since a political position is essentially a bargaining role, which ". . . calls for actions such as compromise, renunciation, face-saving of oneself, which are morally ambiguous or even downright immoral to people with morally rigorous standards" (p. 334).

Personality of Negotiators. In the eighteenth century, Callieres observed that ". . . the passions of princes and of their ministers often overrule their interests . . . men do not act upon firm and stable maxims of conduct . . . as a rule they are governed by passions and temperament more than by reason" (1919, p. 47–48). Two centuries later, a study of seventy-two business, government, and industrial conference groups found systematic evidence consistent with this speculation (Marquis, Guetzkow, & Heyns, 1951). Groups with lower incidence of self-oriented need behavior were better on three relatively uncorrelated measures of group performance: member satisfaction, group productivity, and residual disagreement. Indeed, the most predictive of some one hundred variables were those reflecting the extent to which an individual was motivated by his personal needs rather than by the situation at hand.

Personality may be more or less important, depending upon the circumstances. Snyder and Robinson (1961) report that ". . . when asked if personality plays as great (or greater) a part in behavior as organizational factors such as communication, officials who are at lower echelons tend to say no, while those at high echelons tend to say yes" (p. 158). Two of the conditions influencing the process of negotiation may also interact with person-

ality: It seems likely that personality is more important when information is less and when stress is greater.

One personality characteristic, authoritarianism, has been shown in a number of studies to be related to international attitudes and to cooperative interpersonal behavior. Lane (1955) found those higher on authoritarianism, as measured by four items from the F Scale (Adorno, Frenkel-Brunswik, Levinson, & Sanford, 1950), to be less willing to compromise: They tended to reject, in 1952, the alternative "Keep on trying to get a peaceful settlement" in favor of one extreme—"Pull out of Korea entirely"—or the other—"Take a stronger stand and bomb Manchuria and China." More authoritarian persons are also thought to change their attitudes less readily; for example, Mischel and Schopler (1959) found those who, after the second Soviet Sputnik, still thought the United States would reach the moon first to be more authoritarian. The point is not that nonauthoritarians are better predictors of the eventual landing, but rather that they seem to account for new information more reasonably; nonauthoritarians might presumably also change back to their original attitude more easily, if additional information appeared.

In an experiment employing the Prisoner's Dilemma matrix (Deutsch, 1960), authoritarianism differentiated sharply between those persons who selected the "compromise" alternative (whether choosing before or after the other) and those who selected the "hold out" alternative both times (83 percent of all subjects selected the same alternative whether choosing first or second); of twenty-four subjects choosing "compromise" both times, half were low on the F Scale and only two were high; of those choosing "hold out" both times, none was low, and nine were high. A related scale—also from the *Authoritarian personality*—the E Scale (ethnocentrism), plus some other internationalism items, were found by Lutzker (1960) likewise to predict cooperative choice in a Prisoner's Dilemma game experiment.

Another related personality characteristic, ego control, which refers to the way an individual handles his internal need-tensions and the external demands imposed upon him, was associated in one study (Blum, 1958) with selection of heroes. Among 2680 respondents, all listed in *Who's who in America*, the "over-controllers" (restrained, aloof, rigid), in comparison with the remaining individuals, were more likely (a) to select military men as great leaders, (b) to respond to prestige suggestion, (c) to give high value to maintaining the status quo, (d) to refer to power and prestige factors as reasons for greatness, and (e) to choose socially and politically conservative figures as heroes.

Thus a number of studies consistently find authoritarian individuals to be less willing to compromise and generally less likely to change their position. Paired together in negotiating situations similar to the Prisoner's Dilemma, such individuals seem likely to fare poorly. Paired against a nonauthoritarian, an authoritarian individual might do rather well, at least temporarily, though continued noncooperative choices by another person tend to result eventually in noncooperation on the part of even an originally cooperative person. Whether authoritarianism is generally functional or dysfunctional for the process of negotiation would seem to depend also upon whether the particular negotiating situation calls for rigidity or flexibility; if this is known prior to negotiation, it appears reasonable to select as negotiator a person whose natural disposition fits the role requirement.

A number of other individual characteristics seem also to be related to general performance, either in negotiation situations or in small groups more broadly. The factor most consistently predictive of leadership in small groups is intelligence. Of 182 results relating intelligence and leadership, Mann (1959) finds 92 to be statistically significant, all but one in a positive direction, though the median correlation is only about .25. Less predictive of leadership are adjustment, extroversion, dominance, and nonconservatism.

When selection is made among strategies involving varying degrees of risk, it might be expected, on the basis of several findings reviewed by Atkinson (1957), that ". . . persons in whom the achievement motive is stronger should prefer intermediate risk while persons in whom the motive to avoid failure is stronger should avoid intermediate risk and prefer either very easy and safe undertakings *or* extremely difficult and speculative undertakings" (p. 372). Individuals differ, too, in their reaction to the failure of a risky strategy—as a function of their levels of anxiety and defensiveness. Kogan and Wallach (1964) find that ". . . among the individuals high in both test anxiety and defensiveness, the failure of a risky strategy leads to a heightened affirmation of that strategy. In contrast, for the low test anxious-low defensive persons, just the reverse pattern obtains— failure of a risky strategy leads to an increase in desired shifts toward conservatism" (p. 213). The authors speculate, on the basis of these findings, that, "The failure of a risky policy pursued by political and military decision-makers of a particular personality make-up may well exacerbate their inclination toward risk-taking" (p. 214). Since negotiation requires both the willingness to take risks when appropriate and to persevere when these result badly, basic personality characteristics underlying these dispositions are crucial in a negotiator.

Thus on the basis of considerable empirical evidence, it appears reasonable that different situations, or even different tasks within the same negotiation situation, may demand varying individual characteristics, and the prescription of Francis Bacon in his essay on negotiating remains germane: "Use also such persons as affect the business wherein they are employed, for that quickeneth much; and such as are fit for the matter, as bold men for expostulation, fair-spoken men for persuasion, crafty men for enquiry and observation, froward [sic] and absurd men for business that doth not well bear out itself" (1883, pp. 234–235).

PROSPECT FOR SOCIAL-PSYCHOLOGICAL RESEARCH ON NEGOTIATION

The preceding analysis has suggested ways in which social-psychological factors enter into the goals of negotiation, the ensuing process, and the eventual outcome, as well as contribute to the pre-existing background for negotiation and to the conditions under which it is conducted. In part, these factors relate to questions central to the conduct of diplomacy: How many parties should there be to negotiation? How wide or narrow should the agenda be? Who should the negotiators be? Should proceedings be open or closed? Should the initial position be one the other might accept? How much information should the other party be given? When should threats be employed? But the answers have been partial and of uncertain validity. How can their relevance and validity be increased? Three modes of psychological research stand out as promising approaches; in order of increasing incorporation of reality, these are game experimentation, simulation, and research in situ.

Game Experimentation. Experimental games, like the Prisoner's Dilemma, provide the bare essentials common to conflict situations at any level: two or more parties, each having two or more alternative actions, which jointly determine outcomes of particular utility to each party. By incorporating these elements, such games permit use of formal analysis from game theory and from bargaining theories more generally, which specify standards for rational solution. Game experiments are relatively simple, permit rigid control, yet are rather flexible. Such factors as the kind and extent of communication possible or the information each party has about the values of the other are easily varied. Because these experimental situations are essentially nonverbal, cross-cultural comparisons can be made with relative ease.

Further, by retaining but extending the basic formulation, it is possible to construct a relatively rich experimental situation. In the Interaction Screen (Sawyer & Friedell, 1965), two subjects who cannot see or hear each other may nonetheless engage in a wide range of interactions through an electronic apparatus. Each may by his actions influence in varying degrees both his own reward and that of the other, communicate about his own and the other's proposed actions, and continually display his attitude toward the other. All of this interaction occurs through the equipment and is thus completely objective and simultaneously recorded on IBM cards.

In either simpler or more complex game experimentation, as well as in simulation, it is desirable to incorporate as many as possible of the following characteristics, so that the result may have the desired definitiveness and generality: (a) substantial instrumental motivation by the participants, (b) a situation sufficiently complex so that no ready solution is apparent, (c) a situation permitting negotiation in several areas, (d) imperfect information about the other's values, (e) alternatives and utilities that may change over time, (f) continued negotiation over a considerable period, (g) individual negotiators as representatives of groups, and (h) variations in personality as well as situational conditions, through measurement or selection of participants.

Simulation. The essential element of simulation is the representation of another, usually larger, phenomenon. If it is given context by use of appropriate instructions, an experimental game may become a simulation. Pilisuk and Rapoport (1963) did just this, giving two sets of subjects the identical Prisoner's Dilemma (with twenty rather than the usual two alternatives), but to one set in abstract form and to the other with the choices labeled as degrees of disarmament. That context makes a difference is illustrated by their finding of more cooperation in the disarmament version.

Many simulations, in their attempt to represent reality as fully as feasible, are considerably more complex. The Inter-Nation Simulation (Guetzkow, 1959; Guetzkow, Alger, Brody, Noel, & Snyder, 1963) simulates, through use of five, seven, or nine three-man groups, the interaction among and within a like number of nations. Interaction among these simulated nations includes trade, alliance, and military relations. The procedure incorporates the basic elements of negotiation: Goals are specified for the national decision-makers by making their tenure in office dependent on their continuing ability to satisfy the economic and security needs of the nation; process is realized through written and oral interaction with representatives of other nations; outcomes take the form of election, revolution, or war; conditions of information, timing, and other factors are controlled by such instruments as the simulated world press, which publishes reports of varying veracity; background is represented through instructions that outline previous history.

In simulation *or* game experimentation, the personality of the participants in negotiation is relevant, as previously shown. For this reason, McNeil (1962) has suggested, in commenting upon the use of white, middle-class Protestant children as subjects for research in intergroup conflict, that ". . . a more appropriate analogical model might be found in the study of delinquent children for whom open hostility produces less guilt, the concept of 'fair play' is less cloying, the response to implicit social criticism is more contemptuous, and the drive to power is woven more tightly into the fabric of their being" (p. 78).

In simulation, however, it is sometimes possible for the analogy between diplomat and experimental subject to be much closer than is usual in psychological research on negotiation. In simulating events leading to World War I, Hermann and Hermann (1962) selected subjects whose personality profiles matched those developed for various European principals of July 1914; rather than merely role-taking, however, the participant cast as Kaiser Wilhelm (without being told so) could act out his own needs for dominance, impulsivity, and so forth, as did the German emperor. In addition to personality matching, simulation provides conditions that, through their complexity and representation of reality, are likely to produce motivation at levels more nearly comparable to those of the actual decision-makers. Although the fate of millions does not hang upon the decision of an experimental subject, it is nonetheless possible for a highly involved subject to act with correspondingly great motivation. In evaluating the veracity of simulation, it is thus also crucial to assess the nature and degree of motivation actually existing in each participant.

In further comparison with research in situ, simulation possesses three substantial advantages. First, events that in the real world take months and years may be collapsed into days. Second, experimental conditions may be introduced that would otherwise be impossible, as in Brody's (1963) simulation of the spread of nuclear weapons to a number of nations. Third, in simulation, it is possible to replicate systematically the international system manifold, permitting application of statistical inference.

The crucial question upon which the validity of simulation depends is, of course, its relation to the phenomenon it simulates. Validity can only be established by examining the ability of simulation studies to predict real-world events. As Snyder (1963) suggests, however, the use of simulation is not restricted to verification; it can instead be profitably employed for purposes of discovery.

Research in Situ. Ultimately, international negotiation must also be studied in the actual situation, with the actual participants, as Douglas (1962) has done for labor-management mediation. As is abundantly apparent from the present analysis, virtually no systematic empirical research has been conducted on social-psychological aspects of actual international negotiation.

Initial efforts at systematic research in related areas illustrate a range of possibly fruitful approaches to data collection and analysis. Pruitt (1962) employed a job-sample interview with State Department officials, asking each to list the last four problems on which he had been working. Historical records of gross information on armaments formed the basis for Richardson's (1960) mathematical analyses of the European arms races of 1908–1914 and 1929–1939. Finer analysis, of documents exchanged between major European powers in the summer of 1914, has been conducted by North (1962) by use of content analysis; messages are rated as to the degree of hostility and other characteristics. The General Inquirer (Stone, Bales, Namenwirth, & Ogilvie, 1962) permits relatively ready computer processing of such documents. Analysis of results of such complex phenomena is often facilitated by use of multivariate statistical procedures for examining the simultaneous and independent effects of several variables. Sometimes it is also possible to study the effect of "natural experiments," formed when events of international relations transpire so as to permit inference from comparison of conditions before and after; Campbell and Stanley (1962) describe techniques for analysis of such situations.

Toward a Theory of Negotiation. Cumulative empirical findings resulting from the use of such techniques of observation and analysis as the above should eventually provide sufficient basis for an integrative theory of negotiation. Such a theory, by specifying the critical elements of negotiation and the causal relations among them, would lend coherence to specific findings dealing with particular features of negotiation. The model of negotiation displayed in Figure 13.1 may provide a beginning toward such a theory, though its immediate value lies simply in affording a useful mode of organizing the presentation of research relating to negotiation. This preliminary model might facilitate theory development, however, since it (a) identifies five classes of variables associated with negotiation, (b) suggests certain temporal relations among them, and (c) constructs a framework that accommodates levels of negotiation ranging from interpersonal to international.

Identification of the five broad aspects of goals, process, outcome, background, and conditions has provided a framework that easily subsumed the many variables that have been considered important to negotiation, such as communality of goals, threats, or open vs. secret diplomacy. Though cataloguing of variables within each of these five aspects can by no means be exhaustive at this time, a framework at least suggests where to look. It emphasizes that the study of negotiation involves not only the process within the negotiating chamber but also what occurs around it, before it, and after it.

Distinction of these five aspects also permits their temporal differentiation, with goals and background being antecedent, the process itself and the conditions under which it occurs concurrent, and the outcome consequent. This temporal sequence suggests general directions of influence from which might be developed more specific causal inferences.

Further, because the aspects of negotiation are identified in a sufficiently general fashion, it is possible to apply the model to various levels of negotiation, in which the parties range from persons to nations. Regardless, however, of the level at which negotiation is conducted, crucial variables may variously be psychological, social, economic, cultural, or political, and a satisfactory theory should incorporate each.

REFERENCES

Adams, H. *The education of Henry Adams.* New York: Random House, 1931.

Adorno, T. W., Frenkel-Brunswik, Else, Levinson, D. J., & Sanford, R. N. *The authoritarian personality.* New York: Harper, 1950.

Aronson, E., Turner, Judith A., & Carlsmith, J. M. Communicator credibility and communication discrepancy as determinants of opinion change. *J. abnorm. soc. Psychol.,* 1963, *67,* 31–36.

Atkinson, J. W. Motivational determinants of risk-taking behavior. *Psychol. Rev.,* 1957, *64,* 359–372.

Aubert, V. Competition and dissensus: Two types of conflict and of conflict resolution. *J. Confl. Resol.,* 1963, *7,* 26–42.

Bacon, F. *The essays, or counsels civil and moral.* New York: A. L. Burt, 1883.

Bales, R. F. *Interaction process analysis.* Reading, Mass.: Addison-Wesley, 1950.

Bales, R. F., & Borgatta, E. F. Size of group as a factor in the interaction profile. In A. P. Hare, E. F. Borgatta, & R. F. Bales (Eds.), *Small groups: Studies in social interaction.* New York: Knopf, 1955. Pp. 396–413.

Bales, R. F., & Strodtbeck, F. L. Phases in group problem-solving. *J. abnorm. soc. Psychol.,* 1951, *46,* 485–495.

Bastert, R. H. The two American diplomacies. *The Yale Review,* 1960, *49,* 518–538.

Bauer, R. A. The communicator and the audience. *J. Confl. Resol.,* 1958, *2,* 67–77.

Bauer, R. A. Problems of perception and the relations between the United States and the Soviet Union. *J. Confl. Resol.,* 1961, *5,* 223–229.

Berkowitz, L. Anti-Semitism, judgmental processes, and displacement of hostility. *J. abnorm. soc. Psychol.,* 1961, *62,* 210–215.

Berkowitz, L. *Aggression: A social psychological analysis.* New York: McGraw-Hill, 1962.

Bernard, Jessie Some current conceptualizations in the field of conflict. *Amer. J. Sociol.,* 1965, 70, 442–454.

Bishop, R. L. Game-theoretic analyses of bargaining. *Quart. J. Econ.,* 1963, 77, 559–602.

Bixenstine, V. E., & Wilson, K. V. Effects of level of cooperative choice by the other player on choices in a prisoner's dilemma game. *J. abnorm. soc. Psychol.,* 1963, 67, 139–147.

Black, E. R. The Indus: A moral for nations. *New York Times Magazine,* December 11, 1960, pp. 24 ff.

Blake, R. R., & Mouton, Jane S. Competition, communication, and conformity. In I. A. Berg & B. M. Bass (Eds.), *Conformity and deviation.* New York: Harper, 1961. Pp. 199–229. (a)

Blake, R. R., & Mouton, Jane S. Comprehension of own and of outgroup position under intergroup competition. *J. Confl. Resol.,* 1961, 5, 304–310. (b)

Blanchard, W. H. National myth, national character, and national policy: A psychological study of the U-2 incident. *J. Confl. Resol.,* 1962, 6, 143–148.

Blum, R. H. The choice of American heroes and its relationship to personality structure in an elite. *J. soc. Psychol.,* 1958, 48, 235–246.

Brody, R. A. Some systemic effects of the spread of nuclear weapons technology: A study through simulation of a multi-nuclear future, *J. Confl. Resol.,* 1963, 7, 663–753.

Bronfenbrenner, U. The mirror image in Soviet-American relations. *J. soc. Issues,* 1961, 17 (3), 45–56.

Callieres, F. C. de *On the manner of negotiating with princes; on the uses of diplomacy; the choice of ministers and envoys; and the personal qualities necessary for success in missions abroad.* Paris: Michel Brunet, 1716. (Translated by A. F. Whyte. New York: Houghton

Mifflin, 1919. Reissued, South Bend, Ind.: Univer. Notre Dame Press, 1963.)

Campbell, D. T., & Stanley, J. C. Experimental and quasi-experimental designs for research in teaching. In N. L. Gage (Ed.), *Handbook of research on teaching.* Chicago: Rand McNally, 1962.

Caplow, T. A. A theory of coalitions in the triad. *Amer. sociol. Rev.,* 1956, 21, 489–493.

Caplow, T. A. Further development of a theory of coalitions in the triad. *Amer. J. Sociol.* 1959, 64, 488–493.

Castore, G. F. Number of verbal interrelationships as a determinant of group size. *J. abnorm. soc. Psychol.,* 1962, 64, 456–458.

Chamberlain, N. W. *Labor.* New York: McGraw-Hill, 1958.

Cohen, A. R. Situational structure, self-esteem, and threat-oriented reactions to power. In D. Cartwright (Ed.), *Studies in social power.* Ann Arbor: Institute for Social Research, University of Michigan, 1959. Pp. 35–52.

Cohen, A. M., Bennis, W. G., & Wolkon, G. H. The effects of changes in communication networks on the behaviors of problem-solving groups. *Sociometry,* 1962, 25, 177–196.

Crow, W. J. A study of strategic doctrines using the Inter-Nation Simulation. *J. Confl. Resol.,* 1963, 7, 580–589.

Dahl, R. A. *Congress and foreign policy.* New York: Harcourt, 1950.

Dahl, R. A., & Lindblom, C. E. *Politics, economics, and welfare: Planning and politico-economic systems resolved into basic social processes.* New York: Harper, 1953.

Davison, W. P. *The Berlin blockade: A study in Cold War politics.* Princeton: Princeton Univer. Press, 1958.

Deutsch, M. Trust and suspicion. *J. Confl. Resol.,* 1958, 2, 265–279.

Deutsch, M. Trust, trustworthiness, and the F scale. *J. adnorm. soc. Psychol.,* 1960, 61, 138–140.

Deutsch, M., & Krauss, R. M. The effect

of threat upon interpersonal bargaining. *J. abnorm. soc. Psychol.*, 1960, *61*, 181–189.

Deutsch, M., & Krauss, R. M.   Studies of interpersonal bargaining. *J. Confl. Resol.*, 1962, *6*, 52–76.

Douglas, Ann   The peaceful settlement of industrial and intergroup disputes. *J. Confl. Resol.*, 1957, *1*, 69–81.

Douglas, Ann *Industrial peacemaking*. New York: Columbia Univer. Press, 1962.

Driver, M. *Conceptual structure and group processes in an Inter-Nation Simulation. Part One: The perception of simulated nations*. Princeton: Educational Testing Service, April 1962.

Durant, W. *The story of civilization: Part VI. The Reformation*. New York: Simon & Schuster, 1957.

Durant, W., & Durant, Ariel *The story of civilization: Part VII. The age of reason begins*. New York: Simon & Schuster, 1961.

Edgeworth, F. Y. *Mathematical psychics: An essay on the application of mathematics to the moral sciences*. London: Kegan Paul, 1881.

Erikson, E. *Childhood and society* (ed. 2). New York: Norton, 1963.

Fiedler, F. E.   Leader attitudes, group climate, and group creativity. *J. abnorm. soc. Psychol.*, 1962, *65*, 308–318.

Friedrich, C. J. *Man and his government: An empirical theory of politics*. New York: McGraw-Hill, 1963.

Guetzkow, H.   A use of simulation in the study of inter-nation relations. *Behav. Sci.*, 1959, *4*, 183–191.

Guetzkow, H., Alger, C. F., Brody, R. A., Noel, R. C., & Snyder, R. C. *Simulation in international relations*. Englewood Cliffs, N.J.: Prentice-Hall, 1963.

Guetzkow, H., & Gyr, J.   An analysis of conflict in decision-making groups. *Hum. Relat.*, 1954, *7*, 367–382.

Gyr, J.   An analysis of committee member behavior in four cultures. *Hum. Relat.*, 1951, *4*, 193–202.

Haas, E. B. *The uniting of Europe*. Stanford: Stanford Univer. Press, 1958.

Haas, E. B., & Whiting, A. S. *Dynamics of international relations*. New York: McGraw-Hill, 1956.

Halle, L. J.   The case for quiet diplomacy. *New York Times Magazine*, September 11, 1960, pp. 31, 139–140.

Hamblin, R. L.,   Group integration during a crisis. *Hum. Relat.*, 1958, *11*, 67–76.

Hankey, M. P. *Diplomacy by conference: Studies in public affairs*. New York: Putnam, 1946.

Harsanyi, J. C.   Approaches to the bargaining problem before and after the theory of games: A critical discussion of Zeuthen's, Hicks', and Nash's theories. *Econometrica*, 1956, *24*, 144–157.

Harsanyi, J. C.   Bargaining in ignorance of the opponent's utility function. *J. Confl. Resol.*, 1962, *6*, 29–38.

Hayter, W. G. *The diplomacy of the great powers*. London: Hamilton, 1960.

Heider, F. *The psychology of interpersonal relations*. New York: Wiley, 1958.

Hermann, C. F., & Hermann, Margaret G.   The potential use of historical data for validation studies of the Inter-Nation Simulation: The outbreak of World War I as an illustration. Department of Political Science, Northwestern University, August 1962.

Hicks, J. R. *The theory of wages*. New York: Peter Smith, 1948.

Homans, G. C. *Social behavior: Its elementary forms*. New York: Harcourt, 1961.

Hovland, C. I., Janis, I. L., & Kelley, H. H. *Communication and persuasion: Psychological studies of opinion change*. New Haven: Yale Univer. Press, 1953.

Iklé, F. C. *How nations negotiate*. New York: Harper, 1964.

Iklé, F. C., & Leites, N.   Political negotiation as a process of modifying utilities. *J. Confl. Resol.*, 1962, *6*, 19–28.

Inkeles, A., & Levinson, D. J.   National

character: The study of modal personality and sociocultural systems. In G. Lindzey (Ed.), *Handbook of social psychology*, Vol. II. Reading, Mass.: Addison-Wesley, 1954. Pp. 977–1020.

Janis, I. L., & Feshbach, S. Effects of fear-arousing communications. *J. abnorm. soc. Psychol.*, 1953, 48, 78–92.

Jensen, L. Soviet-American bargaining behavior in the postwar disarmament negotiations. *J. Confl. Resol.*, 1963, 7, 522–541.

Joseph, M. L., & Willis, R. H. An experimental analog to two-party bargaining. *Behav. Sci.*, 1963, 8, 117–127.

Kaplan, M. A. *System and process in international politics*. New York: Wiley, 1957.

Kaplan, M. A., & Katzenbach, N. deB. *The political foundations of international law*. New York: Wiley, 1961.

Kelley, H. H. Salience of membership and resistance to change of group-anchored attitudes. *Hum. Relat.*, 1955, 8, 275–289.

Kelley, H. H., & Thibaut, J. W. Experimental studies of group problem solving and process. In G. Lindzey (Ed.), *Handbook of social psychology*, Vol. II. Reading, Mass.: Addison-Wesley, 1954. Pp. 735–785.

Kennan, G. F. History and diplomacy as viewed by a diplomatist. In S. D. Kertesz & M. A. Fitzsimons (Eds.), *Diplomacy in a changing world*. South Bend, Ind.: Univer. Notre Dame Press, 1959. Pp. 101–108.

Kerr, C. Industrial conflict and its mediation. *Amer. J. Sociol.*, 1954, 60, 230–245.

Kirkpatrick, I. Open covenants—but unopenly arrived at. *New York Times Magazine*, May 15, 1960, pp. 19, 108–109.

Kissinger, H. A. *The necessity for choice*. New York: Harper, 1960.

Klineberg, O. *Tensions affecting international understanding*. New York: Social Science Research Council, 1950.

Klineberg, O. *The human dimension in international relations*. New York: Holt, Rinehart and Winston, 1964.

Kogan, N., & Wallach, M. A. *Risk taking: A study in cognition and personality*. New York: Holt, Rinehart and Winston, 1964.

Krauss, R. M. Motivational and attitudinal factors in interpersonal bargaining. *Amer. Psychologist*, 1963, 18, 392. (Abstract)

Lagos, M. G. *International stratification and underdeveloped countries*. Chapel Hill: Univer. North Carolina Press, 1963.

Landsberger, H. A. Interaction process analysis of the mediation of labor-management disputes. *J. abnorm. soc. Psychol.*, 1955, 51, 552–559.

Lane, R. E. Political personality and electoral choice. *Amer. polit. Sci. Rev.*, 1955, 49, 173–190.

Lanzetta, J. T. Some effects of situational threat on group behavior. *J. abnorm. soc. Psychol.*, 1954, 49, 445–453.

Lenczowski, G. *The Middle East in world affairs* (ed. 3). Ithaca, N.Y.: Cornell Univer. Press, 1962.

Lerche, C. O. The United States, Great Britain, and SEATO: A case study in *fait accompli*. *J. Polit.*, 1956, 18, 459–478.

LeVine, R. A. Anthropology and the study of conflict: Introduction. *J. Confl. Resol.*, 1961, 5, 3–15.

Lieberman, B. *i*-Trust: A notion of trust in three-person games and international affairs. *J. Confl. Resol.*, 1964, 8, 271–280.

Liska, G. *The new statecraft*. Chicago: Univer. Chicago Press, 1960.

Loomis, J. L. Communication, the development of trust, and cooperative behavior. *Hum. Relat.*, 1959, 12, 305–316.

Lorge, I., Davitz, J., Fox, D., & Herrold, K. Evaluation of instruction in staff action and decision making. *Air Res. and Devel. Command Tech. Rep. No.*

16. Human Resources Research Institute, Maxwell Air Force Base, Alabama, 1953.

Luce, R. D., & Raiffa, H. *Games and decisions.* New York: Wiley, 1957.

Lutzker, D. R. Internationalism as a predictor of cooperative behavior. *J. Confl. Resol.,* 1960, *4,* 426–430.

Mack, R. W., & Snyder, R. C. The analysis of social conflict—toward an overview and snythesis. *J. Confl. Resol.,* 1957, *1,* 212–248.

Mann, R. D. A review of the relationships between personality and performance in small groups. *Psychol. Bull.,* 1959, *56,* 241–270.

Marquis, D. G., Guetzkow, H., & Heyns, R. W. A social psychological study of the decision-making conference. In H. Guetzkow (Ed.), *Groups, leadership, and men.* Pittsburgh: Carnegie Press, 1951. (Reissued, New York: Russell and Russell, 1963.)

McNeil, E. B. Waging experimental war: A review of Sherif *et al., Intergroup conflict and cooperation: The Robbers Cave experiment. J. Confl. Resol.* 1962, *6,* 77–81.

Meeker, R. J., Shure, G. H., & Moore, W. H., Jr. Real-time computer studies of bargaining behavior: The effects of threat upon bargaining. *American Federation of Information Processing Societies Conference Proceedings,* 1964, *25,* 115–123.

Messé, L. A., & Sawyer, J. Unexpected cooperation in a game experiment: The Prisoner's Dilemma resolved? Social Psychology Laboratory, University of Chicago, March 1965.

Milburn, T. W. What constitutes effective U.S. deterrence. In D. J. Hekhuis, C. G. McClintock, & A. L. Burns (Eds.), *International stability: Military, economic, and political dimensions.* New York: Wiley, 1964. Pp. 174–186.

Minas, J. S., Scodel, A., Marlowe, D., & Rawson, H. Some descriptive aspects of two-person non-zero-sum games, II. *J. Confl. Resol.,* 1960, *4,* 193–197.

Mischel, W., & Schopler, J. Authoritarianism and reactions to "Sputniks." *J. abnorm. soc. Psychol.,* 1959, *59,* 142–145.

Moore, W. E., & Tumin, M. M. Some social functions of ignorance. *Amer. sociol. Rev.,* 1949, *14,* 787–795.

Morgenstern, O. The Cold War is cold poker. *New York Times Magazine,* February 5, 1961, pp. 14, 21–22.

Morgenthau, H. J. The art of diplomatic negotiation. In L. White (Ed.), *The state of the social sciences.* Chicago: Univer. Chicago Press, 1956. Pp. 404–414.

Morgenthau, H. J. *Politics among nations: The struggle for power and peace* (ed. 3). New York: Knopf, 1960.

Nash, J. The bargaining problem. *Econometrica,* 1950, *18,* 155–162.

Nash, J. Two-person cooperative games. *Econometrica,* 1953, *21,* 128–140.

Newcomb, T. M. Autistic hostility and social reality. *Hum. Relat.,* 1947, *1,* 69–86.

Newcomb, T. M. Individual systems of orientation. In S. Koch (Ed.), *Psychology: A study of a science,* Vol. 3. New York: McGraw-Hill, 1959. Pp. 384–422.

Nicolson, H. *Diplomacy.* London: Butterworth, 1939.

Nicolson, H. *The Congress of Vienna.* New York: Harcourt, 1946.

North, R. C. International conflict and integration: Problems of research. In M. Sherif (Ed.), *Intergroup relations and leadership.* New York: Wiley, 1962.

Osgood, C. E. Cognitive dynamics in the conduct of human affairs. *Publ. Opin. Quart.,* 1960, *24,* 341–375.

Osgood, C. E. *An alternative to war or surrender.* Urbana: Univer. Illinois Press, 1962.

Osgood, R. E. *Limited war: The challenge to American strategy.* Chicago: Univer. Chicago Press, 1957.

Pareto, V. *Manuel d'économie politique.* Paris: M. Giard, 1909.

Pearson, L. B. *Diplomacy in the nuclear age.* Cambridge, Mass.: Harvard Univer. Press, 1959.

Pilisuk, M., & Rapoport, A. A non-zero-sum game model of some disarmament problems. *Peace Research Society (International) Papers,* 1964, *1*, 57–78.

Pruitt, D. G. An analysis of responsiveness between nations. *J. Confl. Resol.,* 1962, *6*, 5–18.

Rabinowitch, E. *The dawn of a new age: Reflections on science and human affairs.* Chicago: Univer. Chicago Press, 1964.

Rapoport, A. *Fights, games, and debates.* Ann Arbor: Univer. Michigan Press, 1960.

Rapoport, A. Formal games as probing tools for investigating behavior motivated by trust and suspicion. *J. Confl. Resol.,* 1963, *7*, 570–579.

Richardson, L. F. *Statistics of deadly quarrels.* Pittsburgh: Boxwood Press, 1960.

Riker, W. *Theory of political coalition.* New Haven: Yale Univer. Press, 1962.

Robinson, J. A. *Congress and foreign policy-making.* Homewood, Ill.: Dorsey Press, 1962.

Rogers, C. R. Communication: Its blocking and its facilitation. *Etc., Rev. gen. Semantics,* 1952, *9*, 83–88.

Rusk, D. Parliamentary diplomacy—debate versus negotiation. *World Affairs Interpreter,* 1955, *26*, 121–138.

Russell, R. B. *A history of the United Nations charter.* Washington, D.C.: Brookings Institution, 1958.

Satow, E. M. *A guide to diplomatic practice* (ed. 4). New York: McKay, 1957.

Sawyer, J. The Altruism Scale: A measure of cooperative, individualistic, and competitive interpersonal orientation. *Amer. Psychologist,* 1964, *19*, 517. (Abstract)

Sawyer, J., & Friedell, M. F. The Inter-action Screen: An operational model for experimentation on interpersonal behavior. *Behav. Sci.,* 1965, *10* (in press).

Sawyer, J., & MacRae, D., Jr. Game theory and cumulative voting in Illinois: 1902–1954. *Amer. polit. Sci. Rev.,* 1962, *56*, 936–946.

Schattschneider, E. E. Intensity, visibility, direction, and scope. *Amer. polit. Sci. Rev.,* 1957, *51*, 933–942.

Schelling, T. C. *The strategy of conflict.* Cambridge, Mass.: Harvard Univer. Press, 1960.

Schelling, T. C., & Halperin, M. H. *Strategy and arms control.* New York: Twentieth Century Fund, 1961.

Schokking, J. J., & Anderson, N. Observations on the European integration process. *J. Confl. Resol.,* 1960, *4*, 385–410.

Scodel, A. Induced collaboration in some non-zero-sum games. *J. Confl. Resol.,* 1962, *6*, 335–340.

Scodel, A., Minas, J. S., Ratoosh, P., & Lipetz, M. Some descriptive aspects of two-person non-zero-sum games. *J. Confl. Resol.,* 1959, *3*, 114–119.

Sharp, W. R. A checklist of subjects for systematic study of international conferences. *Intern. soc. Sci. Bull.,* 1953, *5*, 311–339.

Sherif, M., Harvey, O. J., White, B. J., Hood, W. R., & Sherif, Carolyn W. *Intergroup conflict and cooperation: The Robbers Cave experiment.* Norman, Okla.: University Book Exchange, 1961.

Shubik, M. *Strategy and market structure: Competition, oligopoly, and the theory of games.* New York: Wiley, 1959.

Siegel, S., & Fouraker, L. E. *Bargaining and group decision making: Experiments in bilateral monopoly.* New York: McGraw-Hill, 1960.

Snyder, R. C. Some recent trends in international relations theory and research. In A. Ranney (Ed.), *Essays on the behavioral study of politics.* Urbana: Univer. Illinois Press, 1962. Pp. 103–171.

Snyder, R. C. Some perspectives on the use of experimental techniques in the study of international relations. In H. Guetzkow et al., Simulation in international relations. Englewood Cliffs, N.J.: Prentice-Hall, 1963. Pp. 1–23.

Snyder, R. C., & Robinson, J. A. National and international decision-making. New York: Institute for International Order, 1961.

Stein, M. I., & Heinze, Shirley J. Creativity and the individual. New York: Free Press, 1960.

Steiner, G. A. (Ed.) The creative organization. Chicago: Univer. Chicago Press, 1965.

Stone, P. J., Bales, R. F., Namenwirth, J. V., & Ogilvie, D. M. The General Inquirer: A computer system for content analysis and retrieval based upon the sentence as a unit of information. Behav. Sci., 1962, 7, 92–109.

Taylor, C. W. (Ed.) Creativity: Progress and potential. New York: McGraw-Hill, 1964.

Thibaut, J. W., & Kelley, H. H. The social psychology of groups. New York: Wiley, 1959.

Thomas, E. J., & Fink, C. F. Effects of group size. Psychol. Bull., 1963, 60, 371–384.

Tocqueville, A. de. Democracy in America, Vol. I. New York: Knopf, 1959.

U.S. President's Commission on National Goals. Goals for Americans: Programs for action in the sixties. Englewood Cliffs, N.J.: Prentice-Hall, 1960.

Vansittart, R. G. The decline of diplomacy. Foreign Affairs, 1950, 28, 177–188.

Vinacke, W. E., & Arkoff, A. An experimental study of coalitions in the triad. Amer. sociol. Rev., 1957, 22, 406–414.

Von Neumann, J., & Morgenstern, O. Theory of games and economic behavior. Princeton: Princeton Univer. Press, 1944.

Walton, R. E., & McKersie, R. B. A behavioral theory of labor negotiation: An analysis of a social interaction system. New York: McGraw-Hill, 1965.

Wedge, B. M. A note on Soviet-American negotiation. Proceedings of the Emergency Conference on Hostility, Aggression, and War. American Association for Social Psychiatry, Washington, November 1961.

White, W. L. Cross-cultural bargaining and game behavior. Proc. IX Congr. Interamer. Soc. Psychol. (in press).

Wright, Q. Problems of stability and progress in international relations. Berkeley: Univer. California Press, 1954.

Wright, G. D. Inter-group communication and attraction in Inter-Nation Simulation. Doctoral dissertation, Washington University, St. Louis, Missouri, September 1963.

Zeuthen, F. Problems of monopoly and economic warfare. London: Routledge, 1930.

Zinnes, Dina A. Expression and perception of hostility in inter-state relations. Doctoral dissertation, Stanford University, 1963.

Zinnes, Dina A., North, R. C., & Koch, H. E., Jr. Capability, threat, and the outbreak of war. In J. N. Rosenau (Ed.), International politics and foreign policy: A reader in research and theory. New York: Free Press, 1961. Pp. 469–482.

14

The next chapter continues our exploration of different situations in which face-to-face interactions across national boundaries take place. The chapter focuses on personal contacts occurring in intergovernmental organizations and, specifically, draws on observational and interview data about the United Nations. United Nations diplomats are, of course, representatives of their national governments. Yet, the nature of the setting is such that they also assume, to a considerable extent, nonnational or supranational roles; and, of necessity, they have greater freedom of action and decision latitude than diplomats in more traditional settings. Moreover, international organizations also include—as key participants in the proceedings—multinational secretariats whose members enact nonnational roles. The cross-national interactions that take place in intergovernmental organizations represent, therefore, a complex blending of interactions among national representatives and interactions among individuals participating in a new kind of international society.

What is the nature of the interaction processes in this kind of setting? What patterns of communication tend to develop among the diplomats and with what consequences for intergovernmental relations? What kinds of stresses result from the simultaneous enactment of national and nonnational roles? To what extent do the dual loyalties of secretariat members create conflicts for them? And to what extent do these dual loyalties facilitate the development of trust and consensus within the organization? What do participants in intergovernmental organizations learn from the unique interaction experiences in which they are involved, and what impact do these learnings have on the conduct of foreign policy on the part of their national governments? These are the questions to which Chapter 14 addresses itself.

The author of this chapter, Chadwick F. Alger, is Associate Professor of Political Science and Co-director of the International Relations Program at Northwestern University. In 1962–1963 he served as Visiting Professor of United Nations Affairs at New York University. He is a co-author of *Simulation in international relations* (1963); and has published articles on American foreign policy, the United Nations, international relations, and comparative politics. His major interest is in research on international organizations through interview and long-term observation. To this end, he has done first-hand observations at the United Nations for part of every year since 1958.

H. C. K.

Personal Contact in Intergovernmental Organizations*

Chadwick F. Alger

*T*he best instrument of a Government wishing to persuade another Government will always remain the spoken words of a decent man." In the nuclear age this observation appears to be even more true than when it was written by Cambon over thirty years ago (1931, p. 112). If this is a valid judgment there is some cause for rejoicing, since the number of participants in the dialogue between national governments has increased astronomically since Cambon's words were written. Heads of state, foreign ministers, and other cabinet officials as well, no longer consider personal consultation to be extraordinary. The diplomatic generalist has been joined by the economist, physicist, public relations specialist, and experts in virtually every other field of knowledge in the conduct of intergov-

ernmental conversation. Growth in the number of independent nations has brought an increase in the size of the older diplomatic communities and the establishment of new ones. New international organizations have brought a further expansion of the number of sites of diplomatic activity, and old organizations have had increases in membership.

It should not be surprising that this population growth at the sites of face-to-face contact between different nations is not welcomed by all. Men's images of how intergovernmental relations have been organized in the past serve as restraints on change they are willing to accept. This is particularly true of many who have inhabited the diplomatic "villages" of a passing era. They do not find it easy to accept new

---

* This chapter is based in part on a paper presented at the 40th Annual Meeting of the American Orthopsychiatric Association, Washington, D.C., March 1963, while the author was Visiting Professor of United Nations Affairs at New York University.

inhabitants and transients who bring unfamiliar skills and often violate established customs for the carrying out of intergovernmental relationships. Resistance to this change has brought delays both in the integration of new inhabitants at diplomatic sites and in the integration of "new diplomats" into national foreign services.

Out of personal experience in Lend-Lease and the European Recovery Program, as well as study of the European Communities, Cardozo (1962) has written of the difficulty that diplomatic communities and national foreign services are having in integrating specialists in international economic programs and representatives to international organizations. For example, he describes the difficulty that representatives to the European Communities encountered in their effort to get diplomatic status in Brussels. His account includes the rather humorous eventual disposition of their attempts to get diplomatic license plates.

[After some difficulty,] the permanent representatives to international organizations received diplomatic license plates, but their numbers started from the top of the list, whereas the diplomats accredited to the Belgian government got theirs from the more prestigious lower end (p. 121).

Cardozo deems it necessary to make a plea for broader vision on the part of diplomats, asserting:

They may profit by recalling that reluctant generals ultimately had to accept the tank and the airplane. How much better it would be if the careerists in all fields were the leaders rather than the laggards in developing and accepting the new techniques and training methods that progress demands (p. 136).[1]

Senator Jackson of the United States delivered a widely noted address on the United Nations in early 1962 which revealed antagonism to the developing role of the United Nations, because it was not consistent with Jackson's image of how international relations should be conducted. He asserted that the United States Mission to the United Nations should be staffed "more as other embassies," dissented from the view that the United States Mission has a "unique role," and objected to the role the Mission is playing by arguing: "The Ambassador to the United Nations is not a second Secretary of State, but the present arrangement suggests a certain imbalance in the role assigned to the U.N. in the policy-making process" (p. 110). He also objected to the press, radio, and television coverage of the United Nations, observing that "the space and time devoted to our U.N. delegation does not correctly reflect the relative importance of what is said in New York against what is said in Washington" (p. 110). A similar dissent in Washington from developments in Paris NATO Headquarters was revealed by Sulzberger's explanation of the removal of General Norstad as Supreme Commander Allied Powers Europe. He explained that one of the reasons for removal was Norstad's "belief in the theory that the SHAPE commander was not only an American general but wore fifteen hats as an international Allied servant—a theory discounted by contemporary Washington" (1962, p. 24).

An outburst of negativism toward developments at diplomatic sites of international organizations, particularly the United Nations, has come from some diplomats who have been schooled

---

[1] See the report of the Carnegie Endowment for International Peace, Committee on Foreign Affairs Personnel, *Personnel for the new diplomacy*, especially pp. 54–55, for the most recent commentary on prejudice in the United States Foreign Service against "specialists."

at more traditional sites. For example, Nicolson, who says he was "born and nurtured in the old diplomacy" (1962, p. 1), emits an emotional barrage when discussing the United Nations that is quite out of character with the restrained discourses to be found elsewhere in his works on diplomacy. He sees "lobbies being formed among the smaller countries (as for instance between the Asians and the Latin Americans), the sole unifying principle of which is to offer opposition even to the reasonable suggestions of the Great Powers." And he notes that public debate has led to "all rational discussion being abandoned in favour of interminable propaganda speeches" (p. 120). Another diplomat with similar experience, Thayer, writes approvingly of an Italian diplomat's assertion that lobbying at the United Nations brings "hypocrisy" and "blackmail," and asserts that "the UN's parliamentary diplomacy somehow lacks the quality of reality" (1959, p. 112). There is no doubt some truth in the comments of Nicolson and Thayer, although their extreme form of statement and almost totally negative appraisal does not engender confidence in their judgments. But one problem with commentators such as Nicolson and Thayer is that they have not dug deeply enough into the social fabric of international organizations. It seems that they are so distracted by their image of what ought to happen at diplomatic sites that they never reach an examination of much that is to be found at a site such as the United Nations.

SOME DISTINGUISHING CHARACTERISTICS OF INTERNATIONAL ORGANIZATIONS

One of the reasons why we have been slow to develop a broad sensitivity to the activity in international organiza-tions has been the tendency to perceive this activity selectively, in the light of certain descriptive terms that highlight differences between more traditional diplomacy and international organizations. Activity in international organizations has usually been characterized as "multilateral" diplomacy in contrast to more traditional "bilateral" diplomacy. It is also described as "public" diplomacy in contrast to the more "private" traditional diplomacy. But the customary usage of these terms suggests only some aspects of the diplomatic revolution that is taking place. Diplomacy at the sites of international organizations is "multilateral" in the sense that meetings take place in which a number of nations participate. But it is important to note that much bilateral diplomacy also takes place at these diplomatic sites. Likewise, "public" meetings of councils and assemblies are important activities at international organizations. But much of the work done on items on the agenda of these bodies is done in private. And private diplomacy is conducted on many problems that never get on the agenda of councils and assemblies.

Nevertheless, the regular public meetings of multilateral assemblies and councils are a distinguishing characteristic of international organization diplomacy. For this reason Rusk (1955) has described the activity of these sites as parliamentary diplomacy. This diplomacy is parliamentary not only in the sense that it involves public debates followed by votes on resolutions, but it also requires the diplomat to perform supporting parliamentary tasks, such as lobbying for resolutions and keeping in touch with a wide range of delegates in order to know both how his resolution will be received and what resolutions others are planning to introduce. Attending meetings and discharging these functions require that the diplomat spend much time moving around the "parliamentary" chambers, extending and maintaining contacts with other diplomats.

A second distinguishing characteristic of international organization diplomatic sites is that each national mission has the responsibility of representing its nation to *all* other nations represented at the site. This is quite a different assignment than that of national capital missions, which represent their nation to the host government and protect the interests of their own citizens in the country in which they are located. It is helpful to view the development of missions to international organizations in historical perspective. From one viewpoint the history of diplomacy reveals a gradual evolution toward the establishment and extension of permanent face-to-face links between national governments. The first step took place in the fifteenth century when permanent diplomatic missions in foreign countries began to develop out of temporary missions that had been dispatched for special tasks (Numelin, 1950, pp. 306–307). The development of permanent missions to international organizations can be regarded as a second important step toward this permanency. This step saw the development of permanent international conferences, or international organizations, out of *ad hoc* international conferences. The new sites joined the old ones to provide more extensive permanent social links between national governments. Dag Hammarskjold (1959) gave the following assessment of the importance of the creation of permanent national missions to the United Nations:

A development of special significance is the establishment of permanent delegations at United Nations Headquarters with standing senior representation there for all members of the Organization. While in one sense reducing the practical importance of the public sessions of the various organs, this development has, basically, tended to give these organs greater real weight in present-day diplomacy. The public debate, and the decisions reached, gain added significance when the attitudes presented in public result from practically uninterrupted informal contacts and negotiations (p. 10).

A third distinguishing characteristic is that international organization diplomatic sites also have nonnational features not present at other sites. Secretariat officials are likely to be more numerous than national officials. Much has been written about the "quiet diplomacy" of the Secretary-General of the United Nations. But the work of the Secretary-General provides only one dramatic example of the opportunities afforded thousands of other members of the United Nations Secretariat and secretariats of other international organizations in the day-to-day activity of these organizations. Furthermore, the international organization not only introduces nonnational people, but also nonnational corridors, chairs, tables, and buildings. In a national capital contact takes place either on the territory of the host government or in the embassy of the visiting diplomat. But the international organization headquarters is neutral ground. Since there is common membership in the organization and frequent visits to the "clubhouse," the occasions for contact that is unscheduled (although not necessarily unplanned by one or both parties) are greatly increased.

Description of some easily observable characteristics of international organizations whets the appetite for information that might be gathered from deeper probes into their social fabric. For example: (a) Are communication patterns between nations and the kinds of information that are communicated different in international organizations than they are in more traditional diplomatic settings? And, if they are different, do they have any impact on aspects of international relations that we might call significant? (b) What functions do nonnational roles perform? (c) Do participants in international organizations have learning experiences that are significantly different from those acquired in more traditional diplomacy? The remainder of this chapter will be devoted to throwing some light on these three questions. These have been chosen because observational and interview data are available. Though the data are of modest dimensions, they will provide a sounder basis for hypothesis development than a wider-ranging discussion based wholly on conjecture. The three questions also illustrate three ways in which international organizations affect international systems: through reshaping the patterns of intergovernmental contact, through creating new roles that intervene in these relationships, and through changing the experiences of national officials.

INTERGOVERNMENTAL COMMUNICATIONS IN INTERNATIONAL ORGANIZATIONS

Superficial knowledge of international organizations reveals that participation in them brings extensive changes in intergovernmental communications. In international organizations some nations have continual access to each other that have very slight opportunity for contact elsewhere.[2] The opportunity for interaction between Paraguay and Nepal in the United Nations would offer a striking example. The consideration of a common agenda by virtually all nations in an international system encourages the creation of new coalitions around certain issues. An example would be cooperation in the United Nations between Latin Americans and Afro-Asians on economic development questions. When new coalitions are created around certain issues, they establish new communication networks. The analysis that follows reveals that the creation of international organizations transforms intergovernmental communications in terms of the amount of contact between diplomats, the mode of contact, who communicates with whom, and what is communicated. Discussion will be based on the writer's personal observations at the United Nations over a number of years and responses to a questionnaire administered by Best in 1960 in an effort to assess more systematically hypotheses that developed out of these observations. In these interviews a randomly selected member of each national permanent mission to the United Nations was asked to make comparisons between the United Nations and national capital diplomatic sites.

First, respondents were asked about the amount of contact they had with diplomats from other nations. Responses to the question, "As compared with a post in a national capital, here at the UN do you personally have more contact or less contact with diplomats from countries other than your own?" were distributed as follows:[3]

	Number	Percent
Much more	27	35
More	40	51
Same	6	7
Less	4	5
Much less	1	1
TOTAL	78	99

[2] See Alger, 1965, for fuller discussion.

[3] The following table, and all subsequent tables in this chapter, are reprinted from the unpublished doctoral dissertation of the late Gary Best, by permission of the author's parents, Mr. and Mrs. Donald Best.

Clearly, diplomats at the United Nations have more (or feel they have more) contact with diplomats from other nations, in part because they have fewer responsibilities for citizens of their own nations. Best found the following comment by an Eastern European delegate to be "typical of the majority of all delegates" interviewed:

The contact that you have here with other diplomats is ten or twenty times more than that which you would have in a national capital. This is especially true during the Assembly sessions. You have contacts every day and not with just one person, but rather with many persons. Between sessions, there is still more contact here with diplomats from other countries than there would be in a national capital (p. 121).

The mode of contact was also investigated by asking: "As compared with a post in a national capital, here at the United Nations would you personally be more likely or less likely to communicate orally with representatives of other countries?" The following responses were obtained:

	Number	*Percent*
Much more	7	9
More	55	73
Same	13	17
Less	0	0
Much less	0	0
TOTAL	75	99

It is not only the sharing of U.N. headquarters that encourages increased oral contact, but also the fact that U.N. diplomats perform a different kind of role. One diplomat replied:

In Washington you have few opportunities to meet diplomats from any other country than the U.S. You even meet those from the U.S. infrequently and by appointment. When you do meet someone from another country, such as India, you have nothing in particular to talk about. In Washington, if I were to ask an Indian about some aspect of Indian relations with the State Department, this might be considered improper. Here you can ask an Indian his position on any problem (p. 132).

It is likely that contact between diplomats at the United Nations is predominantly face-to-face, although interview data are not available to document this observation. This contact is at its highest peak during the three months in which the General Assembly is in session. The Assembly's seven committees, which are all committees of the whole with 114 nations represented in each, meet simultaneously throughout the September to December period. Some delegates sit next to each other for three months and engage in long discussions while public debate is in progress. Almost all delegates participate in the public debate in these committees and many participate in the concurrent lobbying, drafting of resolutions, and exchange of ideas that take place in pairs and small groups in the committee rooms, in the corridors, and in missions. Many continue these conversations at the bar in the delegates' lounge and in the delegates' dining room, and at cocktail parties and smaller gatherings. The public debate of the Assembly provides the impetus for much of this activity, but it is only a part of the total dialogue. Though not at such a frenzied pace, the network of conversations continues at United Nations headquarters throughout the year as subcommittees of the Assembly, the Councils and their subcommittees, and sometimes additional sessions of the Assembly itself meet. Even when the Assembly is not in session 51 percent of the members of permanent missions go to United Nations headquarters three or more times a week and 82 percent go twice a week (Best, 1960, p. 98).

Respondents not only judged that they had more personal contact with diplomats from other nations at the United Nations, but also indicated that communication patterns are different in some interesting respects. Because of the considerable attention that the literature on diplomacy has given to diplomatic rank, delegates were asked: "As compared with a post in a national capital, here at the UN would you personally be more likely or less likely to communicate with another delegate without regard for diplomatic rank?" The distribution of responses was:

	Number	*Percent*
Much more	10	13
More	53	70
Same	11	14
Less	2	3
Much less	0	0
TOTAL	76	100

Delegates indicated that the most important reason for increased contact across ranks is the fact that people of differing ranks sit on the same bodies of the United Nations, making contact across ranks a practical necessity. For example, a diplomat who had previously served in London remarked:

Such contacts are much easier here. If an attaché and a minister are both concerned with the same problem here, they will communicate with each other frequently. They will talk almost as equals. This would be unheard of in London. In fact, here very few people even know the ranks of other people with whom they are working. In London, you would definitely know the rank of someone before you communicated with him (p. 125).

Best also learned that diplomats find it easier to make contact with representatives of unfriendly countries at the United Nations than is the case in national capitals. The respondents were asked: "As compared with a post in a national capital, here at the UN would you personally be more likely or less likely to have contacts with delegates from an unfriendly country?" Their replies were:

	Number	*Percent*
Much more	10	14
More	54	77
Same	6	9
Less	0	0
Much less	0	0
TOTAL	70	100

Quotations from two respondents indicate that both the meetings of United Nations bodies and more informal occasions provide the opportunity for increased contact between diplomats from unfriendly countries:

Sometimes we vote for a Soviet resolution and sometimes the Soviets vote for one of ours. The negotiations leading to these votes bring about contacts between the two delegations.

I would be far more likely to talk to Hungarians here than I would in a national capital. Many times this actually happens quite accidentally. You'll be talking with a group of delegates and one will just happen to be a Hungarian (p. 129).

It was found that contact between unfriendly countries did not extend to all unfriendly dyads; one exception mentioned was contact between Arabs and Israelis. However, some governments actually instruct their delegates to have contact with diplomats from unfriendly countries in the United Nations while at the same time instructing their diplomats in national capitals to the contrary.

Contact across ranks and between unfriendly countries are only two ways in which an international organization such as the United Nations alters patterns of communications that exist outside the organization. While serving on subcommittees, cooperating on a resolution, and sitting next to each other in meetings, delegates often initiate contacts that would never be established except for these events. For example, seatmates in General Assembly committees have been observed in conversations that go on for an hour or more and that add up to many days of dialogue during a General Assembly. Such extensive conversations have been observed between diplomats from Hungary and Honduras, from Netherlands and Nepal, and from Afghanistan and Yugoslavia. Perhaps the most intriguing were the conversations of a facile Irish diplomat who alternated between his seatmates on either side—the representatives from Iraq and Israel. It is quite likely that much of this talk is not about business. But it is also most certain that some of it is.

Observers and participants often use the term "informal" to describe United Nations diplomacy. Accordingly, respondents were asked: "In general, as compared with a post in a national capital, here at the UN are your relations with other representatives more formal or less formal?" The responses were distributed as follows:

	Number	Percent
Much more formal	1	1
More formal	2	3
Same	11	14
Less formal	59	77
Much less formal	4	5
Total	77	100

Two comments illustrate contrasting attitudes toward the more informal U.N. society:

> There is none of this silly stuff that there is in capitals . . . . Delegates at the United Nations become colleagues.

> Protocol is not stiff here. In fact there is no protocol at all . . . . The situation is one of anarchy (p. 135).

Although there was probably no common definition of "informal" on the part of respondents, the 82 percent who believe the United Nations to be more informal tend to corroborate responses obtained on the unfriendly-nations and across-ranks communication questions. There is clearly a feeling of much less restraint on the establishment of contact with other diplomats than is the case at national capital sites.

The interview also investigated the diplomat's perception of the exchange of information at the United Nations. Each diplomat was asked: "As compared with a post in a national capital, here at the UN is it more difficult or less difficult to exchange 'off the record' information with another nation?" The following replies were obtained:

	Number	Percent
Much more difficult	0	0
More difficult	3	4
Same	21	28
Less difficult	41	55
Much less difficult	9	12
Total	74	99

The two comments below were made by respondents who thought it less difficult to exchange "off the record" information at the United Nations:

> In a national capital when one ambassador goes to visit another ambassador, each knows that the one has come for some specific reason. It's not just a social

visit. Here two ambassadors can just begin chatting, and one can find out something from the other without the other person knowing that this was the specific purpose of the meeting.

There is a daily exchange of views that goes on at the UN that would be impossible in a national capital. . . . There was just no such common meeting place in Washington as there is in New York. You couldn't just go down to the State Department and sit around chatting with diplomats from other countries (p. 191).

Another dimension of the usefulness of the United Nations as an arena for the exchange of information was also explored by asking: "Is your UN mission more important as a source of information than a post in a national capital?" These were the replies:

	Number	Percent
Most important	9	20
More important	25	57
Same	3	7
Less important	7	16
TOTAL	44	100

It is notable that 34 respondents did not reply to this question, with a number feeling unable to compare the two kinds of diplomatic sites on this basis because they considered them to be so different that they found comparison impossible. As one delegate expressed it:

The UN is our best over-all observation post. This is the best place to find out how the general international winds are blowing. However, if our government wanted to know specifically about something that was going on in Paris, it would contact the ambassador in Paris (p. 188).

One of the qualities of the United Nations as a source of information is the ability of diplomats to contact quickly a large number of countries. As one delegate explained it:

When a piece of news like this takes place it is most useful to just wander through the corridors of the UN or to stroll aimlessly through the Delegates' Lounge. You can talk with a great number of people from a large number of countries to find out how they are reacting. You can't do something like this in a national capital. There is no building, no meeting place, where all these people would just happen to be. And in very few capitals would there be this many people even present (p. 192).

In drawing conclusions from these interview data, it is important to bear in mind that they are based on participant perceptions rather than on direct measures of the phenomena under examination. Furthermore, the comparisons between the United Nations and national capitals were all made by diplomats who were at the time active in United Nations roles. A replication of the study with interviews of national capital diplomats would provide additional data that would permit more reliable comparison. While recognizing these limitations, it seems prudent to probe the potential significance of the characteristics of United Nations communications as perceived by participants. The data presented suggest that, when an issue is inscribed on the agenda of a United Nations body, its consideration is not only affected by the rules of procedure and norms for public debate and decision-making, but it is also introduced into a diplomatic community where the norms for intergovernmental contact and intergovernmental information exchange are different than in national capitals.

There are grounds for speculating that intergovernmental communication systems in international organizations bear an important relationship to their capacity for managing conflict. For example, the communication system at the United Nations brings to mind March and Simon's (1963) discussion of "channelling of information" in their summary of the propositions to be found in the literature on *Organizations*. By channelling of information, they mean "limiting the number of organization members to whom any given bit of information is transmitted" (p. 128). The available data on intergovernmental communications at the United Nations suggest that there is less channelling of information at the United Nations than in national capitals. March and Simon assert that: "The greater the channelling of information processing, the greater the differentiation of perceptions within the organization" (p. 128). Fanelli (1956) reports a strikingly similar finding:

. . . to the extent that the individual is cut off from significant interaction with others he is likely to develop "private" (as opposed to "shared") frames of reference which effectively limit his grasp of social reality.

Extending this idea to the community situation under consideration here, we suggest that high communicators . . . are likely to perceive the community in a different way than do low communicators (p. 443).

March and Simon find that differing perceptions of reality are one of the causes of conflict. This suggests that the United Nations communication system would tend to diminish conflict that is based on differing perceptions of reality.

The greater amount of face-to-face interaction at the United Nations permits the communication of additional information through gesture, facial expression, and tone of voice. It also permits a variety of opportunities for feedback in parliamentary debate,

small negotiation sessions, and impromptu encounters in corridors and lounges. Leavitt and Mueller (1955) offer experimental evidence that both face-to-face contact and feedback resulting from opportunity to ask questions provide a receiver with a better understanding of what a sender is trying to communicate. They also report that when there is opportunity for feedback both "the sender and the receiver can feel, correctly, more confident that they have respectively sent and received accurately" (p. 414). This suggests that conflict generated by inaccurate communications and also by lack of confidence in communication systems would tend to be diminished at the United Nations.

Related also are Kelley's (1950) findings in the study of communication in hierarchies. He found that "communication serves as a substitute for real upward locomotion in the case of low-status persons who have little or no possibility of real locomotion" (p. 55). Hermann (1961) has proposed the application of this proposition to international organizations, suggesting that providing a place "for smaller and developing countries to become high communicators, makes them better able to endure a status position which otherwise can be modified by peaceful means only by a rather long process" (p. 17).

NONNATIONAL ROLES

Though there is much truth in the often repeated assertion that an international organization is nothing more than a composite picture of member nations, this is not entirely true. International organizations have nonnational roles that are performed both by members of secretariats and by national officials. These nonnational roles have limited capacity for affecting international relations, because they operate under the scrutiny of bodies made up of national representatives. Nevertheless, they comprise a social structure that intervenes in relations between national roles from different nations. Discussion will first focus on national diplomats who perform nonnational roles, followed by consideration of the more widely publicized nonnational roles of members of secretariats. Information has largely been obtained through personal observation and discussion with United Nations diplomats.

National Officials

The parliamentary framework of intergovernmental relations in the United Nations, and in other international organizations as well, requires that national officials assume a variety of nonnational roles. Efforts to make collective decisions in committees with as many as 114 members stimulate the aggregation of national interests, division of labor, and the assignment of leadership roles. Some of the roles that are created to serve those purposes, such as those of officials in committees of the General Assembly, are filled by election or formal appointment. In other cases more informal selection takes place, such as the selection of those who serve as intellectual leaders of the diplomatic community, as facilitators of agreement, and as representatives of a number of nations in negotiations. All of these nonnational roles help to make the social structure found at the United Nations more elaborate than that found in national capitals. They make the United Nations and other international organizations more than a society of national officials and secretariats.

The three kinds of more informal roles that were mentioned above will be discussed first: facilitators of agreement, representatives of a group of nations, and intellectual leaders.

A United Nations diplomat may facilitate the reaching of agreement by mediating between two conflicting points of view or by helping to find common ground in a body that has such diverse tendencies that it may be unable to take any action at all. Mediation efforts range from casual individual initiatives in lounge and corridor to more formal sessions in which certain representatives are asked by representatives from other nations to meet singly or jointly with conflicting parties. An example of how national and nonnational roles can be played by the same person was provided in the Special Session of the General Assembly on peace-keeping finance in 1963. The major issue was the apportionment of expenses for the Congo and Suez peace-keeping forces among the members. The Soviet bloc and the French objected to any apportionment at all, saying that the expenditures had been incurred in operations that violated the Charter. Most of the remainder of the membership acknowledged their responsibility but split into two groups with differing views on how the expenses should be apportioned. On one side was a small number of developed nations who would be asked to provide most of the money required and on the other side were the less-developed nations who controlled well over a majority of the votes. Each group preferred methods of apportionment more favorable to the kind of nation in its group. In order to get the necessary money and also the required number of votes, a compromise between the two groups was necessary. An agreement was negotiated in a ten-nation group made up of two teams, five representatives from the developed nations and five from the less-developed nations. A Canadian representative served as chairman of the negotiation sessions and is given much credit by both sides for helping to mediate points of difference between them. However, he also served as a forceful Canadian spokesman and would at these times tell the group that he was stepping out of his role as chairman. In addition, he was chairman of the developed nation negotiating team.

Delegates may also attempt to facilitate agreement through refusing to take a stand in the early stages of debate, in the belief that it is necessary for some to hold aloof so that they are available for mediation. At the same time they may be working hard privately, encouraging others to introduce resolutions and perhaps even writing resolutions for them to introduce. Willingness to accept public anonymity, and even anonymity so far as some of their colleagues are concerned, may permit delegates to exert considerable influence by selecting the one who will take the public initiative on a given item and perhaps even by writing his speech and resolution. Such strategies may, of course, be used as more effective means of advancing national policy than public debate. For example, the United States may decide that certain proposals it wishes to make will be more likely to get a sympathetic hearing if introduced by a small nation rather than by the United States. On the other hand, delegates at times deprive themselves of the opportunity to advance the preferred policy of their own nation in the interest of advancing what seems to be the most feasible basis for general agreement.

Diplomats may also represent a number of nations in negotiations with other diplomats. In one instance in a General Assembly committee in 1962, two diplomats from Western nations met with representatives of Afro-Asian nations in an attempt to arrange a compromise between a resolution favored by the Afro-Asians and Western amendments. The Western diplomats undertook these negotiations not as representatives of their *own* nations but as representatives of a *group* of nations, having the power to commit other Western nations to a compromise within certain specified limits. This successful effort was the conclusion to an intriguing parliamentary drama in which one of the Western negotiators had actually participated in the writing of the Afro-Asian resolution. This was done with the desire to get a moderate Afro-Asian resolution introduced early in the debate that would have sufficient backing to head off possibly more extreme drafts. When other Western nations would not support the resolution, this diplomat then attempted to salvage as much of it as possible through representing the West in negotiations that produced a compromise. In this case the Western diplomat, who played so important a role, was never associated publicly with either the Afro-Asian resolution, the proposed Western amendments, or with the eventual compromise. He played a very minor role in the public debate, and, therefore, he left no public record of his efforts. In fact, only some of the committee members were aware of his significant part in the eventual compromise solution.

Some diplomats become intellectual leaders in certain problem areas because of the information they possess and are able to bring to bear on problems at hand. This superior knowledge may be explained by a variety of factors: long tenure, the importance of a problem area to the diplomat's government, his personal interest, or perhaps his experience on a U.N. subcommittee or special mission that studied the problem in detail. The possession and effective use of information enables some diplomats to exert greater influence than others in United Nations bodies.

Examples of this kind of role are provided by some of the members of the twelve-man Advisory Committee on Administrative and Budgetary Questions, who review the Secretary-General's annual budget before it is presented to the Administrative and Budgetary Committee (Fifth Committee) of the General Assembly each fall. With rare exceptions, the recommendations of this committee are accepted by the General Assembly. Members of the twelve-man Advisory Committee, who serve on it as individual experts, subsequently play prominent roles in the General Assembly committee on matters that have been examined in the Advisory Committee. In the General Assembly committee they speak more than other members, and their advice is often sought. In a study of the Advisory Committee, Singer (1957) describes the "Two-Hat Problem" that results from persons serving both as experts on the Advisory Committee and as national representatives on the larger body. He quotes Trygve Lie's assertion, when he was Secretary-General, that "membership in the Advisory Committee should disqualify a person from service as a member or alternate in the Fifth Committee." Lie saw danger in a situation where Advisory Committee members "also represent their Governments, as representatives or as advisers, in the [General Assembly] . . . where they act as advocates for the Advisory Committee, or may argue or vote against its recommendations" (p. 402). On the other hand, the participation of Advisory Committee members in the Fifth Committee gives them opportunities for injecting their more thorough knowledge of many committee issues into private and public General Assembly debate. They would not have such opportunities if they did not wear two hats.

Thus far the discussion has been about what might be called *ad hoc* roles that are exercised in connection with specific agenda items or problem areas. In addition, there are roles to which diplomats are elected by their colleagues, such as that of chairman, vice-chairman, and rapporteur of committees, and President of the General Assembly. These roles are generally exercised with considerable detachment from national roles by diplomats from all regions of the world. The chairman of a committee, for example, normally satisfies even those from countries unfriendly to his own that he has tried to give a fair hearing to all and has not steered debate in ways advantageous to his own nation. One reason a chairman finds it necessary to do this is that retaliation for unfair treatment could be quickly applied in other bodies where diplomats from other nations have the chair. But it is also the case that unfairness might wreck the proceedings of his own committee by encouraging unnecessary argument and wrangling. This route is avoided, it seems, because there is a desire on the part of chairmen and other elected officials to be recognized as good performers. As a result, chairmen are concerned with such things as getting through the agenda on time, having a full list of speakers for each meeting, and getting resolutions in on time. Thus, the institutional norms for a "good" chairman cause diplomats to behave much differently than they would if sitting at their country's seat in the body concerned.

Diplomats are also called upon to fill other nonnational roles when small groups are asked to draw up recommendations or reports for the consideration of larger bodies. Examples of such tasks are visiting missions to colonial territories and the Committee on Contributions of the General Assembly which recommends how the expenses of the United Nations should be apportioned. Involvement in such tasks seems to have an effect on the behavior of national delegations when reports are submitted to the parent body. Participation provides a delegate's government with new information that may affect policy. Furthermore, there is a tendency for national delegations to support reports and recommendations for which their own diplomats share some responsibility. For example, possibly because of preoccupation with the India-China border dispute, the Indian delegation was most inactive in the Administrative and Budgetary Committee of the General Assembly in 1962. However, when the Committee on Contributions made its report, suggesting a formula for making budgetary assessments on members, the Indian delegation became quite active in efforts to obtain support for the report. This appeared to be related to the fact that the Committee on Contributions' report was presented by its Indian chairman, a former Indian Ambassador to the United Nations.

Though there is evidence to indicate that United Nations diplomats handling both national and nonnational roles are adept at wearing more than one hat, there is also indication of stress between different roles that are being handled by one person. For example, during recent private negotiations in the United Nations General Assembly, in which a few delegates were trying to find a solution acceptable to the entire Assembly, a delegate said to me: "If some of our governments knew in detail what we are doing here, we would be fired." William J. Goode (1960) draws attention to the fact that

"conflicting [role] strains frequently result in changes in the social structure." It is clear that the nonnational roles that national diplomats perform at the United Nations are bringing change in the intergovernmental social structure, though as Goode concludes, "whether the resulting societal pattern is 'harmonious' or integrated, or whether it is even effective in maintaining the society, are separate empirical questions" (p. 494).

The nonnational roles held by national officials at the United Nations would appear to integrate the membership through developing capacity for making common decisions. It has been described how occupants of these roles help to aggregate diverse interests around a common policy and how they sometimes provide information and standards of judgment that are independent of any particular national interest. In addition, the exercise of these roles by national officials permits them to inject new information and perspectives into their own national systems. Sometimes their involvement in an international enterprise brings their government to support an activity that they might not otherwise have supported. Thus, there is some indication that the exercise of nonnational roles has an effect on national policies.

Secretariat

Secretariat roles at international organization diplomatic sites have received more attention than nonnational roles occupied by national diplomats. Interest is usually focused, however, on certain dramatic activities on the part of high secretariat officials, such as mediation efforts of the Secretary-General of the United Nations in the Cuban crisis of 1962 and the Suez crisis of 1956. But the functioning of secretariats, like that of national missions, also includes the continuous participation in an intergovernmental society by hundreds and sometimes thousands of international civil servants engaged in a multitude of activities. It is this aspect of the performance of secretariats that will be considered here.

As members of a secretariat take part in the daily life of an international organization, they provide a continuous flow of messages into its society. They (a) inform others of past practice and accepted norms of the organization, (b) provide background information through documents and the spoken word, and (c) serve as nonnational monitors of relations among national representatives and of the health of the organization. Like some of the nonnational role activity of national diplomats, much secretariat activity is more effective if few know about it.

Secretariat officials, along with national diplomats having long terms of service in an international organization, serve as reservoirs of knowledge on past practice and accepted norms in a variety of ways. One example that can be publicly observed in the case of the United Nations is the support provided by the secretariat during public meetings. On the dais of a General Assembly committee the chairman, a national diplomat, has on one side of him the undersecretary responsible for secretariat activities on the problems being debated and on the other side a committee-secretary provided by the secretariat. Committee chairmen change each year, but there is considerable continuity in the undersecretary and committee-secretary posts. There is also continuity in the staffs that assist these officials and sit behind them on the dais. Even if a chairman has served in the committee on previous occasions, he has not had experience in guiding the work of the committee and must

rely a great deal on experienced members of the secretariat when the intricacies of both substance and procedure are faced.

The chairing of a General Assembly committee thus becomes a cooperative project between secretariat and chairman. Particularly crucial is the function of the committee-secretary, who helps the chairman keep an eye on the pace at which the committee is handling its work; maintains a list of delegates having indicated a desire to speak; prods those who have not yet signed up to do so, if they intend to speak; and encourages those intending to propose resolutions to submit them. During meetings the conversations between chairman and committee-secretary are frequent. Their cooperative judgments about committee pace can be important to final outcomes on issues. To push an item to a vote too soon may stop the private negotiation that takes place alongside public debate in any parliamentary body before it achieves a fruitful consensus. To fail to close debate at the appropriate time may permit an existing consensus to disintegrate during subsequent public argument. Committee-secretaries play a role in these decisions. In the rapid interaction that takes place as a committee reaches the point of decision on an agenda item, the committee chairman sometimes neglects to turn off his microphone before consulting his secretary. On one occasion the meeting room of a General Assembly committee echoed the hurried advice of a committee-secretary to his chairman: "Have them vote now!"

An important part of the role of any secretariat is the gathering of information on substantive issues for the use of the councils and assemblies that it services. This pool of information may be considerable. In the case of the United Nations, the documentary product is often more than participating diplomats can consume. Secretariats thus are common information agencies for participating nations, thereby tending to increase agreement on what the facts are and what the significant problems are. H. G. Nicholas, in *The United Nations as a political institution* (1959), asserts:

The collection, ordering and providing of information at the points where it is most needed and can produce its greatest effect is one of the most important services that U.N. officials discharge. It is much more than an archivist's or statistician's function; it is political in the highest degree, calling for qualities of political judgment and forethought no less than of accuracy and integrity (p. 147).

The documentary product of the secretariat is particularly important for the small national missions which cannot afford research staffs. Information is not only provided in documents, but also in a continual round of discussion between secretariat and national diplomats, in lounges and corridors, in secretariat offices, and during public meetings. Two United Nations diplomats have written:

Many international civil servants have better technical qualifications for discussing some of the subjects within the jurisdiction of ECOSOC than do the government representatives attending particular meetings. It is sometimes difficult to avoid feelings of inferiority on the part of delegates, and of superiority on the part of the Secretariat caused by a misunderstanding of the nature of their functions (Hadwen & Kaufmann, 1962, p. 21).

On occasions the secretariat provides nonnational pools of information that erode away some of the more extreme information products of national governments. An example has been the information supplied by secretariat and national diplomats who have gone to colonial territories on visiting missions. Information provided both by nations administering territories and by nations attacking their colonial administrations has received effective challenge by information collected under United Nations auspices.

There are a variety of ways in which secretariat personnel can act as nonnational monitors of an international system represented in an organization. This may simply mean correcting a message garbled in transit between two nations, or making certain that antagonists stay in contact through the good offices of the secretariat. Secretariats cannot always help, do not always seize all opportunities, nor do they act with desired effect in all situations. But the nonnational element they provide in the continuing conversation in an international organization is different than the contribution of any nation. From their nonnational posture they sometimes see undesirable consequences of certain projected actions that more partisan diplomats do not see in the heat of battle. They are a continuing source of suggestions on how things might be done. Not infrequently there is an available national diplomat willing to take credit for advancing their ideas. On occasion the "suggestions" of the secretariat may consist of texts of resolutions and have even included speeches introducing resolutions.

This brief discussion of secretariats has highlighted some of their less publicized, though not necessarily less significant, contributions. In particular, it has demonstrated that secretariat participation in the political process in international organizations is not confined to the dramatic mediation or "quiet diplomacy" of a few high-ranking officials. Many members of secretariats are also vital participants in the continuous debate and discussion in which national officials are engaged. Because of their tenure, expertise, and detachment (from national roles), they are able to exert influence on decisions. In this respect they have an impact on policy in much the same way as members of national bureaucracies.

Like national officials who also occupy nonnational roles, members of secretariats can also occasionally inject information and perspectives gained in their roles into the foreign affairs apparatuses of their own nations. While from one viewpoint it may be regretted that the national origins of members of secretariats may inhibit loyalty to an international organization, national affiliations permit secretariats to have lines of communication to resident national diplomats that are at times quite useful. On some occasions contact between secretariat officials and national diplomats is looked upon with suspicion. One occasion received much note in the press when the United Nations Undersecretary for Political Affairs, a Soviet citizen, passed several notes to the Soviet representative during a Security Council meeting. The assumption by the press that the Undersecretary was engaging in improper conduct was never supported by information about the content of his messages. There could be alternative explanations of his behavior. For example, he could have been communicating information consistent with his U.N. obligations but which the Soviet delegate would not have deemed reliable had it come from a secretariat official of any other nationality. This is a kind of role not peculiar to international politics. Executives in the U.S. government sometimes serve as useful links to officials in their native states. For example, it might be recalled that Assistant Attorney General Louis F. Oberdorfer, an Alabaman, helped to mediate the Birmingham racial dispute in May 1963.

There has been much discussion of the importance of developing loyalty to international organizations on the part of secretariats and of national officials who assume such posts as President of the United Nations General Assembly. In addition, there is naturally concern that they have necessary *expertise* on substantive questions. It is, indeed, crucial that occupants of these roles not receive instructions from governments and that they have a high degree of substantive *expertise*. But the preceding discussion reveals that these are not the only necessary attributes of effective performance of nonnational roles. Particular attitude and skill requirements must be appraised in the context of social processes in which nonnational roles are involved. Technically competent and loyal secretariats can achieve little without the development of a high degree of consensus, on specific issues, among member nations. This requires the continual redefinition of the interests of particular nations in the context of the developing interests of other nations. Observation indicates that nonnational roles encourage the development of consensus through the part they play in linking nations in a common political process. Though it may in some ways seem paradoxical, the nationalism of the occupants of some nonnational roles may provide indispensable links between this political process and national governments.

It is sometimes forgotten that bureaucrats in many settings are, to some degree, representatives as well as experts. The performance of the United States Foreign Service, to use a national bureaucracy example, has been appraised with suspicion and severely criticized by legislators and citizens from other areas of the United States because it recruits a disproportionate number of its officers from a few North-eastern schools. In response, the Foreign Service is intensifying recruitment in other areas and is also encouraging officers to spend their leaves among the people in their native states. It is hoped that this program will extend the links between the implementation of United States foreign policy in the field and the population throughout the nation. Is it reasonable to expect that links between secretariats and their constituent national governments are any less important?

LEARNING EXPERIENCES OF PARTICIPANTS

The flow of information, patterns of contact, and exercise of and contact with new roles provide new kinds of experiences for participants in international organizations. The members of national missions are, like members of all diplomatic missions, extensions of national bureaucracies. However, broader geographic scope of contact, more numerous discussions with diplomats from other nations, and perhaps exercise of nonnational roles require them to see a broader panorama of the world than before. Members of secretariats have similar experiences, usually with more intense effect, because of their greater independence from the governments of their own nations. The learning experiences of individual participants in an international organization are a factor that contributes to the quality of its society. The images that participants acquire of the organization itself and of the international system that is represented in it affect the communication patterns that these individuals establish and the kind of social environment that they help provide for other participants. In addi-

tion, when these individuals move on to other roles, probably elsewhere in their national governments, they may apply their learning at other sites.

Addressing themselves to the effects of participation in the United Nations, two career diplomats wrote as follows, after serving for several years in the missions of Canada and the Netherlands to the United Nations:

In the U.N. . . . the word "diplomat" is rapidly losing its old connotation of elegance and wealth. As the U.N. security services have noted, "It is difficult to tell the delegates from the visitors." Thus the U.N. has had an effect even on the appearance of U.N. delegates, and by its methods of operation possibly on their characters. There is no doubt that the personal and parliamentary experience which delegates get at the U.N. may have long run consequences of value to the international community (Hadwen & Kaufmann, 1962, p. 54).

B. F. Matecki (1957) offers a supporting observation when he mentions "the profound changes that the personal contact of members of United States delegations to international institutions has wrought in their thinking and outlook" (p. 143). He also cites examples in which United States delegates have, as a result of changed attitudes, been able to get United States policy changed (pp. 92, 142–143, 159–160). Alexander Dallin (1962) writes the following about Soviet officials:

While there are wide variations, one gains the impression that Soviet personnel stationed at the U.N.—be it with the U.S.S.R. mission or on the United Nations staff—tend to be more practical and pragmatic in outlook than those in the "home office"; at times, they seem less concerned with doctrine than with success. And while it is easy to exaggerate such nuances, there are occasional suggestions of different perceptions of reality (p. 96).

The writer has investigated the dimensions of learning experiences acquired through participation in the United Nations by means of interviews, discussions with delegates, and by observation. The interviews were conducted in 1959 with twenty-five General Assembly delegates both during the first two weeks of their service in the General Assembly and two months later.[4] The sample includes nine delegates from the Far East, three from the Middle East, six from Europe, three from Africa, and four from the Americas. These delegates all had their first experience in the United Nations during the period between the before-and-after-experience interviews. Thirteen came to the General Assembly from other foreign affairs posts (eight from their respective foreign offices and five from overseas posts). Of the remaining twelve, three came from other government posts, four were parliamentarians, and five were private citizens.

The interviews revealed that, after only two months at the United Nations, the participants were aware of an expanded number of issues and nations. Of the twenty-three who were asked to select an agenda item for discussion, only seven felt able to do so on the pretest. At least eleven of the twenty-three, and probably more, did not feel informed enough to discuss an agenda item. However, all delegates but one were willing to discuss an agenda item with the interviewer in the posttest, providing evidence of change from very little information on certain issues to greatly extended knowledge. A dramatic example of expanded awareness was the delegate from a Middle East foreign office who indicated that he had never even heard

of some of the African countries that his committee discussed. As an example, he cited the North and South Cameroons, still dependent territories at the time. He indicated that he now knew "how they emerged, what factors concerning them have political significance, and what the role of various blocs is in relation to such countries as these."

Scattered throughout the interviews are occasional comments by delegates in which they indicated surprise at positions taken by other nations on certain issues. An Eastern European delegate was surprised to find that the Scandinavian nations sometimes "lined up with the colonial powers" on colonial questions. An African delegate from one of the newer countries was extremely surprised to find that the United States voted with his nation on the South West Africa issue. A Far Eastern delegate who had served in his foreign office for twelve years was surprised to find that the white dominated nations of the Commonwealth did not vote as a bloc in his committee.

Several commented on the value of learning about the problems of other nations and the effect of the policies of their own nation on these problems. A number of delegates volunteered comments on how informative it was to hear delegates from other nations explain their policies and viewpoints. Two United States congressmen who have served in the General Assembly have written of their estimate of the effect of the exchange of such information on individual viewpoints:

One reason for the importance of these contacts was that many delegates coming from distant countries, relying on their own press and on diplomatic channels for their background information, frequently did not understand why the United States

---

[4] For a full report on these interviews see Alger, 1963c.

took the position it did on many issues. In a surprising number of instances, delegates altered their views on matters under discussion after acquiring additional background as a result of talks with representatives of the United States and of other nations (Carnahan & Judd, 1958, p. 3).

Although the interview did not have a question on the point, four delegates emphasized the importance of opportunities to establish face-to-face contact with officials of other nations. At the end of his interview a Western European delegate volunteered this statement:

On my committee men come year after year, and friendly relations continue despite disagreement over policy. It is very important that people in international conferences know each other well. It permits the reaching of compromises. One has choices of many kinds of words for stating the same thing in either very polite or very rash words. With friends, you are more likely to use friendly words. Therefore, it is useful to have friends negotiating in international conferences.

Some delegates had seen some nations as negative stereotypes whose policies were grossly simplified and exaggerated. Under these conditions face-to-face contact in the United Nations is much like other intercultural exchange in which "contact will provide richer and more accurate information about other people and will show them to be much like members of one's own group" (Katz, 1960, p. 193). Not all stated the effects of face-to-face experience as dramatically as an African delegate who said of the delegations of some nations: "It has helped me to realize that they are, after all, human beings."

Although the interviews were not designed to test the proposition, evidence gathered in the interviews and other information available leave little doubt that participation in the United Nations expands the number of nations as well as the number of issues of which the delegate is aware. Interview material suggests that this awareness extends the number of nations and number of issues in which the delegate feels involved and sometimes for which he even feels some responsibility. There is also evidence to indicate that there is sometimes a change in the delegate's affective map of the world, that is, in whom he designates as the "good guys" and the "bad guys." As the positions of nations become known on a wider range of issues, it becomes more difficult to evaluate these nations as being either all good or all bad.

Thus it appears that participation in an international organization tends to give the participant a more extensive and more realistic image of the system of nations represented and perhaps a feeling of more extended involvement.[5] The intergovernmental society in the organization provides a microcosm of this system that enables the delegate to see the total system in operation, look into the faces of officials from all its units, and direct words to those faces and see and hear their response. In the United Nations he may feel that 113 other nations are too many to contend with at one time and might wish not to try, but he is nevertheless continually reminded of their presence. Delegates from all countries have votes, and delegates from countries he might consider insignificant may have influence by virtue of talent or elected post. The "good guys" are not always

---

[5] Cardozo concludes that experiences of national officials serving as permanent representatives to the European Communities "have made them likely to be more devoted to international cooperation than many of the officials with whom they deal in their own government departments" (1962, p. 108).

voting with him and the "bad guys" sometimes are. Thus the pointed walls of certitude that isolate the "good" and "bad" may be eroded round. In the interviews, a Norwegian parliamentarian stated: "I will go back with a clearer view of the fact that my nation belongs to the whole world."

Interviews with General Assembly delegates, before experience in the body, also revealed considerable ignorance of how the General Assembly operates. One revelation of this was the posttest question that asked how experiences in the General Assembly were different than had been expected. Three delegates indicated that they had had no clear expectations at all; two of these were from foreign offices. Of the twelve who experienced differences from what they had expected, three delegates from smaller nations were surprised at the prominent roles small nations play in the Assembly. A parliamentarian had thought that the General Assembly "would be a forum for speeches." But during his Assembly experience, he found that "draft resolutions involve a good deal of lobbying and negotiation." He had "had no idea of this." A delegate from a foreign office found that "things that go on in the corridor seem more important" than he had anticipated. Ten of the twenty-five responded that their experiences were no different than expected. It was remarkable to find, however, that one of these had said in the pretest that his duties would not differ much from his obligations in the foreign office, while in the posttest he said that his duties in the General Assembly were much different from those in the foreign office.

In responses to other questions, there was some indication that participation in the General Assembly would permit more effective use of the United Nations by governmental posts at home. A delegate whose permanent post was in a foreign office said that he would now be able to suggest policy for his nation's General Assembly delegation "that can really be carried out." A delegate from another department of the government said that "before I came I knew that there were committees and I knew the general organization, but I didn't know precisely what they were doing and how things were done. Now I know procedure better, and this will enable me to make better recommendations to the Foreign Office." The interviews revealed initial lack of information, vagueness, and even erroneous information about how the United Nations actually operates on the part of General Assembly delegates, some of whom were in positions in which they could directly affect their nation's United Nations policies.

Finally, material in these interviews and more general discussion with United Nations diplomats suggest that participation permits diplomats to learn social skills that they did not have before. For example, a career foreign service officer said: "It made me more tolerant of long speeches." Some adaptation is required to develop the patience and perspective necessary for handling a problem in the context of 113 other nations instead of just one. Pursuing national objectives and collecting information as a mobile "parliamentarian" requires a quite different pattern of behavior than most diplomats have engaged in before. It may be significant both that these new skills are learned and that they are learned in a society whose norms are the product of the combined participation of representatives from most national governments of the world.

CONCLUSION

In the introduction to this chapter, it was pointed out that some of the terms used to describe activity in international organizations, such as "multi-lateral" and "public," offer only partial images of these institutions. Material drawn from interviews and personal observations at the United Nations has been presented as evidence supporting this assertion. After explicating how international organizations affect intergovernmental communications, we suggested some potential consequences of these effects for international conflict. Following description of nonnational roles in international organizations, it was indicated how these roles provide a social structure that helps to link nations in a common political process and how these roles have subtle effects on national policies. While reporting on the broadened perspective of the international system and the new social skills that are acquired by participants in international organizations, it was indicated that these learning experiences contribute to the distinctive milieu of international organizations. Since most officials who participate in international organizations eventually move on to other posts in their national governments, these learning experiences are later fed directly into governments.

On the basis of these three probes into the social fabric of one international organization, more general conclusions will now be drawn as a contribution to the development of international organization theory. An international organization is a microcosm of an international system that is created through involving representatives from national governments in parliamentary-like activity. These microcosms differ from the international systems they represent, however, in that they are in some respects more like small societies and parliaments than international systems. Participants in the organization learn about the

other units in the system primarily through direct contact with human beings rather than through indirect means. Communications are less like those usually found between large organizations and more like those within decentralized organizations or in parliaments. This not only permits the development of new contacts and an increase in quantity of communications, but also extends the kinds of information that can be exchanged, permitting greater "off the record" exchanges.

International organizations are also more than microcosms of international systems in that they become new units in these systems. Not only do they develop norms for intergovernmental communications and for the development of consensus that are different from the rest of the system, but they also have an array of nonnational roles that become involved in intergovernmental relations. There is a body of permanent officials who participate in the definition of norms and in monitoring intergovernmental relations. National officials are also co-opted into nonnational roles. One important way in which international organizations are different from nation units is the fact that they overlap these units. The exercise by national officials of international organization roles is one manifestation of this overlap. It is important that what Guetzkow (1961, p. 61) calls an "exclusiveness norm" does not inhibit national officials from performing nonnational roles in the way an exclusiveness norm inhibits an individual from serving two national governments at the same time. Since the existence of a relatively small quantity of overlapping memberships is one of the distinguishing characteristics of international systems, this feature of international organizations attracts our attention. Overlapping group memberships have been cited by a number of writers as restraints on intergroup conflict.[6]

Participation in international organizations tends to produce national policies that are responsive to total systems represented in organizations rather than policies responsive to individual units. Effective response to the parliamentary decision-making milieu of an international organization creates pressure for greater decision latitude on the part of representatives in international organizations. This suggests that there are pressures on nations that participate in international organizations for responsiveness to the external environment that are in some respects greater than those in more traditional diplomatic relations. Max Beloff (1961) supports this line of speculation when he concludes, after examining recent developments in British participation in foreign affairs:

> In bilateral negotiations national objectives are pre-determined; the object of negotiation is to reconcile those of one party with those of the other, by compromising, where necessary, on their respective demands. In multilateral negotiations, the national interest cannot be settled in advance, but is worked out co-operatively in a "seminar" atmosphere, more like that of an interdepartmental committee. One of the features of the new type of multilateral negotiation is that one can never be certain what is going to come up next. This makes detailed instructions on tactics impossible (p. 176).

Senators Hickenlooper and Mansfield also offer supporting evidence in a report to the Senate after serving in the United States delegation to the United Nations General Assembly in 1959. They complained that the links between Washington and New York cause United States participation to be "cumbersome and slow to respond to changing situations." They concluded:

> If policy is to be pursued effectively in a General Assembly which includes over 80 other nations—nations whose differing views as well as the idiosyncrasies of their representatives must be reckoned with—the Ambassador and the members of the permanent mission must have a measure of freedom for parliamentary maneuver (pp. 6–7).

The foregoing suggests that the character of the intergovernmental society in an international organization may have important bearing on the capacity that the organization has for handling international problems. The addition of such a society to an international system greatly increases the number of intergovernmental linkages and provides a different kind of milieu for contact. The occasions for exerting influence on other governments and for responding to other governments are greatly increased. International organizations, such as the United Nations, therefore, increase the size of the "influence pie." This is similar to Likert's (1960) finding, in the study of business organizations, that more productive departments were characterized by "greater amounts of reciprocal influence" between managers and subordinates. This is made possible because both leaders and members *learn more complex and different forms of social interaction*" (p. 11). Likert indicates that his findings may have relevance for international relations, suggesting that the "sovereignty pie" (a synonym for

---

[6] For example, see Gluckman, 1955, pp. 4, 68, 74; Fortes & Evans-Pritchard, 1940, p. 14; and Williams, 1951, p. 531. For fuller discussion of the relevance of overlapping group memberships to international relations see Alger, 1961, pp. 139–140; 1963a, pp. 417–418; 1963b, pp. 42–46.

"influence pie") may be increased in the same way.

In handling problems, the United Nations not only offers decision-making bodies, such as the Assembly and councils, but builds an intergovernmental society around a problem. When a problem arises, such as the Congo or the financing of peace-keeping operations, this society is continually active on the problem, whether more formal bodies are in session or not. It facilitates continual adjustments in national policies, tending to substitute a host of small adjustments for extraordinary confrontations that require adjustments of great magnitude. Thus, relations are conducted more through a host of capillaries and less through a few main arteries. When a problem eventually reaches the public arena in the Assembly or one of the councils, the outcome will be importantly shaped by the nature of the intergovernmental society that has developed around the issue.

REFERENCES

Alger, C. F. Non-resolution consequences of the United Nations and their effect on international conflict. *J. Confl. Resol.,* 1961, 5, 128–145.

Alger, C. F. Comparison of intranational and international politics. *Amer. pol. Sci. Rev.,* 1963, 57, 406–419. (a)

Alger, C. F. Hypotheses on relationships between the organization of international society and international order. *Proc. Amer. Soc. Int. Law,* 1963, 35–46. (b)

Alger, C. F. United Nations participation as a learning experience. *Publ. Opin. Quart.,* 1963, 27, 411–426. (c)

Alger, C. F. Decision-making theory and human conflict. In E. B. McNeil (Ed.), *The nature of human conflict.* Englewood Cliffs, N.J.: Prentice-Hall, 1965. Pp. 274–294.

Beloff, M. *New dimensions in foreign policy. A study in administrative experience, 1947–1959.* New York: Macmillan, 1961.

Best, G. Diplomacy in the United Nations. Unpublished doctoral dissertation, Northwestern University, 1960.

Cambon, J. *The diplomatist.* London: Philip Allan, 1931.

Cardozo, M. H. *Diplomats in international cooperation: Stepchildren of the foreign service.* Ithaca: Cornell Univer. Press, 1962.

Carnahan, A. S. J., & Judd, W. H. Report on the twelfth session of the General Assembly of the United Nations. U.S. House of Representatives, Committe on Foreign Affairs, 85th Congress, 2nd Session, House Report No. 1611. Washington: U.S. Government Printing Office, 1958.

Carnegie Endowment for International Peace, The Committee for Foreign Affairs Personnel *Personnel for the new diplomacy.* New York: Carnegie Endowment, 1962.

Dallin, A. *The Soviet Union at the United Nations.* New York: Praeger, 1962.

Fanelli, A. Extensiveness of communication contacts and perceptions of the community. *Amer. sociol. Rev.,* 1956, 21, 443–445.

Fortes, M., & Evans-Pritchard, E. E. *African political systems.* New York: Oxford, 1940 (reprinted 1961).

Gluckman, M. *Custom and conflict in Africa.* New York: Free Press, 1955.

Goode, W. J. A theory of role strain. *Amer. sociol. Rev.,* 1960, 25, 483–496.

Guetzkow, H. *Multiple loyalties: Theoretical approach to a problem in international organization.* Princeton: Center for Research on World Political Institutions, 1955.

Hadwen, J. G., & Kaufmann, J. *How United Nations decisions are made.* New York: Oceana; Leyden: A. W. Sythoff, 1962.

Hammarskjold, D. The developing role of the United Nations. *United Nations Review*, 1959, *6*, 8–18 (reprint of introduction to the annual report of the Secretary-General on the work of the organization, 1959).

Hermann, C. Some findings on the nature of communication relevant to international organization. Unpublished paper, Northwestern University, 1961.

Hickenlooper, B. B., & Mansfield, M. Observations on the United Nations. U.S. Senate. 86th Congress, 1st Session, Senate Document No. 26. Washington: U.S. Government Printing Office, 1959.

Jackson, H. M. Do we rely too much on the U.N.? *New York Times Magazine*, April 1, 1962, *12*, 112–113.

Katz, D. The functional approach to the study of attitudes. *Publ. Opin. Quart.*, 1960, *24*, 163–204.

Kelley, H. Communications in experimentally created hierarchies. *Hum. Relat.*, 1951, *4*, (1), 39–56.

Leavitt, H. J., & Mueller, R. A. H. Some effects of feedback on communications. In A. P. Hare, E. F. Borgatta, & R. F. Bales (Eds.), *Small groups*. New York: Knopf, 1955. Pp. 414–423.

Likert, R. Influence and national sovereignty. Ann Arbor: Institute for Social Research, University of Michigan, (1960). (Mimeographed)

March, J., & Simon, H., with Guetzkow, H. *Organizations*. New York: Wiley, 1963.

Matecki, B. E. *Establishment of the International Finance Corporation*. New York: Praeger, 1957.

Nicholas, H. G. *The United Nations as a political institution*. New York: Oxford, 1959.

Nicolson, H. *The evolution of diplomacy*. New York: Collier Books, 1962. (First published London: Constable & Co., 1954; and New York: Macmillan, 1955.)

Numelin, R. *The beginnings of diplomacy*. New York: Oxford Univer. Press, 1950.

Rusk, D. Parliamentary diplomacy. *World Affairs Interpreter*, 1955, *26*, 121–138.

Singer, J. D. The United Nations Advisory Committee on Administrative and Budgetary Questions. *Publ. Admin.*, 1957, *35*, 395–410.

Sulzberger, C. L. When and why the rug was pulled. *New York Times*, August 13, 1962, p. 24.

Thayer, C. *Diplomat*. New York: Harper, 1959.

Williams, R. *American society*. New York: Knopf, 1951.

15

The next chapter concludes our exploration of situations involving direct interactions among persons of different nationality. The chapter focuses on personal contacts that occur in the context of international exchanges—specifically, contacts between foreign students and nationals of the host country. Here we are dealing with cross-national interactions in which the participants function as individuals, rather than as official representatives of their countries. In an unofficial sense, however—and sometimes even in a semi-official sense—foreign students may very well see themselves as "ambassadors" of their countries, and are often treated by their hosts as national representatives. This is, in fact, one of the characteristic features of a great deal of the informal interaction that takes place between traveler and host.

In Chapter 4 we were primarily concerned with the effects of personal contact on the images of the traveler and his host. Chapter 15 draws, to a considerable degree, on the same sources of data. The emphasis, however, is on the nature of the interaction processes that occur in this type of contact situation. What are some of the special problems that arise in interpersonal relationships when these take place across national boundaries? What factors determine the degree of tension, the ease and openness of communication, and the level of understanding in such relationships? How are interactions affected by the visitor's perception of the relative status of his own nation and the host nation; by the cultural differences between the two nations; by the visitor's commitment to his own country; and by the goals that he brings to the experience? What kinds of contact are conducive to the development of long-term relationships, based on common interests and tasks? These are the questions to which Chapter 15 addresses itself.

Successful international exchanges have the potential of creating international networks, based on common interests and experiences, that cut across national boundaries. Such networks could complement, on an unofficial level, some of the developments inherent in the growing importance of international organizations, as discussed in Chapter 14. Both of these types of development represent contributions to an international society, existing alongside of and in perfect harmony with national societies, but cross-cutting national lines in organization and function.

The author of Chapter 15, Anita L. Mishler, has been doing research on the effects of cross-national educational experiences since 1960. Between 1960 and 1964 she was Research Associate in the Laboratory of Social Relations, Harvard University. At present she holds an appointment as Research Associate at the Center for Research on Conflict Resolution, University of Michigan, although she continues to live and work in Massachusetts. She has also taught sociology and participated in research on socialization in mental hospital wards. Her major interests include cross-cultural research, and the study of alienation and adult socialization.

H. C. K.

Personal Contact in

International Exchanges*

Anita L. Mishler

A long with the increase in international tensions that has characterized the years since the end of World War II, there has also been a striking increase in direct international contacts. Ever increasing numbers of people choose to sojourn in another country for varying periods of time. Not only have cross-cultural contacts increased but they are qualitatively different from what they were at other points in time.

The present situation is unique in several ways. There are large numbers of people who spend upwards of a year living and working outside of their own countries. There is a greatly increased variety in the forms of sojourn available and therefore in the segments of the population for whom opportunities to participate in such experiences arise. The activities of the United Nations and its committees require the recruitment of people of various skills who are

assigned to work in foreign settings and in collaboration with members of other nations. The technical aid activities of the United States and of other powers involve large numbers of experts and technicians who establish working relations with their counterparts in other nations. Organizations such as the Peace Corps, which involves thousands of Americans, add to the scale and introduce a new form of cross-cultural contact.

In this chapter we will be primarily concerned with the veritable army of students and scholars who travel to another country to pursue their studies and research and who become sojourners abroad. While the United States and other powers view the educational exchange programs as part of their foreign policy activities, these programs are among the ones least likely to be conceived as weapons in the Cold War. Therefore the goals of the so-

* This chapter is a product of a research program on social influence and behavior change, directed by Herbert C. Kelman and supported by Public Health Service Research Grant MH–07280 from the National Institute of Mental Health. The chapter has benefited from the suggestions of Lotte Bailyn and Herbert C. Kelman.

journer are likely to be defined in individual terms and the contacts that he develops are likely to be viewed as ends in themselves rather than instruments of national policy.

STUDENT EXCHANGES

For centuries students have traveled to centers of learning in other lands. However, the great numbers of people involved in exchange programs at present and the variety of countries from which they come do in fact change the character of the population that participates in foreign study. Exchange students do not yet represent all the strata of their respective societies, but they are much more representative than was the case before World War II. There are many institutional and organizational supports available so that recruitment is not limited to those who can themselves finance their education and travel abroad. It should be noted, however, that for visitors to the United States the English language requirement still selects students from the elite groups, particularly in the newly developing nations.

In addition to recruiting a wider range of participants, exchange programs today take place in an internationalized world. The milieu into which the exchange student or scholar returns makes it possible for him to act in terms of the new experiences he has had, the new views and wider commitments he has developed. Prior to World War II most international students who came to the United States, England, or Germany came for specific training not available in their home countries. Once they acquired this training and returned home, the experience abroad rarely entered into their personal or professional lives. They had little occasion to pursue interna-

tional contacts and there were few paths or occupational structures that offered opportunities for individuals to develop careers in an international context. At the present time there is a greater likelihood that exchange scholars will take back not only the specific training for which they ventured abroad but also a view of their job in an international context and a personal and professional involvement in an international network. Moreover, they are more likely to bring these new learnings to a more accepting milieu than was the case heretofore. Bennett, Passin, and McKnight (1958), in their study of the Japanese exchange student, discuss the milieu into which the student returns as being crucial in affecting not only his readjustment to his home country but also his view of the value of his experiences abroad. It can be assumed that the more accepting the milieu, the greater the likelihood that the returnee will build upon the experience in concrete ways.

It is likely that under these new conditions, exchange students will develop new views of the host country (as discussed in Chapter 4). These new views do not necessarily imply wholly favorable attitudes toward the host. For example, there is little evidence that cross-cultural contacts per se lead to *favorable* attitudes towards the foreign policies and activities of the host nation. Riegel (1953), in his study of Belgians who had studied in the United States, indicates that "while personal popularity of Americans was greater among former student exchangees than among other Belgians, no significant evidence could be found that this friendliness permanently affected attitudes to American national policies and behavior" (p. 322). But it is likely that a more *complex* and *differentiated* image of the host country will develop. The possibilities do exist in this new situation for individuals to spend enough time in the other country to learn about it in its varying dimensions and aspects through developing contacts and establishing relationships. They are then able to respond more in terms of a differentiated view and less in terms of a simple stereotype which can by definition only be relevant to one aspect of a nation and its people.

In addition to learning something of the complexities of another society, participants in these new forms of cross-cultural contact have the opportunity of coming together with people who share specific tasks, professions, and interests. These shared tasks could form the basis of continuing relationships that are extranational in content and perhaps supranational in commitment.

The quality of the experience abroad, what the sojourner learns about the host country, and most particularly the development of lasting relationships with members of that country depend on his opportunities for developing contacts and on the nature of these contacts. This chapter is concerned with examining the processes of face-to-face contact and some of the peculiar problems that arise in interpersonal relationships when these take place across national boundaries.

For each student and for each relationship there are many variables that affect these processes. We will be particularly concerned here with four factors *antecedent* to the trip abroad that can determine the exchange student's opportunities to establish contacts and the quality of these contacts: the sojourner's perception of the relative positions of his nation and the host nation; cultural differences between the two countries; the sojourner's commitment to his own country; and the goals with which he comes to the experience.

RELATIVE POSITIONS OF HOST NATION AND OWN NATION

Nationality is the symbol around which many historical grievances and political realities cluster, and cross-cultural contacts take place within the framework imposed by these issues. A key set of factors that have a significant effect on interaction in the cross-national situation is the nature of the relationship between the visitor's nation and the host nation. For most people the fact of their nationality is rarely an item of concern or a major determinant of behavior, except in times of national emergency or crisis. In a situation of sojourn in another country, however, national identification is likely to become a salient consideration. Even the cosmopolitan, who in his own country is accustomed to think of himself as a citizen of the world, must respond in part as a national of his own country when he is a visitor in another land. While it is true that individuals do not often confront each other as symbols of the histories of their respective national positions, these factors do come into play in the course of their contact. The initial structuring of the situation of contact is often in terms of nationality, irrespective of the individuals involved. Thus, it will vary depending upon whether there has been a history of dependency or colonialism, whether one nation is considered to be more advanced or affluent than the other, and whether the two nations are currently allies or adversaries.

These factors are likely to affect what the sojourner brings to the interaction: his attitudes towards the host, his expectations of how he will be regarded and treated, his areas of sensitivity, his feelings of status threat or security. For each national group there are aspects of the home country vis-à-vis the host country that elicit particular sensitivities. Thus, Watson and Lippitt (1955), in their study of Germans visiting America in 1949, report defensiveness on the part of the Germans about their country, which was not simply due to cultural differences but was related to the recent defeat of Germany by America. Lambert and Bressler (1956) found that Indian students were likely to respond strongly to certain statements and questions by Americans from which they inferred an American view of India as a backward country. This was particularly true for those students who adopted an ambassadorial role during their sojourn, that is, who saw themselves as representatives of their country. These areas of sensitivity are rooted in a long history of relationship between India and Western nations based on the assumption of India's lower status and inability to govern itself. Even students who come from developed Western countries are sensitive to certain questions asked by Americans about their countries. In interviews with Scandinavian exchangees in the United States (currently being analyzed by the writer), many respondents expressed resentment at American "ignorance" about the differences among the Scandinavian countries. They regarded this lack of information as a deprecation of the importance of their home countries. During the course of their sojourn, however, many of them came to explain the Americans' lack of information on the basis of the size of the Scandinavian countries. They indicated that they, after all, did not know much about the differences between Texas and California. Some areas of sensitivity are thus more easily overcome than others, particularly when the nations are more nearly equal and the sensitive areas therefore less crucial.

The exchangee's experiences with respect to his areas of sensitivity will determine his behavior and his contacts. If he encounters people and situations that elicit these sensitivities, he is likely to minimize contact, generalize feelings of resentment to larger parts of the host nation, and turn inward towards members of his own group. Lambert and Bressler (1956) indicate that one of the most powerful influences upon the Indian student was the American view of India as the Indian understood that view.

Morris (1960) studied exchange students at the University of California (Los Angeles) with the purpose of testing "the proposition that national status is an important determinant of the adjustment of foreign students during their stay in another country" (p. 13). Several aspects of national status were considered: perceived accorded national status (the status the visitor thought Americans assigned his nation); actual accorded national status (national status actually assigned by Americans); and objective status (national status based on the criterion of level of education in the country). The four indices of adjustment were: favorableness to the United States; personal satisfaction with stay; satisfaction with educational and training facilities; and amount and kind of social contact with Americans. Of particular interest here is the relationship between national status variables and contact with Americans. Morris reports a high relationship between perceived accorded national status and the depth of contact with Americans. Those students who perceived that Americans accorded their nation high status were more likely to develop deep friendships than were those who perceived that Americans accorded their nation low status. These findings suggest very clearly that the experience of national status deprivation (the perception that his nation is accorded a lower status than he feels it deserves) will not only affect the visitor's general attitudes to the host country, but also reduce the possibilities of positive experiences during the sojourn by limiting the nature of his personal contacts.

A visitor who comes to the host country with wide areas of sensitivity is particularly likely to experience a sense of status deprivation for several reasons. First, his threshold for perceiving slights to his nation is likely to be lower because, given his sensitivity, he fully expects such slights. Secondly, his very expectation of slight may elicit confirming behavior on the part of the host. In addition, inasmuch as sensitive areas have historical roots in the relationship between the host nation and the sojourner's nation, there is a likelihood that the host will in fact treat the sensitive sojourner in a way that communicates low accorded status.

The status deprivation hypothesis could account for the observation by Selltiz, Christ, Havel, and Cook (1963) that European students in the United States are likely to have more frequent interactions with Americans and to make more American friends than are non-Europeans. It can be presumed that European visitors are less likely to bring strong sensitivities to their American experience and that European nations are more likely to be accorded high status by the American hosts.

The Selltiz *et al.* data show that the effect of the national and regional factor on the amount and nature of interaction *can* be outweighed by other factors, but only under extremely favorable conditions. They compared groups of exchange students differing in their opportunities for interaction with Americans (provided by the nature of their living arrangements) and in their motivations for such interaction. The findings indicate that living arrangements with high interaction potential do in fact lead to greater interaction. Furthermore, those students who do interact more with Americans, learn more about America and are more aware of differences among individuals and subgroups within the American scene. However, the differences between Europeans and non-Europeans in their interaction with Americans disappear only under the joint conditions of highest interaction potential of the living arrangement and highest motivation for interaction.

Although it is true that the relative positions of the visitor's nation and the host nation and the history of their relationships tend to determine the degree to which a visitor will experience feelings of status loss or gain and thus to define the nature of the initial contacts he is likely to establish, these effects are not inevitable. The specific experiences encountered in the host country can have a profound impact and may reverse the course of the relationship. Lambert and Bressler (1956) suggest:

In view of the close personal identification of the student with the prestige of his home country, it seems reasonable to assume that any assault on the status of India will be perceived as an implicit attack on the student himself. However, it seems equally plausible that the converse is true: the elevation of the status of the student will be interpreted by him as an expression of good will toward India. If this hypothesis is correct, the student who is accorded overt individual status recognition may as a consequence alter his perceptions of America's attitudes toward India and relax the set of mechanisms which he erects in defense and praise of his country (p. 102).

CULTURAL DIFFERENCES

In a world of power, differences in national status and the perception of status create problems for relationships among people. In day-to-day interactions certain other differences may seriously impede genuine efforts to establish and maintain contacts. The sojourn situation is inevitably a situation in which the individual is confronted with a culture different from his own, in terms of customs, values, standards, and expectations. Thus another set of factors that is likely to play a significant role in the nature of the interaction between host and visitor is the degree and nature of the cultural differences between the two societies. Here we are not dealing with the fact that the two societies *represent* different cultures and nationalities, but with the direct effect of these very differences themselves, in other words, with the way in which these differences affect the course of the contact and interaction.

The greater the cultural differences the greater is the likelihood that barriers to communication will arise and that misunderstandings will occur. Visitors to America from more traditional societies, for example, will have particular difficulty in dealing with problems that arise out of status differentials. Bennett *et al.* (1958) suggest that among the Japanese the culturally accepted mode of interaction with individuals of higher status is withdrawal or passive acceptance of the other's definition of the situation. Very different expectations, however, are communicated by Americans who often attempt to deny status differences. These divergent views can cause confusion for the Japanese visitor, who may respond by minimizing his contacts with Americans and limiting the nature of his interactions.

Many visitors to the United States experience difficulties due to differences between American and European norms with regard to the development of friendships. The casual, open, and immediate hospitality of Americans is often interpreted by the visitor as an overture to close friendship in line with the meaning that such intimacy has in his own society. When the contact is not continued or does not develop into a close relationship, the visitor often concludes that Americans are hypocritical and superficial in their personal relations.

In addition, the more different the cultures, the greater the problems for the visitor in adjusting to his daily life situation, which in turn limits his freedom to engage in even superficial or minimal contacts. Under certain circumstances, wide differences in food habits may absorb the energies of the visitor and limit his freedom. Language differences and the attendant difficulties can create almost insurmountable barriers to contacts. Morris (1960) reports relationships between language facility and the extent of social contact for the foreign students in the UCLA study. Deutsch and Won (1963) indicate that, for foreign trainees, English language facility was an important factor in satisfaction with the total social experience in the United States as well as with the training experience.

There is yet another way in which cultural differences may inhibit interaction. Studies of Indian students (Lambert & Bressler, 1956) and Japanese students (Bennett *et al.*, 1958) indicate that some sojourners are afraid of becoming too Westernized because they anticipate adjustment problems upon return to their home countries. This may lead to great concern with the dangers of assimilation and to consequent avoidance of exposure to and contact with the life of the host country.

Cultural differences are not necessarily inhibiting factors. Under some circumstances and for some students, these differences can provide the most fruitful beginnings of a cross-cultural relationship. The visitor is confronted with new and sometimes confusing things around him, and is meeting people who are different from him in some ways though the same in others. By contrast he may become newly aware of values and standards implicit in his own culture. The host, in contact with the visitor, may also become more attentive to aspects of his own culture that are of importance to him. He can become interested in how his culture appears to a stranger and may attempt to see it from this other perspective himself. The beginnings of a real contact between them could develop from the mutual exploration of their differences. This, however, is not a usual pattern. In order for friendships to develop out of differences certain preconditions are required.

One of these factors is likely to be a personality disposition to respond favorably to differences rather than to perceived similarities. Some of the data available from a study of Scandinavian students in the United States (Kelman & Bailyn, 1962) indicate that perceptual sharpeners and levelers experience their sojourn in America in different ways. The data suggest that sharpeners are more likely to compare their country with America and themselves with Americans and to be involved with their American experience. The levelers, on the other hand, are more likely to feel like visitors while abroad and to be less open to new experiences. Clearly, different processes are involved for those visitors who seek out and relish differences than for those

who prefer similarities and need to perceive similarity before they can feel comfortable.

VISITOR'S RELATIONSHIP TO HIS OWN NATION

The problems of cultural differences and of national status affect the conditions of contact differentially for different students. The sojourner is placed in a position of acting as a national of his own country, but the course of his interaction in this situation is affected by the nature of his own relationship to his nation. National identifications vary for different nations and regions, but they are also likely to be determined in important ways by the personal characteristics of the individual citizen. The position of the individual in his own country, his previous experiences with other cultures, as well as his personality characteristics are likely to affect his commitment to his own country and his reaction to cultural and national differences.

Lambert and Bressler (1956) point out that those Indian students who suffered the "least ego assault" had come to favorable terms with the West before arriving in the United States. Each of these students had grown up in an atmosphere of family commitment to the West. In some cases their fathers had positions in the colonial civil service; some had attended missionary schools and some were members of ethnic or religious minorities. "As people who were partially alienated from the mainstream of Indian culture they were less involved with its prestige" (p. 82). Students such as these are prepared or predisposed to interact with mitments, particularly ones that are tablish contacts with them.

Alienation from one's own culture does not necessarily lead to greater openness in the new situation. There are students who are so uncertain about their places in their own societies that they are unable to develop new commitments, particularly ones that are likely to bring into focus their own conflicts and dissatisfactions.

There is some evidence that confrontation with a different culture and with new opportunities does create greater problems for some travelers than for others, depending on the nature of their relationships to their own nations. In a study of changes in attitudes of Scandinavian students during their stay in the United States, Kelman and Bailyn (1962) discuss two patterns that characterize responses to the experience abroad. In one, more characteristic of exchangees who are established in the occupational structures of their home countries, there appears to be an ambivalence and yet a commitment to one's own society. These individuals are likely to be defensive about their own countries, while indicating a global, undifferentiated satisfaction with them. This view of their own countries is accompanied by a general resistance to the American experience and by avoidance of interaction with Americans. The second pattern is more characteristic of less-established visitors, who express increasing awareness of some limitations of their own countries, but also indicate a differentiated appreciation of their special qualities. Many of the students in this group take longer to adjust to America, but their adjustment is deeper and they become personally involved in their American experience and with the people they meet. The authors suggest that this latter pattern may reflect a greater willingness to engage in self-examination and self-criticism and to be open to the sojourn experience.

The quality of the individual's relationship to his own country can, thus, be important in his mode of orientation toward the experience abroad and his motivation for making new contacts and establishing new commitments. In modern differentiated societies an individual can have varying degrees of commitment to his own country and varying degrees of disaffection from major aspects of his society. The existence of these complex patterns of national identification makes for wide differences in the nature of the contacts established by individuals while abroad, but it also increases the likelihood that each visitor will be able to establish meaningful contacts with nationals of the host country *at some level*. Thus, it would appear that international educational exchange has the potential of providing students who have wide varieties of national commitment the opportunity to develop contacts and relationships with nationals of other countries on the basis of other-than-national loyalties.

GOALS OF THE SOJOURN

Among the factors that are important determinants of the sojourner's experience are the goals with which he comes to the host country. The purposes of the trip as seen by the student will affect many aspects of his orientation to the experience, the efforts he makes to establish relationships with members of the host country, and to some extent the actual situations in which he finds himself and the potential of these situations for facilitating interaction.

Most agencies that sponsor educational exchange in the United States have as their goals international understanding, friendship for the United States, and aid in the economic and social development of other nations. The exchangees, however, are more likely to have individual goals of personal and professional development.

Students who go to another country for an extended period of study usually do so for combinations of reasons. Of special interest, however, are the differences between those for whom professional or academic purposes are primary and those for whom general "socio-cultural" purposes are primary. Scott (1956), in a report on the American experience of Swedish students, notes that "there has been a change of purpose of study between students of the 1920–1940 period and those of the post 1945 period. Specialized study was the predominant or sole purpose of about three-quarters of the pre-war group, but only of one-third of the post-war group" (p. 49). It is likely that this shift from specialized study to a more socio-cultural interest is more characteristic of European students than of students from Asia, Africa, and Latin America. To be sure, there are probably few students who select themselves to study in another country who are not at least in a minimal way curious about that country and its people, but students differ in their *primary* goals.

There are students who are not or not yet professionally committed to specific training and for whom study abroad is particularly attractive because of the opportunity to be in a foreign country. We might therefore expect differences between the professionally committed and the professionally uncommitted in what they hope to gain, which part of the experience is viewed as important, which part as most satisfactory and which aspects of the experience have the most relevance for impeding or facilitating cross-cultural contacts and effecting changes in attitudes.

There appears to be some evidence that those students who do not come for specific occupational objectives but for socio-cultural reasons, that is, those who indicate that they are primarily interested in seeing the country and meeting people, are actually more likely to have contacts and establish relationships with members of the host country. Lambert and Bressler (1956) indicate, in their study of Indian students, that among the group of occupationally uncommitted are found the ones with the most frequent and most amicable relations with Americans. Similarly, Sewell and Davidsen (1961), in a study of Scandinavians on an American campus, report that the more socio-cultural the purposes of the sojourn, the greater is the student's participation in American life, the more favorable is his impression of the United States, and the more likely he is to be satisfied with the visit.

There is some evidence that these socio-cultural interests do not simply develop in the course of extended participation with Americans, but rather can be considered to be in some respects antecedent to the trip abroad. An analysis of interviews of Scandinavian exchange students in America (Mishler, 1963) reveals that those students who manifested socio-cultural interests even before leaving for America, as indicated by the extent of general preparation for the trip (reading about America, talking to people who had been there, studying the language), tended to participate more with Americans after arrival. The individuals in this socio-culturally oriented group who actually engaged in a high degree of participation with Americans also showed—on post-return interviews, conducted after the respondents had been back home for a year—that the American trip had considerable impact on them and had become an integral part of their daily lives.

It appears that not only do students with "socio-cultural" interests participate in activities to satisfy these interests, but that those whose interests are primarily occupational or academic tend to avoid such activities. Bailyn (1963), in an analysis of changes in work orientation among Scandinavian students during their year in the United States, found that the greatest increase in professional commitment occurs in the group least involved in their American experience. It is this same group whose primary motivation for the trip centered on work.

On the other hand, exchange scholars, as contrasted with students, are more likely to have opportunities for satisfying interactions within a professional milieu and with professional colleagues in the host country. The Gullahorn and Gullahorn (1963) studies of American Fulbright grantees are of interest here. They found that in their sample (of professional Americans) there was a "significant positive relationship between number of professional contacts a grantee reported having abroad and his own degree of satisfaction with his award experiences. Furthermore, there was a significant difference among the satisfied as contrasted to the dissatisfied grantees in the frequency of their contacts with professionals abroad" (p. 42). The Gullahorns' interpretation of their interview data indicates that the high satisfaction of the grantees was due to

. . . their initially sharing professional values and goals with their foreign colleagues so that their shared endeavors led to increased positive sentiment and more frequent interaction. In some cases, however, the interaction and sentiment variables were reversed. That is, the structured research positions the grantees occupied in their host institutions required a high frequency of interaction. To the extent that the interaction was constructive, it led to an increased appreciation of the congruence between their own and their hosts' goals and thus increased positive sentiments (p. 42).

The structural characteristics of the work setting can require varying degrees of interaction with members of the host country. Coming as a professional with more specific occupational interests, the exchangee is likely to meet co-professionals in a work-oriented setting. Such situations increase the possibilities for exchangees to participate as equals with opportunities to contribute as well as receive in the work setting. Kelman (1963), Watson and Lippitt (1955), and others point to this as an important aspect of the sojourner's experience. The development of joint work in specific occupational areas can often provide the means for contacts to continue over time and beyond the extent of the exchange visit.

CONCLUSION

We have discussed some of the factors that seem to be important in the process of developing personal contacts by exchange students who come to study in another land. We have mainly emphasized material available for students who come to the United States.

Although the support for student exchange is international, the goals of the various sponsoring governments and private groups are as varied as the goals of the individual students who participate in these programs. In general, there is the hope that the visitors to another land have an opportunity to establish contacts and make friends among members of the host country.

These contacts seem to have several important values. First, it is quite clear that those students who do make contacts and friends learn, through these relationships, to see the host country in new ways. More particularly, they are likely to view America, for example, from several perspectives and to see it as a complex and differentiated society. In a sense they give up their responses to it in terms of one dominant image in exchange for a view of the parts, which they learn to see as having differing degrees of value and with which they can be in differing degrees of sympathy.

The establishment of contacts and friendships can, however, have another and related value. Under certain conditions and for certain people, the contacts developed in America with Americans have within them the possibility of becoming long-term relationships based on common interests and tasks. The interests that are most likely to develop in this direction are those based on professional and career concerns, which do persist over time. The people most likely to become involved in such long-term relationships are scholars who go abroad with work and professional commitments already established. It is members of this group who are most specific about their personal goals for the sojourn and who are in the best position to enter into situations in which they can participate as equals, and can contribute as well as receive in the professional contacts that are established.

Although we have no real evidence on this point, it may very well be that the experiences of foreign students in America can best be understood by hypothesizing that there are two types of outcomes which refer to two relatively separate groups of students. One type of exchangee is the younger undergraduate who is interested in seeing America and meeting Americans. He is looking for an international identity and is free of home-country attach-

ments to the point of being available for a variety of relationships with new people in a new situation. He is likely to take back home a great deal of information about America and a differentiated view of American society, as well as American patterns of life that are congenial to him. Another type would be the older, more established exchangee, who comes for more specific training or professional experience and who may be in a position to develop more specific contacts.

In both groups, it would seem that certain predisposing factors or factors antecedent to the exchange experience itself are important in affecting the kinds of contacts made and their potential for becoming long-term relationships. Our consideration of the various studies in this field indicates the special importance of one of these factors: the nationality or the world area from which the exchangee comes. Differences in the experiences of the exchangees due to this factor arise for a variety of reasons but have the over-all effect of reducing the degree to which non-Europeans make contacts with Americans and therefore the possibilities of their sharing in the values deriving from such contacts. There are indications, however, that the effects of such antecedent factors can be overcome, at least in part, by the way in which the visitor's living and work situations are structured.

REFERENCES

Bailyn, Lotte   Orientation to work: A study of Scandinavian students in America. Cambridge: Harvard University, 1963. (Dittoed)

Bennett, J. W., Passin, H., & McKnight, R. K. *In search of identity: The Japanese scholar in America and Japan.*

Minneapolis: Univer. Minnesota Press, 1958.

Deutsch, S. E., & Won, G. Some factors in the adjustment of foreign nationals in the United States. *J. soc. Issues,* 1963, *19*(3), 115–122.

Gullahorn, J. T., & Gullahorn, Jeanne E. An extension of the U-curve hypothesis. *J. soc. Issues,* 1963, *19*(3), 33–47.

Kelman, H. C. (with Victoria Steinitz) The reactions of participants in a foreign specialists seminar to their American experience. *J. soc. Issues,* 1963, *19*(3), 61–114.

Kelman, H. C., & Bailyn, Lotte Effects of cross-cultural experience on national images: A study of Scandinavian students in America. *J. Confl. Resol.,* 1962, *6,* 319–334.

Lambert, R. D., & Bressler, M. *Indian students on an American campus.* Minneapolis: Univer. Minnesota Press, 1956.

Mishler, Anita Predisposition and experience as related to post-return integration. Cambridge: Harvard University, 1963. (Dittoed)

Morris, R. *The two way mirror.* Minneapolis: Univer. Minnesota Press, 1960.

Riegel, O. W. Residual effects of exchange of persons. *Publ. Opin. Quart.,* 1953, *17,* 319–327.

Scott, F. D. *The American experience of Swedish students.* Minneapolis: Univer. Minnesota Press, 1956.

Selltiz, Claire, Christ, June R., Havel, Joan, & Cook, S. W. *Attitudes and social relations of foreign students in the United States.* Minneapolis: Univer. Minnesota Press, 1963.

Sewell, W. H., & Davidsen, O. *Scandinavian students on an American campus.* Minneapolis: Univer. Minnesota Press, 1961.

Watson, Jeanne, & Lippitt, R. *Learning across cultures.* Ann Arbor: Institute for Social Research, University of Michigan, 1955.

Conclusion

16

Social-Psychological Approaches to the Study of International Relations

THE QUESTION OF RELEVANCE

Herbert C. Kelman

We are now ready to return to a question that was raised in the introductory chapter to this volume and repeated, in a variety of contexts, in some of the chapters that followed: What relevance, if any, do social-psychological approaches have to basic problems in international relations? Specifically, what is their potential relevance to the analysis of issues underlying policy formulation? And what is their potential relevance to the development of theory in international relations?

In Chapter 1, two different kinds of research were distinguished to which social-psychological approaches have made contributions: the study of the international behavior of individuals; and the study of international politics and foreign policy. The question of relevance has rather different implications for these two types of research, and it will be easier, therefore, to examine them separately. It must be noted, however, that there is considerable overlap between these two types of research. They do not represent a sharp distinction along methodological lines; thus, the second type very definitely draws on analyses of the behavior of individuals, and the first type is by no means restricted to analyses at that level. Nor do they represent a systematic conceptual distinction. They are simply a convenient way of grouping two types of studies differing in general content and purpose. "The study of international politics and foreign policy" refers to research that is designed to understand and predict the behavior of nation states or other political units and of the individuals acting for these bodies.

"The study of the international behavior of individuals" refers to research
on behavior in an international context
that is not directly linked to the spheres
of political decision-making or state-to-
state interaction—although, as we shall
see, it may have considerable bearing
on these.

THE RELEVANCE OF RESEARCH ON THE INTERNATIONAL BEHAVIOR OF INDIVIDUALS

It is much easier to establish the
relevance of social-psychological approaches insofar as they are concerned
with studying the "international behavior" of individuals—that is, the ways
in which individuals relate themselves
to their own nation and other nations,
to the international system as a whole,
to foreign policy issues, and to the
broader questions of war and peace;
and the actual interactions between individuals of different nationalities. As
was pointed out in Chapter 1, these
problems are specifically and inherently
of a social-psychological nature. Regardless of how relevant such research
might be to problems of international
politics, it represents a legitimate area
of social-psychological investigation,
meaningful and justified in its own
right. In other words, it can be said to
have "face relevance" for anyone who is
interested in exploring the direct and
indirect interactions of individuals with
national and international objects.

At the same time, it can hardly be
denied that studies, for example, of the
structure of attitudes toward foreign
policy issues or of individuals' conceptions of their national roles, can provide
general background information useful
in the analysis of foreign policy and
international politics. The *specific* usefulness of such research depends on
one's view of the role of public opinion

in the foreign policy process—a question to which we shall return later. But
even those analysts who assign a minimal role to public opinion are likely to
agree that public conceptions and reactions are part of the context within
which foreign policy is carried out, and
that an understanding of these factors,
therefore, contributes to mapping out
the background for international relations.

But does the study of the "human
dimension" in international relations
have any *direct* relevance to questions
of foreign policy, and particularly to
those fundamental aspects of foreign
policy on which war and peace depend? I shall try to show, first, that
there are certain specific aspects of
foreign policy to which the study of
individual attitudes and cross-national
interactions does have direct relevance.
As for its relevance to the broader questions of war and peace, this depends in
part on our judgment of the significance of certain general attitudinal factors in creating the conditions for peace.
I shall, therefore, proceed to examine
whether (a) international cooperation
and (b) changes in nationalist and internationalist ideology have some bearing on the conditions for peace, and
hence whether research on these problems has potential political relevance.

Relevance to Specific Foreign Policy Goals

The foreign policy repertoire of national governments is not taken up entirely by the conduct of international
conflict and activities directly related to
it. Foreign policy also concerns itself
with a wide range of international activities that constitute ends in themselves, or means toward certain specific
goals that may have only a remote connection with the pursuit and resolution

of internation conflict—activities such as foreign trade and foreign aid; participation in various international bodies of a largely nonpolitical nature, such as the specialized agencies of the United Nations; international communication and information services; educational and cultural exchanges; special cooperative international projects, for example of a scientific nature; and ongoing cooperative international arrangements in such diverse areas as postal procedures, fishing rights, and weather prediction. Some of these activities are, of course, linked to broader foreign policy goals with potential implications for war and peace. Foreign aid, to take the prime example of this point, can be seen as a foreign policy tool designed to assure the stability of emerging nations, or to reward allies, or to attract neutrals or at least keep them from joining "the other side." Other activities, such as cultural and scientific exchanges, are often deliberately pursued as means of reducing international tensions. In the atmosphere of the Cold War it is particularly likely that almost any international activity will be converted into a tool for either pursuing or assuaging the dominant conflict, or at least that it will be presented in the rhetoric that characterizes this conflict. Nevertheless, these activities do have a life of their own, and their successful execution represents a foreign policy goal in its own right, regardless of their possible implications for the broader issues. To these more specific goals, social-psychological research on the international behavior of individuals has obvious relevance.

Enhancing the Effectiveness of International Activities. Such international activities as educational and cultural exchanges, technical assistance, international conferences, specialized agencies and committees, and joint ventures in scientific and other domains involve interaction between individuals of different nationalities. If these activities are to be successful—in other words, if the specific foreign policy goals represented by these activities are to be achieved—the interacting individuals have to communicate effectively with each other, develop patterns of cooperation, and be prepared to accept some degree of change in their attitudes and habits. Activities of this sort are bound to create some difficulties, resistances, tensions, and misunderstandings among the participants even when they are all of the same nationality. One can readily think, for example, of the adjustment problems experienced by a student coming to a new community, the resistances engendered by attempts to introduce changes in farming methods, and the interpersonal difficulties that interfere with task attainment in conferences, committees, and work-groups.

Such difficulties are greatly magnified when the participants differ in nationality and cultural background (cf. Chapter 15). Thus, communication may be hampered and misunderstandings may arise because of cultural differences among the participants. For example, they may misinterpret one another's actions because these have different meanings in their respective cultures, or they may continue to interact at a polite superficial level because they lack shared signals for communicating readiness to enter on a genuine exchange. Sensitivities, particularly about one's national status relative to that of participants from other countries, are another source of difficulties that may limit the effectiveness of international activities. National status sensitivity has been found to be a major variable in shaping the experience of exchange students (cf. Lambert &

Bressler, 1956; Morris, 1960), and is especially likely to color reactions to foreign aid programs on the part of the aid recipients. Distrust of nationals of other countries is, of course, another barrier to effective interaction around specific tasks. Such distrust may be based on the specific relationship between the nations represented, such as the mutual distrust between Americans and Russians; or on generalizations from earlier experiences, such as the distrust of Africans for Europeans.

Social-psychological and related research have obvious relevance to problems of this sort. General studies of communication and group interaction, or of attitude change and adjustment to novel situations, can provide useful background for studies that specifically address themselves to these processes in an international context. To complement research on the nature of the *processes* involved, there is a need for understanding the values, customs, communication patterns, and social institutions that characterize the different countries represented in various international activities. Such understanding can be gained through a variety of techniques, such as anthropological field studies, cross-cultural surveys, or comparative institutional analyses. These two types of research—that is, research on the processes and problems of cross-national interaction, and research on the cultural characteristics of the various participants in such interaction—can jointly contribute to enhancing the effectiveness of international activities. The former would do so by identifying barriers to communication and cooperation that are likely to arise in such situations and suggesting ways for overcoming them; the latter, by providing the participants specific information about each other that would help to reduce misunder-

standing and to facilitate productive exchange. (On the last point, cf. Klineberg, 1964, Chapter 13.)

Studies of students who go abroad for training, of the nature of their experience, and of the types of adjustment problems they face while living in the foreign country and upon returning home (cf. Chapters 4 and 15), are an example of social-psychological research that has direct relevance to efforts to enhance the effectiveness of international exchanges of personnel. Equally relevant are studies that focus on individuals who go abroad primarily to serve in the country they are visiting rather than to be trained there, such as the Peace Corps Volunteers (for example, Smith *et al.*, 1963). The attitudes that these individuals bring to the experience abroad and the satisfactions that they derive from it can have an important bearing on the success of the entire venture. In this connection, research on the selection of personnel for assignments abroad or in international agencies (cf. Klineberg, 1964, Chapter 12) can contribute directly to increased effectiveness of international programs. Such research would provide a basis for assessing the characteristics of individuals who can perform effectively in specific types of international settings.

Another type of applied research that has direct relevance for improving international activities is evaluation research, involving systematic study of specific technical assistance projects, exchange-of-persons programs, information campaigns, international conferences, or cooperative ventures. On the basis of such research, it should be possible not only to conclude whether the program under study achieved its goals, but also to gain some insight into ways of enhancing the effectiveness of similar programs in the future. For example, in an intensive evaluation study of a multi-national seminar for communications specialists (Kelman, with Steinitz, 1963), a partial analysis of interviews held with participants led us to identify seven general conditions that are likely to enhance a participant's satisfaction: (a) relevance of the experience to the participant's specific professional concerns; (b) the participant's opportunity for colleague-like relationships with his counterparts in the host country; (c) the participant's opportunity to make personal contributions; (d) availability to the participant of choice in activities and arrangements; (e) arrangement of the participant's schedule and facilities in line with his desired pattern of activities; (f) the participant's opportunity for informal social contacts with nationals of the host country; and (g) enhancement of the participant's national and personal status (pp. 104–114).

If sufficient cooperation on the part of operating agencies can be obtained, it is possible also to do more ambitious types of research, such as field experiments in which different program procedures (for example, two different ways of conducting an international conference) are developed and systematically compared; or action research projects, in which program participants join research personnel in successive evaluation and revision of the program as it proceeds. These types of research have been carried out in other settings and can certainly be applied to efforts to enhance the effectiveness of international activities.

So far, I have been speaking primarily about the contributions that basic and applied social research can make to the overcoming of barriers to communication and cooperation and thus, in turn, to the productivity of international activities and the satisfactions they provide for their participants. Typically, the goals of international activities also include the production of change in the behavior and attitudes of participants, although the degree and kind of change involved will vary considerably.

There are certain kinds of international activity—of which technical assistance and aid to developing countries are the prime examples—whose success depends on producing fundamental changes in the action patterns, attitudes, and even values of individuals and communities. Such programs may presuppose, for example, changes in the work habits and group loyalties of the individuals involved, and changes in the power structures and reward systems of their communities. Given the existing cultural patterns, values, and institutional structures of the societies in question, it is understandable that innovations will often (a) represent a threat and thus arouse strong resistances, (b) be difficult to institute because of the absence of essential psychological and institutional preconditions, and (c) have disruptive consequences for the target community. These problems are likely to be exacerbated when the change agents come from other countries, are unfamiliar with the existing patterns and channels for instituting change, and arouse suspicion, resentment, and feelings of inferiority in the target population.

Clearly, the success of such programs can be aided by an understanding of resistances to attitude change (cf. Chapter 6) and of processes of change-induction in individuals, organizations, and communities; and by research that focuses specifically on the induction of change in this type of situation—that is, a situation in which the change agents represent other countries or international organizations, and in which the induction itself is part of a larger process of national economic and political development in the context of an international system in which level of industrialization represents a major dividing principle. To facilitate social change in this kind of situation, it is necessary to combine knowledge about general principles of planned change with knowledge about the specific ideological systems and institutional structures of the societies in question. A mapping of the existing values and institutions must precede any attempt to induce change, if we are to (a) understand precisely what the change would involve, what readinesses for it exist, and what barriers would have to be overcome; (b) identify existing values and institutions that can be used to facilitate change; and (c) find ways of minimizing disruptive consequences. Such a mapping would require not only a study of traditional culture patterns and institutions, but also an exploration of emerging power relationships and belief systems, in recognition of the fact that we are dealing with societies in flux. It would be important to focus, among others, on those ideological dimensions that relate directly to the program itself—such as the target population's conceptions of economic development and social change, and of foreign aid and international cooperation.

Another type of change that is frequently desired by a government that initiates various kinds of international activities is a change in the images of the initiating country or the attitudes toward it held by other populations. Whatever other goals they may have, foreign aid projects, personnel exchanges, and information campaigns are partially designed to transform the hostile, suspicious, or indifferent attitudes of other peoples into favorable ones, or at least to increase their understanding and correct their misconceptions of the initiating country. There are many barriers to change in these attitudes and images, similar to the ones that have already been discussed, and again social-psychological research has clear implications for understanding these barriers and finding ways of overcoming them. General principles of attitude change (as discussed in Chapter 6), combined with study of the specific situations involved, can thus contribute to the achievement of this particular set of goals. In a paper devoted to a more detailed analysis of this general problem (Kelman, 1962a), I tried to develop the proposition that favorable attitude change is most likely to result from various international activities if they make possible the joint occurrence of two conditions: (a) the provision of genuinely new information about the country and people in question, in the context of (b) a positive interaction with and friendly behavior toward representatives of that country. Any attempt to create these conditions must confront the special resistances to change that are likely to arise in a particular situation. For example, foreign aid projects may fail to provide conditions for favorable attitude change because "there are strong forces in the direction of hostility toward the donor country that are inherent in the very nature of the aid situation. The fact that nationals from the donor country have come to his country to give aid is concrete evidence, from the recipient's point of view, of his own inferior status. The situation has obvious implications of an unfavorable comparison, damaging to the recipient's self-esteem. The very fact that he finds himself in this situation with its negative implications for the evaluation of his country and himself may generate hostility. This hostility is most naturally directed at the one who, by giving, underlines the recipient's inferiority" (Kelman, 1962a, p. 79). In this situation, therefore, meeting the conditions for attitude change will depend on the extent to which status-enhancing features are built into the project itself as well as into extra-project relationships.

Research on the selection of personnel, evaluation studies, and action research, which were discussed above, are equally applicable to questions of inducing change—whether this be the often fundamental changes in habits and values that constitute the goals of technical assistance programs, or the changes in images and attitudes held by other peoples that governments hope to produce through many of their international activities.

Assessing and Influencing Public Attitudes. Whatever we may assume about the role of public opinion in the determination of foreign policy—a question to which I shall return later—there is little doubt that governments are concerned with attaining public support for the policies they are pursuing. Even if we were to take the extreme position that governments can and do effectively ignore the preferences of the public at large in the *formulation* of foreign policy, we would have to grant that the *execution* of foreign policy is often affected by the nature of the public's reaction to the steps proposed or taken. An obvious example would be any foreign policy move that re-

quires a certain amount of sacrifice on the part of the population. If the public does not support the move with sufficient enthusiasm, then it cannot be carried out as effectively. Moreover, lack of public support reduces the credibility of the move and thus its effectiveness in influencing other nations.

It becomes important, therefore, for governments to assess public response toward foreign policy moves that they are contemplating or that they have carried out, and to exert influence on the public when support for these moves is insufficient. Studies of attitudes on foreign policy issues thus have direct relevance to certain specific foreign policy goals. Of similar relevance is knowledge about ways in which attitudes are influenced (cf. Chapter 6) and public support is mobilized (cf. Chapter 8). On the broader level, the study of people's general orientation toward foreign policy issues and of their relation to the nation state (cf. Chapter 10) can provide useful background for understanding their reactions to specific foreign policy moves and the conditions under which their loyalties can be aroused and their support elicited.[1]

The concern of governments with assessing and influencing public attitudes also extends beyond their national boundaries. One of the foreign policy goals of most governments is to create a favorable image abroad. The emphasis on this goal may vary for different governments and at different times.

---

[1] In my judgment, the relationship between public opinion and foreign policy decisions involves a considerably more complex and reciprocal process than the above paragraphs imply. I would assume that governments do not merely assess public reactions to their policies and, if they find the level of acceptance to be insufficient, proceed to shape these reactions in the desired directions. To a large extent, the process may indeed take precisely this form, but the decision-makers are also influenced by public opinion. This influence is often indirect and is more likely to derive from the opinions of important elites than from those of the "man in the street," but it does suggest the existence of a two-way process. We shall examine this possibility in greater detail when we discuss the relevance of social-psychological research to the study of foreign policy.

Moreover, a government is by no means equally concerned with all foreign populations: it will be particularly anxious to produce a favorable image and acceptance of its policies among those nations whose support it deems crucial to the successful achievement of its foreign policy objectives. Research on the attitudes of foreign populations and on the effectiveness of various efforts designed to influence these attitudes thus also has direct relevance to certain specific foreign policy goals.

Relevance to Broader Questions of War and Peace

We have seen that social-psychological research on the international behavior of individuals—specifically, on their interactions in the context of various international programs, and on their attitudes toward foreign policy issues—has not only intrinsic interest for the social psychologist fascinated by these problems, but also direct relevance to certain specific, if limited, foreign policy goals. But does it have any relevance to the broader questions of war and peace? Certainly, the oft-quoted statement from the constitution of the United Nations Educational, Scientific, and Cultural Organization implies such relevance: "Since wars begin in the minds of men, it is in the minds of men that the defenses of peace must be constructed." According to this view, research on motives, images, and beliefs of individuals, and on the modification of these in the direction of greater international understanding and cooperation would have the highest relevance to the basic issues of war and peace.

If, however, one regards war—as I do—as essentially a societal and inter-societal process, then the political relevance of what we are here calling the study of the international behavior of individuals is not as obviously apparent. In an ultimate sense, I would subscribe to the "minds-of-men" formulation, because societies and institutions are, after all, created by men, controlled by men, and subject to change by the actions of men. Their effects "work in and through human beings; they are altered as the result of human relations" (Klineberg, 1964, p. 6). The actions of men in the international arena, however, take place with reference to organized political systems, and they can have an impact on matters of war and peace only insofar as they affect these systems and are mediated by them. Thus, it cannot be assumed that activities designed to promote international understanding and world-mindedness necessarily contribute to creating the conditions for peace. It is not enough that they alter the minds of men; we must also be able to show that they enter into those political processes whereby international conflicts are conducted and decisions for war or peace are made. Let us examine the effects of international cooperation from this point of view, taking international cooperation (broadly defined) as the prototype of activities designed "to construct the defenses of peace in the minds of men."

International Cooperation. There is considerable disagreement about the potential contributions of such activities as international exchanges, cooperative ventures, or the Peace Corps—whatever their intrinsic merits may be—to creating the conditions for peace. Proponents of such activities often argue that they increase international understanding and improve mutual attitudes. We have already seen in Chapters 4 and 15 that there is no clear-cut evidence that international travel and exchange in fact produce more favorable attitudes. But even if they did, there is some reason to question how much bearing such favorable attitudes are likely to have on the prevention of war. Is it reasonable to suppose that favorable attitudes developed through personal contact can overcome the realities of a conflict of interests? If conflicts between nations are based primarily on incompatible goals rather than on lack of understanding, it is doubtful that increased understanding can contribute greatly to their resolution. Despite these limitations, it seems to me that international cooperation does have political relevance, though its contribution to creating the conditions for peace may be largely indirect and long-range.

One can distinguish four types of effects of international cooperation and exchange that may have an impact on the relations between two nations and may reduce the likelihood that conflicts between them will take violent forms: (1) an increased openness, among key individuals in each nation, in their attitudes toward the other nation; (2) a reduction in the level of tension between the two nations; (3) an increased commitment to an internationalist ideology; and (4) a development of a network of relationships cutting across national boundaries. What is the potential relevance that each of these four interrelated effects might have for international politics?

1. Participants in international exchanges and other forms of cooperation do not universally and necessarily come away from these experiences with wholly favorable attitudes toward the other nation or nations involved. Yet the indications are that such experiences can and usually do produce some very important attitude changes—provided the experiences themselves are personally and professionally satisfying to the participants. These are not necessarily changes in general favorableness toward the host country, but rather changes in the cognitive structure—for example, in the complexity and differentiation—of images of the host country (cf. Kelman, 1965). Such changes are probably more meaningful in the long run than total approval of the country would be; they indicate a greater richness and refinement of images and a greater understanding of the other society in its own terms. Moreover, participants in such activities are likely to develop personal ties to the other country and to certain individuals within it, and thus a sense of personal involvement in its fate. As we have already noted, this increased understanding and involvement are not likely to overcome real conflicts of interests that exist between the nations. They are likely, however, to create a greater openness in individuals' attitudes toward the other nation.

If there is a continuing pattern of cooperation and exchange between two nations, involving many individuals who are in leading positions within their own societies, then there should be a greater *predisposition within each nation to trust the other nation, to perceive it as nonthreatening, and to be responsive to it* (cf. Chapter 11). Thus, while it would be naive to assume that a pattern of cooperation and exchange is a sufficient condition for peace between two nations, such a pattern should decrease the likelihood that the nations will resort to violence in resolving their conflicts. If conflicts arise between nations whose citizens have a history of close and friendly contact, there should be less of a tendency to perceive threatening intent in the other and to formulate the issue in black-and-white terms, and a greater readiness to communicate with one another and to seek accommodation.

2. If two nations that are in conflict with each other are, at the same time, involved in exchanges and cooperative ventures, the level of tension that marks their over-all relationship is likely to be reduced. They are more likely to engage in at least some inteactions that are free of hostility and mutual threat, and that provide opportunities for communication and for the discovery of common values and interests. Needless to say, these more positive interactions will not cause the basic conflict between the two nations to vanish and will not persuade them to abandon the pursuit of incompatible goals. They can, however, contribute to the creation of an *atmosphere in which these basic conflicts can be negotiated more effectively and political settlements can be achieved.*

It has been extremely difficult, for example, for the United States and the Soviet Union to negotiate disarmament agreements, even though such agreements would be beneficial to both sides, because of the absence of mutual trust, without which the disarmament process cannot be initiated. Negotiation of more basic settlements of Cold-War issues is even more difficult under these circumstances. Positive interactions between two nations in areas outside of those on which their conflict centers, by reducing the level of tension, may help to build up some degree of mutual trust and thus at least make it somewhat more likely that serious negotiations on the issues in conflict will get under way. Moreover, the establishment of cooperative relationships in some domains may help to counteract tendencies toward complete polarization of the conflicting nations and may thus make it easier to find ways of "fractionating" the conflicts be-

tween them. Fisher (1964) has argued very persuasively that fractionating conflict—"dividing up the issues and considering them separately in small units" (p. 109), rather than treating each as part of a total ideological confrontation—may reduce the risk of war and at the same time facilitate achievement of specific national goals.

3. International exchanges and cooperative ventures—provided they are intrinsically useful and satisfying—are likely to increase world-mindedness and commitment to an internationalist ideology among the participants. Wide adoption of this type of value framework would seem to be necessary to provide the ideological underpinnings to a peaceful world order. In the short run, peaceful settlement of conflicts is more likely where there is an acceptance of the legitimacy of supranational organizations and a willingness to surrender some degree of national sovereignty to them. In the long run, the stability and effectiveness of such supranational organizations depend on the acceptance—as fundamental values governing the relations between nations—of the concepts of international (in contrast to strictly national) security, nonviolence in the settlement of conflicts, and responsibility for human welfare on a world-wide basis. As the rate of international exchange and cooperation increases, it seems reasonable to suppose that ideological changes in these directions will become more widespread.

Such changes in the belief systems of individuals, in and of themselves, are not likely to produce major changes at the institutional level. New institutional arrangements are likely to be developed when their functional significance becomes apparent to important segments of the societies involved. Thus, for example, it can be argued that the major impetus for the development of the European Economic Community came, not from an ideological commitment to the idea of a united Europe, but from the recognition that economic operations can be made more efficient and profitable if they can be planned and coordinated with reference to a wider geographical area. Nevertheless, it is probably true that the existence of supporting beliefs within the societies —such as, in the case of EEC, the belief in the idea of a united Europe, along with the postwar disenchantment with traditional nationalism—facilitates the establishment of new institutional arrangements by providing an ideological framework ready to incorporate them. In the same sense, then, international exchange and cooperation may contribute to the development and strengthening of international political institutions by increasing the *ideological readiness for them among influential segments of the participating nations,* even though the major force toward the development of such institutions is likely to come from functional requirements rather than from an abstract commitment to an internationalist ideology.

4. The most important source of the political relevance of international exchange and cooperation, in my opinion, is its contribution to the development of human networks that cut across national boundaries. Participation in such activities, if they are successful, is likely to lead to the establishment of ongoing relationships around common professional concerns among individuals representing different nationalities. These relationships have functional significance for the individuals in the sense that they are directly relevant to their professional interests and the effective performance of their professional roles. Thus, individuals and groups from different countries become

committed to international cooperation not as an abstract value, but as a concrete vehicle for carrying out personally important activities and pursuing their immediate and long-range goals. They become involved in a network of interdependent individuals and groups, without reference to national differences, and are likely to develop a sense of loyalty to it. What is crucial here is that this loyalty cut across national lines; it need not be antagonistic to or competitive with national loyalty, but simply independent of it.

Insofar as international exchange and cooperation contribute to the development of such cross-cutting loyalties, they help to create the conditions for peace. We have seen, in Chapter 2, that the existence of cross-cutting ties created by multiple overlapping loyalty groupings tends to promote integration and internal peace within preliterate societies. Coser (1956) points out that modern pluralistic societies are "sewn together" by the existence of multiple group affiliations of individuals, which "make for a multiplicity of conflicts crisscrossing society" (p. 79). Individuals are members of various groupings, involved in diverse conflicts along divergent lines. Thus, for example, individuals who are members of antagonistic groups in the economic sphere may, at the same time, be members of the same religious group and thus stand together in a conflict with other religious groups. Because the lines of conflict between these multiple groups do not converge, deep cleavages along a single axis are prevented. "The interdependence of conflicting groups and the multiplicity of noncumulative conflicts provide one, though not, of course, the only check against basic consensual breakdown in an open society" (p. 79). It is in this same sense that the development of *networks, based on professional and other interests, that cut across national boundaries* can contribute to the stability and integration of the international system. It would do so, not by eliminating conflicts, but by counteracting tendencies toward complete polarization—toward subordinating all relationships to a single basic conflict along national lines.

To put it in other terms, the development of cross-cutting networks that have functional significance for many individuals in the enactment of their various roles should create a widespread vested interest in maintaining both the pluralism and the integrity of the international system. Insofar as groupings that cut across national lines are important to individuals in the enactment of their various roles—in other words, insofar as individuals have become tied into a pattern of genuine interdependency—they will resist a definition of the international system along strictly national lines, in which national affiliations supersede and subsume all other affiliations. Moreover, they will have something at stake in maintaining the integrity of the international system, since its breakdown would also mean the breakdown of the cross-national networks in which they are involved. Ultimately, the maintenance of a stable international system will probably require the development of political and even military institutions (cf. Kelman, 1962b) that cut across national lines and that make, not for an elimination of national loyalties, but for a diffusion of loyalties that would counteract total cleavages along national lines. International exchange and cooperation can, however, contribute to this process in a small but cumulative way. As more and more cross-cutting ties develop, the vested interest in a pluralistic and stable international

system is likely to increase and ever stronger barriers to the breakdown of the system are likely to arise.

Ideologies of National and International Systems. In discussing the political relevance of international cooperation, I suggested that it may produce certain ideological changes among influential segments of the participating nations. This raises the larger question of the role of ideological factors—particularly of nationalist ideology—in international politics. To the extent to which such ideological factors enter into the relations between nations, their study has obvious political relevance. In particular, an understanding of the conditions that facilitate change from a narrowly nationalist to an internationalist ideology would have important implications for the broader issue of war and peace. But do such ideological factors really have any significant impact on the relations between nations?

Before attempting to answer this question, let me indicate briefly what I mean by nationalism and the social-psychological study of it. (See Chapter 10 for a more detailed discussion of related issues.) One can describe nationalism as an ideology that views the nation as the unit in which paramount political power is vested. The nation state, being the embodiment of the nation, is placed at the pinnacle of power and entitled to overrule both smaller and larger political units. The modern nation state derives its legitimacy and cohesiveness from the fact that it is seen as representing the nation —in other words, from the correspondence of the political entity with an ethnic, cultural, and historical entity with which at least large portions of the population identify.

The social-psychological study of nationalist ideology focuses on the belief systems of individuals. It is concerned with the ways in which individual nationals and subgroups within the population relate themselves to the nation state, their definitions of the role of national and of the expectations that go with it, their level of commitment to and degree of involvement in the nation, and the nature of the satisfactions with which their national identification provides them. The study of political ideology at the social-psychological level, however, must be closely linked to an analysis of this ideology at the system level. That is, in studying political ideology we are not simply dealing with the beliefs of individuals, but with a set of beliefs that is inherent in the political system itself, communicated to individual citizens in the course of socialization and throughout life, and adopted by them (with individual variations in nature and degree).

Nationalist ideology, at the system level, must be seen in terms of the functions of the nation state. The performance of these functions and the effective operation of the system presuppose consensus about national institutional arrangements, the relation of the nation state to other states, and the relationship of the individual to the nation state. This set of assumptions by which the system runs constitutes its ideology, which is built into its institutional structures and its constitution, and transmitted through its basic documents and elite communications. The ideology built into the national system and communicated by its leaders may take different forms, depending on the level of development of a particular state, on its international position, its power and success in the international

arena, and its internal political structure. These variables would determine the *particular* functions that a given nation state must perform at a given historical juncture (such as the unification of tribal elements or the maintenance of bloc leadership), in addition to the *generic* functions common to all nation states.

There are many variations in the way in which the system ideology is interpreted and incorporated into the belief-systems of individuals and subgroups within the population. Depending on their demographic and personality characteristics and on their positions within the social and political structure, individuals may vary in the components of the ideology that they emphasize or deemphasize, the intensity of their commitment to the nation state, their definition of the national role and the expectations that go with it, and the way in which they enact this role.[2] While there may be such variations, it is essential to the effective functioning of the nation state that the basic tenets of its ideology be widely accepted within the population. For example, the system cannot operate successfully unless the population accepts the authority of the state as legitimate and shares the assumption that, in times of national crisis, the national role becomes paramount in the citizen's hierarchy of roles. The wide acceptance of these assumptions depends, in turn, on the extent to which individuals and groups are—in one way or another—integrated into the national system (cf. Katz, Kelman, & Flacks, 1964; and Chapter 10 in this volume).

These ideological assumptions, pro-

---

[2] According to the present view, the chauvinistic, exclusive type of nationalism would be one variant of nationalist ideology, which for a given nation may be the dominant form of the ideology at certain times (at certain historical junctures or certain periods of national crisis), and a deviant form at other times.

vided they are widely accepted by the population, constitute the terms on which a nation state relates to other nation states and on which international institutions are established. When viewed in this way, then, ideological factors clearly have a significant impact on the relations between nations. We sometimes tend to forget this fact because these ideological assumptions are so solidly built into our national and international structures that we come to regard them as givens, as part of the structure of reality. The feeling that ideological factors are irrelevant may be due to a concentration on the modern Western nation state to such an extent that the ideological assumptions that define that particular type of political system are seen as universal and inevitable, rather than as representing one position on a range of possible ones. We need a more comparative perspective, which takes into account a wider range of historical periods and of societies. It would then become apparent that the nation state was not always and is not everywhere the basic political unit; that it may take different forms, associated with different ideological assumptions; that it does not always function adequately, in part because some of its basic assumptions may not be widely accepted by a population that is poorly integrated into the national system; and that the functions, structures, and ideological assumptions of even the Western nation state are now changing in significant ways.

A comparative perspective makes it quite apparent that ideologies different from those that govern the modern nation state are possible, and that they would have important implications for the relations between nations. Of particular relevance to questions of war and peace.would be the possibility of developing a more internationalist ide-

ology, in which the nation state would not be regarded as the paramount political unit in all respects. Such an ideology would not presuppose the complete abandonment of the nation state and its ideology, but might represent a variant of nationalist ideology for which some precedents already exist. There is no inherent reason why loyalty to international institutions should be incompatible with loyalty to the nation state, provided the two "are furnishing compatible solutions to different needs" (Guetzkow, 1955, p. 39).

The key question, of course, is how changes in ideological assumptions can be brought about. I would assume, in general, that such changes are most likely to arise, not through a direct attack on underlying values, but as a consequence of the adoption of new institutional arrangements that incorporate new values and ideological assumptions. "A specific institutional structure may be accepted on pragmatic grounds without requiring, in the first instance, a radical reorganization of national and individual values (although such a reorganization may evolve from the institutional structure in action)" (Kelman, 1962b). As the nation state itself becomes committed to certain supranational arrangements and in fact becomes dependent on these arrangements for the performance of some of its basic functions, it can be expected that its ideology will change and that this will be reflected in the belief systems of the citizens. As a matter of fact, given the many changes in the functioning of nation states that have already taken place in the postwar period, what is involved here is probably not so much the development of an entirely new ideology, as the encouragement of an already existing variant of nationalist ideology.

The development of the United Nations and its various affiliates, and of nonnational roles within these organizations (cf. Chapter 14), is contributing to this process of institutional change from which ideological changes are likely to flow. Similarly, international exchange and cooperation are contributing to this process insofar as they lead to the development of institutionalized networks cutting across national boundaries (as described above). To be sure, it may be a long time before these developments will lead to ideological changes sufficient to have a major impact on the relations between nations. They do suggest, however, an alternative set of assumptions by which nation states in their interaction with each other can operate. An exploration of such alternative assumptions, in comparison with the currently dominant ones, may thus have profound relevance to long-range questions of war and peace.

THE RELEVANCE OF RESEARCH ON INTERNATIONAL POLITICS AND FOREIGN POLICY

When we turn to social-psychological research that deliberately addresses itself to issues of international politics and foreign policy, the question of relevance takes on a different character. It may be intrinsically interesting to study the patterning of public opinion on foreign policy issues, or the images that important decision-makers have of their own and other countries, or the interactions of college students who are simulating actors in an international system. No matter how interesting and worthwhile these studies may be in their own right, however, insofar as they are presented as contributions to the understanding of international politics and foreign policy, it is entirely fair

to apply more stringent criteria of relevance to them. It becomes important to ask whether they have any relevance to the actual conduct of international affairs and whether they tell us anything about the factors that enter into foreign policy decisions.

It is usually not very fruitful to pose the question in such absolute terms—that is, to debate whether these studies have any political relevance *at all*. It would be unreasonable to insist that public opinion plays no role at all in the foreign policy process, or that the images of decision-makers have no effect whatsoever on the actions they take in the name of the state, or that one can learn nothing about international processes from observing the simulation of these processes in a group of college students. The real question concerns the *kind* of relevance that such studies have for international politics and foreign policy and the *limits* of this relevance. What is it that one can and cannot learn from them, and how does the information they yield help to order and explain the phenomena with which the student of international politics is concerned? And here there is room for genuine disagreement about the kinds of conclusions that can legitimately be drawn from such studies and about the importance of these conclusions. These disagreements may be due to differences in evaluation of the importance of certain kinds of variables —such as public opinion or images of decision-makers—in determining international political processes, and of the validity of certain types of research methods—such as simulation or content analysis—as sources of information about international political processes.

One can distinguish four ways in which social-psychological approaches can contribute to the study of international politics and foreign policy:

(a) They can contribute directly to the study of one *substantive problem* that is in large part within the domain of competence of the social psychologist—the role of public opinion in the foreign policy process. (b) They can provide analytical tools for investigating the individual decision-maker as the *unit of analysis* in the study of state behavior. (c) They can provide concepts and methods for the detailed study of *processes* that are centrally involved in internation relations, particularly foreign policy decision-making and international negotiation. (d) They can address themselves to some of the *assumptions* that are frequently made—explicitly or implicitly—in formulation of theory as well as policy in international relations.[3]

The relevance of these four types of contributions is a matter on which students of international relations disagree, depending on the substantive and methodological assumptions they make. In the pages that follow, I shall review each of these four types of contributions and the kinds of questions that can be raised about them, and attempt to show in what ways they are relevant to the study of international politics. My intention is not only to show that these contributions are indeed relevant, but also to point to the necessary limits of their relevance.

Public Opinion in the Foreign Policy Process

The role of public opinion in the foreign policy process is a substantive problem to whose exploration social-psychological concepts and methods can make clear and direct contributions. The political relevance of such research, however, rests on the assumption that public opinion does indeed play an important role in the foreign policy process—an assumption that some observers would question. They point out that the general public has very little information about foreign policy matters and very little interest in them, and that opinions in this domain tend to be simple, undifferentiated, and poorly structured. (See Chapters 3 and 8 for discussions of the structure of opinions and images relating to foreign policy matters.) A public opinion so impoverished can hardly have a major impact on foreign policy decisions. Moreover, these observers point out, foreign policy issues do not enter significantly into the electorate's choice between candidates, nor do decision-makers lose public support as a consequence of their actions in the foreign policy arena. Decision-makers can, therefore, carry out foreign policy without fear of electoral punishment or decline in their popularity.

There is little question that foreign policy attitudes among the population at large are marked, to a great extent, by apathy, ignorance, and a general lack of structure and stability. It does not follow, however, that public opinion therefore plays no role in the foreign policy process. It would be a mistake to equate public opinion with the distribution of answers to questions about specific foreign policy issues

---

[3] The first three ways in which social-psychological approaches can contribute correspond roughly to the three types of research relating to international politics and foreign policy that were described in Chapter 1 (pp. 13–17): public opinion in the foreign policy process; individual actors in the foreign policy process; and processes of interaction in international conflict and conflict resolution. The fourth kind of contribution is related to the development of theory and methodology in international relations and the formulation of policy recommendations, as discussed in Chapter 1 (pp. 17–20).

on the part of a cross-section of the general population. If we focus on public moods and broad orientations, rather than on specific policy issues, we can readily see that even the opinions of the general public may help to direct and constrain foreign policy decisions. Furthermore, if we think in terms of an *effective* public opinion, in which different segments of the population carry different weights, rather than in terms of cross-sectional opinion distributions, we can see more clearly the ways in which publics enter into the foreign policy process. Let me elaborate these two points and comment briefly on their implications for the study of public opinion along lines that would be maximally relevant to problems of foreign policy.

The Role of the General Public in the Foreign Policy Process. The moods of the general public and their broad orientations toward national and international affairs are an essential part of the climate within which foreign policy decision-making takes place (cf. Chapter 9; also Almond, 1950). Decision-makers are likely to be influenced by widespread sentiments within the population that may favor hostility or friendliness toward certain other nations, involvement in or withdrawal from international affairs, militancy or conciliation in response to external pressures, and expansionism or cooperation in the pursuit of national goals. They are also likely to take into account, in the formulation of policy, such underlying dispositions as "the population's mood of pessimism or optimism about their own institutions, their level of confidence in the government, [and]

their desire for peace or readiness for war" (Kelman, 1958, p. 2).

In part, these moods and orientations within the population exert a "positive" influence on the process of policy formulation, in the sense that they impel decision-makers toward perceptions and actions that reflect public sentiments. Often, decision-makers are not only influenced by these pervasive moods, but actually share them with the rest of the population. In fact, these moods may originate in the very elites from which the decision-makers are recruited and then spread among the rest of the population, so that it becomes difficult to specify who is influencing whom. To the extent to which the orientations of decision-makers and the public overlap, studies of public opinion can serve as a valuable source of information about the predispositions of the decision-maker himself.[4] At the very least, however, studies of public opinion ought to reveal the kinds of actions that express popular moods and for which the public is ready; it can be assumed that these states of readiness constitute one of the inputs into the policy process to which decision-makers are not entirely unresponsive.

Moods and orientations within the population also exert a "negative" influence on the process of policy formulation, in the sense that they serve as constraints on the decision-maker (cf. Chapter 8). Even though the decision-maker may have a great deal of latitude (as far as public response is concerned) in foreign policy matters, there may be certain broad limits set by public opinion within which he must operate. There are many specific policies that

---

[4] The degree of overlap varies, of course, in different societies, at different times, and for different issues. See Chapter 7 for a discussion of the question of how much one can generalize from public images to leader images with special reference to the Soviet Union.

he could adopt without losing public support, but he may well be in difficulty if he violates certain pervasive assumptions and dispositions. Thus, to be assured of support, he must assess the state of public opinion before formulating policy and take its underlying moods into account.

The loss of support may take the form of electoral punishment. Despite the fact that specific foreign policy issues do not seem to play an important role in American voting behavior, there is some indication that general concern with avoiding war has had some impact on recent presidential elections. In 1952 and 1956, the Republican Party apparently gained some votes because it was seen as better able than the Democratic Party to keep the United States out of war; in 1964, with Senator Goldwater's candidacy, the Republican Party clearly lost this advantage.[5]

But the risk of losing electoral support is not the only source of constraint on the decision-maker. The very execution of foreign policy often requires wide public support, particularly if it calls for extensive sacrifices on the part of the population. Such support contributes vitally to the success of foreign policy moves, not only by providing active and enthusiastic participation in them at home, but also by lending credibility to them abroad. Decision-makers will be reluctant, therefore, to initiate important actions if they are not assured of public support. The difference between democratic and totalitarian societies with respect to this type of constraint is only one of degree, for even the totalitarian decision-maker cannot carry out foreign policies without public support and cannot ignore,

therefore, pervasive moods in his population.

It is, of course, possible for decision-makers to mobilize public support for a policy that they consider to be desirable though unpopular. Undoubtedly, those observers who maintain that public opinion does not determine foreign policy, but is determined by it, are often correct. Decision-makers may very well manipulate public opinion in order to bring it into line with decisions that they have already made—and here again the difference between totalitarian and democratic systems may be only one of degree. The possibility of mobilizing and manipulating public opinion, however, may be available to the decision-maker only within certain broad limits. He may be unable to mobilize support for policies that go counter to the general moods and broad orientations that we have been discussing. Sometimes, ironically, these inhibiting moods and orientations may themselves be the products of earlier efforts to mobilize public opinion in a very different direction; once they have been created, however, they may offer powerful resistances to a reorientation of foreign policy. In any event, there are likely to be at least some limits to the manipulation of public opinion, and these too serve as constraints on the decision-maker: he will be reluctant to initiate actions for which it will be difficult to mobilize public support.

But even when decision-makers choose actions that go counter to the public's preferences, in the expectation that they will subsequently mobilize support for them, this does not mean that public opinion—in the sense of broad orientations—plays no role in the policy process. The ability to mobilize

---

[5] Evidence for this conclusion comes from data obtained by the Survey Research Center, University of Michigan, and subjected to the type of analysis reported in Stokes, Campbell, and Miller (1958).

support depends on the presence of certain general dispositions within the population on which decision-makers can draw. For example, decision-makers may choose a policy that involves a serious risk of war in the expectation that they will be able to mobilize public support for it. This expectation rests, however, on certain assumptions about public dispositions—such as the assumption that the public accepts the legitimacy of the government and of its authority to decide on questions of war and peace, or that nationalist sentiments will readily be aroused when a situation is defined as one of national crisis, or that there is a readiness for belligerency which can be touched off by informing the public of a slight to national honor or prestige. The existence of these dispositions is usually taken for granted in modern nation states, but there is no reason to assume that they will always be present and certainly not that they will always be present to the same degree. The variability becomes even greater when situations other than those defined as national crises are involved. In short, whenever decision-makers choose actions in the expectation that they will subsequently mobilize public support, they must assess (though this is often done implicitly) the degree to which the public is disposed to respond to such mobilization, and must know on what public moods, images, and other dispositions they can draw in order to attain support.

In many foreign policy actions, the decision-makers are not so much concerned about mobilizing active support, as they are about avoiding active opposition. They may often feel free, therefore, to make decisions on the assumption that the public is largely ignorant and apathetic about the issues involved, and thus quite readily manipulable: when presented with a *fait accompli*, the public will accept the decision without protest. But even this situation involves an assessment of public opinion and its degree of manipulability. ". . . the fact that the population is poorly informed on foreign-policy issues, that its attitudes are poorly structured, and that it has little interest or commitment on these matters does not mean at all that public opinion is unimportant; for this state of apathy, or whatever else we wish to call it, is very clearly a state of public opinion, and one which has profound effects on the conduct of foreign affairs" (Kelman, 1958, p. 3).

In considering the effects of public opinion on decision-making, we must keep in mind not only the "objective" constraints imposed by public sentiments, but also the constraints as *perceived* by the decision-maker. There is good reason to believe that decision-makers often have an exaggerated view of the strength of public opposition to certain policy innovations. To be sure, such statements as "the public will never go along with this policy" or "the public insists on this response" are often techniques used by decision-makers to buttress the position that they themselves prefer. No doubt, however, there are times when decision-makers genuinely believe these statements and—rightly or wrongly—feel that their hands are tied.

Whether or not these statements are genuine, they may constitute a self-fulfilling prophecy: they may create the very public opinion that they predicted and thus introduce constraints that did not exist before. When this happens, the decision-maker in turn may exaggerate the strength and rigidity of the public's feelings. The victim of his own propaganda, he may be unaware of the extent to which his own communications contributed to the state of public opinion that now ties his hands. Under these circumstances, he would be likely to underestimate his own ability to mobilize public support for innovative policies. For example, the indications are that the American public would be much more willing to go along with a policy of diplomatic recognition of Communist China than many decision-makers believe or claim. Thus, in a recent survey (Patchen, 1964), respondents were asked how they would feel if "the President suggested that we exchange ambassadors with Communist China the way we do with other countries." Fifty-one percent indicated that they would favor following his suggestion and 34 percent that they would oppose it. Even among those respondents who, earlier in the interview, had said that the United States should not deal with the Communist Chinese government at all, 28 percent favored exchanging ambassadors if the President suggested it. If the *hypothetical* introduction of a mere presidential *suggestion* can make so much difference, it seems reasonable to predict that an *actual* pronouncement by the President that changing circumstances *require* a new policy toward China would meet with widespread acceptance.

The study of public opinion can thus be useful as a check on the assumptions of decision-makers about the constraints under which they are operating. It can provide relevant information not only for the decision-maker himself in his choice of actions and his efforts at mobilizing public support, but also for groups concerned with influencing foreign policy. Public opinion data—such as those regarding Communist China—can potentially be brought into the foreign policy debate as evidence that certain policy innova-

tions are indeed feasible. When public opinion data are used for these purposes, however—either by decision-makers or citizen groups—it is important to keep in mind that the current distribution of opinions on an issue is generally a poor indicator of what policies the public would be prepared to accept *if their adoption were strongly urged by national leaders*. More often than not the general public favors the official policies of the moment, so that projections based on poll data may systematically underestimate the possibilities for change. If more valid conclusions are to be drawn from opinion surveys, it will be necessary to introduce methodological refinements that will help us assess the structure, stability, and motivational bases of public attitudes, and predict the effects of changing circumstances and authoritative communications on them (cf. Chapter 8; also Katz, 1960, and Kelman, 1961). Moreover, it will be necessary to assign different weights to the opinions of different segments of the population, depending on their roles in the total foreign policy process—the issue to which I shall turn next.

Effective Public Opinion and the Structure of National Leadership. When decision-makers speak of public opinion, they generally think in terms of influential congressmen, or newspaper editors, or leaders in various nongovernmental organizations. Individuals who occupy these positions of national leadership can exert direct influence on the decision-maker in part because they control some of the means —such as financial or editorial support —that he needs for successful execution of his policies, in the short run or in the long run. Much of their power, however, stems from their relationship to public opinion. Rosenau (1963) uses the term "national leaders" in this connection interchangeably with "opinion-makers," whom he defines as "those members of the society who *occupy positions which enable them to transmit, with some regularity, opinions about foreign policy issues to unknown persons*" (p. 6). By virtue of their positions, these national leaders can impede or facilitate the achievement of consensus. They perform, in Rosenau's terms, a "veto-support function": decision-makers are constrained by their opposition, and turn to them for help in the mobilization of public support.

It is clear that decision-makers are sensitive to public opinion, as personified by the national leaders, and that public opinion thus plays an important role in the policy process. It is equally clear, however, that *effective public opinion* in the sense that I have been speaking of it is not identical with the distribution of opinions on foreign policy issues among the population at large. What we are most interested in, when we wish to assess the impact of public opinion on foreign policy decisions, are the opinions of the leaders or opinion-makers. As Rosenau (1963) points out, "except perhaps when mass passivity diminishes in extreme emergencies or when votes are cast in elections, the views of national leaders *are* public opinion insofar as foreign policy issues are concerned" (p. 28). "They guide and mold mass opinion and they also reflect it, and in this dual capacity the flexibility, intensity, and depth of their opinions constitute the essential subsoil in which foreign policy alternatives must be rooted" (p. 17).

To study public opinion in the foreign policy process it is necessary to analyze the structure of national leadership in order to determine *whose* opinions count. Examination of the power structure within the society would help to identify those positions from which influence on foreign policy decisions can be exerted, "and to determine the degree to which they are influential, the issues over which they have some control, and the way in which they exert their influence. . . . Study of the communication structure would reveal which groups have access to the information enabling them to play a role in foreign policy and to communication channels enabling them to exert influence" (Kelman, 1955, p. 48). In Rosenau's (1963) terms, we are concerned—when analyzing the structure of national leadership—with "the pattern of positions which are likely to generate opinion-making on various issues" (p. 10).

It is important to note that the composition of the leadership can be expected to differ from issue to issue. The likelihood that an opinion-maker will become activated by a given issue depends on the relevance of this issue to the concerns of the group that he represents and the degree to which it touches on his group's interests. Thus, for each issue "one could plot a set of positions in the society out of which opinion-making activity is likely to emanate irrespective of the identity of the particular persons who occupy them. It is hardly surprising, for example, that an embargo on the importation of Cuban tobacco produced opinion-making activity on the part of the president of the Tampa [Florida] Cigar Manufacturers Association" (Rosenau, 1963, p. 10).

Depending, then, on the issue, the leaders of different groups within the population are likely to make their influence felt and to become influential. "This is true for direct influence, as expressed for example in pressure groups: the Catholic Church may be more influential than military groups in legislation regarding censorship, but will probably be considerably less influential in matters relating to war and peace. It should also be true for indirect influence in the sense of 'whose opinions have to be taken into account': the opinions of college administrators may be more important than those of industrial workers when it comes to decisions on military training, but considerably less important when it comes to decisions on defense production" (Kelman, 1954, p. 5). Decision-makers will be most responsive to those leaders who have a stake in a particular issue —provided they also have a base of power—since these are the individuals whose opposition they fear and whose support they need with respect to this issue.

In short, then, in studying the role of public opinion in the foreign policy process, we must first ask *whose* opinions count *on what issues*. Such an analysis would enable us to assign different weights to different segments of public opinion and thus provide a bridge between the opinions of the population and the actions of the decision-maker. We would then be able to view the distribution of opinions on various policy issues in the context of the opinion–policy relationship as a whole. On the one hand, we would be able to deal more effectively with the *dynamics of opinion formation* on foreign policy issues—the psychological and social processes by which opinions become crystallized and public sentiments mobilized. Here we would be concerned with "downward" communication from the opinion-makers, with the mechanisms and processes by which they reach attentive publics and thus in turn the mass public (cf. Rosenau, 1961). On the other hand, we would be able to examine the ways in which public opinion enters into the

dynamics of decision-making on foreign policy issues—the effects that it has on the assumptions and constraints under which decision-makers operate, and on the types of actions they choose and the manner in which they present them to the public. Here we would be concerned with "upward" communication from the opinion-makers, with the mechanisms and processes by which they reach decision-makers, whether it be at their own initiative or at the initiative of the decision-maker himself. When the study of public opinion is embedded in these ways in the study of opinion-making and decision-making processes, its relevance to foreign policy becomes more readily apparent.

Individual Actors in the Foreign Policy Process

Students of international relations have been quite concerned with the question of what constitutes the proper unit of analysis for the study of international politics (see, for example, Wolfers, 1959). One approach to this problem is based on the "conviction that the analysis of international politics should be centered, in part, on the behavior of those whose action is the action of the state, namely, the decision-makers" (Snyder, Bruck, & Sapin, 1962, p. 173). According to this approach, the state is seen as the basic actor in international politics, but it is assumed that state actions can be analyzed most effectively by focusing on the behavior—specifically, the decision-making behavior—of those individuals whose responsibility it is to act for the state. Insofar as the study of international politics follows this kind of approach—taking the individual decision-maker as the unit of analysis and his behavior as the object of systematic observation—social-psychological concepts and methods are clearly relevant.

Focusing on the individual decision-maker in the foreign policy process has several advantages: (a) It counteracts and corrects for the tendency to reify the state and treat it as if it were a human agent. Analyses of state behavior typically involve such notions as perceptions, expectations, and motivations, taken from the vocabulary of individual behavior. If such concepts are going to be used, then there would seem to be advantage in using them more precisely and systematically. This can be accomplished by focusing on the individuals who are the carriers of perceptions, expectations, and motivations. (b) When the individual decision-maker is used as the basic unit of analysis, it becomes possible to analyze in detail the processes that produce state behavior. By contrast, when the state is used as the basic unit of analysis, we are much more dependent on inference if we wish to understand the precise ways in which certain state actions come about. (c) Observations of individual decision-makers provide an empirical handle for the study of international relations. In the field of international relations it is much more difficult to develop indices of macro-level variables than it is in the field of economics. To the extent to which we are able, therefore, to conceptualize in terms of the behavior of individuals and their interaction, we are in a better position to develop suitable measurement procedures.[6]

Whatever its advantages may be, the study of individual decision-makers is politically relevant only if one accepts the assumption that the individual de-cision-maker is a relevant unit of analysis for the study of international politics. This assumption has on occasion been challenged on one of two grounds. Some critics have argued that the study of individual decision-makers is inappropriate because these men do not operate as individuals in their decision-making positions. The outcomes of their decisions are not determined by their psychological characteristics or by the nature of their interactions with each other. It is, therefore, misleading—according to this argument—to focus on individuals as if they were independent actors in international politics and as if their preferences really made a difference. According to this type of criticism, then, observations of the decision-maker are entirely irrelevant. A second type of criticism, while accepting the *relevance* of the behavior of decision-makers in the determination of state action, is concerned about the *equating* of state action with the behavior of decision-makers. By focusing entirely on the decision-maker—according to this view—we tend to ignore the fact that he is part of a larger process. We may thus obscure the role of certain societal forces in the determination of state behavior, which would emerge more clearly if we took the state as the basic unit of analysis, or if we focused not only on the decision-makers, but on all elements within the society that contribute to the policy process.

In sum, questions can be raised about two assumptions that underlie—or may appear to underlie—the study of individual decision-makers: the assumption of the individual decision-maker as independent actor, and the assumption of the individual decision-maker

---

[6] As a matter of fact, even when propositions stated in terms of macro-level variables are put to the test, the actual indices used to measure these variables may be based on observations of individual behavior. For example, one might use public opinion data to obtain an index of the stability of a regime or of the tension level that characterizes the international system.

as sole actor in international politics. Let us proceed to examine each of these two assumptions.

The Decision-Maker as Independent Actor. In questioning the relevance of studying individual decision-makers, some critics point out that the foreign policy decision-maker operates under very severe constraints. It is misleading, therefore, to treat him as an independent actor who contributes importantly to the choice between alternative state actions. It certainly cannot be denied that the behavior of the foreign policy decision-maker is severely constrained. It does not follow, however, that a social-psychological analysis focusing on the individual decision-maker is *ipso facto* irrelevant.

The relevance of psychological analysis is sometimes dismissed because of the mistaken notion that such an analysis is identical with the attempt to explain decision-making in terms of the idiosyncratic characteristics of the decision-maker. Before we examine, therefore, some of the ways in which a focus on the behavior of decision-makers may be politically relevant—despite the existence of powerful constraints—it is important to spell out exactly what such a focus entails. When we speak of images, motives, and values of decision-makers we refer to much more than their idiosyncratic characteristics (cf. Snyder, Bruck, & Sapin, 1962, pp. 153–173; and Chapter 12 in the present volume). One can distinguish at least four major sources of the images, motives, and values that a decision-maker brings to any given situation:

1. The role that he is enacting within his decisional unit and within the larger structure of which this unit is a part: This role carries with it certain expectations that will determine, to a

large extent, the incumbent's definition of the situation and the goals that he will pursue. As Snyder *et al.* (1962) point out, the behavior required by this role reflects in part the functions and objectives of the total foreign policy-making structure and of the particular unit to which the individual decision-maker belongs; and in part norms and values internal to the decisional unit—relating, for example, to the interest of this unit in maintaining its peculiar traditions and its structural position within the total organization. While different role incumbents are likely to differ in the way in which they interpret the requirements of their roles, the broad outlines of the role behavior will be similar regardless of the individual characteristics of the decision-maker.

2. Norms and values that he shares with most of the members of his society: The images and motives that determine the choices of the decision-maker are derived, in part, from the predispositions that he brings to any given situation as a member of his particular society and culture. These are in no sense idiosyncratic to him as an individual, but they may have a great deal to do with the way in which he defines the situation and the kinds of goals he tries to pursue. It can be assumed that, given the same "objective" circumstances, decision-makers with different sociocultural backgrounds would make different choices.

3. Norms and values that he shares with those subgroups within the population to which he belongs: Images and motives derived from this source are likely to be quite important since they are often held in common by the decision-making elite as a whole. The segment of the population from which decision-makers—particularly members of a given decisional unit—are recruited

tends to be somewhat restricted. Insofar as this is true, the same subgroup norms and values may affect the preconceptions and preferred strategies of the entire decisional unit, and may even be built into its definition of the decision-making role.

4. His personality: Images, motives, and values derived from this source are, of course, unique to the individual decision-maker. Even here, however, we are not only concerned with extraneous frustrations, hostilities, and so on, that the individual displaces from other areas of his life onto the decision-making situation. It is also possible to look at personality factors that play a direct role in the way in which the individual handles the problems inherent in the decision-making situation itself—for example, the way in which he interprets the role of decision-maker, the kind of problem-solving skills that he brings to it, and the kind of decision-making style that he displays. Snyder *et al.* (1962) distinguish, in this connection, between "organizationally relevant personality factors and . . . idiosyncratic factors (those stemming from ego-oriented needs and conditions)" (p. 173). No doubt, both types of factors operate; the former, however, can be applied more readily to a systematic analysis of the decision-making process. Insofar as we are dealing with personality factors relating to a specific type of situation we should be able to identify a limited number of patterns and develop propositions about their differential effects on the process.

A social-psychological analysis of the decision-maker is concerned, then, with the effects that his images, motives, and values, *derived from all of these sources,* have on his behavior. His behavior, in turn, is seen within the organizational context in which it occurs, and as part of a process of communication and interaction among the various members of the unit that is responsible for the final decision. With this conception of the study of the individual decision-maker in mind, let us return to the question of the political relevance of this kind of approach. I shall attempt to show that focusing on the individual decision-maker has considerable relevance for international politics, despite the fact that the foreign policy decision-maker operates under powerful constraints.

I would like to propose, first of all, that, even though the constraints under which the decision-maker labors are very severe, they are not so severe that he is left with no latitude whatsoever. It seems unlikely that external realities force the hands of the decision-makers to such an extent that their reactions are completely determined by these realities and entirely unaffected by their own predispositions and the social processes within their decisional unit. The decision-maker's freedom of movement is likely to vary, of course, as a function of a number of different factors. An obvious one, for example, is his position in the political hierarchy: decision-makers at higher echelons have more opportunities to make their preferences felt, although even lower echelon officials may influence the process by the type of information they feed to their superiors and the way in which they carry out their assigned tasks. Another variable is the nature of the decision involved. Wolfers (1959) suggests, for example, that decision-makers experience strong "compulsion" on issues where national survival is at stake. "Where less than national survival is at stake, there is far less compulsion and therefore a less uniform reaction" (p. 96). Even in situations in which the broad directions of decisions are determined by external realities (as these relate to what are deemed to be vital national interests), the decision-maker may have some latitude in the way in which he carries out these decisions and this, in turn, may have important long-run consequences. For example, even if one assumes that the general direction of U.S. policy toward the Soviet Union in the 1950s could not have been altered by decision-makers' preferences, Holsti's (1962) analysis suggests that Secretary Dulles' beliefs and images had an important effect on the form that this policy took—for example, on the intensity with which the Cold War was pursued and on the lack of openness of the U.S. government to possibilities of settling Cold-War issues.

In short, since constraints are not perfect, the perceptions and motivations of decision-makers contribute—in varying degrees—to the final outcome. These perceptions and motivations derive from the various sources that have already been discussed. The decision-maker's actions are determined, in part, by his personality characteristics. But these are by no means the only source of the predispositions that he brings to the decision situation nor are they the determinants of action with which a social-psychological analysis is most actively concerned. Of special interest are the determinants of the decision-maker's actions that derive from norms and values he shares with the rest of his society. Insofar as these include such conceptions as what represents the national interest and what constitutes a proper reaction to certain moves by other countries, they actually contribute to the decision-maker's sense of constraint and compulsion under certain circumstances. Of similar interest as determinants of action are the images and motives—the assumptions and role definitions—that are common

to the decision-making elite in general. Thus, the characteristics of the decision-making elite—and of the particular segment of the population from which it tends to be recruited—become key factors in the choice of national action. Finally, a social-psychological analysis is concerned with the characteristics of the particular decisional unit in which the decision is vested—the norms and values, the patterns of interaction, and the leadership structure that it has developed. These, of course, are partly a function of the particular combination of individuals that constitute the unit and partly a function of the structure and objectives of the unit and of its place within the larger foreign policy organization. How much these various factors contribute to the choice of action on the part of decision-makers—and thus reduce the role of constraints imposed upon them by external realities—would seem to be at least an open question.

I have been speaking of constraints as imposed by external realities, and of the images and motives of the decision-maker—deriving from the society, the subsegment of that society, and the decisional unit to which he belongs— as factors that reduce the effect of constraints. The relationship between these two sets of factors, however, may equally well be reversed. We have already seen in the last paragraph that societal norms may set constraints on the individual decision-maker by specifying the issues that involve vital national interests and the reactions that are appropriate in certain international situations. Thus, the decision-maker would feel constrained by his assessment of public expectations and of the range of reactions that would be "politically safe." Similarly, the norms of the groups from which the decision-maker comes and of the unit to which he belongs may limit the range of actions that he can take—or even the possible range of alternatives that he can perceive. To the extent to which his reference groups consist of people like himself, he is subject to a normative environment that is far more homogeneous than the society at large, and may therefore perceive constraints to an exaggerated degree.

In other words, it may often be true that external realities would permit the decision-maker considerable freedom of movement, but the social norms and values by which he is guided impose constraints upon him. In decision situations of this sort, a social-psychological analysis—far from being irrelevant—is in fact imperative. An analysis of the objective realities alone would not be sufficient for an understanding of the vital national interests that the decision-maker feels compelled to take into account, for in large part these are vital national interests only because they are socially defined as such.

In general, it is evident that a sharp distinction between constraints based on external realities and constraints based on group norms is difficult to maintain. Thus, even in a situation in which the decision-maker feels that he has no freedom of action, we are dealing in part with a social-psychological problem. In the most extreme case, the definition of situations that involve the national interest and the proper reactions in such situations may be written into the decision-maker's role to such an extent that the particular individual enacting the role may be entirely unable to bring his personal preferences into play. Even under such extreme circumstances, however, a social-psychological analysis is not precluded. It would be continuous with the analysis of *role behavior* in other kinds of social situations.

It can be assumed that in any kind of social situation—even the most casual encounter between strangers or the most intimate relationship between personal friends—the participants are enacting socially defined roles and are responsive to the requirements of these roles. The degree to which role considerations govern a given situation of interaction will vary, of course. Foreign policy decision-making situations may often be extreme in that participants are subject to highly structured role requirements with little room for variability. They are still, however, within the total range of social situations, in all of which the analysis of role behavior is at the heart of the social psychologist's concern. In other words, the fact that foreign policy decision-makers function under special circumstances—that they operate as representatives, rather than as individuals, and that their behavior is often highly structured and circumscribed—does not mean that social-psychological considerations are irrelevant; it simply means that social-psychological analysis must focus on the special type of role behavior that occurs under these special circumstances.

An analysis meeting these requirements would start out with the attempt to define just what the crucial circumstances in this type of situation are. What are the demands to which the foreign policy decision-maker is subject? How are these built into the larger political system and its ideology? What are the organizational patterns that were set up to carry out foreign policy functions and what is the organizational context within which a given decision-maker enacts his particular role? Given the demands of the system and the organizational patterns set up to meet these demands, what is the nature of the processes by which decisions are made? What forms do these processes take as a function of different situational factors, including domestic and international events? How does the individual decision-maker define his role and its requirements? What goals does he pursue within this role? How do decision-makers react and interact as they arrive at decisions in the face of different situations?

These questions refer not to the decision-maker as a person, but to the *role* of the decision-maker. In studying the general characteristics of this role—and whatever variants of it the situation permits—we ask questions about the motives and images of individuals. These questions are not concerned, however, with their personal goals or preferences, but with their conceptions of national objectives and the requirements for achieving them and of their own roles within this process. Thus, in order to predict, for example, how the decision-makers of Nation X would respond to a particular provocation from Nation Y, we would be more interested in learning their views of what constitutes a threat to the national interests of X and of the responses to various kinds of provocations that are prescribed by their roles, than we would be in assessing the level of hostility or the attitudes toward Y of individual decision-makers. In sum, the political relevance of focusing on individual actors in the decision-making process becomes apparent once we recognize that a social-psychological analysis is as much concerned with the behavior of roles—and attitudes within and about these roles—as it is with the behavior of persons.

The Decision-Maker as Sole Actor. The second type of criticism that may be raised against approaches that focus on individual decision-makers is that

they provide an incomplete picture of state action by equating it entirely with the behavior of individual decision-makers. An excessive concentration on the decision-maker may cause us to neglect the fact that, while he is the locus of state action, he is not the state; and while he has the final responsibility for state action, he is by no means the sole actor contributing to the process. There are many elements within any society that play more or less direct roles in determining the policies pursued by the state—in general or on certain specific issues—even though they have no formal responsibility for formulating or executing foreign policy. Moreover, there are certain societal processes (such as those discussed in Chapters 9 and 10), formed by the aggregation of social interactions among many individuals and groups throughout a national population, that serve to create a state of readiness for certain kinds of state action. To be sure, all these influences *culminate* in the actions taken by the responsible decision-makers, but they may be obscured if we *restrict* our analysis to the actions of the decision-makers.

In part, this criticism points to the need for a detailed analysis of the total policy process and all of the elements within the society that contribute to it, along the lines suggested in the earlier discussion of public opinion in the foreign policy process. This kind of analysis would supplement rather than supplant the analysis of decision-making behavior itself. There is a more fundamental implication, however, in the above critique of the decision-making approach. It may well be that the societal processes that culminate in state action would emerge more clearly if we took the state, rather than individual actors, as the basic unit of analysis and searched for relationships between variables at that level. For example, it might be proposed that as bureaucratic elements within a society gain in political influence, foreign policy decision-making takes on a more pragmatic character. It is quite unlikely that a proposition of this kind would emerge out of a microanalysis of the decision-making process or that it would be capable of confirmation by such an analysis. To study the effects of such broad societal processes we would have to examine historical and comparative data (along with data about the power structure and the dominant ideology within the societies in which we are particularly interested). For quantitative analysis, we would have to develop indices of such societal variables as rate of bureaucratization and of such structural variables as the relative political influence of the bureaucratic segment of the population.

While it is evident that a microanalysis of the decision-making process would probably not reveal and might perhaps even obscure the operation of certain larger societal processes, it constitutes an important part of the total research strategy on such problems. The illustrative proposition about the role of bureaucratic elements is based on the assumption that, as these elements gain political influence, the decision-making process will take on a different form. Once the reasonableness of this proposition has been established, it would become important to check out whether—in a situation in which bureaucratic elements are politically influential—the decision-making process does indeed take the form that has been postulated. Here, then, a detailed examination of precisely how decisions come about becomes essential, and the results of such an examination may lead to some modification or refinement of the original proposition. In short, criticism of the decision-making approach, insofar as this approach assumes the decision-maker to be the sole actor, is well taken. What it suggests, however, is certainly not an abandonment of this approach, but a combination of analyses at different levels (cf. Chapter 1, p. 34).

There is another type of criticism that is not directed at the decision-making approach per se, but at the dominant tradition in the study of international relations that views nation states as the sole actors in the international system. The decision-making approach, by focusing on national decision-makers who speak for the state, is part of that larger tradition even though it uses the individual rather than the state as its basic unit of analysis. The assumption of the state as the sole actor has been criticized because it does not allow for "corporate bodies other than nation-states [that] play a role on the international stage as co-actors with the nation-states" (Wolfers, 1959, p. 101). These include both subnational bodies—"parties, factions, and all sorts of other politically organized groups" within the state that "can take a hand in matters transcending national boundaries" (p. 102)—and various international and supranational bodies, such as "the United Nations and its agencies, the Coal and Steel Community, the Afro-Asian Bloc, the Arab League, the Vatican, the Arabian-American Oil Company, and a host of other non-state entities [that] are able on occasion to affect the course of international events" (p. 104). The importance of this criticism is particularly apparent if one regards the fully sovereign nation state as only one of a range of principles by which the international system can be organized, and is alert to the indications of change within the international system, including the possibility of "a steady deterioration and even ultimate disappearance of the national state as a significant actor in the world political system" (Singer, 1961, p. 90).

This criticism, however, is not directed at the emphasis on individual actors as such. As a matter of fact, by focusing on individual actors, we may be able to achieve a different perspective on the international system, with less exclusive emphasis on the nation state. Alger (1963) proposes, in this connection, that we "look upon those persons, from whatever nation, who carry on international relations as a society of individuals. In this society there are groups—religious, professional, ethnic, national, etc. The importance of nation groups is a matter that must be empirically verified since it will vary in different parts of the society and change through time" (p. 408). And Wolfers (1959) stresses that attention to individual actors is essential as a check on the basic assumption of those who criticize the exclusive concern with the nation state. This type of criticism presupposes that men do not identify themselves and their interests "completely and exclusively with their respective nation-states," but with other corporate bodies as well. "But to discover how men in the contemporary world do in fact identify themselves . . . attention must be focused on the individual human beings for whom identification is a psychological event" (p. 105).

Processes of Interaction in International Relations

One way of investigating foreign policy decision-making is to study the individuals and organizations that participate in the process. In this way we can learn about key factors that shape the process—the assumptions and pre-

dispositions that decision-makers bring to it, and the organizational channels within which it is acted out. Of special significance, however—particularly in light of our emphasis on role factors in foreign policy decision-making—is the observation of these individuals and organizations as they are actually engaged in the process of arriving at decisions. Systematic observations of this sort are usually very difficult to obtain. Investigators have, therefore, attempted to reconstruct the process involved in past decisions through interviews with major participants in these decisions (cf. Snyder & Paige, 1958) or through content analysis of relevant documents (cf. North et al., 1963).

Similar considerations arise in the study of negotiation and other processes of interaction between nations. The constraints under which the negotiator typically operates are even more severe than those of the decision-maker. How much latitude the negotiator has in a given situation and what impact his images and goals are likely to have on the proceedings depend on his status and on the nature of the negotiation in question. The negotiator functions primarily, however, as a representative of his government. Much of what we would want to know about his contribution to the process can only be gleaned from observing him in this role—from observing the process of negotiation as it unfolds. To the extent to which international negotiations are carried out publicly, such observations should be easier to obtain than those of intragovernmental decision-making, yet there are many aspects of international negotiation that are not readily accessible to observation.

The problem of inaccessibility is one (though by no means the only) reason for turning to general social-psychological research on such processes as decision-making and negotiation. The assumption is that study of these processes in other settings, though removed from the context of international politics, can provide valuable insights to supplement those obtained from more direct observations. Thus, research on various aspects of intergroup relations within a society—particularly in the areas of race relations and labor-management relations—could be used for these purposes. Such studies could be based on systematic observations, intensive interviews with representatives of the interacting parties and onlookers, and perhaps, on occasion, even some degree of experimental manipulation. On the whole, these situations are likely to be somewhat more manageable than comparable situations in international relations. The number of actors is usually more limited, the relevant elements can be identified more readily and more comprehensively, and the key participants and situations are more likely to be available for observation. This is not to minimize the complexity of intergroup relations within a society but, compared to international relations, they do offer more opportunities to social scientists for detailed observation (particularly participant observation) of interaction processes and "unofficial" questioning of participants.

A second source of indirect data about the kinds of interaction processes that are involved in international relations are laboratory experiments on interpersonal and intergroup relations.[7] Prime examples of such research are bargaining experiments of the Prisoner's Dilemma variety and studies of interaction in the small-group tradition.

(Many such studies are reviewed in Chapters 11 and 13.) A more recent development is the laboratory simulation of international relations (cf. Guetzkow et al., 1963), which—though carried out in a setting far removed from international politics—attempts to reproduce in the laboratory some of the essential conditions of international relations. (See Chapters 12 and 13 for a discussion of some simulation research.) Experimental studies have the advantage, not only of making certain processes of interaction more accessible to the investigator, but also of providing types of information that are not available by any other means. It is possible to manipulate variables that are of interest to the investigator and to study their effects on the interaction, while keeping extraneous factors under experimental control. Such studies are capable, therefore, of yielding causal information and of testing theoretical propositions in a relatively controlled fashion. Simulation studies, in particular, can also provide some empirical bases for predicting the effects of certain changes in the international system—such as the introduction of new kinds of weapons, the use of new strategies, or the development of new institutional arrangements—on the course of international relations. By contrast, nonexperimental studies can only provide inferential information about causal relationships. Moreover, they can tell us very little about the effects of conditions that have occurred only rarely in real life, and nothing about the effects of conditions that have never occurred.

These advantages of experimental re-

---

[7] Field experiments, combining some of the advantages of experimental control with a greater real-life flavor, are potentially also a very rich source of such data, but there has been relatively little work in this direction. An example of a study that is somewhere between a field experiment and a laboratory experiment is the Robbers Cave experiment (Sherif et al., 1961).

search, however, must be weighed against its disadvantages, of which the most obvious is the problem of generalization. When we attempt to generalize, for example, from the two-person game that is so often used in bargaining experiments to international negotiation situations, we are immediately confronted with the wide gap between interpersonal relations and international relations, and between laboratory settings and real-life settings. The danger of personification is ever-present when we transfer findings from such studies to international relations: one must beware of thinking of the nation state as if it were an individual reacting, as an individual would, to promises and threats and various other tactics and strategies. Nor can one resolve this problem by generalizing from the behavior of the experimental subjects to individual negotiators or decision-makers, rather than to nation states. The subject in a bargaining experiment, who acts for himself, is in a very different situation from the national official, who acts as a representative of his government and is part of an elaborate structure involving many other elements of his society—including various governmental units, pressure groups, and public opinion. To understand the actions taken by such national officials, one must take into account the contributions of all of these elements, both in terms of their direct participation in the decision-making process and in terms of the constraints that they impose on the responsible actors. One can legitimately question to what extent it is possible to generalize to this situation from a situation like the two-man game, which is so differently structured.

Studies of intergroup relations—both field studies (such as those dealing with racial or industrial relations) and ex-

perimental analogues—are less vulnerable to this criticism, since the participants do act as representatives of groups rather than as individuals acting entirely for themselves. Even these studies, however, provide problems in generalization, because the composition of the responsible actors in intergroup relations at "lower" levels is far less complex than it is in international relations, and because much of the relevant interaction in intergroup relations—in contrast to international relations—is of a face-to-face nature.

The Inter-Nation Simulation (Guetzkow et al., 1963) is designed to deal with this very problem by building into its structure some of the elements that would permit more ready generalization to the international situation. Specifically, the participants in this simulation do not act as individuals, but take the roles of responsible decision-makers representing their nations. Experimental procedures involve not only negotiations between participants representing different nations, but also negotiations among decision-makers within each nation; there is even an opposition leader in each nation who enters into the process. Thus, there is an attempt to simulate the intranational interactions that play such a crucial part in foreign policy decision-making. Feedback from the constituency of each decision-making unit also enters into the simulation through the programming of intranational reactions, such as electoral defeat or revolution, as consequences of various decisions.

These features of the simulation procedure meet some of the major criticisms of experimental analogues of international relations, but they do not by any means dispose of the problem of generalization. Critics of simulation point out that there are certain major differences between the simulated world and the real world which make generalization difficult. Participants in simulation studies are usually students who do not have the experience or the responsibility of actual decision-makers; they are engaged in a make-believe situation, in which very little is at stake; the intensity of their involvement and the level of stress are considerably attenuated; and the interactions are highly simplified and the time period over which they extend is greatly compressed. (Cf. Verba, 1964, for a discussion of some of these criticisms.)

Certainly it cannot be denied that laboratory simulations are very different from the real world, and social-psychological experiments on interpersonal and intergroup relations even more so. The question of generalization, however, involves much subtler issues than the mere degree of similarity or difference between the artificial situation created in the laboratory and the real-life situation to which one hopes to generalize. An experimental study is designed to investigate the effects of one or more variables on a particular process or its outcome—let us say, for illustrative purposes, on the probability that negotiation between two conflicting parties will lead to a cooperative resolution, satisfactory to both. If such a study is to be relevant to international politics, it must test the effects of variables that actually play a significant role in international relations. Whether or not a particular variable plays a significant role may itself be a matter of controversy, but the investigator who wishes to make a relevant contribution must at least attempt to analyze the situation to which he hopes to generalize and select variables that appear to play a role in that situation. Thus, for example, a study of interpersonal bar-

gaining may show that cooperative solutions are more likely to emerge when the two parties have personal affection for each other. It is quite likely that this study has relatively little bearing on international negotiation because it focuses on a variable that does not play a significant role in that setting. On the other hand, an experiment that shows that cooperative solutions are less likely to emerge when the two parties make extensive use of threats ought to be relevant because it deals with a variable that—at least on the face of it—would appear to be significant in international relations. In short, then, a study conducted in a very different setting than that of international politics may still be highly relevant if it has isolated a variable that is crucial in international relations.

Assuming that a crucial variable has been identified, the question arises as to whether the experimental situation is so structured that it allows this variable to operate in the way in which it is likely to operate in the real world. Returning to the example in the last paragraph, it might be suggested that reactions to threat take a rather different form in a situation in which the negotiator acts as a representative of a group than they do in a situation in which he acts for himself. To the extent to which this is true, generalization from an experiment involving a two-person game to the international situation becomes questionable, even though the experimental variable itself is clearly relevant. In other words, it is necessary to incorporate into the laboratory situation the significant *conditions* of the international situation that affect the way the experimental variable under study is likely to function. Our ability to generalize, then, depends on the adequacy with which we have identified and reproduced in the laboratory situation the relevant background conditions.

The mere fact that an experimental situation differs in obvious ways from the real world does not *ipso facto* make it irrelevant as a possible source of valid generalizations. As Verba (1964) points out, the experimental model does not need to "look like" the real world. "What is important is the question of whether it *operates like the real world in the respects that are relevant to the study at hand*" (p. 502). And there is no general a priori answer to this question. The relevant conditions that need to be built into the laboratory situation are likely to be quite different, depending on the particular variables under investigation. What these conditions are must be determined through a combination of analytic and empirical procedures. For example, if we want to evaluate the extent to which one can generalize from the reactions to threat on the part of student participants in a laboratory simulation to the reactions of experienced decision-makers, we would have to analyze the situation in detail and see whether there is any reason to believe that threats would have a differential effect on experienced versus inexperienced decision-makers. If there is reason to suspect that this factor might make a difference, it would probably be best to seek an empirical answer, by running two versions of the simulation—one with experienced and one with inexperienced participants—and observing the reactions of the two types of participants to variations in threat. In any event, the fact that there is a difference in degree of experience between decision-makers in the simulation and in the real world is not a sufficient basis for rejecting the relevance of the simulation, unless there is some

reason to believe that this difference makes a difference with respect to the variables under investigation.

I have tried to show that it would be unwarranted to dismiss a laboratory situation as irrelevant *in general,* without reference to the particular problem with which it is concerned. It would be equally unwarranted, however, to accept a particular laboratory procedure as relevant in general and suitable for all purposes. That is, it is impossible to establish the validity of a laboratory procedure in such a way as to allow us to generalize indiscriminately from it to the real world of international relations. A procedure that is valid for the study of some problems may be quite invalid for the study of others. This is true not only for the more simplified and stylized types of laboratory situations, such as those used in Prisoner's Dilemma studies, but also for the more elaborate attempts to simulate the international system. A procedure like the Inter-Nation Simulation has a great advantage in that it is based on a detailed analysis of foreign policy decision-making and international politics and is deliberately designed to incorporate many of their crucial features in the laboratory model. As a result, the Inter-Nation Simulation not only resembles the real world more closely than simpler experimental situations and thus has greater face validity, but also contains the crucial background conditions necessary for testing the effects of a wide range of variables. Nevertheless, one cannot assume that it would be relevant for all purposes.

It may very well be that, for certain purposes, the simulation procedure is *more* elaborate and complex than necessary. Simpler situations may be available that incorporate the crucial conditions necessary for testing the hypothesis in question, and that have the advantage of being less costly, more flexible, and more capable of yielding unambiguous results (Pruitt, 1964). In other words, the simulation procedure may incorporate more background conditions than necessary for a given purpose. For other purposes, however—and this is most germane to our present discussion—it may fail to incorporate the crucial background conditions that would permit valid generalization. While many features of international relations are built into the Inter-Nation Simulation, others are *of necessity* excluded. Other types of laboratory procedures would therefore have to be devised to test the effects of those variables whose functioning in the real world depends on conditions that the current Inter-Nation Simulation does not incorporate.

The question of generalization from experimental studies to the real world, then, cannot be settled once and for all. There is no laboratory situation that can have universal validity. The conditions on which valid generalization depends have to be reexamined for each specific problem that an investigator is pursuing. By the very nature of experimental work in the social sciences, there must be some degree of tension between the laboratory and the real world. Concern about the possibilities and limits of generalization is therefore an inherent and ubiquitous part of the entire investigative process.

In view of these considerations, the political relevance of experimental studies depends very heavily on the way these studies are used—the way they fit into the total effort to gain systematic understanding of international relations. Two points become particularly important if we grant that our ability to generalize from laboratory studies is necessarily a matter of some continuing ambiguity: the need to use laboratory studies in conjunction with other types of research, and the need to view these studies as contributions to systematic thinking about international relations rather than as final scientific verifications of propositions about international relations.

1. Experimental studies are most likely to be useful if they are part of a combined research strategy, attempting to close in on problems in international relations from different angles through the use of different methods. Data from experiments and simulations (as well as data from field studies of intergroup relations) must be taken in conjunction with data of all kinds obtained directly at the level of international relations. While experimental research can complement direct observations or historical reconstructions of international interactions, it cannot substitute for them. It must turn to such studies in order to identify significant variables that ought to be manipulated in the laboratory and crucial conditions that ought to be built into the laboratory situation if it is to produce generalizable findings. Furthermore, findings from experimental studies must be checked out by means of *in situ* research, in order to determine how well propositions established in the laboratory hold up in the real world. There is a need then, for continued movement, back and forth, from the one type of research to the other. Insofar as laboratory studies are integrated into such a larger research strategy, investigators can come to grips with the problem of generalization. They can maximize the unique contributions of experimental research while minimizing its major limitation.

2. Given the ambiguities inherent in any attempt to generalize from the laboratory to the real world of international relations, it would be much more appropriate to regard experimental techniques "as a flexible mode of dis-

covery and clarification rather than as a mode of rigorous test or validation" (Synder, 1963, p. 11). We are severely limited, at least at the present stage of development of the field, in our ability to obtain experimental verifications of propositions about international relations. If we recognize these limitations and view experimental work, instead, as a special type of contribution to the process of systematic thinking about international relations, then its potential relevance becomes more readily apparent.

In developing a suitable experimental situation, the investigator is forced to clarify his theoretical notions and is likely to become aware of some of their implications. In a discussion of experimental bargaining games, for example, Schelling (1961) notes that "To build a game of this sort, and especially to build into the game particular features that one wishes to represent, requires that one define his concepts operationally. A game of this sort imposes discipline on theoretical model-building; it can be a test of whether concepts and propositions are meaningful, and a means of demonstrating so when they are" (p. 57). Experimental situations, moreover, permit detailed observations of interactions and provide opportunities for discovering unexpected phenomena. Above all, relationships observed in experimental studies can cut into commonly held assumptions about international relations by demonstrating the *possibility of the impossible* and the *questionableness of the obvious*.

Even though an experiment or simulation cannot establish with any degree of certainty that a relationship observed in the laboratory holds true in the real world, it *can* establish that such a relationship is at least possible under certain circumstances. If the existence of this relationship has previously been deemed completely im-possible, its demonstration in the laboratory may constitute an important new input into theoretical and sometimes strategic thinking. For example, if we have shown in a laboratory simulation of international relations that the use of Osgood's (1962) strategy of graduated reciprocation in tension-reduction (GRIT) produces a reversal in the arms race, we have certainly not proven the efficacy of this strategy in the real world. The laboratory demonstration does, however, suggest some new possibilities worthy of consideration when we theorize about international influence processes or examine policy alternatives. Experimental studies can thus contribute to theoretical and strategic innovations by forcing onto the agenda certain possibilities that might not otherwise have been considered.

Similarly—and, again, without proving anything—experimental studies can demonstrate that what is deemed obvious may not be obvious at all, at least under certain circumstances, and that results may be quite different from those that are commonly expected. If an "obvious" proposition is disconfirmed in the laboratory, its validity in the real world is not destroyed, but it is at least thrown into question. Again, then, experimental studies can contribute to systematic thinking about international relations by making it necessary to reexamine certain assumptions about the nature and functioning of the international system that were previously taken for granted.

Perspectives for the Formulation of Theory and Policy

In recent years, some international relations specialists have been turning to social psychology and related disciplines for propositions and interpretations relevant to theoretical and policy questions in the field of international relations. Moreover, some social psychologists have themselves entered into the debate of these questions. Social-psychological contributions are based in part on the kinds of research that were discussed in the preceding three sections, and in part on extrapolations from general social-psychological principles and from research designed for other purposes. It is to be hoped, of course, that social-psychological inputs will increasingly come from research specifically designed to answer questions about international relations, but even extrapolations from other areas can provide a useful perspective on the assumptions that enter into the formulation of theory and policy.

These extrapolations refer to the behavior of nation states and thus involve the application to state behavior of principles and findings based on the behavior of individuals. When such extrapolations are made, therefore, one either assumes that more or less similar principles apply at these different levels of analysis; or that approximate, but still adequate, predictions of state behavior can be made from a knowledge of the reactions of those persons (decision-makers and to a lesser extent various members of the public) whose individual behaviors aggregate into state behavior.

Insofar as these assumptions are untested and controversial, the extrapolation from individual to state behavior is open to the charge of personifying the nation state. Thus, critics may point out, for example, that it would be misleading to suppose that B's perception of and reaction to a conciliatory move on the part of A would take the same form in the relations between two nations as it would in the relations between two individuals. The relations between nations, they would argue,

cannot be understood simply in terms of the motives and perceptions of individuals, but must be analyzed within their historical and political context. This may lead, then, to the related criticism that too often attempts at extrapolation from psychological data are not informed by the historical and political realities impinging on internation behavior and do not take these adequately into account.

The temptation to personify the nation state, and the glossing over of historical and political factors that constitute the conditions within which state actions are carried out, represent real dangers to which we must always remain alert—as I have already indicated in several contexts, both in the present chapter and in Chapter 1. Yet the existence of these dangers is not a sufficient reason for the social psychologist to rule himself out of the debate on theory and policy in international relations. In exercising justifiable scientific caution, we must beware of becoming *over*cautious; it would be regrettable if we chose to make *no* contribution simply because we cannot make an *unambiguous* one. Given the limited development of international relations theory, the scarcity of measurable concepts at the macro-level of analysis, and the difficulty in devising investigative tools, it would be unwise to close off any avenues from which contributions to international relations thinking can potentially come. Social-psychological extrapolation, if carried out responsibly —with due regard for the dangers it entails and for the importance of placing it in its proper context—is one such avenue.

The value of extrapolations on the part of the social psychologist—despite the fact that he typically works with concepts rooted in the study of interpersonal relations, and has limited *ex-*

pertise in historical and political spheres—must be assessed, not simply in terms of the extrapolations themselves, but in relation to the other inputs into theoretical and policy thinking in international relations. When this is done, it becomes apparent that social-psychological analysis can actually perform a *corrective* function with respect to some of the thinking in the field: (a) it can address itself to the psychological assumptions—often unexamined or even unstated—that underlie many theoretical and policy formulations; and (b) it can counteract some of the special biases that seem to be built into the more traditional historical and structural analyses of international relations. Let us examine these two possibilities in turn.

Psychological Assumptions. The tendency to generalize from psychological principles, based on interpersonal relations, to matters of international relations did not originate with the professional psychologist. Personification of nation states seems to pervade much of the thinking about international relations, not only among average citizens, but also among practitioners and students of foreign affairs. Even as sophisticated a decision-maker as Secretary of State Rusk seems on occasion to use a street-fight as his model for the relations between the United States and the Soviet Union. Thus, he was quoted as saying to the reporter John Scali, at the height of the Cuban crisis: "Remember, when you report this—that, eyeball to eyeball, they blinked first" (Hilsman, 1964, p. 20). And W. W. Rostow, Chairman of the State Department's Policy Planning Council, wrote in the *New York Times* (1964): "Behind all the elaborate mechanisms of diplomacy, behind the in-

credible complexity and sophistication of the world of nuclear weapons and delivery vehicles, the cold war comes down to this test of whether we and the democratic world are fundamentally tougher and more purposeful in the defense of our vital interests than they are in the pursuit of their global ambitions" (p. 113).

Systematic efforts at conceptualizing international relations—whether these be at the level of theory construction, policy formulation, or choice of strategy —vary in the extent to which they personify the nation state and the extent to which they impute to it reactions based on some simplified model of interpersonal relations. Central to most of these conceptualizations, however, are certain assumptions about social-psychological processes—about the goals of nation states, about their perceptions of each other, and about their probable reactions to various types of influence attempts.

Thus, for example, Morgenthau (1954) is clearly making a psychological assumption when he states, as the basic proposition of his theory of international politics, "that statesmen think and act in terms of interest defined as power" (p. 5). Power in this context refers to "man's control over the minds and actions of other men" (p. 26). Morgenthau makes additional psychological assumptions in explaining the readiness of the mass of citizens to support the foreign policies of their nation state. "Not being able to find full satisfaction of their desire for power within the national boundaries," he writes, "the people project those unsatisfied aspirations onto the international scene. There they find vicarious satisfaction in identification with the power drives of the nation" (p. 95).

The formulation of policy vis-à-vis

other nations, and in particular the choice of strategies in the execution of these policies, invariably involve a whole series of social-psychological assumptions. Assumptions are made, first of all, about the way in which other nations are likely to react to such influence attempts as threats or promises (cf. Singer, 1963). These predictions, in turn, are based on assumptions about the goals and perceptions of these other nations. At a more specific level, various psychological assumptions govern the procedures followed in international negotiations. For example, the importance of negotiating from strength, and the advantage of starting with a large demand and then allowing it to be whittled down, are often stressed. Clearly, these involve assumptions about the effects of various kinds of bargaining behavior on the reactions of one's partner.

These different assumptions underlying theory and policy can be tested—more or less readily and more or less directly—through social-psychological research. But even in the absence of specific empirical tests, the social psychologist should be able to contribute to the debate insofar as the validity of certain psychological assumptions is at issue. Through extrapolation from general principles and from research on other problems, he should be able to say whether a particular assumption seems reasonable, whether it is consistent with the accumulated knowledge of the field, whether it would require some modification or qualification, whether there are some prior conditions on which its validity rests, or whether an entirely different set of assumptions ought to be considered. Thus, by bringing his professional perspective and relevant *expertise* to bear on the issue, he can help to advance the process of thinking about it.

A good example of a problem area that could benefit from social-psychological inputs is the debate about deterrence strategies. Much of the thinking about deterrence is based on certain psychological assumptions that are seldom made explicit—for example, assumptions about probable reactions to threat, or about the rationality of decision-makers. These assumptions do not only represent—at least in part—generalizations from interpersonal relations whose applicability to international relations has not been tested, but they are based on conceptions of interpersonal relations that are themselves of doubtful validity. Clearly, social psychologists could contribute to the thinking about these strategies, at the very least by offering informed evaluations of the psychological soundness of certain commonly held propositions about human behavior.

It may be worth noting that much of our strategic thinking is open to question not only with respect to its psychological assumptions, but also with respect to its reading of the historical and political context. To be sure, strategies based on military force are backed up by historical precedent and are readily seen as politically "realistic." There is good reason to believe, however, that—given their heavy emphasis on military and game considerations—they often overlook significant historical and political *realities*. Thus, for example, the "missile gap" episode of a few years ago provides some evidence that American deterrence strategies were based on estimates of Soviet intentions that were not supported by subsequent events; it would appear that intentions were assessed on the basis of information about Soviet capabilities, rather than on the basis of detailed analysis of Soviet purposes and the nature of Soviet leadership. Those aspects of strategic thinking that are still based on the model of a bilateral game (particularly a two-person zero-sum game) are especially open to question for their failure to take into account the emergence of new historical forces and the transformation of political realities —as exemplified by the growing importance of the emerging nations, and the probable proliferation of nuclear weapons.

These last examples were designed to illustrate that a social-psychological perspective and a historical-political one are not necessarily opposed or alternative to each other. Some of our thinking about international relations suffers from the absence of both. Moreover, a combination of these two types of perspectives may actually enhance the value of each. Thus, for example, the calculation of Soviet intentions in any given situation must be based on what is known about the history of the Soviet Union and the structure of its political system, but it cannot be based entirely on these considerations. The social-psychological dimension must also be brought into the analysis, through an examination of such data as the current images, values, and expectations of Soviet leaders and citizens, despite the obvious methodological difficulties in the acquisition of these data.

Historical-Structural Assumptions. A social-psychological perspective may complement a historical and structural analysis, not only because it can introduce new dimensions and data relevant to these, but also because it represents a different analytic approach. It can thus help to counteract some of the difficulties that are inherent in a historical-structural approach.

Analyses based largely on historical and structural considerations are often characterized by a static emphasis—an emphasis on how things are and, by implication, on how they therefore must be. This kind of analysis is very useful as long as the situation remains relatively stable, but it is less adequately equipped for dealing with changed situations requiring different kinds of responses. Thus, while American and Soviet societies have been undergoing major changes, scholars have tended to lag somewhat behind reality in their perceptions of the adversary. As Bauer (1961) points out, "the American student of the Soviet Union uses a model largely based on Stalin's reign, particularly during the periods of purges. The Soviet view of America . . . is based in part on the state of American society during the great depression of the 1930's" (p. 226). Similarly, foreign policy formulation has not quite caught up with the revolutionary changes in weapons systems and in the power relationships within the international system.

If policy thinking with a historical-structural emphasis is slow in responding to changing circumstances, it is even slower in the discovery of new approaches and the development of new strategic possibilities. There is a tendency for this kind of thinking to be caught in a closed circle, particularly when it involves policy formulation in a conflictual relationship between two nations. "Political realities" are defined, in large part, in terms of the existing relationship between the conflicting nations; it is not surprising, therefore, that political realities, so defined, require policies that perpetuate the existing relationship.

The special contribution of a social-psychological perspective is that it regards any particular historical-structural situation as only one of a range of possibilities, and that it is concerned with propositions about the conditions under which different kinds of effects emerge. Let us say, for example, that we want to predict how Nation Y is likely to react to a particular policy move on the part of Nation X. Typically, such a prediction would be based largely on what is known about Nation Y's political structure and leadership, its past behavior, and its relationship to X. A social-psychological analysis, however, would attempt to identify the various conditions—such as those surrounding the projected policy move and those characterizing the general relationship between X and Y—on which the predicted outcome depends. Such an analysis—by focusing not on "what reactions can be expected," but on "what reactions can be expected under what conditions"—can more readily suggest possible ways of changing outcomes by changing the underlying conditions. It goes without saying that a social-psychological analysis can never substitute for a political and historical one, but it can complement it in a unique way. In contrast to the more static historical-structural approaches, it is set to recognize hypothetical variants of the existing situation, to see possibilities for changing it, and to come up with new policy orientations.

A social-psychological perspective can, thus, help in the development of alternative policies and innovative strategies that fail to emerge as long as our thinking is bound by traditional assumptions about actions and reactions in the international arena. Moreover, a social-psychological perspective would regard the very set of assumptions on which our international system is currently built as only one of a number of possible sets of assumptions, and hence potentially open to change. Thus, such a perspective would help in the development of alternative institutional arrangements for the international system, characterized by new ideological orientations, new types of loyalties, and

new patterns of relationship among different societies. The importance of such contributions to systematic thinking about these problems is particularly apparent when we recognize that we find ourselves today in a novel world situation, for which there is no adequate historical precedent, and in which many traditional assumptions are no longer relevant.

REFERENCES

Alger, C. F. Comparison of intranational and international politics. *Amer. pol. Sci. Rev.*, 1963, 57, 406–419.

Almond, G. A. *The American people and foreign policy.* New York: Harcourt, 1950.

Bauer, R. A. Problems of perception and the relations between the United States and the Soviet Union. *J. Confl. Resol.*, 1961, 5, 223–229.

Coser, L. A. *The functions of social conflict.* New York: Free Press, 1956.

Fisher, R. Fractionating conflict. In R. Fisher (Ed.), *International conflict and behavioral science.* New York: Basic Books, 1964. Pp. 91–109.

Guetzkow, H. *Multiple loyalties.* Princeton: Princeton Univer. Press, 1955.

Guetzkow, H., Alger, C. F., Brody, R. A., Noel, R. C., & Synder, R. C. *Simulation in international relations.* Englewood Cliffs, N.J.: Prentice-Hall, 1963.

Hilsman, R. The Cuban crisis: How close we were to war. *Look*, August 25, 1964, 28(17), 17–21.

Holsti, O. R. The belief system and national images: A case study. *J. Confl. Resol.*, 1962, 6, 244–252.

Katz, D. The functional approach to the study of attitudes. *Publ. Opin. Quart.*, 1960, 24, 163–204.

Katz, D., Kelman, H. C., & Flacks, R. The national role: Some hypotheses about the relation of individuals to nation in America today. *Peace Research Society*

(*International*) *Papers*, 1964, *1*, 113–127.

Kelman, H. C. Public opinion and foreign policy decisions. *Bull. Resch. Exch. Prev. War*, 1954, *2*(4), 2–8.

Kelman, H. C. Societal, attitudinal and structural factors in international relations. *J. soc. Issues*, 1955, *11*(1), 42–56.

Kelman, H. C. Introduction: Studies on attitudes and communication. *J. Confl. Resol.*, 1958, *2*, 1–7.

Kelman, H. C. Processes of opinion change. *Publ. Opin. Quart.*, 1961, *25*, 57–78.

Kelman, H. C. Changing attitudes through international activities. *J. soc. Issues*, 1962, *18*(1), 68–87. (a)

Kelman, H. C. Internationalizing military force. In Q. Wright, W. M. Evan, & M. Deutsch (Eds.), *Preventing World War III: Some proposals.* New York: Simon & Schuster, 1962. Pp. 106–122. (b)

Kelman, H. C. (with Victoria Steinitz) The reactions of participants in a foreign specialists seminar to their American experience. *J. soc. Issues*, 1963, *19*(3), 61–114.

Kelman, H. C. The effects of participation in a foreign specialists seminar on images of the host country and the professional field. *J. appl. behav. Sci.*, 1965, *1* (in press).

Klineberg, O. *The human dimension in international relations.* New York: Holt, Rinehart and Winston, 1964.

Lambert, R. D., & Bressler, M. *Indian students on an American campus.* Minneapolis: Univer. Minnesota Press, 1956.

Morgenthau, H. J. *Politics among nations* (ed. 2). New York: Knopf, 1954.

Morris, R. T. *The two-way mirror: National status in foreign students' adjustment.* Minneapolis: Univer. Minnesota Press, 1960.

North, R. C., Holsti, O. R., Zaninovich, M. G., & Zinnes, Dina A. *Content analysis: A handbook with applications for the study of international crisis.* Evanston, Ill.: Northwestern Univer. Press, 1963.

Osgood, C. E. *Alternative to war or surrender.* Urbana: Univer. Illinois Press, 1962.

Patchen, M. *The American public's view of U.S. policy toward China.* New York: Council on Foreign Relations, 1964.

Pruitt, D. G. Some comments on the use of simulation in the study of international relations: A discussion of papers presented by Richard A. Brody and Lawrence Solomon at the Symposium on Psychology and International Relations. Georgetown University, June 26–27, 1964. (Mimeographed)

Rosenau, J. N. *Public opinion and foreign policy.* New York: Random House, 1961.

Rosenau, J. N. *National leadership and foreign policy: A case study in the mobilization of public support.* Princeton: Princeton Univer. Press, 1963.

Rostow, W. W. The test: Are we the tougher. *The New York Times Magazine*, June 7, 1964, pp. 21, 111–113.

Schelling, T. C. Experimental games and bargaining theory. In K. Knorr & S. Verba (Eds.), *The international system.* Princeton: Princeton Univer. Press, 1961. Pp. 47–68.

Sherif, M., Harvey, O. J., White, B. J., Hood, W. R., & Sherif, Carolyn W. *Intergroup conflict and cooperation: The Robbers Cave experiment.* Norman: Univer. Oklahoma Book Exchange, 1961.

Singer, J. D. The level-of-analysis problem in international relations. In K. Knorr & S. Verba (Eds.), *The international system.* Princeton: Princeton Univer. Press, 1961. Pp. 77–92.

Singer, J. D. Inter-nation influence: A formal model. *Amer. pol. Sci. Rev.*, 1963, *57*, 420–430.

Smith, M. B., Fawcett, J. T., Ezekiel, R., & Roth, Susan A factorial study of morale among Peace Corps teachers in Ghana. *J. soc. Issues,* 1963, *19*(3), 10–32.

Snyder, R. C. Some perspectives on the use of experimental techniques in the study of international relations. In H. Guetzkow *et al., Simulation in international relations.* Englewood Cliffs, N.J.: Prentice-Hall, 1963. Pp. 1–23.

Snyder, R. C., Bruck, H. W., & Sapin, B. Decision-making as an approach to the study of international politics. In R. C. Snyder, H. W. Bruck, & B. Sapin (Eds.), *Foreign policy decision-making.* New York: Free Press, 1962. Pp. 14–185.

Snyder, R.C., & Paige, G. D. The United States decision to resist aggression in Korea: The application of an analytical scheme. *Admin. Sci. Quart.,* 1958, *3,* 341–378.

Stokes, D. E., Campbell, A., & Miller, W. E. Components of electoral decision. *Amer. pol. Sci. Rev.,* 1958, *52,* 367–387.

Verba, S. Simulation, reality, and theory in international relations. *World Politics,* 1964, *16,* 490–519.

Wolfers, A. The actors in international politics. In W. T. R. Fox (Ed.), *Theoretical aspects of international relations.* Notre Dame, Ind.: Univer. Notre Dame Press, 1959.

Index of Authors

Index of Subjects

Achievement motive, 444, 498, 510
Actors in international relations, individuals as, 5–7, 10–12, 14, 17–18, 565–576, 586–594
nation states as, 13, 566, 586, 593–594, 601
nonnational bodies as, 51, 578–579, 593
Aggression, 250, 253
Communist, 241, 245, 250, 253, 259
displacement of, 46–47, 50, 267–268, 323, 589
and prejudice, 46, 57, 97, 208, 301, 367
in foreign policy attitudes, 90–91, 97–99, 210
and international attitudes, 90, 97, 172
intersocietal, 5, 21, 46, 53, 57
intrasocietal, 46, 53–54, 55, 57, 58, 59
control of, 58–59, 63
Russian accusations of U.S., 244, 245, 253, 254
socialization of, 46, 57, 63, 65–66
Altruism, 323, 470
Arms race, 246, 249, 376, 387, 391, 420–421, 427, 600
Richardson equilibrium model of, 422–423, 429, 513
Atomic weapons, 75, 174, 205, 246, 381, 403
Attitude, 292, 294–295, 447
component of image, 25, 26
determined by social system, 23, 240
externalization function, 205, 208, 210
on foreign policy issues
of businessmen, 122–123, 446
and personal aggression, 210–211
and religiosity, 312, 313, 314
and social mobility, 312
functional approach, 169, 203–207, 208, 262, 286, 302, 321
intensity of, 206–207
object-appraisal function, 205, 205n, 208, 230
personality factors in, 203–211, 262, 301, 322
social-adjustment function, 204–205
Soviet toward World War II, 241, 246, 248, 251, 259n, 260, 262, 271
stability of, 196–208, 296
toward other nations
as a function of childhood socialization, 43, 46, 50–52, 64, 240

Attitude (*Cont.*)
toward other nations (*Cont.*)
generalized evaluative tendencies, 45, 47–48, 72, 73, 89, 117, 295, 410–414
generalized optimism/pessimism, 87, 88, 89, 209
value-expressive function, 206
see also Image
Attitude change, 188, 204, 216, 221, 296, 569, 570, 574
see also Image change
Attitude structure, 213, 293, 295, 296, 302, 328, 566
Authoritarianism, 51, 178, 204, 209, 322, 411, 509–510
and international attitudes, 209, 315, 322, 367
studies of, 81, 90, 124, 209, 210, 324, 325, 326, 327–328, 509, 510
see also Ethnocentrism

Bargaining, 375, 383, 450, 451, 464, 467, 481, 489, 496, 509, 596, 597
studies of, 406, 478 ff., 483, 493–494, 496, 512, 513
tacit, 380, 403, 404, 477, 487
Belief, factors in stability, 261–264
intensity of, 361
see also Attitude; Image
Britain, attitude toward, 72, 87, 87n

China, People's Republic of, 199, 241, 254, 291, 296, 353, 379, 384, 396, 402, 411, 418, 427, 437, 509, 584
Churchill, Sir Winston, 136, 174, 267, 369, 384, 397, 472, 485, 508
Civil defense, 279, 308, 311–312, 316
Coalition formation, in multiparty negotiation, 493–494
Cognitive balance, 25, 82, 83, 95, 118, 133, 169, 208, 213, 219, 224n, 262, 262n, 294, 295, 298, 410, 506
and dimensional complexity of images, 83, 100, 213
and nationalism, 258
re-establishment of, 95, 118, 151–152, 215, 219, 227, 257
and relations among image components, 82, 100, 132–133

616